TEXT AND DRUGS AND ROCK 'N' ROLL

TEXT AND DRUGS AND ROCK 'N' ROLL

The Beats and Rock Culture

Simon Warner

BLOOMSBURY

NEW YORK · LONDON · NEW DELHI · SYDNEY

Bloomsbury Academic
An imprint of Bloomsbury Publishing Inc

1385 Broadway
New York
NY 10018
USA

50 Bedford Square
London
WC1B 3DP
UK

www.bloomsbury.com

First published 2013
Reprinted 2013

Library of Congress Cataloging-in-Publication Data
A catalog record for this book is available from the Library of Congress.
Warner, Simon, 1956–
Text and drugs and rock 'n' roll: The Beats and Rock Culture/by Simon Warner
p. cm.
Includes bibliographical references and index.
ISBN 978-0-8264-1664-3 (hardcover: alk. paper) 1. Music and literature. 2. Beat generation.
3. Rock music—20th century—History and criticism. 4. Authors, American—20th century.
5. American literature—20th century—History and criticism. I. Title.
ML3849.W288 2013
700.973'09045–dc23

2012037315

ISBN: HB: 978-0-8264-1664-3

Typeset by Fakenham Prepress Solutions, Fakenham, Norfolk NR21 8NN
Printed and bound in the United States of America

CONTENTS

ACKNOWLEDGEMENTS

Some sections of this book have appeared elsewhere in different forms. The publishers would like to credit the original sources and thank them for permission to use this material:

'Sifting the shifting sands: Allen Ginsberg, "Howl" and the American landscape in the 1950s', *Howl for Now: A Celebration of Allen Ginsberg's epic protest poem*, edited by Simon Warner (Pontefract: Route, 2005), pp. 25–52.

'Filming "Howl": A cinematic visualisng of the text – Ronald Nameth', *Howl for Now: A Celebration of Allen Ginsberg's epic protest poem*, edited by Simon Warner (Pontefract: Route, 2005), pp. 73–85.

'A soundtrack to "Howl": First thought, best thought – Bill Nelson', *Howl for Now: A Celebration of Allen Ginsberg's epic protest poem*, edited by Simon Warner (Pontefract: Route, 2005), pp. 103–115.

'Raising the consciousness: Re-visiting Allen Ginsberg's 1965 trip to Liverpool', *Centre of the Creative Universe: Liverpool and the Avant Garde*, edited by Christoph Grunenberg and Robert Knifton (Liverpool: Liverpool University Press, 2007), pp. 95–108.

'The Sound of the Summer of Love? The Beatles and *Sgt. Pepper*, the hippies and Haight-Ashbury', *Summer of Love: The Beatles, Art and Culture in the Sixties*, edited by Joerg Helbig and Simon Warner (Trier: WVT, 2008), pp. 5–21.

'Tuli Kupferberg', obituary, *The Guardian*, 26 July 2010.

'Peter Orlovsky', obituary, *The Guardian*, 4 July 2010.

'Jim Carroll', obituary, *The Guardian*, 22 September 2009.

'Steven Taylor: A Beat Englishman in New York', *Beat Scene*, No. 58, 2009.

'Return to Lowell: A visit to the Commemorative and Kerouac's grave', *Beat Scene*, No. 60, 2009.

One Fast Move or I'm Gone: Kerouac's Big Sur, DVD review, *Beat Scene*, No. 60, 2009.

'Jim Carroll: Poetry prodigy, post-Beat and punk rocker', obituary, *Beat Scene*, No. 61, 2009.

One Fast Move or I'm Gone: Kerouac's Big Sur, CD review, *Beat Scene*, No. 61, 2009.

CREDITS

I would like to thank the following for their help in making this volume possible. My partner Jayne Sheridan; my father Lionel and late mother Joyce for their decades of support; my long-time friend Paul Morgan and my first travelling companion in the US, Nigel Haddon; Dave Moore for his helpful input; Simon Morrison, for his work on the index, and Jed Skinner and Charlie Heslop for their assistance; colleagues Derek Scott and Kevin Dawe and former colleague Allan Greenwood for their encouragement; students on my Beat and rock course at the University of Leeds for their enthusiasm; my editor at Bloomsbury, David Barker, for providing this opportunity, and also members of his team, Ally Jane Grossan and Kaitlin Fontana, for their efforts along the way. Last, but not least, I pay tribute to the input of the press production house, particularly copy editor Dawn Booth and project manager Kim Storry at Fakenham Prepress Solutions, for their diligent contribution to this project.

I also want to pass on my appreciation to a number of key individuals who lent me their time and thoughts as I researched, prepared and wrote this book: David Amram, Michael Anderson, Levi Asher, Michael Beasley, Mark Bliesener, Victor Bockris, Michael Brocken, Pete Brown, Bart Bull, Jim Burns, Bill Byford, Mike Chapple, Jim Cohn, David Cope, Ian Daley, Dick Ellis, Royston Ellis, Christopher George, Holly George-Warren, David Greenberg, Christoph Grunenberg, Peter Hale, Joerg Helbig, Clinton Heylin, Michael Horovitz, Barney Hoskyns, Vic Juris, Bob Kealing, Larry Keenan, Harvey Kubernik, Chris Lee, Edward Lucie-Smith, Michael McClure, David Meltzer, Sharon Mesmer, Barry Miles, Pete Molinari, Ronald Nameth, Bill Nelson, Lucy O'Brien, Frank Olinsky, Brian Patten, Joyce Pinchbeck, Genesis P-Orridge, Jonah Raskin, Kevin Ring, George Rodosthenous, Jim Sampas, Philip Shaw, Pete Smith, Steven Taylor, Chris T-T, Anne Waldman, Sheila Whiteley and David Sanjek (1952–2011).

Dedicated to the memory of an old friend and colleague
Geraldine Connor (1952–2011)

… and also to a young friend
Tom Arnold (1984–2012)

PREFACE

Texts and Drugs and Rock 'n' Roll is a book which considers the ways in which two different artistic worlds found common ground in the final third of the last century. The rock musicians who came to the fore at the heart of the 1960s and a radical community of writers, who had originally made their mark in the 1950s, forged friendships and alliances that would challenge the traditional divide between that mass cultural form called popular music and the realm of the literary, a world that would have, conventionally, aimed its output at an elite rather than a mainstream readership. The fact that a maturing brand of rock music was, from around 1965, able to build connections with various Beat Generation novelists and poets suggests that, in a time of great change, this was another symbol of fluidity and transformation, an era when barriers were being broken and the long-established cultural model, constructed on notions of high and low art, was being re-visited, re-ordered and understood anew. Nor would this be merely an esoteric sideshow to the main event we now recall as the Swinging Sixties. On the contrary, the period would witness the two greatest musical acts of the day – the Beatles in the UK and Bob Dylan in the US – developing associations with various leading names from the Beat community: initially with its most voluble figurehead Allen Ginsberg and later with novelist William Burroughs, poets Lawrence Ferlinghetti and Michael McClure and others. Ginsberg would befriend Dylan then Paul McCartney and John Lennon; McCartney would become linked to Burroughs; Dylan would build connections with Ferlinghetti and McClure; and there were other Beats and other musicians who would form relationships as the years went by. Of the principal Beats, Jack Kerouac, author of *On the Road* and perhaps the movement's key text, was the only significant absentee from this network of inter-action. He took a quite different view of the social, cultural and political trends that would unfold during the decade and felt little, if any, affinity with them. Yet, even as he largely withdrew from view, occasionally to re-appear to comment negatively on the mindset of the new decade and the actions of its young people, his inspirational presence to the maturing rock culture and the hippies, in many senses the post-Beat heirs, who attached themselves to it was, nonetheless, plainly evident. Kerouac may have tried to un-link himself from the changing times, but the times would not disconnect themselves from his powerful influence and the ideas he had shared in his many novels over the previous ten years.

For many of the other Beats the notion of cooperation held more appeal and these ambitions appeared mutual, too. Rockers courted poets and poets convened with rockers, and this development would be more than just a fleeting gesture. On the contrary, the links between the Beats and rock musicians would be sustained in the decades that followed. A host of key acts who would emerge in the later 1960s and beyond – from the Doors to the Velvet Underground, David Bowie to Patti Smith, the Clash to Tom Waits, U2 to Nirvana – would follow in the footsteps of Lennon, McCartney and Dylan and demonstrate a similar inclination to acknowledge and maintain a connection to this literary community, and a number of the Beat writers would also continue to participate in this relationship with enthusiasm. This volume will trace that pattern of inter-relationship, identify numerous key examples of the trend, endeavour to understand why this connection was sealed, and how it managed to survive the vicissitudes of cultural – and sub-cultural – change at a time when society's motors appeared to accelerate at an extraordinary pace.

We might see this study as an indication not just of recent historical shifts but also academic ones, too. The academy is rarely an early adopter of new trends: they may be ephemeral and pass too quickly to be of substance, so scholarly departments are cautious and bide their time. Yet universities in the West have, in the last half century or so, begun to acknowledge two things: that popular culture is not outside nor beneath its consideration and also that the long-standing structure of subjects and disciplines within the traditional academy is not as immoveable as may once have been thought. In terms of the status of popular culture, the post-Second World War years have witnessed areas of creative production from film, from around the 1950s, to television and radio, from around the 1960s, enter the academic realm. It has taken longer for popular music to join this elevated pantheon but, over the last 30 years, the subject has increasingly made its mark, either as part of media studies or communication studies or black studies courses or, particularly in the UK, as a field of study in its own right. We might see also, within the terrain of Popular Music Studies, an example of that movement away from an older disciplinary rigidity. For this subject is, in essence, a gathering of disciplines or sub-disciplines rather than a unified topic of enquiry. Thus musicology and sociology, anthropology and history, business and cultural studies are just some of the approaches employed to make sense of this network of aesthetic, social and industrial ideas that criss crosses the field of exploration. The consideration of music and literature as an inter-disciplinary project is a newer concept still – at least for popular music scholars. In art music, there has been a gradual trend in the later twentieth century towards an examination of the relationship between orchestral or symphonic sounds and signs of a specific musical period and the literary ones – novels, poetry, plays – that may display a connection in style or spirit or a commonality in some other fashion.[1] The argument proposes that we can learn more by looking at such artistic practices in association rather than in isolation. Such associations have been considered less, at least to date, in terms of popular music and the literary. This volume hopes to help that process of investigation along by asking how musical expressions and written ones, in tandem, might share a relationship within a historical period. How does one area of practice stimulate, inspire or even change the other? The case of rock music and the Beats seems to be a promising instance in which such questions can be examined further.

In this collection, these associations will be considered in a variety of different ways. A number of longer essays will reflect on the ways in which Jack Kerouac, Allen Ginsberg and William Burroughs share links to this history. It will reflect on how Kerouac's broad rejection of the cultural scene of the 1960s did not mean he avoided his own adoption as an influential icon by the rock culture that followed; it will contemplate how Ginsberg became a guru of the post-Beat counterculture, befriended many of its principals and emerged as both spokesman and activist in an era of political ferment; and how Burroughs, despite his distinct lack of empathy with the hippies and their ethos, would later emerge as a hero of punk and new wave in the 1970s. There are extended accounts of the manner in which seminal rock stars have involved themselves with the Beat community: Dylan's crucial connections to the Beat chronology will be addressed; the Beatles' relationship to the hippies of Haight-Ashbury and the Summer of Love will be considered; Tom Waits' passion for Kerouac will be explored, as will the impact that the Beat scene has had on Patti Smith's career.

There are sections on the place of Ginsberg's poem 'Howl' in mid-1950s America as rock 'n' roll initially erupted, on Ginsberg's trip to Liverpool in 1965, and on recordings and cinematic tributes that have paid homage to Kerouac. There is also a chapter considering the place of women in the Beat Generation and how the seeds they sowed in the 1950s may have helped to create opportunities for women in rock in subsequent decades, and an overview of the way musicians and poets in the UK responded to the primarily American phenomenon of Beat. Furthermore there are portraits of some of significant yet less celebrated players in the Beat-rock story, such as poet David Meltzer – the first Beat to meet Dylan

---

[1] Texts that have explored this field include Delia da Sousa Correa (ed.), *Phrase and Subject: Studies in Literature and Music* (Oxford: Legenda, 2006) and Michael Allis, *British Music and Literary Context: Artistic Connections in the Long Nineteenth Century* (Woodbridge: Boydell Press, 2012). The UK's Open University also has a Literature and Music Research Group which considers this inter-section. See http://www.open.ac.uk/Arts/literature-and-music/index.shtml [Accessed 16 December 2012].

– Steven Taylor, Ginsberg's guitarist and Fugs member for decades, poet rocker Jim Carroll and the British musician and artist Genesis P-Orridge, who enjoyed a long-term association with Burroughs.

In addition there are a number of other ways in which this history is reviewed – extended interviews with some seminal Beat characters, including poet Michael McClure, musician and composer David Amram, and an important photographer of this scene, Larry Keenan; obituaries of poet Peter Orlovsky and musician Tuli Kupferberg; shorter sketches of Lawrence Ferlinghetti and Neal Cassady; conversations with experimental film-maker Ronald Nameth, rock guitarist Bill Nelson and Cream lyricist Pete Brown; and a series of Q&As with a string of individuals with close connections to the Beat-rock crossover, as academics and magazine editors, record producers and rock band managers, poets and songwriters, offer some personal reflections and original insights on the ways in which this literary form and that musical style find common ground.

Rock and rock 'n' roll: A short note to the reader

The terms rock and rock 'n' roll[2] inevitably appear many times in the pages of this volume and I would just like to share some thoughts on the use of these terms in this collection. Applying these descriptions of a musical style with accuracy is complicated by a number of factors: rock has been an abbreviation for rock 'n' roll from the earliest days of this form; rock as a stand-alone term began to mean something distinctive from the mid-1960s; and the ways in which UK and US journalists – and indeed fans – use the phrase rock 'n' roll require some differentiation. I would argue that a quite separate title, dedicated to this very subject, is overdue. Here, however, I will have to be necessarily brief and as economic as possible, as I share some remarks on the matter.

From a British standpoint, I would propose that the full phrase rock 'n' roll refers essentially to a brand of US-derived popular music, a hybrid marrying of white country and black blues, that emerged in the mid-1950s and survived as a commercial force into the early 1960s. For a range of personal, cultural and industrial reasons,[3] the original musical sound of Elvis Presley and Bill Haley, Little Richard and Chuck Berry, lost impetus as the new decade commenced.

In the UK, as the Beatles – a one-time rock 'n' roll group – began their meteoric ascent from 1962, the new popular music attracted adjectives such as pop and

---

[2] Even rock 'n' roll itself has multiple forms, e.g. Rock 'n' roll, rock and roll, rock & roll, rock + roll.
[3] Presley's entry into the army, Little Richard's religious conversion, Buddy Holly's death and Berry's jailing are often cited as reasons for early rock 'n' roll's decline.

beat.[4] As the Beatles' self-composed work then grew in range and sophistication, and particularly after Bob Dylan's decision to amplify his formerly acoustic folk repertoire in 1965, the term rock was used more widely to define the latest stage in a sonic revolution centred on the electric guitar. We might also claim that the term rock became ideologically loaded with information that transcended mere music, exhibiting social and political signs that extended well beyond teenage concerns with the best-selling singles of the Top 40. As I have suggested myself, post-British Invasion, and certainly in the wake of Dylan's Newport transformation, 'rock underwent a profound change as it became more involved in the headline issues of the times: the US Civil Rights movement, anti-Vietnam War protests, the counterculture and drugs'.[5]

In the US, however, while the term rock definitely existed with this fresh sense of invigorated meaning, the older version from which it was derived – rock 'n' roll – survived, and almost interchangeably. For reasons possibly linked to nostalgia or connected to notions of a natural artistic continuum, rock 'n' roll continued to be utilised generally as an umbrella term for post-mid-1950s, group-oriented, popular music – and it remains an appellation that is used quite sweepingly and often with little precise discrimination in its American homeland, even today.

Thus, this potent, yet sliding, signifier – possessing different transatlantic nuances – creates a small difficulty for a book like this, one that is attempting to cross the oceanic divide and consider both US and UK responses to developments in half a century and more of popular music evolution. The issue is further complicated by those Americans interviewed here who quite legitimately use the language with which they are familiar – and, if rock 'n' roll means to them what rock may mean to a British reader, I have decided to bypass the debate by simply adopting the terminology the interviewer has personally applied in our conversation and hope that context will tend to reveal meaning.

I have even permitted myself a little creative licence, too. While this book is entitled *Text and Drugs and Rock 'n' Roll*, its contents focus predominantly on what I, as a UK-based commentator, would certainly describe as rock rather than rock 'n' roll (though the latter in its original form is not entirely absent from these pages). I hope you will allow my non-doctrinaire choice of title and that drawing on a phrase made most famous by Ian Dury's memorable post-punk anthem 'Sex & Drugs & Rock & Roll' from 1977 is, under the circumstances, excusable!

---

[4] There is no evident, or at least direct, connection between beat – as in beat music, beat group or Merseybeat and a common adjective in UK popular music between c.1961 and 1965 – and Beat – as in the Beat Generation and Beat writing in the 1950s US. Apart from the connotation of musical rhythm that informs, to a greater or lesser extent, both uses of the term, it seems that these applications were independent and perhaps merely an example of the *Zeitgeist* at work on both sides of the Atlantic and in slightly different time frames.

[5] Simon Warner, 'Rock', *Rockspeak!: The Language of Rock and Pop* (London: Blandford, 1996), p. 266.

INTRODUCTION

i) How the Beats met rock: Some history and some context

Close to the end of 1965, a key event, bridging two cultural movements, occurred in the city of San Francisco, that great coastal frontier of radical thinking, novel politics and adventurous art. There in California, above the Bay, in the heart of the established bohemian enclave at North Beach, the poets and novelists of an earlier era came face to face with an icon of a new age: representatives of the Beat Generation, like disciples welcoming a young prophet, gathered around a critical figurehead of the arriving rock generation, a guitar-wielding wordsmith with the power to reach a mass audience. In doing so, those writers appeared to pass the baton of possibility from the 1950s to the 1960s. The poems and prose that had challenged the stultifying air of an anxious, perhaps paranoid, America, in the decade or so after the Second World War had concluded, had loosened the latch of the door to fresh opportunity of expression. But it would take a wave of literate rock 'n' rollers, plugged-in folkies and hallucinogenic mavericks to push that portal fully open and discover, beyond, a garden of mysteries, a palace of delights beckoning, and lead the West – certainly its maturing young – into a mind-stretching moment, casting off the confines of conformity along the way. That December summit meeting at City Lights bookshop, which saw Lawrence Ferlinghetti, Allen Ginsberg, Peter Orlovsky, Richard Brautigan, Michael McClure and other luminaries of the pen spend time with Bob Dylan, has sometimes been dubbed 'the Last Gathering of the Beats'. But, if it was a symbolic swansong for an extraordinary concentration of literary talent,[1] it also represented a seal of approval from an established generation to a folk singer whose vision now lay

---

[1] It is worth noting that while the Last Gathering of the Beats featured a remarkable convention of talents, several of the key players – Jack Kerouac, William Burroughs, Gregory Corso and Neal Cassady among them – were not involved in this cameo.

beyond the acoustic excursions of Woody Guthrie and Ramblin' Jack Elliott and looked towards a new – if controversial – electric era.

The friendly and informal convention on the sidewalk of Columbus was wonderfully captured by a young photographer called Larry Keenan and, if the most famous shot from this session, a massed throng outside Ferlinghetti's bookstore, did not include Dylan – he declined the invitation to join the main group – other pictures from the day confirmed that the one-time Minnesota troubadour now turned global pop guru was there or thereabouts. The other photographs that Keenan snapped – Dylan plus his guitarist Robbie Robertson, Ginsberg and McClure in an adjacent alley which divides City Lights from its next-door-neighbour, the renowned bar Vesuvio's, and later re-christened Jack Kerouac Street in 1988 – appeared to frame the transfer of countercultural power from the Beat realm to its transgressive, if more carnivalesque, successor, the peace and love terrain of the hippies, even if, it must be said, Dylan would have a distinctly ambivalent relationship with that rising psychedelic creed. The singer had originally intended to use the City Lights images as the cover for a forthcoming album, rock's first double set, called *Blonde on Blonde* which would eventually appear in the following June. In the end, the singer-songwriter, ever enigmatic, decided not to utilise the pictures that were generated that day on his forthcoming record sleeve and so deny a worldwide audience a pictorial record of a significant meeting.[2]

But the frozen moments that Keenan captured assumed an enduring subterranean power: evidence that the ethos of the protesting poets shared something in common with the resisting rock stars who were rapidly becoming the most famous faces on the planet as the Swinging Sixties evolved from a site of flighty fashion and teenage kicks into a seat of political punch, rallying an increasingly sophisticated community of adolescents to struggle for a new sheaf of rights – social and racial, sexual and narcotic. If Dylan would spend the later 1960s in a somewhat ambiguous relationship with the electric wave of change – cultural and political – that would follow, on that December day in San Francisco he seemed the king-elect of a movement with liberal, even radical, perspectives at its heart and the power of amplified rock music at its back.

But, whatever hopes and dreams were driving the former Robert Zimmerman at the fulcrum of a momentous decade – and the singer's mind and soul had been stretched and strained, bashed and beaten, in the previous months by inner and outer pressures, ranging from self-induced drug forays to widespread fan disenchantment at his shifting artistic strategy[3] – to present himself as the thinking

---

[2] Some of the pictures from the session would be utilised on the much later 5 LP/3 CD Dylan retrospective *Biograph* released on Columbia in 1985.

[3] On 25 July 1965, Dylan has surprised many fans by including an electric set in his appearance at that summer's Newport Folk Festival.

man's popular musician or merely as a capricious rebel, constantly out of step with the expectations of both a demanding media and his swelling flotilla of follower-fanatics, the influence of Beat culture had been a shaping force in the years leading up to the City Lights gathering. Work by Kerouac and Ginsberg, Corso and Ferlinghetti, had already had a permeating effect on his life by the time he shook hands and exchanged smiles with a number of these now maturing poets, a gang who had, around ten years before, initially, and severely, rattled mainstream US sensibilities, from coast to coast, through their words and actions, their taboo-breaking verse and unconventional prose, their society-challenging doctrines and behaviour.

Where was the appeal? What was the connection? On what foundations were these associations based? Why, at a time when the young of the First World were so fervently looking forward, did one of their shining lights seem so capable of looking back? What could an older generation of writers, all close to, or well past, that age that baby-boomer rock 'n' rollers appeared to fear most – the onset of the dreaded 30 – impart to this open-minded, loose-limbed, long-haired superstar who had caught the attention of a billion disciples. What could the crusty, curling leaves of a book of verse, the thumb-eased, dog-eared pages of a well-turned novel, teach this freewheeling, folk-strumming general at the head of much younger battalions raised on the television's magic eye, the arrival of the space age and the mesmerising cacophony of a new music that promised dreams of love, of life, of liberty. How could the grey 1950s, broadcast in monochrome and cowering in the Cold War shadows, lend any energising spark to the glowing 1960s, shot in Technicolor and screened in Cinemascope? And why would Dylan's attachment to this antecedent crowd soon be echoed by other key individuals for whom rock was their first language?

There are a number of responses we might offer to such questions and the aim of the heart of this account, the tentacles of which stretch from a time some way prior to Dylan's regal pomp and on to subsequent eras when his crown would be tilted at by several waves of up and coming young pretenders, is to explore the reasons why this most dominating of late twentieth-century performers, as singer and composer, was so taken with the style and spirit of those boho writers and why others would join him to also warm themselves in the Beat slipstream. What was it that attracted, even entranced, in a variety of manners and fashions, those other undisputed giants of this domain, John Lennon and Paul McCartney, not to mention a string of other major players in popular music's widening and unfolding drama – from folkies to psychedelic rockers, then punks and new wavers, industrial innovators and adherents of grunge to rappers, new country stars and riot grrrls – particularly from the mid-1960s, through the succeeding decades and on to the start of the next century? Why, in the years that followed, did bands and performers as diverse and as important as the Grateful Dead and the Velvet

Underground, Tom Waits and David Bowie, Patti Smith and Joe Strummer, U2 and REM, Sonic Youth, Kurt Cobain and Death Cab for Cutie, all tip their hats in some way to this literary line? How did Beat writers and their ideology manage to speak to a series of musical generations, a range of subcultures – some of which, like the hippies and the punks, appeared to share a deep antipathy – and even cross racial and gender boundaries with their literary messages, their artistic philosophies?

These associations of ground-breaking literary style and multifarious forms of popular musical expression in the post-war, babyboom rush and after, represent a fascinating, if rather paradoxical, theme. Why paradoxical? Well, in these relationships we appear to witness an intersection of creative practices that had been traditionally divided by a long-evolving and essentially solidified arts hierarchy: that established code that saw certain artistic activities as the preserve of the elite and learned and a distinctive brand of pursuits that were regarded as strictly for the proletarian and less-educated masses. Thus orchestral music, opera, the theatre, fine art and literature were considered the stuff of finer minds, patronised over many epochs by the aristocracy and the church, and enjoyed by a narrow segment of the population. Meanwhile, the wider populace – the agricultural workers then the factory toilers of the Industrial Revolution – had their own entertainments and distractions, ones regarded as less substantial and certainly less important by society's upper-tiers. Thus from the folk songs and dances of the rustic scene, with their roots in the Medieval, even pre-Medieval period, to later urban forms that arose from industrialisation and new social formations – the on-stage presentations of vaudeville and music hall, brass band concerts and public house singalongs, for instance – popular expression was deemed fleeting and insignificant by those elevated tastemakers who had set the art standards in a pre-modern age and whose worldview persisted even as the Western world began to change fundamentally and rapidly. There were some disruptions to this seamless divide – Shakespeare's plays were attended by ordinary theatregoers in the late sixteenth century and opera in seventeenth century Italy was a style enjoyed by the all strata of that society. But, even by the mid-twentieth century, older codes largely held sway – there were clear splits between art perceived to be serious and enduring and those superficial fripperies of the proletariat, pleasures considered to be ephemeral and of minimal worth by establishment commentators, a separation perhaps underpinned, reinforced even, by those profound transformations wrought by a surging, swelling industrial society.

The relentless rise of cities during the nineteenth century, in Western Europe and the US particularly, and the spread of technology were key here: urban communities, premised on the need to concentrate workers in places where burgeoning manufacture was centred, provided a possibility for the masses to gather and forge an entertainment programme that was for them, by them and of them, and major new inventions in this area meant that those forms of pleasure the public desired, craved even, could be disseminated, consumed and enjoyed more widely than ever. First cinema and sound recording from the 1890s, then later radio in the 1920s and television from the 1940s, provided new means of production and presentation, new frameworks of control that often circumvented those older institutions which had both controlled arts distribution – through concert halls and traditional theatres – and sustained and defended long-standing ideas about what art – good art – might be. The new outlets challenged the controlling hand of the establishment – the powerful in both secular and religious circles – to designate what was worthwhile and what was not. The first half of the twentieth century saw these processes intensify in the US as radio stations prolif-erated, records and gramophone players became commonplace, and Hollywood became a talking medium and quickly a key platform for music, too, after 1927. In the UK, the wheels of change turned more slowly as broadcasting was a monopoly held by the BBC, an independent body from its earliest days but one that relied on government funding. Yet even in Britain, gradual shifts in society's weft and weave were underway.

The Second World War would disrupt these processes in many ways, assist it in others – for example, the appearance of vinyl records, which would boost the phonographic business massively at the end of the 1940s, was linked to war-time research into plastics – but once the industrial West had staggered from the devas-tating effects of that global conflict, mass entertainment would return to continue its challenge to the long-standing cultural order. Disputes in the American radio industry in the early 1940s would allow doors to open to marginalised musical forms – from jazz to blues, R&B and country – and the speedy post-war rise of television in the US would see hundreds of radio licences cheaply sold off to new broadcasters, often at the ethnic margins, which would spread so-called 'race' music to new audiences. The deep divisions in US society drawn by history, geography and skin colour could not be upheld as easily once the airwaves promiscuously spread sounds that could reach almost anyone, anywhere, with suitable transmitters, which became increasingly powerful, and receivers, which by the early 1950s became increasingly portable, as transistor radios released adolescent consumers from the family wireless and the living room and allowed them to make their own listening choices, in their bedrooms or even in the street.

During this very period surrounding the end of the war in 1945, the young men, who would in time comprise the core of the Beat fraternity, were meeting and shaping their literary hopes in New York City. Musically, these tyros were drawn to a new and exciting brand of jazz – the sound of bebop, a style suffi-ciently radical to resist easy incorporation by the mass media. Its cerebral density, its rejection of accessible melody and standard rhythms, set it apart from jazz's earlier incarnations – forms such as ragtime and tailgate, then swing – which had, by the 1930s, been gradually adopted and integrated into mainstream popular culture and, as importantly, appropriated and, some would argue, diluted by a generation of white musicians. The big band with its jazz-inspired syncopated tempos provided dance-hall accompaniments and many of the larger ensembles had white leaders, such as Tommy Dorsey, Benny Goodman and Glenn Miller.

The revolutionary complexity of bebop was a music more of the concentrating mind than the romantic soft shuffle and proved a potent drug to the young Beats; as they shaped their own evolving aesthetic in cafés, bars and late-night conversations,[4] they dreamed of producing literary work that was both as thrilling and intellectually stimulating as this mentally invigorating style of jazz, now beginning to attract an admiring, if essentially underground, crowd. Thus the nascent, rebellious words of Kerouac, Ginsberg and Burroughs – gestating in their heads, gradually appearing in draft – were comparable, in some ways, to the angular notes, the furious solos, the instrumental duels, that Charlie Parker, Dizzy Gillespie and Thelonious Monk were propagating at venues such as Minton's Playhouse in Harlem[5] during the first half of the 1940s and which the proto-Beats were devouring, with great relish, as listeners. Later writers have compared Parker, Gillespie and Monk to the Beat triumvirate of Kerouac, Ginsberg and Burroughs. Certainly all were large and original talents who pursued their experimental expressions with a rare fervour; two of them died young; four of them became addicts of various kinds – only Gillespie and Ginsberg appeared to escape a period of reliance on drugs or alcohol. Critic Richard Meltzer saw Kerouac as Parker, 'the meteoric alpha soloist [...] blowing chorus after chorus of personal asymmetries into art that was neither happy nor sad'; Ginsberg as Gillespie, 'self-promoter [...] deceptively brilliant under the showman's spiel'; and Burroughs as Monk, 'sphinxlike [...] deconstructing paragraphs rather than chords'.[6] That said, whatever apparent congruencies this pair of creative triangles may have shared, the contrasting power relation between the two sets of trios was unavoidable. While these white university students, graduates and drop-outs, and would-be writers, were lured by the frenetic excitements of black life and, specifically, the energy of a new black art, bebop was at the heart of a marginalised music scene still infused and infected with the pressures, stresses and alienations of pre-Civil Rights days, some two decades before Martin Luther King's campaigns for equality made its

---

[4] Around 1944, Kerouac, Ginsberg, Burroughs and their friend Lucien Carr compiled a shared manifesto which they called the 'New Vision', a statement which expressed a commitment to experimental art, approved of the derangements that drugs might stimulate and rejected both censorship and conventional morality as barriers to the creative impulse. See Steven Watson, *The Birth of the Beat Generation: Visionaries, Rebels and Hipsters, 1944–1960* (New York: Pantheon, 1995), p. 40.

[5] Kerouac, as a Columbia undergraduate, had an apartment at 118th Street close to Minton's at this time.

[6] Richard Meltzer quoted in John Leland, *Hip: The History* (New York: Ecco, 2004), p. 137.

first dents in the superstructure of institutionalised prejudice. Socially, politically and economically disenfranchised, radical black artists like the beboppers used new approaches to music-making to not only make their creative mark but also challenge the codes and expectations of orthodox society. The sounds they made were both personal statements but also provided a critical, if oblique, commentary on the state of the US racial order. As Nat Hentoff commented:

> Jazz, after all, is a medium for urgent self-expression, and the young insurgents of the 1940s could no longer feel – let alone speak – in the language of [Louis] Armstrong. Aside from musical needs, the young Negro jazzmen, who at first formed the majority of the modernists, felt more assertively combative about many issues apart from music than did Armstrong and most other Negro jazzmen of earlier generations; and this change in attitude to their social context came out in their music.[7]

Thus, no matter how intriguing Parker and his fellow instrumentalists were as innovators, they remained caught in the net of an often legalised ostracism based on skin colour. The emerging Beats, meanwhile, were free to taste the exotic fruits of black New York, romanticise them, even over-romanticise them, and then return to the safe haven of white normality. They could, we might argue, choose the deprivations of a bohemian hand-to-mouth existence; their black jazz heroes had many fewer options. It would take essentially until the mid-1950s, around a decade later, for the Beats to see their literary ideas made published flesh and for the novelist and critic Norman Mailer to address some of these racial tensions and social contradictions in his 1957 essay 'The White Negro',[8] originally published in *Dissent*, in which the attractions of black subcultural life to the white hipster were investigated.[9] In that sense, the Beats were precursors of a later and longer revolution that would see white music fans drawn to subsequent black musical genres such as R&B and soul, funk and hip hop, and the language and lifestyles linked to them, in the decades to come.

There is another chain of connection we might add: an entertaining, perhaps apocryphal story, in which there appears to have been an impressively direct,

---

[7] Nat Hentoff quoted in Leon Ostransky, *Understanding Jazz* (Englewood Cliffs, NJ: Prentice Hall, 1977), p. 201.

[8] Norman Mailer, 'The White Negro: Superficial reflections on the hipster', *Protest: The Beat Generation and the Angry Young Men*, edited by Gene Feldman and Max Gartenberg (London: Panther, 1960), pp. 288–306.

[9] There were, of course, eventually black Beats, too, but some would have a complicated affiliation to the literary community. Leroi Jones, the most prominent African-American to be identified as Beat, detached himself from the scene when he became Amiri Baraka and turned his energies to radical black politics in the mid-1960s.

chronological line joining several phases in the subterranean world of New York City over two decades: Lester Young, the great jazz tenor-man, is said to have turned Kerouac onto marijuana in the 1940s; Kerouac, it is alleged, did the same for a rising, young Manhattan journalist for the *New York Post* called Al Aronowitz in the 1950s;[10] Aronowitz, we are led to believe, did the same favour for Bob Dylan in the early 1960s; and Dylan, soon after in 1964, shared his herbal bounty with a group called the Beatles. In that genealogical track, traced through the New York underground, we see dope – both stimulant of a rising alternative society and badge of social transgression – move, in around 20 years, from the cellars of Harlem to the poets of the Village to the clued-up newspaper folk of mid-town, to the folk singers of Washington Square and on to an upper storey suite of the luxury Hotel Delmonico (today called Trump Park Avenue), a narrative with extraordinary racial, cultural and social mobility at its core, if ever there was one.[11]

But, to move forward, the link between the Beats and jazz is a subject, quite probably an extended volume, in itself, and this book, while acknowledging the deep importance of that musical style to Kerouac, Ginsberg, Ferlinghetti and others, is about those other brands of popular musical expression that take hold after the mid-1950s and reach a potent point in their development around ten years on. Jazz, as we have suggested, is an umbrella term covering a multitude of forms – from the Broadway ballad to New Orleans tailgate, the sound of white swing bands to the compelling rhythms of the Latin scene – and bebop, the music forged by Parker, Gillespie and their kin, had a somewhat complicated connection to that generic centre. Bebop was a cerebral mode of expression from the outset, and, arguably the antithesis of a standard mass entertainment model, an outlet sharing more in common with twentieth-century modernism and the contemporaneous, canvas outpourings of the Abstract Expressionist painters of the period – Jackson Pollock, Mark Rothko and Barnett Newman – than a mainstream record-buying, concert-going audience.[12] When the Beats chose bebop as a key soundtrack to their personal and artistic lives, they were, in part, attracted by its thrilling contemporaneity, drawn

---

[10] Aronowitz interviewed Kerouac in 1959.

[11] Some of these links are more verifiable than others. Sam Charters refers to the Young and Kerouac connection in the 1940s in his lecture 'Jack Kerouac and jazz', '*On the Road*, 25th Anniversary Conference', Naropa Institute, Boulder, Colorado, 1982, http://www.archive.org/details/On_the_road__The_Jack_Kerouac_conference_82P261 [accessed 28 February 2012]. Al Aronowitz certainly met Kerouac in the 1950s and also interviewed Neal Cassady in jail in 1960; Aronowitz introduced Ginsberg to Dylan in 1963; and he was present at the Dylan and Beatles meeting in 1964. See also Al Aronowitz, *Bob Dylan and the Beatles: The Best of the Blacklisted Journalist, Vol. 1* (Bloomington, IN: Authorhouse, 2004).

[12] In New York in the 1940s and into the 1950s, the musicians, painters and writers engaged in new creative approaches often gathered in the same bars and cafés, such as the White Horse and the Cedar Tavern in Greenwich Village. Another, the San Remo, was a social haunt of Pollock, jazz trumpeter Miles Davis, composer John Cage, artist Larry Rivers, Kerouac and many others. See Bill Morgan, *The*

to the flame by its very rejection of convention, elements they hoped that they may, eventually, be able to distil into the lines of an essay, the paragraphs of a novel the stanzas of a work of verse.

The relation of the Beats to the popular musical voices that would rise to a crescendo from the mid-1950s onwards was rather different: in the 1940s, those novelists and poets-to-be sought out jazz and its new breed of inventive purveyors; in the mid-1960s, and in the years that followed, the process would, in the main, be reversed – practitioners of the new rock sounds would tend to seek out the Beats, even if Ginsberg was a frequent catalyst and willing bridge. Jack Kerouac may have reflected on the emergence of a new kind of male star in his 1957 essay 'America's new trinity of love: Dean, Brando, Presley'[13] and he may even have briefly considered calling his imminent novel *Rock 'n' roll Road*[14] instead of *On the Road*, but the Beats would not convene with rock, in any substantial sense, for around a decade, by which time the dance-oriented stylings of the original rock 'n' roll, a largely teen-targeted music led by Elvis Presley and Little Richard, Chuck Berry, Buddy Holly and Bill Haley, had been supplanted, certainly from around 1965, by a more mature, socially and politically conscious version, penned and performed most notably by Dylan in the US and the Beatles in the UK, and then scores of others who would aim to follow their lead and join this transatlantic trend.

How may we perceive that rock music was becoming deeper and more serious? In the hands of some of the key, cutting-edge artists, the music was assuming added weight and scope, something that had been quite unexpected of the form when it had initially made its mark in the heart of the 1950s. A decade on, the Beatles and the Beach Boys, both of whom had been willing, just a handful of years before, to replicate the quite primitive sounds and structures of early rock 'n' roll, started to exploit new studio technologies and production techniques – from stereo to multi-tracking, sound effects to unfamiliar instruments – to create work that moved the popular song into a new and elevated realm and also made the assumption, in part, that the wider palette of their music would be aimed at the album format rather than the singles market, with the extra implication that their audiences would be older and with tastes that were more developed than mainstream radio and the Top 40 could accommodate. In landmark collections such as the Beatles' *Revolver* (1966) and *Sgt. Pepper's Lonely Hearts Club Band* (1967) and the Beach Boys' *Pet Sounds*

Beat Generation in New York: A Walking Tour of Jack Kerouac's City (San Francisco, CA: City Lights, 1997), p. 89.

[13] Richard Lewis reads the essay on the tribute CD, *Kerouac: Kicks Joy Darkness* (Rykodisc, 1997).

[14] Douglas Brinkley, 'The American journey of Jack Kerouac', *The Rolling Stone Book of the Beats: The Beat Generation and the Counterculture*, edited by Holly George-Warren (London: Bloomsbury, 1999), p. 115.

(1966) the stakes were raised – there was a hardly concealed, if amicable, contest between the main protagonists, Paul McCartney and Brian Wilson for instance, to out-do the other in this intense, creative head-to-head struggle. Their two groups had that rare ability to move from the commercial – complex, experimental productions such as 'Good Vibrations' (1966) and Lennon and McCartney's double A-sided 45 'Strawberry Fields Forever' and 'Penny Lane' (1967) were huge popular hits – to longer, sustained compositions on the albums that ran alongside them and asked different questions of the listener. Bob Dylan was embroiled in different strategies – his controversial experiments of 1965, when he moved from acoustic to amplified recordings and performances, never saw him abandon the rough and ready rawness of folk, country or, indeed, rock 'n' roll. Dylan had stated from the start that his tastes were wide – from Woody Guthrie to Little Richard and Hank Williams – but his desire to produce a sound that communicated authentic emotions rested more on his voice, simple instrumentation and basic arrangements rather than the new tricks of the recording engineer, the swelling arsenal of studio devices and the gloss that technical breakthroughs could add to the process of record-making.

Yet the sound of the new music was not all the audience would hear. Lyrics, too, were gaining in purpose and sophistication – and words, of course, were the same essential raw material of the novelist and the poet as they were of the song-writer. It was on this plane that the literary voices of the Beats and the lyrical spokesman of rock had their most obvious opportunity to share a dialogue. Dylan had been amazing his followers with songs that spilled words, told tales and cast opinions with glorious facility, insight and wit since his earliest recording forays – from 'Talkin' New York' (1962) to 'A Hard Rain's a-Gonna Fall' (1963), 'Masters of War' (1963) to 'With God on Our Side' (1964) – and his amplified phase saw few signs that plugging-in would mean he abandoned the central role of the lyric in his work, as 'Mr. Tambourine Man', 'Maggie's Farm' and 'Subterranean Homesick Blues' (all from 1965) signalled a fresh style, a less direct narrative approach, but no compromise on that alchemic fusing of both musical and lyrical elements. The Beatles, and Lennon for sure, seemed most affected by Dylan's output as wordsmith. Two pieces principally credited to Lennon, 'In My Life' and 'Norwegian Wood' (both 1965), are often regarded as early attempts to apply Dylan's approach to heartfelt slices of autobiography. McCartney's more objective song-writing mode – frequently adopting the voices of characters other than himself – may have been in contrast to his composing partner's more earnest pursuit of self-exposure. But it is hard to see how important pieces like the McCartney-conceived 'Eleanor Rigby' (1966) could have occurred without Dylan's adventurous and literate push towards words that transcended common themes of plain and simple love and romance and delved instead into darker, more dramatic and sometimes disturbing places for their inspiration.

Yet if the words of rock songs were being transformed in the middle of this decade – affected by the politics of the day, the loosening stays of sexual liberation or the impact of mind-altering of drugs, for example – it was a gesture by the Beatles, as they released *Sgt. Pepper*, that changed the playing field crucially. By including a full transcript of the album's lyrics on the LP sleeve, the group gave their words special and expanded status: no longer were the stanzas and verses mere embroidery to the main tapestry of the musical soundtrack. Instead, they were accorded a stature as a stand-alone text. We might argue that it was at that moment that the lyric-as-poetry debate, one that Dylan had already triggered, was propelled forward significantly. Before that, Dylan had included his own Beat-like prose on several of his sleeves but had eschewed the notion – before and after *Sgt. Pepper*, in fact – that his words would be displayed in a verbatim way on the album sleeve.[15] Yet the Beatles' decision to do so was hugely influential. Richard Goldstein's book *The Poetry of Rock*[16] even bracketed an earlier hero of the wordsmith's art Chuck Berry and Allen Ginsberg together. 'Berry', Goldstein said, 'was sex, speed and see-you-later-Alligator jive. While Ginsberg howled, he rocked. Remembering them both in the cultural hereafter, we will probably dig Ginsberg and dance to Berry'.[17] But his volume principally celebrated the latest generation of rock lyrics as legitimate examples of verse in their own right, showcasing work by Jim Morrison and Van Morrison, John Sebastian and Grace Slick, Donovan and Paul Simon, alongside Dylan and the Beatles, their lines and stanzas imprinted on the paperback page to be clearly read, not only listened to. Certainly the collection confirmed a trend and a late 1960s rush of confessional singer-songwriters, largely collected under a new hybrid which had grown out of folk rock, simultaneously assumed the roles of latterday lyric poets, at least in the eyes of those listeners who flocked to devour their work.

From James Taylor to Joni Mitchell and Carole King, Paul Simon and Leonard Cohen, Jackson Browne to Randy Newman, not to mention all four individual members of early supergroup Crosby, Stills, Nash and Young, from Van Morrison to Cat Stevens and Elton John (even if his words were penned by Bernie Taupin) and many more besides, these singers privileged the popular lyric in a way that it had not been positioned before *Sgt. Pepper*'s eye-catching packaging, words and all, changed the rules of the game. Folk, in the first half of the 1960s, may have valued the messages of its words, but the crowd of new singer-songwriters possessed an appeal, a sensitivity, a directness, that transcended the earnest broadside style of their socially conscious, acoustic predecessors. Stokes explains the term singer-songwriter: 'The term is something of a catch-all, designed to include anyone who in an earlier era would likely have been called a folkie […] write his or her own songs, and perform them in a way that implied the lyrics were

---

[15] Dylan in a long career, spanning 35 studio albums, has very occasionally shared his lyrics on the sleeve – for example, *Empire Burlesque* (1985) and *Under the Red Sky* (1990).

[16] Richard Goldstein, *The Poetry of Rock* (New York: Bantam, 1969).

[17] *Ibid.*, p. 15.

more important than (certainly) the beat and (maybe) the melody.[18] But Maslin personalised and humanised this phenomenon. 'What was most important [...] was presenting one's musical persona with a persuasive semblance of straightforwardness and simplicity' often employing 'the sheer allure of personality.'[19]

The words these songwriters conjured were no longer regarded as detached celebrations of or commentaries on love or loss but, rather, fragments of an artist's private life laid bare. Whether it was James Taylor's stay in rehab – hinted at in 'Fire and Rain' (1970); Joni Mitchell's passion for Graham Nash – in 'Willy' (1970); Stephen Stills' mourning for lost love Judy Collins – in 'Suite: Judy Blue Eyes' (1969); or David Crosby's tragic hymn to the assassinated Robert F. Kennedy – 'Long Time Gone' (1969) – there was a powerful sense that the stories being related were an open window into the crises, the crushes and concerns of these composer-performers. Whether these were always personal exposés, or not, barely mattered; it was the perception that counted. Such understandings and interpretations echoed themes at the heart of the Beats' own revelations, so often based on actual experience and all the more credible and convincing for that. We might argue that in the hands of Kerouac, Ginsberg and their fellow travellers, the novel and the poem distanced themselves from what we had, previously, described as fiction; the new singer-songwriters distanced their songs from fiction, too, cladding their melodic stories in more than a layer of felt life.

So, in the wake of the Beatles' decision to include a lyric sheet, the printed words became a central part of the album experience with that strong suggestion that the words had value in themselves, could be enjoyed separately from the music they accompanied, and had, by clear implication, poetic qualities of their own. Whether this was true or not – and Dylan would long continue to attract serious analysts who saw poetry in his lyrical art[20] – rock's words were regarded as far superior to the bubblegum banter of assembly-line crafted pop songs. And in time, many of the acclaimed artists' words would be promoted further, appearing in anthologised book-form, much like poetry collections in fact.[21] This

---

[18] Geoffrey Stokes, 'Trimming the sails', *Rock of Ages: The Rolling Stone History of Rock and Roll*, edited by Ed Ward, Geoffrey Stokes and Ken Tucker (Harmondsworth: Penguin, 1987), pp. 447–63 (p. 452).

[19] Janet Maslin, 'Singer songwriters', *The Rolling Stone Illustrated History of Rock & Roll*, edited by Jim Miller (New York: Random House, 1976), p. 312.

[20] Respected academics such as Christopher Ricks, a Briton at Boston University, has been one such advocate for Dylan's words. See the entry in *The Bob Dylan Encyclopedia*, edited by Michael Gray (London: Continuum, 2006), pp. 571–4.

[21] Bob Dylan's *Writings and Drawings* (London: Panther) would first appear in the first of several editions in 1973, collecting his lyrics in one substantial paperback. Other later examples include *The Lyrics of John Lennon* (London: Omnibus, 1997), whose author had already seen his humorous verse published while still a Beatle, Paul McCartney's *Blackbird Singing: Poems and Lyrics 1965–1999* (London: Faber and Faber, 2001) and *Joni Mitchell: The Complete Poems and Lyrics* (New York: Crown Publishing, 1997).

foregrounding of popular music's words was a further sign of rock's claim to share messages, even manifestos, which went well beyond the tittle tattle of adolescent courtship. By doing so, rock marked out its territory as a serious and substantial form, and one with literate intentions. Many of the Beats found this development appealing because they admired the aims of the project – the dissemination of often challenging ideas through an innovative medium to large audiences – and could see ways in which their poetry – personal, political and often proselytising – might benefit from a friendly association with the potent momentum of rock and its leading lights. It is perhaps not without irony that as the rock lyric escaped its musical bonds, a number of the Beat writers, in the years that would follow, would see their poetry, even their prose, enveloped in a musical wrapping. As rock moved closer poetry, so would literature move closer to rock.

This was not necessarily welcomed by all – early popular music historians like Nik Cohn, with typically entertaining hyperbole, accused mid-1960s rock of 'third-form poetics, fifth-hand philosophies, ninth-rate perceptions'.[22] But Pichaske, much more content to use a term like rock poetry, says that 'twentieth-century poets have had precious little to do with music – at least until Ginsberg, Ferlinghetti and the Beats. Most modern poets have discarded the regularities of stanza and meter imposed on poetry by its early associations with music and virtually discarded all vestiges of poetry as an oral art [...] Which just may explain why modern poetry has fared so poorly and rock so well, and which of the two is closer to traditional poetic art.'[23]

But to return to those earlier notions of changing cultural patterns and the onset of a series of increasingly fluid intersections, from above and below, which had been testing the once formidable barricades that had segregated high and low art practices for so long, we may well point to the blurring of those lines in the relationship between Beat and rock as a pertinent example of this phenomenon. In the mid-1960s, as high profile writers and widely recognised popular musicians appeared to identify common interests and a mutual benefit in sharing notes, was this not merely the latest sign of that enduring, but now embattled, artistic order under attack? If that is the case, how might we characterise the key features of this process, this two-way street? We might begin with this premise: that we are identifying the meeting of a recognised literary grouping – essentially well-read, college educated and primarily middle class – with an emerging wave of popular musicians – generally less literate, less educated and often from a lower levels of the class pyramid – and extrapolate to suggest that this is merely the latest symptom of that high-low cultural wall being threatened and even dismantled.

---

[22] Cohn quoted in David Pichaske, *The Poetry of Rock: The Golden Years* (Peoria, IL: The Ellis Press, 1981), p. 3.
[23] Pichaske, pp. 4–5.

If that is the case, we could perhaps further interpret this phenomenon in two ways: the Beats, many of whom had been the beneficiaries of high-level US educations, often with Ivy League associations,[24] and a serious interest in what we might define as elite literature,[25] had actually managed to create a body of writing that had the potential to appeal beyond the upper echelons of the academy and the narrow confines of the avant garde. While the Beat writers as a community had a powerful motivation to espouse experiment, they were also committed to work that was either socially relevant, politically aware or explored matters of concern to a contemporary consciousness. In the meantime, emerging rock artists took advantage of the shifting ground in society – with class petrification beginning to melt, not to mention those previously embedded stratifications of religion and race – and their own attendant upward mobility, to make their music and messages more serious, more substantial, more intellectual. Let us not forget, either, that a number of the frontline rock musicians who would engage in these of acts of cultural co-operation had also experienced levels of education that their pre-war equivalents would never have done. For example, Dylan had briefly been a student at the University of Minnesota at Minneapolis in 1959 before departing for New York, while Lou Reed attended Syracuse University, New York in 1960 and Jim Morrison studied on the UCLA campus from 1964. In the UK, John Lennon, Eric Clapton, Keith Richards,[26] Ray Davies and Pete Townshend, all of whom would connect in various ways with the unwinding literary thread, had attended UK art schools at the end of the 1950s and beginning of the new decade. They would bring their own thoughts and theories – shaped by literary, film and art studies – to the new forum.

It may be proposed then, to put the idea in the most basic terms, that the Beats saw these informal alliances, these arrangements with the erupting rock culture, as an ideal opportunity to share their work with considerably bigger audiences than had enjoyed their output so far. Simultaneously, rock musicians looked upwards and aimed higher, employing the format, power and accessibility of a mass musical form but framing, within their work, serious ideas and even political comment. As the Beats reached out more widely and rock artists raised the bar of their ambition, a meeting of minds and possibilities ensued. For the novelists and poets this was no dumbing down or artistic compromise – their often experimental works of the late 1950s and early 1960s were not adapted or bowdlerised

---

[24] Kerouac had attended Columbia even if he did not graduate; Ginsberg did graduate from Columbia, despite twice having experienced expulsion; Burroughs had earlier graduated from Harvard; Ferlinghetti graduated from Columbia and later studied at the Sorbonne in Paris.

[25] The proto-Beats of the 1940s who clustered in New York had reading lists that ranged from Shakespeare to the Romantic poets, Dostoyevsky to the Symbolists, Proust to Joyce, Melville to Genet, Céline to Spengler.

[26] Keith Richards adopted the name-style Richard from the early 1960s to the early 1970s.

for an expanding readership; democratisation did not imply that this literary art had been watered down in any sense. Rather, rock's endorsement of Ginsberg, Burroughs, Kerouac and others encouraged fans of the great singers and groups of the day to familiarise themselves with Beat literature. If you were listening to *Blonde on Blonde* or *Revolver*, you were most likely also intrigued to know what 'Howl', *Naked Lunch* and *On the Road* may offer by way of background.

The time was also ripe, in other ways, for such integrations to occur. College opportunities had grown in the US in the post-war period and even in the UK there was a gradual rise in university openings for those who came from less privileged backgrounds. A better-educated, young adult population, in that key late adolescent and twenties demographic, was hungry for cultural offerings that provided more heft than the pubescent, romantic doodlings of the singles-based Top 40. Thus notions that popular music may take a grown-up course and reflect that in its lyrics, its music and its broader manifesto – with politics and literate expression both featuring in that scheme – did not seem strange to the new youth and post-youth segment of Anglo-American society.

There were also important industrial and media signals that the change was happening – and quickly. By 1967, the long-playing album had begun to replace the 45rpm single as the principal commercial product of the music business, a sign that rock music had moved into a fresh phase and was aiming its output at new, older and more prosperous demographies. Further the period would see magazine launches responding to and reflecting these transformations. In the US, *Crawdaddy*[27] (1966), *Rolling Stone* (1967) and *Creem* (1969) would report the dynamic, and often combustible, mix of new sounds and new ways – from political activism to the rising profile of the drug culture.

Of *Rolling Stone*, Lindberg *et al.* comment that 'with its in-depth articles, substantial interviews and reviews, had succeeded in becoming *the* authoritative voice on popular music for most of the Western world'.[28] Yet, there were quickly interesting tensions about the ideological status of the magazine, most relevant at a time when the counterculture was challenging most establishment positions, and the cultural fluidity of rock's intertwining with literature was providing an example of radical interaction that tested standard notions of social expectation. 'The mainstream media and probably part of its readership viewed *RS* as an

---

[27] Founder Paul Williams claimed in the first issue he produced that 'you are looking at the first issue of a magazine of rock and roll criticism'. See Ulf Lindberg, Gester Gudmundsson, Morten Michelsen and Hans Weisethaunet, *Rock Criticism from the Beginning: Amusers, Bruisers and Cool-Headed Cruisers* (New York: Peter Lang, 2005), p. 106.
[28] Lindberg *et al.*, p. 133.

underground magazine, but in reality it was planned and has always functioned as a commercial venture', Lindberg *et al.* suggest.[29]

It would take a little longer for the British popular music media to catch up but, by 1968, *Melody Maker* had trumpeted intentions to add serious coverage of developments in rock music – particularly the emerging progressive rock – to its first-rate treatment of folk and jazz. Says Frith of *MM*: 'Its features got longer, the interviews more serious; the core of the paper became the album and concert reviews.'[30] In 1973, the *New Musical Express*, an out-and-out pop paper in the 1960s with few perspectives beyond the singles chart, would shift also and begin a new and successful phase as a commentator on broader socio-cultural happenings – from films to literature – alongside its main focus on rock, with its earlier obsession with pop and the courting of a younger teenage following now shelved. Thus, as the texts covering rock music became more discursive and sophisticated, literate voices, and literature itself as a concept, could be more easily accommodated in the pages of these print outlets but also, therefore, in the minds and imaginations of their consumers.

Alongside more mainstream titles, the underground press in both countries would also play its part in reporting a cultural moment that was able to accept the elision of rock and politics, drugs and literature within its remit, with the Beats enjoying significant recognition, seen as important pieces in the jigsaw of the counterculture. In the US, *Fuck You: A Magazine of the Arts* emerged as early as 1962 while *The East Village Other* and *Berkeley Barb* were both founded in 1965. By the mid-decade, Sukenick states, the underground culture was starting to attract a big popular audience. 'The underground press [...] were starting to define a large hip audience. By the end of the sixties, one of the radical underground press-syndication services alone served an audience of twenty million.'[31] In the UK, *International Times*, which became *IT* after a dispute with the owners of the name of the daily London-published newspaper the *Times*, premiered in 1966 to be followed by *Oz* the next year and then *Friends*, later *Frendz*, in 1969. Comments Lindberg *et al.*: 'The British underground press was, like its American counterpart, passionately devoted to provocation, alternative living and "revolution" in a broad sense.'[32]

Out of these conjunctions, various significant interactions arose which helped confirm a connection between cutting-edge popular music and accompanying literary forces, with the Beats a regular and prominent factor. Magazines such

---

[29] *Ibid.*
[30] Simon Frith, *Sound Effects* (New York: Pantheon, 1981), p. 171.
[31] Ronald Sukenick, *Down and In: Life in the Underground* (New York: Collier Books, 1987), pp. 168–9.
[32] Lindberg *et al.*, *Rock Criticism from the Beginning*, p. 197.

as *Rolling Stone* and *Creem* would provide platforms for journalists with Beat interests like Greil Marcus and Lester Bangs and publish emerging writers like Hunter S. Thompson and Tom Wolfe, as novel and vivid brands of subjective reportage earned the epithets gonzo and new journalism. The British underground press would provide seeding grounds for writers such as Nick Kent, Charles Shaar Murray and Mick Farren, who would all see rock as part of a wider social and cultural context, and become the banner names of the revitalised *New Musical Express*. Other scribes on the magazine – like jazz writer Brian Case and punk evangelist Tony Parsons – would show a particular interest in the Beat realm.[33] In the US, Ed Sanders' *Fuck You* would become a vital and controversial link between the Beats and the new cultural explosion – he would publish Beat writers, promote the new arts and eventually form his own band the Fugs, whose style would be an amalgam of electric rock and polemic folk, subversive politics and radical poetry.[34] Barry Miles would play a similar role as connective tissue in the UK. A founding editor of *IT*, friend of Ginsberg and McCartney and later *NME* journalist, he would be an energetic promotional fulcrum for a scene where rock music joined forces with a bigger, bolder gathering of ideas and ideology. Miles played a central role in creating the International Poetry Incarnation at the Albert Hall in London in June 1965 when Ginsberg, Ferlinghetti and Gregory Corso joined a line-up of British poets – Michael Horovitz, Adrian Mitchell, Pete Brown and others – and an international contingent of readers. He would later commission pieces by Burroughs and Ginsberg for *IT* and helped to make amicable links between the Beat writers and the British rock aristocracy, the Beatles and the Rolling Stones most notably.[35]

So, for Ginsberg, McClure and other Beats who joined a caravan that linked rock and literature and identified areas of common interest and purpose, there seemed to be various possibilities at stake: a credibility by association with Dylan, Lennon, McCartney and others and the promise that doors would be open to bigger, younger audiences of listeners and readers. By linking in this manner, the Beats, whose literary output was often quotidian in content and frequently concerned with the experience of the common man, opened up the possibilities of their serious ideas reaching a readership that may otherwise have barely been aware of their existence. Meanwhile, as rock musicians moved above and beyond the traditional materials of the popular song – primarily, the joys and angst of

---

[33] Case, joined by fellow *NME* contributors Roy Carr and Fred Dellar, would later collaborate on a book-length account of this scene in *The Hip: Hipsters, Jazz and the Beat Generation* (London: Faber, 1986).

[34] See Ed Sanders, *Fug You: An Informal History of the Peace Eye Bookstore, the Fuck You Press, the Fugs, and Counterculture in the Lower East Side* (Boston, MA: Da Capo, 2011).

[35] See Barry Miles, *In the Sixties* (London: Jonathan Cape, 2002).

young romance – and into the realm of social and political commentary, raising questions about war, freedom and equality, they were able to feel the validation of poets who had long experience of challenging society's conventions. This not only provided confidence to songwriters like Dylan and Lennon, then Jim Morrison and Patti Smith, but also dressed their work in a reflected gravity and intellectual respectability. In addition, by connecting with the Beats, Dylan, the Beatles, the Grateful Dead, the Doors and others who made their great mark in the mid- to later 1960s, there was the strong sense that these musicians and songwriters were joining forces with or paying tribute to their literary heroes, writers who had inspired them as adolescents in the later 1950s and early 1960s. Dylan's link to McClure, McCartney's ties to Burroughs, Jerry Garcia's connection to Cassady, for example, enabled this younger generation of music-makers to acquire artistic status and a vein of seriousness that popular music alone could not invest in isolation. As we have stated, popular music from the mid-1960s was increasingly a dollar-drenched business as lucrative album sales superseded the far less profitable singles market. However, alliances and friendships with Beat poets brought a benefit that a magnified royalty cheque and a healthy chart position could not confer – cultural capital.

By the mid-1960s, then, the descending horizon of an earlier writing community and the ascending perspective of a new musical grouping had become aligned in a fine example of the *Zeitgeist*. There were various catalysts required for this experiment to proceed apace: the face-to-face meeting of Dylan and Ginsberg at a house party in New York City in December 1963 was one; Ginsberg's backstage meeting with the Beatles at a Dylan gig in London in May 1965 was another. But the clearest public sign that this alliance had been made flesh was, as we have described, the Last Gathering of the Beats on that December day in San Francisco in 1965 when singer mingled with poets and novelists in the north Californian rain.

Not all Beats, as we have stated, would identify with this merging of energies and interests – Kerouac would reject the whole premise of the 1960s counterculture, while Burroughs would be particularly unsympathetic to the peace and love postures of that hippy subculture most connected to the developments in rock music at this time, just as these cross-cultural connections were being forged. But this would not stop rock and its subcultural followings, from then on, identifying with and appropriating Beat ideologies from its figurehead authors. If Ginsberg quickly became a leading countercultural guru, present in person at many of the historical events that marked the testing course of the later 1960s,[36] if Cassady

---

[36] Ginsberg would be present at the Oakland anti-war demos in late 1965, the Human Be-In in San Francisco in early 1967 and the Chicago Democratic Convention riots of the summer of 1968. Burroughs, alongside French writer Jean Genet and US new journalist Terry Southern, would join the latter event.

became embroiled personally, too, in high profile ways with the social revolution,[37] those writers who had attempted to distance themselves from these changes could not disconnect their reputations from the movement's forward momentum. The spirit of Kerouac, as traveller and seeker after truth, and Burroughs, as a living embodiment of narcotic adventure, would still be adopted as guides and heroes by musicians and their fans alike, even if they, as writers, could find little of value in these alliances and transformations.

We have been discussing, then, a continuing process by which art forms or practitioners from different rungs of the cultural ladder have found common purpose, grounds for agreement or collaboration, in the modern period. What would once have been regarded previously as a strictly high art form – the novel, the poem, maybe the play, the stuff of intellectual fibre – with what has generally been considered a standard bearer of the low arts – the song, the lyric, the tune, and escapist and light entertainment. We might also characterise this binary opposition in other ways – as the cerebral versus the visceral, the mental versus the physical. We have, in addition, invoked issues of education and class to explain the division that had existed between these two particular worlds for much of their development and how, in this instance, that separation between literature and popular music, Beat and rock, had begun to establish a form of resolution by the mid-1960s.

But, then again, we should stress that this specific entente was by no means a one-off in the mid-twentieth century and after. We need to point as well to the rise of a general relativism that infused cultural interpretation in the post-Second World War era, a trend that saw the status of modernism – a radical and experimental period in the visual arts and architecture which stretched from around 1880 to 1970 but was arguably at its height between 1914 and 1950, one that might be further described as the epoch in which the avant garde dominated – gradually eroded by a condition dubbed postmodernity, a development that recognises the decline, the dissolution perhaps, of the high-low divide. This new philosophical critique tended to abandon the old terms of judgement: the regimented idea of good art or bad art – with the practices of the cultural elite generally linked to the former and the activities of the ordinary and lower tiers of society usually associated with the latter – became passé and discredited. No cultural movement played a bigger role in establishing the postmodern drift – its ideas have hardly become the consensus even half a century and more later – than the style known as Pop Art.

From the mid-1950s in the UK and a little later in the US, a new wave of painters rejected the abstraction that had become the ultimate statement of the modernist creed by the end of the 1940s and decided instead to return to the representational,

---

[37] Cassady's involvement with Ken Kesey's Acid Tests when he became a driver of the Merry Pranksters' bus saw him engaged directly in a countercultural project.

but not in the conventional pre-photographic sense. Rather, British painters such as Richard Hamilton, Eduardo Paolozzi, Peter Blake and David Hockney and Americans like Jasper Johns, Andy Warhol, James Rosenquist, Claes Oldenburg and Roy Lichtenstein adopted and adapted the objects of mass manufacture and entertainment – cartoons and comic books, movie stars and pop singers, magazine advertisements and the products of the supermarket shelf – and re-utilised them in paintings and collages, sculptures and silkscreen prints, presenting them as totems, mirrors perhaps, of the contemporary world but also offering them as the very material of a new fine art, displacing the dense, existential abstraction of Pollock and his brotherhood with symbols that were familiar to all. This sleight of hand, shocking at first, was speedily accepted by the galleries and dealers of the establishment and this latest acclaimed school, either celebration of or assault on the booming consumer society, was praised for its bold wit and inherent irony. Thus, rock 'n' roll's negotiated marriage with the land of letters, a mass art joining forces with an elite one, may quite possibly be considered another example, alongside Pop Art, of that same postmodern impulse.

ii) Charting the Beats: Background and impact

So, that celebrated San Franciscan crossroads – Dylan on tour, dropping into the Bay Area as part of his end of year tour, and the city's purveyors of the new prose and verse, radical re-workers of the post-war word, keen to meet and greet the musical Messiah – is an intriguing junction on a compelling musical journey, and *Text and Drugs and Rock 'n' roll* aims to provide a wider guide through this odyssey of interaction and engagement. Its essays try to make sense of a number of themes and threads, alliances and collaborations, people and places: transgenerational connections which would inspire creativity on both sides of this fresh artistic contract, for the writers *and* the musicians. In fact, popular music in its post-Presley incarnation has, on both sides of the Atlantic, drawn quite richly, on the font of literature. Writers, poets and novelists as diverse as William Shakespeare and John Donne, William Blake and Samuel Taylor Coleridge, Percy Bysshe Shelley and Alfred Lord Tennyson, Edward Lear and Lewis Carroll, J. R. R. Tolkien and Graham Greene, James Joyce and Samuel Beckett, Norman Mailer and George Orwell, James Baldwin and Nelson Algren, Anthony Burgess and Nik Cohn, Hubert Selby Jr. and Ayn Rand,[38] to cite only a few, have been referenced or seen their works called upon as points of inspiration. In addition, a host

---

[38] See Simon Warner, 'Culture shock: The arts in rock', *Rockspeak!: The Language of Rock and Pop* (London: Blandford, 1996), pp. 73–133.

of fiction genres – from the folk tale and ancient myth to the gothic saga and sci-fi adventure – have provided sources for composers and bands in various ways.

Yet it is the Beat Generation that has provided quite possibly the most fertile and frequent literary nourishment for rock musicians, whether as a hook for band names, album or track titles, as a starting point for songs, as a trigger for subject matter, or as a catalyst for a particular approach to penning lyrics. Yet we might also suggest that it is the pervading spirit of Beat writing – its interests in freedom of the individual, in candour of expression, in the lure of the road and the adventures it may hold, in its hunger for stimulations of the mind and the body, in its range of campaigning issues in the fields of sexual identity, personal politics and the ecology – that has provided a general infusion to those musicians and songwriters who have followed. From the powerful attraction of the tour in rock culture – the enduring gig trail of one-nighters across countries and even continents, suggests an equation with the constant, yearning travels of so many of the Beats from the 1940s to the 1960s – to the many waves of confessional singers baring their own experiences, their own lives, in an autobiographical, singer-songwriter manner, it is hard not to see a potent echo of the Beat ethos, the Beat ideal, transcending the decades and still informing popular music's mythology well into the twenty-first century, close to 70 years after these notions took root.

Various commentators at various points have commented on this association. Bruce Cook, as early as 1971, was speculating on the relationship between rock and the Beats. Suggesting that the jazz poetry experiments had never really delivered a satisfying marriage, he says that by the later 1950s and early 1960s '[j]azz had ceased to be sung, was no longer danced to, and could only be appreciated by those with a musical education. And that was where rock came in. It was the most accessible of music, offering a heavy beat to dance to and easy melodies to sing.'[39] But he believes, at first, it was 'so limited musically and emotionally'[40] before gradually showing signs of maturity and improvement and among the influences that musicians began to incorporate were 'the prose and poetry of the Beats'.[41] Among the ingredients he felt were absorbed were the notions of 'poetry as song'[42] and ideas of poetry as a public utterance rather than a solemn, socially isolated, academic one. Cook adds: 'It would not be too much to claim, then, that if the Beats had not given poetry a firm push in the direction they did [...] then what many are now calling the rock poetry movement might never have happened. Beat, in this, was a necessary precondition to rock in its present form.'[43]

---

[39] Bruce Cook, *The Beat Generation* (New York: Charles Scribner's Sons, 1971), p. 222.
[40] *Ibid.*, p. 223.
[41] *Ibid.*
[42] *Ibid.*
[43] *Ibid.*, pp. 225–6.

Steve Turner makes more general points about the connection between Beat writing and the emergence of a new musical culture. He says that '[o]ne of the achievements of Jack Kerouac and his Beat contemporaries was in making literature, whether spoken or printed, as '"sexy" as movies, jazz and rock 'n' roll'.[44] And, as he extrapolates this alchemical process, this social and artistic transformation, to the next two decades, he states: 'Everything that the archetypal rock 'n' roll star of the 1960s and 1970s experienced – marijuana, amphetamines, hallucinogenics, homosexual experimentation, orgies, alcoholism, drug busts, charges of obscenity, meditation, religious engagement – had already been experienced by the Beats during the previous two decades.'[45] Choosing an enduring rock star as a potent example of just a few aspects of Beat's engrained impact, Turner remarks: 'Bruce Springsteen, who shared with Jack a working-class, East Coast, Catholic upbringing, also shared his love of fast cars and the open American landscape. It is hard to imagine Springsteen existing without Jack. Even his stage clothing of a check shirt and blue jeans – once unthinkable attire for a performer – are straight out of *On the Road*.'[46]

Furthermore, Ted Gioia, in his survey of cool in the post-war decades, talks about the power of the spiritual in the Beat consciousness, from Catholicism to Buddhism and 'the Edgar Cayce[47]-influenced spirituality of Neal Cassady'.[48] He comments:

[I]f we jump ahead to 1969 (the year of Kerouac's death at age forty-seven), we see how the spiritualised tone permeates the new youth culture, shaping a whole generation's sense of what is cool and defining the emerging lifestyle – setting it apart from the typical varieties of licentiousness and rebellion. We find it in the unconventional opinion leaders of the post-Kerouac generation (who often acknowledged his influence), from the Beatles to the Doors, Bob Dylan to Simon and Garfunkel, Ken Kesey to Carlos Castaneda.[49] Indeed almost every aspect of the new movement would take on a transcendental tone, following the cues set by Kerouac and his confreres: sex moves from the clinical detachment of Kinsey to the higher vibes of Summer of Love ecstasy; narcotics lose their social stigma and are now a pathway to opening the 'doors of perception'; ecology morphs from *Silent Spring*[50] alarmism to back-to-nature

---

[44] Steve Turner, *Jack Kerouac: Angelheaded Hipster* (London: Bloomsbury, 1996), p. 19.

[45] *Ibid.*, p. 21.

[46] *Ibid.*

[47] Edgar Cayce (1877–1945) was a US Christian whose alleged psychic powers drew followers to his philosophies including Cassady.

[48] Ted Gioia, *The Birth and Death of the Cool* (Golden, CO: Speck Press, 2009), p. 122.

[49] Anthropologist Carlos Castaneda, who died in 1998, wrote a series of books, commencing with *The Teachings of Don Juan* in 1968. Their interest in shamanism, sorcery and the out of body experiences prompted by drug use chimed with the hippy interests of the period.

[50] Rachel Carson's *Silent Spring* (1962) was an early and influential call to manage the global environment.

grooviness; social protest shifts from the strikes and labour conflicts of earlier decades, with their battlefield overtones, to sit-ins and love-ins, everyone mouthing the word *peace*, wearing its now ever-present symbol on shirts and patches, pendants and placards.[51]

Holly George-Warren expresses this view: 'As a cultural phenomenon, the Beat Generation changed us more than any other twentieth-century movement; its effects are still being felt today. As a literary movement, the Beat Generation gave us a cacophony of fresh, new American voices; the common thread running through the work was this: to say what hadn't been said in a language as unique as one's own thumbprint.'[52] Her comments were made as editor of *The Rolling Stone Book of the Beats*, and the alliance revealed, in that very title, is most significant itself. Here was a magazine, founded at the height of a historic shift in 1967 in the city of San Francisco, most associated with a strident countercultural moment and with the sounds of a new and alternative rock music at its core, lending its name to a later collection that would celebrate and commemorate the Beats from a number of perspectives, but, importantly and frequently, through the lens of rock music and rock musicians. Patti Smith and Richard Hell, Graham Parker and Lee Ranaldo. Lou Reed and Eric Andersen are all among the cast of contributors, evidence in itself of the rich Beat-rock vein. George-Warren stresses the association when she comments that 'the Beat filter has added texture to the recordings of numerous artists whose music gave the magazine its *raison d'être*: from the Beatles, Dylan and the Velvet Underground in the sixties, to David Bowie, Tom Waits and Patti Smith in the seventies, to Sonic Youth and Beck in recent years.'[53] Her book, she asserts, 'should make it clear how such a small group of individuals could affect us so powerfully – how one group could spawn both the Summer of Love and the Blank Generation'.[54]

Who then were the Beats? The core figures in this group initially met in 1943 in New York City when William Burroughs first made the acquaintance of two younger men, Allen Ginsberg and Jack Kerouac, who had moved to the city as university students. Burroughs, born in St. Louis in 1914, had graduated from Harvard in 1936, then spent time in Vienna studying medicine before the Second World War. But, by the early 1940s, his life had become a shiftless, peripatetic affair. Rejecting his patrician Midwest roots, he had done a number of drudge jobs, including time as a pest exterminator in Chicago, before arriving in New York. His

---

[51] *Ibid.*, pp. 122–3.
[52] Holly George-Warren, 'Introduction', *The Rolling Stone Book of the Beats: The Beat Generation and the Counterculture*, edited by Holly George-Warren (London: Bloomsbury, 1999), p. ix.
[53] *Ibid.*, p. x.
[54] *Ibid.*

interests in drugs and firearms led him to rub shoulders with the city's criminal fringe as he survived on a monthly cheque from his wealthy family, a member of which, his uncle, had created great riches from the invention of the adding machine in the late nineteenth century. Jack Kerouac, born in Lowell, Massachusetts in 1922, was a young student at Columbia University when the decade commenced, a good scholar whose additional sporting prowess had helped him to win a scholarship. But when a broken leg brought his college football career to an early close, he spent some time in the war-time merchant marine, before befriending and finding himself in the same apartment as Burroughs, and also Ginsberg.

Ginsberg, younger still and born in Newark, New Jersey, in 1926, had also attended Columbia with aspirations to eventually be a labour lawyer. Expelled after an expletive-fuelled row with his anti-Semitic dorm cleaner, he would also be drawn to the same accommodation as Burroughs and Kerouac and begin a lifelong association with his two senior associates. Early on in their friendship they shared long conversations about life and art, and both Kerouac, a would-be novelist, and Ginsberg, drawn to writing poetry, shared their literary hopes and ambitions. Burroughs' writing vision was less clear but together they drew up a creative manifesto called the 'New Vision', a radical statement of artistic intent which praised experiment, discounted conventional morality and, at heart, responded to the psychic crisis of a world torn by conflict.

Other individuals would form part of this circle, including an aspiring journalist Lucien Carr, another writer John Clellon Holmes, a Times Square hustler called Herbert Huncke and Joan Vollmer, who had embarked on a relationship with Burroughs, despite the man's avowed homosexuality, and would live with three principals in the same property. In 1944, Carr became embroiled in a fatal incident in which a predatory older man called David Kammerer, who had been making homosexual advances to him for some years, was stabbed and murdered. Carr would be jailed for this act of manslaughter; Kerouac would become entangled as an accessory as he had disposed of the knife. The killing would have a marked effect on various members of the group: it exposed the sexual tensions that were present in this circle in which heterosexuals like Carr and Kerouac rubbed shoulders with homosexuals like Burroughs and Ginsberg. But it also gave a dark lustre to their lives and provided material experience that some would use in their later writing. A contemporaneous novel written by Burroughs and Kerouac, *And the Hippos Were Boiled in Their Tanks*, not officially published until 2008, drew, in part, on this drama.

In 1946, another important player in the story would enter the room. Neal Cassady, son of a hobo, a compulsive car thief and an occasional railway brakeman from Denver, turned up in New York, keen to meet Kerouac and his crew after hearing about them from Hal Chase, a mutual friend. Cassady's handsome gait and freewheeling personality brought a new spark to the Manhattan clique. Kerouac found his stories and style inspirational; Ginsberg was sexually drawn to this physically rapacious wanderer. By 1947, Kerouac and Cassady had embarked on the first of several of their journeys across North America which would form the basis for important sections of his later fiction, including *On the Road*. In 1948, while Kerouac was back in New York, Clellon Homes and he discussed the nature of the world and the relation of this band of young writers to it. Drawing on a term that Huncke had taught them – 'beat'[55] – the pair conceived themselves part of a Beat Generation, the phrase echoing, to an extent, the Lost Generation of the inter-war years. After this, the loosely gathered set of friends gradually began to describe themselves as members of the Beat Generation, although the appellation was quite casual in some ways and certain members never felt entirely comfortable with the name. Kerouac would see his first novel, *The Town and the City* – an epic family saga inspired by Thomas Wolfe – published in 1950 but it would be Clellon Holmes' book *Go*, which appeared two years later, that would be considered the first Beat novel, a recounting of some of the unorthodox adventures and philosophical attitudes of their literary crowd with many of the real participants present in the fiction, each in loosely veiled disguise. His article for the *New York Times* on 16 November 1952, entitled 'This is the Beat Generation', would spread the news of these new socio-literary developments to a wider public.

During these early years, Allen Ginsberg had continued to pen poetry, but verse of a more traditional kind. However, a number of matters would change his approach to his art. In 1948, he claimed the long dead English mystic William Blake had addressed him while in a quasi-hallucinatory state. This auditory visitation would be followed by a meeting with William Carlos Williams, an established poet from his home town of Paterson, whose style rejected the formal parameters of the poetic and, instead, described the world he saw in a more informal, almost conversational tone. He encouraged the younger poet to try this, too. As significantly, Ginsberg's involvement with Huncke and his criminal associates led to his arrest for holding stolen property in his home. Tried for this crime by implication, he was sentenced, in 1949, a stay in a psychiatric hospital in the hope that both his homosexual tendencies could be stemmed and his attraction to the underworld exorcised. While in hospital, Ginsberg would meet Carl Solomon, another inmate with literary talents, who would further inspire his creative cause.

Burroughs led an unsettled life in the late 1940s. He became involved with various business propositions, one with his common law wife Joan Vollmer, in

---

[55] Beat was defined in a number of ways. It was used to mean 'down and out, poor and exhausted' by jazz musicians such as Mezz Mezzrow, who also coined dead beat or beat-up. See Ann Charters (ed.), *The Penguin Book of the Beats* (London: Penguin, 1993), p. xvii. Ginsberg, interpreting hustler Herbert Huncke's street usage, said beat meant 'exhausted, at the bottom of the world, rejected by society, streetwise' (*ibid.*, p. xviii). Kerouac later stressed Beat's beatific, saint-like sense in his June 1959 essay 'The Origins of the Beat Generation' in *Playboy*. See: http://xroads.virginia.edu/~ug00/lambert/ontheroad/response.html [accessed 9 November 2012].

1947: a marijuana farm in the lost wilds of Texas. But the project was a conspicuous failure. In late 1949, they eventually headed to Mexico to avoid the attention of the law. But in 1951, in Mexico City, Burroughs, while attempting a drunken William Tell act with Vollmer and a spirit glass, shot his partner in the head. The killing had a devastating impact on Burroughs. Although he managed to escape the grip of the Mexican police authorities, he was deeply haunted by this accident in the years that followed. While he had written some fiction prior to this incident – a co-penned novel with Kerouac and some of the material which would appear much later as *Queer* (1985) – he has claimed that it was Vollmer's death that would be a crucial trigger to his life as a novelist. It would force him, he has said, to write his way out of the depression that befell him. In 1953, with Ginsberg's connections and support, he published his first novel *Junkie*, a pulp-like account based on his links to the drug and crime worlds.

For Kerouac the first half the 1950s saw him travel and write almost constantly. The relative failure of his debut work to make a mark had left him demoralised. Yet he was not undeterred as a novelist. In spring 1951, back in New York, he produced a manuscript in three weeks of round-the-clock typing, a fictionalised account inspired by his travels with Cassady at the end of the 1940s, that would form the basis for *On the Road*. But publisher interest was limited and it would be six years before a version of the text was issued. Ginsberg had a similar fallow period. He moved to California where he took a conventional job in the growing market research sector and even had relationships with women. In 1954, however, he met Peter Orlovsky, who would become his life partner, and commit himself to a homosexual route. The next year was more significant still when, on 7 October 1955, he gave a first pubic reading to a lengthy and hard-hitting poem called 'Howl'. The event, at the Six Gallery in San Francisco, was a key moment in the dissemination of the Beat project. Four other poets would take part, including Michael McClure and Gary Snyder,[56] each linked to the city's ongoing Poetry Renaissance, a revival that had been steered by the man who would MC at the event, Kenneth Rexroth. All readers at the gathering would also then secure an association with a West Coast expansion of the Beat idea. Vital to this was the poet-publisher Lawrence Ferlinghetti, whose bookshop City Lights had been founded in the city in 1953. Hearing Ginsberg recite at the gallery – an occasion that also saw Kerouac in the audience – he speedily invited the poet to publish the work in the Pocket Poets series he had launched. *Howl and Other Poems* would emerge in 1956. A year later it would face obscenity charges but the court threw out of the claims arguing the poem had redeeming social value. The

---

[56] Philip Whalen and Philip Lamantia would be the other contributors.

judicial proceedings would bring national and global publicity to the poem and widespread recognition of Ginsberg and his Beat fraternity.

In 1957 also, Kerouac would secure his major breakthrough, too, when *On the Road* appeared, gaining critical acclaim and enjoying a spell as a best-selling title. The success would open the door to publication of a string of manuscripts that had been in preparation for several years. *The Dharma Bums* (1958), a story based on Kerouac's friendship with Gary Snyder, an important Buddhist Beat, *The Subterraneans* (1958) and the poem cycle *Mexico City Blues* (1959) were notable arrivals. Burroughs meanwhile had left the US for North Africa and the liberal city of Tangiers. Drawn by the prospect of rent boys and severely drug-addicted, he nonetheless continued his writing efforts. When Kerouac, Ginsberg and Orlovsky visited him in 1957, they found his room littered with hundreds of sheets of typing, chaotically distributed. Ginsberg's energetic dedication saw the pages assembled in a presentable form and, in 1959, Burroughs' taboo-testing narrative, a parade of sexual perversity and rampant narcotic habit, was published in Paris as *The Naked Lunch*. By then, the author was living in the French capital at the so-called Beat Hotel,[57] with Ginsberg and Gregory Corso, a poet who had become part of the Beat community in 1951 after meeting Ginsberg, and who, in 1958, produced his own collections *Bomb* and *Gasoline*.

By the end of the 1950s, the leading triumvirate of Beat writers had shared their key works with the world. Yet the decade to follow would see them follow highly individual and, in some ways, conflicting tracks. Ginsberg, with Orlovsky, would spend the early 1960s travelling to countries and cultures quite different from their US experience, including territories that had been marked out of bounds to Americans – Cuba, the USSR and Eastern Europe – as the Cold War intensified. But the poet also visited South America and India in an odyssey that balanced spiritual questing with his more politically driven strivings. From the mid-1960s, however, he would bring his blend of Buddhist allegiance and commitment to social change to the fore, linking with the drug radicals such as Timothy Leary and Ken Kesey and the anti-Vietnam movement, to become one of the most prominent activists on the frontline of the American counterculture. Having published a tribute to his late mother in 'Kaddish' in 1961, Ginsberg would develop a long series of what he called 'auto-poesy' from 1965, sketches and phrases recorded on tape when he toured the US. Burroughs would leave Paris and head for London, one of the vibrant centres of the new cultural scene. But if his writing continued apace – book titles like *The Soft Machine* (1961), *The Ticket that Exploded* (1962) and *Nova Express* (1964) would appear during this period – and his interests in film

---

[57] The Beat Hotel was at 9, rue Git-le-Coeur, a basic rooming house on Paris' bohemian Left Bank. See Barry Miles, *The Beat Hotel: Ginsberg, Burroughs, and Corso in Paris, 1958–1963* (New York: Grove Press, 2000).

as a medium grew, he took little direct interest in the cultural revolution, broadly rejecting the pacific messages and spiritual content of the hippy insurgence and maintaining a low profile. Kerouac would also reject the counterculture's thrust, attacking its un-American values and regarding the introduction of a psychedelic drug like LSD to the US as a Communist plot to destabilise the nation's youth. He found the anti-war movement equally distasteful and criticised it in print and on television. He published fiction, too – *Big Sur* (1962), *Desolation Angels* (1965) and *The Vanity of Duluoz* (1968), for instance – but the flare of fame that had engulfed him at the end of the 1950s left him with deep psychological wounds. Turning increasingly to drink, he became a hermit-like figure, tied to his mother's hearth and ragingly conservative in his views, even upsetting Ginsberg with his anti-Semitic remarks. In 1969, aged 47, the ravages of drink led to organ failure and his death was recorded in St. Petersburg, Florida on 21 October.

Ginsberg and Burroughs would last much longer. By the early 1970s both were living in New York City again. Ginsberg remained a social activist, arguing fervently for causes that pursued peace and campaigns that supported sexual rights for gay men and women. Once the hippy flower had faded, Burroughs' more dystopian visions, now expressed more and more in a science fiction mode, chimed with the punk and new wave insurrection in popular music and the wider arts, and he was seen as a guiding light to many working in those areas. In 1974, Ginsberg would establish the Jack Kerouac School of Disembodied Poetics, attached to the Naropa Institute in Boulder, Colorado, where he, Burroughs and Corso[58] would all teach. Ginsberg and Burroughs would continue to write, to publish and to read, until their deaths within months of each other in 1997 – Ginsberg, aged 70, in New York on 5 April and Burroughs, aged 83, by now in Lawrence, Kansas on 2 August. By then, the Beat impulse had been throbbing for more than half a century and a major exhibition mounted in 1995–6, a couple of years before their passing, called *Beat Culture and the New America 1950–1965*, staged at the Whitney Museum of American Art in New York, then in Minneapolis and San Francisco, sent the clear message that this radical force in literature and the broader arts, even if it had never quite been incorporated into the cultural establishment, had left a deep and enduring impact on the US and global landscape, a thorn in the side of mainstream thinking and the complacencies of convention and a powerful thread in the changing of the nation's consciousness. There remain, still, debates about who or what the Beat Generation precisely was – which individuals require inclusion, who may be merely at the fringes of the core – but Bill Morgan has some useful reflections, citing the central importance of Ginsberg to our understandings and perception

---

[58] Gregory Corso, born in New York City in 1930, lived until 2001.

of this literary community. He explains: 'The history of the Beat Generation is really the story of [Ginsberg's] desire to gather a circle of friends around him, people he loved and could love him. What united these people most was not only a love of literature but also Ginsberg's supportive character, a trait that often verged on obsession. It was their friendship that they shared and not any one common literary style, philosophy or social theory.'[59]

What though has been the appeal of this gathering of writers to the rock musicians who have followed in their wake? It is, quite possibly, the over-arching ideas of the Beats, or maybe an idealised view of what they were and what they did, as much as the high quantity of actual literary work they produced, that have been most pervasive in shaping rock consciousness. Just as the Beats valorised jazz and its soloists in a manner that was frequently over-idealised, perhaps the rock generation have repeated that feat with the Beats, setting their artistic ancestors on a pedestal in a fawning, less than critical, manner. After all, for all their fascinating lives, their substantial legacy in words, the Beats were flawed individuals: some may have sought the status of saints or gurus or guides, at least, with admirable persistence, as Kerouac chased a beatification of sorts, Ginsberg tracked nirvana and Burroughs aimed his vitriolic attack on the power of authorities of all kinds. Yet their biographies are so often haunted by self-doubt, desperation, despair, fear of failure, even tragedy, as much as success, acclaim and self-actualisation. Their life narratives may read like a raging stream of thrills and excitement, factuality moulded into barely-disguised fiction. But, along the way, their picaresque tales were scored by the thorns of death, murder and manslaughter, addiction, obsession and frustration, terms in jail and spells in the asylum, lurking criminality often at the fringes and obscenity battles in the courts, unfulfilled sexualities and unhappy relationships with partners, and even large-scale fallings-out between many of the main players in this extended drama. Kerouac and Burroughs were early accessories to a gay murder by Lucien Carr; Ginsberg was incarcerated in a mental hospital after his links to a gang of thieves were exposed; Cassady was a regular prisoner and Corso had been locked up, too. Burroughs shot his common-law wife. Both he and Ginsberg had desired Cassady as a sexual ideal, but he spent a lifetime chasing women at the ultimate expense of his marriage to Carolyn. Kerouac rejected his only daughter for many years; Burroughs saw his own son die of drink-linked causes; Ginsberg's mother's mental health and early death had a powerful impact on his maturing worldview. Ginsberg and Burroughs faced the courts who wanted to ban their work – a mixed blessing when judicial attacks brought global publicity but also large personal stresses on them as artists. And none of this considers the

---

[59] Bill Morgan, *The Typewriter is Holy: The Complete, Uncensored History of the Beat Generation* (New York: Free Press, 2010), p. xvii.

dubious sexual pursuits of boy lovers by Burroughs nor the political opinions of Kerouac who, later in life, backed the war in Vietnam, adopted staunchly Republican positions and even anti-Jewish ones, a barbed riposte maybe to Ginsberg's leftist philosophies and enthusiastic participation in the hippy counterculture, as alcohol became his great crutch and creeping destroyer.

But what did this literary group convey which stirred the imagination of later performing and composing creatives? As we have suggested, the lure of travel, the notion of the open road, the sense of movement, moving on and heading for the next horizon, that permeates most forcefully the works of Kerouac, has provided popular music, and most often its rock fraternity, with an ethos, a model, to follow. Turner has dubbed Kerouac 'the James Dean of the typewriter'[60] while Miles refers to him as 'a cultural icon along with the young Marlon Brando, the young Elvis and James Dean'.[61] Central themes in many of his key works – from *On the Road* (1957) to *The Dharma Bums* (1958), *Lonesome Traveller* (1960) to *Desolation Angels* (1965) – are transience, impermanence and the prospect of fresh excitements. In Neal Cassady, Kerouac's Dean Moriarty in *On the Road* and Cody Pomeray in *Visions of Cody* (1973) and several others, there seems to be a living embodiment of Kerouac's vision: in Cassady's frenetic speech and impulsive style, the existential hero, avaricious in his sexual desire, is personified, caring only for gratuitous pleasure, the needs of now and, almost immediately after- wards, the forthcoming adventure. As Kerouac most famously states in *On the Road*: '[T]he only people for me are the mad ones, the ones who are mad to live, mad to talk, mad to be saved, desirous of everything at the same time, the ones who never yawn or say a commonplace thing, but burn, burn, burn like fabulous yellow roman candles exploding like spiders across the stars and in the middle you see the blue centrelight pop and everybody goes "Awww!"'[62] In Cassady, or at least in Moriarty, he appears to have found that explosive concoction.

We may argue that the theme of the road – a spine that dominates the Kerouac/ Cassady mythology or that of their fictional alter egos Sal Paradise and Moriarty – is powerfully sustained in the machismo legend that surrounds rock as a live medium: the tour, the travels from town to town, the brief and intense salvation of the stage and the post-gig availability perhaps of new and willing women, ravaged fleetingly, and then forgotten in a haze of adrenalin, alcohol and pills. No one would suggest that the code of the musician on the highway was created by Kerouac's stories alone but his central novel, *On the Road*, and much of his other writings intensified the hope, the dream, that the chance to move, the urge to go, would bring multiple experiences and many fresh, sensory opportunities. As Carr *et al.* comment: 'Kerouac's spiritual

---

[60] Steve Turner, 1996), p. 13.
[61] Barry Miles, *Jack Kerouac: King of the Beats* (London: Virgin, 1998), p. xii.
[62] Jack Kerouac, *On the Road* (London: Penguin, 1972), p. 11.

desperation crash-coursed him through Zen, Roman Catholicism, mysticism and hip. Drugs, sex and jazz fuelled the hot rod go-go-go prose style.'[63]

In Burroughs, rock perceives the terror and the thrill of narcotic experiment, the possibilities and the pitfalls. The creator of *The Naked Lunch* (1959) and *The Soft Machine* (1961) seems to prompt the extraordinary – and quite conceivably misleading – presumption that the drug user and abuser can manage, and therefore survive, his excesses. In that sense, he provides an example of survivor who has tasted most poisons, never apparently cowered from the challenge of chemical or organic disorientation and, by living to a grand age, virtually proved that indulgence and early death are not necessarily indivisible bedfellows. As Leland opines, in a view that stretches across the undercurrents of several ages and numerous countercultures and frames the dark appeal of this form of transgression, neatly if bleakly: 'Though most people take drugs for pleasure, hip clings more to the downside: the furtiveness of copping, the risk of harm, the compulsions of the addict.'[64] Bono comments that Burroughs 'was a great, walking bad example of doing junk and he lived to be 84'.[65] Yet this novelist is much more than a mere receptacle for artificial stimulation who endured a life-long toxic storm: he is also a fervent anti-authoritarian, an enemy of systems of control – whether the state, the law or the church – and is thus a committed, if hardly conventional, libertarian. His interest in radical art and experiment is also particularly notable and his literary innovations, from the cut-up to the fold-in, mark him as one of the true ground-breakers in late twentieth-century literature and the wider arts.

In 1962, fellow writer Norman Mailer said: 'Burroughs is the only American novelist living today who may conceivably be possessed by genius.'[66] Caveney claims that 'no writer has proved as eclectic as Burroughs in his influence on pop, leaving his mark on a whole range of movements from punk to techno, hip hop to grunge',[67] while Miles comments: '[H]is ideas, images and language have reached the general population by non-literary means: through films, videos, records and tapes or through artworks by the many artists who have been influenced by his images and ideas.'[68]

Ginsberg may be regarded as the radical politico, as interested in broader social causes as his own personal ambition, but also as a sexual pioneer, libertine and

---

[63] Roy Carr, Brian Case and Fred Dellar, *The Hip*, p. 105.

[64] John Leland, *Hip: The History* (New York: Ecco, 2004), p. 262.

[65] Quoted in Tommy Udo, 'He was a great advertisement for doing everything you shouldn't do', *New Musical Express*, 16 August 1997.

[66] Jed Birmingham, 'William Burroughs and Norman Mailer', 14 October 2009, Reality Studio, http://realitystu.dio.org/bibliographic-bunker/william-burroughs-and-norman-mailer/ [accessed 16 October 2011].

[67] Graham Caveney, *The 'Priest', They Call Him: The Life and Legacy of William S. Burroughs* (London: Bloomsbury, 1997), p. 189.

[68] Barry Miles, *William Burroughs: El Hombre Invisible* (London: Virgin, 1993), p. 5.

even exhibitionist. Said Mikal Gilmore in his 1997 obituary: 'Allen Ginsberg not only made history – by writing poems that jarred America's consciousness and by insuring that the 1950s Beat movement would be remembered as a considerable force – but he also lived through and embodied some of the most remarkable cultural mutations of the last half-century.'[69] He may have been a campaigning homosexual – his signature poem 'Howl' (1956) was, in part, a premature gay *cri de coeur* – but, in his own declamatory way, in his bold public persona, he helped to open up a door to the wider sexual revolution of the 1960s – even that one eventually enjoyed by the heterosexual population, too – by raising questions about issues of libido and repression and liberty in the decade before, when it was not just a rebellious gesture to explore such topics, but actually an act of inherent danger to the individual, in an era when the US state was determined to homogenise the thinking of its populace and excise the dangers of leftist insurgence. We might also point to his 'auto-poesy', which emerged after 1965, like those examples in *The Fall of America: Poems of These States 1965–1971* (1973), many of which are travelogues akin, in some ways, to Kerouac's, records of energetic odysseys, but fragmentary, picaresque and kaleidoscopic. Adds Gilmore: 'As much as Presley, as much as the Beatles, Bob Dylan or the Sex Pistols, Allen Ginsberg helped set loose something wonderful, risky and unyielding in the psyche and dreams of our times. Perhaps only Martin Luther King Jr.'s brave and costly quest had a more genuinely liberating impact upon the realities of modern history, upon the freeing up of people and voices that much of established society wanted kept at the margins.'[70] This did not please all and certainly not even those in his closest circle. Kerouac, he said, was 'mad at me for working in relation to the political scene' because he thought that 'was a betrayal or a diversion or a complete divagation from what he had in mind and what I had in mind' which was 'the attempt to open up the heart'.[71] Ginsberg's determined course damaged the friendship but did not deflect him from the wider project on which he had embarked. For other would-be movers and shakers, the poet had sparked intense dreams of possible transformation beyond the literary sphere: 'Howl' would trigger hope and intent in the hearts and heads of a wave of younger artists. Diane di Prima felt that Ginsberg and 'Howl' 'could only be the vanguard of a much larger thing. All the people who, like me, had hidden and skulked, writing down what they knew for a small handful of friends…all these would now step forward and say their piece'.[72]

---

[69] Mikal Gilmore, 'Allen Ginsberg, 1926–1997', *The Rolling Stone Book of the Beats: The Beat Generation and the Counterculture*, edited by Holly George-Warren (London: Bloomsbury, 1999), pp. 227–40 (p. 228).

[70] Gilmore, *ibid.*

[71] Ginsberg quoted in Sukenick, 1987, pp. 81–2.

[72] Quoted in Sukenick, 1987, p. 94.

Future Fug Ed Sanders spent 50¢ on Ginsberg's book, and purchased two issues of *Evergreen Review*. 'I absorbed all that information and, you know, that was it. My life changed overnight.'[73] His collaborator-in-waiting, Tuli Kupferberg, was similarly awakened by the poem's astringent manifesto. 'It was political and it was personal and it seemed to free the forms up. It was certainly what was needed at the time. It really came as a great cleansing shower, something that opened up everything again.'[74]

Yet there are various other Beat threads, too, that would feed into the history that follows – from the Buddhist affiliations of Kerouac, Ginsberg and Gary Snyder; interests in the ecology exemplified by Snyder and Michael McClure; the DIY enterprise of publishers of books and journals, characterised most prominently by Lawrence Ferlinghetti and City Lights, but also in the many poetry magazines produced by Leroi Jones, Hettie Jones, Diane di Prima and others, representing entrepreneurial action outside the commercial mainstream; and the black radicalism of Leroi Jones, assuming the name Amiri Baraka in 1965, and essentially abandoning his Beat associations for the African-American struggle.

But if we are painting a portrait of the essence of Beat and its sustaining injection to the succeeding rock culture, it is hard not to home in on factors other than the literary or the political or the spiritual. For it is surely in its taboo-breaking, its rule bending and its risk-taking, that Beat provides a model of engagement to so many of rock 'n' roll's protagonists. As Leland comments:

> One indisputable fact about the Beats is that they were a divisive force, and however benign or inoffensive the language they wrapped around themselves, the truth – 'Go fuck yourself with your atom bomb'[75] – was more exciting, more threatening and more commercially viable. Through their writings, often about themselves, they promulgated the hip promise that society's margins held more of its life than the mainstream. They were the circus that some children ran away to join, others wished they had the nerve, and even more parents feared lest their children run next. Dislodging themselves from the complacency of the Eisenhower era, the Beats indulged in the horror, sadism, sexuality or unbridled irresponsibility that lay just outside the average Joe's grasp.[76]

Turner has already emphasised the fact that whatever rock's principal cast members played out in the decades from the 1960s onwards, the Beats had

---

[73] *Ibid.*, p. 95.
[74] *Ibid.*, p. 96.
[75] From Allen Ginsberg, 'America', *Collected Poems, 1947–1997* (London: Penguin, 2009), pp. 154–6 (p. 154).
[76] Leland, 2004, p. 148.

already experienced. So it is perhaps that draw of transgression that holds the most magnetic pull. The social forces that had held the West in a particular grip for several hundred years – those controlling monoliths of church and state, the power of the law and the persuasive threat of social ostracism generated by family or peers or community – were challenged in a particularly direct fashion during those post-Second World War years and the Beats were a concentrated, and articulate, embodiment of that challenge. Society's failings, its horrifically self-destructive tendencies, its ethnic intolerances, had all been exposed by the terrors of global conflict, by the horrifying emblems of industrial-scale genocide and the utter devastation of great cities obliterated by unfettered application of irresistible technologies on unarmed civilians. The Beats were keen to take on these injustices but they also believed that in the liberation of self – through life and art – that there were other ways to test the frayed fabric of a civilisation in crisis. Says Bill Morgan:

> The Beats of the forties and fifties were the catalysts who precipitated the more widespread social rebellion of the sixties and seventies. As a small group of kindred spirits determined to practise absolute personal freedom within a society governed by stifling conservative attitudes, they set an example embraced by the next generation. The period of general upheaval we call 'the sixties' might well have taken place without the Beat Generation, but it would have certainly had a different flavour and moved at a different pace. When the Beats broke free from the status quo in life and art, they set the stage for the future.[77]

Rock itself would, in time, take on some of the major issues of the day, harnessing its phenomenal power to call for peace at Woodstock in 1969, place the flood victims of Bangla Desh in the spotlight in 1971, back anti-racist policies through vehicles like Rock Against Racism in the later 1970s, bring environmental concerns to the fore by questioning the credibility of nuclear strategies through agencies like MUSE[78] in 1979, drag the obscenity of world hunger up the diplomatic agenda via events such as Live Aid in 1985, help bring down the apartheid regime in South Africa via records and concerts during the 1980s, draw attention to issues of social injustice in territories like Tibet in the 1990s and contest the morality of the war in Iraq in the 2000s, for instance. In that sense, we might see a continuing narrative between the political consciousness of the Beats and the campaigning

---

[77] Bill Morgan, 2010, p. 247.
[78] Musicians United for Safe Energy (MUSE) was formed by musicians Graham Nash, Jackson Browne, Bonnie Raitt and others, in part as a response to the nuclear accident at Three Mile Island at Harrisburg, Pennsylvania in March of that year.

sensibility that rock would occasionally, and often with great impact, display over several decades.

Yet to reiterate, I do believe that it was rather the power that the Beats granted to the individual that was most important to the flame of rock 'n' roll: that power to choose a course that was not mapped out, petrified even, by the oppressive certainties of power, class, race, gender and sex, those certainties that had ossified society and drained the freedom of choice for men and women to plot a route that was unconventional, unexpected or resistant to the norm. As Pountain and Robins emphasise: 'The Beats regarded jobs, families, security, indeed any form of deferred gratification as dull and conformist. They opted out of work and civic duties to pursue immediate pleasures, claiming to be chasing a higher truth through oriental philosophies and experimentation with mind-expanding drugs.'[79] If that behaviour was indeed what we could characterise as transgression, then it was such an ideological inflection the Beats helped to bring to generations who followed in their wake. Whether it was the music-makers themselves or their subcultural followers – the hippies or the punks, the goths or the b-boys, the followers of grunge or the ravers – it was this sense of opportunity, of possibility, a freeing of the imagination, a releasing of the spirit – which, if it meant transgressing social codes or deviating from legal rules, then so be it – that the Beats most effectively passed on as their legacy. They gave permission to those who followed to step outside the confines of restriction and limited expectation and extend their scope of personal, artistic and creative aspiration. It is on that principal notion, I would assert, that the connection between Beat ideas and rock expressions most convincingly rests. But such a claim has strong hints of the impressionistic about it. How can we substantiate and demonstrate these links?

iii) Beat and rock: A survey of association

If we are to go looking for more specific evidence of rock's engagement with Beat, or Beat's engagement with rock indeed, what are the signs that might help us to establish that such connections exist? These signs may appear in a variety of forms: there may be actual artistic evidence of association on recordings or in collaborative performances; there may be examples of social interaction or informal mixing; or there could be fragments of information garnered from a range of other media sources – interviews, for instance, in

---

[79] Dick Pountain and David Robins, *Cool Rules: Anatomy of an Attitude* (London: Reaktion Books, 2000), p. 67.

which writers or musicians are mentioned as friends or influences, on-stage comments, videos or photographs. There may be references to Beat writers in songs; there may be references to rock artists in Beat poetry or prose. Further, there may be actual recorded tributes to the writers, celebrating their literary work in a musical setting. In this section I would like to explore some examples of the kind of evidence that could help us make these assessments and then proceed to offer an overview of some of the instances in which Beat and rock have joined hands in various complementary fashions. Let us initially use brief examples below, a number of which will be explored more fully in the chapters that follow.

Bob Dylan's connection to the Beats may be evidenced in a variety of ways: his autobiographical statements that he read work by these writers from the end of the 1950s; via information gleaned from biographical accounts and the informants who feed into those histories; from the social contacts he forged during the 1960s, with particular reference to his meeting with Allen Ginsberg in 1963 and his attendance at the Last Gathering of the Beats in 1965; and Dylan's contribution to various Ginsberg recordings in the 1970s and 1980s. This is before we even consider the work that Dylan produced himself – at first centred on the traditional folk repertoire with some self-penned compositions in the style of his heroes like Woody Guthrie, then followed from 1963 by song-writing that was more political, and then, from 1965, by recordings that were more personal, poetic and even abstract, a mode which sees the artist leave behind the historical past and the political present to produce songs that no longer confront an everyday realism but begin to deal in more obscure lyrical avenues of the psychological and the unconscious, a major step away from the narrative accounts of folk and the romantic concerns of the popular song. Ginsberg's simultaneous physical presence as these shifts occur – in the short film accompanying 'Subterranean Homesick Blues', at the filmed San Francisco press conference in December 1965, and in the movie *Don't Look Back* – can hardly be discounted. Nor can we ignore the apparent, and regular, reference to Kerouac's titles – such as *Desolation Angels* and *Visions of Gerard* – in Dylan's output – 'Desolation Row', and 'Visions of Johanna', for example – in the performer's key work of this mid-1960s period. In addition, Dylan's own ambitions as a novelist, perhaps in the cut-up mode of Burroughs, are revealed when he belatedly issues his fictional work *Tarantula* in 1971.

Ginsberg's presence at various important junctures we have already mentioned but we might add further relevant fragments to this picture. The new poems he develops after 1965 when Dylan buys the poet an expensive tape recorder, allowing him to gather this thoughts on the move; the various references he makes to Dylan in his poems after the mid-1960s; his inclusion on the major Dylan tour, the Rolling Thunder Revue,[80] from 1975–6 and, most particularly, when the poet joins the singer at the grave of Kerouac in Lowell, Massachusetts. There, the pair pay homage to the novelist in poetry and song, a scene that appears in the movie record of the tour *Renaldo and Clara* (1978). Let us also mention Ginsberg's appearance in Martin Scorsese's *No Direction Home* (2005) when the poet is a central witness to the songwriter's life and impact and, finally, the tribute that Dylan pays from the stage to Ginsberg shortly after his death in 1997.

As for the Beats and the Beatles, we have strong suggestions that the group adopted the very spelling of their name as a result of a conversation between John Lennon and Liverpool Beat poet Royston Ellis. Before then, Lennon had produced a satirical newspaper in school titled *The Daily Howl*. The group would not meet Ginsberg until May 1965, after a Dylan concert at the Albert Hall, but Paul McCartney would quickly become a friend of the poet. Not only would Ginsberg visit the singer's home in London, but by the later 1960s, McCartney, Ginsberg and their mutual associate Barry Miles had also agreed to create a spoken word record label called Zapple, a project echoing, and under the auspices of, the Beatles' new record label Apple. In the mid-decade, too, with William Burroughs now living in London, McCartney was helpful to the writer and his associates who had various recording projects they hoped to develop at the time. As for Lennon, the songwriter would include Ginsberg in the chorus of his great anti-war anthem, 'Give Peace a Chance', in 1969 and, as the early 1970s unfolded and Lennon moved to New York, Ginsberg's home city, the two would meet on a number of occasions as their various political concerns, particularly in relation to the on-going Vietnam War, coincided. But Ginsberg would also be a Lennon ally as the Beatle fought to gain a Green Card and permit him to stay in the US as the very real threat of deportation hung over him. In the mid-1990s, McCartney joined Ginsberg on one of his last recording ventures. 'The Ballad of the Skeletons' would include the Beatle on guitar, and musical contributions from Patti Smith Group member Lenny Kaye and composer Philip Glass.

As for Ginsberg's interest in the Beatles, it seems plain that he was caught up in the same musical excitement that gripped the world from 1964 but desired a taste of it that went beyond merely hearing their records; he craved a first-hand experience of what had created this extraordinary phenomenon. Not only did Ginsberg become an early convert to their sound, once Beatlemania had spread like wildfire across the US, he was also sufficiently interested in the band's background to visit their home city of Liverpool in 1965. His engagement with

---

[80] Sukenick writes: 'Some of Ginsberg's friends say that in some ways he always wanted to be a rock star [...] Once he told me with a sense of awe that he's recently read a poem to twenty – or was it forty? – thousand people. Anne Waldman says it was with the Rolling Thunder Revue, and Bob Dylan let him read to the outdoor crowd because it was raining' (1987, p. 82).

the Mersey poets and musicians and his celebrated praise of the city, dubbing it 'at the present moment the centre of the consciousness of the human universe'[81] were clear evidence of the poet's excitement at this regional cultural eruption. While the Beatles had well and truly put Merseyside on the global map by this time, Ginsberg's appearance in person in the city was not an insignificant factor in drawing attention to Liverpool's other creative voices such as Adrian Henri, Roger McGough and Brian Patten, Beat-linked Britons, whose anthology *The Mersey Sound* would create a huge new – and young – readership for contemporary poetry when it was published in 1967. Very shortly after his Mersey sojourn, Ginsberg would appear at the International Poetry Incarnation at the Albert Hall in London, in June 1965, when more than 7,000 attended a reading also featuring Gregory Corso, Lawrence Ferlinghetti and a number of new British poetry voices such as Michael Horovitz, Adrian Mitchell, Spike Hawkins and Pete Brown, an event often considered the birthing pool of the UK underground.

So the case for Ginsberg's connection to the rock scene and the countercultural flow, even if we only outline his links to Dylan and the Beatles, the two major acts, after all, to come to the fore in the mid-1960s, is hard to dispute. Nor can we dismiss the proactive efforts of the singer and the group to trigger and strengthen their links with the poet over many years. Ginsberg's death prompted tributes from both rock critics and artists. Gilmore believed that '"Howl" was one of the most incandescent events in post-World War II literary history or popular culture, and its arrival later insured the Beats their place on the map of modern time'.[82] Yoko Ono added that Ginsberg 'was intelligent in a way that influenced a whole generation'.[83] Bono commented: 'Allen was extraordinary. There's a much more minimal style, sort of post-[Raymond] Carver sense for literature right now. But that drunk language still survives. If you think about it, the headiness of the Sixties and the dizziness of it all, I think his position is safe.'[84]

We might also point to some of the tributes that have been paid to Ginsberg by artists as diverse as They Might Be Giants – their 1994 song 'I Should Be Allowed to Think' refers to 'Howl' and gently lampoons it; Rage Against the Machine, whose live version of the poem 'Hadda be Playing on the Jukebox' formed part of the CD single 'Bulls on Parade' in 1996; Patti Smith and her 1997 work 'Spell' is based on 'Footnote to Howl'; and Black Rebel Motorcycle Club's 'Howl', from the 2005 album of the same name, considered to be a reference to both the Beat

---

[81] Allen Ginsberg quoted in Edward Lucie-Smith (ed.), *The Liverpool Scene* (London: Donald Carroll, 1967), p. 15.

[82] Mikal Gilmore, 'Allen Ginsberg: 1926–1997', obituary, *The Rolling Stone Book of the Beats: The Beat Generation and the Counterculture*, 1999, pp. 227–40 (pp. 233–5).

[83] Yoko Ono, 'Memories of Allen', *The Rolling Stone Book of the Beats*, pp. 275–83 (p. 278).

[84] Bono, *ibid.*, p. 276.

Generation and their home city of San Francisco, where the poem was first presented. So, these are useful examples of Ginsberg's presence in this muso-literary setting. But in what other ways can we pinpoint this intersection and this interaction? How else did Beat touch rock and how did rock impact on Beat?

While Kerouac was distanced from many of the social transformations that arose in the last decade of his life – he would die in 1969 – and was actually highly critical of the countercultural forces of the 1960s which he regarded as fundamentally anti-American, his personal position had little effect on his status as iconic hero for that immediate rock generation and subsequent ones beside. Lester Bangs wrote on his passing: 'Jack was in so many ways a spiritual father of us all, as much as Lenny Bruce or Dylan [...] He was among the first artists to broadcast to the world this new sensibility aborning these last two decades, a sensibility that first began to take shape about the time many of us were born.'[85] He adds: 'The first hipsters were a far cry from the affected zombielike "cool" stance that came to predominate later. Like the best aspects of the Sixties' hip movement and Kerouac himself, they represented the apotheosis of American individualism and rascally exuberance ...'[86]

Kerouac would become the subject of many dozens of namings in songs, that would follow his demise, by artists spanning many rock genres – from Willie Alexander and the Boom Boom Band's 'Kerouac' (1976) to Tom Waits' 'Jack & Neal' (1977), King Crimson's 'Neal and Jack and Me' (1982) to the Blue Oyster Cult's 'Burnin' for You' (1982), Graham Parker's 'Sounds Like Chains' (1983) to the Smiths' 'Pretty Girls Make Graves' (1984), 10,000 Maniacs' 'Hey Jack Kerouac' (1987) to Steve Earle's 'The Other Kind' (1990), Weezer's 'Holiday' (1994) to Guided by Voices' 'Kerouac Never Drove, So He Never Drove Alone' (2002), the Go-Betweens' 'The House that Jack Built' (2004) to Sage Francis' 'Escape Artist' (2005), the Hold Steady's 'Stuck Between Stations' (2006) to Frank Turner's 'Poetry and the Deed' (2009), to name only a small selection. In addition, Kerouac's travelling companion Neal Cassady has also made many appearances including in songs by the Grateful Dead, the Washington Squares, Fatboy Slim and the Maple State.

Yet the most concentrated tributes arise in two albums which appeared in the late 1990s. *Kerouac: Kicks Joy Darkness* from 1997 was a wide-ranging homage to the writer in words and music and gathered a major line-up of singers who wished to pay tribute to his life and work. Two years later, *Jack Kerouac Reads On the Road,* had a different context and a contrasting texture, featuring much more of Kerouac's own voice as reader and singer, but did contain significant new work by jazz composer and arranger David Amram – settings of the novelist's

[85] Lester Bangs, 'Elegy for a Desolation Angel', *The Rolling Stone Book of the Beats: The Beat Generation and the Counterculture*, pp. 140–3 (p. 140).
[86] *Ibid.*, pp. 140–2.

re-discovered poems – and by long-time Kerouac follower Tom Waits who, joined by Californian funk rock band Primus, provided his own version of a Kerouac song, named in honour of his breakthrough novel, 'On the Road'.

Yet it was *Kicks Joy Darkness*, taking its adapted title from Kerouac's oft-quoted *On the Road* passage, 'At lilac evening I walked with every muscle aching among the lights of 27th and Welton in the Denver coloured section, wishing I were a Negro, feeling that the best the white world had offered was not enough ecstasy for me, not enough life, joy, kicks, darkness, music, not enough night',[87] that would provide the most engaging and multi-faceted survey of the writer's output, re-interpreted by singers and bands operating in many different rock modes – indie bands, grunge artists, dance acts, folk performers, hippies, punks and new wavers among them – a clear reflection of the way that Kerouac, and Beat writers more generally, have been able to cut across the divisions that have so often separated singers and bands by genre and subculture in the popular music world. The appeal of these writers appears to have transcended the historical rock camps, which have been regularly seen to be in competition or in binary opposition, for example, the hippies and the punks.

Among those who participated in the project, produced by Jim Sampas with Sonic Youth's Lee Ranaldo as associate producer, were Michael Stipe of REM, Eddie Vedder of Pearl Jam, Steven Tyler of Aerosmith, Joe Strummer of the Clash, the Velvet Underground's John Cale, Rob Buck of 10,000 Maniacs, Thurston Moore of Sonic Youth, the group Morphine and Patti Smith. They were further joined by actors Johnny Depp and Matt Dillon, comic Richard Lewis, Grateful Dead lyricist Robert Hunter, the writer Hunter S. Thompson, Lydia Lunch, Lenny Kaye, Warren Zevon, Jeff Buckley, Juliana Hatfield and surviving Beat originals Allen Ginsberg, William Burroughs and Lawrence Ferlinghetti. The album release appeared also in a double CD version in Japan, adding four pieces to the original set, with acid jazz act UFO (United Future Organization) and Graham Parker joining the line-up in the expanded edition.

Commenting on the collection, Robert Elliot Fox says: 'There are twenty-five tracks in all, and all of them are interesting, although they inevitably vary in importance and effectiveness of presentation.'[88] He adds, however, that 'while the associated music on *Kicks Joy Darkness* often does provide an interesting counterpoint to the spoken text, there are times when the music overwhelms the words or distracts us unnecessarily from the tonalities of voice as an instrument in itself. This is true, for example, where Kerouac is reading from "MacDougal

---

[87] Jack Kerouac, *On the Road*, p. 169.
[88] Robert Elliot Fox, 'Review essay: *Kerouac: Kicks Joy Darkness*', *Postmodern Culture*, Vol. 7, No. 3, 1997, sourced at http://muse.jhu.edu/journals/postmodern_culture/v007/7.3r_fox.html [accessed 2 January, 2011].

Street Blues". The dubbed-in rock music by Joe Strummer of the British band the Clash doesn't add anything to the performance and in fact makes it harder to hear what Kerouac is doing vocally; at the very least, the instrumental track should have been less prominent in the mix. For a much more successful amalgamation, compare the way Aerosmith singer Steven Tyler's background vocal is handled on his reading of "Dream: 'Us kids swim off a gray pier'", or how Kerouac quietly scats in the background while Grateful Dead lyricist Robert Hunter reads from *Visions of Cody*.'[89]

More recently, there have been film projects that have seen artists engaged to write music for Kerouac-centred productions. In 2009, Jay Farrar, formerly of Uncle Tupelo and Son Volt, and Ben Gibbard of Death Cab for Cutie combined to create and perform the accompanying soundtrack to the documentary *One Fast Move or I'm Gone: Kerouac's Big Sur*. The film, which was released to coincide with the fortieth anniversary of Kerouac's death, featured an ingredient that was unusual. While Gibbard and Farrar devised a score that drew heavily on indie rock and alt.country, the lyrics they utilised were drawn verbatim from Kerouac's own 1962 novel *Big Sur*. Gibbard has had a long-standing attraction to Kerouac's work and Death Cab for Cutie have included songs referencing the writer on earlier albums. 'Lowell, MA' and 'Title Track' from the band's 2000 album *We Have the Facts and We're Voting Yes* and 'Bixby Canyon Bridge' from the 2008 album *Narrow Stairs* provide examples of this interest.

William Burroughs' work has been the fertile source of band names – the Mugwumps, Soft Machine, Steely Dan and the Nova Mob among them – not to mention one of rock's most enduring and prolific genres – heavy metal – a phrase that first appeared in *The Soft Machine* in 1962, the reference linked to the character Uranian Willy dubbed 'the Heavy Metal Kid'. The phrase 'heavy metal thunder' would later appear in one of the decade's climactic rock anthems, Steppenwolf's 'Born to Be Wild', a song that would feature most famously in the soundtrack to the movie *Easy Rider* (1969). In addition, Burroughs' creative techniques based on the cut-up, an approach developed from the end of the 1950s with Brion Gysin, has had its own impact on rock music. He has also collaborated with a number of key artists. Yet his interest in the 1960s counterculture was severely restricted and he found no affection for the peace and love messages of the hippies. Nonetheless, by the early 1970s, he had made a connection with David Bowie, a novel and outrageous musical icon whose ambiguous gender play and theatrical showmanship had caught headlines on both sides of the Atlantic. Bowie had passed through several incarnations over the previous few years – London mod and electric folkie included – before shaping an act that combined kitsch glamour, indeterminate

---

[89] *Ibid.*

sexuality and abrasively energetic rock 'n' roll, an Anglicised take on the Manhattan posturings of Warhol's Factory and the Velvet Underground.

In 1973, Burroughs met Bowie in London for a conversation that would form the core of a feature article in *Rolling Stone* in February 1974.[90] The singer's career was at its acclaimed height as the album *The Rise and Fall of Ziggy Stardust and the Spiders from Mars* (1972) and its stage incarnation caused a major stir. Furthermore, as he shared in this exchange with Burroughs, the rock singer had forthcoming projects in mind including an adaptation of George Orwell's novel *Nineteen Eighty-Four*. Although the latter production did not eventually proceed under that name, *Diamond Dogs* (1974) would present some of the novel's themes but place them in a post-apocalyptic, glam rock-illuminated world. More significant here though was Bowie's move towards a cut-up approach to his lyric construction, a clear nod to Burroughs. Bowie acknowledges in Buckley that he was 'heavily into the whole idea of Brion Gysin/William Burroughs "cut-ups"',[91] and the same biographer states: 'Burroughs would provide a resonant paradigm for Bowie. His books were nightmarish visions of a society populated by desensitised mental and physical cripples – his was the world of drug addicts, criminals and sexual "deviants" [...] What Burroughs did was to try and incorporate a different realm of experience, the experience of low-life culture, into the mainstream.'[92]

As for Burroughs' own creativity of this period, the decade would see him working on a series of dystopian stories that may have been the antithesis of the hippies' peace and love programme but nonetheless chimed much more closely with the more menacing and pessimistic mood of the punk, post-punk and new wave eras and he has been dubbed, in some circles, the Godfather of Punk. His return to New York City from London in 1974 coincided with the emergence of new, energetic and frequently transgressive musical styles which would soon hatch the much-hailed punk sounds of CBGBs. In fact, Burroughs' science fiction that followed in the early 1980s, including a trilogy that begins with *Cities of the Red Night* (1981) and continues with *The Place of Dead Roads* (1983) and *The Western Lands* (1987), is credited as one of the inspirations of a new sci-fi form called cyberpunk which blended futuristic tale-telling, hi-tech components and elements of punk, pulp and noir, with William Gibson and Bruce Sterling among the style's prime creators.

The novelist's re-location to his once familiar New York City, after years of movement between Europe and North Africa, was greeted with particular joy by

---

[90] See Craig Copetas, 'Beat godfather meets glitter mainman: Burroughs and David Bowie', *The Rolling Stone Book of the Beats: The Beat Generation and the Counterculture*, edited by Holly George-Warren (London: Bloomsbury, 1999), pp. 193–202.

[91] David Buckley, *Strange Fascination: David Bowie – The Definitive Story* (London: Virgin, 2005), p. 24.

[92] *Ibid.*, p. 184.

Patti Smith and she shared her pleasure directly from the stage of the St. Mark's Poetry Project during a performance. Smith was a prime mover in the nascent punk and rock poetry scene and she would befriend Burroughs. Although he appeared to have little genuine interest in rock music, he was taken by its cultural power and as a social phenomenon. His New York return had seen him engaged as a monthly columnist with the noted popular music magazine of the day *Crawdaddy* and one of his 1975 contributions was a celebrated interview with Led Zeppelin guitarist Jimmy Page.

In 1978, the Nova Convention, presented at various locations in New York, would place Burroughs in the context of the cutting-edge art of the day and its growing relation to rock culture. The event was a celebration over several days, from 30 November to 2 December, of the novelist, his work and ideas and an impressive gallery of serious musical artists would participate in the venture. Poet John Giorno and Burroughs' assistant James Grauerholz played a part in conceiving the homage. Ted Morgan says that they saw the occasion as 'a gathering of the counterculture tribe which would enshrine Burroughs as its leader'.[93] Among those who attended and contributed were Patti Smith and Frank Zappa – who had replaced the legally entangled Keith Richards – Ed Sanders of the Fugs, Allen Ginsberg, Peter Orlovsky and Brion Gysin, composers Philip Glass and John Cage, poets Anne Waldman and Giorno himself, novelist and new journalist Terry Southern, LSD guru Timothy Leary and performance artist Laurie Anderson.[94]

A British rock musician and radical artist called Genesis P-Orridge, whose background combined agit-prop theatre, installation art and Situationist happenings, not to mention the explosion of punk, would develop his connection with Burroughs in the 1980s, although the pair had been in conversation in the past through mailart, a network of communication that had originally been engineered by the New York art collective Fluxus in the late 1960s. P-Orridge's interest in the cut-up as a principle of art-making had made Burroughs a natural mentor and ally. In 1980, the death of the writer's associate Antony Balch led to strong likelihood that important Burroughs films in his care would be removed from his London office and simply thrown away. Brion Gysin, in Paris at the time, urgently contacted P-Orridge asked him to physically salvage the rare archive and thus he became, at Gysin and Burroughs' request, its custodian.[95] P-Orridge had

---

[93] Ted Morgan, *Literary Outlaw: The Life and Times of William S. Burroughs* (London: Bodley Head, 1991), p. 547.

[94] A double-album recording of the event was released by Giorno Poetry Systems in 1979. See: http://globalia.net/donlope/fz/related/The_Nova_Convention.html and visit 'The Dial-A-Poem Poets: The Nova Convention', http://www.ubu.com/sound/nova.html [accessed 30 January 2012].

[95] See Genesis P-Orridge, '"Thee Films": An account by Genesis P-Orridge', *Naked Lens: Beat Cinema* edited by Jack Sargeant (London: Creation, 1997), pp. 184–96 (p. 187).

made his reputation with the two rock bands he founded and led – Throbbing Gristle and Psychic TV – although his UK notoriety rested on a 1976 exhibition at the ICA (the capital's Institute of Contemporary Arts) when he and his then partner Cosey Fanni Tutti had presented a multi-media event called *Prostitution*. In 1982, P-Orridge brought Burroughs to the UK on a reading tour called the Final Academy. This event would underpin their friendship and bands linked to the P-Orridge circle, like Ministry and Coil, would collaborate with Burroughs during this period. The 1990s would see Burroughs further engaged with the rock world and with artists and bands who were regarded as some of the most significant of the day. Kurt Cobain, whose band Nirvana had become the leaders of the Seattle-centred grunge movement, would join forces with the novelist on a recording. Released in 1992, 'The "Priest" They Called Him' married a reading by Burroughs of a short story and an excoriating guitar response by Cobain. To Burroughs' low key rendition of a section of his novel *Exterminator!*, in which the 'priest' of the title, an un-named addict seeks to score heroin on Christmas Eve, the Nirvana frontman shaped a dissonant feedback-drenched riposte based on 'Silent Night' and 'To Anacreon in Heaven'. Although the spoken and musical tracks were laid down separately, Burroughs and Cobain did meet later. In 1993 Cobain would invite Burroughs to feature in a video the band were making as a tie-in to 'Heart-Shaped Box' but the writer resisted the guitarist's request to join the cast. Says Charles R. Cross: '[E]xactly what Kurt hoped to achieve by casting the writer was never clear: In his attempt to convince Burroughs to participate, he had offered to obscure the writer's face, so that no one other than Kurt would know of his cameo. Burroughs declined the invitation.'[96] Cobain's heroin-scarred life was ended when he shot himself in 1994.

In 1991, U2 began their Zoo TV tour, a highly ambitious, multi-media production that would promote their new album *Achtung Baby* and continue on its global trek until 1993. The project was about more than merely showcasing new, recorded product. Zoo TV was a deconstruction, a satire, of the mass media in its many forms. Burroughs was invited to contribute, and his reading, on film, of his acerbic lampoon of 'Thanksgiving Prayer', formed an integral part of a televised version of the in-concert presentation in 1992, screened at Thanksgiving time that year. He would later make a fleeting appearance in another U2 concept, the video which accompanied their 'Last Night on Earth' single in 1997, shortly before his death.

In his obituary in *New Musical Express*, Stephen Dalton said that Burroughs was 'one of the most revolutionary writers of the century, whose influence spread through

---

[96] Charles R. Cross, *Heavier than Heaven: The Biography of Kurt Cobain* (London: Sceptre, 2002), p. 271.

rock 'n' roll from Lou Reed to Joy Division to Kurt Cobain'.[97] Lewis MacAdams believed he 'came to embody a Luciferian spirit to generations of musicians from Lou Reed to David Bowie to Patti Smith to Trent Reznor'.[98] Bono, lead singer of U2, dubbed him 'the sting in the tale of WASP'.[99] Writing in a fiftieth anniversary collection commemorating *Naked Lunch*, DJ Spooky remarked: 'In Burroughs' world, like the realm of the DJ, the acoustic imagination is a place we can all think of as a liberated zone – a place where the mix can absorb any pattern, any sequence, and any text'.[100]

If we consider the patterns of engagement between Beat and rock from a periodic point of view, the mid- to later 1960s saw a number of acts beyond Dylan and the Beatles make connections with this literary terrain. The Fugs, named subversively in honour of the sanitised term Norman Mailer was forced to euphemistically employ in his celebrated novel of the Second World War, *The Naked and the Dead* (1948), as the soldiers' realistic use of the word 'fuck' was deemed inadmissible at the time, were an early example of the Beat spirit being re-formulated in a popular music context. In his 1971 account, Cook asks, 'Did the Beats influence rock?' and answers the question in this way: 'Yes. A direct link of sorts can be established through the Fugs, that notorious trio of scato-porno-rockers who have a large following in and outside New York, even though their record cannot be played on air'.[101] The band continued in a different form well into the new century, some 40 years after Cook wrote that but when the band emerged, around 1965, they were built on a triple core of Ed Sanders, a poet, publisher and political activist whose *Fuck You: A Magazine of the Arts* ran in New York for 13 issues from 1962–65, its mimeographed format, certainly, and its provocative title, also, alluding to the approaches – both tactically and linguistically – that the Beats had pursued in the previous decade; Tuli Kupferberg, who had already made a mark as a minor Beat writer and publisher in his own right in the 1950s and had been memorialised in Ginsberg's 'Howl' as the man who jumped off the Brooklyn Bridge and survived; and a younger drummer from Texas named Ken Weaver.

Sanders not only edited a journal which attracted a stellar line-up of contributors – Ginsberg, Burroughs, Orlovsky, Mailer, Warhol, Herbert Huncke, Diane di Prima and Frank O'Hara among them[102] – but also, eventually, controversy. The

---

[97] Stephen Dalton, 'Bill's excellent adventure', William Burroughs obituary, *New Musical Express*, 16 August 1997.

[98] Lewis MacAdams, 'William S. Burroughs (1914–1997)', obituary, *The Rolling Stone Book of the Beats: The Beat Generation and the Counterculture*, edited by Holly George-Warren (London: Bloomsbury, 1999), pp. 171–3 (p. 171).

[99] Quoted in Tommy Udo, 1997.

[100] DJ Spooky, 'All consuming images: DJ Burroughs and me', *Naked Lunch @ 50: Anniversary Essays* (Carbondale, IL: South Illinois University Press, 2009), pp. 233–7 (p. 237).

[101] Cook, 1971, p. 224.

[102] For more information and images see 'Ed Sanders and the Fuck You Press', Verdant Press, http://www.verdantpress.com/fuckyou.html [accessed 4 January] and Jed Birmingham, 'Fuck You

intervention of the police, at his Peace Eye Bookstore in the East Village in early 1966, saw the force seize an edition of the publication on grounds of obscenity. The police action would close both the magazine and the bookshop but, by now, Sanders and Kupferberg had devised a new outlet for their ideas with the creation of the Fugs whose first album, *The Village Fugs*,[103] appeared in 1965 to be followed by a rush of LP releases, including re-packaged variations, over the next two years.

Sanders recalls the genesis of the group, who were formed at the venue called the Dom in New York's St. Mark's Place owned by legendary proprietor Stanley Tolkin:

> We'd go there after poetry readings. I remember I think it was after a Robert Creeley reading at the St. Mark's, we all went over there. There was Joel Oppenheimer and Leroi Jones and I think Creeley was there, all kinds of people were there, Ted Berrigan. The place was packed and there was this strange music, you know, by the Beatles, this was late '64, so the Beatles had hit, there was Wilson Pickett, and all those black dance groups [...] We used to go there dancing after the readings [...] So Kupferberg was there one time and I said, 'Hey, you know. This is it. We'll set it to poetry and see what happens.'[104]

Cook said the band 'in a peculiar way [...] are a most literary kind of group: the words do count with them. Their melodies, such as they are, serve only to support their crudely witty poem-lyrics.'[105] Sanders remarked: 'We came to music through literature, through being well read and literate. A lot of poetry was written with regard to music and meter. Most of the ancient poetry was sung. We've put a lot of good poetry into rock – Ginsberg's, Matthew Arnold's, Ezra Pound's, Sappho's and so forth.'[106] They also paid tribute to a hero of the Beats and a particular inspiration to Ginsberg, William Blake, and produced their own setting of 'Howl'.

Miles described the Fugs as 'a natural product of the downtown music scene'[107] and quotes Sanders' aims for the group: 'This is an era of civil rights, sexual & consciousness expansion revolutions, & those are the banners under which the Fugs are going to present themselves to America.'[108] In autumn 1968, there was a famed encounter between Kerouac and Sanders on William F. Buckley's television

---

press archive', Reality Studio, http://realitystudio.org/bibliographic-bunker/fuck-you-press-archive/ [accessed 4 January 2012].

[103] The album's full, original title was *The Village Fugs Sing Ballads of Contemporary Protest, Point of Views* (sic), *and General Dissatisfaction* (Folkways). It was then re-issued as *The Fugs First Album* (sic) on ESP-Disk in 1966.

[104] Ed Sanders quoted in Sukenick, 1987, p. 166.

[105] Cook, *ibid.*, p. 225.

[106] Sanders quoted in Cook, *ibid.*

[107] Barry Miles, *The Hippies* (London: Cassell Illustrated, 2003), p. 68.

[108] *Ibid.*, p. 158.

show *Firing Line* when the subject of the hippies was debated. Kerouac was drunk and Sanders' friendly attempts to engage with his hero on camera and off were met by the novelist's surly rejection. The Fugs would dissolve by the end of the decade but then re-form in 1984 when Ginsberg's guitar player Steven Taylor joined the expanded band. They would then continue working into the next century, although Kupferberg would die, aged 86, in 2010.

Sanders' activities would continue alongside the band's schedules. In 2002, he published a narrative poem, *The Poetry and Life of Allen Ginsberg*, as Edward Sanders, commenting in the 'Afterword': 'I did not plan to write a book on Allen Ginsberg, but rather an extended elegy, which I began at the time of his death in April 1997 when for a while grief seemed to course without limit. I would be walking down the street and suddenly weep thinking about him [...] I loved him and he is in mind almost as if he were alive even as I type on this warm spring day ...'[109]

Emerging at a similar time to the Fugs, and also in New York City, were the Velvet Underground, a band's whose history would take impetus from the broader Beat nexus. Formed in 1965 and fronted by two songwriters, Brooklyn-born singer Lou Reed and British viola player and composer John Cale, with guitarist Sterling Morrison and drummer Mo Tucker, they would become the in-house rock group at Andy Warhol's Factory, the artist's headquarters and studio where an entourage of film-makers and photographers, artists and dancers, models and musicians, freaks and hangers-on would gather from early 1964. The Velvet Underground's first regular engagement was at the end of the following year at the Café Bizarre in Greenwich Village. Although in their short sets they were making little impression – Tucker was relegated to tambourine as the club owners wanted to restrict noise levels[110] – the coming months would see their fortunes change. Warhol had become involved in a new discothèque and light show project which he intended to use as material for a filmed venture. Paul Morrissey, Warhol's principal lieutenant in respect of movie creation, made a different proposal. Says Watson: 'Paul Morrissey suggested a bigger plan: Warhol should emulate Brian Epstein and sponsor a band. Showing Warhol movies behind the band would give them a chance to re-cycle movies that had had very limited distribution ...'[111]

Film-maker and Ginsberg associate Barbara Rubin, who had also played a key part in sparking the International Poetry Incarnation in London the previous June where Beat poets had filled one of the capital's most prestigious venues, would now perform an important role in connecting the Velvet Underground and the

---

[109] Edward Sanders, 'Afterword', *The Poetry and Life of Allen Ginsberg* (London: Scribner, 2002), pp. 239–40.
[110] Steven Watson, *Factory Made: Warhol and the Sixties* (New York: Pantheon, 2003), p. 251.
[111] *Ibid.*

Warhol community. Rubin had heard the band in rehearsal and, explains Watson, 'believed they could be cultural heroes of a new age. In her mind, that select group included Allen Ginsberg, Bob Dylan, the Beatles, and [*film-maker*] Jack Smith. She directed her energy in exposing all of them to one another.'[112] Ginsberg said of this: 'She saw us as spiritual men, heroes of a cultural revolution involving at first mainly sex and drugs and art. Her genius was sympathising with everybody's desire to get together in work with their fellow geniuses.'[113]

The Velvet Underground, a four-piece until a new Warhol-recommended singer called Nico joined the act, would participate in the *Exploding Plastic Inevitable*, a multimedia extravaganza that debuted in New York on 8 April 1966, travelled also to a number of cities in the US and Canada and was filmed in Chicago. They released their debut album *The Velvet Underground & Nico* in spring 1967, just weeks before the Beatles' *Sgt. Pepper's Lonely Hearts Club*, including material on the debut album that would both excite and surprise – a signal to the countercultural underground that taboo lyrical topics, in an often dishevelled and stark rock setting, could challenge the more conventional tropes of mainstream popular music, particularly with a hallucinogen-fuelled Summer of Love imminent. But the release was out of sync with that sunny and optimistic mood and arguably some way ahead of its time. Its controversial and dissonant devices would prove a turn-off in terms of its commercial reception.

The album, with its memorable Warhol banana cover, would sell poorly but still become enormously influential, particularly to the post-1960s bands who shaped the punk and new wave movements of the next decade and beyond. Yet it is hard to see how songs like 'Heroin',[114] 'Waiting for the Man', 'Venus in Furs' and 'The Black Angel's Death Song' – with their themes of narcotics, sado-masochism and death – could have been created without the new and liberated climate that the Beats had helped to construct with their own candid expressions, particularly Ginsberg in ground-breaking works like 'Howl', where homosexuality had been dealt with in an honest and uncompromising manner, and Burroughs' writings on drugs and perverse sexual practices in *Naked Lunch*, for example. The work of the Velvet Underground had been influenced by other forces that may be loosely grouped under a newly fermenting trash aesthetic and Warhol's effect in shaping this revolutionary style – in his visual art, in his movies – cannot be under-stated. But the lyric texts that Reed utilised on the debut record, and on later songs, had a definite Beat taint based, we may assume, on degrees of personal experience –

---

[112] Watson, p. 252.

[113] Ginsberg quoted in Watson, *ibid.*

[114] Lewis MacAdams comments that 'Heroin' was 'probably the most powerful and moving drug song ever written', *Birth of the Cool: Beat, Bebop and the American Avant-Garde* (New York: The Free Press, 2001), p. 244.

life as art – and often transgressive in subject – conventional codes broken and standard moralities unheeded.

In 1971, by which time the original impetus of the band had dissipated and Reed would be starting to shape a solo career, he would give a high profile poetry reading at St. Mark's Church alongside a rising star of the Downtown poetry scene, Jim Carroll. Bockris describes the scene: 'In front of an avant garde audience of rock writers and poets, including Allen Ginsberg, Lou rose to the occasion, leading off with "Heroin" and going on to read "Sister Ray", "Lady Godiva's Operation" and "The Black Angel's Death Song" to considerable acclaim.'[115] So taken was Reed by the audience's response that 'he announced he'd never sing again, because he was now a poet.'[116] He was not true to this claim: he would return to rock music and spend the next 40 years pursuing a largely musical route in various distinct fashions, up to and including a surprising and extraordinary collaboration with heavy metal band Metallica in 2011 on their joint venture *Lulu*. But the influence of poets and literature – the writer Delmore Schwartz was another of Reed's notable inspirations – was ever there. When Ginsberg died in 1997, the Velvet Underground singer said: 'His poetry was so American and so straightforward, so astute, and he had such a recognisable voice. Modern rock lyrics would be inconceivable without the work of Allen Ginsberg. It opened them up from the really mediocre thing they'd been to something more interesting and relevant. He was very brave and he was also very honest – a no-bullshit person.'[117] John Cale, who would also contribute a piece called 'The Moon' to the Jack Kerouac tribute *Kicks Joy Darkness* the same year of Ginsberg's passing, also emphasised the importance to him of the late poet: 'Allen Ginsberg, John Cage and La Monte Young were the first three figures of the New York avant garde I met when I arrived in the city in 1963 [...] Allen was the conscience of the underground/avant garde to whom we all deferred.'[118]

If the Beats had established their main beach-head in New York City in the 1940s and 1950s, the West Coast of the US, and specifically San Francisco, would prove a new and fertile planting ground for this literary style, with Lawrence Ferlinghetti's mould-breaking bookshop and publishing house City Lights and the drive of individuals like Kenneth Rexroth steering what would become known by the mid-1950s as the San Francisco Poetry Renaissance. The Beats both fed into this and off it, with Ginsberg's unveiling of 'Howl' in 1955, the obscenity trial that City Lights would face in 1957 after publishing *Howl and Other Poems*, and a number

---

[115] Victor Bockris, *Lou Reed: The Biography* (London: Hutchinson, 1994), p. 207.
[116] *Ibid.*
[117] Lou Reed, 'Memories of Allen', *The Rolling Stone Book of the Beats: The Beat Generation and the Counterculture*, edited by Holly George-Warren (London: Bloomsbury, 1999), p. 278.
[118] John Cale, *ibid.*, p. 277.

of Bay Area writers becoming linked to the movement. Poets like Ferlinghetti, Michael McClure, Gary Snyder and David Meltzer and the novelist Richard Brautigan would all be seen as part of the broad community that comprised the Beat Generation. In the 1960s, just as New York's radical music community began to make its mark, growing out of the creative innovation and bohemian mentality that the Beats had most helped to engender, so San Francisco's music-makers began to make their voices heard as the new decade unfolded.

A fascinating link between the Beats of the later 1950s and the rock developments of the early to mid-1960s was a writer who felt he was too young to be an original Beat but too old to be one of the new hippy brigade. Yet the success of Ken Kesey as author – his debut 1962 novel *One Flew Over the Cuckoo's Nest* had been one of the most acclaimed of the year and quickly became a Broadway theatre hit the following year – would provide a significant catalyst for a distinct Californian scene, engaged with new music, art and literature and outsider social codes, to arise. Kesey had been a writing student at Stanford in 1959 and had also worked as a medical orderly to fund his studies. The latter experiences were important raw material in conceiving the mental asylum at the heart of his novel, where Randle McMurphy, a rebel and criminal, finds himself after a brush with the law, which sees him deemed insane. The asylum and its chief nurse become a metaphor for authoritarian society, McMurphy the resistant force and an apparently deaf mute, native American Indian, the narrator and quiet conscience of the story.

But the power of this allegorical fable would be only a part of Kesey's contribution to the new decade. While studying, he had also been paid to take part in CIA-backed medical experiments linked to the effects of psychedelic drugs. So intrigued was he by the impact of LSD that he strove to maintain these experiences outside the laboratory and shared samples with friends. The fact that powerful forces in the academic psychiatric world like Timothy Leary were concurrently being lured by the promise of psychedelic drugs and their revelation, and arguing that LSD could be a door to a positive social transformation, suggests that the *Zeitgeist* was guiding a number of influential individuals – in science and the arts – simultaneously and in different locations. Leary, sacked from his prestigious Harvard University post, would continue his campaign and Kesey would also pursue his intentions to spread the psychedelic gospel across the wider nation.

Having completed his second novel, *Sometimes a Great Notion*, Kesey planned a US tour, funded by his substantial earnings from his first book. Its scheme was to take the novelist and a small group of his friends on an LSD-fuelled adventure across the continent to New York City, all aboard a pre-war school bus they dubbed Furthur and decorated in eye-catchingly luminous, proto-psychedelic colours. The drug was not illegal – it would not be banned in the US until 1966 – so Kesey's bold experiment was not outside the law as it stood. The trek was fully documented – photographs were taken and sound recordings and a filmed record were created – with the intention that the odyssey would be turned into a feature-length documentary. In fact, it would take more than 40 years for a version of the account to appear, in the 2011 movie production *Magic Trip*. But the trip – both geographically and chemically – that Kesey and friends undertook in 1964 would have an impressive bearing on the counterculture's evolution. It was a potent emblem of personal liberation, played out not in the subterranean environs of downtown but via a psychedelic carnival in the full glare of the summer highway, that seemed to distil, in its transgressive open-ness the spirit of a new time, a new consciousness arriving.[119]

The notion of travel and the road, powerfully embodying those themes of freedom and excitement which had so engaged many of the Beat Generation and its followers, was regenerated in Kesey's journey and the thread connecting his escapade to those that the earlier novelists and poets from that writing community had undertaken, in the previous decade and a half, could hardly have been better founded. While the travelling party, dubbed the Merry Pranksters, would embrace artists, photographers and film-makers, it would also include a living literary legend. That legend was Neal Cassady, not famous for his own writing, at least his own *published* writing,[120] still a young man, but already immortalised in the pages of Jack Kerouac's *On the Road* as the fictional adventurer Dean Moriarty and a Beat icon in his own right. Dennis McNally discusses his link to Kesey and his crew, recalling that Cassady had spent time in San Quentin jail after a 1958 drug bust saw him incarcerated for two years. Shortly after his release, McNally states: 'Neal turned up at Kesey's home [...] He'd read *One Flew Over the Cuckoo's Nest* and felt a spiritual kinship with Randle Patrick McMurphy, the novel's protagonist and indeed there was a bond. "Speed Limit" became his nickname, and he formed an integral part of Kesey's circle.'[121] When the school bus set out on its trans-continental route, Cassady was at the wheel and, to add to the Beat associations, when the Merry Pranksters arrived in Manhattan with a celebratory party in mind, Jack Kerouac was among those who would be invited to join the revelries. However, the novelist, now distanced from his friends and former lifestyle and deeply sceptical of developments in US society, seemed in no mood to condone the liberal attitudes and freewheeling behaviour of Kesey and his cohorts, even if his one-time great friend Cassady

---

[119] The Beatles' *Magical Mystery Tour*, their 1967 film, while distinctly English in content, seemed, in part, to pay tribute to the exuberant escapism of Kesey's earlier American adventures.

[120] Neal Cassady had become famous among his Beat friends for his long, frenetic, effusive letters, uncensored and highly descriptive. The most celebrated of these, running to around 13,000 words in length, was sent to Kerouac in 1950 but it was later lost. A surviving section was published as Cassady's *The First Third* (San Franciso: City Lights, 1971). See Barry Miles, 1998, pp. 147–8.

[121] Dennis McNally, *A Long Strange Trip: The Inside Story of the Grateful Dead* (London: Bantam Press, 2002), p. 109.

was present.[122] When Kerouac arrived and was invited to take a seat on a sofa, overlain with the Stars and Stripes, he picked up the flag and carefully folded it before sitting, a clear symbol of the tensions that existed between the new wave of roisterers and a man whom they would have considered a definite role model.

Returning to California, a series of parties would evolve from summer 1965 at Kesey's La Honda property and at other venues in the locale, including the Santa Cruz home of his friend Ken Babbs,[123] that would see further experimental LSD gatherings occur – what became dubbed the 'Acid Tests'. Not only were Cassady, Allen Ginsberg and Peter Orlovsky attenders on occasion, a rising journalist called Hunter S. Thompson and even members of the local Hell's Angels chapter, but a musical crowd, too, who were friends of Kesey's, a band formerly known as the Warlocks, a combination of jug-band folkies and John Coltrane addicts with a dash of conservatoire expertise, who would become a key part of many of these celebrations, contributing extraordinary free-form soundtracks – embracing rock and country, blues and jazz – to accompany these radical social experiments. By now, playing as the Grateful Dead, guitarists Jerry Garcia and Bob Weir, bassist Phil Lesh, drummer Bill Kreutzmann and keyboard player Bill 'Pigpen' McKernan, would become a further strand entwining the Beat culture of Cassady, the new literary counterculture of Ken Kesey and the nascent stirrings of hippy life in the city of San Francisco, soon to blossom brilliantly, and briefly, as the utopian centre of 1967's Summer of Love, with a recently coined rock 'n' roll offshoot – acid rock – at the heart of the new experience.

The Dead would be particularly drawn to Cassady, a tragic casualty by 1968, and works like 'That's it For the Other One' on *Anthem of the Sun* (1968) and 'Cassidy' – recorded by Bob Weir on his solo album *Ace* (1972) – and by the group themselves on 1981's *Reckoning*, would celebrate their hero. Says McNally: 'Disguised as a loony, mad-rapping speed freak, Neal Cassady was very possibly the most highly evolved personality [the band] would ever meet, and was certainly among their most profound life influences other than the psychedelic experience itself.'[124] In January 1967, at the Human Be-In, there was an intriguing collusion between those musical groups leading the acid rock charge – the Dead, Jefferson Airplane and Quicksilver Messenger Service – and the Beat poets – Ginsberg and Michael McClure, Lawrence Ferlinghetti and Gary Snyder – when all shared a stage in Golden Gate Park in San Francisco.

---

[122] Relations between Cassady and Kerouac had soured, particularly as a result of the 1958 drug bust that had led to his two-year prison sentence. There were suggestions that Cassady's reputation as the wild spirit Dean Moriarty had preceded him and actually contributed to particular police interest in his activities and his arrest and charge.

[123] McNally, 2002, pp. 110–11.

[124] *Ibid.*, pp. 107–8.

Furthermore, if the catalyst of Kesey, and the revolutionary cultural milieu he manufactured and largely stage-managed, would prove to be an important springboard in the extended career of the Grateful Dead and a distinguished chapter in the history of rock music, we should not ignore the verdant conditions he stimulated and that helped to spawn an extraordinary body of literature as well. Although Kesey himself never produced sustained work on the scale of his first two novels, others created accounts of these episodes, these scenes, in remarkable number. Hunter S. Thompson's *Hell's Angels: The Strange and Terrible Saga of the Outlaw Motorcycle Gangs* (1966) was an early example of what would be described as a non-fiction novel and would also come to be associated with the new journalism, a brand of writing that would see the reporter – previously assumed to be an impartial, arm's length observer of news or trends – become a more engaged player in the drama, jettisoning the long-standing divisions between objective and subjective approaches to reportage. Another writer linked to the new journalism phenomenon, Tom Wolfe, would pen *The Electric Kool Aid Acid Test*, an acclaimed – if outsider – description of the Kesey/Acid Test moment which appeared in 1968. Allen Ginsberg's celebrated 1965 poem 'First Party at Ken Kesey's with Hell's Angels' was an eye-witness reflection of this eclectic countercultural nexus, while *Freewheelin' Frank: The True Story of a Hell's Angel by a Hell's Angel* (1969) was an autobiographical volume recounting the story of Frank Reynolds, a project on which Michael McClure closely collaborated.

There are other seminal American bands of the later 1960s who also found overlapping associations with the Beats. The Doors' frontman Jim Morrison would particularly acknowledge interests in poetry and the influence of the Beats. His family moved to the Bay Area of San Francisco in autumn 1957 when he was a teenager and he paid visits to City Lights in those adolescent years, once briefly engaging with Lawrence Ferlinghetti himself. As biographers Jerry Hopkins and Danny Sugerman recall: 'Ferlinghetti was one of Jim's favourites, along with Kenneth Rexroth and Allen Ginsberg [...] also fascinated by Dean Moriarty.'[125] They add that he 'read the great French Symbolist poet Arthur Rimbaud, whose style would influence the form of Jim's short prose poems. He read everything Kerouac, Ginsberg, Ferlinghetti, Kenneth Patchen, Michael McClure, Gregory Corso and all the other Beat writers published.'[126]

Morrison would share a friendship with McClure after meeting in 1968. The Beat poet said, in a 1990 interview, that he 'liked Jim [...] I liked his intelligence. I liked his style. I liked the way his mind moved and I like the way he moved. He was a pretty well integrated human being, both physically adept and mentally

---

[125] Jerry Hopkins and Danny Sugerman, *No One Here Gets Out Alive* (London: Plexus, 1982), p. 12.
[126] *Ibid.*, p. 17.

adept, the whole individual working in one direction. You could sense the poet there. You've got to remember that at this point I was not interested in rock 'n' roll. I had already been through it. So Jim being in the Doors meant just about nothing to me. I mean, it certainly wouldn't have been in his favour. It was through the artistry of [keyboardist] Ray Manzarek and Jim that I became interested in music again.'[127] Morrison produced his own published poetry, too. Two collections, *The Lords and the New Creatures* (1969) and *An American Prayer* (1970), would appear before his death in 1971. Later McClure would join forces with Manzarek for a long-running project featuring recordings and live performances. *Love Lion* (1991) captured McClure and Manzarek collaboratively on both CD and video and the film *The Third Mind* (1997) explored the two men's artistic interaction. McClure would feature, too, alongside Lawrence Ferlinghetti, when the Band, Dylan's principal collaborators at the end of the 1960s and after, announced their decision to separate in the mid-1970s and gave a valedictory performance alongside a vast and impressive cast of friends and supporters, in November 1976. Their on-stage farewell celebration at Winterland, San Francisco, filmed by Martin Scorsese, would be released as *The Last Waltz*, one of the most celebrated of all in-concert rock movies, in 1978.

Nor was the impact of Beat literature limited to the musical artists of the US: there was a transatlantic effect, too. In the UK, a diverse range of performers and songwriters drank from the Beat cup. As we have mentioned, David Bowie's early 1970s experiments saw him tap into the cut-up methods of William Burroughs to shape his lyrical texts, but there were others significant acts from a range of styles and genres who would include reference to the Beat writers in their work. Van Morrison's 1982 song 'Cleaning Windows' name-checked Kerouac and so did 1993's 'On Hyndford Street', while Mike Heron, once of the Incredible String Band, wrote 'Mexican Girl' (1979), a reference to a Kerouac love interest in *On the Road*, and 'Jack of Hearts' (2005), a song inspired by the autobiography of Kerouac's first wife Edie Parker. Progressive rockers Jethro Tull referred to Kerouac also in the song 'From a Dead Beat to a Greaser' (1976) while King Crimson went further still by releasing an album-length work dedicated to the literary brotherhood, *Beat*, in 1982. The latter was a 25th anniversary celebration of the publication of *On the Road* and included various references to the main Beat protagonists – 'Neal and Jack and Me', 'Heartbeat' (a nod to Carolyn Cassady's early memoir *Heart Beat* (1980)), 'Sartori [sic] in Tangier' (a tribute that managed to merge both elements of Kerouac's novel *Satori in Paris* (1966) and Burroughs' North African bolt-hole

---

[127] Michael McClure quoted in interview with Frank Lisciandro, 1990, 'Nile insect eyes: Talking on Jim Morrison', *Lighting the Corners: On Art, Nature, and the Visionary – Essays and Interviews*, Michael McClure (Albuquerque, NM: University of New Mexico Press, 1994), pp. 237–56 (pp. 237–8).

of the mid- to late 1950s), 'The Howler' (with Ginsberg's 'Howl' its hook) and 'Neurotica', a comment on the Beat magazine of the same name.

Notable singer-songwriters from the mid-1960s who were attracted by the notion of Beat included the Canadian Leonard Cohen, at first a poet and novelist who then turned to music with his debut album in 1967. His poetry collections *The Spice-Box of the Earth* (1961) and *Flowers for Hitler* (1964) were supplemented by his novels *The Favourite Game* (1963) and *Beautiful Losers* (1966), but it was when he turned to recording his words in a musical setting with his LP *The Songs Of Leonard Cohen* that his reputation as a melancholic and lyrical song-smith spread. Richard Fariña, whose post-Beat novel *Been Down So Long It Looks Like Up to Me* (1966) emerged in the year of his premature death, was originally a folk-singer in Greenwich Village. He married two women from that circle: Carolyn Hester, whose 1961 album featured Bob Dylan on harmonica, and Mimi Baez, sister to Joan. As Richard and Mimi Fariña they made their first live appearance at the Big Sur Folk Festival in 1964 and recorded and released three albums. Joan's then relationship with Dylan, and Fariña's association with her sister, saw the foursome develop close friendships between 1963 and 1966. Tragically, however, two days after the publication of his debut novel, Fariña was a passenger fatally injured in a motorcycle accident. The Scottish-born performer Donovan, whose Dylan-like work won him widespread acclaim – a link cemented by his appearance in the Dylan documentary *Don't Look Back*, based on the American's UK tour of 1965 – would later release the album *Beat Café* in 2004, the title track of which would pay warm tribute to the Beat era and its atmosphere.

We have commented on Beat's ability to rise above subcultural divides and the output of Kerouac, Ginsberg and Burroughs seemed just as capable of triggering empathetic feelings in the punk and new wave bands that rose to prominence from the mid-1970s. While many of those acts seemed determined to knock over the traces of the hippy era, its psychedelic legacy and its failed utopian promises, the new rock bands also appeared to have few reservations about aligning with the Beat writers themselves, even if that same literary movement had also offered inspiration to that earlier subculture, one most often linked with a peace and love credo. Burroughs, to an extent, as we have seen and certainly Ginsberg were capable of understanding, even reciprocation, in this re-ordered landscape, as punk actively and aggressively supplanted hippy as a revolutionary mouthpiece. When Victor Bockris asked Burroughs about his feelings toward punk rock, there was a certain ambivalence. He described it as 'an important phenomenon'[128] but he stressed that: 'I am not a punk and I don't know why anybody would consider

---

[128] William Burroughs quoted in 'Burroughs on punk rock' in Victor Bockris, *New York Babylon: From Beat to Punk* (London: Omnibus, 1998), pp. 181–2 (p. 181).

me the Godfather of punk [...] I think the so-called punk movement is a media creation. I have, however, sent a letter of support to the Sex Pistols in England because I've always said that the country doesn't stand a chance until you have 20,000 people saying bugger to the Queen. And I support the Sex Pistols because this is a constructive, necessary criticism of a country which is bankrupt'.[129] As for Ginsberg, Miles makes this point with particular reference to the poet's talent to cross boundaries regardless of culture or age:

> Again Allen was able to transcend the generation gap. He wrote 'Howl' just after rock 'n' roll was invented, but a decade later was able to relate to Lennon, McCartney, Jagger, Dylan and the other Sixties musicians. Now there was a new wave of rock musicians, who saw the previous generation as boring, lifeless and irrelevant, yet they regarded Ginsberg as a source of inspiration and as someone who could understand exactly what they were doing – as he did.[130]

In the US, rock artists to be – from Patti Smith to Tom Verlaine and Richard Hell of Television – arrived in New York in late 1960s and early 1970s harbouring poetic aspirations with the French Symbolists and the American Beats among their role models. Hell, who would leave Television in 1975 and then form part of subsequent influential acts such as the Heartbreakers – with New York Dolls Johnny Thunders and Jerry Nolan – and the Voidoids, saw Burroughs as an heir, of sorts, to Arthur Rimbaud. Hell has argued that 'Burroughs was the real Rimbaud, or at least the one who stayed the course.'[131] However, by the time Smith and Verlaine and Hell[132] made their most imposing mark, the punk scene had fermented and erupted and their main mode of expression had become not verse but rock in live hothouses such as CBGBs[133] in the Bowery. In spring 1974, writes Bernard Gendron, the venue's owner Hilly Kristal 'agreed reluctantly to take in the fledgling band Television, led by the poets Tom Verlaine and Richard Hell [...] But it was the Patti Smith group, already notorious in local rock and art circles, that really set the CBGBs scene in motion when they were paired with Television on a two-month residency in spring 1975.'[134]

---

[129] Burroughs in Bockris, *New York Babylon*, 1998, p. 182.

[130] Barry Miles, *Ginsberg: A Biography* (London: Viking, 1990), p. 492.

[131] Richard Hell, 'My Burroughs: Postmortem notes', *The Rolling Stone Book of the Beats: The Beat Generation and the Counterculture*, edited by Holly George-Warren (London: Bloomsbury, 1999), pp. 216–19 (p. 216).

[132] Verlaine and Hell had published poetry jointly under the single name Theresa Stern. See Robert Palmer, *Dancing the Street: A Rock & Roll History* (London: BBC Books, 1996), p. 269.

[133] Originally the bar was called CBGB and OMFUG: Country, Blue Grass and Blues and Other Music for Uplifting Gourmandisers. See Palmer, 1996, p. 268.

[134] Bernard Gendron, 'The Downtown music scene', *The Downtown Book: The New York Art Scene 1974–1984*, edited by Marvin J. Taylor (Princeton, NJ: Princeton University Press, 2006), pp. 41–65 (p. 53).

Yet the broader, so-called Downtown Scene, that flourished in Manhattan from the mid-1970s to the mid-1980s, embracing music of many kinds, visual art of multiple varieties and eclectic modes of live perfomance, clearly had a continuing awareness of the Beat tradition. Of this period, Robert Siegle explains that 'one quality that kept the Beats on the mental horizon [...] was their problematic mixture of elements: women writing the body (Diane di Prima, Hettie Jones, among many others), issues of class and ethnicity (Allen Ginsberg and Gregory Corso), and the importance of race (Bob Kaufman, Amiri Baraka and Ted Joans). Politics was everywhere, as was the primacy of oral performance over the written page.'[135]

At a similar time in Britain, as punk assumed a highly politicised tone, the London-based Clash carried a particular punch, rising alongside the headline-seizing Sex Pistols but outlasting the latter's briefly incandescent flare. The band proved to be not only the most credible and enduring bands of the initial UK punk eruption, but also one that forged a connection with Allen Ginsberg in the early 1980s. The group were making a live appearance at Bond's International Casino in New York in June 1981, and Ginsberg engaged vocalist and songwriter Joe Strummer in a backstage conversation. When the poet expressed aspirations to collaborate with the band, Strummer proposed that he should join them on stage, which he did. The result was 'Capitol Air', a track that would appear on Ginsberg's career-spanning compilation set *Holy Soul and Jelly Roll* in 1994. Commenting on the experience, Ginsberg later stated: 'They're all good musicians, [guitarist] Mick Jones particularly, and they're very sensitive and very literate underneath all the album-cover roughneck appearance. I don't know of any other band that would, in the middle of a big heavy concert, be willing to go on with a big middle-age goose like me, who might or might not be able to sing in tune, for all they know.'[136] As a partial consequence of this impromptu live piece, Ginsberg joined the Clash in the recording studio the following January to lay down the track 'Ghetto Defendant', a piece which became a stand-out cut on the band's 1982 album *Combat Rock*. Joe Strummer's Beat adventure would be further expended when he lent his talents to the 1997 Kerouac tribute *Kicks Joy Darkness* (1997), overlaying his idiosyncratic rendition on the novelist's own reading of his work 'MacDougal Street Blues'.

Among those post-punk performers emerging in the 1980s, who would continue to engage with the Beat cause were Sonic Youth, also later graduates of the febrile Downtown Scene. During a career stretching to three decades, they dedicated songs to Ginsberg – 'Hits of Sunshine (for Allen Ginsberg)' (1998) – and Corso – 'Leaky Lifeboat (for Gregory Corso)' (2009). In addition, individual members Thurston Moore and Lee Ranaldo would also play roles in the *Kicks Joy*

---

[135] Robert Siegle, 'Writing Downtown', *The Downtown Book: The New York Art Scene 1974–1984*, edited by Marvin J. Taylor (Princeton, NJ: Princeton University Press, 2006), pp. 131–53 (p. 136).
[136] Miles, 1990, pp. 491–2.

Darkness homage. Moore would contribute to the track 'The Last Hotel' with Patti Smith and Lenny Kaye; Ranaldo would act as the album's associate producer and contribute to two of the cuts – 'Letter to John Clellon Holmes' with Morphine saxophonist Dana Colley and 'Woman' with Jim Carroll and Lenny Kaye. Ranaldo, who would take a production credit on the subsequent tribute album *Jack Kerouac Reads On the Road*, would also issue a series of Beat-like books – prose, stories and journals, including *Bookstore and Others* (1995), *JRNLS80S* (1998), *Road Movies* (2004) and *Against Refusing* (2010) – alongside his 1993 solo recording *Scriptures of the Golden Eternity*, the title echoing Kerouac's 1960 prose poem collection *The Scripture of the Golden Eternity*.

Ranaldo talked about his relationship with the Beats at the Sonic Youth website in 1998. He says that 'ever since reading *On The Road* in '74, just out of college and on my first road trip, NY to California, at the time, the Beat writers have had a strong influence on me. I just loved the way Kerouac in particular wrote, the muscular energy and enthusiasm for life and love and travel. Ginsberg and Burroughs, Snyder, etc. came later as more acquired tastes, but Kerouac was so easy to read and so simple to identify with.'[137] As for the Beats' impact on alternative culture in a general sense, he remarks: 'I think the influence they had is immense. Kerouac and the "rucksack revolution", popularising (not inventing) the notion of travel and freedom; Burroughs bringing in more transgressive and sinister, heady elements; Ginsberg most influential in the long run though, or most effective proselytiser, espousing way back in the '50s ideas of a transcendant drug culture and later being ahead of the curve on Eastern religious exploration, and political activism, homosexual freedom, etc. His life really had a great impact on so many aspects of youth culture, from the '50s right through to '80s–90s. The more I explore his biography, the more apparent it becomes.'[138]

There are other rock artists we might mention who have included Beat references in their output or found common spirit with the writers' philosophical or artistic approaches. REM were inspired by Kerouac's spirit, well reflected in guitarist Peter Buck's remarks on the matter. 'I'm probably one of the few people who's read everything the guy wrote,'[139] he explains. The group felt an affinity with the lure of movement as they toured in their early days. 'It's like *On the Road*', says Buck. 'We all read it when we were 14 or 15. It was a real thing, where you could spot the heart of America. The heart wasn't in a constitution or a government-

---

[137] Lee Ranaldo, 'Interview – Beat Generation questions', Steve Appleford, 4 August 1998, Sonic Youth website, http://www.sonicyouth.com/symu/lee/2011/09/08/i-view-beat-generation-questions-1998/ [accessed 28 February 2012].

[138] *Ibid.*

[139] Peter Buck quoted in David Perry's notes in the booklet accompanying CD box set *The Jack Kerouac Collection* (Rhino Records Word Beat, 1990).

type thing, but it was in a collection of people. And that's what we found.'[140] REM would collaborate with Burroughs on the 1996 track 'Star Me Kitten', while the group's vocalist Michael Stipe contributed a track – 'My Gang' – to *Kerouac: Kicks Joy Darkness* (1997). Stipe also took a Beat-like cue in his photographic collection *Two Times Intro: On the Road with Patti Smith*[141] (1998), when he joined his fellow singer on tour in 1995 and featured, among the images he shot, a concentrated gathering of artists who have been linked to Smith herself and this wider literary circle, from Ginsberg to Lenny Kaye, Tom Verlaine, Thurston Moore and Kim Gordon, the monochrome document even hinting at Robert Frank and his 1959 account *The Americans*. Rob Buck – no relation to REM's Peter – was part of 10,000 Maniacs, whose song 'Hey Jack Kerouac' became one of their best-loved numbers, expressed similar sentiments to his namesake. 'When I was 18, I read *On the Road* and *The Dharma Bums* and I went out to try and imitate [Kerouac's] experience. He wrote like a lot of music influenced him – he always sounded like the bebop players he loved. To me, his writing was an extension of that music. It was very improvised yet very together.'[142]

Beck's interest in Ginsberg was confirmed in their 1997 conversation for the Buddhist online publication *Shambhala Sun*.[143] He also revealed an affection for the Beats in Jerry Aronson's film portrait of Ginsberg, commenting that he likes 'their idea of America; it's kind of romantic. There's a certain romanticism about the lifestyle that they led: travelling, going wherever life took them, in search of relationship, connection, interaction with people and finding some piece of America that still has individuality and humanity in it'.[144] One figure who has been less positive towards the Beat tradition, even if his spoken word forays would suggest a stylistic connection, is Henry Rollins, one-time frontman of Black Flag. Although he has admitted affection for Ginsberg's output and has praised 'Howl' and 'Kaddish', he has less time for Burroughs and Kerouac. He told website *The Modern Word* in 2005: 'I remember reading *On the Road* by Kerouac in '82 and the only thing that occurred to me was, "Kerouac, what a pussy", because it was so nothing like what I was enduring on the road. I was watching people get stabbed and I was seeing some pretty rough stuff.'[145]

---

[140] *Ibid.*

[141] Michael Stipe, *Two Times Intro: On the Road with Patti Smith* (New York: Ray Gun Press, 1998).

[142] Rob Buck quoted in David Perry, 1990.

[143] *Shambhala Sun*, 'The late Allen Ginsberg and Beck in conversation: A Beat/Slacker transgenerational meeting of minds', January 1997, http://shambhalasun.com/index.php?option=com_content&task=view&id=2050&Itemid=244 [accessed 27 February 2012].

[144] Beck quoted from *The Life and Times and Allen Ginsberg*, directed by Jerry Aronson, 2007.

[145] Henry Rollins, 'You can't dance to a book', interview with Neddal Ayad, *The Modern Word*, 20 November 2005, http://www.themodernword.com/interviews/interview_rollins.html [accessed 28 February 2012].

Other acts, too, have referenced the Beats or worked with them, been inspired by their writings, drawn on their artistic devices or even adapted their work, from American artists such as the Byrds' Roger McGuinn, Iggy Pop and the Blue Oyster Cult, Laurie Anderson, the Dead Kennedys' Jello Biafra and Red Hot Chili Peppers, Loudon Wainwright, Tom Russell and David Dondero to British performers like Mott the Hoople, Al Stewart and Marillion, Throbbing Gristle and Cabaret Voltaire, the Fall, Joy Division and Radiohead, not forgetting Australia's Go-Betweens. We may add further the tributes bands have paid to Beat associates, like Mercury Rev's 1993 musical setting of Robert Creeley's 'So There', and homages to Charles Bukowski,[146] whose name has been revered and celebrated by the Manic Street Preachers, the Boo Radleys and Modest Mouse among others.

Nor does this summary take account of that remarkable stream of cultural activity that has poured forth from the African-American community over the last 75 years and more and with specific reference to the hip hop and rap styles which emerged from the 1970s and owed such a debt to the spoken word tradition, stretching back to poet-songwriters such as Gil Scott-Heron, groups such as the Watts Prophets and the Last Poets, and further still those significant black voices who made their mark within the Beat community – most pertinently Leroi Jones/Amiri Baraka,[147] but also Ted Joans and Bob Kaufman. There are fuller histories to be related which forensically connect the Harlem Renaissance of the 1920s and the jazz poetry of Langston Hughes to the ongoing Nuyorican Poets of the new century, via the black voices of the Beat Generation and hip hop stars like Chuck D and KRS-One, Michael Franti, Mos Def and DJ Spooky. Mark Kemp states that 'the looping rhythms of hip-hop contain the very core of the "Beat" in Beat Generation: More than any popular youth counterculture since the 1960s […] hip-hop's cut-and-paste interpretation of modern life can be directly traced to Burroughs. Moreover, the swinging, bopping cadence of its words juxta-posed against the thump-thump-thump of the music have kept alive the spirit of Kerouac's reading backed by jazz musicians.'[148] In the subsequent club culture, too, there are fragments worth mentioning – from the slick acid jazz of UFO's 1991 cut 'Poetry and All That Jazz' to Bomb the Bass' florid Beat celebration 'Bug Powder Dust' from 1994.

---

[146] Charles Bukowski (1920–94) never fraternised with the Beats but his brand of gritty realism saw him often bracketed with the writers of that community.

[147] See Simon Warner, 'Amiri Baraka in Manchester', Beat Scene, No. 69, 2013.

[148] Mark Kemp, 'Beat Generation in the generation of beats', The Rolling Stone Book of the Beats: The Beat Generation and the Counterculture, edited by Holly George-Warren (London: Bloomsbury, 1999), pp. 415–19 (p. 417).

iv) The Beats' own recordings: A selective discography

While rock artists have paid many tributes, in a variety of contexts, to the Beat Generation novelists and poets in their songs and albums, it is also worth noting that there is a substantial body of recordings made by the Beat writers themselves, often involving musicians. Some of these projects have emerged in the public domain but much has not. In fact, there is a significant body of spoken word material, sometimes accompanied, that was laid down, which has never been made commercially available. Stephen Ronan's 1996 volume[149] was the most impressive attempt to collate this work and he included 'selected unreleased recordings'[150] in his survey, a rare document in itself which only appeared in a print run of 60. Since then, of course, the output has grown, swollen by recordings made by the Beats themselves and also those other acts who have paid homage to those writers. In this short section, I would like to list key recordings made by the Beats or paying specific tribute to them and released in an official form, alongside principal compilations. I stress again that this is a selective process and that Ronan's rare edition lists hundreds of recordings, both mainstream issues and much more obscure tapes which have never been formally released.

To consider first Jack Kerouac, who recorded and released three principal albums in his life-time. With pianist Steve Allen he made *Poetry for the Beat Generation*[151] (1959) and, with the saxophonists Al Cohn and Zoot Sims, *Blues and Haikus*[152] (1959). *Readings by Jack Kerouac on the Beat Generation*[153] (1960) is a production that sees the author read prose and poetry. These albums were later gathered in *The Jack Kerouac Collection*[154] (1990) on three CDs. We might also add the soundtrack to the short movie *Pull My Daisy*[155] (1959) with Kerouac's narration and David Amram's score. In the 1990s, two albums that paid tribute to Kerouac were issued: *Kerouac: Kicks Joy Darkness*[156] (1997) and *Jack Kerouac Reads on the Road*[157] (1999). The first was a series of homages to and musical settings of

---

[149] Stephen Ronan, *Disks of the Gone World: An Annotated Discography of the Best Generation* (Berkeley, CA: Ammunition Press, 1996). Note: This section draws extensively on Ronan's detailed listings. Each recording (and variations) is catalogued by number but the book has no page numbers.

[150] *Ibid.*, title page.

[151] Released on Dot, then Hanover. See Ronan, 1996, A-250.

[152] Released on Hanover. See Ronan, 1996, A-256.

[153] Released by Verve. See sleeve notes, *The Jack Kerouac Collection* (Rhino Records Word Beat, 1990), p. 27.

[154] Released on Rhino Records. See Ronan, 1996, A-276.

[155] The film can be viewed at http://www.youtube.com/watch?v=mYtfNu9O3dc [accessed 12 February 2012].

[156] Released by Rykodisc, 1997.

[157] Released by Rykodisc, 1999.

Kerouac's prose and poetry by artists drawn from a range of popular music genres, from folk to punk, indie to grunge and more, alongside key figures from the Beat circle: Ginsberg, Burroughs and Ferlinghetti. The second had, at its core, a series of re-discovered Kerouac recordings – examples of the writer reading his own prose and recordings of song standards the novelist made himself. In addition, two poems were given new musical arrangements by David Amram. Finally two versions of a song called 'On the Road' were presented: a home-recorded version by Kerouac, who was the actual composer of the piece, and a new version by Tom Waits with the band Primus.

Allen Ginsberg's recordings include his 1959 release *Allen Ginsberg Reads Howl and Other Poems*,[158] a 1966 edition *Allen Ginsberg Reads Kaddish*,[159] and *Songs of Innocence and Experience by William Blake*[160] from 1969, on which he is joined by Peter Orlovsky on vocals, guitarist Jon Sholle, trumpeter Don Cherry and drummer Elvin Jones, among other musicians. On the album *First Blues: Rags, Ballads and Harmonium Songs*[161] from 1981, Ginsberg accompanies himself on harmonium. A further recording from 1983 carries a similar, though abbreviated, title, *First Blues*,[162] but features a much wider gathering of players – from Bob Dylan to Jon Sholle, violinist David Mansfield, Steven Taylor on guitar and Arthur Russell on cello. *The Lion for Real*[163] from 1989 sees Ginsberg joined by guitarist Bill Frisell, bassist Steve Swallow, guitarist Marc Ribot and composer Arto Lindsay and several others, including Todd Rundgren in a subsidiary role. In 1994, a four CD compilation of the poet's work appeared as *Holy Soul, Jelly Roll: Poems and Songs 1949–1993*.[164] Two years later, in 1996, Ginsberg issued his last important collaborative work when he made the single 'The Ballad of the Skeletons'[165] with Paul McCartney on guitar and drums, Lenny Kaye on bass and Philip Glass on keyboards plus, on guitars, Marc Ribot and David Mansfield.

William Burroughs' recorded output has been more extensive even than that of Kerouac and Ginsberg, with *Call Me Burroughs*[166] in 1965 an early gathering of the writer reading his work. Ten years later *William S. Burroughs/John Giorno*[167] was a similar collection of readings, as poet Giorno and founder of the label

---

158 Released by Fantasy Records. See Ronan, 1996, A-118a.
159 Released in the Atlantic Verbum Series. See Ronan, 1996, A-128a.
160 Released by MGM/Verve Forecast. See Ronan, 1996, A-141a.
161 Released by Folkways Records. See Ronan, A-170a.
162 Released by John Hammond Records. See Ronan, 1996, A-184.
163 Released by Great Jones/Island Records. See Ronan, 1996, A-201.
164 Released by Rhino Word Beat. See Ronan, 1996, A-218b.
165 Released by Mercury Records. See GlassPages, Philip Glass on the Web, http://www.glasspages.org/skeleton.html [accessed 12 February 2012].
166 Released by The English Bookshop, Paris. See Ronan, 1996, A-6a.
167 Released by Giorno Poetry Systems Records. See Ronan, 1996, A-20.

Giorno Poetry System Records joined Burroughs as a co-contributor. *The Nova Convention*,[168] a double LP, appeared in 1979 and was a document based on the Burroughs celebration – a conference cum seminars and live performances – of the previous year in New York City, with Frank Zappa, Patti Smith, Ed Sanders, John Cage, Philip Glass, Allen Ginsberg and Laurie Anderson all participating. *The Elvis of Letters*[169] (1985) was a joint venture with film-maker Gus van Sant, who added a musical accompaniment to readings by Burroughs. In 1990, *Dead City Radio*[170] combined the novelist's spoken word contributions with musical arrangements by a diverse range of music-makers: Sonic Youth, John Cale, Steely Dan's Donald Fagen and Blondie's Chris Stein all featured in the credits. Three years later, Burroughs joined forces with Nirvana frontman and grunge icon Kurt Cobain to release a track entitled 'The "Priest" They Called Him',[171] although neither writer nor guitarist worked in the studio together, each creating their spoken and musical tracks separately. In 1993, also, *Spare Ass Annie and Other Tales*[172] saw the Disposable Heroes of Hiphoprisy add a soundtrack to Burroughs' words. A prolific year would see *The Black Rider*,[173] too, issued, an album which brought together the creative skills of playwright/director Robert Wilson, Burroughs as librettist and Tom Waits as musician, a recording based on a music theatre piece first staged in Hamburg in 1990. In 1996, *10% File Under Burroughs*[174] was a homage album to both Burroughs and Brion Gysin, with an eclectic array of contributors – from Marianne Faithfull, Herbert Huncke and Chuck Prophet to Bomb the Bass, the Master Musicians of Joujouka and Material. Material would also release a Burroughs-centred album, *The Road to the Western Lands*,[175] in 1999, with the novelist's words and narration showcased.

Which other recordings and artists might we include in this brief survey? We should mention Lawrence Ferlinghetti's *Poetry Recordings in the Cellar with the Cellar Jazz Quintet*[176] (1958), a work which co-credits Kenneth Rexroth. Much later, in 1999, Ferlinghetti would record *A Coney Island of the Mind*[177] with Morphine's saxophonist Dana Colley and then, in 2005, *Pictures of the Gone World*[178] with David Amram. Leroi Jones/Amiri Baraka would record versions of

---

[168] *Ibid.*, see Ronan, 1996, A-26.
[169] Released by T.K. Records. See Ronan, 1996, A-46a.
[170] Released by Island Records. See Ronan, 1996, A-64.
[171] Released by Tim Kerr Records. See Ronan, 1996, A-75.
[172] Released by Island Records. See Ronan, 1996, A-76a.
[173] *Ibid.*, see Ronan, 1996, A-79.
[174] Released by Sub Rosa. See Ronan, 1996, A-85.
[175] Released by Triloka Records, 1999.
[176] Released by Fantasy Records. See Ronan, 1996, A-103a.
[177] Released by Rykodisc, 1999.
[178] Released by Synergy, 2005.

his poem 'Black Dada Nihilismus' on the New York Art Quintet's eponymously-titled album[179] of 1966 and, 20 years later, with Paul Miller/DJ Spooky on *Off Beat/A Red Hot Sound Trip*.[180] Gary Snyder's *Turtle Island*[181] (1991) was realised as a poetry-with-music work accompanied by the Paul Winter Consort. Michael McClure's collaboration with former Doors keyboardist Ray Manzarek is represented by the 1993 album *Love Lion*.[182] Gregory Corso's *Die On Me*[183] from 2002 sees him joined by Ginsberg, Peter Orlovsky and Marianne Faithfull on a final recording released a year after his death. David Meltzer's *Poet w/Jazz 1958*[184] is a further work which was not released until 2005. In addition, there are a number of further recorded examples by Beat or Beat-linked writers gathered by Ronan's *Disks of the Gone World*, among them two compilations: *The Beat Generation*[185] (1992) and *Howls, Raps and Roars*[186] (1993). The first is a three CD set, the second a four CD collection. Both bring together elements of the poetic and the musical and feature many of the principal Beats alongside rarities and curiosities. The first covers a wide expanse of ground from the Rod McKuen-penned song 'The Beat Generation' to Kenneth Patchen and Lord Buckley alongside both popular and jazz musical examples. The second is more poetry-inclined but does include work by Lenny Bruce and re-issues Ferlinghetti and Rexroth's jazz poetry recordings in San Francisco's Cellar.

---

[179] *New York Art Quintet* (ESP-Disk, 1966). See Ronan, 1996, A-238a.
[180] Released by Red Hot/Wax Trax. See Ronan,1996, A-221.
[181] Released by Living Music Records. See Ronan, 1996, A-319.
[182] Released by Sanachie. See Ronan, 1996, A-285.
[183] Released by Koch Records, 2002.
[184] Released by Sierra Records, 2005.
[185] Released by Rhino Records. See Ronan, 1996, A-1a.
[186] Released by Fantasy. See Ronan, 1996, A-234.

1 SIFTING THE SHIFTING SANDS: 'HOWL' AND THE AMERICAN LANDSCAPE IN THE 1950s

On 7 October 1955 in the Six Gallery in downtown San Francisco, an emerging but little known poet called Allen Ginsberg stood to deliver a new, long poem he had been working on over the previous months. 'Howl', read to a small, if packed, crowd of friends and supporters, would-be novelists and ambitious young poets, was an immediate sensation. The listeners greeted the piece, an impassioned statement touching upon issues as broad as the Cold War, homosexuality, Buddhism and jazz, drugs, the supernatural and suicide, with a huge and enthusiastic ovation. Said Jonah Raskin in his book *American Scream: Allen Ginsberg's 'Howl' and the Making of the Beat Generation*: '[T]he audience was transformed [...] indifferent spectators becoming energetic participants [...] No one had been to a poetry reading that was so emotional and so cathartic'.[1]

Several of the writers in attendance would actually go away and write their own first-hand account of what had gone on that evening – Jack Kerouac would fictionalise the occasion in his 1958 novel *The Dharma Bums*, for example – a suggestion in itself that there was a strong sense a piece of history, a memorable literary moment, had been played out on that autumn night. 'In all of our memories no one had been so outspoken in poetry before', wrote another poet Michael McClure after the reading. 'We had gone beyond a point of no return – and we were ready for it, for a point of no return. None of us wanted to go back to the grey, chill, militaristic silence, to the intellective void – to the land without poetry – to the spiritual drabness. We wanted to make it new and we wanted to

---

[1] Jonah Raskin, *American Scream: Allen Ginsberg's 'Howl' and the Making of the Beat Generation* (London: University of California Press, 2004), p. 18.

invent it and the process of it as we went into it. We wanted voice and we wanted vision.'[2] An underground gathering of subterranean scribes and street philosophers, the so-called Beat Generation, had raised its head above the parapet.[3]

With 'Howl', Ginsberg marked his arrival as a writer of profile and status. His previous decade, and more, of uncertain progress – acceptance then expulsion from the Ivy League campus of Columbia in New York, his involvement with the under-classes of Manhattan and his fringe contributions to their criminal activities, a period under the scrutiny of the asylum, his visionary episodes in which he believed he had heard the voice of William Blake, and his time as an employee of the Madison Avenue advertising industry – was behind him; his life as poet had commenced. The day after the Six Gallery reading, Lawrence Ferlinghetti, the proprietor of City Lights bookshop and its emerging publishing operation, would acknowledge Ginsberg's achievement with scant delay. Ferlinghetti, referencing words that Ralph Waldo Emerson had penned to Walt Whitman in praise of *Leaves of Grass* in 1855, exactly 100 years before, wrote to Ginsberg: 'I greet you at the beginning of a great career. When do I get the manuscript?'[4]

While this new era would not be without its accompanying difficulties – the acclaimed piece would indeed be published by City Lights the following year, as *Howl and Other Poems*, only to face obscenity charges and a high profile court case within months – the breakthrough that 'Howl' represented was enormous, not only for the writer of the poem but also those in Ginsberg's circle. His friends Kerouac and William Burroughs would gain immensely from the poet's national, then international, recognition. Ginsberg had been and remained a tireless promoter of his fellow writers' novels. He had helped Burroughs to publish his debut book, *Junkie*, in 1953, and would continue to push his much more difficult, experimental works like *The Naked Lunch* as the 1950s turned into the 1960s. For Kerouac, 'Howl' was like the fanfare before the curtain rose and the stage illuminated, for Ginsberg made mention of his friend's numerous unpublished novels in the preface to the poem and included him among several dedicatees. In 1957, *On the Road*, the major novel of this tight-knit gathering of writers, would appear and cause a sensation. The Beats, a community known essentially to its core members only before the mid-1950s, would swiftly become a literary grouping familiar to hundreds and thousands of readers around the globe in the months and years that would follow.

Yet, if writers and poets of a fresh vein were beginning to make their mark at this moment, there were other significant forces at play on a shifting American landscape. By the time Ginsberg premiered his soon-to-be published poem, a

---

[2] Michael McClure, *Scratching the Beat Surface* (San Francisco, CA: North Point Press, 1982), p. 13.
[3] Joining Ginsberg and McClure as poets who read that night were Philip Lamantia, Gary Snyder and Philip Whalen, in an event introduced by Kenneth Rexroth. See Raskin, 2004, pp. 15–16.
[4] Ferlinghetti quoted in Raskin, 2004, p. 19.

significant record was coming to the end of a six-month stay in the Top 40, the American *Billboard* chart which had become the standard weekly sales listing for pop songs from 1940. Bill Haley and His Comets' single '(We're Gonna) Rock Around the Clock' – also widely described in its shortened version of 'Rock Around the Clock' – had entered the chart on 15 April 1955 and would remain in that list for the next 24 weeks.[5] During its stay it would also enjoy eight weeks in the number one position, a significant indicator that this record had entered and remained part of the national psyche for some considerable time.

Why was this of importance? This was not Haley's first chart entry: Palmer credits his 1953 release 'Crazy Man Crazy' as 'the first white rock and roll hit'[6] and, at the end of 1954, Ward states that 'Shake, Rattle and Roll', a bowdlerised version of a Big Joe Turner hit, 'shot up the Top Ten – not only in the United States but also in England, where teenagers were apparently awaiting this blast of new music just as avidly as Americans were'.[7] But '(We're Gonna) Rock Around the Clock' left a deeper imprint because, not only was it heard on record players and radios, but had also been featured in an acclaimed and widely-seen movie of 1955, *The Blackboard Jungle*, a school-based drama starring Glenn Ford which had utilised music – jazz versus rock 'n' roll – as a metaphor for the generation gap. The film, based on a novel by Evan Hunter concerned 'a new teacher at a high school in a "bad" section of town [who] is taunted and abused by a group of his students (including a black one played by Sidney Poitier)'.[8] A fellow teacher also endures the ignominy of having his jazz records smashed by members of his class.[9]

Why though should we attempt to elide these two works, 'Howl' and 'Rock Around the Clock', a piece of poetry and a song? Why should a connection be made between an un-minted poem, known to but a dedicated few, and a hugely successful pop record, familiar to millions across the States? This chapter will argue that both of these expressions were symptomatic of an America that was undergoing a period of dramatic transition. While Ginsberg's verse and Haley's song were coming from different intellectual places, and appealing to different sections of society, they were symbols of that metamorphosis. These two distinct tributaries in America's cultural stream gushed freely, and largely independently, during the latter 1950s and early 1960s yet, by the middle of the 1960s, appeared to find confluence. By then, the jump and jive innocence of rock 'n' roll had matured into the earnest exhorting

---

[5] Joel Whitburn, *The Billboard Book of US Top 40 Hits – 1955 to Present* (New York: Billboard Publications, 1983), p. 129.

[6] Palmer, 1996, p. 25.

[7] Ed Ward, 'The Fifties and before: Streetcorner symphony', *Rock of Ages: The Rolling Stone History of Rock and Roll* edited by Ed Ward, Geoffrey Stokes and Ken Tucker (Harmondsworth: Penguin, 1987), pp. 83–97 (pp. 89–90).

[8] *Ibid.*, p. 106.

[9] *Ibid.*

of a new rock, no longer merely concerned with the boy-meets-girl obsessions of adolescent-oriented pop, but now spreading its creative net to embrace sex and psychosis, politics and pot, as the Beatles and Bob Dylan replaced the early heroes of rock's pantheon. And, with that transformation, some of the key Beats would take the view that rock was something they could feed into and bounce off; the musicians and the poets could and would discover common ground. But that coming-together is a tale for another place in this volume. Here we will examine the US context in which Beat literature, with 'Howl' as its unravelling and uncompromising standard, and original rock 'n' roll, both symptom of, and cure for, post-war teen neurosis perhaps, were initially recognised.

Let us consider the national setting that applied in the middle of the 1950s and the kind of America that felt the psychological tremors that Ginsberg's vociferous assault sent scurrying across the nation, first among the literati, then the media, then the courts and, with remarkable speed, among ordinary men and women in the street. What had been happening socially and politically prior this to thought-quake; what had been unfolding in the worlds of literature and popular music, art and art music? The decade after the end of the Second World War, concluded first in Europe then devastatingly under atomic clouds in the Far East, was a time of extraordinary contrast for the US. On the one hand, the economic troubles, that had so scarred the 1930s, troubles that had only been exorcised by a combination of Roosevelt's Keynesian plans to rebuild America and the arrival of the war which had galvanised industry and seen off the last remnants of Depression, evaporated and by the early 1950s economic boom was bringing prosperity to large portions of the nation: the white middle classes, particularly, saw standards of living rise and the home become a haven for an abundance of newly available consumer goods – fridges and other kitchen appliances, radios and televisions. There was a sense, certainly among the advantaged sections of American society that the cruelty of war had at least been followed by the balm of material comfort, the cooling breeze of financial security. As Bradbury writes: '[R]eal incomes doubled, the rewards of a mass consumer society spread even further and America became a land of unprecedented affluence, an example to others.' But, he counsels, 'the age of affluence was also an age of materialism and conformity'.[10]

However, we should be cautious of these broad brush-strokes; the picture was far from rosy in all aspects. The Civil War, that traumatic scarification of the American soul, was not yet a hundred years past and the promises the bloody conflict had intended to deliver – emancipation of the American Negro from the yoke of brutalised slavery, in particular – had only been partially fulfilled. If the barbarisms of plantation enslavement had legally ended with the war's conclusion,

---

[10] Malcolm Bradbury, *The Modern American Novel*, 2nd edn. (Oxford: Opus, 1992), p. 159.

even by the 1950s the lot of most black men and women was only marginally improved. Mass Negro emigration to the northern states from the 1930s and into the 1940s had seen cities like Chicago and Detroit, cradles of the US industrial recovery, employ large numbers of black workers on their production lines. In this sense there were economic prospects – jobs and homes in cities on the rise – for those who left the south even if their social position remained on the lowest reaches of the ladder. However, in the southern states, where the wounds of the Civil War had barely healed even after the Second World War, the emancipated classes remained third class citizens, bound in a straitjacket of so-called Jim Crow laws.[11] Voting rights and educational opportunities existed in theory but, in practice, the discriminatory attitudes that persisted in Georgia, Alabama, Mississippi and other members of the former Confederacy meant that blacks had little chance of genuine advancement.

Not that the whites, enjoying the fruits of consumer overflow, had lives of complete security and contentment. The peace won after VE Day and VJ Day had been built on curious alliances which would quickly strain, then burst, at the seams. The enforced entente with Soviet Russia to combat Nazi Germany in Europe was rapidly revealed to be a marriage of convenience. Stalin's bootprint remained firmly planted in most of the Eastern European states that had been the battleground in the closing years of the war, the tide of Communism now spread across half the continent.[12] Meanwhile, the US retained a powerful military presence in the West of that continent. Germany was split, four ways between the principal Allies and the old capital Berlin, the microcosm which echoed that broader arrangement, soon emerged as the cracking point in this diplomatic stand-off. The USSR's blockade of the German capital in 1948 led to the famous air-lift to relieve those West Berliners under the administration of the Americans, French and British.[13] And, of course, this was just a symptom of a wider malaise: an ideological divide between libertarian capitalism and authoritarian socialism which would become the setting for a protracted contretemps during the whole of the 1950s. Once the Rosenbergs, Julius and Ethel, had passed US nuclear secrets to the Soviets, in a bid to balance the military arsenals on each side of the split,[14] the American populace spent at least a decade fearing that atomic weapons, used with such devastating event on Japan, would be targeted at them at some early stage. Nor was this fear merely a metaphorical one, simply haunting the inner psyches of America. The claims of the notorious Senator Joseph McCarthy appeared to go a long way to justifying these anxieties. The House Un-American Activities

---

[11] Bruce Wetterau (ed.), *Concise Dictionary of World History* (London: Robert Hale, 1984), p. 419.
[12] Norman Davies, *Europe: A History* (London: Pimlico, 1997), pp. 1062–3.
[13] *Ibid.*, p. 1067.
[14] Wetterau, 1984, p. 678.

Committee (HUAC), which pre-dated the rise of McCarthy investigations but shared a similar agenda, suggested that Communist sympathisers were secreted in every avenue of everyday life – from politics to business, trade unions to the entertainment industry – and that these earmarked individuals were, in essence, traitors whose plotting would leave the US backdoor open and allow the Soviets to infiltrate, bringing the capitalist citadel to its knees, either through entryist stealth or invading missiles. 'Fears about communism', says Hamilton, 'encouraged people to distrust reformers while the emergence of the prosperous suburbs, where every house looked the same, everyone watched identical television shows, and everyone dressed alike, solidified conformist views'.[15]

Yet Lhamon balances the scales:

> Without denying their recent agonies, Americans were distinctly more optimistic following World War II, after taking a decade to think it all over, than during the wallows of despair that followed the trench warfare of the first war and the dislocation of the Depression. In spite of the overwhelming impact of Belsen and Nagasaki, and their warning demonstration of human capacity – mass genocide and world incineration – contemporary American culture has tried to find alternatives rather than bewail the obvious. It has tried therefore to escape the modern feeling of confinement, of complete determination, which Jean-Paul Sartre's *No Exit* so succinctly epitomised. Indeed in many of the central contemporary artefacts – *Catch-22*, Elvis Presley's 'Mystery Train', Robert Rauschenberg's combine paintings, for instance – are about this process of finding new ways to overcome despair, reassembling old feelings in new ways so to feel possibility again in the world.[16]

For black Americans, there were hints of possibility, too – the chance that they may be able to emerge from the long, dark night of political, social and economic disadvantage. For the first half of the twentieth century, the NAACP (National Association for the Advancement of Colored People), founded in 1909,[17] had been striving on behalf of the Negro population, presenting its case but making only modest headway. However, two developments in the middle of the decade would provide the catalyst for potential change. On the national stage, a Supreme Court ruling in the summer of 1954 would order that schools could not pursue a policy of racial segregation, a landmark decision that would still result in black

---

[15] Neil A. Hamilton, *The ABC-CLIO Companion to the 1960s Counterculture in America* (Santa Barbara, CA: ABC-CLIO, 1997), p. 58.
[16] W.T. Lhamon, Jr, *Deliberate Speed: The Origins of a Cultural Style in the American 1950s* (Washington, DC: Smithsonian Institution, 1990), p. 7.
[17] Wetterau, 1984, p. 540.

schoolchildren becoming pawns in a grim game in the years that followed, as whites with a separatist inclination challenged the ruling on the streets and at the gates. But the fact was that the judiciary had backed the principle of non-discrimination, prompting a sea change in Southern American life. As Lhamon puts it: '[A]n agency of conservation, affirmed the radical changes already ongoing'.[18] The following year, when Rosa Parks refused to give up her seat to a white man 'as Southern custom demanded'[19] on a Montgomery, Alabama, bus, the pebble she dropped into the pool would soon build a tidal wave of activism known as the campaign for Civil Rights. That rolling programme of debate and peaceful demonstration would become a prominent focus for progressive energies, black and white, until the murder of its figurehead Martin Luther King in Memphis in 1968.

But what were the forces at play in the cultural world by the middle years of the 1950s? We have already hinted at the state of flux, but Raskin provides a lively overview to support such a proposition:

> There were visible cracks in the culture of the Cold War and sounds of liberation in rock 'n' roll, in Hollywood movies like *Rebel Without a Cause*, and in plays like Arthur Miller's *A View From the Bridge* and Tennessee Williams' *Cat on a Hot Tin Roof*. There were popular novels like Sloan Wilson's *The Man in the Gray Flannel Suit* that presented a critical perspective on American corporate culture, and there was provocative and innovative fiction like Vladimir Nabokov's *Lolita* first published in Paris. In baseball, the Brooklyn Dodgers defeated the New York Yankees in the 1955 World Series, an upset that showed Americans that the raggle-taggle team of bums could defeat the seemingly all-powerful machine and the men in the pinstriped uniforms.[20]

Hollywood, at this time, was facing its biggest crisis since the boom days of the 1930s with the arrival of a new challenger to its hegemony. Television was an infant to cinema's adult at the start of the 1950s but it was quickly apparent that the small screen was going to be a significant threat to the much bigger one. Entertainment on TV proved to be a compelling draw to the traditional customers at whom the movie-makers had aimed their product before – adults. Consequently, the Dream Factory's agenda shifted and its studios began to make pictures which another section of the society – teenagers – would want to see. It is no coincidence that this period saw cinema walk hand in hand with James Dean, Marlon Brando and rock 'n' roll. *Rebel Without a Cause*, *The Wild One*, *The Blackboard Jungle* and

---

[18] Lhamon, p. xii.
[19] James J. Farrell, *The Spirit of the Sixties: The Making of Postwar Radicalism* (London: Routledge, 1997), p. 92.
[20] Raskin, 2004, pp. 10–11.

Rock Around the Clock were as much about Hollywood's yearning for adolescent dollars, a means of exchange in ample supply, as a representation of the *Zeitgeist* at play, though Maltby reminds us that Hollywood also proved adept at finding other ways to manage the upstart TV. The film studios, he tells us, also 'entered television production and rapidly colonised it.'[21]

In the theatre, the most important play of the time was Arthur Miller's *The Crucible* (1953), ostensibly an account of the 1692 Salem witch trials but in reality a lightly-veiled allegory for the McCarthy-ite investigations which had not only harried high profile people from positions of influence but demonised their friends and colleagues who had been pressurised into denouncing them. Wardle admires the playwright's technique of 'commenting on the present from the vantage point of historical melodrama.'[22] The fact that Miller would later be called to appear before the investigating authorities lent this brave exhibition of artistic resistance extra moment still.

In literature, in the fields of poetry and the novel, what had been the trends in the years before Ginsberg's 'Howl' exploded? Bradbury talks of the situation at the end of the Second World War as the beginning of 'the age of American hegemony.'[23] Modernism had died, he argues, with the passing of Yeats and Freud in 1939, Joyce and Woolf in 1941. In the US, the fall-out from the war's paradoxical political alliances had a bearing on the way the written word evolved. He remarks: 'It is significant that the very best of the post-war American writers were those who had acquired their political education in the left-wing atmosphere of the 1930s and were now in the process of coming to terms with the atmosphere of moral ambiguity that ran so strongly through the post-war, cold war atmosphere of the late 1940s and 1950s, when writers throughout the west felt writing needed to begin again.'[24] The searing jolt of the Holocaust prompted a string of Jewish intellectuals, who had tarried with Communism and then left it behind, to express their feelings through fiction. He cites Saul Bellow, Norman Mailer, Bernard Malamud and Philip Roth as important examples of this trend. 'Now the theme was no longer the immigrant victim struggling for place and recognition in the New World, rather that of the Jew as modern victim forced by history into existential self-definition, a definition that was not solely religious, political, or ethnic.'[25] Cunliffe suggests that Bellow, Malamud, Mailer and Ginsberg 'all of them in their individual ways [...] developed techniques of writing-as-talk (confession, harangue, invective)'

---

[21] Richard Maltby, *Hollywood Cinema* (Oxford: Blackwell, 1995), p. 72.
[22] Irving Wardle, 'American Theatre since 1945', *American Literature Since 1900*, edited by Marcus Cunliffe (London: Sphere, 1988), pp. 205–36 (p. 210).
[23] Bradbury, 1992, p. 159.
[24] *Ibid.*, p. 164.
[25] *Ibid.*, p. 165.

that departed 'radically from the well-behaved, consistent locutions of the genteel tradition'.[26] Mailer would, a little further down the road, publish his widely read essay 'The White Negro' in 1957, which contemplated the white need to emulate black behaviour and values. Meanwhile, black fiction, represented best by Ralph Ellison's *Invisible Man* (1952) and James Baldwin's *Go Tell it On the Mountain* (1953) and *Giovanni's Room* (1956) also revealed the rise of a Negro voice that explored a morality that was charged with a sense of political outrage, as identity, religion and sexuality were addressed from the other side of the racial tracks.

Yet there is little doubt that the book which would cast most light on the crisis facing neurotic, affluent white America would come from the pen of J. D. Salinger in the form of 1951's *The Catcher in the Rye*. Bradbury says that 'the moral and realistic novel of the 1950s was always a novel under strain, under pressure from ethical change, sexual expectation, and changing attitudes to personal fulfilment, and above all from the ever-complicating American reality'[27] and it was Salinger's book that perhaps best expressed this quality of tension. He calls it 'the strongest novel of the Fifties; it caught its mood and became a universal student classic'.[28] Cunliffe says that the novel 'seemed to speak for an era which distrusted public attitudes but had nothing very certain to put in their place'.[29] Salinger 'seemed *the* voice of the youthful, middle-class urban American' whose central character Holden Caulfield 'surveys Manhattan and its hinterland through the eyes of an incoherent but likeably honest teenager'.[30]

As for poetry, those pillars of modernism, Ezra Pound and T. S. Eliot, still cast long shadows over the years that followed the Second World War, yet their status and reception was confused, perhaps compromised, by their allegiances, political and national. Pound's dalliance with fascism tarnished his poetic reputation; Eliot's decision to take British citizenship in 1927 would alter perceptions among those of his original homeland. It is intriguing that William Carlos Williams should criticise the pair suggesting that by 'kowtowing to Europe' they had both harmed American poetry.[31] Williams, from the same New Jersey town Paterson, as Ginsberg, would not only leave his own mark on American verse but would become friend of, mentor to and influence on this younger poet.

While we might mention rising poetic figures of this period – Robert Lowell, John Berryman and Marianne Moore and the emerging nexus at Black Mountain College – the importance of Williams, a practising doctor who remained a

---

[26] Marcus Cunliffe, *The Literature of the United States*, 4th edn. (Harmondsworth: Penguin, 1986), p. 401.
[27] Bradbury, 1992, p. 180.
[28] *Ibid.*
[29] Cunliffe, 1986, p. 392.
[30] *Ibid.*, pp. 413–14.
[31] *Ibid.*, p. 419.

working poet throughout his life, to Ginsberg should not be underestimated. Williams was also more than a versifier; his theorising on poetry affected a number of young poets including the individual to whom he was especially close and who would eventually unveil 'Howl'. Explains Mottram:

> Williams' example was effective right through the 1950s and into the 1960s – a long example by poetry and writing on poetry [...] Poetry for him [...] was not simply personal lyricism and imitations of regular measures and stanzas: it was an innovating function of society. The line of speech is the basic measure, a form which excludes no possibility of intelligent resource. The form is not 'free verse' but the measure and spatial control of cadential lengths and the varied placing of a wide range of information.[32]

He refers to Williams' own cycle, *Paterson*, in five books between 1946 and 1958, to typify this manner of expression and adds: 'In 1948 Williams wrote of a poem as "a field of action"; these works carry the sense of a constructed place to work, into which the poet's experience is continuously articulated, becoming synonymous with his life, rather than in the sense of the alchemist engaged for life in his work.'[33] William Carlos Williams became a supporter of and guide to the young Ginsberg and, when 'Howl' was published as the centrepiece of Ginsberg's debut collection, the older man would pen the foreword.

In the visual arts, the 1950s would see seismic shifts in aesthetic attitudes. At the start, the predominance of Abstract Expressionism, the ultimate statement of the abstract concerns of the modernist ethos as represented by Jackson Pollock, Barnett Newman and Mark Rothko, was evident. The decline of the representational, the realistic or figurative, had been in progress for the first half the century but when Pollock, specifically, pursued a new style from 1947 involving the pouring or dripping of paint on to the canvas, 'he dissolved the customary compositional focus on a central image and broke down the illusion of objects in space, arriving at an "allover" composition in which the seemingly limitless intricacy of surface texture creates a vast, pulsating environment of intense energy, completely engulfing the viewer'.[34] Yet if this loosely tied American school retained kudos in the opening years of the decade, by the mid-point, a counter revolution would gain crucial momentum. Pop Art would challenge the notions of existential abstraction, adopting rather than rejecting the objects of mass society. Robert Rauschenberg, whose early work at Black Mountain College owed much more to

---

[32] Eric Mottram, 'American Poetry, Poetics and Poetic Movements', *American Literature Since 1900*, edited by Marcus Cunliffe (London: Sphere, 1988), pp. 237–82 (pp. 242–3).
[33] *Ibid.*, p. 243.
[34] Jonathan Fineberg, *Art Since 1940: Strategies of Being* (London: Laurence King, 2000), p. 86.

abstraction than the semiotics of Pop, would eventually, alongside Jasper Johns, help trigger a movement that would draw freely on the imagery of the movies and billboards, comic books and supermarket shelves. Their heirs, Andy Warhol, Roy Lichtenstein, James Rosenquist and others would produce artworks which represented 'the first cultural flowering of postmodernism',[35] as the processes of high art became fervently engaged with the semiotics of mass production and consumption, paying homage and lampooning them in an intriguing sleight of hand.

Musically, the early 1950s would see John Cage, another Black Mountain activist, as the exemplar of the modernist impulse. His *Music of Changes* had been a ground-breaking experiment in 1951. The following year, his production *Theater Piece #1*, which also incorporated Rauschenberg's minimal 'White Paintings' and Merce Cunningham's choreography, became regarded as the first 'happening'.[36] Yet in less rarefied circles – in the cities, on the streets, in the bars and concert venues – the sounds of America were undergoing a thrilling evolution. Dramatic developments such as bebop, the chosen style of most of the Beat circle, would maintain its momentum as the cutting-edge of jazz. In the 1940s, and Kerouac and his Manhattan friends were first-hand witnesses to this process, Charlie Parker and Dizzy Gillespie, Charles Mingus and Thelonious Monk brought a new frenetic sound to the clubs of Manhattan's 52nd Street and the concert venues of Harlem. Their tempestuous improvisation left the formal features of swing and the big band far behind, a sign that the Negro artist could still speak with a voice that was fiercely individual, determinedly original, in the face of widespread artistic appropriation by white band-leaders and musicians. For Ralph Ellison bebop marked nothing less than 'a momentous modulation into a new key of musical sensibility; in brief, a revolution in culture'.[37] When Kerouac and Ginsberg sought means to reflect the fracture and fury of the world around them in their writing, the pulse and patter of jazz phrasing served their prose and poetry well.

Yet, to return to earlier themes in this essay, if bebop, and the bigger umbrella of modern jazz, was the soundtrack to a particular cool urban clique, a crowd aware of Miles Davis, of marijuana and maybe the attitudes framed in the French existential literature of the time – Sartre and Albert Camus – then younger, mainstream audiences across the US were discovering a musical hybrid that veered toward the visceral rather than the cerebral. Rock 'n' roll, long-time black slang for the sexual act, represented a cross-fertilisation of genres that had not

---

[35] John Storey, 'Postmodernism and popular culture', *The Icon Dictionary of Postmodern Thought*, edited by Stuart Sim (Cambridge: Icon, 1998), pp. 147–57 (pp. 147–8).
[36] Fineberg, 1940, p. 176.
[37] Ralph Ellison quoted in Scott DeVeaux, *The Birth of Bebop: A Social and Musical History* (London: Picador, 1997), p. 1.

found common ground until the early 1950s. Blues and R&B, the sounds of Negro America, had been broadly confined to black audiences, segregated in their own 'race' chart. Country music, a style which had been dubbed hillbilly in its early incarnations then called Country & Western as the form expanded from its roots in the South to the younger states in the West, was associated with white consumers. Yet this period was ripe for change and the barriers would not remain in place for long. When musicians and managers, producers and promoters, black and white, blues and country, intermingled in centres like Memphis, where the North met the South, the chemistry would forge alliances and provide new opportunities. As Palmer states: '[A] new breed of American musicians and entrepreneurs found the literal and imaginative space to create something fresh'.[38]

The stimuli for this changing climate had been triggered in the 1940s. A number of industrial and technological factors had paved the way for a transformed popular music scene. At the start of that decade the four national radio stations became embroiled in a dispute with the biggest performance rights society ASCAP – the American Society of Composers, Authors and Publishers. When the artists' body sought higher rates for airplay, the radio companies refused and a strike ensued. The vast majority of the most significant song repertoire became unavailable to the airwaves. But the radio stations did not capitulate. Instead they set up a new royalty collection operation called BMI, Broadcast Music Incorporated.[39] This new agency did not restrict itself to songwriters in the dominating Broadway tradition of Gershwin, Porter and Kern. Blues, R&B, country and Latin composers had the chance to be played and earn from their music in a way that would have been quite unlikely without the ASCAP dispute. When the industrial disagreements were settled – and the process took around two years – the old monopolies were broken and BMI artists had their foot in the door.

Other factors would play their part – the re-emergence of independent labels, the rise of television and its surprising side effects and the invention of a versatile and long-lasting material, vinyl, an offshoot of war-time plastics research, for the creation of records. Independent labels were first called so in the 1940s. The Wall Street Crash of 1929 had seen dozens of small record labels collapse. Only the biggest players, companies like RCA, Decca and EMI – eventually dubbed the majors – would survive. As the Depression ebbed and war erupted, a new generation of immigrant businessmen moved into the sector creating small operations which took particular interest in musical styles at the edges – blues, jazz and R&B. Thus the Bihari brothers from Lebanon established Modern in Los Angeles, the Turkish Ertegun brothers founded Atlantic in New York and, in Chicago, the

---

[38] Palmer, 1996, pp. 16–17.
[39] *Ibid.*, p. 136.

Chess brothers from Poland, built their eponymous record company.[40] Through these outlets, performers such as Muddy Waters, Big Joe Turner, Ruth Brown, Little Walter and John Lee Hooker would gain national profiles.

Television would play a curious and accidental role in opening up the musical channels. When TV's foothold grew at the end of the 1940s, there was a widespread assumption that radio would go into quick decline – who would want to merely listen when images and sound were available in tandem? 'Many experts,' says Peterson, 'reasoning that no one would listen to a box when they could listen to a box that also showed moving pictures, thought that TV would completely replace radio.'[41] One result of this was that radio licences, previously highly prized, expensive and hard to obtain, were now off-loaded much more cheaply and easily in a bid to squeeze out a last gasp return before their value collapsed.[42] The consequence was that many licences were issued to smaller, niche operators whose interest lay in playing fringe musical styles. This gave further impetus to the rise of genres that had previously been marginalised. Radio transmitters became more powerful, too. When Cleveland radio DJ Alan Freed – the man who claimed to have coined the term rock 'n' roll in a musical context – presented his *Moondog House* show replete with R&B sounds, favourable weather conditions could carry the Ohio broadcast to New York listeners. Crucially, white teenagers could hear black records on air for the first time constructing a new market for sounds that had been previously enjoyed only in Negro parts of town. This novel interplay, this cross-cultural alchemy, would open avenues in the early to mid-1950s quite unthinkable in 1945.

So, in our bid to consider the environment in which Ginsberg's 'Howl', and 'Rock Around the Clock', too, made their initial impressions, we have contemplated, by way of summary, the social and the economic, the political and racial, the artistic, literary and theatrical, entertainment interests as represented by Hollywood, by radio and television, the poetical and the musical. We may have gone further, of course, and weighed up the role of matters as diverse as sex and sexuality, drugs and spirituality, for instance, in the shaping of a fresh consciousness, but the areas examined, I would argue, provide a useful framework of understanding. In what ways, then, can we draw lines between the poetic and musical texts under scrutiny and the broader setting outlined within this account? How did issues of black and white, middle-class affluence and consumer boom, Cold War stresses and political witch-hunts, the rise of television and a new wave of movie star rebels, teenage

---

[40] Charlie Gillett, *The Sound of the City: The Rise of Rock and Roll* (London: Souvenir, 1987), pp. 67–118.
[41] Richard A. Peterson, 'Why 1955? Explaining the advent of rock music', *Popular Music*, 9/1, 1990, pp. 97–116 (p. 102).
[42] *Ibid.*

identity and adolescent spending power, have a bearing on what Ginsberg recited or Haley sang? In short, the poem and the song teased out many of the tensions, many of the concerns, many of the excitements that the new America was experiencing. Old certainties – racial groupings, political alliances, respect of the flag and authority and deference to age – were no longer so well-founded and these cultural landmarks suggested as much.

Bill Haley's release reflected the move from the white ballad to a more rhythmic style propelled by an insistent backbeat. Those characteristics owed much to the R&B and jump jive traditions of the black community of the 1940s and early 1950s, but there had been a softening, a smoothing out of the Negro qualities: the earthier elements had been toned down. This was something that Haley had already engaged in on earlier recorded outings. When he took Big Joe Turner's 'Shake, Rattle and Roll' in 1954, a track which shared similar musical and production ingredients to 'Rock Around the Clock', he had followed a familiar route by sanitising lyrics that were felt too sexually explicit in their original form. But the fact that these stylistic features or hints of innuendo could feature in a white artist's repertoire, and then be propelled into the charts, were clear indicators of change. The message of 'Rock Around the Clock' was certainly subversive. Stepping away from the debate around the word rock – did it mean dance or was there a sexual sub-text to that term? – the song expressed that adolescent ambition to escape the restrictions of the clock and curfew, home life and respectability. When the film *The Blackboard Jungle* utilised Haley's song and live performance to personify the new concerns of American youth – a desire to knock over the old, an aspiration to independence, a keen-ness to create a distinct identity from the adult world – a platform for the song's widespread exposure was well and truly built. Little Richard or Chuck Berry, already enjoying some success by this time, may have better represented this new youthful fervour but their blackness would have been too threatening for the Hollywood companies making the picture and the vast majority of the audience which came to view it. Haley, kiss-curled but far from youthful, leading a group which through its horns also featured unprovocative hints of a white swing act, became the conduit by which more potent representatives of the black/white crossover – like Berry, Elvis Presley and Jerry Lee Lewis – could later raise their performing and recording profiles. 'Rock Around the Clock' was a pervasive, accessible courier of a new spirit, heard by tens of millions, but it was more emblem than manifesto.

Allen Ginsberg's epic work was more complex, more densely wrought, more fraught, more personal in tone and content. It eschewed the metaphorical, refused to side-step the unsayable, and confronted in a direct, not to say courageous, fashion the crisis facing the outsider in America. Ginsberg, as son of Socialist father and Communist mother and someone who had held earlier ambitions to become a labour lawyer, had sufficient leftist credentials to place himself, potentially, in McCarthy's very firing line. If the poet had emerged five years earlier he would have very likely faced the wrath of the House Un-American Activities Committee and maybe suffered the kind of fate that the great, campaigning folk singer Pete Seeger endured during the 1950s – banned from the airwaves, banned from performing, facing the constant threat of imprisonment. But Ginsberg, in 1955, was more than just a political agitant, a potential speck of grit in the establishment's eye. As a Jew and as a homosexual man – and 'Howl' is, among so many things, a baring of the poet's sexual soul – Ginsberg was doubly, triply, cursed in the mainstream view of this WASP-dominated society. Yet, typically, Ginsberg does not pen a verse merely bemoaning his own dilemma – he includes himself in this drama, inspired by those very principles William Carlos Williams had discussed with him as he sought to break away from formal poetics and develop his own voice – but presents a universal appeal on behalf of the marginalised, disenfranchised, the dispossessed, the lost American, black or white, clinging by broken finger-nails to the last carriages of the affluence express. Yes, 'Howl' is also a celebration of that listless, anxious, wandering America which seeks new truths, fresh hope, through music, drugs, spirituality and travel, away from the threat of arrest, of surveillance, of banishment. The work is an eclectic gathering of the ancient and the modern, which gives a poem that was the height of contemporary commentary in 1955, a timeless durability. As Mottram states: 'His measure is frequently a large inclusive line, reaching sometimes paragraphic proportions, a major inventive rhetoric of the time, and eminently suited to declamation. It incorporated Melville's sentence structure [...], Hebraic scripture, Blake's long lines and Whitman's chants.'[43]

How might we then sum up this meeting of two diverse artefacts of expression and the extraordinary period into which they were thrown? How can we measure their impact? There is no doubt both 'Howl' and 'Rock Around the Clock' left a heavy thumbprint on that decade. The poem – its reading and publication, its obscenity trial and the subsequent acquittal – gave the Beat writers an opportunity to present and explain their philosophies nationally and globally. The impact of those ideas on cultural and sub-cultural life in the next 15 years were huge, informing the growing folk revival and Civil Rights movement, the rock revolution of the mid-1960s, the rise of the hippies and the anti-Vietnam War struggles. Ginsberg's ideologies and his active presence formed a cornerstone to the counterculture in the US and in Europe. As for the song, it enjoyed transatlantic success and, as we have proposed, opened doors for more captivating, more charismatic, performers than Haley. It is hard to see how rock 'n' roll would have won such a following, so quickly, without that artist and without that release. By extension, it is also difficult to see how figures of the stature of Bob Dylan and the

---

[43] Mottram, 1988, p. 270.

Beatles could have emerged without the conjunctions of Beat verse and rock 'n' roll music, without the 1955 successes of 'Howl' and 'Rock Around the Clock'. By the end of the 1950s, Dylan was as interested in Kerouac and Ginsberg as he was in Little Richard and Woody Guthrie; John Lennon was an art-school follower of both Beat writing and Gene Vincent. By the mid-1960s, Ginsberg was warmly welcomed into their near regal circles.

But, to step into the present, half a century or so later, does the distant pulse of those happenings still register on our cultural Geiger-counter? In these postmodern times, can we retrospectively see that poem and that song, as important contributors to our contemporary condition, our latterday frame of mind? For Jameson postmodernism's existence rests on 'the hypothesis of some radical break [...] generally traced back to the end of the 1950s or he early 1960s. As the word [postmodernism] itself suggests, this break is most often related to notions of the waning or extinction of the hundred-year old modern movement [...] Thus abstract expressionism in painting, existentialism in philosophy, the final forms of representation in the novel, the films of the great *auteurs*, or the modernist school of poetry [...] all are now seen as the final extraordinary flowering of a high-modernist impulse which is spent and exhausted with them.'[44] In the early twenty-first century, in an age when older understandings of cultural – and social – order have been rent asunder, certainly reshuffled almost beyond recognition, was the mid-1950s the time when those realignments were well and truly set in train?

Rock 'n' roll, the marrying of white and black styles, country and blues, has been occasionally posited as a moment when popular music and the postmodern initially converged, ideas outlined by Strinati.[45] Here were two separate threads – each borrowing from the other – and producing a collage of styles. Strinati suggests that rock 'n' roll was 'a novel and original fusion' and therefore not postmodern but if we are to widen the scope of our analysis and put the stress, instead, on Jameson's 'radical break', then the production and consumption of this new music, both of which side-stepped the long-standing racial boundaries, did represent a very significant break with older working traditions. The Beats, in a different way, could be regarded as precursors of the postmodern, too. Their radical approaches to literary content and form, their methods of presentation and dissemination, have contributed to the crumbling of the walls between high and low art. How did they do this? They celebrated the anecdotal and autobio-graphical; they favoured the candid and confessional; they rejected the formalism

---

[44] Fredric Jameson, *Postmodernism or the Cultural Logic of Late Capitalism* (Durham, NC: Duke University Press, 1999), pp. 1–2.
[45] Dominic Strinati, *An Introduction to Theories of Popular Culture* (London: Routledge, 1995), pp. 233–5.

of the academy; they took their poetry to bars and cafés; and they self-published and spread their work through little magazines outside the publishing establishment. In short, they kicked over the traces of convention at every turn.

Ginsberg's poetry, never unhappy to reflect on and include the symbols and signs of the everyday, has, in that sense, a relationship to the Pop artists, another creative community whose work has helped to shape the debate on the shift to postmodernity, as we have already mentioned. The mid and latter years of the 1950s were a time when American society was still repressed and rigid – the presence in the White House of Dwight Eisenhower, a military man with powerful links to the triumphs and traumas of the Second World War embodied this – but the artistic shifts, a series of potent undercurrents, were strongly suggesting the decade to follow would be somewhat different. 'Howl' and 'Rock Around the Clock' were, undoubtedly, significant, early signs. So was Arthur Miller's marriage to Marilyn Monroe – the avatar of legitimate theatre marrying a screen goddess and, perhaps *the* popular icon of the era – and so were Miles Davis' new takes on Joaquín Rodrigo and Manuel de Falla when the *Sketches of Spain* sessions began at the very end of the decade. The *ancien regime* of high-brow and low-brow, elite and popular, was gradually crumbling, a preface to a moment, not far off, when Ginsberg and Dylan could establish shared agendas and Andy Warhol would feel able to invite the Velvet Underground into his own palace of mysteries.

INTERLUDE A

Lawrence Ferlinghetti: A survivor surveys

The poet and publisher Lawrence Ferlinghetti was deservedly the subject of a ninetieth birthday profile on BBC Radio 4 on 15 March 2009. Deservedly? Because here is a man whose long life spans most of the vast arc of the twentieth-century and his achievement is large: as writer but also as catalyst. It is hard to see how American letters would have developed in the closing decades of the last Millennium without his input and insight.

He is a significant survivor because he was both senior to and has out-lived so many of that generation of US penmen who called themselves Beat, yet, without his contribution, they would, for sure, have been a much more minor footnote in recent literary history rather than key players in a celebrated writing movement that both reflected, but also helped to instigate, a psychological insurrection, a rejection of the mediocrities and mundanities of the mainstream.

I only met Ferlinghetti once, back in early summer 1978, not long after I had arrived in San Francisco for the first time. It was glimmering day, the northern Californian sun golden on the street, the sidewalk cast in the cool overhang of charcoal shadow. I'd just visited City Lights bookshop, Ferlinghetti's place of business. As I left and wandered down Columbus, I spotted him coming towards me and said hello. I asked him to sign the very item I'd just purchased – a postcard from the shop.

He smiled graciously, modestly and wrote his name in a broad-nibbed felt pen. I only wish I'd had more wherewithal to chat longer. Or invite him for a drink in that marvellous corner bar called Vesuvio's, next door to the store. But youth is all too often awestruck and unable to tap into the luck of the moment. I ambled downhill, he back uphill and we never spoke again. But I do still have the autograph, somewhere.

The weekend radio show was entitled *A Reluctant Beat*, reflecting on Ferlinghetti's arm's length relationship with that community of poets and novelists who emerged from the mid-1940s in New York City and spread their gospel to the Bay Area by the mid-1950s, led principally by Allen Ginsberg, Jack Kerouac and William Burroughs but joined by a string of other friends and fellow travellers as the years unfolded and their ideas spread.

Why was Ferlinghetti significant? And why was he reluctant? He was crucial because it was he who heard Ginsberg read an unpublished poem called 'Howl' in October 1955 at the Six Gallery in San Francisco and quickly offered to publish the writer in his Pocket Poets series, thus providing the Beats with a platform to attain a national, then international, profile. But the publisher felt too closely tied to longer, older socio-political traditions – the left, the unions, anarchism – to fully embrace the newer gathering, activists in their way but less interested in the notions of organised action and more concerned, arguably, with an existential individualism.

Eventually, in fact not so long after, Ferlinghetti was forced to fight an obscenity battle over 'Howl', a long verse that addressed far too many taboos – sex, drugs, race, religion and more – to avoid the attention and then interrogation of the authorities, still numbed by a paranoia inculcated by McCarthy's recent witch-hunts.

Ginsberg's résumé – Jewish, homosexual, second generation Russian immigrant with a Communist mother and a Socialist father – was probably enough to set the establishment alarm bells ringing even before he shared his intense opinions in print. But, in the end, the courts declared that the poem possessed sufficient artistic merit to evade the censor's knife and Ferlinghetti's independent publishing house had won a notable victory in the struggle for freedom of expression.

But Ferlinghetti was, and is, a poet, too, and his collections – *A Coney Island of the Mind* and *Pictures of the Gone World* – became celebrated in their own right. Nor was he a sycophant of the Beat circle. He turned down Kerouac's manuscript for *Mexico City Blues*, when the author of *On the Road* was at the peak of his earning potential, because he didn't consider his spontaneous sketches to be poetry at all.

Ferlinghetti, who has always been a fan of jazz and an innovator in the field of jazz poetry, made musically-accompanied recordings of both of his most recognised verse collections when Dana Colley, saxophonist with Morphine, joined him on *A Coney Island of the Mind* in 1999, and, in 2005, when the poet linked with a long-time ally of the Beat community, the jazz musician David Amram on *Pictures of the Gone World*. Both recordings were produced by Jim Sampas, whose Beat recording CV is long. Sampas also included the City Lights man's contribution to *Kerouac: Kicks Joy Darkness*, the 1997 CD tribute to the novelist.

As Ferlinghetti enters his tenth decade, many of the giants of the Beat era have gone – Kerouac in 1969, Ginsberg and Burroughs in 1997 – but City Lights, the first such shop in the US dedicated to paperbacks alone, continues despite the prediction of another renowned, and sadly late, seer of the San Francisco literary scene, Kenneth Rexroth, that Ferlinghetti's plan to avoid traditional hardbacks was doomed to commercial failure. The proprietor of, quite conceivably the world's most famous bookstore, still, I am sure, finds that little detail something to smile about.

INTERVIEW 1

David Amram, jazz musician and Beat composer, including the *Pull My Daisy* soundtrack

David Amram, is a jazz musician, orchestral composer and arranger, who has been associated with the Beats for more than half a century. Born in 1930 in Philadelphia, he is a French horn player, pianist and multi-instrumentalist who has worked with Dizzy Gillespie, Charles Mingus, Leonard Bernstein and many other giants of US music. He also lends his name to a number of significant movie soundtracks including *Splendor in the Grass* (1961) and *The Manchurian Candidate* (1962). He first met and befriended Jack Kerouac in 1956, then joined him on his earliest live jazz poetry ventures. In 1959, he penned the music to the legendary Beat film *Pull My Daisy*. Later he worked with Allen Ginsberg in the recording studio, joining sessions which also included Bob Dylan in 1971 and 1981. In 1999, he was one of the principal contributors to the album *Jack Kerouac Reads on the Road*, arranging scores to accompany taped work by the novelist that had been discovered decades after his death. In 2004, he accompanied Lawrence Ferlinghetti on a musical setting of his poem *Pictures of the Gone World*. His books include three volumes of autobiography – *Vibrations: The Adventures and Musical Times of David Amram* (2001), *Offbeat: Collaborating with Kerouac* (2003) and *Upbeat: Nine Lives of a Musical Cat* (2007). I met Amram at his upstate New York home in the rural Putman Valley in summer 2004.

SW   I know that you have been involved in music all your life and rock music hasn't been at the centre of what you've done, but I would like to get some sort of sense of the way you feel, first of all how music fitted into these experiences in the 1950s – you were very much part of that – and I'd like to try and get your views on rock 'n' roll, for example. **Was it affecting you or was it being rejected by people like you and your literary colleagues. Let me first of all ask the wide question, how do you feel music and Beat literature connected in the 1950s and why did they make a connection?**

DA   There were two people, in my opinion who were central to what we would call Beat today: the two people who coined that expression, John Clellon Holmes, whose book *The Horn*, which we all felt had even more insight, as its own entity, than anything that has been written and, of course, Jack Kerouac, whose descriptions of jazz are unparalleled. There was also someone who's left out of the Beat pantheon who was just as important, someone we all read, Ralph Ellison, whose *Invisible Man*, which we all considered to be a masterpiece, even though I've never seen, to my knowledge, anybody saying that in print. Jack certainly felt that way and I did and every musician I knew, Dizzy Gillespie, Charlie Parker, Monk, everyone read Ralph Ellison, not because he was a black author, but because he was a great author who was black, who wrote about all this so beautifully and was a musician himself. Also Langston Hughes, who had extraordinary poetry and essays about jazz and history. Langston Hughes wrote so beautifully about that and influenced us, as well.

There was another writer, of equal importance, Seymour Krim, whose collection of essays, *Views of a Near-Sighted Canoneer*, had some amazing insight into Harlem of the 1940s and early 1950s, and the fact that so much of this great music came out of these terrible, oppressive experiences. And he realised, as a white person there, he could not only enjoy the spirituality and the beauty of the music, but he also had to understand the pain and suffering and chaos it came out of. He said you should not to allow yourself to be in a false state of ecstasy about something that came out of such a terrible situation – and it was about music of overcoming. But basically, the people that we would associate with the word Beat, Kerouac and John Clellon Holmes, had a real understanding; John, sociologically, intellectually and humanistically, could see what that life was like for those musicians and through the dreariness and the horror, the neglect and the wretched working conditions, some great music was being played.

Lord Buckley, another key figure of our time, who Kerouac and I loved, another who has also been virtually ignored until recently, was himself of course the great jazz poet improviser. But Kerouac, above all, not only could write about the music, he could play it and he could sing it, so when we did our collaborations, it was like being with a wonderful jazz musician and a singer as well as a brilliant writer.

We also both knew, certainly Jack knew and I knew, that this music was about overcoming, about improvising, about yea-saying, about celebrating life and about dealing with catastrophes and turning them around into positive situations. So, understanding that jazz also came so much from the African-American church experience, from field hollers, from all kinds of other music – it was something that was easy for us to relate to, those other musics, that were the source of jazz.

The case in point being that Stravinsky and Bartók, as much as any rock 'n' roll, were two central figures that Charlie Parker, Dizzy Gillespie, Monk, always spoke about, that Jack always spoke about, that I was interested in. And, in addition to Stravinsky and Bartók, we also had the wonderful blues singers, starting with Bessie Smith and Lead Belly and harmonica players like Little Walter, people like that who came later on, all the way up to the great South Side Chicago blues players, who were themselves the foundations of rock 'n' roll. And we were aware, although I know it certainly hasn't been written about that much, I know I was certainly aware, of Screaming Jay Hawkins, the Platters, the Flamingos, the Coasters, Little Richard. These were tremendous players of music.

Interestingly enough, when I saw Charlie Parker play, and I told Jack about it, in 1952, when I met Charlie Parker, he was on the bill with the Clovers – and the Clovers had a guitarist named Bill Harris who arranged their music who also played unaccompanied Bach on the guitar in 1952. So when they talk about rock 'n' roll, we usually begin that discussion with the Beatles and the Rolling Stones, the opening acts for these giants. When Charlie Parker played at the Apollo Theatre, rather in Washington DC at the Howard Theatre, which I described in my book *Vibrations*, he said to me 'Listen to the Clovers!', in addition to telling me to listen to Bartók and Stravinsky and Delius, Frederick Delius, he also said, 'Listen to The Clovers and if you don't understand what I am doing, hear what the Clovers are doing!'

The point being that early rock 'n' roll, the seminal rock and roll, came out of the same sources as jazz. Chuck Berry was a tremendous jazz fan. The blues are the blues regardless of who plays them and to the credit of the English musicians of the 1960s, the Beatles, the Rolling Stones, Eric Burdon, Eric Clapton, Joe Cocker and so on, had much more knowledge of and respect for these old blues players and seminal fathers of rock 'n' roll than most people in the United States did. And in England, as everyone knows, the Beatles and the Stones were often opening acts for these people, who in the United States worked what was called the Chitlin Circuit, named after the chitlins which is a dish made out of old parts of the pig and all cooked up and fried up, which was a very popular dish among African-Americans and white people who lived in the South that ate the same food as well.

But the Chitlin Circuit was where most of these people worked. Many of them had day jobs and just played on weekends and to the credit of the Rolling Stones and the Beatles, those groups mentioned these great old players so often that they jump-started their careers in the United States, as a result of the Beatles and the Stones taking this music and re-energising it, repackaging it and re-doing it for their own expression, their own pleasure. Now all of this was alike to jazz but in the 1960s when the rock 'n' roll industry was truly born, and suddenly there was a fortune being made from this music, not only jazz was put on the back-burner, but most of the people who were the creators of rock 'n' roll didn't get credit until the 1990s.

Little Richard and Chuck Berry and a few of the survivors who lived long enough, are now considered to be icons and one of the wonderful things was seeing the Chuck Berry tribute where they had some of the great players like Eric Clapton and Keith Richards, who loved Chuck Berry, playing with Chuck Berry and you could just see in their expressions on their faces the homage that they held for these people. Well Chuck Berry himself and these rockers were very close to people in jazz and all of us had a kind of communal respect and appreciation for one another's music.

SW   **So in the 1950s there wasn't a snobbery among jazz players and rock 'n' roll players?**

DA   There was a lack of snobbery to the point where Charlie Parker did one of his famous gigs and during intermission he disappeared and people said, 'Oh my gosh, is he out partying and forgot to come back, or did he have to pawn his horn, or did he have to get his own saxophone out of the pawn shop, or did a friend get him into conversation and he got so interested that he forgot to come back to play!?'

So finally they were looking and walking all around the streets and someone walked across the street where there was a polka band playing and Charlie Parker was sitting with the polka band during intermission and he had such a good time playing polkas that he forgot to come back to his job!

So, there was an appreciation. I mean how would Charlie Parker in 1952 get a 21-year-old kid like me, or Dizzy Gillespie, in 1951, come with his band and crash in my basement apartment and give me a whole lesson for life on how they tried to live if they didn't have appreciation for other people. Our whole era was based on mutual respect, open-ness, egalitarianism and warmth.

SW   **What happened when Elvis Presley came along in the mid-1950s? He was providing the big headline, 'White man singing like a black man'. How did Kerouac, how did you feel about someone like Presley, did Kerouac ever say anything about Elvis?**

DA   No, we all enjoyed his singing; he was a wonderful singer. He was coming right out of that Southern tradition where white people and black people were brought up together. When I lived in Washington, which was officially segregated, I lived in what was called a checkerboard neighbourhood. That meant that even though there was segregation, black and white people lived in the same block, we hung out with each other, played with each other's kids, played music together and had a closer relationship than a lot of people do today, where there is no awareness of the cultural commonality, that every human being on Earth shares with every other human being, because of the changing times and the fact there is not that cultural tie.

     What's happened now is that rap has become so predominant that now a lot of white kids are trying to imitate rappers. But that doesn't really get you into the culture by pretending to be something that you are not born into. What gets you into another culture is living together, playing music together, collaborating together, eating together, hanging out together, arguing with one another, playing sports with one another, and this was something that was very much of the 1950s world, it was part of a whole community.

SW   **Yes, but wasn't there still a divide in America that you were sort of changing? It would be idealised, wouldn't it, to say that there was this wonderful melting pot? You were at the forefront of the change in some ways.**

DA   Well we never thought of it as a melting pot; that was a sociologist's idea to reduce everything to one big fast food, disgusting bowl of slop with no identity. We were celebrating, certainly Jack was and I was, I don't think Allen [Ginsberg], Burroughs was, or indeed a lot of the other people, but certainly Jack and myself, and every musician I knew, and almost all the painters that I knew, were celebrating the treasures of European culture and the treasures of the New World which included American Indian art, painting, music, philosophy, and Latin American music, Afro-Cuban music with Machito and Mario Bauza, the great arranger, and Tito Puente, the young percussionist who got people to learn about the mambo and had a whole extraordinary excitement created around the Afro-Cuban sound and the music of Puerto Rico, all of which became combined with jazz as a cousin, just as rock 'n' roll was a cousin of jazz.

All of this was happening at the same time. It was a time of collaboration and, as far as saying, in my opinion, we were stretching the envelope, what we were doing was trying to survive harmoniously and be creative in a very oppressive situation. So we were not interested in trying to oppress other people or trying to jam some fake, quasi-political rhetoric down other people's throats with a manifesto of *The Ten Days that Shook the World*, or being like the Trilateral Commission, or official founding fathers of the Beat Generation. That famous picture of Allen, Gregory Corso, Kerouac, myself and the painter Larry Rivers, when we were all sitting round. And now we're on the covers of all these books now.

SW   **I saw it in Boulder, Colorado, only yesterday. Peters, the book shop there, had a signed edition.**

DA   When that picture was taken, we were making the film *Pull My Daisy*. The one thing that is interesting is, first of all, we were all smiling and having fun, which doesn't fit into the Beat, gloomy, negative, sour picture of, like, a bunch of angry rock 'n' rollers because their stock portfolio failed! We weren't into that because we didn't have any money, number one, and, number two, we were having fun being with each other and, number three, all of us looked and dressed completely differently, none of us looked like beatniks and none of us were in uniform because we didn't do that. And Jack and Larry and myself had been in the service so we had already been in uniform previously; we had already done that.

But the thing, I think, that is one of the distinguishing factors is that there was not that snobbism and we were trying to bring everyone to be welcome at the table and hoping that we would be allowed. I used to talk to Jack about that wonderful scene in the great Dickens novel, *Great Expectations*, that was made into such a wonderful movie where the little boy is sitting at a dinner table with all these wealthy people he's been adopted by. And the father is standing outside in the snow looking through the window, wishing that he could be part of it. And we almost felt that we wished we could be sitting at that table and welcome everyone to our table.

That's what made the times so wonderful, that was the energy that Jack Kerouac wrote about and reported about, because he was really a reporter. And without Jack Kerouac there would have been no so-called Beat Generation. He was the engine that pulled the train. It was the phenomenal success of *On the Road* that made all the other people, now considered to be of the Beat Generation, even rise above the level of obscurity. Otherwise, in my opinion, no one would have ever heard of them today. And Carolyn Cassady would concur with that.

SW **In the late 1950s then when you first performed jazz poetry with Kerouac, am I right in thinking that the initial season that you did together in New York actually wasn't that well received?**

DA Oh people loved it. We used to do it before we even did the very first, what you might call an official reading at the Brata Art Gallery, on East 10th Street, in October of 1957 and I had the date wrong in my first book because I couldn't remember that accurately, that particular date, and there was no hard evidence. But I did get some of the second one which was right up towards the end of December and the first one that we did, someone just put out some flyers right, never been able to get a copy and Philip Lamantia, Howard Hart, Jack and myself decided to actually to do it. I described all that in detail in *Off Beat: Collaborating with Kerouac*, how we went up to see Frank O'Hara at the Museum of Modern Art and the person didn't even think Kerouac could have written this: he was sort of a crude truck driver and he couldn't have written a book, that someone else wrote the book for him, because they didn't like the way he dressed and spoke.

But before that, Jack and I used to do that at parties, on park benches, coffee houses, anytime we were together and a lot of other people did, some of whom would have an instrument. Someone would read a poem and somebody would accompany him and this has been going on since Homer did *The Iliad* and *The Odyssey* on a boat accompanied by a lyre player. And Langston Hughes told me they did that all the time during the Harlem Renaissance but they didn't call it jazz poetry and they never gave a kind of an official New York jazz poetry reading.

Ours was just something we did for a bunch of friends because the art gallery thought it would be fun and it created such a stir, the Circle in the Square Theatre said, 'Let's do it there', and fortunately I had the old poster, so that's kind of the hard evidence, you know the paper trail that I guess historians need to show that it actually happened.

But when it was called the Jazz Poetry Trio, Jack and I used to call it music poetry/poetry music because it wasn't exclusively jazz. It was music to fit the poem and, very often, I would just improvise and rhyme raps myself and Jack would do the same and I never knew whether he was reading something that he wrote or just something that he made up on the spot, or if it was something by Baudelaire or Céline or Gregory Corso or Langston Hughes or some of the other people whose work he loved and admired.

SW **Am I right in thinking that once *On The Road* had been published, Kerouac's fame was obviously on the rise and didn't you do a short residency together at one of the Village jazz clubs ...**

DA No, there was a famous one that he did at the Vanguard for which I was not available and after that we played our jazz poetry reading at the Circle in the Square. But at the Vanguard he came in, the musicians had no idea who he was, what he was doing …

SW **It was the Vanguard that didn't work then …**

DA And that was because he came in and the musicians, who Jack loved and knew about, didn't really know who he was. There was a tiny dressing room about the size of a phone booth and Jack came in not dressed up and the jazz players would always get dressed up because they were conscious of the bad image that jazz had amongst so many people, so they figured that, if they would dress up to the nines, people would take them more seriously as artists. And Jack came in as he always did just looking as if he had come from working as a lumberjack for the day and he looked elegant in his own way but he wasn't dressed up that way so people would look and say, 'Who the hell is this guy?', and he, being so sensitive, thought that perhaps these people who he admired and loved didn't really want to do that with him. So he drank a lot as a result and felt insecure and I wasn't there as a security blanket as someone who loved him.

    Steve Allen came to one of those shows and Jack was reading finally by himself and Steve said, 'You know, let me try and play some music for you', so Bob Thiele, who made records, happened to be sitting in the audience and said to Steve, 'Why don't you guys make a recording' so Jack as a result was able to make a recording with Steve. We were going to do a recording several times but we never got around to is except for the recording of the film *Pull My Daisy* and years later I did one for Rykodisc. Fifty years after Jack had narrated into a tape recorder, I added the music.

SW **That was a fantastic, the work you did on the *Jack Kerouac Reads On the Road* CD. That epic section, about 18 minutes long, is it 'Washington Blues'? That is magnificent.**

DA Well, thank you. Actually I used that theme in the second movement of my flute concerto that I wrote for James Galway, which is dedicated to Kerouac, and I used that melody again as the principal theme, because I liked it so much I decided it should have a life of its own. Thank you.

SW **It has so many colours, so much richness, so many styles.**

DA Well interestingly enough, what I did for that one, I used two different groups and I orchestrated and wrote the whole thing as a 20-minute piece with two different groups so that I had to record them separately so one could fit into the other. That's where I used my skills as a classical composer as if I was…

SW **How was that edited?**

DA It was very simple because I had it all figured out. I said this is the first piece, this is the third piece, this is the second piece, this is the eighth piece, just put them together. I had everything timed with a stopwatch so that one thing flowed into the other and it fit the poem perfectly.

But the second one that we did called 'Orizaba 210 Blues', I did it the opposite way. I wrote nothing down and I did everything improvised, one track after another, and created the whole track out of my head, like Jack often did when he typed and the nice thing is people listening to both of those can't tell which is written and which is improvised – and the point being that what Jack tried to do was edit in his head, to plan and then to let it happen.

When I compose I sit there, sometimes all day, working on one measure but at the very end what I decide to use is something that is correct but also sounds effortless. So you have to work real hard to sound effortless. Kerouac did that too, that is one of the big secrets. And by being spontaneous and being formal, that's the magic of his work and that is why his work towers above everyone else of the so-called Beat Generation. Because he really had that ability to combine that jazz philosophy.

Now I think in the rock world, Jim Morrison was the heir to that, certainly with the Doors, and the Last Poets, of course, who were fantastic and those are people in rock that we all love. Certainly, Jack appreciated, before he died, as we all did, Carlos Santana, who was extraordinary and still is today, and a lot of Jim Webb, the great songwriter also we appreciated. Jack loved a lot of the country artists, too, because they were so sincere, beautiful and musical and honest.

SW **Were there any particular country heroes Kerouac ever mentioned to you?**

DA They weren't heroes, but we all loved Jimmie Rogers and Patsy Kline, of course, and Hank Williams who we used to say was the Texas haiku master because his miniatures said everything. Willie Nelson, way back then, we were aware of through the grapevine, even though he was an obscure songwriter.

SW **He wrote 'Crazy' didn't he?**

DA Yes, and Willie also, of course, had that jazz inflection in everything that he ever did. Jazz musician Miles Davis loved Willie. There was always this connection between the different people who were coming from a truly soulful place.

SW **Yes, there is a tendency isn't there in music, certainly in popular music, to pigeonhole and say, 'Miles Davis does this, Willie Nelson**

does this', and you feel as if the barriers are more divisive than useful?

DA   Oh, of course. We were interested in the music. Jack was revolted by what became the rock 'n' roll industry, combining the promulgation of young people getting stoned out on drugs, not reading books, not writing, nor being creative, not having respect for anyone else, not studying and not being more open and inclusive, but just being blasted out and saying that was a revolutionary move, being irresponsible and despising the country that had offered us so much.

Jack had an immigrant sense of appreciation for America because it had offered himself and his family a better opportunity. He saw the beauty part of all the people in this extraordinary country who make such an unpredictable, wild, crazy place, and like all musicians who travel like we do, we are all patriotic in the sense that we appreciate that beauty and the unsung heroes and heroines of our culture and the early rock 'n' rollers who led that same nomadic life of being on the road.

When rock 'n' roll became an industrial phenomenon and was taken over by substance-abusing, criminal type people who were looking for some fast money, it changed the feeling of it because the people in charge, unlike in the world of jazz, were not the musicians and the fans who loved them, but other people who were using the powers of corporate America to manipulate people into buying something that they themselves didn't appreciate and respect.

So they say that the tree dies at the top, so if somebody is controlled by a bunch of philistine ignoramuses, the chances are the artist will find a way to make it beautiful anyway! Just as Michelangelo painted the Sistine Chapel – it took him four years – where he was being screamed at every week, 'Hurry Mike you're behind schedule'. He managed it anyway.

But in the case of a lot of rock 'n' roll, it was so tainted by the people who ran it that they used these poor young musicians really in the way that purveyors do and pimps do when they take a 15-year-old off of a bus coming from the Midwest and turn her into a prostitute and then when they are 21 years old, discard them because they are no longer commercially viable.

SW   **Do you think this had happened before the 1960s were over or was this was a post-1960s phenomenon – had this already happened in the 1960s?**

DA   No, this happened in the 1960s when the record companies had drug abusers and opportunists who saw progressive politics, because of the devastation of the Vietnam War, as a way of tapping into the youth dollar. All that, together with a highly inflated economy, handed the country over to the right wing where it still is today. It was irresponsible on the part of a lot of people and a lot of the icons who were created themselves became victims as a result of that.

SW **Hendrix, Joplin and so on.**

DA Yes and fortunately the music of Janis Joplin and the Band, and some of the other great early rockers, still survives and is appreciated more than ever by younger rockers because it has integrity and substance and quality and creativity and imagination. Songwriters like Fred Neil, the extraordinary work that they have done and …

SW **Yes, you were making this very interesting point about the rock industry exploiting young musicians and you made this parallel with prostitution or whatever. But do you feel as if there was some kind of continuity between what Beat had been and what rock became after the mid-1960s?**

DA No.

SW **OK.**

DA How's that for a short answer? I think there were some people … Allen [Ginsberg] was very attracted to rock because of the gigantic audience that it reached and some people tried to attach themselves to the rock industry just to get the exposure that rock offered. The famous statement was that the head of Columbia Records told Miles Davis that by using that machinery, if he would change his attitude and what he did to an extent, he could make him into a pop star. And Miles, who had spent his whole life making all this magnificent music for little record companies that probably gave him a thousandth the level of appreciation for what he did, went along with it and he became a rock star.

On the other hand, Dizzy Gillespie, with whom I played up until he passed away, continued on his chosen path. Doesn't mean one's better than the other. There is no question of what anyone should do or how people should conduct their lives, but ultimately the music and literature and art and painting have to come from a very private place, and I have always admired people like Willie Nelson and Dizzy and Eubie Blake, who finally got famous when he was 80 years old, and Picasso and people who stayed their course and whatever phases they went through they never tried to be something that they weren't publicly.

They were always open to doing many, many different things, but everything was done with integrity, with love, with devotion, with humility and it wasn't done in public: no one was charged to buy a painting, commission a symphony, commission an opera, see a jazz concert, see anything, if people were merely experimenting. The idea of experimental art is you experiment at home. When you are out there playing for people you are creating something.

[Charles] Mingus said: 'Man, you practise at home. When you come on the gig you come to create.' He also said, 'We were playing in this really funky bar where the guy behind the bar, who was also a part-manager, he would come out and beat up the customers if he didn't like their attitude.' Mingus remarked: 'It doesn't matter how ratty these joint are, every night with me is Carnegie Hall.' The first time I heard that expression.

Basically what all these artists and musicians and the early rockers did was to create wonderful music, wonderful art, wonderful entertainment, wonderful oral history through music, of their life experiences in sometimes the most wretched conditions and when they finally got to an exalted condition, they still did it and still do it to this day.

So Little Richard and Chuck Berry and Ray Charles, until he passed away, and Willie Nelson still, people who are in their 70s, are a lifetime of continuity, of excellence and warmth and inclusiveness. And Kerouac was very much like that and that's the way that I try to be. Ultimately, the people who really last come not because of their image, or because they are hot just for a moment, but because what they did has enduring value and we were interested, certainly Jack and myself, in enduring value. We both knew, just as Carlos Santana knows and the great early rockers know, that there are no short cuts.

SW **So would you be critical of Ginsberg for pinning his colours to that rock flag in the 1960s?**

DA No, because he felt that was the thing to do and he was struggling as an American poet, to try to get poets to feel they could go out to read their work, that they could be taken seriously, that they could be popular, that they could make money, that they could have celebrity.

Allen opened up the doors for a lot of other people to think that they could write poetry and go out and read it and that's why I played on all those recordings that he asked me to because I said regardless of what they are like it is a good thing to open up the door for a young songwriter to say, 'Gee, Allen Ginsberg is supposed to be a famous poet and he's trying to get out there and sing what he wrote, maybe as a songwriter, I can consider myself to be a poet too.'

Conversely for a lot of musicians like [Ginsberg guitarist] Steven Taylor, who is a brilliant accompanist, just as brilliant as they get. He could show other musicians that you can play with someone who is a reader, you can play sensitively and softly, to honour the music that is already in the poetry and the words.

To be an accompanist is the highest level of artistic achievement and to be an ensemble player and to reinforce those basic principles of art which is so important in an ego-driven world, instead of everyone blasting each other off the stage and to be sensitive and musical and giving. Steven was great at that and when he and Allen played together it was terrific. And I always enjoyed it, and I was the one who got Bob Dylan …

SW   **I wanted to ask you a little more about Bob Dylan …**

DA   Well I was asked recently to work on that *Masked and Anonymous* movie. Jeff Rosen [Dylan's manager] called me up and Dylan and Larry Charles, the director, wanted me to do the score similar to the one I had done for *The Manchurian Candidate*, back in 1962. I felt that seemed to show that sometimes when something has value, it will retain the value. In Dylan's case, what he did so long ago still is resonant to people because it has intrinsic value and beauty to it. Quite some time ago, Dylan called me up and we went to a poetry reading at NYU with Gregory Corso and Allen reading.

SW   **When was this then, David?**

DA   I think it was 1971 but it might have been 1970, I have the dates confused, but it was in the fall of either 1970 or 1971 and it was in all the books, sometimes October, sometimes November.[1] I'm pretty sure it was October and it's in my own book, but I can't remember whether it was '70 or '71, but it's one of those two dates. I was living on Sixth Avenue, 11th Street. Dylan said, 'Let's go hear, Allen and Gregory', because Dylan loved Gregory's poetry, as we all did, and Ginsberg himself said, 'The poet I like more than my own work is Gregory.'

We all were crazy about Gregory's work and it's always great to see Allen, cause he was so much fun and so argumentative and so interesting to be with and you never knew what he was going to do, say, what phase he was in, so it was always enjoyable to be with him, especially then. And he was always full of life and he was in his guru phase, where he was all dressed up in the white robes.

During intermission, Bob and I went back, Allen took me to one side. He said, 'Please man, get Dylan to come over tonight, come and see me, I've been trying for ten years to get him to do something with me

---

[1] Author's note: It seems most likely the reading occurred in September 1971.

musically. Please David, I beg you, please, please.' I said, 'Well sure, I'll ask him.' So I said to Dylan, 'I'm free, I'm just writing some music, I can take the time off and just hang out.' So I said to Dylan, 'Yeah, why not?'

After the reading was over we went to Nathan's, one of those places that was in the Village, one of those fast-food places and had some fried, crankcase, oil-cooked food and then walked over to Allen's place. We walked up the stairs, we opened up the door and right in the doorway, Allen had a guitar that he handed to Bob, who said, 'Key of G, Bob, G'. And he took his harmonium out and played a note, which I think was a B, it wasn't even a G anyway, and Dylan was looking non-plussed.

So he took the guitar and played a G chord and then, snap I heard a sound. Allen already had a tape recorder set up in the hallway and Dylan said 'Turn that fucking thing off!' and that was the beginning of Allen's musical career.

So then we sat around in the living room and he said, 'I've always wanted to do this.' So we were there for about two hours and Allen was reading some of the things that he had written and pushing down his one note on his harmonium and croaking away, he had a natural beautiful voice and even though it wasn't singing in the key that we were playing, and he'd never done that before, and it was still, it was interesting, and he was having such a good time.

So, as we left, he said, 'I've been trying to do this David for years.' The next day he called up and Channel 13, PBS – it was then called WNET, I believe still – which was a local free broadcasting corporation station in New York. WNET had a programme called *Free*,[2] I believe the name was, and Allen had already set up something with them ahead of time, just in case Dylan did come over and agree to do it. He had approached the show, so Allen had it all figured out, I guess, the minute I said I would try to bring Bob, get him to come over with me. About three weeks later, we did this television programme, that was really pretty scary and Dylan was standing there in the greenish suit looking really sour and playing the guitar ...

SW **Did you play something yourself?**

DA I played French horn, piano, everything you know ... and Dylan was looking really sour and saying, 'How in God's name did I ever get into this?!' And suddenly, they had something shone upon the screen, an AP dispatch about Cambodia, Laos, exporting opium through Air

---

[2] The show was actually called *Freetime*.

America, which was owned by the CIA, and that this was a way to keep Communism spreading to those countries in exchange for us supporting their major drug dealers.

So there was this news agency dispatch and Allen was kinda chanting it, with us playing music in the background. I look up at the television screen and I said 'My gosh, watching this dispatch with someone reading it with music in the background was so effective, so much more effective than just reading it in the newspaper, hearing somebody saying it or reading it, and hearing someone say it without the music'.

The three combined, regardless of what the level of the music was, which was pretty funky, still was really interesting and I thought that this could really open up the door for a lot of kids to say let's get together with musicians and collaborate and poets and writers and maybe they could come up with something a whole lot better. They couldn't have come up with something much worse!

But that didn't matter, because it was an idea and I said the idea's more important than the quality or the why it was done, you know it was more than just a publicity stunt. In my opinion for Allen, he was making a point that people can collaborate, so we made some recordings which were so awful. I think John Hammond tried to put some of them out.

SW **Was that the album *First Blues*?**[3]

DA This was a long time ago.

SW **Yes.**

DA At the recordings, I said to Allen, 'Why don't you let Bob play at least four measures introduction?' He said, 'What?' I said, 'Well in music you don't just have the one person singing wall to wall, non-stop with nothing else happening, you vary it.' But Allen didn't know about that cause he was more of a solo personality and didn't basically pay attention to what was around him, which is okay cause that's just the way Allen is, his loveable self, that the way he was.

But you see Jack was completely the opposite. He was like, totally sensitive of everything that was happening and always tried to be responsive as a whole. Over the years Allen would do different

---

[3] *First Blues* was a 1983 double album gathering tracks from Ginsberg recording sessions in 1971, 1976 and 1981 and produced by John Hammond. This should not be confused with a mid-1970s Chelsea Hotel recording entitled *First Blues, Rags, Ballads and Harmonium Songs*, produced by Ann Charters, although the two releases share some song titles in common. See items A-170 and A-184 in Stephen Ronan, 1996.

programmes that ran out of money and I would come in. In 1981 when my daughter was born there was a place called ZBS Studios in Fort Edwards, New York – I was involved living at my father-in-law's in his living room with my first baby, waiting for my wife to have her second child delivered and Allen called up.

He was out of money and I went to the studio and played trap drums – you notice how I never played trap drums on a record! – and put on some French horn and flute parts, piano parts, too, and even sang a background part, over-dubbing stuff but it wasn't finished and they didn't know what to do with it. They'd run out of money and I kinda finished it for them, cause having all the experience of composing and writing and playing and everything, it wasn't that hard to do and I had some really nice stuff on them, I had some nice things.

Years later Hal Willner, went through all of those tapes and cut out about 80% of the stuff they played that was in a different key, with the wrong notes and everything else – and they sounded quite good. At the very end, Allen really started getting good with his singing, and the last time we played together in San Francisco, at the de Young Museum, I believe, when they had the travelling Beat exhibition, I said Allen, I said, 'Yes, me and you are really getting that music together'. He said, 'Well I think I'm getting closer, David'. He was really getting an idea – and Steven [Taylor] was an enormous help. He was always a terrific performer and always an amazing kinda personality, but he was really starting to sound wonderful, I was really proud of him.

SW **Was this in 1996 or 1995, not long before he died?**

DA Yeah, I think it was 1996. I believe it was the fall of '96 – we could look in the book – after the Whitney Museum show of '95, when Allen and I did a whole bunch of stuff together at NYU and in concert and had a great, great time. We even did a jazz poetry performance at the A&S [Abraham & Strauss] department store in Brooklyn. It was really, really fun.

I always had it, and he used to come and sit in with my band and play the finger cymbals cause he was able to do that. He had a good rhythmical sense and he used to have so much fun. I would introduce him as one if my favourite finger cymbal players and he used to come and sit in with the band and bash away and have a ball. And I was like, you know, to see him enjoying himself and when he was in that situation he really had fun, loved to be with musicians.

I think that, sometimes, he really didn't necessarily spend time with the level of musicians that he could artistically because he wasn't really that concerned about that. It was more a way of getting visibility to survive and that's certainly understandable. But he had improved, I think, once he started working with Steven and I think I did things I could to encourage him, too, to improve artistically as well in combining words and music, cause it is a responsibility when you are out there to try and inspire young people to aspire to excellence.

Not just to be a celebrity but to be out there inspiring a search for excellence and respect for your fellow artists and a lot of rock 'n' roll has nothing to do with that. It is all cynical and jaded and the idea that it is all just supposed to be a joke and that everything sucks.

That's fine for people who feel that way and I respect that feeling, that particular adolescent rage, but when you get a little older you have a responsibility to society and to art and to history and to your own work and to all those who came before you, to try to put out excellence. And that's not being a snob, that's being for real and that's what Jack talked about, about Beat being beatitude, trying to really be soulful and beautiful in everything that you do, whether you are playing in a prison, a street corner or at the White House.

SW **Do you think Bob Dylan was a Beat or at least a carrier of the Beat?**

DA No. No, Bob Dylan was himself. He was a kid from Hibbing who used to listen to radio late at night. I've been in Hibbing, his home town, and he had the same Jewish background I did and he dreamt of doing something more than he was told he could do, and to be something different than he was told that he could or should be.

And he went on a search, which I think he's still on, on those road trips that he takes, looking for some kind of a higher meaning. Becoming a world famous figure in his early twenties and being able to survive that is in itself extraordinary and to be out there now in his 60s still making people feel good and playing music and still writing and being creative is a wonderful thing. And I always had a great time with him, playing with him and certainly he helped to upgrade the standards, in many respects of popular music, and bring it to another whole other level.

I was with him the night that he was inducted in the Songwriters' Hall of Fame. There's a great picture of us and he was kind of non-plussed. All these great old songwriters like Sammy Cahn and people who were smoking cigars and the old Tin Pan Alley songwriters inviting Bob Dylan into the Hall of Fame was very, very touching.

He has made a tremendous contribution and I always felt he had an enormous respect and appreciation for Jack Kerouac. I think that's the closest probably he could come to him, because he was too young to have known Jack and Jack wasn't in New York that much by the early 1960s – he was away – was probably to know Allen and to know me.

So I think because of that, he probably had an interest in both of us but I think, I always had the feeling, that his true love of the period were the works of Jack Kerouac and that, like I say, is probably 95% of everyone else who is interested in the word Beat. Not to denigrate everyone else, but the fact that it was really about Jack that all of this happened, and is happening today.

Those of us who were blessed to know him were fortunate just as those of us who knew Charlie Parker and Dizzy and the painters Franz Kline and Joan Mitchell and the other wonderful writers of that period Norman Mailer, John Updike, who loved Jack's work, who Jack loved, who never mentioned the word Beat, but were there and are still here, writing up a storm and Kurt Vonnegut. There is a great picture of Kurt and me at George Plimpton's place.

It turned into a kind of memorial for *The Paris Review* where we were talking and Kurt said he was the same age as Jack would have been, and Ferlinghetti, if he was still here. All these people were such wonderful artists, who still go out and inspire people.

I was at Dizzy Gillespie's seventieth birthday party about four in the morning and he said to me, 'I was on *The Cosby Show* a bunch of times and *The Tonight Show*. America can see who I am because of my being able to transcend the ghetto that they tried to put all the jazz musicians into regardless of our achievements.' Then he looked very sad which he very seldom did and he said, 'Most of the other cats never had that chance.' He was here long enough.

Chuck Berry, B.B. King and Ronnie Spector, so many of the great gospel artists and blues artists, Little Richard, are still here to be able to receive the acknowledgement that they were due and some of the jazz artists, like the great pianist Hank Jones, Barry Harris, Billy Taylor, these magnificent people, some of these great, great people, are still with us and are now getting the appreciation that they deserve. Many people didn't.

Jack passed away way too young. Allen and Gregory both lived long enough to get a little bit of that and I mention that because there is an obligation to bear witness to others not just to yourself and they say in the Bible, 'By your words ye shall be known.' My hope is not only that my music, which is now getting played and recorded all over the world, the flute concerto I wrote for James Galway, the first movement in memory of Charlie Parker, who I met in 1952, the second movement in memory of Jack Kerouac who I met in 1956, and the third for Dizzy who I met in 1951.

I played with all three of them, they all knew each other. Each movement of the piece reflects a genre of music that was an area that they worked in. Every note was written out but it sounds, sometimes, as if the musicians are actually improvising or jamming.

So I combined the formal and the spontaneous into something that very much was what Jack was about and what I had been about and Jack and I both got that from jazz artists, painters, poets, playwrights and everyday people who were part of that wonderful hidden world that Jack wrote about.

So what became Beat in my opinion was actually Jack's reporting of some extraordinary collaborations and some extraordinary people who otherwise would never have been documented. Also *Atop an Underwood*,[4] a wonderful book of his early writing, shows he would have been just as great a writer if he had never come to New York.

All of us who knew him in New York were blessed to know him and he can be considered to be one of our great writers of our English language without even using the word Beat, because his work transcends all that and God knows, I know, I believe mine does as well.

---

[4] Jack Kerouac, *Atop an Underwood: Early Stories and Other Writings*, edited by Paul Marion (New York: Viking, 1991).

2 CHAINS OF FLASHING MEMORIES: BOB DYLAN AND THE BEATS, 1959–1975

Allen Ginsberg is the only writer I know [...] I know just two holy people. Allen Ginsberg is one[1]

BOB DYLAN

Dylan really does belong in a rack with Kerouac[2]

DAVE VAN RONK

There is no question that Bob Dylan's evolution as one of the most important singer-songwriters in the popular music firmament was marked, particularly in its early phases, by a connection with the writers of the Beat Generation. Between the very end of the 1950s and the mid-1970s, Dylan had various influential encounters with this literary cell – either as a close and enthusiastic reader of their texts as a college student or, a little later, as a friend of (and sometime collaborator with) various members of this writing community. The friendship was best defined, perhaps, by his association with Allen Ginsberg, with whom he would have an enduring connection, but his interest in Jack Kerouac's writing style was perhaps just as important to his development as an artist. There would be others in the Beat circle who would make links with Dylan – among them Michael McClure, Lawrence Ferlinghetti and David Meltzer – and William Burroughs would have an impact on the musician's voice as a novelist when he published his own work of prose fiction at the start of the 1970s. It maybe goes without saying

---

[1] Dylan quoted in Robert Shelton, *No Direction Home: The Life and Music of Bob Dylan* (London: New English Library, 1986), p. 353

[2] Van Ronk quoted in Shelton, 1986, p. 99

that Dylan himself would have a reciprocal effect on many of the writers with whom he found empathy. Says Michael Gray of the Beats: 'It was an artistic storm that Dylan [...] seemed so avant garde in visiting upon a mass market and a new generation. The Dylan of 1965–66 swims in a milieu taken from these men and their contemporaries.'[3] In this chapter I want to explore some of the key intersections in the Beat-Dylan odyssey, with particular reference to the singer's initial discovery of this radical trend in literature in the coffee houses of Dinkytown close to the University of Minnesota through to the visit by the songwriter and Ginsberg to Kerouac's grave during the Rolling Thunder Revue tour of 1975–76.

There are various ways in which this relationship is identified and described. Dylan, in particular, has been the subject of numerous biographical accounts, of course, by writers in the US and the UK – Anthony Scaduto and Robert Shelton, Clinton Heylin Richard Williams, to mention only a few. He has also offered himself, in more recent times, the first part of an autobiographical account. All of these volumes have drawn attention, to various degrees, to the impact of the Beats on this performer and his creative progression. While Kerouac's effect is widely referenced as an inspirational, yet almost ethereal, force by those commentators offering life stories and critical surveys of the singer, Ginsberg's tangible role, as friend and sounding board to the artist, has been more straightforward to chart. Of all the Beats, the poet's personal links to Dylan are most evident and the most subject to scrutiny. A 2006 essay by Richard E. Hishmeh, 'Marketing genius: The friendship of Allen Ginsberg and Bob Dylan', is a most useful insight into the connected lives of these two individuals, and a piece that conveys a potent notion through its title alone. We will return to various of those sources as we consider this engaging overlap of artistic output – song and music, prose and poetry – and the transgenerational issues raised by this interplay, as older artists and a younger one, in the case of Dylan, identified value in sharing energies and outlook.

The Beats are an amorphous crowd – from their debut steps in the early-1940s to their self-naming in the latter years of that decade to their first national trumpeting in a *New York Times* Sunday magazine of 1952, this so-called generation of writers has provided a loosely-knit net for individuals cast across the US, based in Europe and even further afield. Kerouac baulked when the Beats became linked to ideas of the beatnik and a particular brand of subcultural cool or anti-social delinquency; Ginsberg went as far as to state that there was no such thing as a Beat Generation. And Gregory Corso remarked that 'three writers does not a generation make'.[4] But, even if the principals of the Beat Generation felt contained and constrained by the their bracketing within a specific clan and wanted to resist

---

[3] Michael Gray, 2006, p. 42.
[4] Corso quoted in the film *What Ever Happened to Kerouac?*, directors Richard Lerner and Lewis MacAdams (New Yorker Films, 1986).

such pigeon-holing, for the cultural historians and literary critics of the second half of the twentieth century, there was a discernible gathering of poets and novelists, generally men with rare exceptions only, who shared a certain brotherhood, one linked more closely perhaps to ideology – concerns about personal freedom, expressive honesty and artistic candour – than to a common creative style. So if we accept there is a Beat community, then we can also accept that there are those who follow in their wake. The term post-Beat, by no means a universal denomination, has gained some retroactive stature, as we look back at the recent era of social change and progress in the arts and culture.

With that point in mind, declaring Dylan a post-Beat may seem to have certain credence. It places him within a broader tradition without signing him up to the central credo, a set of philosophical ideas that had peaked by the mid-1950s and pre-dated Dylan's emergence, even from his teenage phase. So it was with some surprise when, in 1992, the *grande dame* of Beat history, Ann Charters, placed Bob Dylan within the Beat family itself when she produced her edited volume *The Portable Beat Reader*, a digest of Beat writing. For this respected commentator – the first to produce a biography of Kerouac in 1973 – to cite Dylan, at least by implication, as a core figure in the movement, was not only brave but also charged with meaning. It proposed that Beat was not a merely descriptive term whose potency had largely evaporated as the 1960s commenced, but one that could still be pinned to the most important solo singer-songwriter of the epoch even if his debut album did not emerge until 1962.

How does she make this case? Charters draws attention to Dylan's resistance to studio re-takes quoting the singer thus: 'I can't see myself singing the same song twice in a row. That's terrible.'[5] In his 'insistence on spontaneity', Charters sees the Beat spirit alive and well. Further she cites Joseph Wenke who proposes that the singer shares 'the Beats' attitudes toward social authority, politics, and drugs, emphasizing the primacy of the self and rejecting institutionally prescribed norms'.[6] Charters further supports this by suggesting that in the decade following his emergence, Dylan 'continued to be influenced by the Beats – through his reading, through his association with [...] Allen Ginsberg and Michael McClure, and by his visions of himself as a solitary creative artist in the rebellious and liberating atmosphere of the 1960s, which the Beats partly inspired and helped to sustain.'[7]

Wenke adds extra perspective, too, in his longer biographical account of the artist, saying:

---

[5] Quoted by Ann Charters, 'Bob Dylan', *The Portable Beat Reader* (New York: Viking, 1992), p. 370.
[6] Joseph Wenke cited in Charters, 1992, p. 370.
[7] Charters, 1992, p. 370.

Throughout his career Dylan has shared with the Beats the aesthetic assumption that true artistic expression is the result of a spontaneous outpouring of the soul and that revision often leads to over-refinement and falsification. In addition he is indebted to the Beats for having combined poetry with music, thus creating an audience that was ready to respond to unconventional lyrics sung to rock accompaniment, a combination folk-music purists were unwilling to accept [...] Finally, and most important, from the beginning of his rock period, the style of Dylan's most characteristic lyrics unmistakably reveals that Beat poetry was a strong influence on him as he developed into the most provocative and imaginative lyricist of his generation.[8]

So let us think about the various ways in which this relationship was forged and built over around a decade and a half, the period when Dylan arguably produced his most important recorded work – from his signing to Columbia Records and his debut record, through Civil Rights engagement to his amplification at Newport, from the motorcycle accident to the Isle of Wight and then an epic return to form in the shape of *Blood on the Tracks* in 1975, followed by the Rolling Thunder Revue, a celebrated live project and a much less praised, *cinema verité* movie document that emerged from the months of that concert odyssey.

For Dylan's initial Beat associations, we need to return to the very close of the 1950s as the would-be English student, having graduated from Hibbing High School in June 1959, enrolled at the University of Minnesota. Says Richard Williams: 'The best thing about Minneapolis was the access to a ready-made coffee-house social life, most of which was centred on a district called Dinkytown. This is where the local Bohemians [...] congregated. They were the last flowering of the Beat Generation, the sort of people still fired by Jack Kerouac and Lenny Bruce, Zen and Existentialism; still holding jazz-and-poetry concerts and happenings; still wearing baggy sweaters and goatees; mimicking the Greenwich Village of the early fifties (itself a mimicry of the Left Bank).'[9]

Dylan played the bars and coffee shops and increasingly became drawn to the fringes where the poets and the loners, the writers and drop-outs spent their time. Such was the appeal of this semi-subterranean zone that it was not long before his university studies were essentially neglected. He comments: 'I suppose what I was looking for was what I read about in *On the Road* – looking for the great city, looking for the speed, the sound of it, looking for what Allen Ginsberg called

---

[8] Wenke, 'Bob Dylan', *Dictionary of Literary Biography*, Vol. 16, 'The Beats: Literary Bohemians in Postwar America', Part 1, http://www.bookrags.com/biography/bob-dylan-dlb/ [Accessed 24 August 2011].

[9] Richard Williams, *Dylan: A Man Called Alias* (London: Bloomsbury, 1992), p. 23.

the "hydrogen jukebox could this be world".[10] By the autumn of 1960, his days as a student were over and it was the university of life, the academy of alternative literature and the realm of the folk singer, that was increasingly driving him on. Dylan later remembered the Dinkytown scene: 'There was unrest ... frustration ... like a calm before a hurricane ... There were always a lot of poems recited ... Kerouac, Ginsberg, Corso and Ferlinghetti ... I got in at the tail end ... and it was magic ... every day was like Sunday.'[11]

At the very start of 1961, Dylan left behind the Midwest of his home, his family and his abandoned studies and headed for a bitter-cold, frozen-out New York City where he hoped to make music, yes, but also connect with a number of singers he knew only by their recordings. In his autobiographical *Chronicles*, Dylan said: 'I was there to find singers, the ones I'd heard on record – Dave Van Ronk, Peggy Seeger, Ed McCurdy, Brownie McGhee and Sonny Terry, Josh White, The New Lost City Ramblers, the Reverend Gary Davis and a bunch of others – most of all to find Woody Guthrie.'[12] Some of these people he would quickly meet up with – via Dave Van Ronk he even gained a prestigious spot at the Gaslight as he found his feet as a newcomer performer in Greenwich Village – yet amid the hubble bubble of the folk scene – thriving in some ways as the tourists came to listen, clandestine in others in the more secret corners of Izzy Young's Folklore Center – Dylan scoured the radio for music that excited him, stimulated his ears and his mind.

He liked some Ricky Nelson, Roy Orbison for certain, yet he was also clearly seeking something of substance, something under the radar, that the literary life of Dinkytown had previously furnished for him. He found a heap of human stories in his new home of New York City but still sought meaning below the bustling surface, yet the radio appeared bland and shallow. 'The *On the Road*, "Howl" and *Gasoline*[13] street ideologies that were signalling a new type of human existence weren't there, but how could you have expected it to be?' Dylan asks. '45 records were incapable of it.'[14]

Early on in *Chronicles,* there are small chinks of light that hint at Dylan's continuing concern with the Beats. He mentions the jazz musician, and close Kerouac associate, David Amram and the poet Ted Joans as characters who might wander the Village streets, past the bars and cafés that the singer was either performing in or taking a break in between sets. And he compares a fellow singer on the scene, Bobby Neuwirth, as reminiscent of Neal Cassady, a man able, like

---

[10] Bob Dylan, *Chronicles: Volume One* (London: Pocket Books, 2005), p. 235.
[11] Quoted in Robert Shelton, 1986, p. 70.
[12] Dylan, 2005, p. 9.
[13] Gregory Corso's poem collection *Gasoline* was published by City Lights in 1958.
[14] Dylan, 2005, p. 34.

Kerouac's Dean Moriarty, to 'talk his way out of anything'.[15] But he also makes the point that '[t]he Beats tolerated folk music but they didn't really like it. They listened exclusively to modern jazz, bebop'.[16] In that respect, Dylan's remark was close to the truth yet it is intriguing that he declares an interest himself in the musical style the Beats most espoused. He states: 'I'd listen to a lot of jazz and bebop records, too. Records by George Russell or Johnny Cole, Red Garland, Don Byas, Roland Kirk, Gil Evans [...] I tried to discern melodies and structures. There were a lot of similarities between some kinds of folk music and jazz'.[17] He even recalls a day-time encounter with Thelonious Monk, sitting at the piano in the Blue Note. 'We all play folk music', Monk had said to Dylan.[18]

Yet, if Dylan's musical universe was quite eclectic, he hints that the literary heroes that may have sparked his fire in Dinkytown just a year or so before had begun to lose their allure. Not yet 20, the singer's teenage world-view was being modified, it appeared, by the maturing power of the big city. 'Within the first few months that I was in New York,' he explains, 'I'd lost my interest in the "hungry for kicks" hipster vision that Kerouac illustrates so well in his book *On the Road*. That book had been like a bible to me. Not anymore, though. I still loved the breathless dynamic bop poetry phrases that flowed from Jack's pen, but, now, that character Moriarty seemed out of place, purposeless – seemed like a character who inspired idiocy. He goes through life bumping and grinding with a bull on top of him.'[19]

John Hammond, the great talent-spotter of twentieth-century American music, would soon encounter the new arrival in the city and take a fancy to his sound and style. Signing him to Columbia Records, Hammond would oversee the release of Dylan's eponymous debut in March 1962 – a gathering of covers with a smattering of originals, including the deeply autobiographical 'New York Talkin' Blues' and 'Song for Woody', his touching homage to his principal musical hero Woody Guthrie – and, even if the premiere album did not set the world alight, it would be a platform on which to build. By the time of his second album in May 1963, *The Freewheelin' Bob Dylan*, Dylan's folk sensibilities, and with his increasingly personal, self-composed and politically tinged compositions to the fore, had been adopted by the burgeoning Civil Rights movement and he would appear on the stage at the event that would form the historic climax of the March on Washington, on 26 August 1963, that great rally for racial quality attended by some 250,000 marchers, when Martin Luther King delivered his 'I have a dream' speech. Yet, before 1963 was out, dramatic changes were afoot. President John F. Kennedy's

---

[15] *Ibid.*, p. 48.
[16] *Ibid.*
[17] *Ibid.*, p. 94.
[18] *Ibid.*, p. 95.
[19] *Ibid.*, pp. 57–8

assassination in November while campaigning in Dallas was the most tragic of all but, for Dylan, the killing would have personal reverberations beyond mere grief.

Invited to accept the Tom Paine Award of the Emergency Civil Liberties Committee in New York for his Civil Rights endeavours, Dylan was drunk and far from gracious during the evening's proceedings. He made snide remarks about the older faces in the audience and then added comments – about issues of race, politics and class and about the assassination itself – that outraged. 'There's only up and down,' he said, adding: 'I'm trying to go up, without thinking of anything trivial such as politics.' He mentioned the Washington march and stated: 'I looked at all the Negroes there, and I didn't see any Negroes that looked like none of my friends. My friends don't wear suits.' But it was his lack of respect for the late president that inflamed most. 'I got to admit,' he said, 'that the man who shot President Kennedy […] I don't know exactly what he thought he was doing, but I got to admit honestly that I, too – I saw some of myself in him.'[20]

Drink-fuelled rhetoric aside, it seems evident that some of the political zeal that fuelled the Dylan motor had begun to retreat. Some say he considered that a gunman could be aiming his sights at him at a time when temperatures were running high – particularly in the South, as the Freedom Rides of the early decade made symbolic challenges to the white racist strategies of those deeply traditional, and once slave, states often leading to bloody violence – in the debate about racial status and opportunity. But perhaps the singer had also embarked on one of those decisive and dogmatic shifts that have marked his career over many years: when Dylan appears to have finally found his cultural niche and the press have pigeon-holed him as a folk interpreter, electric rocker or a country musician, as a politico or a Jew or as a Christian, he frequently performs a striking *volte face* to throw the media off the scent.

Whatever drove this shift – fear, boredom, a psychological claustrophobia, or mere caprice – a meeting he would make as the year finally faded would certainly help set the songwriter on a fresh and distinctive course over the next few years. It would prompt a change in his approach to writing songs, it would cement his aura as an autonomous artist rather than a contracted troubadour singing songs for a particular and narrow audience or at the behest of a label, and underlie his increasingly apolitical nature, separating him, in most respects, from the countercultural fury that would fire the latter years of the 1960s, particularly that surrounding the ongoing war in Vietnam and the various forces of revolt – from the hippies to the Yippies and Black Panthers and the Weather Underground – that would transform the non-violent struggle of the earlier period into a time

---

[20] Quoted by Robin Denselow, *When the Music's Over: The Story of Political Pop* (London: Faber, 1989), p. 42.

of direct action, civil disobedience, angry street protest and even conspiratorial terror.

Whom did Dylan befriend? Well, it was his first face-to-face encounter with Allen Ginsberg, set up by the always-proactive *New York Post* music and culture journalist Al Aronowitz, that would prove significant indeed. We have already touched upon the various signs of Dylan's Beat sympathies as late adolescent and novice music-maker, and the singer makes first published reference to Ginsberg on the sleeve notes of the album *The Times They are a-Changin'*. Says Gray: 'Dylan mentions Ginsberg in an early poem: a section of the *11 Outlined Epitaphs* that made up Dylan's sleevenotes for his third album.'[21]

But here now was a crucial development: an actual link to the one of the principal names of the movement, one that arose at 'a pivotal moment in the lives and careers of both men'.[22] Gray comments that 'Ginsberg, perhaps more than any other individual writer of the Beat Generation, opens up for Dylan, and for *his* whole generation, a bright, babbling, surreal, self-indulgent, sleazy, intensely alert modern world no predecessor had visited'.[23] The initial in-the-flesh encounter was, for sure, a connection each would value to the end of Ginsberg's life in 1997.

Aronowitz, who had written about the Beats and was, by now, also writing about Dylan, heard of a party that 8th St Bookshop co-owner Ted Wilentz was hosting in New York on Boxing Day, 1963, at which Ginsberg and his lover Peter Orlovsky would be present. Aronowitz, playing intermediary, also made sure that Dylan was invited, and poet and songwriter made contact. 'Allen had never spoken to Dylan before', says Michael Schumacher, 'but he [...] was familiar with his music [...] Dylan displayed a sense of social consciousness that Allen found admirable.'[24] The pair, he adds, 'seemed to be travelling on the same path – to the extent that Dylan was now playing his folk and blues-flavoured music in some of the same venues that Allen had used for his poetry readings only a few years before. And Ginsberg was delighted to be introduced to the musician.'[25]

Says Ted's son, Sean Wilentz:

At [Ted] Wilentz's apartment, Ginsberg and Dylan discussed poetry and, according to Aronowitz, Ginsberg came on sexually to Dylan. Dylan, unfazed, invited Ginsberg to join him on a flight to Chicago where he was scheduled

---

[21] Gray, 2006, p. 256. *The Times They are a-Changin'* was recorded between August and October 1963 and released at the very beginning of 1964.

[22] Sean Wilentz, *Bob Dylan in America* (London: Bodley Head, 2010), p. 50.

[23] Gray, 2006, p. 255.

[24] Michael Schumacher, *Dharma Lion: A Biography of Allen Ginsberg* (New York: St Martin's Press, 1992), p. 405.

[25] *Ibid.*

to play at the august Orchestra Hall the following night. Ginsberg declined, worrying he recalled, that 'I might become his slave or something, his mascot'.[26]

Schumacher explains that the early basis for the Ginsberg-Dylan association was 'mutual admiration' even if they had quite different personality traits. While Dylan was 'an elusive personality, sometimes withdrawn and sometimes egotistical, always changing, as hard to grasp as mercury', Ginsberg was 'gregarious and inquisitive'. But the two 'shared a common interest in poetry and music, and their initial encounter was a positive one', he states.[27] In fact, Scobie, in his Ginsberg profile at the Dylan website *Expecting Rain*, says that the association of poet and singer is, subsequently, often characterised as one akin to father and son. Yet he makes the interesting point that, although they appeared to be of two quite different eras, their birth-dates were only 15 years apart, a chronological fact that actually undermines such a parent-child notion.[28] The timing of their breakthrough work – Ginsberg's first published collection, *Howl and Other Poems* in 1956, only pre-dating Dylan's eponymous debut album by six years – skews the generational lens still further, as the poet was a mature 30 when he made his name initially while the singer was only 20. Speaking of 'Howl', the epic cornerstone of Ginsberg's debut collection, Gray states: 'There is not one line from this huge, sprawling poem that cannot claim to be the deranged, inspired midwife of Dylan of the mid-1960s'[29] but he adds that the process was also two-way. 'Dylan's achievement has included the remarkable fact of his being able to turn right round and become a major influence on Allen Ginsberg.'[30]

Soon after the Wilentz party, Dylan would conceive one of his most important songs to date, 'Chimes of Freedom', which saw him apply a lyrical technique which would be later described as 'chains of flashing images'.[31] Wilentz argues that such an approach marked 'both Dylan's reconnection to Beat aesthetics and the transformation of those aesthetics into song. In the two years that followed Ginsberg and Dylan influenced each other, as both men recast their public images and their

[26] Wilentz, p. 69.

[27] Schumacher, p. 405.

[28] Stephen Scobie, 'Ginsberg, Allen', 'The Bob Dylan Who's Who', *Expecting Rain*, 18 April 1997, http://expectingrain.com/dok/who/g/ginsbergallen.html [accessed 4 September 2011].

[29] Gray, 2006, p. 256

[30] *Ibid*.

[31] Ginsberg told Seth Goddard in a c. 1994 interview in *Life*: 'So those chains of flashing images you get in Dylan, like "the motorcycle black Madonna two-wheeled gypsy queen and her silver studded phantom lover", they're influenced by Kerouac's chains of flashing images and spontaneous writing'. The interview, 'The Beats and the boom: A conversation with Allen Ginsberg', was published at *Life*'s website, 5 July 2001. It can be found at http://www.english.illinois.edu/maps/poets/g_l/ginsberg/interviews.htm [accessed 20 December 2011].

art'.[32] It is surely not inconsequential either that the sleeve notes of *The Times They are a-Changin'* – Beat-like verse richly strewn with name-checks from Guthrie to Robert E. Lee and Piaf and Modigliani – would be echoed on subsequent album covers, too, enigmatic poetic statements or idiosyncratic reflections in the mode of journal entries and signed by Dylan himself.[33] Yet it is not without irony that at a point Ginsberg was becoming, if anything, even more politicised – his long-term poetic concerns with honesty, peace and freedom now galvanised in an increasingly high-profile public role, in which the media took an increasing interest – Dylan would find the solace of his own personalised lyric-writing a way to distance himself from the more obvious frontline campaigns, as the Civil Rights struggle segued into an anti-war one from around 1965.

Ginsberg's most significant poetic work may have been behind him by the mid-1960s yet, from this point, he assumed a status that actually transcended his reputation as notorious, alternative versifier, the writer who had faced *in absentia* the censorious scorn of the US courts in 1957 when 'Howl' was unsuccessfully tried for obscenity. In fact, his role as countercultural guru would be secured for several decades to come, adopted as an inspirational figure by several subsequent subcultural streams in the years that followed. Hishmeh sees the new close association with a renowned songwriter, a man whose stature as pre-eminent protest singer was firmly cemented by 1964, as crucial to this momentum: 'Ginsberg's friendship with Dylan provided the catalyst that facilitated his movement into mainstream recognition from a new generation of youth culture. His affiliation with Dylan allowed Ginsberg, with some acumen, to dabble in mediums beyond just poetry ...'[34]

In the meantime, as a fêted figurehead of the anti-war coalition – that energetic marriage of middle-class, white students, political liberals, social rebels and even committed revolutionaries – Ginsberg would be physically present at numerous flashpoints in the years that followed: early street clashes in Oakland in 1965, the Human Be-In in San Francisco in 1967 and in the heart of the Chicago Democrat Convention demos in 1968. Almost simultaneously, Dylan would be scheming an escape from the hullabaloo of the rising fire-storm, heading almost literally for the family kitchen to evade the rising political heat, domestically ensconced, from 1966, with his new wife and growing brood in the rustic back-water of Woodstock in upstate New York. Speaking of this volatile period, Dylan says:

---

[32] Wilentz, p. 69.

[33] See sleeve notes on the LPs *Another Side of Bob Dylan* (Columbia, 1964), *Bringing It All Back Home* (Columbia, 1965) and *Highway 61 Revisited* (Columbia, 1965).

[34] Richard E. Hishmeh, 'Marketing genius: The friendship of Allen Ginsberg and Bob Dylan', *The Journal of American Culture*, Vol. 29, No. 4, December 2006, pp. 395–404 (p. 396).

America was wrapped up in a blanket of rage. Students at universities were wrecking parked cars, smashing windows. The war in Vietnam was sending the country into deep depression. The cities were in flames, the bludgeons were coming down. Hard-hat union guys were beating kids with baseball bats [...] Maoists, Marxists, Castroites – leftist kids who read Che Guevara instruction booklets were out to topple the economy. Kerouac had retired, and the organised press was stirring things up, fanning the flames of hysteria. If you saw the news, you'd think the whole nation was on fire [...] Truth was I wanted to get out of the rat race. Having children changed my life and segregated me from just about everybody and everything that was going on.[35]

In what ways did the emerging Dylan-Ginsberg affiliation present itself then, if not in a directly political context? We might identify a number of events in 1965 that would reflect the shared admiration, in some senses overlapping agendas, of the pair. In March, Dylan's fifth album *Bringing It All Back Home*, appeared and its cover paid lightly-veiled tribute to the Beats in the free-form, automatic writing of Dylan's own sleeve notes[36] plus to Ginsberg himself in one of the cover photographs, which showcased the poet in sartorial style: neck-tied and top-hatted. Paul Williams acclaims the collection and with specific reference to a trio of the album's songs – 'Mr. Tambourine Man', 'It's Alright Ma (I'm Only Bleeding)' and 'Gates of Eden' – places his admiration of the pieces in a quite specific Beat context. He remarks: 'It is as though all three songs came out of him in one breath, easily the greatest breath drawn by an American artist since Ginsberg and Kerouac exhaled "Howl" and *On the Road* a decade earlier.'[37] According to Gray, Dylan, in these highly-productive, mid-decade years, was able to take the Beat spirit, the Beat idea, and 'put it up on stage with a guitar. His greatness lies in the way he did that, the cohesive, individual voice with which he re-presented it and the brilliance of his timing in doing so.'[38]

In May, there was more interaction to follow as Dylan and Ginsberg linked up in the UK. The poet's appearance in England, after a sojourn in Europe and a widely reported expulsion from Czechoslovakia on grounds of his homosexuality, allowed him to make almost immediate contact with Dylan. On tour, the singer was playing live dates at London's Albert Hall. Ginsberg attended and was not only

---

[35] Dylan, 2005, pp. 113–14.
[36] In this passage, rendered in lower-case, Dylan states: 'why allen ginsberg was not chosen to read poetry at the inauguration boggles my mind', sleeve notes, *Bringing It All Back Home* (Columbia, 1965).
[37] Paul Williams, *Bob Dylan – Performing Artist 1960–1973: The Early Years* (London: Omnibus, 2004), p. 128.
[38] Gray, 2006, p. 42.

able to catch up with Dylan after the concert but also meet the Beatles, who were present at an after-show gathering, for the first time.

The tour was being filmed by the celebrated new documentary maker D.A. Pennebaker – a core member of a fledgling *cinema verité* movement in the US and France, exploiting the exciting possibilities that newly developed hand-held cameras were offering to innovative movie minds. When, around this very time, the cameraman recorded a promo piece to support Dylan's forthcoming single 'Subterranean Homesick Blues', who should join the singer, in the alley down the side of the capital's prestigious Savoy Hotel, as he peeled lyric sheets in nonchalant fashion, but Ginsberg himself plus another folk performer Bobby Neuwirth, the two figures placed in the background of this ground-breaking sequence. In fact, the trio of Dylan, Ginsberg and Neuwirth are credited with the actual creation of the hand-etched cue cards, the inspiration for many homages and lampoons in other short films, video and advertisements in subsequent years. The eye-catching promo would itself eventually form the opening section of Pennebaker's feature-length account, *Don't Look Back*,[39] issued in 1967.

This would not be the only important reunion that Dylan and Ginsberg would enjoy in 1965 and we shall return to another resonant occasion quite shortly. But the mention of 'Subterranean Homesick Blues' raises some other relevant issues linked to various Kerouac influences becoming evident in Dylan's output around this time. There are a number that can be identified during this formative period as the singer moved from being an acoustic player (even if *Bringing It All Back Home*, the March 1965 album, had featured some electric performances) to an artist committed to adding amplification to his sound, with the July 1965 Newport Folk Festival show the most high-profile and controversial attempt to share this news with his fans in a live situation. Nat Hentoff says of of Dylan's decision that he was 'after the biggest possible audience he could get, and he saw where rock was going and he too wanted to be part of it'.[40] While he felt by the standards of a folk stalwart like Peter Seeger this may have been regarded as a sell-out, Hentoff believes Dylan's 'music did get better'.[41] Ginsberg backs Dylan still further, according to Sukenik, 'praising his changes as a paradigm of fluidity in contrast to the crippling ideological rigidity of the old radical left'.[42] The poet later argued that selling out is:

... one of those cornball ideas that people who didn't have anything to do got hung up on. I wouldn't have minded doing it if I could find what to sell out

---

[39] Pennebaker's film is actually, if ungrammatically, titled *Dont Look Back*.
[40] Nat Hentoff quoted in Sukenick, 1987, p. 121.
[41] *Ibid.*
[42] Sukenick, 1987, p. 121.

to. Geniuses don't sell out, in the sense that genius bursts the bounds of either selling out or not selling out. When somebody has real inspiration like Dylan, the move to electric is just simply the expansion of his genius into more forms, wilder forms. He's got that sense of negative capability being able to go all the way in, without necessarily losing himself. Committing himself at the same time, doing it like a poet, landing like the cat with nine lives.[43]

Steve Turner believes that 'Subterranean Homesick Blues' can be connected, by way of titular inspiration alone, to Kerouac's 1958 novel *The Subterraneans* (about his love affair with a black woman) and cites further examples: the epic song 'Desolation Row' referencing Kerouac's *Desolation Angels* (his 1965 book which offers an account of his fire-watching brief in the Rockies in the mid-1950s) and the composition 'Visions of Johanna' borrowing from *Visions of Gerard* (the tribute that Kerouac penned to his older brother who died as a child). Turner adds: 'Dylan was the first songwriter to attach the language and interests of the Beats to the power and influence of rock 'n' roll and, by following his example, many who loved both Elvis Presley and Jack Kerouac, Little Richard and Allen Ginsberg or Chuck Berry and William Burroughs were able to conceive a reconciliation of their passions.'[44]

Further, if we consider the actual texts from which Dylan drew influence, British independent Beat scholar Dave Moore pinpoints some quite specific examples.[45] Says Moore in the online publication *Dharma Beat*: 'Two of the songs,[46] "Desolation Row" and "Just Like Tom Thumb's Blues" include direct quotes from Kerouac's novel *Desolation Angels*, including the phrases "the perfect image of a priest",[47] "her sin is her lifelessness",[48] and "Housing Project Hill".[49] Additionally, he mentions other examples of this trend.[50] Dylan's 'with his memories in a trunk' in 'Desolation Row' compares to Kerouac's *Desolation Angels* phrase 'with cabinets with memories in them'[51] and Dylan's 'mama's in the factory, she ain't got no shoes' in 'Tombstone Blues' – from *Highway 61 Revisited* – has a

---

43 Ginsberg quoted in Sukenick, 1987, pp. 121–2.
44 Steve Turner, 1996, p. 20.
45 See Dave Moore, 'Was Bob Dylan influenced by Jack Kerouac?', *Dharma Beat*, http://www.dharmabeat.com/kerouaccorner.html#Bob%20Dylan%20influenced%20by%20Jack%20Kerouac [accessed 29 August 2011].
46 Both from *Highway 61 Revisited* (Columbia, 1965).
47 The lyric appears in 'Desolation Row' and in Jack Kerouac, *Desolation Angels* (London: Panther, 1972), p. 199.
48 The lyric appears in 'Desolation Row' and Kerouac, 1972, p. 363.
49 The phrase appears in 'Just Like Tom Thumb's Blues' and Jack Kerouac, 1972, p. 163.
50 Dave Moore, independent Beat scholar, personal communication, email, 26 August 2011.
51 Kerouac, 1972, p. 82.

resonance with 'my mother ... skiving in shoe factories',[52] again from Kerouac's *Desolation Angels*. We might note, as well, the song title 'Desolation Row' and a further phrase in another *Highway 61 Revisited* song 'From a Buick 6' – 'junkyard angel' – which together spawn the book title *Desolation Angels*. In addition, we might add the song 'On the Road Again' from *Bringing It All Back Home* (1965) as a very likely nod to Kerouac's *On the Road*.

In a connected sense, too, we can also see Ginsberg and Dylan cross-referencing each other with various name-checks of the other in work of this time. Ginsberg first includes Dylan's name in a poem in 'Beginning of a Poem of These States' in September 1965, and refers to the song 'Can You Please Crawl out Your Window?', stating then 'first time heard'.[53] Dylan appears again towards the end of this piece, too, in which Ginsberg seems to reference, if misquote, a line from 'Positively Fourth Street' – 'you'd see what a drag you are'.[54] Dylan turns up, too, in passing in 'Hiway Poesy: LA-Albuquerque-Texas-Wichita'[55] which is dated January 1966. The following month, reference is made to Dylan and his song 'Queen Jane Approximately' in 'Wichita Vortex Sutra'.[56] Later in 'Crossing Nation',[57] from June 1968, the poet appears to chide his protégé – 'Dylan silent on politics, & safe' – at the height of the political street conflict, and he also rates a fleeting mention in 'Ecologue'[58] from Fall, 1970. As for reciprocity, Ginsberg's name appears in a throwaway Big Pink recording of summer 1967 with the Band entitled 'See You Later Allen Ginsberg' which Clinton Heylin says 'is more of a rhyme than a song'. He adds that it is 'a little piece of spontaneous wordplay around the idea of "See You Later Alligator", changed to "See you later croco-gator" before they give the nod to the basement boys' mutual friend, Allen Ginsberg, who had recently shared a stage with the Band in New York'.[59] Greil Marcus dubbed it 'a longtime hit in Ginsberg's office'.[60]

But to return to the closing months of 1965, Ginsberg was in California,[61] linking up with Ken Kesey, successful novelist with *One Flew Over the Cuckoo's Nest* (1962) and by now probably best-known as the architect of the Acid Tests

---

[52] *Ibid.*, p. 289.

[53] Allen Ginsberg, 'Beginning of a Poem of These States', *The Fall of America* in *Collected Poems 1947–1980* (Harmondsworth: Viking, 1985), p. 369.

[54] *Ibid.*, p. 372.

[55] Ginsberg, 'Hiway Poesy: LA-Albuquerque-Texas-Wichita', *The Fall of America* in *Collected Poems*, p. 390.

[56] Ginsberg, 'Wichita Vortex Sutra', *The Fall of America* in *Collected Poems*, p. 409.

[57] Ginsberg, 'Crossing Nation', *The Fall of America* in *Collected Poems*, p. 499.

[58] Ginsberg, 'Ecologue', *The Fall of America* in *Collected Poems*, p. 542.

[59] Clinton Heylin, *Revolution in the Air – The Songs of Bob Dylan Vol. 1: 1957–73* (London: Constable, 2009), p. 329.

[60] Greil Marcus, *Invisible Republic: Bob Dylan's Basement Tapes* (London: Picador, 1997), p. 259.

[61] Ginsberg states that Peter Orlovsky and he had come to San Francisco 'some time early in mid '65' in his article 'Coming to terms with the Hell's Angels', *The Sixties*, edited by Lynda Rosen Obst (New York: Random House/*Rolling Stone* Press, 1977), pp. 160–3 (p. 160).

which had seen the writer travel by bus, from 1964, with his friends around the US spreading the gospel of LSD, a drug which would actually remain legal in the States until 1966. In October 1965 the Free Speech Movement, associated with rising anti-Vietnam feeling, was taking shape on the university campus at Berkeley. A march was organised from Berkeley to Oakland, the industrial, working class port close to San Francisco. 'Their target was the Oakland Army Terminal', says Doggett, 'where new recruits were inducted into the service.'[62] But the demo was blocked by the police and marked by the intimidating threat of intervention by local Hell's Angels.

The following month a further march was planned and Kesey and Ginsberg[63] became engaged in tense negotiations as there had been further strong suggestions that the Hell's Angels would protect, what the bikers saw as, patriotic American honour by physically attacking the demonstrators. But Kesey, who had developed relationships with some of the Angels and their chapters, hoped he could persuade them not to carry out their threats. Ginsberg's involvement and his utter commitment to non-violent methods added an extra ingredient to the scenario. The poet describes a difficult meeting at the home of Angel Sonny Barger to discuss the demo and the wider ramifications:

> [Neal] Cassady, myself, Kesey and several of Kesey's Prankster friends gathered together with about 20 Hell's Angels at Barger's house with his wife, in Oakland [...] I was scared but they were all gung-ho for it. I brought along my harmonium and everybody was in a relatively excited state [...] We finally did get into a discussion of what to do about the march and I was trying to discourage Barger from attacking; so was Kesey, very manfully, trying to talk sense to Barger. He told Barger that it wasn't really a communist plot, the main thing that he kept telling him was that it wasn't *just* communists. The Angels' argument was we gotta fight 'em here or over there.[64]

In the end, Ginsberg embarked on an audacious strategy, encouraging a Buddhist chant to which all gathered eventually contributed. He feels that this communal act played a crucial part in defusing the stand-off. 'I was absolutely astounded. I knew it was history being made. It was the first time in a tense, tight situation that I relied totally on pure, mantric vocalisation, breath-chant, to alleviate my own paranoia and anxiety, resolve it through breathing out long breaths', he

---

[62] Peter Doggett, *There's a Riot Going On: Revolutionaries, Rock Stars and the Rise and Fall of '60s Counter-culture* (Edinburgh: Canongate, 2007), p. 24.

[63] Another Beat poet, Gary Snyder, also attended the demonstrations. See Doggett, p. 24.

[64] Allen Ginsberg, 1977, pp. 160–3 (p. 161).

states.[65] Ultimately, the Hell's Angels responded to Ginsberg and Kesey's coaxing, announcing, several days later, that they would not mount an assault as 'it would demean them to attack the filthy marchers'.[66]

A potential head-to-head battle on the streets of Oakland had been averted and the Angels had saved face. Ginsberg comments, 'That "happy ending" came mostly from Ken Kesey's statesmanship and common sense, because he'd been the one enlightened person on the scene – he wasn't on the left or the right. Instead of banning and denouncing the "outlaw" Angels, he socialised with them and let a little light into their scene'.[67] A little later, Kesey strengthened his links to the infamously violent bikers by inviting members to a house party at his home at La Honda. The occasion was celebrated in one of Ginsberg's best known poems of the period, 'Party at Ken Kesey's with Hell's Angels'.

Very shortly afterwards, at the start of December, Dylan's current tour reached Berkeley Community Theater.[68] Ginsberg, who remained in San Francisco, recalls 'I saw a lot of him, and he gave me 30 or 40 tickets for opening night. A fantastic assemblage occupied the first few rows of Dylan's concert: a dozen poets, myself, Peter [Orvlosky], Ferlinghetti, Neal, and I think Kesey, Michael McClure; several Buddhists; a whole corps of Hell's Angels led by Sonny Barger [...]; and then came Jerry Rubin[69] with a bunch of peace protestors. Fantastic.'[70]

Ginsberg and Dylan spent extra time together both appearing at the singer's press conference on 3 December 1965 then convening to forge an intriguing allegory for the joining of these two scenes – poetry and rock – when musicians and writers rubbed shoulders outside City Lights bookshop on 5 December for a series of photographs, framing what became dubbed the Last Gathering of the Beats. Why did this happen? Well, there were reasons of fraternity and solidarity as Dylan and his guitarist Robbie Robertson, Ginsberg and McClure, to name some of the notables, stood together for these shots, some of which were taken in Adler Alley, the passage adjacent to the bookstore, dividing City Lights from Vesuvio's bar on the next corner, a thoroughfare later re-christened Jack Kerouac Street in 1988[71] and eventually restored as Jack Kerouac Alley in 2007.[72]

---

[65] *Ibid.*

[66] *Ibid.*

[67] *Ibid.*, p. 162.

[68] Dylan played Berkeley on 3 and 4 December. The next night he performed at the Masonic Memorial Auditorium in San Francisco. See Clinton Heylin, *A Life in Stolen Moments – Day by Day: 1941–1995* (London: Omnibus, 1996), p. 87.

[69] Jerry Rubin was a Berkeley student and campaigning activist. He would later found the radical political hippy wing, the Yippies (the Youth International Party), with Abbie Hoffman, in 1967.

[70] Ginsberg, 1977, p. 162.

[71] See Steve Turner, 1996, p. 212.

[72] See Carl Nolte, 'Kerouac Alley has face-lift', *San Francisco Chronicle*, 30 March 2007, http://www.sfgate.com/cgi-bin/article.cgi?f=/c/a/2007/03/30/BAG4NOUONC1.DTL [accessed 29 September 2011].

Dylan had in mind that these images could well be used as sleeve illustrations for his next album, *Blonde on Blonde*. So there was both an artistic and a commercial imperative for this session. Yet Dylan was not completely exploitative of the circumstances. There were many more Bay Area writers present as part of this informal convention: Lawrence Ferlinghetti, owner of City Lights, Peter Orlovsky, poet David Meltzer, novelist Richard Brautigan and others. When Dylan was invited to join the larger group outside the North Beach store, the exercise a tribute to an earlier shot of jazz musicians in New York City, he declined. Whether this was out of respect for the elder statesman, whether it was modesty, whether it was because he was happy to be with the hippest of the crew in Ginsberg and McClure and not, maybe, with the less current crowd, we will never know. But the collection of images became iconic, a powerful suggestion that the powers of a preceding countercultural wave in literature had been passed to a literate songwriter and rising rock star. In the end, the pictures were not used as the feature spread on *Blonde on Blonde* anyway, but they still became a memorable record and a historical document – a monochrome fusing of two generations of artistic mavericks.

For Ginsberg, the days shared with Dylan were not just a useful rallying point, a morale-boosting sharing of ideas, a regenerative West Coast parley. The poet also asked the singer if he might buy him a state-of-the-art tape recorder, an expensive, industry standard machine of the day used by radio broadcasters. Miles comments: 'Feeling generous, Dylan gave Allen $600 to buy himself a top-of-the-line portable reel-to-reel Uher tape recorder, which would run for 10 hours on batteries and could be plugged into a socket to recharge. Dylan also bought an amplifier for Peter [Orvlovsky] and an autoharp for Michael McClure.'[73] For McClure the gift opened up the possibility of adding music to his lyrics,[74] and he reciprocated by giving the singer 'one of the 600 privately printed copies of his long howl of outrage against the Vietnam War, "Poisoned Wheat"';[75] for Ginsberg, Dylan's gesture opened up a new and fertile period as he conceived stream of consciousness travelogues, such as 'Wichita Vortex Sutra', that would form part of the wider collection *The Fall of America* (1973), which he began to record on tape. Explains Alex Houen: 'Wired for sound, the stage was thus set for the poet to try and loop automation and lyrical biography into a new circuit. On 15 December 1965, Ginsberg, Peter Orlovsky, Peter's brother Julius, and their friend Steven Bornstein left San Francisco to commence a series of road trips around the US. With Peter driving, Ginsberg

---

[73] Miles, 1990, p. 381.

[74] 'San Francisco poets were poor in 1965 and it was an impressive present and it committed me to music' says Michael McClure, 'Bob Dylan: The poet's poet', *Lighting the Corners: On Art, Nature and the Visionary – Essays and Interviews* (Albuquerque, NM: University of New Mexico Press, 1993), p. 26. He would later write the song 'Mercedes Benz'.

[75] Peter Doggett, 2007, p. 28.

experimented with dictating into the tape recorder. So began Ginsberg's foray into what he called "auto poetry" – flashes of lyrical observation spoken spontaneously and sporadically into the Uher while travelling.[76]

Thus, for Ginsberg, the December encounter had opened the door to a fresh vein of creative productivity. But how did these developments work in Dylan's favour? Dylan realised, post-Newport, that his reputation with the die-hard folk crowd anyway, had been seriously damaged.[77] Yet Hishmeh recognises, in his connection to Ginsberg, a device by which he could wriggle free of at least some of these demons. He believes that 'Dylan was able to use this friendship to negotiate his transition from folk music hero to the poet-laureate of rock and roll. His bond with Ginsberg put Dylan's folk purist dissenters in an awkward bind. While they could easily reject and disparage his decision to go electric, they would find it much more difficult to reject a rock icon who held court with poets and, through such allegiances, became a poet himself.'[78]

In July 1966, Dylan was the victim of a motorcycle accident and was laid low for a number of months. But he had already begun to withdraw from the whirlwind of publicity that chased his every move. Ginsberg nonetheless visited his injured friend in August, spending the afternoon with him and, reports Miles, 'taking a pile of poetry for him to read: Rimbaud, Blake, Shelley, and Emily Dickinson',[79] although Shelton places the visit later in September, adding Brecht to the list of texts.[80] The retreat to Woodstock by Dylan and his desire to commit himself to his domestic projects would not deter either fans or reporters. His next few years would be played out in a haze of a stalking media and a barrage of questions about his political position, particularly as the campaign against US involvement in the conflicts of South East Asia intensified. For Ginsberg, the escalation of protest prompted a quite different response: he joined many of the crucial moments where the forces of countercultural action – whether politicos, performers or writers – shared platforms, stages or even the streets.

On 14 January 1967 a significant joining of the forces of poetry and the new psychedelic rock culture occurred, once again in the city of San Francisco. The Human Be-In, staged in Golden Gate Park, was one of the biggest demonstrations to date against the war and in favour of a rising peace and love ethos that had trans-fixed much of the Bay Area, and particularly the city district of Haight-Ashbury.

---

[76] See Alex Houen, ' "Back! Back! Back! Central Mind-Machine Pentagon …": Allen Ginsberg and the Vietnam War', *Cultural Politics: An International Journal*, Vol. 4, No. 3, November 2008, pp. 351–73 (p. 355).

[77] The following spring Dylan faced new controversy when he took his amplified tour to the UK. Cries of 'Judas' greeted him at Manchester's Free Trade Hall in May 1966.

[78] Hishmeh, 2006, p. 396.

[79] Miles, 1990, pp. 391–2.

[80] Shelton, 1986, p. 375.

Anti-war sentiment, hallucinogenic drugs and a mass influx of young people from across the country were all underpinning a powerful stand against the military policies of the government. The Human Be-In brought together four of the figure-heads of the Beat world and three of the great acid rock bands beginning to make their mark. With Ginsberg and Ferlinghetti, Michael McClure and Gary Snyder providing the poetic dimension, the Grateful Dead – who had already formed part of Kesey's earlier live LSD-inspired projects – Jefferson Airplane, Country Joe and the Fish and Quicksilver Messenger Service offered the musical component, and a crowd of some 20,000 celebrated communally in an event that is generally regarded as the catalyst for the Summer of Love that would follow just a few months later.

While Dylan continued to record and release regularly, his later 1960s output did not attract the same critical acclaim that his work between 1963 and 1966 had garnered. But he had other ventures in mind – one, a longer prose work that would develop into the stream of consciousness account entitled *Tarantula*, finally issued in 1971, and a sign that he had ambitions beyond the song, the concert hall and recording studio and wanted to be seen not just as a singer with poetic inclinations but as an artist with a literary voice of his own. The work had been gestating for some time and had actually been written as early as 1966, but the motorcycle accident that would sideline the singer would also postpone the launch of the project for several years. Oliver Trager comments: 'In this collection of urban prose poems, Dylan echoes the wordplay and street-savvy rhythms of his mid-1960s songs and liner notes.'[81] The book, he says, 'found Dylan at a point in his artistic evolution when word games and spontaneously combusting ideas were as naturally to him as breathing'.[82]

Robert Shelton referred to *Tarantula* as 'an enigma wrapped in a question mark'[83] and dubbed it 'difficult reading'. He said: "It is howlingly funny, at times very violent, but is original, inventive and challenging [...] Play "Highway 61" a few times before you plunge in.'[84] Gray saw it in these terms: 'A singular item in, but an honourable part, of Bob Dylan's work, *Tarantula* combines lengthy prose-poem sections broken up by shorter, more readily comprehensible passages in the form of comic letters written by, and addressed to, different sharply drawn, vividly recognisable kinds of contemporary people: mostly risibly shallow young ones.'[85] But he also stressed the Beat qualities of the piece. 'Both parts of the book draw

---

[81] Oliver Trager, '*Tarantula*', *Keys to the Rain: The Definitive Bob Dylan Encyclopedia* (New York: Billboard Books, 2004), p. 606.
[82] *Ibid.*
[83] Shelton, 1986, p. 235.
[84] *Ibid.*, p. 238.
[85] Gray, 2006, p. 651.

heavily on upon the oeuvre of the Beats – the "letters" perhaps especially seeming to echo some of the work of Kenneth Patchen[86] and Gregory Corso. But the long prose-poem sections are also awash in slick, playful allusions to, and puns upon, a vast range of books, films and other items sucked inside the knowing maw of Anglo-American culture, from the blues to nursery rhymes.'[87] He considers the book to be 'fitfully, exhilaratingly acute about greed, corruption, manipulation, ugliness and threats to the social fabric'[88] and is surprised at how little the volume has registered with the wider Dylan community. 'Granted that *Tarantula* comes from the very period in Dylan's creative life that most people value most […] it's remarkable how much his audience too has neglected this orphan.'[89]

By the stage *Tarantula* made its belated bow, Ginsberg had chanted his Buddhist mantras on the terrifying streets of Chicago in August 1968, joined by the French writer Jean Genet, the American new journalist Terry Southern – whose uncredited screenplay would form the narrative heart of the great independent movie hit of the following year, *Easy Rider* – and also William Burroughs, a most unlikely participant in a cutting-edge political fray, as the forces of law and order rained their blows on the countercultural alliance, determined to persuade the Democrats to choose an anti-Vietnam War presidential candidate in an election year, just weeks after Robert F. Kennedy, the expected frontrunner in this race, had been gunned down in Los Angeles in June. The following year, Ginsberg would also make links with the most politicised of the Beatles, too, as John Lennon included the poet in the choral crowd that would feature on the recording of his own anti-war anthem 'Give Peace a Chance' in Montreal in June 1969.

At the start of the new decade, even though Dylan was in a continuing personal and artistic trough, he reunited with Ginsberg on a musical project which would see the duo enter the recording studio and produce some of the poet's first songs with a band. When the opportunity came to spend time in the studio with Dylan, he seized the chance to lay down his own poetry and his songs with musicians. The offer and opportunity arose out of a Ginsberg reading which Dylan attended at the Loeb Centre at New York University at the end of September 1971 and, at which, the poet had impressively improvised some verse. So taken was the singer by the poet's ability to extemporise, he telephoned Ginsberg, after the show, to congratulate him on this talent. Says Schumacher: 'Dylan had always wanted that feeling of spontaneity in his recorded music and he had gone to some lengths to assume a rough-edged, made-up-on-the-spot feeling on his albums. Ginsberg

---

[86] Kenneth Patchen (1911–72) was 'typical of the jazz-influenced […] generation of writers who ended up being called the Beat Generation', Gray, 2006, p. 529.
[87] Gray, 2006, p. 651.
[88] *Ibid.*
[89] *Ibid.*

had taken it a step further. By improvising his poetry onstage, he was, in essence, working without a net.[90] Dylan proposed they make an immediate attempt to record some tracks built on such an approach and they gathered later that same evening. Dylan had co-opted long-time Kerouac friend and collaborator David Amram, who had also attended the New York reading, to join the informal session. The rehearsal featured Dylan on a guitar borrowed from Peter Orlovsky's girlfriend[91] and Amram played his French horn.

Schumacher adds: 'Allen played harmonium and improvised lyrics [...] After Dylan taught him several new chord changes he found that he could play and improvise in a standard twelve-bar blues structure.'[92] Says Stephen Scobie, at the acclaimed Dylan website *Expecting Rain*, of the affair: 'If Ginsberg had been, to some extent, Dylan's teacher in the field of poetry, here the roles were reversed; Ginsberg regarded Dylan as his musical "guru", and deferred to him for advice and assistance.'[93] At the end of the next month, on 30 October, Ginsberg and Dylan, backing on guitar, first performed together in a filmed item for *Freetime*, a show screened on a PBS-TV station shortly afterwards. Orlovsky and Warhol Factory lynchpin Gerard Malanga were also involved.[94]

Days later, in early November, they entered the studio,[95] New York City's Record Plant, joined by another raft of supporting musicians – folk artist Happy Traum and respected guitarist Jon Sholle among them – and kindred spirits, including Gregory Corso and Anne Waldman. Over two sessions, they laid down Ginsberg songs, including 'Vomit Express' and 'September on Jessore Road' plus an extended William Blake jam. Traum, who played banjo on 'Vomit Express', said: 'The Record Plant was packed with musicians, poets and friends of musicians and poets (many of them beatnik legends from my youth) in a scene of socialising hubbub, cacophonous tuning-up, excited conversation, musical anarchy, and occasional flashes of brilliance.'[96] Unfortunately, the results would have patchy exposure and it would not be until the much later, four CD Ginsberg retrospective *Holy Soul and Jelly Roll*, issued in 1994 and overseen by Hal Willner, that some of the tracks would be experienced by a wider audience.[97]

---

[90] Schumacher, 1992, p. 557.

[91] *Ibid.*

[92] *Ibid.*

[93] Scobie, 1997.

[94] Gray, 2006, p. 257.

[95] John Lennon is thought to have provided funding towards this recording project. See Peter Doggett, 2007, p. 460.

[96] Happy Traum quoted on the sleeve notes to the Ginsberg compilation *Holy Soul Jelly Roll* (Rhino World Beat, 1994).

[97] Note that the book, *First Blues: Rags, Ballads & Harmonium Songs 1971–74*, (New York: Full Court Press, 1975), by Ginsberg, includes lyrics to songs recorded with Dylan in November 1971, among them 'Vomit Express'. It also includes the poems 'On Reading Dylan's Writings' and 'Postcard to D----'.

It would be some while before Dylan and Ginsberg made their next and perhaps greatest connection when singer asked poet to join the Rolling Thunder Revue, an extraordinary gathering of musicians and performers, friends and hangers-on, who would set out like a roaming caravan in the autumn of 1975 to take Dylan's music and an eclectic range of supporting entertainment to smaller theatres across the US. The early 1970s, post-Woodstock, had seen the rise of the mega-concert: stadium gigs and festivals played out in front of tens of thousands, sometimes hundreds of thousands, as rock moved from the teen pop single experience of the earlier 1960s to an album-oriented, multi-billion dollar global business. Dylan himself had joined the Band on a tour of such magnitude in 1974, a trek that would visit Madison Square Garden, Los Angeles Forum and other large venues, and spawn an uneven live double album *Before the Flood*. So, Rolling Thunder, perhaps most for its figurehead, Dylan himself, was a return to roots, not actually to bars, but to mid-scale venues which could accommodate many hundreds or low thousands of attendees. Says Richard Williams of the timing of the plan: 'There was an energy around: the young bands that were appearing didn't want to sound like Led Zeppelin or the Eagles. There was a new kind of radicalism in the air, a reaction against the way rock and roll had been commodified, turned into an industry. Dylan was from the older generation, but that was how he saw it, too. His answer was to put together a touring outfit that stood a chance of reproducing the spirit that music had possessed before every successful musician was presented with three roadies and a couple of tax shelters.'[98]

The tour would include a core backing band, essentially musicians who had been involved in the rehearsal and recording sessions for Dylan's latest album *Desire*, laid down that summer, but then expanded by numerous Dylan associates, including Ramblin' Jack Elliott, Joan Baez, Bobby Neuwirth, David Blue and many others, including wife Sara and various offspring of the participants. While the playwright Sam Shepard was engaged to provide a written account of the event, Ginsberg – as well as Peter Orlovsky and Anne Waldman – became part of the live jamboree. It should also be remembered that this remarkable convention was also the raw material of a movie – part documentary, part fictionalised commemoration, part surreal drama – that would eventually appear as the epic, near four-hour *Renaldo and Clara* in 1978.

The Rolling Thunder odyssey commenced at the end October and played its opening two shows at the War Memorial Auditorium in Plymouth, Massachusetts. But it was the fourth show, on 2 November, and events the day after, that are of particular pertinence here. The live performance was staged at the Technical University in Lowell, also Massachusetts, a key location in Kerouac's life story – his boyhood town, mythologised specifically in *Doctor Sax* but also a setting for

---

[98] Williams, 1992, p. 135.

other semi-autobiographical novels in, for instance, *The Town and the City*, and the place where he had been buried in 1969. For Dylan as long-term Kerouac enthusiast and Ginsberg as close friend for around 25 years up to his death, Lowell had special resonance.

The gig at the university saw Dylan, Baez, Neuwirth, Bowie guitarist Mick Ronson and others join the near two-hour set. Alan Bershaw, writing at *Wolfgang's Vault*, says that events that would occur the next day have been widely reported but comments: 'What, up until now, has not been known is just what a fantastic performance the Lowell show actually was.[99] It goes without saying that hometown hero Jack Kerouac was certainly on the mind of all concerned this night, so it's no surprise that the performance leaned heavily toward an *On the Road* theme. In terms of Bob Dylan, the Lowell show stands out as being one of his most exuberant performances ever, and thanks to this particularly crisp and dynamic recording, every nuance can now clearly be heard.'[100] He adds: 'Dylan's choice of material, much like the album *Desire*, has a distinctive unity. The songs that Dylan chose to perform and the way he chose to perform them on this tour displays one of his greatest strengths – a beautiful disregard for professional songwriter polish. This elasticity in his approach to his material is what makes these performances so immediately engaging, not only for the audience, but for Dylan himself.'[101]

The day that followed would see one of the most significant junctures in the Dylan story, certainly a key occurrence in the Dylan-Ginsberg relationship, when both men, joined by Orlovsky, paid a touching, autumnal, noon visit to the simple grave of Kerouac in one of Lowell's vast Catholic cemeteries. The episode would be filmed and form part of the *Renaldo and Clara* saga in due course. But the sight of poet and singer forming a brief, if symbolic, triumvirate with a late hero and friend, was compelling evidence that the power of the Beat movement remained an enduring inspiration to Dylan. Ginsberg's presence at this quiet homage made the occasion special indeed for both men. Writes Nat Hentoff in *Rolling Stone*: 'Ginsberg had brought along a copy of *Mexico City Blues* and Dylan read a poem from it. The three sat on a grave, Dylan picking up Ginsberg's harmonium and making up a tune. When Dylan pulled out his guitar, Ginsberg began to improvise a long, slow, 12-bar blues about Kerouac sitting up in the clouds looking down on these kindly wanderers putting music to his grave. Dylan is much moved, much

---

[99] The entire Lowell performance, from the night of 2 November 1975, can be heard at the live concert website *Wolfgang's Vault*. Visit: http://www.wolfgangsvault.com/the-rolling-thunder-revue/concerts/technical-university-november-02-1975.html [accessed 5 September 2011]. It was posted in early 2011.

[100] Andy Bershaw, 'Concert summary', The Rolling Thunder Revue Concert, Technical University (Lowell, MA), 2 November 1975, *Wolfgang's Vault*, http://www.wolfgangsvault.com/the-rolling-thunder-revue/concerts/technical-university-november-02-1975.html [accessed 5 September 2011].

[101] *Ibid.*

involved, closely captured by the camera crew that has also come along.'[102] Sam Shepard, the scribe of this tour and of this moment, reflects, too, on the scene: 'I try to look at them both head-on, with no special ideas of who or what they are but just try to see them there in front of me. They emerge as simple men with a secret aim in mind. Each of them opposite but still in harmony. Alive and singing to the dead and living. Sitting flat on the earth, above bones, beneath trees and hearing what they hear.'[103]

For Schumacher, the visit to the grave and the nearby grotto with various haunting statues of religious figures, was important because it seemed to offer opportunities to reflect on the motivations that lay behind the Dylan-Ginsberg association. During the tour, Dylan expressed feelings about the burden of myth and image that haunted him wherever he went. Schumacher believes that their friendship, which had attracted detractors, 'extended beyond their mutual artistic influence. Dylan admired Ginsberg's ability to handle his celebrity [...] Conversely, Ginsberg admired Dylan's ability to guard his privacy. Dylan had been a public figure for more than a decade [...] but he was always keen to keep a portion of his life for himself. Through his music, he had given a fragment of his life to the public, but not so much that he would pay Kerouac's dear price for celebrity.'[104]

Yet Hishmeh takes a less idealised, we might claim less sentimental, view of the Kerouac grave set-piece and harks back to the idea at the heart of his thesis that there was a strong and knowing marketing project underlying this tender tribute, its choreography carefully schemed and its impact, as a media event, quite intended. He draws attention to Shepard's own observation 'that on that particular day a red Galaxy driven by a reporter for *Rolling Stone* magazine followed Dylan's car'.[105] Hishmeh comments further on this: 'Although made in passing, this remark importantly signals that the day's activities in Lowell, Massachusetts were premeditated, unspontaneous and destined for public display. Yet, Shepard's descriptions and photos of Ginsberg and Dylan at the gravesite of Kerouac in this section seemingly elide the twin narratives of premeditation and publicity. The event appears so spontaneous, so natural and authentic, that any accusation suggesting artifice would fall on deaf ears.'[106]

That said, while Hishmeh's comments may dispel that most fanciful of notions that the Dylan-Ginsberg link up in the cemetery was somehow forged in heaven,

---

[102] Nat Hentoff, 'The pilgrims have landed on Kerouac's grave', *Rolling Stone*, 15 January 1976, p. 36.
[103] Sam Shepard, 'Singing on the grave', *Rolling Thunder Logbook* (New York: Viking Press, 1977), p. 95.
[104] Schumacher, 1992, p. 603.
[105] Hishmeh, 2006, p. 401.
[106] *Ibid.*

130 TEXT AND DRUGS AND ROCK 'N' ROLL

the more cynical, maybe worldly, reading of the occasion merely confirms what most of us already knew: that rock culture by the 1970s was increasingly part of a sophisticated public relations machine and that nothing, or virtually nothing, was being left the chance. If Dylan was not engaging a high-powered publicist to orchestrate this sequence, the singer himself was canny enough to know the synergy that such a combination of people and places would fire. Yet the grave visit could have been schemed in a more calculating way still. Shelton points out that 'some of the most affecting moments of the autumn tour were visible only to the camera crew'[107] – and we must presume *Rolling Stone*.[108] Dylan could have turned the occasion into a bigger press scramble and invited the world's media to the graveside. Further, he could have turned it into a solo Dylan visit, though the absence of Ginsberg, with his obvious and moving connection to the proceedings, would have surely lessened the impact, the poignancy, of the plan. Whatever, it seems that Dylan recognised the significance of this spiritual sojourn, this brief detour from the rock 'n' roll road, and wanted it to figure as an important episode in the movie he was creating and, indeed, it would form a section in the released version of the production.

Ginsberg would continue with the Rolling Thunder Revue after Lowell but the prominent place he may have envisaged for himself in the real-life drama, the celluloid drama, too, was never really cemented: for the poet, the re-connection with Kerouac and with Lowell must have been the most warming experience of the whole jaunt. Shepard's part as day-to-day documenter, in prose and verse, snapshots and sketches, may have been a role that Ginsberg would have relished. As Scobie remarks: 'Perhaps because his contributions to the concerts were so limited, Ginsberg flung himself with even greater enthusiasm into the improvisational atmosphere of the making of the film. He was certainly much more at home in the free-floating, slightly crazy process of improvisation than was the more script-oriented Sam Shepard.'[109] But the tour itself was also much more about the music and the extraordinary gallery of stars who would take to the stage. In 1976, the package would enjoy a second lease of life without Ginsberg but, by now, the original ethos of the autumn edition – smaller venues, secret gigs – had been displaced by a harder-headed, commercial outlook and the following spring expedition would be booked into larger halls and even stadiums with the admirable, founding idea undermined by the cost, the sheer scale, of taking dozens on the road.

Before the autumn dates were through, however, Ginsberg would sign off with an essay written for the cover of a new record which would see the light of day

---

[107] Shelton, 1986, p. 455.
[108] We must assume that it was Nat Hentoff, the great jazz and culture critic, who was present as *Rolling Stone* feature writer to witness the graveside events. The magazine appears to carry no other contemporary, first-hand reportage of the occasion.
[109] Scobie, 1997.

early in 1976. *Desire* would see Dylan's reputation, substantially revived by 1975's outstanding *Blood on the Tracks*, upheld: the dead-ends of the late 1960s, the unfulfilled intentions of the early 1970s, seemed now behind him, and the fresh material on the album would, of course, form a core ingredient in the live reper-toire of the Rolling Thunder Revue as he played with the musicians who had been instrumental in recording the work. The notes that Ginsberg would compile were headed 'Songs of redemption' and we might wonder whose redemption or the redemption of what? Dylan tarnished status certainly seems to have been buffed up by the fresh body of work and the tour, too. The poet, not surprisingly makes reference to the Rolling Thunder adventure and to the new song 'Isis', which had become one of the highlights of the concert dates. In fact, the dateline he adds to his piece is 10 November, just a week after the Lowell trip. Says Ginsberg:

> 'Isis' here recorded. the singer later developed onstage sung for weeks whiteface, big grey hat stuck with November leaves & flowers – no instrument in hand. thin Chaplinesque body dancing to syllables sustained by Rolling Thunder band rhythm following Dylan's spontaneous ritards & talk-like mouthings for clarity.[110]

The poet also makes reference to his long-standing belief that a long-held dream of his – perhaps Dylan, too – that poems and rock music could somehow find a comfortable communion and reach a mass audience had been attained both on the album and during Rolling Thunder itself. He states: 'Big discovery. These songs are the culmination of Poetry-music as dreamt of in the 50's & early 60's – poets reciting-chanting with instruments and bongos – Steady rhythm behind the elastic language. poet alone at microphone reciting-singing surreal-history love text ending in giant "YEAH!" when minstrel gives his heart away & says he wants to stay.'[111]

The relationship between Dylan and Ginsberg, and by implication the broader Beat corpus, would not end in that autumn of 1975, but its zenith was quite probably struck during those months. The two would return to the recording studio in 1981 for smaller scale projects than had featured ten years before, as Dylan played bass on a small number of tunes, but the close encounters that saw the friendship peak in the decade from 1965 to 1975 would be barely repeated. In 1991, Dylan re-visited more than several of his back pages, when he released the song 'Series of Dreams', a pleasing, yet fairly routine, compositional work-out but

---

[110] Allen Ginsberg, 'Songs of redemption', album sleeve notes, Bob Dylan, *Desire* (Columbia, 1976), sourced at 'Bard on bard', 9 June 2011, *The Rock File: Notes on the Rock Life*, http://therockfile.wordpress.com/2011/06/09/bard-on-bard-1975/ [accessed 6 September 2011].
[111] *Ibid.*

one brought to vivid life by the black and white, occasionally colour-tinted, video that accompanied it. Among the many fleeting vignettes realised the in the short film, from all eras of the Dylan career arc, are evocative frames from the Kerouac grave episode, clearly a fragment of the past the singer holds in some regard, and the title of the piece has echoes of the novelist's own 1961 experimental volume *Book of Dreams*.

When Ginsberg died in New York City from complications linked to liver cancer in April 1997, Dylan was on tour in the Maritimes, the Eastern provinces of Canada. The night after the poet's passing, he dedicated a version of 'Desolation Row',[112] a song infused by the dense lines and interweaving themes, peopled by a menagerie of freaks and outsiders from present and past, reality and imagination, an extended work of contemporary verse for sure and a most appropriate tribute from one musician with high poetic ambitions to another poet with his own musical aspirations. 'What they did share, ultimately,' says Scobie, 'was a conception of the poet as prophet. Both of them saw the poet's role as far more than the expression of purely personal feelings, but rather as a public statement of a morally responsible position.'[113]

---

[112] Scobie, 1997.
[113] *Ibid.*

INTERVIEW 2

Michael McClure, poet and author of *The Beard*

Michael McClure is a poet, playwright, novelist and essayist who was at the heart of the San Francisco Poetry Renaissance and a key player as the Beat flame grew in the city with the Six Gallery poetry event in 1955, an occasion at which he read. He has issued many poetry collections including *The New Book/A Book of Torture* (1961) and *Love Lion Book* (1966), published writings and essays gathered in *Scratching the Beat Surface* (1982) and *Lighting the Corners* (1994), penned a novel *The Mad Club* (1970) and his 1965 play *The Beard* attracted both critical praise and official sanction. He has various links to some of the leading rock names of recent decades. He was a friend of Dylan – he famously gave the poet an autoharp – and also Jim Morrison, wrote 'Mercedes Benz' which Janis Joplin sang and has developed a long and successful working relationship with ex-Doors keyboard player Ray Manzarek. Together they have toured and recorded their collaborations in music and poetry.

I spoke to McClure at his home in the Oakland Hills in July 2004.

SW   **I'm trying explore the similarities and the dissimilarities between the Beat culture of the 1950s into the 1960s and the rock culture that followed in various forms: original rock 'n' roll and then this more sophisticated style that emerged in the mid-1960s from Dylan and the Beatles and so on. I want to try and establish what continuities there were and what discontinuities there were.**

        The Beats might be described as having a certain apolitical side whereas the rock culture had pinned upon it, at least, a politicised condition and maybe we could touch upon those things. The Beats seemed less willing to use, in a sense, mass media techniques to disseminate their material, whereas rock culture gripped the mass

media opportunity with both hands and reached a global audience. There are all sorts of connections and maybe disconnections, but if I could start off by asking you this question …

In the mid-1950s when the Six Gallery gathering happened in 1955 when Kerouac's *On the Road* was published, and so on, there was, alongside, this the emergence of rock 'n' roll as a recognised national phenomenon and I just wondered, Michael, whether you could say a few words about the rise of rock 'n' roll culture alongside what you were doing as a poet, what you and your fellows were doing. What impact did that have on your work, did you tune it out or did you tune into it?

MM There was a group in England, four young men called the Beatles. I believe, at first, they were called the Silver Beatles and played basement venues. They were profoundly aware, among other things, of American black music. This was a movement that was going on, of young men forming groups that were playing music that was roughly based on black music from earlier in the century. This particular group, the Beatles – the B-E-A-T-L-E-S [*spells out the word*] – shifted from the word, spelt Beetles, B-E-E-T-L-E-S, because clearly as we watched them and listened to them, we could see that they were taking advantage and using the great openings provided to them by what they were hearing in Beat poetry and it changed the nature of their lyrics. Probably the same is true of the Stones though the Stones didn't take the name the Ginsbergs or something! So, from the very beginning I see the black music and Beat poetry, which I see as highly political – if you had been at the Six Gallery you would have found five readers, five of the most radical, outspoken, politically directed people you are ever likely to meet, in that age group.

SW **That's an interesting point you've made but if we go back a little way and mention a name like Elvis Presley.**

MM I didn't have anything to do with Elvis Presley.

SW **Why do you say that?**

MM I didn't care for him.

SW **You didn't like him?**

MM It's not that I liked or didn't like him. To me, Elvis Presley represented white kids trying to be free by imitating black music – and that wasn't the only way to be free – and it caught on. It was a rage and it probably helped a lot, but I didn't need that help and the people I knew didn't need that help and we listened to others.

SW **OK, so the original rock 'n' roll surge in the late 1950s?**

MM No, nothing doing.

SW   **That's extremely interesting, but once this British Invasion occurred, and obviously Bob Dylan was part of that, too …**

ST   We formed a great kinship with the British Invasion. What I know about rock 'n' roll … my meeting with rock 'n' roll was in my house, I lived at 264, Downey Street in San Francisco, three blocks from Haight-Ashbury, a block and a half from where the Grateful Dead was living. Country Joe and the Fish moved in across the street from me. The Charlatans, which were my favourite group, local group, moved in half a block down the street and I'd been living in the neighbourhood for several years.

       I saw a really great and interesting community happening around me, but not just a community of musicians. It was a radical community, a radical, visionary, political community, of the kind that Marcuse talks about in his essay on liberation. It made a lot of foolish mistakes, had a lot of genius, had a lot of beauty, and a lot of meaningfulness came out of it. And rock 'n' roll was simply a part of it. I found myself being talked to by young rock 'n' rollers who wanted me to help them write songs.

       Consequently I had to learn to write songs to show them, or develop techniques. But the musicians were no more important than the sandal makers or the poets originally. It wasn't until the musicians were thrust up on the stage and made into idols, which we all enjoyed because we loved dancing in the Fillmore and having them up on those stages play. That's where I learned to dance. I didn't learn to dance … I'd not had much interest in dance either. It was at the Fillmore that I learned to dance and at the Fillmore dances where you'd go dancing with one person looking like Billy the Kid and another one looks like Jean Harlow and another one looks like Florence Nightingale and another one's the Princess of Araby, and you're all dancing on the floor together making up your own dance. That's an extraordinary experience.

SW   **So you were saying a little earlier that you were living in Haight-Ashbury from around 1960?**

MM   1961.

SW   **And the arrival of the bands like the Grateful Dead, the Charlatans and so on …**

MM   Also the Jefferson Airplane and let's not forget the Quicksilver Messenger Service, and Big Brother and the Holding Company.

SW   **And all of these bands were living in the Haight?**

MM   Not necessarily were they living in the Haight but they would come there for their social life, rather than North Beach which had been the traditional social reservation. Although come to think about it, I think

I could safely say, yes, that most of them were living within a mile of the Haight.

SW **So you had moved to the Haight from North Beach?**

MM No I hadn't, I'd moved out of North Beach very early. North Beach became a tourist centre and they had buses driving up and down the street showing beatniks to the tour bus people. And the beatniks that they were looking at were people who were wearing rubber tyre sandals – like Mexican sandals were made in those days – wearing berets, had long beards, with spaghetti and were drinking warm wine and playing conga drums. These were not me or Allen Ginsberg or Jack Kerouac, these were people wearing pirate costumes offering to write a poem for you for 25 cents.

SW **These were charlatans with a lower case 'c'!**

MM You said it … They were the creations of the media. But a lot of interesting things were done by us and we still used North Beach for a centre to meet in because we were accustomed to meeting there. It's the first place I lived when I came to San Francisco. And the Cellar was there where David [Meltzer] played for example. So there were legitimate things out there but it was a place to get out of pretty damn quick. So people got out into what's called the Western Addition of Haight-Ashbury or over onto Fillmore Street or even into Marin across the Bay.

SW **Did the community of poets who were based in San Francisco feel a certain sense of intrusion when the new wave of musicians began to arrive in the Haight?**

MM No not at all. If you want to know about a sense of intrusion, America's most famous academic poet Robert Lowell. I took Robert Lowell to hear rock 'n' roll about 1967, '68. He was grossly offended and intruded upon. But I wanted him here because I thought it was wonderful and beautiful and new.

There's not a competition between poetry and rock, not with my generation, but the following generation – I do know that a number of writers suffered severely by being over-awed by rock 'n' roll and worshipping it, to the extent their poems suffered. I don't know of any instances, aside from the formalist conservative poets of say the ilk of Lowell or people like that, who had anything against rock 'n' roll, not while rock 'n' roll was still in its revolutionary phase. We were for it, we were part of it.

I had their posters all around me with me reading with the Grateful Dead and reading with different rock groups and when my play *The Beard* was done, the first major performance of it was done at the

Fillmore Auditorium with a rock group. I considered it my milieu, but I didn't consider rock 'n' roll my milieu.

I considered that revolutionary community my milieu and rock 'n' roll was an important and delightful and pleasurable part of it, for the music, which I didn't like listening to as much as I liked dancing to. I pretty much began to lose interest in rock 'n' roll when the dances were turned into sit down affairs, when people sat down and listened to it.

SW   **So this would have been after 1968 or something like that?**

MM   Yes and also when it commercialised itself. You'd be sitting in a restaurant and the scouts would be there from New York and London wanting to know if you were a part of a rock 'n' roll group, because I had my hair down to my shoulders, and, if not, who did I know who was. And they had almost blank contracts getting names signed at the bottom of it.

SW   **So I suppose, in a sense, if I had been a poet I may have been concerned ...**

MM   You do have a pretty weird opinion if you think that poets were competition, or if you think that poets weren't political and music was. Those are two places you are the most far out of anybody I've ever heard in my life.

SW   **OK, I mean this is a hypothesis ...**

MM   Well your hypothesis is bizarre.

SW   **... which requires challenge. This is how a piece of research develops. I think there are these stereotypes drawn by some readers, writers, commentators who have seen the Beats as a group of poets and writers who were partially interested in disengagement rather than engagement.**

MM   That's quite wrong!

SW   **If you read someone like Kenneth Rexroth ...**

MM   Rexroth was just pissed off.

SW   **This is one of the things I'm driving at because if someone like Rexroth who talked about disengagement this is one of the premises I'm interested in talking through or challenging.**

MM   Well Rexroth, there's personal issues involved here. You've got to understand that I knew Rexroth during this crisis that he was having. He often visited the community we were living in, the commune. You could say we were living in because it was only about two and a half blocks from his house.

Kenneth was going through a terrible crisis. Because a poet of the same age group as the Beats, and a friend of the Beats, but from the East Coast had run off with his wife and taken the two children and he had nearly a nervous breakdown as many people might do in an instance like that. Quite a bit of hallucinating, a very sensitive and brilliant man, but very far over the edge. Kenneth went very far over the edge and he decided that Jack Kerouac, and then he decided that the Beats, had something to do with it. And he denounced the Beats from then on. What he left behind him were four or five articles denouncing the Beats. I remember in one of them he talked about me, running around making all the money I could, off of readings for colleges and making big money at the college circuit. We were extremely poor! And our feelings were hurt very badly by that kind of stuff, which was just plain laughable, depending on where it appeared.

I would thank Kenneth for being one of the patriarchs, as you have patriarchs in Zen, and warn you that he had a crazy streak and that accounts for all the bad things that he said about us, and he continues to hold his bad feelings, and yet we are the ones who still, today, are honouring him. I just wrote a piece called 'Seven Things about Kenneth Rexroth'[1] which I delivered at the celebration of his collective poems. We have all been lamenting the fact that his poems were disappearing. That takes care of Rex, who else said that we were politically disengaged?

SW **I think in some ways, Michael, I'm thinking about two different kinds of politics.**

MM I have a very hard time forgiving the rock 'n' roll groups who were really part of that revolutionary beginning for just giving it up completely and giving themselves over to wish wash and never mentioning another political thing in their existence. Now that does not include the Doors, that does not include the Grateful Dead, that does not include Jefferson Airplane or Country Joe. But for most of the rock 'n' roll groups, that either continued to have a revolutionary basis or were created by scouts from large corporations after the revolutionary period, I really feel some contempt for them, for selling their asses out.

SW **So I suppose in some ways then we've got an issue of perception here because the Beats decided not to engage with some of the traditional political processes, you weren't very interested in the party systems, for instance you didn't care if it was the Democrats or Republicans.**

MM That's because we were anarchists, communists, socialists, who did

---

[1] Michael McClure's piece, 'Seven Things about Kenneth Rexroth', *Big Bridge*, http://www.bigbridge.org/issue10/elegymmcclure.htm [Accessed 22 December 2011].

not believe in the system. We didn't disengage from it; we proposed another system and we still do to this day. Don't think of the Beats as something that's gone away. The Beats are still here as a presence, and a much stronger presence politically, generally speaking, than the disappointment of popular music. You've got it really twisted around.

SW **Michael, I haven't got it twisted around. I'm trying to find a way through some of the perceptions that have arisen in recent times because the rock groups in the 1960s appeared to create a mass revolution; they appeared to create a change in mass consciousness because they were able to sell millions of records, they were able to reach millions of listeners around the world, whereas something like poetry it doesn't do that.**

MM That isn't the function of poetry.

SW **So if that isn't the function of poetry …**

MM At least not in the short term, not in a short period of time. But what it is you're talking about, you're talking about the triumph of advertising, you're talking about the triumph of commodification and the triumph of commercialisation. You're not talking about politics, you're talking about slavery, you're fucking talking slavery and many of those people enslave themselves. These are people I greatly admired and loved as fellow artists and many of them, the ones who remained true to something, I still do.

SW **Who do you consider to be those people, who stayed true to those principles?**

MM The Grateful Dead, Country Joe, the Jefferson – whatever they are now – the Starship and Big Brother, who were almost driven out of existence by another great act of commercialisation … erm, what was his name? He was also Dylan's agent. I liked him, too. He wheedled Janis away from Big Brother and the Holding Company.

But if you want to see something revolutionary, you go back to the Monterey Pop Festival and you look at the extravagant mind-breaking event of Big Brother and the Holding Company dancing while they performed with Janis Joplin – there's a piece of revolution.

And then to hire Janis away and commodify her into trillions of little fucking round, skinny flat records that people could listen to and get light-hearted kicks out of is not fucking revolutionary or fucking politics, and let me say that this all started because you said, 'What are the groups that you still believe in?'

I would believe in Big Brother and the Holding Company, if anybody ever saw them anymore, but because Janis got ripped off from them, and gave into whatever depths in her psyche caused her to do, they hardly exist anymore. But the ones that do are pretty fucking great and they were also so revolutionary that they used no lyrics but were moving people in a very intense way with their music, which was the most difficult thing for me to get around. But I admire them greatly, even more greatly, in retrospect, people like Quicksilver Messenger Service.

I saw a real revolution and I saw real politics and I saw real politics taking place as a community and I see, looking back, I hate to tell you how goddamn important it was. Because it astonishes, and it's pathetic, but so much has come of that community of artists and thinkers and philosophers, dunderheads, astrologers, deep thinking, deep feeling, deep drugging people that it's one of the primary influences on society today. So that's where the politics is …

SW **I completely agree.**

MM … not with some fucking rock 'n' roller, who says Iraq once on the entire side of an album and people say 'That's so exciting, they're so political'. That's shit, that's shit. It's commercialisation, it's commodification, it's a further lowering of human consciousness to think that that's something, to be so half assed, that you're so simple minded that you go ga ga over discs pressed and sold for vast amounts of money. Hey, I've made some albums and I know what it costs to make them. And I know how much advertising goes into it to sell them. Furthermore, I've done a lot of writing for the *Rolling Stone*, I know people at the *Rolling Stone* or I used to, I know that inside and out too.

As a matter of fact I remember the day when Michael Lydon came to my door when I was living over on Fillmore Street and said, 'Michael I want to show you' – he was working for *Newsweek* back then – and he said, 'I want to show you something I just did. It's a rock 'n' roll newspaper'. And he showed me the first *Rolling Stone*. I said: 'Why the fuck does anybody want a newspaper about rock 'n' roll?' I mean, I couldn't understand why rock 'n' roll would be splintered off from the other magazines of cultural revolution going on, like the *Berkeley Barb*, which had enormous amounts of rock 'n' roll in it, too.

But here's Jann,[2] takes it over and you can sell records, the record companies can sell your magazines and you can all sell each other. It's a big fucking commercial endeavour. So it's not political, it is not revolutionary.

---

[2] Jann Wenner was the founder, publisher and editor of *Rolling Stone* in San Francisco in 1967.

There was a revolution; the revolution still continues spread out through society and, once in a while, you can find it in music, sometimes you can find it in painting. Like here, out of all these people who are painters in New York and sculptors in New York, who are making vast amounts of money, which is something I don't care about. But look at that – that's the back cover of *The Nation* paid for and drawn by Richard Serra.[3] I'd be a lot happier if I saw a lot more people who were in the arts doing that, whether they're in music or whether they're in sculpture or painting. That means something, and if you think that I wasn't in politics, you're fucking wrong.

Like all my plays were politics, they were politics that accompanied the Vietnam War; they absolutely broached the subject that this society is just fucking cuckoo. And if you think that Gary Snyder wasn't political or you think Allen Ginsberg wasn't political or you think Joanne Kyger wasn't political or you think Diane di Prima wasn't political, it's because you never read a fucking word of them

SW **But what if I said William Burroughs or Jack Kerouac?**

MM They're unfortunates. William Burroughs and Jack Kerouac – let me say a) they're friends; b) they're both brilliant writers. I admire them both enormously and they are, unfortunately, apolitical. And that may be one of the reasons why both are best known today, so they can be pointed to, is the fact that they are apolitical. Essentially they are harmless.

Burroughs has all this talk about viruses against our society and so on. That's science fiction. Kerouac's *On the Road* sells cars; it sells camping equipment to high school kids. Good. That's why they're popular. But do you want to know who Jack Kerouac wanted to be like? Jack Kerouac wanted to be like Gary Snyder.

SW **Well that's an interesting way of putting it.**

MM After the Six Gallery reading when he heard Allen Ginsberg read 'Howl', he heard me read, Rexroth's introduction to us, which was beautiful and appreciative of what was really going on, and so forth. He didn't go away and write the story of Allen Ginsberg, he went away and wrote darker poems, because it's revolutionary to go out into nature, and it's revolutionary to take another viewpoint on society from that standpoint. Jack was a great, great man, great, great writer, too, and I've got to say also a great, great, great Buddhist visionary.

---

[3] The back cover of the magazine *The Nation* on 5 July 2004 featured a Serra artwork which formed part of a campaign that was critical of George W. Bush and encouraged individuals to use their voting power.

SW   **Could I ask where the figure of Bob Dylan fits into this? Clearly he
      was someone you had much to do with.**

MM   First of all David Meltzer had given me Dylan's, probably first, album
      and I took it home and said, 'Oh God! I grew up listening to these
      people in high school', particularly people who would come down from
      the University of Chicago while I was in high school, singing fucking
      Appalachian folk songs – 'It's shit!' I said, this is a nice kid, but I've
      heard all this stuff till I'm ready to gag it up.

      The next time I heard Dylan, Larry Keenan[4] came by my house, and
      this was when I was living in the Haight-Ashbury, and I had a record
      player in my hallway and he put on that song that goes: 'At dawn my
      lover comes to me/And tells me of her dreams/With no attempts to
      shovel the glimpse/Into the ditch of what each one means'.[5] And he
      didn't tell me what he had put on and I said, 'That's William Blake'.
      I thought it was William Blake singing and it was coming out of the
      walls. And he said, 'No, no, no – that's Bob Dylan'.

SW   **So you had a sort of transcendental moment?**

MM   Yeah, and then the next thing I know, Allen Ginsberg, to do Dylan a
      favour, has invited a bunch of people to his first concert – no it wasn't
      his first concert, it was his first electric concert – in San Francisco at the
      Masonic Auditorium[6] in 1965 and I was invited along with a bunch of
      Hell's Angels and Joan Baez, a couple of poets.

      We were all sitting in the front row listening to Bob and I thought it
      was like a cross between Marilyn Monroe and Charlie Chaplin; I loved
      him. I think he's great. I think his songs … I believed in his poetry, his
      work rides above song-writing, in the same way somebody like Bob
      Hunter's work. I don't belittle song-writing, I like song-writing, I like
      to do it, I like songs – but it isn't poetry usually, and there are a few
      mighty, strange and wonderful exceptions.

      We got to become pretty good friends. He gave me an autoharp and
      I learned to play that autoharp. I wrote a bunch of songs, including
      'Mercedes Benz', and I wrote them at the same time as I was writing
      the autobiography of my Hell's Angel's brother, Freewheelin' Frank,
      secretary of the Angels, who I met at the Bob Dylan concert and who
      was a big Bob Dylan/Joan Baez fan.

---

4 Larry Keenan was a student of McClure's and would-be photographer.
5 From Bob Dylan's 'Gates of Eden' (Columbia, 1965).
6 Dylan performed at the Masonic Memorial Auditorium in San Francisco on 5 December 1965. He
returned to the same venue on 11 December. See Clinton Heylin, *A Life in Stolen Moments – Day by
Day: 1941–1995* (London: Omnibus, 1996), p. 87.

SW **So there are other connections, but if I was to play devil's advocate again …**

MM I don't like devil's advocate.

SW **Well sometimes devil's advocate needs to be in the room to stimulate the kind of commentary we're making, I mean I'm not here to provoke you Michael. I'm here because I am very interested in your view.**

MM It just makes me realise what a world of shit that's been created out there when I hear you say this stuff.

SW **Well I'm here to challenge some of those perceptions. If I do play that advocate and say, Bob Dylan came along in 1965 and hi-jacked some of the cultural capital that the Beat writers had.**

MM Nonsense, what did he hi-jack? He came along and he was a superb poet, who didn't hi-jack, didn't take anything from me. That inspires me! My friends inspire me. Ginsberg inspired me, he didn't fucking take something from my cradle. Gary Snyder, because he writes about nature, didn't take nature away from me; Philip Whalen because he writes about Zen didn't take Zen away from me. These people are feeding me – it's wonderful. And suddenly poetry just had another dimension that it's had many times, many times in human history.

SW **Well what happens when a poet like Dylan does sell huge numbers of CDs or records as they were at the time? What happens to poetry at that moment? Is there still this problem that poetry is becoming commodified? Is it a triumph of advertising, as you suggested?**

MM No. Not in this case because he doesn't lend himself to it strongly. He doesn't beg for it. I know all of his tricks and games.

SW **So there are some artists who are able to transcend that?**

MM Well they're able to transcend it by keeping their teeth. They don't say, 'Can I suck your cock now that you're putting out my records in a million copies?'

SW **And few artists have got the courage to resist that?**

MM They love it. It's what they want. And then hip-hop learned how to do it from the way rock 'n' roll did it – and they did it even faster. They were smarter than the white boys. Because it took those fucking white boys about six months to learn how to sell out and all it took hip hop was about three.

SW **OK, so Dylan was able to rise above the …**

MM He didn't sell out. He didn't sell out. If he's that popular, it's a miracle, a fucking miracle and he played the game a little bit. I would have played the game that much. I'm not talking about Puritan, let's draw the line, and put people on one side of the line and give medals to people on the other. Everyone slides back and forth. But Dylan didn't slide back and forth very much – he stayed right out there.

SW **Do you still listen to his work?**

MM Not so much. What happened with Dylan was his popularity became so enormous that he now has imitators of imitators of imitators. It's become a milieu. We're going to have to wait for the milieu to go away to really hear Dylan. Now, he's been whited out by his imitators and the children of his imitators. It's unfortunate, because what he has to say is so great.

I listened to that new album a couple of years ago when he actually changed his style; that was very interesting. I listened to that carefully. He went from using imagery to using figures of speech – very, very strange. My fantasy of it was that he was trying to shake the people running after him, imitating him, by making a total change from the kind of poetry he was writing to poetry composed of figures of speech. You know, John Ashbery writes his poetry composed almost entirely from figures of speech, too.

SW **So Dylan, an important figure about whom you've said some significant things. Jim Morrison, with whom you also had a close friendship, a young man cut down in his prime.**

MM I wouldn't say cut down … dead!

SW **OK, dead in his prime. How does he fit into this process? He was influenced by Beat poetry to a degree; he was influenced by earlier writers as well. Was he a figure who resisted commodification or was he someone who was doomed to this terrible early end anyway? What is the Morrison link to this world we are discussing?**

MM Well, if we talk about commodification, I don't think the Doors … the Doors were a kind of high-up-the-heap success. But I don't believe commodification happened until after Morrison's death. I believe that they probably…it's entirely possible that the Doors sold far more albums now than they did when Jim was alive. He certainly didn't do anything to lend himself to commodification. He was outrageous!

SW **But is he almost a symbol of what you needed to do to not fall into that trap?**

MM There isn't anything you need to do to fall into that trap – just don't fall into it in your own way. Just be you and not fall into it; there's no trick. Different people have different temptations, sometimes temptation comes in the form of Al Grossman, which must be very hard to deal with.

SW **Well Albert Grossman had a reputation. Thanks for those comments on Jim Morrison. Did rock culture have any influence on your own work, do you think? Do you think it made you different in any way as a writer?**

MM Oh yes, but I don't think rock culture is the right word.

SW **Rock music or rock lyrics, maybe …**

MM The revolutionary milieu of the early days of the Haight-Ashbury and the development into rock 'n' roll as a high art is one of the most influential things in my life. But included in that is the drug culture of the Haight-Ashbury, and my own drug culture long before the Haight-Ashbury, and the dances, the fucking dances, at the Avalon and the Fillmore, and the clothing, and the open-ness of sexuality and body freedom.

SW **So you enjoyed the viscerality that rock culture brought. There was a cerebral dimension but you enjoyed the visceral almost …**

MM Yes. I had come in by way of jazz. I was listening to jazz and I was listening to Monteverdi and I was listening to Vivaldi, and I was listening to Miles Davis, especially Thelonious Monk. I appreciated that music cerebrally as well as physically.

SW **The beat of rock set your body free, did it?**

MM But that's it, you see. You're trying to attribute it too much to rock. It wasn't rock culture – it was counterculture with rock as the figurehead. Did it influence me? Did it look like it? I had my hair down to here.

SW **So would you say, probably, Ginsberg and yourself were the most moved, most attracted by this new cultural moment when rock emerged, as you say, as the figurehead in the counter culture? Did you feel as though Ginsberg and yourself were drawn into this new moment?**

MM Of the Beats, yes.

SW **And some other Beats felt that this wasn't such a great development?**

MM No I wouldn't say that.

SW **Kerouac certainly didn't, did he?**

MM I've got to tell you – I've got to separate off Kerouac. You very rightfully pointed to the apoliticality of Jack and Burroughs. But I point to the fact that the reason they're known, and it can be used to point at them, is because of their commodification. Jack certainly didn't seek the commodification. Burroughs didn't avoid it. They were a little older than me. Jack was ten years older than me. Allen was seven years older. Burroughs must have been fifteen. The rest of us were pretty much between Ginsberg and myself. If you include [David] Meltzer in, which is only fair, he would be the youngest.

SW **Yes, there's this curious turnaround which happens in the 1970s when punk arises and Burroughs is then dubbed the godfather, there are some strange twists. What did you make of that, that post-hippy**

moment when punk came along. Is that relevant, or irrelevant, to the story you've been mapping out?

MM Well I wasn't interested in that many punk groups. I liked Black Flag and some people like that. But they were really out there. They were putting their beliefs out there. But, in general, I sympathised with punk because it was a grail quest, and I sympathise with anybody who is on a grail quest, but it doesn't mean I have to be interested in them and there just weren't that many punk rockers of interest to me.

3 MUSE, MOLL, MAID, MISTRESS? BEAT WOMEN AND THEIR ROCK LEGACY

Quite recently, I had a female student, who was investigating the social upheavals of the 1960s, comment, with some surprise, that such a tumultuous era, for all its promise of liberation, seemed to be a time during which women remained essentially under the thumb. Freedom may have been an appealing target for a number of groups of that noted period of transformation – white, middle-class students attacking the military industrial complex, blacks struggling for Civil Rights, gays calling for legal recognition of their own after centuries of ostracism, not to mention ethnic communities of all kinds resisting the global hand of colonialism. Yet women participants, though often present in these campaigns, were generally assumed to be outside the vanguard of change. These huge cultural, racial and political tussles were usually perceived as men's work: involved females were there not to mount the barricades or theorise the revolution but merely to tend the psychologically – and even physically – wounded, but hardly lead the way.

In fact, even when headway was made, there was scant sense that the bounty of these hard-fought efforts was equally available to both men and women anyway. Hippy chicks or black girlfriends were not necessarily seen as the natural heirs to anything; they remained, in most cases, the hand-maidens of the patriarchy, at the demo or the festival, in the church or on the street. Yet, if the 1960s was a period when such imbalance was still broadly taken as a given, it was also a decade when women began to slowly, then vociferously, challenge such casual assumptions. American writers such as Betty Friedan and Gloria Steinem and, a little later, Kate Millet and the UK-based, Australian feminist Germaine Greer would start to express their dissatisfactions with the undemocratic rebellion that was raging in Washington and Chicago, Paris and London, and demand that women's rights be also part of the radical agenda for change and progress, improvement and justice.

Step back ten years further and the place of female players in the dramas of the day was still more diminuated. In the US, the 1950s represented an epoch in which many of the seeds that would flower in the decade to follow would take root. Yet it was a time when the nation's economic comfort – cars, televisions, fridges and transistor radios became the norm, for large swathes of the white population at least – was in sharp relief to the country's psyche, haunted by fears of Communist entryism and nuclear wipe-out. Such schizophrenia was played out alongside a soundtrack of rock 'n' roll – itself a symbol of racial miscegenation, as black blues met white country, and a deeply worrying one to conservative forces – and against a backdrop of general unease, generated by signs that the Negro would no longer accept the restrictions of his manacled role, nor would leftist artists, socialist folkies and liberal intellectuals simply condone this absurd truce between fiscal boom and Cold War paranoia as a complacent excuse for contentment.

J. D. Salinger in his 1951 novel *The Catcher in the Rye* and Norman Mailer in his 1957 essay 'The White Negro', for example, distilled some of these tensions – the outsider adolescent and the white desire to ape black codes – in their writings. On the folk front, Woody Guthrie and Pete Seeger pleaded the cause of the worker when unionism was attracting profound suspicion and judicial harassment from the authorities. Movies reflected the generational divide as older teenagers left their parents at home watching TV to catch Marlon Brando in *The Wild One* (1953) and James Dean in *Rebel Without a Cause* (1955) and the real political melodramas of the day were mirrored by thinly-veiled dramatic satires like Arthur Miller's powerful stage-play *The Crucible* (1953).

Then, a more integrated group of writers, the Beats, rocked the boat still further, preaching escape from norms, from respectability, by abandoning traditional work for the pleasures of creativity, replacing the suffocating demands of domestic aspiration with the joys of the road, the exotic pleasures of the ghetto, mind-altering odysseys on drink and drugs, and the passions of passing, soon forgotten, girls, all to the pulse of bebop. The men who made this mark – and they did avidly record their adventures in a flood of poems and novels – had scant regard for the part that women might actually *contribute* to this narrative of rebellion. Jack Kerouac, for all his roistering, constantly felt the tug of his mother's apron-strings and disowned a daughter for many years; William Burroughs and Allen Ginsberg were homosexual with competing inclinations; Neal Cassady was an inveterate womaniser who married several and slept with hundreds of others. But none was encouraging of the female as artist, as writer. When women did appear, in the lives or lines of these individuals, they were for sex or soup or temporary escape from the thrills and the spills, the self-generated insanity of the search.

The small number of women remembered – perhaps the poet Diane di Prima[1] alone was able to establish an autonomous literary standing in the wake of the initial Beat upsurge – were part of that life support system which permitted the men to booze, to brawl, to ball, and still find something warm, both in the oven and in bed – and space to write when the inspiration came. Yet, in the last couple of decades or so, we have seen a swelling, retrospective literature penned by female figures who were not at the very core of what went on but have important memories to share of both the Beats they knew but also their part of the history that unfolded; how they, as women, fitted into these unreformed times. Some were lovers even wives, some muses, some little more than servants; even if they had talents, they were submerged by notions that they were merely bit-part players, hand-maidens to those male characters doing the real toil which would lead to the genuine art. Some of these accounts are recent arrivals; others have been resurrected after decades in the shadows, blotted out by the dominating power of men's poetry and men's novels of that period. As Ann Charters states:

> The second wave of feminism, which began in the late 1960s, occurred after the publication of Kerouac's, Ginsberg's and Burroughs' most influential books. Although in her pioneering *Sexual Politics* (1970) Kate Millet had challenged Norman Mailer's misogynistic portrayal of women (Mailer was then often associated with the Beats), it took at least twenty years of feminist literary criticism before attention began to be paid to the complex role played by Beat women as writers themselves. When Beat writing first appeared, it was attacked acrimoniously by critics in both the popular press and conventional intellectual journals, who were appalled by the social and stylistic challenges of Beat poets and novelists. The more recent attacks by feminist critics claiming that Beat males didn't support Beat women have been similarly heated. It is now widely acknowledged that many of the Beat males were no more sensitive to the needs of the intellectual women in their midst than many other males of their generation were to the needs of the women they worked and lived with.[2]

In this section, I want to both examine the place of Beat women participants in this cultural revolution – how they were largely ignored at the time but have since enjoyed something of a latterday revival – but also to extrapolate their efforts to gauge how far their influence sowed the seeds of later creative assertions by members of the so-called 'second sex'.[3] And I particularly wish to expand the canvas

---

[1] Diane di Prima published her first poetry collection, *This Kind of Bird Flies Backwards* (New York: Totem Press), in 1958.

[2] Ann Charters, 'Foreword', *Girls Who Wore Black: Women Writing the Beat Generation*, edited by Ronna C. Johnson and Nancy M. Grace (New Brunswick, NJ: Rutgers University Press, 2002), pp. ix–x.

[3] Simone de Beauvoir's 1949 feminist history was entitled *The Second Sex* (London: Vintage, 1997).

of consideration by thinking to what extent those female novelists, memoirists and poets helped to shape an environment in which women musicians and songwriters of subsequent decades may have been inspired by their lower profile sisters of the 1950s and early 1960s. To what extent can we pinpoint a legacy – how have subsequent players on the rock 'n' roll stage taken intellectually, artistically and sartorially from their female Beat forebears; how have their lives, their style, their politics or, indeed, their sexual politics been shaped by the shadow cast by a previous generation of women who broke the mode of expectation and ploughed an unconventional furrow, even if their statements and achievements were buried in a long drift of amnesia, to be uncovered some time down the line. In essence, I hope to identify some later artists who seem to keep alive the flame of female Beatdom in the later years of the twentieth century and even into the post-Millennial phase. First though, some reflections on women who were around during that original era but whose abilities or contributions were only belatedly exposed to a wider readership.

Joyce Johnson was, for a time, a girl-friend to Kerouac. She was his partner on the day the first editions of the *New York Times* hit the news-stands heralding the arrival of his novel *On the Road* in September 1957. Thirty years on, in *Minor Characters* (1987), Johnson told the story of their relationship. It was acclaimed as an important record of a crucial moment in the writer's life – long-sought fame realised and the beginning of his all too speedy decline – but also of how she felt about her role on the fringes of the bohemian boys' club. As interestingly, Johnson was someone who went on to publish herself – she had novels before *Minor Characters* emerged – and a rather more recent memoir, 2004's *Missing Men*, re-visits other episodes in her past. It only fleetingly refers to Kerouac in its near-300 pages but is a sensitive and insightful reflection of an intriguing life: early years as a Broadway child understudy in which she lived out her mother's, rarely her own, dreams and later as the wife of two painters who struggled and strove without ever making a breakthrough. *Missing Men* is not only a slice through a rich seam of twentieth century life – her family had been East European, Jewish émigrés to America – but also an individual account of a woman of ability having to pander, until her later years, to the ambitions, and generally frustrated ones at that, of men who found it hard to accommodate her as an equal partner. The machismo mood of the these post-Abstract Expressionists, while barely misogynist, left her feeling, eventually, as if the solo course was the only way she could be a fulfilled writer in his her own right.

Another more recent addition to this expanding, if esoteric, archive, not issued until 2008, appears from a different angle, another perspective: a sister who saw her elder brother rise to the ranks, initially as a friend of Kerouac and Ginsberg and then as the first in the group to publish a novel fictionalising the new Manhattan scene at the end of the 1940s. John Clellon Holmes' *Go* (1952), although it actually comes after Kerouac's published debut, is still usually cited as the first Beat novel and is a convincing, and rather undeservedly sidelined, outline of the febrile world in which visions of a new world were plotted on the subway, on bridges, at all-night parties and in downtown bars, and with the principal architects of this artistic mêlée all present, if disguised, in the text. Holmes' junior sibling Elizabeth Von Vogt was a teenager during the time her story unfolds. *681 Lexington Avenue: A Beat Education in New York City 1947–1954* revolves around an apartment that becomes the occasional haunt of Kerouac and Cassady and the place where brother John shares his wit and wisdom and, most importantly, his knowledge of jazz with his kid sibling.

Von Vogt is not a writer in the sense that Johnson is: there is only occasionally art in her telling of these days. But the material is of sufficient moment to justify its recounting. What is fascinating is that this young woman, in her tender mid-teens, is living a relatively unfettered life in the most exciting city on earth – attending jazz gigs galore, making friends and lovers with both boys and older, more worldly, men returning to study under the GI Bill, and meeting the nascent Beats in cafés, in lofts and basements around the island. In one memorable moment, she comes across Herbert Huncke, junkie and thief and gutter guru to all of her brother's pals, at a dubious party, fuelled by wine and harder stuff, before John whisks her from the half-light of degradation to the safety of her mid-town home. She wanders on the edges of this twilight land, a bright post-pubescent, protected by a circle of brilliant college drop-outs, Village geniuses, white Negroes, who long for a dangerous draught of nocturnal spirit.

Both Johnson and Van Vogt are determinedly independent forces in the autobiographies they map out. Yet each is quite clearly bound by the contemporary rules and expectations that confront them. They see Kerouac and company, running wild, running free, while they have their moralising, quite sanctimonious, mothers, keen to guide their daughters to some kind of formal path – marriage, mortgage, children – before it's all too late. Ironically, it was Kerouac, particularly, who soon found himself increasingly drawn to the maternal home, the umbilical cord tugging him back. As the 1960s unfolded, as women stood up for their rights and opened the gates of opportunity to the successors of Johnson and Van Vogt, the individual dubbed the King of the Beats was pickling his liver in his mother's sitting room, railing against the progressive activists who battled for change and drinking himself finally into oblivion in the autumn before the decade concluded.

But let us think now of a range of other women who were also attached to or associated with, in various fashions, this predominantly phallocentric literary scene. Di Prima we have mentioned, a poet who would publish from the later 1950s, share relationships with significant Beat writers – like Leroi Jones – and have a number of offspring along her picaresque way. But she also produced a significant body of work despite the domestic calls that she addressed, generally as a solo parent. Carolyn Cassady would largely tolerate the wild infidelities of husband Neal, even embark on her own brief relationship with Kerouac in the early 1950s with Cassady's tacit encouragement, and then, eventually, produce an account of those years in *Off the Road: Twenty Years with Cassady, Kerouac and Ginsberg* (1990) somewhat later. Hettie Jones was wife to Leroi Jones – later self-identified as Amiri Baraka – and an active editor and publisher in the poetry journal world that would promote the new wave of writers, generally male but occasionally female, too.

Two of Kerouac's wives, Edie Parker and Joan Haverty, would, in time, pen autobiographical accounts of their part in the writer's life; so would another girlfriend Helen Weaver.[4] Elise Cowen would court Ginsberg at a time when he was still caught between the pull of homosexual inclination and the possibility that he may find stability in a heterosexual guise. That girlfriend would write poetry, too, and then commit suicide after the pressures her family placed upon her to conform and reject the Beat orbit. After she died, her parents destroyed virtually all her written verse. Another fascinating freewheeler was ruth weiss, a young Jewish escapee from Nazi terror in the Austria of the 1930s, who rejected her Teutonic roots in powerful, emblematic fashion, abandoning the capital letters that mark all nouns in the German tongue, a rejection of the dark shadows of the past and an assertive expression of a self-determining future once she arrived in the US.

Other women writers should be included in this listing. Bonnie Bremser, a wife to Beat poet Ray Bremser, suffered harder conditions than most in a situation where her jailbird partner's violence and the spectre of drugs were constantly present. But she still published work. Lenore Kandel was a woman who carried the Beat impulse forward to the flower power era of her home city of San Francisco and particularly in her poetry volume *The Love Book* (1966), and Janine Pommy Vega. Joanne Kyger and Joanna McClure are others who deserve mentions. Furthermore, Anne Waldman, Ann Charters and Jan Kerouac are potent examples of younger women who for a variety of reasons – as friends, academics and family members – kept the Beat spirit alive, all important links in this historic chain, whose poetry, biography and prose preserved the potency of the 1950s literary line for post-1970 generations.

Waldman as Ginsberg associate and director of the St. Mark's Poetry Project in New York City's Lower East Side from 1968[5] would enable young talents like Jim

---

[4] Parker's volume, *You'll Be Okay: My Life with Jack Kerouac* (San Francisco, CA: City Lights), appeared in 2007; Haverty's memoir, *Nobody's Wife: The Smart Aleck and the King of Beats* (Berkley, CA: Creative Arts Book Company), was published in 2000; Helen Weaver's *The Awakener: A Memoir of Kerouac and the Fifties* (San Francisco, CA: City Lights) was issued in 2009.

[5] Waldman was assistant director from the project's commencement in 1966. Two years later she became director and held this position for the next ten years.

Carroll and Patti Smith to bring their post-Beat verse to the stage of that remarkable seventeenth-century church. She would also maintain her own, significant identity as poet and become one of the founding forces of Ginsberg's Buddhist-inspired Jack Kerouac School of Disembodied Poets in Boulder, Colorado in 1974. Charters was very important. A young university researcher when the mid-1950s surge occurred, she met Kerouac in his fading years, created his first bibliographic account and then produced his first biography, simply entitled *Kerouac*, four years after his passing, in 1973. Jan Kerouac's links to this arc are more tortured, more traumatic, yet still intriguing. Rejected for a decade and a half as his daughter, father Jack would eventually meet and acknowledge his offspring. In time, she would publish herself, Beat-like trials and trails captured in *Baby Driver* (1981) and *Trainsong* (1988). Ultimately she would be caught up the struggle for the Kerouac estate, as another biographer of the older writer, Gerald Nicosia, author of *Memory Babe* (1983), supported her in her legal arguments with the Sampas family, a member of which, Stella, had become Kerouac's third and final wife in 1966. Jan's early death from kidney disease in 1996 was a desperate tragedy but it did not end the often bitter dispute; the battle for the inherited rights has continued for decades.

Apart from the writers we have mentioned, other women featured large in the lives of the Beat Generation menfolk. Kerouac's mother Gabrielle, the woman he called Mémère and the person to whom he ran for cover and comfort and cash when his personal or financial resources were running on empty, would outlive her son, surviving until 1972. Without that maternal force – a figure represented as his aunt in his most famous tale *On the Road* – it is hard to see how Kerouac would have written all he did, even lasted as long as he did, even though his death at the age of 47 was premature in any terms. His many years of penury when his writing was earning him close to nothing, his hard-living, hard-travelling times were frequently softened by his mother's hearth, her apparently unconditional love, even when this Catholic matriarch disapproved of much of what he did, and despised many of those with whom he congregated. We should also highlight Ginsberg's bond to his mother Naomi, too, a woman who stood well outside the bounds of convention herself as a 1930s Communist and naturist but whose life crumbled after the war when her uncertain mental health led to her long-term incarceration in an asylum. Her death in 1956 became the prompt for 'Kaddish', the poet's most revered work after 'Howl'. The title was drawn from the Jewish mourning prayer and was a powerfully sustained poetic mantra to his departed parent. Burroughs had a generally negative view of women – his dogged brand of homosexuality meant he regarded them as threats rather than complements to his life – yet, from 1946, he spent a number of years in a common law partnership with Joan Vollmer before he accidentally killed her with a gun-shot in 1951. For all the horrors of that William Tell-like shooting – Burroughs aimed a gun to dislodge a spirit glass from the top of her head but the echoes of the historical crossbow and the apple were unavoidable, even if the outcomes were quite different – it has to be said that remorse the would-be writer felt was so deep that it triggered a reaction in his mind, in his soul, so profound that he felt forced to use story-telling as a way out of his deep and lasting disturbance at this apparently drunken folly.

For Cassady, too, women were his constant quarry – the teenage LuAnne Henderson, who became his bride in 1945 three years before he wed Carolyn, was just one of many, many dozens, perhaps several hundreds, who partnered him, slept with him, even, on occasion, married him bigamously. He was, in short, during his 41 years of hyper-frenetic life, obsessed with girls, women and sex. Which is not to say that in the homosocial ring that formed the fulcrum of the Beat caucus, that Cassady, like all the other principals, was not interested in sexual encounters with men, too. The network of liaison and tension that criss-crossed this fraternal gathering was one of the enduring features and fractures marking their various and multiple connections and collusions, interpersonal and intellectual interplay, over half a century. It might be asserted that there were a number of things that kept thinking, creative women at arm's length from this core crew – the ongoing sexual hunger that Cassady and Kerouac had, too, for fleeting and rapidly forgotten satisfactions in the bedroom; the homosexual energies that drove Ginsberg and Burroughs; and that complicated intersection where mainstream heterosexuality was impinged upon by the calls of homosexual and bi-sexual attraction and engagement. In this circle most of the games, most of the options, were explored at certain times and often to the disadvantage of stable relationships with female associates.

But let us return to that notion of Beat women and the legacy they may have handed down to succeeding generations and, specifically, to subsequent female musical singer-composer-performers, particularly, during the final third of the last century. This provides a problem that is difficult to address and disentangle without a certain degree of speculation. For, while male musicians from the mid-1960s, as this book firmly asserts, displayed the influence and impact of the Beat writers on their lives and work, there is no simple gender symmetry here: we cannot begin to claim that Beat women had a similar effect on female singers and songwriters because most of the written work those novelists and poets had produced in the 1950s would lie largely undiscovered and unheralded until several decades later. One thing we might propose, however, is that the themes in male Beat literature – travel, independence, artistic experiment, sexual adventure – did affect forward- and free-thinking women musicians, too. Couple those thoughts to the swelling tide of feminist ideas that would prosper just before and after 1970 and we can conceive of a climate, an environment, in which it was more possible for female artists to shape autonomous creative careers. We might see those women who picked up guitars, sang on stages or entered the male preserve of the recording student as equivalent to the Beat women who tried to share their art in the earlier era. However while the 1950s saw manhood – in the shape of Kerouac and Ginsberg, Cassady and Burroughs, for instance – utterly overshadow female ability and industry, within a decade and a half, while men like Dylan and Lennon may well have continued to lead the way, the door had been left sufficiently ajar for women singer-songwriters to creep through and also share some of the spotlight. There had been creative women in both periods; the difference for those who came later was that the social chains on the woman as homebound domestic had been considerably loosened and there were actual opportunities for expression and exposure, if the female singer had the talent and determination to carve out a niche.

Still, those brave women who counted themselves a part of the Beat revolution – even if the men who drank in cafés and bars alongside them undervalued their presence and the broader blocs of mainstream society saw them, perhaps, as immoral jezebels chasing the idle and unwashed – must be regarded as trend-setters. They may be considered harbingers, or at least early adopters, of a later rebellion which eventually recognised that women did not have to be chained to the kitchen sink and household chores and could be a great deal more than that: achievers in society, in the professions and the arts, on a par with their male counterparts. As Brenda Knight, whose celebrated collection of the writings of Beat women came out in 1996, shining a torch almost anew on this mostly buried, or at best obscured, archive, remarks:

> Women of the fifties in particular were supposed to conform like Jell-O to a mould. There was only one option: to be a housewife and mother. For the women profiled here, being Beat was far more attractive than staying chained to a brand-new kitchen appliance. For the most part, the liberal arts educations these young women were given created a natural predilection for art and poetry, for living a life of creativity instead of confining it to the occasional hour at the symphony. Nothing could be more romantic than joining this chorus of individuality and freedom, leaving behind boredom, safety and conformity.[6]

The quiet, frequently anonymous, gestures of the women of the 1950s, barely acknowledged at the time by male Beat protagonists and critically regarded by sanctimonious and illiberal commentators outside the scene, would form a base, a potential platform, a Trojan horse, for more strident feminist voices to crack the glass ceiling within a decade or so. Anne Waldman provides a pertinent foreword to Knight's anthology, describing it as 'a kind of resurrection [...] a

---

[6] Brenda Knight, 'Sisters, saints and sybils: Women and the Beat', *Women of the Beat Generation*, edited by Brenda Knight (Berkeley, CA: Conari Press, 1996), p. 3.

necessary reckoning'. She comments: 'This book is a testament, primarily, to the lives of these women, lest they be ignored or forgotten. For what comes through the searing often poignant hint or glimpse of an original – often lonely – tangible *intellectus* – a bright, shining, eager mind. And these very particular "voices" as it were form in unison a stimulating and energetic forcefield of consciousness that manifested at a rich and difficult time in cultural history, spanning half a century.'[7]

So, to move forward a little, how might we recognise a Beat shade, a Beat strain, in the women singers, songwriters and musicians who made their mark in the latter stages of the last century and beyond? There are a number of possible ways in which we might approach such a question and even attempt an informal assessment. But, let me stress, that accurate measurement is hardly the intention. Rather, the aim of this section of the chapter is to use a broad palette of evaluation and extrapolate across several time periods. This survey will try to describe some of the characteristics which defined the Beat writers' artistic philosophy; touch upon a wider sense of what the Beat ethos may have expressed; and also offer an impressionistic view of the manner in which mores and codes, outlooks and even looks, may have been transgenerationally shared by the women we consider. This method may sometimes appear more suggestive than scientific, but I hope to argue that Beat traces survive in a number of significant women artists from the later 1960s to the present time.

Let us begin with some criteria, some benchmarks, for comparison. The Beats' 'New Vision' of 1944 presents a useful codification of the ideas that sparked this writing community's project, even if its formation pre-dated, by some four years, the naming of the Beat Generation itself. Kerouac, Burroughs, Ginsberg and their inner circle of associates framed a set of ideas that would drive them forward, certainly for the next decade and a half, even if not every proto-Beat or each subsequent member of this grouping signed up, in any formal sense, to this bold ideological statement of creative intent. Steven Watson summarises the principal tenets of this early thinking here:

1) Uncensored self-expression is the seed of creativity. 2) The artist's consciousness is expanded through non-rational means: derangement of the senses, via drugs, dreams, hallucinatory states, and visions. 3) Art supersedes the dictates of conventional morality.[8]

We might underscore this with notions of experimentalism in life and art; a desire to challenge taboos; and interests in sexual adventure or libertarian behaviour.

---

[7] Anne Waldman, 'Foreword', *Women of the Beat Generation*, edited by Brenda Knight (Berkeley, CA: Conari Press, 1996), pp. ix–xii (pp. x–xi).
[8] Steven Watson, 1995, p. 40.

We could add further to our defining exemplars of a Beat ethos by referring to an almost existential inclination towards movement and travel; concerns with ideas of the spirit and the spiritual; and consider also later interests in ecological issues and political campaigning. Of course, not all Beats subscribed to all of these ideas but they offer a more than helpful sketch of some key concepts which bound many Beats together over a quarter of a century or so. Further we might draw attention to the sartorial style that the Beats passed on, intentionally or not: a bohemian chic adopted and adapted in various fashions – from berets, sunglasses and sandals to striped Breton fishermen's shirts and duffel coats, black skirts and dresses, leg-ins and stockings and kohl eye-liner – more superficial a signifier conceivably but also a more obvious and blatant one. So, we have a range of signs we might use as guides to assess the presence of a Beat quotient in those women artists who have followed, whether in their behaviour, their statements or in their art – on record, on album sleeves, in photographs, on stage, or on screen.

That very creative material may hold clues of various kinds when we consider the extent to which those singer-performers are referencing what we may recognise as Beat themes or Beat practices or Beat style. This could potentially be revealed in a range of ways: the lyrical content; the lyrical form; the poetic qualities of the words the artist produces; and the extra curricular output beyond the framework of the rock song, such as stand-alone poetry, prose, novels, short stories and so on, which may be appear as extras on a singer's résumé. That singer or songwriter may even stray into that hybrid field of spoken word where music and verse combine in a manner that is neither simply song nor mere oration but presents something of each. Then there may be more obvious connections: when singers work with Beat writers, credit Beat writers or name-check them as influences in credits, in performances or in magazine interviews. Let us initially consider a small number of suitable examples from different decades and then offer a longer list of candidates more briefly.

Joni Mitchell has been a constant presence since the middle of the 1960s, regarded widely, says Coupe, as 'the most important female singer-songwriter'[9] to emerge in that decade, occasionally announcing her intention to withdraw from music-making in more recent times but still active as a creative individual well past the Millennium. In fact, her art school roots and her lifelong dedication to painting have marked her as a woman of multiple talents, though it is for song-writing that she is has been best known, even if many of her album sleeves feature her own artworks. That detail alone immediately marks a Beat shade to the Mitchell oeuvre; the relationship between the visual arts and the Beats of the

---

[9] Laurence Coupe, *Beat Sound, Beat Vision: The Beat Spirit and the Popular Song* (Manchester: Manchester University Press, 2007), p. 174.

1950s[10] and the link between art colleges and rock music-making, particularly in the 1960s, immediately suggests more than a passing connection between these two worlds.

A Canadian who moved to the US to become a darling of the Californian music boom of the later 1960s and early 1970s, her hippy style – long blonde hair, simple back-to-nature attire, a golden girl indeed of the musical community that settled in Laurel Canyon – also had a strong hint of the boho about it. But her appearance was quite secondary to the talent she possessed as vocalist, songwriter and guitarist. Her songs, from the start, set her apart from the standard folk fare, though she originally grew out of that musical scene. She added her remarkable singing range to a series of intriguing guitar tunings, both of which made her a special figure at a time when female singer-songwriters – from Judy Collins to Janis Ian and Judee Sill, Laura Nyro and Carole King to Carly Simon and others beside – were carving out a new space.

Her songs, however, quickly transcended the quotidian fare of the pop-folk setting. With 'Woodstock' (1970) she celebrated most famously the key gathering of the hippy tribes and arguably the apex of what the Beats had begun a decade and a half before, even if the horrendous traffic queues over that astonishing weekend prevented her from playing her scheduled set at the event. But she also brought the confessional manner of Beat expression to her love songs – 'Willy' and 'My Old Man' were tributes to her then partner Graham Nash, whose band Crosby, Stills, Nash and Young became one of the most potent political charges on the rock scene as one decade faded and another one began. Yet if her album *Blue* (1971) became almost a symbol for the time, featuring extraordinarily personal songs – the title track and 'River' among them – there was also a sense that she could tell a wider story in works like 'California'. She could have, if she had desired, ploughed this furrow for years – yearning, fragile acoustic arrangements – but she quickly moved on, and several times. *Court and Spark* (1974) saw her link with jazz saxophonist Tom Scott and his band the LA Express and the work became bigger and deeper in scope. Then, *The Hissing of Summer Lawns* (1975), a supremely ambitious reflection of life in the West and the many worlds beyond, showcased 'The Boho Dance', a tender portrait of a gone land where she had begun her journey, in the basement haunts of the bohemian folk milieu. The following year, Mitchell's appearance at the Band's final concert at Winterland, San Francisco, which would become Martin Scorsese's movie tribute *The Last Waltz* (1978), also marked her as part of that community of Beat-linked musical performers – from the act at the very heart of the farewell to guests like Van

---

[10] The New York Abstract Expressionists of the mid-century inhabited many of the same Village social scenes as the Beats, while Larry Rivers emerged as one painter with particularly strong Beat associations. Rivers appeared in the Kerouac-penned film *Pull My Daisy* in 1959.

Morrison, poets Lawrence Ferlinghetti and Michael McClure, of course, Bob Dylan, linking with his long-time accompanists.

On her album *Hejira* (1976), joined by fretless jazz bass *wunderkind* Jaco Pastorius, the theme of travel was visited with a keen eye and the material was infused by the roaming spirit – from 'Refuge of the Roads' to 'Coyote' and the title track, this collection seemed to embody the very urge to move, and move on, that had so obsessed Kerouac and Cassady 30 years before, a very rejection of the home-making domesticity towards which women were still guided. An outstanding effort again, she would re-group to make a sprawling double album, *Don Juan's Reckless Daughter* (1977), which framed in its title the artist's fervent female autonomy, and then a much less accessible record called *Mingus* (1979), a sturdy and unsentimental paean to the recently deceased Charles Mingus, bebop upright bass player supreme and one of that very circle that the Beats had so fawned over in the New York of the 1940s and 1950s. The jazz twist was maintained into the early 1980s as guitarist Pat Metheny signed up and ex-Miles Davis saxophonist Wayne Shorter took time out of Weather Report (like Pastorius, who held his place in her later ensembles) to accompany Mitchell, amazing accolades to a non-jazz artist but an indication of how seriously the instrumental masters of that cerebral and essentially non-commercial field regarded this versatile, sometimes visionary, performer.

Thus we might mark Mitchell as an important songwriter and lyric poet within a popular music setting. But she was more than that: her guitar-based, singer-songwriter categorisation did not exempt her from experiment, incorporating a wide range of styles, from jazz rock and bebop, including composing, arranging and collaboration, to global music styles exemplified by the Burundi drums employed on 'The Jungle Line' and the Latin percussion details of *Don Juan's Reckless Daughter*. Nor have her writing themes been confined to the realm of romance: her commentaries extended broadly across social, cultural and political reflection, and her concern with that existential lure of movement certainly sets her in a Beat framework. As Lucy O'Brien states: 'Working in minor keys as much as major, experimenting with cadence and inflection, layering her songs with deft touches of jazz, rock and folk, Mitchell thrives on difference, on the unpredictable.'[11] A remarkable homage to the singer's output emphasised the respect of the jazz establishment when Herbie Hancock, a keyboardist who connects the cool school of Miles Davis to the age of jazz rock, unveiled *River: The Joni Letters* in 2007.

Furthermore, her paintings, an increasingly significant part of her output as the century turned, confirm her determination not to be confined by the limitations of

---

[11] Lucy O'Brien, *She Bop II: The Definitive History of Women in Pop, Rock and Soul* (London: Continuum, 2002), p. 182.

the music industry and align her with a more general artistic sensibility, while her determinedly bohemian/hippy style, from the oft-worn beret to the long dresses and the constant cigarette, little changed over half a century, places her in that historical continuum. We should not ignore her ecological flavour either as one of her earlier and most recognised pieces, 'Big Yellow Taxi' (1970), was a prophetic, green treatise on the over-use and abuse of the planet's natural resources, a song that convincingly interweaves notions of rustic destruction under the heel of urban spread with the spiky fading of a love affair. Coupe connects Mitchell's efforts, too, to the Beat poet Gary Snyder who has both commitments to Zen spirituality and eco-centred ideas. He says that Mitchell, like Snyder, is 'interesting for her attempt to maintain Beat values in the midst of the widespread dilution and/or distortion of them in the name of the "counterculture"'.[12]

Patti Smith is another woman who carries Beat credentials and, arguably, in a more explicit way. An artist with many faces, she was actor and painter in her early years in New York City at the end of the 1960s. But it was as a poet that she made her first significant splash in Manhattan, debuting her poems live at St. Mark's Church on the Lower East Side in 1971, an opportunity afforded by a later Beat poet Anne Waldman, who had directed the hugely influential poetry project at the venue since 1968 and offers a crucial connection between the literary and musical periods. Smith's debt to the Beat impulse runs deep even if she privileges a host of other artistic talents who have shaped her work, first as a writer and subsequently as one of the most important rock artists, regardless of gender, of the final quarter of the last century. The French Symbolist Arthur Rimbaud, the Abstract Expressionist painter Jackson Pollock and the musicians James Brown, Bob Dylan, Jimi Hendrix and the Rolling Stones are often cited as shaping forces in her life, which saw her transform her talent as versifier into fully blown rock talent with the release of her debut album *Horses* in 1975.

But her interest in, and debt to, some of the major Beat names is undeniable. She met Ginsberg when she was struggling and striving, living with her friend and lover Robert Mapplethorpe, in something close to cold-water poverty. The poet bought her a sandwich, a tiny but not insignificant moment in Smith's ascent, more emblematic than substantial perhaps, it nonetheless prefaced closer associations with both Burroughs and Gregory Corso when she and the now rising photographic star Mapplethorpe moved to the Chelsea Hotel in 1971. There she became part of one of the most eccentric and dynamic collectives of the era, befriending musicologist Harry Smith, meeting Dylan sideman Bobby Neuwirth, finally graduating to the fringes of Andy Warhol's febrile crowd and, ultimately, forging a powerful identity of her own with a full electric band.

---

[12] Coupe, 2007, p. 174.

How does Smith carry the Beat torch? We might catalogue a series of signs that appear to link her to that earlier brotherhood. A determined experimentalist who has worked across an impressive span of activities – poetry, the stage, on record, in the visual arts, on film – she has been informed by that modernist, avant garde imperative to stretch the bounds of art, oral, sonic and visual, and, in that sense, we can see a close alliance with the New Vision of the original Beats. We might also point to ideas of uncensored self-expression: her poetry and spoken word canon, generally linked to amplified music after 1975, has been taboo-breaking and a challenge to conventional mores. Her debut single featured the song 'Piss Factory', its title immediately inflammatory, and its contents, highly autobiographical in the Beat tradition, were full of candour and confession – shots at organised religion, a strong odour of adolescent sex musking the track, and a high charge of recollected teen anger and frustration present. 'Horses', the title piece on her first LP, was a more confusing collage of heightened sense and obscure revelation, a cut-up with Burroughsian nuances, the subject matter a hallucinatory ode to sex and derangement, violence and mortality. Still more unnerving was the later 'Rock 'n' roll Nigger', a taboo-busting song which still, decades after release, has the coiled power to unsettle and shock. Smith attacks the sacred cow of propriety, of acceptable language, with a bludgeon and, echoing earlier speculations about the so-called 'white Negro', classifies Christ, Pollock, herself, even Hendrix, most bizarrely it might be claimed, as 'niggers', a term that in 2012 continues to be one of the most contested, combustible, and jagged shards of slang in English, packed with a racist history which now needs unpacking all over again after the pejorative word's recent reclamation by sections of the African-American community.[13] In 1978, its power to offend was greater still and its subversion by a white woman, already breaking boundaries as an all-out, unrepressed female rock 'n' roller, added to the cultural confusion as much as 'Howl' might have done in 1955.

The fact that Smith has lauded Dylan – the great link in many ways between Beat and rock sensibilities, once he had assumed his electric persona and, before that even, when his acoustic guitar was still his main weapon of choice – worn the garb of a timeless bohemian – black, white and striped T-shirts, and inevitably androgynous – and also penned poems and sung tributes to the Beats, further adds to this aura of connection. Her verses to Burroughs and Ginsberg, her recorded homage to 'Howl' on the latter's death on *Peace and Noise* (1997) and her appearance on the tribute album of the same year, *Kerouac: Kicks Joy Darkness*, also suggest this ongoing affection for the Beat family and its philosophies. Her sympathies for this grouping have not occurred without criticism in some quarters

---

[13] The reclaimed version of the term has been re-conceptualised as 'nigga', a subverted form of resistance rather than a symbol of subordination, best exemplified in the name of late-1980s rap group NWA (Niggaz With Attitude).

and the section in this book dedicated to Patti Smith as a post-Beat figure explores that subject in more detail. But, says Carrie Havranek: 'More than any other artist of her generation, [she] embodies a downtown New York City aesthetic sensibility. She is artist/singer as poet, one whose integrity is unquestioned and whose ambitious, unconventional approach to music took her through various phases, genres and sounds.'[14] Although the distorting effects of powerful narcotics have not been part of Smith's artistic strategy, her eclectic and inventive résumé charts a course that appears to chime resonantly with the Beats' own New Vision.

Rickie Lee Jones, whose star burnt most brightly at the end of the 1970s and at the start of the 1980s but sustains a credible career into the new century, cultivated a boho appearance and twilight lifestyle that placed her very quickly in the post-Beat bracket. Her eponymous 1979 debut album was marked by its themes and threads of the urban night, notions of movement and travel and peopled by a cast of characters, real and imagined, who seemed to step straight out of the bohemian milieu – in bars and cafés, on gas stations, on the street and at the roadside. 'Chuck E.'s in Love', a jaunty folk rock ballad, touched upon a genuine figure in her circle, while another mutual friend of both singer and subject, Tom Waits, would form part of Jones' scene and particularly tag her as a Beat woman by association. As Mick Farren wrote at the time Jones emerged: 'The similarities between Ms Jones and the aforementioned Waits are more than a little marked. Both have a basis in Forties jazz nostalgia, both seem to be trying to turn themselves into characters from some beat-generation/Damon Runyon world where Nick the Greek slips through the shadows and Jack Kerouac could show up any moment in a beat-up Hudson. The resemblance doesn't even stop there. On stage, in a beat-up cocktail dress, pink beret pulled down over one eye and a Sherman brown cigarillo hanging out of the corner of her mouth, Rickie Lee slugs back drinks with the confidence of someone who believes she has a cast-iron liver. Just to complete the Waits connection, she even hung round with the same LA bohemian street crowd, in the bars of Hollywood and Venice.'[15]

Waits, the archetypal musical heir to that literary generation's code, would be her romantic partner for a time, as well, as her premiere LP won her the Best New Artist prize at the 1980 Grammys. Such auspicious beginnings were darkened by her growing drug habits and the Waits affair would come to an end. Afterwards, she told *Rolling Stone*: 'Tom and I were living like characters from the movies when we were together. Tom really wanted us to be poor Mexicans with our kids screaming on the back seat at a drive-in. And it was impossible. He really is a

[14] Carrie Havranek, *Women Icons of Popular Music: The Rebels, Rockers and Renegades*, Volume I (Westport, CT: Greenwood Press, 2009), p. 420.

[15] Mick Farren, 'Rickie Lee Jones', *New Musical Express*, 9 June 1979, *Rock's Backpages*, http://0-www.rocksbackpages.com.wam.leeds.ac.uk/article.html?ArticleID=1554 [accessed 25 November 2011].

character, you know. It's like the old bohemian poet who has to suffer and be broke, like Charles Bukowski.'[16] But Jones, in the wake of the split, appeared to distance herself from this métier, remarking: 'I don't find it romantic being poor or being an alcoholic or a junkie or a whore. People think I'm a real down-and-outer, but it wasn't a character I chose. It was the position I was in.'[17] Yet this short period would pigeon-hole her, perhaps unfairly, perhaps not. Nonetheless, her career would continue through numerous collections, all marked by the same maudlin, streetwise nostalgia that had marked her first release. The boho wardrobe, the beret at cocky angle and the enduring recollection that she and Waits had been for a time the beauty and the beast of the Beat after-ball, have all continued to place her in that distinctive camp, 30 or more years and more than a dozen albums later, best distilled in the 2005 triple CD set, *Duchess of Coolsville*, an anthology that casts a torch on her musical interests – from folk to jazz, European chanson to Broadway ballad – and, in its title, frames the kind of Beat-flavoured legacy she has carried and maintains, willingly or not.

More recent performers who may also carry a Beat badge, include Ani DiFranco – one of that small brigade of artists who usually adopt the lower case style in their name – who has led a resolutely independent course, as singer, guitarist, songwriter and label proprietor since she first came to wider attention in the late 1980s and has been prolific, from her eponymous debut in 1990 through remarkable live work captured on *Living in Clip* (1997), her well-received double CD collection *Revelling/Reckoning* (2001) to *Which Side are You On?* (2012). She represents various aspects of Beat consciousness: her autonomous artistic nature and fierce determination to resist the restraints of the corporate, symbolised by the DIY ethos of her long-running record label Righteous Babe;[18] her frequent dependance on spoken word techniques within her song-writing structures; her publication of poetry alongside her lyrics in book-form; and her insistence that she plays out a confusing game of sexual ambivalence, winning huge support from women and the nascent riot grrrl movement when she appeared to pin her colours to the lesbian flag and then outraging many former followers by twice marrying men. Her own attachment to bisexuality reveals a level of sexual adventure, or at least a rejection of sexual convention, that certainly Beat men of the 1950s saw as a necessary part of their experience. As she told Lucy O'Brien: 'People talk about […] the issue of *queer* sexuality. But to me they are not issues. This is my life. I've never felt like watering my experience down to make it radio-friendly.'[19] Her

---

[16] Jones quoted in Timothy White, 'Rickie Lee Jones: The Great Disconnected's leading lady flirts with happiness', *Rolling Stone*, 6 August 1981.

[17] *Ibid.*

[18] Founded as Righteous Records in 1989, it was re-named Righteous Babe Records in 1994.

[19] Ani DiFranco quoted in O'Brien, 2002, p. 402.

self-belief in her art, in herself, and her resistance to compromise in this area has echoes of the same risks that Ginsberg, particularly, was taking with homosexual revelation half a century before. Comments Havranek: 'Her intensely personal music, by and large, is situated at the threshold of folk and punk, reflecting a heavy dash of social consciousness with humour and self-righteousness thrown into the mix. In short, politics and art are inseparable for this artist.'[20] She adds that DiFranco has offered an 'open roadmap' to her personal and emotional life and dubs her lyrics both 'poetic' and 'stream of consciousness.'[21]

Jason Ankeny dubs her 'a folkie in punk's clothing' who 'battled successfully against the Goliath of corporate rock to emerge as one of the most influential and inspirational cult heroines of the 1990s'. He adds that her songs tackle 'issues like rape, abortion, and sexism with insight and compassion.'[22] Such details – candour, confession, outspoken and empowering activism and the use of poetry formats, not to mention the support and promotion of other outsider, muso-poetic spirits like Utah Phillips through her own label – mark DiFranco as a recognisable heir to the Beat project with a potent dash of old-fashioned folk radicalism and more contemporary riot grrrl attitude.

We might also consider other women who, for a variety of reasons and connections, fit, or connect with, the Beat template. British singer Marianne Faithfull, who has enjoyed a bold recording career with collections of self-penned songs and tributes to European composers such as Brecht and Weill, also worked at Naropa in the 1970s and contributed to Gregory Corso's 2002 album *Die on Me*. Nico, singer with the Velvet Underground, was involved also in experimental film and made albums that drew on the continental chanson tradition, and Debbie Harry, of Blondie, paid homage to Beat dress codes in various ways in the group's early days, before extending her more experimental activities into art film productions by David Cronenberg and Jonas Åkerlund. Kathy Acker, principally a novelist and poet, also worked in a rock context and performed with British post-punks the Mekons, while Karen Finley, poet and performance artist, maintained the Beat spoken word style on stage and on record. Punk rocker Lydia Lunch, a member of Teenage Jesus and the Jerks, emerged as a prominent performing poet and also appeared on albums that paid tribute to Kerouac and Burroughs. One time member of Nervus Rex, a punk band, Lauren Agnelli re-emerged in the 1980s as a central member of the post-beatnik/folk group the Washington Squares. Laurie Anderson, a major US performance artist since the 1980s, worked with Burroughs and, in her private life, married Beat follower and Velvet Underground singer and lyricist Lou Reed.

---

[20] Havranek, 2009, p. 86.
[21] *Ibid.*
[22] Jason Ankeny, 'Ani DiFranco – Biography', *All Music Guide*, http://www.allmusic.com/artist/ani-difranco-p38383/biography [accessed 28 February 2012].

Exene Cervenka of LA rock band X had spoken word interests and Kim Gordon, bass player with Sonic Youth, was at the centre of an extended new wave musical experiment which saw her and her colleagues Thurston Moore and Lee Ranaldo acknowledge various links with the Beat tradition. Singer-songwriter Julianna Hatfield appeared on *Kicks Joy Darkness*, while Natalie Merchant, lead singer of 10,000 Maniacs, has maintained a boho demeanour as band member and, in more recent times, as solo artist and she was partially responsible for the group's track 'Hey Jack Kerouac'. Courtney Love, leader of the riot grrrl band Hole, would appear in the Joan Vollmer role in Gary Walkow's 2002 Beat bio-pic *Beat*, singer-songwriter Dayna Kurtz penned a Kerouac tribute in 'Just Like Jack' while British singer P. J. Harvey has pursued a career which links to a wide swathe of rock literati from Marianne Faithfull to Nick Cave and acquired something of a reputation as a UK version of Patti Smith.

Another individual we have mentioned as a key connection between Beat and post-Beat, and to whom we should return, is the poet Anne Waldman, a woman who has seen important action at vital points in the story – from her role as early director the St. Mark's Poetry Project through to her founding contribution to the Jack Kerouac School of Disembodied Poetics in Boulder, Colorado, alongside a constant stream of poetry, essay, film and spoken word ventures over more than four decades. But she has also been consistently involved in music-making, too, collaborating with various composers over many years, including Ginsberg guitarist Steven Taylor and with her own pianist son Ambrose Bye. With Taylor, she continues work on an ambitious operatic re-telling of poet Ezra Pound's controversial life and, with Bye, her latest collection of spoken word recordings with musical accompaniment, *The Milk of Universal Kindness*, was released in 2011. It joined a lengthy sequence of collections where the oral and melodic have been married-up dating back to the 1970s, well reflected in her collection of readings and performances, *Battery: Live at Naropa 1974–2002*, issued in 2003. We might see her as the one of the most direct heirs of the Beat poetry spirit carrying it forward in a range of revitalised jazz or rock or popular music settings.

Waldman can certainly see a line of association between what Beat women may have done in the 1950s in a largely unreported sense and what later female artists and musicians managed to achieve in a more high profile fashion. She comments: 'I agree that the Beat legacy – in many of its various possibilities and aspects – continued through the orality and performance of many women artists coming after and, in some cases, overlapping. It was as if a kinetic energy had been let out of the bag (a "high energy construct" in Charles Olson's phrase), and the way for more assured women artists to ride it was through an expressive larger/grander poetics in forms that could be political, personal, improvisational, and also work alongside popular musical forms and structures – and instrumentation. And they were able to succeed in public spaces and flourish. The public spaces were opening in the sub-culture or counter-culture and you had those alternatives where you could get your start, test the waters.'[23]

She points to the folk legacy as a central bridge between these worlds and 'obviously, the singularity of Joan Baez', whose mark on that genre was large and deep even before she embarked on a two-year affair with Bob Dylan which anointed them, for a time, King and Queen of that musical scene. The fact that Dylan had a link to both folk and Beat communities is notable in itself but we should not forget that Baez's younger sister Mimi was also embroiled in similar musical and literary groupings as wife of novelist Richard Fariña, whose comical and picaresque work, much in the bohemian campus mode, *Been Down So Long It Seems Like Up to Me*, was published in 1966, just two days before he was killed in a motorcycle accident. The inter-woven lives of Dylan, Fariña and the two Baez women is vividly related in David Hajdu's 2001 book, *Positively Fourth Street*,[24] revealing aspects of the merging muso-literary terrain in which Dylan was predominant and where Fariña would have prospered had he lived. All four of these people were engaged in folk practices yet all were informed and well-read, applying literary thoughts in musical settings, musical ideas in literary ones.

With Baez and her oeuvre in mind, Waldman says she was familiar with the environment in which the folk community arose. 'The small cafés and folk clubs – and you get links, too, back to Harry Smith's anthology, too. I grew up on MacDougal Street and frequented the cafés and other music places. My brother was a folkie who used to hang out in Washington Square Park. I sat on Lead Belly's lap as a child, went to Peter Seeger's Hootenannies', she remembers.

She adds that 'the Poetry Project, founded in 1966 and I was there from day one, was also an example of more public space and rhizomic possibility, where Laurie Anderson and Patti both read/performed early on. Then there was the Nova Convention, in New York City in 1978, where Laurie truly had her debut, on a programme with William, Allen, John Giorno, myself and others, where women could be heroic, as well – or heroine-etic. Taking a stance and, in my case, a more vatic stance. Orator, prophet, etc. Upping the amp, so to speak. Because Allen Ginsberg, William Burroughs, Kerouac had galvanised the culture with a torqued vision that woke its audience to itself.'

Waldman returns, too, to the seminal place of Dylan in this unfolding setting, as a specific inspiration for her own musical excursions. 'And there was also Bob Dylan whose words you could always hear! That's certainly what I wanted to do. What were the skilful means? A more encompassing panoramic voice, a body willing to take a stand. I always worked with musicians up and down the spiral

---

[23] Anne Waldman, personal communication, email, 28 September 2011.
[24] David Hajdu, *Positively Fourth Street: The Lives and Times of Joan Baez, Bob Dylan, Mimi Baez Fariña and Richard Fariña* (London: Bloomsbury, 2001).

over many years. The Kerouac School, established in 1974 was a place to also work in collaboration with the likes of jazz giants Don Cherry or Steve Lacy. And Steven Taylor, multi-gifted poet, musician, Allen's accompanist, of the Fugs. Marianne Faithfull also a guest at Naropa, and consider her friendship with William, Allen and Harry Smith, too.'

Yet she is disinclined to find a single cause for the changes and evolutions that occurred and opened gates to women that had appeared shut, if not bolted, for so long. 'Rock and folk were involved here', she adds, 'but also experimental trajectories. And there are consociational overlaps here, too.' Waldman stresses: 'I would want to be very specific about the individual paths and directions this cultural explosion or intervention took, and not just lump the huge variety of talent and fruition to one cause or point, because you also need to reflect on what was going on in the culture: the anti-war movement and the liberating strokes of feminism. And all the other tides of the culture. Something had to give.'

She adds: 'Interesting to contemplate Patti watching Jim Morrison and thinking, "I can do that too". Also thinking about Janis Joplin singing the Michael McClure-penned song, "Mercedes Benz". So the influences from the guys but also very strongly from the women, as well. I met Diane di Prima when I was 18 or younger, saw her in her milieu, and also as activist, publisher, engaged with the Poets' Theatre. Then there was Hettie Jones, too, as editor, memoirist. And I also think of the additional arenas that gave space and grace – historical literary and performance movements. Fluxus with Yoko Ono, the permission John Cage gave, and a sense of mantra through Allen. I had also studied Indian singing with LaMonte Young at one point. It seemed quite radical to combine mantra with political activism.'

Women who did emerge also had contact and connection with Waldman. She recalls that 'Joni Mitchell gave me a dulcimer when we were on the Rolling Thunder tour in the mid-Seventies and said, "It might work – be interesting –with your poetry". She even gave me my first lesson but the sound was too mild and sweet for what I was vocalising at the time. I remember also that Carly Simon wrote to me as a fan of my work.' In conclusion, she does believe that 'the Beat thrusts are powerful triggers, alchemic, decidedly, and in many ways a reclamation for women of some original bardic place that's also inherently there for us already. But also there was an invitation from the culture, needing its powerful women, setting the stage, asking us to stand up, perform and correct the imbalance.'

Sharon Mesmer is from a later generation, a more recent figure in this landscape – an acclaimed New York-based poet who studied with Ginsberg in the early 1990s. Born in Chicago, she has lived in Brooklyn in more recent times and includes the verse collections *Half Angel, Half Lunch* (1998) and *Annoying Diabetic Bitch* (2008) and the short fiction volumes *The Empty Quarter* (2000) and *In Ordinary Time* (2005) among her publications. She has been in rock bands – the

Mellow Freakin' Woodies who issued the album *In a Mellow Freakin' Mood* in 1994 – and has an enduring connection to that popular musical culture. If women were marginalised in the original Beat community of the 1950s, did the Beat spirit eventually energise or galvanise later women to use popular musical forms – rock, folk and so on – to carry that earlier legacy forward? Says Mesmer: 'Well, certainly for me the women who were part of the original Beat community, like Diane di Prima, for instance, inspired me toward creating a means of expression for myself, and I'm talking when I was 14, which is when I started reading and writing poetry and actually thinking of myself as a poet. That said, I should say that when I was 14, I wasn't aware of women being marginalised in the arts – that came later, for sure! For me, the women "in the arts" *were* the women in rock 'n' roll, the very individuals under consideration here.'[25]

So who were the women music-makers most significant to Mesmer as younger rock 'n' roller and later as writer and how did that musical and poetic impulse connect in her particular case? 'First of all, there were the women singer-songwriters like Carly Simon – I loved "That's The Way I've Always Heard It Should Be" – and Joan Baez and Joni Mitchell. They were, you know, sensitive and poetic, and appealed to that part of my brain that responded to Sylvia Plath and Anne Sexton. Then there were performers like Suzi Quatro and the band Fanny; Quatro's sister Patty was in Fanny. They played tough, sexy, rockin' guitars, low-slung and cool, and I wanted to *be* them. Carly Simon's beauty was kind of too much to aspire to. Also Maggie Bell of Stone the Crows and Genya Ravan of Goldie and the Gingerbreads and, of course, Janis Joplin. They weren't beautiful but they had those strong presences, great songs, great voices and, probably even more important, great clothes and cool. Later, Nico. When I discovered Patti Smith – in a tiny article in *16* magazine, of all places – she eclipsed all of them. She connected the poetry with the rock 'n' roll, and plus she was skinny and weird-looking, and that appealed to me immediately.' Does she feel that some kind of transgenerational influence or force passed from that under-recognised colony of Beat women to the next three generations of sister artists and feed their musical art in some fashion? 'Certainly in the person of Patti it did, since she had exposure to the Beats. And there was no way she was going to be marginalised because she had written for *Creem* magazine and had friends within the music journalism community who, by the way, were also inspirations to me – people like Lisa Robinson, Lillian Roxon,[26] for example.' Did the

---

[25] Sharon Mesmer, personal communication, email, 31 October 2011.
[26] Lisa Robinson was a key member of the staff of magazine *Hit Parader* in the 1970s and also wrote about music for the *New York Post*. She has been contributing editor to *Vanity Fair* since 1999. Lillian Roxon was the creator of rock's first encyclopedia, which carried her name, published in 1969. She died, aged 41, in 1973.

lack of recognition for women writers in the earlier era find some compensation in the emergence of independent creative females in areas such as rock and folk, punk and riot grrrl? Mesmer comments: 'I don't know about in the 1970s, which was my "coming of age" era – I don't know if the lack of recognition in the field of writing spilled over into rock 'n' roll *then*, though I'm sure it was a factor later, with women like Karen Finley and Kathy Acker and Anne Waldman.'

Was the liberating power of Beat, plainly hibernating for women originally, somehow made available, in a delayed, alchemic manner, to subsequent female performers? 'There's a parallel here, a funny one, I think: artists take over "bad neighbourhoods" because the rents are low and the spaces are big, and then a couple of years later the affluent people move in because the area has been made "safe". And the artists move out because the low rents have become way too high. It used to be that what you were seeing happening in the arts was a bellwether for what you'd be seeing soon in the general culture, though in a watered-down way, of course. It always seemed to me that trends in the arts would filter into life in general, and I do agree that the liberating power of art, made available to, or claimed by, women – "claimed by" being the phrase that rings true to me – had a huge influence on the culture, emboldening teenage girls to claim power.'

She adds: 'With a contemporary artist like Lady Gaga, for instance, it's hard to pin that kind of influence on her because I don't see her as being that original. Great artists steal, mediocre ones borrow – we all know that – but that "borrowing", under the influence of post-modernism and all its discontents, has become fetishised. There's a hopelessness now about being original', Mesmer asserts. 'There's a hopelessness in general that has to be dealt with and transcended.'

David Meltzer has wandered most avenues where literature – poetry and prose, commentary and criticism – and popular music – from jazz to folk and rock – intersect. As a young arrival in San Francisco as the Poetry Renaissance unfolded in that city and the challenging rhythms of 'Howl' lent momentum to that community's creative upturn, Meltzer wrote and read poetry, delivered his verse to a live jazz soundtrack in the late 1950s, and, as a song-writing guitarist in the 1960s, mixed with the West Coast folk revivalists like Jerry Garcia, David Crosby, Janis Joplin and Quicksilver's Dino Valente, before finally forming a psychedelic folk rock band called the Serpent Power, with his wife Tina, in 1967. Meltzer has always been an astute observer and critic of these scenes as well as participant. He produced a seminal set of interviews in *San Francisco Beat: Talking with the Poets* (2001), edited *Reading Jazz* (1993) and *Writing Jazz* (1999) and issued a sweeping reflection on Beat history in his long poem *Beat Thing* (2004).

Meltzer has a particular take on the interface between women and Beat and rock music, as he explains: 'Realistically, and in service of accurate history, women suffered the same delimiting in the 1950s as in the 1920s. Sex radicalism was always male-centred. And in dealing with the Beats, even more phallocentric. The mythos is invariably about sons and men fleeing the hearth, going on the road as guys bonded and bound to male fraternity, the female as mother/bride. I always felt idea of "the Women of the Beat Generation" was an attempt at revisionist history of the essentially all-male cast of characters. Typically, many of the women included were "wives of" A-list bards.'[27]

He continues: 'Diane di Prima was and remains the lone female in the all-male pantheon. Bonnie Bremser's memoir of life with Ray sets one narrative in place of poet as pimp. The two best histories of that period from a female perspective are Joyce Johnson's aptly titled *Minor Characters* and Hettie Jones' *Becoming Hettie Jones*. Di Prima's memoirs – the one for Girodias[28] and her recent first volume of her autobiography – nail it down. Lenore Kandel's so-called "shocking" *The Love Book* is another statement challenging the male privilege so dominant in the Beat arena.'

He adds: 'All the post-Beat songwriters you name may be the aftermath of that same mythos now skewed from a female perspective but still essentially doing the guy thing by honouring that movement. What was the Beat? Its virtues and complicities? How does, for instance, Nellie McKay fit into the neo Beat boogie? I always thought the Shangri-Las were emblematic of tough love and Mary Weiss, their lead singer, returned to the studios after decades and her album resonates with skewed romantic love glossolalia that Shadow Morton produced in their signature recordings.'

Meltzer has some other ideas to suggest in this debate about a continuing thread. 'What about Annie Lennox? What about Ani DiFranco? Both address the inequities of the romantic fairytales of Beat guys who were subsumed in movies, pop records, at the time almost totally focused on romantic love, from the male purview. Pop culture and jazz culture were essentially male projections. What about my friend Janis Joplin who struggled and fought and submitted and died before realising how alive she was? Trying to negotiate the tightrope over Grand Canyon's Identity theme park should be a fascinating adventure into either adding onto the myth or challenging it.'

Although the genealogical line from Beat women to the more intellectually adventurous and personally autonomous female rockers of more recent times is more crooked than straight, it seems that Waldman, Mesmer and Meltzer – three individuals from different time zones in the span of Beat expression – can see

---

[27] David Meltzer, personal communication, email, 16 February 2009.
[28] Maurice Girodias was a Paris-based publisher who founded the Olympia Press and also issued work by Henry Miller, Willam Burroughs and Vladimir Nabokov. Di Prima's *Memoirs of a Beatnik* was published by him in 1969.

a relationship between the barely heralded efforts of the 1950s, when women tried to raise their heads above a parapet built and protected by men, to the later decades when female musicians were able to fight their corner, raise their profile and establish, in some cases, significant reputations in a rock 'n' roll realm, still generally assumed to be the natural terrain of the male performer.

While feminism in its various forms – the second wave that began as women's liberation at the end of the 1960s and the third wave of the later 1980s, sometimes regarded as post-feminist, which saw female writers and musicians attain a confidence that maybe even superseded the efforts of their activist predecessors and found expression in post-punk derivatives like riot grrrl – was plainly a bridge, a catalyst, for women to secure their status within the patriarchy, it would be a mistake not to credit those pre-liberation writers, those female Beats who were only belatedly given recognition for their output, who were in essence, we might argue, the underground of the underground. If the male Beats could regard themselves as subterranean, operating in the underbelly of the mainstream, the women novelists and poets who formed a fringe part of their circle, were buried deeper still in the subcultural sediment, constructing their own whispering revolution that would only find its full voice when re-discovered in the feminist glare of the later twentieth century and, as importantly, in a delayed artistic personification, through the creative brilliance of figures like Joni Mitchell, Patti Smith and other members of their bold sorority.

4 RAISING THE CONSCIOUSNESS?: RE-VISITING ALLEN GINSBERG'S 1965 TRIP TO LIVERPOOL

In the very heart of the Swinging Sixties, a decade the influence of which has continued to vibrate luminously through the last years of one Millennium and into the first years of the next, a high-profile poet and campaigning activist of Jewish-Russian-American background came to Liverpool, a place where the ley lines seemed to hum most loudly and warmly in the late spring and early summer of 1965. At the end of that May, Allen Ginsberg, Beat-politico-Buddhist-performer-poet, extended his ongoing and impromptu world tour – Cuba, Russia, Eastern Europe and on to the UK – to take in a northern English city that had, only quite recently, unleashed on the world nothing short of a musical sensation. Yet the visitor had more to praise than just an all-conquering quartet who had left such an indelible impression across the Atlantic and beyond. But more of that later.

The Beatles, following their arrival in New York in February 1964, had sparked little less than a cultural revolution. Until then, British pop had been a virtual irrelevance to the US, the most powerful and lucrative marketplace of all. But the group's spearheading of the British Invasion would, in the next few years, leave a lasting brand on the American rump. The Fab Four seized the keys to the rock 'n' roll citadel and opened gates that would eventually admit home-grown artists from Herman's Hermits to the Rolling Stones, the Dave Clark Five to the Who, the Animals to the Kinks, Led Zeppelin and Van Morrison, Fleetwood Mac, David Bowie and Elton John, the punks and the New Romantics.

So, the Beatles were one convincingly powerful reason for such outside interest in their home city at the mid-point of a momentous decade. But what would prompt Allen Ginsberg, the voluble guru of the Cold War silence and the garrulous precursor of the hippy generation, to not only spend a near week in Liverpool but also coin an iconoclastic phrase that would both delight – and maybe even haunt – the city for the next four decades. For Ginsberg concluded during that amiable and frenetic stay – in box-rooms and bars, in bookshops and basements – that Liverpool was 'at the present moment the centre of the consciousness of the human universe'.[1] Although Edward Lucie-Smith, whose 1967 volume *The Liverpool Scene* would become a broadside for the city's new vibrancy, was later reported to be the recipient of that comment,[2] it seems much more likely that he said it, during his stay, to fellow writer Adrian Henri, one of a community of poets who would provide another appealing lure for Ginsberg to spend some time by the banks of the Mersey.

In this chapter I aim to contemplate that 1965 visit from a number of positions, attempting to historically re-describe the Ginsberg stay from personal and reported accounts, drawing on interviews, histories and biographies. I want to try and establish what Ginsberg made of Liverpool and attempt a reading of what the Liverpool Poets and the wider community made of this exotic guest. And, perhaps crucially, I would like to try, through more recent responses by critics and commentators, to make sense of the poet's widely remembered and oft-quoted remark, one that continues to resonate through the recent Merseyside mindset and offers ongoing succour and encouragement to the city's artists, its enduring bohemian quarter, even its officially sanctioned arts sector.

But first: who was Allen Ginsberg and why did he count? From the late 1940s through the early 1950s, Ginsberg was a central figure in a dynamic sub-cultural grouping, self-dubbed the Beat Generation – beaten down but also beatific, aspiring to saintliness – which had forged literary, artistic and musical cells in Greenwich Village, in North Beach, San Francisco and Venice Beach, LA. Yet it would take Ginsberg's live debut, in 1955, of his long poem 'Howl', and the subsequent acclaim then furore, raised by obscenity charges eventually dismissed, to propel the Beats into a national then international phenomenon, becoming 'familiar to hundreds and thousands of readers around the globe in the months and years to follow'.[3] Before that decade had ended, further members of this creative clan – novelists Jack Kerouac and William Burroughs, poets Michael McClure, Lawrence Ferlinghetti, Gregory Corso, and others – would see their writings appear in print as the Beat phalanx, for a period, surrounded the literary establishment.

---

[1] Ginsberg quoted in Edward Lucie-Smith (ed.), *The Liverpool Scene* (London: Donald Carroll), p. 15.
[2] Michael Schumacher, 1992, p. 446.
[3] Simon Warner, 'Sifting the shifting sands: "Howl" and the American landscape in the 1950s', *Howl for Now: A Celebration of Allen Ginsberg's Epic Protest Poem*, edited by Simon Warner (Pontefract: Route, 2005), pp. 25–52 (p. 29).

By the early 1960s, the US, and by implication the wider world, was entering a period of tremorous drama. As the American Civil Rights movement battled for racial equality, the tensions between political blocs in the West and East intensified. First a 1962 diplomatic crisis saw Soviet attempts to site missiles on Cuba leaving President John F. Kennedy's finger hovering over the nuclear button. Then Kennedy's killing in Dallas in 1963 prefaced a new war in South East Asia that would set the capitalism of America against the Communist aspirations of North Vietnam, the following year.

Against this extraordinary backdrop, Ginsberg became a dynamic link between the Beats of the 1950s and the emerging hippies of the 1960s. By 1965, Ginsberg's prescient messages of freedom and individualism – an anti-war manifesto underpinned by Eastern spirituality – chimed roundly with the *Zeitgeist*. He would meet and befriend Bob Dylan then John Lennon and Paul McCartney – he was 'welcomed into their near regal circles'[4] – and an informal alliance of folk singer, rock group and Beat poet would take shape. In time, Ginsberg would perform and record with them all.[5]

In the weeks before he came to Liverpool he had been briefly based in middle Europe, famously spending time in Czechoslovakia still, at this point, a satellite and puppet state of the Soviet regime. Here he was ritually crowned King of May by the students of Prague. But the authorities were less impressed, disturbed by Ginsberg's infectious notions of self-determination not to say his unconventional sexual mores, and he was expelled from the country.[6]

Ginsberg headed for London, in time to catch the first of two performances by Dylan at the Albert Hall on 9 May, meeting the Beatles in the singer's hotel suite after the first show.[7] Shortly afterwards the poet left London for a re-charging English odyssey, determined to celebrate his thirty-ninth birthday in the company again, he hoped, of the Beatles, back in the capital, on 3 June. His train trip, at the start of the last week of May, carried him northwards to Lime Street railway station,[8] where a figure representing another vital stream in Liverpool's reviving

---

[4] Warner, 2005, p. 48.

[5] Examples of these collaborations include: Ginsberg's recording sessions with Dylan in 1968, 1971 and 1981 gathered on the compilation *Holy Soul Jelly Roll: Poems and Songs 1949–1993*; an informal musical gathering with John Lennon at the ex-Beatle's birthday party of 1971 and on-stage with Lennon in New York in 1972 (see Schumacher, 1992, pp. 556–7, 569); and Ginsberg's own collection *The Ballad of the Skeletons* (1996) which would involve contributions by Paul McCartney, on record and on stage.

[6] Miles, 1990, pp. 362–8.

[7] Schumacher, 1992, pp. 445–6.

[8] The precise days Allen Ginsberg spent in Liverpool are a matter of certain conjecture, but the poet did write to his father Louis on 1 June 1965 saying, 'I spent the last week in Liverpool where the Beatles come from', which helps to place the date of the trip with some accuracy. See Allen Ginsberg, Louis Ginsberg, *Family Business: Selected Letters Between a Father and a Son*, edited by Michael Schumacher (New York: Bloomsbury, 2001), p. 236.

cultural life – poetry – would greet him. Brian Patten was the youngest member of a trio of poets who would later be gathered in *The Mersey Sound*, that much celebrated volume, published in 1967, in the Penguin Modern Poets series.

On the day of Ginsberg's arrival in the city 'it was so cold that [Patten] lent him a multi-coloured jumper his grandmother had knitted him long before the coming of flowerpower', Bowen reports.[9] According to the same account, Patten had no room for the visitor to stay but he said in a 2006 interview that the visitor did reside in his flat for the first days of the trip. 'He stayed with me at 32, Canning Street in Toxteth, Liverpool 8, in an attic room I shared with a student called Tim Dawson. Allen would sit in the box room with a skylight, sing his Buddhist chants and say his Buddhist mantras. He was a bit of a showman. Tim and I were great fans but we were more fans of "Howl" than all his chanting and bell-tinkling!'[10]

How had the Ginsberg visit to Liverpool come about? Patten explains the background: 'The American poet Robert – Bob – Creeley, had been up to Liverpool to do some readings. He enjoyed Liverpool and mentioned to Allen that the city had a great buzz. Bob had been published in the poetry magazine I was running, *Underdog*. In fact, we had published both Ginsberg and Creeley. Bob came to the city some months before; it may have been late 1964. He did two appearances – one at Sampson & Barlow's in a London Road cellar where I used to do readings and at the university. At the university, Creeley had maybe four or five people there; university people weren't interested – they were into the Movement poets. But at the other reading at Sampson & Barlow's, the place was buzzing and full of people.'[11]

Certainly Creeley's crowded reception augured well for Ginsberg's subsequent visit: there *was* an audience for US poets and poetry which remained, in Britain at least, at the avant garde fringe. But Ginsberg's time in Liverpool appears to have been more of a social whirl than a performing occasion. He seems to have desired a taste of the sights and the sounds rather than a platform for himself and his poetry. He did, however, perform once during his six-day stay, at 'Parry's Bookshop […] next to the Philharmonic Hotel' according to Bowen.[12] But Patten recalls differently: 'Allen did a small reading in a bookshop called Wilson's at the bottom of Hardman Street, it was a kind of family-run bookshop. It was a very crowded reading in a very small space with about 50 people packed in. It was not really well publicised but Allen was quite happy to do a little reading.'[13]

---

[9] Phil Bowen, *A Gallery to Play to: The Story of the Mersey Poets* (Exeter: Stride Publications, 1999), p. 62.
[10] Brian Patten, personal communication, telephone conversation, 6 July 2006.
[11] *Ibid.*
[12] Bowen, 1999, p. 63.
[13] Patten, telephone conversation, 2006.

Adrian Henri claimed that there had been some tension caused by the presence of the London-based Beat and jazz poet Michael Horovitz who 'totally monopolised proceedings'.[14] Horovitz responds to this accusation: 'Adrian clearly resented that I [...] should be there at all on his home turf and presumably somewhere he felt he might be more central, though "monopolising" was no part of my intention – for all that it may have looked like that to him and perhaps, via Adrian, to Allen.'[15] Horovitz's part in establishing links between the American Beats – like Ginsberg, Ferlinghetti, Corso, Burroughs, Creeley and others – and the UK throughout the early 1960s, via his publication *New Departures* and live readings, had been crucial. Horovitz stresses that both he and fellow London poet Pete Brown had been engaged 'to provide substantial support performances'[16] at Ginsberg's Liverpool reading. He feels that audience members would have been as familiar with his and Brown's work as with Ginsberg's.[17] But, despite these hints of discontent, Henri later enthused that the bookshop appearance 'had been one of the best poetry readings I've ever been to, certainly the best I've ever heard Allen do. It was late spring evening, sunlight coming through the window, and he sat cross-legged and just read and it was totally intimate and beautiful and it just flowed out, not even preaching, just talking to you, but talking like some sort of prophet.'[18]

Patten recalls a less meditative encounter, a more psychedelic one, during Ginsberg's Liverpool sojourn. 'I spent some time with Allen on acid,' he reveals. 'We both took a tab and spent hours and hours in the Walker Art Gallery walking around. We saw it in a new light, in fact many different lights.'[19] What did he feel Ginsberg made of his time in the city? 'He loved the excitement of the city, full of boy bands, sweaty, tiny stages. It was paradise. He was drawn to the energy of Liverpool – there was youthful buzz in the clubs, we were hearing lots of music, lots of groups. We went drinking in the Phil and the Cracke.'[20] The visitor wrote to his lover Peter Orlovsky: 'I spent all week in Liverpool home of the Beatles and heard all the new rock bands and gave a little reading and had a ball with longhair boys – it's like San Francisco except the weather is greyer – lovely city, *mad* music, electronic hits your guts centres (*sic*).'[21] But Patten, in his reveries with Ginsberg, recalls a human and humane figure rather than a poetic superstar. 'He was a

---

[14] Bowen, 1999, p. 63.
[15] Michael Horovitz, personal communication, email, 24 July 2006.
[16] Horovitz, personal communication, email, 29 July 2006.
[17] *Ibid.*
[18] Bowen, 1999, p. 6.
[19] Patten, telephone conversation, 2006.
[20] *Ibid.* Note that the Philharmonic and Ye Cracke are both famous city hostelries.
[21] Quoted in Miles, 1990, p. 371.

genuinely accessible, nice man, friendly. Lots of people who were not interested in poetry found him quite fascinating, too.'[22]

After initially staying at Patten's tiny premises, Ginsberg transferred to the slightly more roomy surroundings of Henri's home at 64, Canning Street. 'It was more comfortable there,' comments Patten.[23] Ginsberg's new host was slightly anxious at what to expect. Bowen reveals that fellow Beats Ginsberg and Gregory Corso had previously stayed at the home of the celebrated Liverpudlian critic, writer and jazz singer George Melly, who had been 'appalled' when 'they behaved very badly'.[24] But Henri need not have feared. 'He duly arrived and was charming [...] the morning after we'd been to the Cavern [...] there was Allen washing the dishes and singing one of those Buddhist chants to himself. It really was an amazing revelation.'[25]

While Ginsberg was in Liverpool, he was also taken to the city's Art College by poet-painter Henri, who taught there and would, some years on, win the prestigious John Moores Art Prize in 1972. They later visited a church in Everton in Albion Street and the incident prompted Henri's first poem of significance, 'Mrs. Albion You've Got a Lovely Daughter', a piece that refers to William Blake, a crucial figure in the life of Ginsberg who believed he had heard the great English mystic in a supernatural encounter in the late 1940s.[26] Henri later told interviewer Stephen Wade that 'Allen noticed this street called Albion Street; and of course he was entranced, because it was a Blakean sort of sign'.[27] Ginsberg spent time in other places – drinking dens and rock haunts, most famously the Cavern, where the sexually voracious and uninhibitedly adventurous American was said to have had a liaison with a drummer he encountered.[28] 'He jammed with Trevor, drummer with Faron and the Flamingos', as the Liverpool émigré, now Baltimore-based, poet Christopher George says in his verse work 'Allen Ginsberg in Liverpool', a tribute on Henri's death in 2000 and published online four years later.[29] Henri said that the musicians thought Ginsberg was 'great'[30] and 'the feeling was mutual', Cook states in his book *The Beat Generation*.[31]

---

[22] Patten, telephone conversation, 2006.

[23] *Ibid.*

[24] Bowen, 1999, p. 62.

[25] *Ibid.*

[26] See Miles, 1990, pp. 99–105.

[27] Stephen Wade, *Gladsongs and Gatherings: Poetry and Its Social Context in Liverpool since the 1960s* (Liverpool: Liverpool University Press, 2001), p. 90.

[28] Bowen, 1999, p. 63.

[29] Christopher George, 'Allen Ginsberg in Liverpool' (For Adrian Henri 1932–2000), poem at http://chrisgeorge.netpublish.net/Poems/AllenGinsberginLiverpool.htm, originally published in *Electronic Acorn* 16, September 2004 [accessed 21 July 2006].

[30] Edward Lucie-Smith (ed.), *The Liverpool Scene* (London: Donald Carroll, 1967), p. 17.

[31] Cook, 1971, p. 154.

So, beer and verse, LSD and art, sex and music, enjoyed in the rarefied atmosphere of a Liverpool glowing in its associations with the world power who were the Beatles and a swelling poetry scene that had not only pre-dated the Merseybeat boom but, by 1965, was maturing into a movement that would soon test the thesis that the regional could not take on the metropolitan – something the Fab Four had already effectively challenged in the musical sense but one the city poets would challenge in matters literary. In many ways, as Ginsberg toured the city streets, these literary aspirations were still to be made flesh – Lucie-Smith's book would be two years in the publishing, as would *The Mersey Sound* – so, in early summer 1965, this American guest, we might propose, was tasting the early juice of the harvest before it passed to the lips of the nation. What though of this iconoclastic statement, this resounding comment, identifying the city as 'the centre of human consciousness'? What made the great Beat bard deliver a sentence of such dogmatic certainty, a description of the place that seemed to ring of headline-seeking hyperbole? The comment has certainly been the subject of much conjecture since.

Bowen suggests in saying what he said 'Henri and others knew he was talking about the Beatles'.[32] The ubiquitous power of the group meant, for a long time and perhaps well into the 2000s, that the name of the city and the name of the band had become synonymous: to praise Liverpool was to praise the Fab Four. The world's gaze was so fixed on the most outrageously gifted of songwriters, the most prolifically productive act of the era, that the attention of the people of Planet Earth was plausibly, on that basis alone, focussed on that location; to know of the group was to know what the world was listening to during these times. Jonah Raskin of Sonoma University, California, leading Ginsberg scholar who penned the 2004 'Howl' history *American Scream*, supports this analysis: 'I would say that it was the Beatles that brought the comment. And [Ginsberg] was in the habit of making grandiose and global statements and wanted to sound like a sage and an oracle, all at the same time. The Beatles did put Liverpool on the map of the world for most Americans – even hip Americans.'[33]

But there are other explanations, other interpretations. Melly in his much-praised account of the 1960s insurgence *Revolt Into Style* – a quote in itself from Thom Gunn on Elvis Presley – commented of Ginsberg's remark: 'A typical exaggeration, just the thing to set the middle-aged teeth on edge, and yet if you substitute "the young" for "the human universe" it was surprisingly accurate.'[34] Poet, critic and *Beat Scene* contributor Jim Burns admits that 'years ago I

---

[32] Bowen, 1999, p. 67.
[33] Jonah Raskin, personal communication, email, 5 July 2006.
[34] George Melly, *Revolt into Style: The Pop Arts in the 50s and 60s* (Oxford: Oxford University Press, 1989, orig. pub. 1970), p. 238.

commented, probably a bit sourly, on Ginsberg's remark and was taken to task by George Dowden, his early bibliographer, who reckoned I'd taken him too seriously and the comment was only meant lightly, perhaps a little variation on Jung's statement about Liverpool being "the pool of life".[35] There are still more grounded, maybe cynical, takes on the Ginsberg description. Some have suggested – even Patten has hinted at it – that the visiting poet may have been liable to make such sweeping claims for other places he went to, as well. Poet Christopher George understands that Ginsberg may have made similar remarks on at least two other cities[36] – possibly about Milwaukee, maybe about Baltimore – unlikely candidates, it could be argued, in the pantheon of seminal, globe-shaping communities.

Then there are the earthier, sexual spins on Ginsberg's words, derived principally from the comments that follow the first section of the quotation: 'They're resurrecting the human form divine there – and those beautiful youths with long, golden archangelic hair,'[37] recalling St Augustine's reference to the Angles as angels when he visited England on a Christian conversion mission in the sixth century. Although we must assume the poet is making no direct allusion to the Beatles on this occasion, the long-haired fashion and implied androgyny, that was part of that new age, must have had an appeal to the sexual inclinations of the arriving Ginsberg. In *Bomb Culture*, Nuttall makes a connection in a different, broader context: 'American reporters thought that the Beatles were queer because of their hair-cuts.'[38] Maybe Ginsberg, at this point, shared the view of those members of the US media. He may have known, too, about Brian Epstein's submerged sexual preferences and the strong innuendo that he had been drawn to manage the Beatles, not because they were outstanding musically, but because he had found Lennon physically and compellingly attractive.[39] Steven Taylor, who has taught at the Beat-associated Naropa University in Boulder, Colorado, and spent around 20 years as Ginsberg's guitar player up to the poet's death in 1997, hints strongly at the sexual sub-texts underpinning these matters. 'Ginsberg would have said Liverpool was the centre of consciousness or whatever because of the Beatles,' he states. 'He had a crush on them, just as he had on Dylan. Young men of obvious talent and massive fame. Al was what we call a star fucker. And he was right. Liverpool was a vortex of consciousness, on account of Lennon, for my money.'[40]

Michael Horovitz, a key catalyst of the period who would also help assemble the renowned Albert Hall poetry event a week and a half after Ginsberg's Mersey

---

[35] Jim Burns, personal communication, letter, 15 July 2006.
[36] Christopher George, personal communication, email, 6 and 7 July 2006.
[37] Schumacher, 1999, p. 446.
[38] Jeff Nuttall, *Bomb Culture* (London: Paladin, 1970, orig. pub. 1968), p. 229.
[39] Albert Goldman, *The Lives of John Lennon* (London: Bantam Press, 1988), pp. 139–42.
[40] Steven Taylor, personal communication, email, 5 July 2006.

trip, brings his own first-hand insight to the poet's remark. 'It seems quite likely that Allen was asked for a quote by one or more of the bevy of media folk he attracted wherever he went, sometimes by his own design'. Horovitz adds: 'I suspect the geographical and relatively provincial aspects of parallelism between Merseyside/Lancashire (in relation to London), and the Bay Area/California – where Ginsberg hit his major-key voice and big-time stride – (in relation to New York City), seemed related to the delight he took in tracing trails and haunts of the Beatles *et al.* while hanging out around Liverpool those May 1965 days and nights.' Horovitz also recalls the sexual charge the visiting American seemed to be experiencing in the city with such enormous and endearing relish. 'He had been drawn to Lennon in particular from way back, and swiftly came to fancy and adore Patten and various longhairs, musos, popsters, beatniks and dope-freaks who came his way via the Merseybeat/Liverbard wavebands, worldwide, so the city from where many of them sprang was bound to be a sort of Mecca.'[41]

Surviving Beat, Bay Area-based poet and musician David Meltzer, a friend and collaborator with Ginsberg over many years, suggests that the 'consciousness' quote may have had its roots, in part, in a volume of prose published that same year by the Black Mountain College poet Charles Olson. His *Human Universe and Other Essays* came out close to that time and Meltzer thinks that this fragment may have fed into Ginsberg's remark in an inter-textual way. Adds Meltzer: 'In 1965 Allen was still amazingly tone-deaf and rhythm-challenged but was always alert to the "new thing" – certainly the Beatles were and remain a one-of-a-kind revolution that will not be repeated. In a couple of years they advanced from a cover band to a banal song-writing duo into something that changed, forever, pop music. I honestly don't know how "musical" Allen was. I remember playing behind him in Allendale, Michigan and realising that, curiously, he didn't get it, he didn't swing, even though his desire was strong. Allen, McClure and Ferlinghetti were caught up in the fantasy of rock stardom. Yet Dylan told me early on that it was the poets who "had it" not the songwriters. The real movers were the Beatles who opened up the sizzle of a "scene" that the Liverpool Poets like Henri easily affiliated with.'[42]

Perhaps, though, the final reflection should fall to Edward Lucie-Smith, a significant commentator and critic who was deeply influential in placing the poetry of the city in a wider context, lifting it from the parochial to a nationwide readership through his edited volume *The Liverpool Scene*. He believes that Ginsberg's comment arose on two counts: 'The rise of the Beatles, and the sense that Adrian Henri and the other Liverpool poets represented a commitment to

---

[41] Horovitz, personal communication, email, 7, 24 and 29 August 2006.
[42] David Meltzer, personal communication, email, 9 July 2006.

Modernist, internationalist values missing from the British poetry being written elsewhere at that time. Philip Larkin and Kingsley Amis thought all that was rubbish and, of course, they much preferred jazz to rock. You've got to remember that Adrian was interested in popular culture, including rock, but also very much interested in the whole early Modernist culture represented not only by the Cubist Picasso, but also by Apollinaire, the Dada writers in Zurich and so on.'[43] Ultimately, however, we might speculate that in the heady rush of rock music and popular verse immersing the city at the time, the consciousness most raised during the visit to the shores of the Mersey in 1965 may well have belonged to Ginsberg himself.

Author's note: I am indebted to the letters, emails and conversations shared with me on this subject during July and August 2006. Thank you to Jim Burns, Royston Ellis, Christopher George, Michael Horovitz, Edward Lucie-Smith, David Meltzer, Brian Patten, Jonah Raskin, Steven Taylor and Mike Chapple (features writer, *Liverpool Echo*).

---

[43] Edward Lucie-Smith, personal communication, email, 4 July 2006.

Q&A 1

Michael Horovitz, poet, publisher and British Beat

Michael Horovitz has been a tireless publisher and promoter of poetry in the UK for well over half a century. He published work by Beat writers in his magazine *New Departures* – Kerouac and Burroughs were in early issues – and then took the project on the road as Live *New Departures*, combining poetry and jazz in performances reminiscent of American spoken word experiments. He read at the legendary Albert Hall poetry event in London in 1965, joining Ginsberg, Ferlinghetti and Corso, has published numerous collections of his own – including *Bank Holiday: A New Testament for the Love Generation* (1967), *Growing Up: Selected Poems and Pictures 1951–1979* (1979), *Wordsounds and Sightlines: New and Selected Poems* (1994) and the epic *A New Waste Land: Timeship Earth at Nillennium* (2007) among them – and edited a landmark anthology of the new British underground poetry *Children of Albion* (1969). In 1980, he launched the Poetry Olympics which, for more than three decades, has seen him continue to present, project and anthologise verse by writers of all backgrounds and often in settings where popular musicians participate. His own gigging William Blake Klezmatrix Band reflects his passions for Blake, jazz and Jewish klezmer.

You have always had a close interest in jazz, of course, and that was one of your passions that linked you to the Beat writers from the start. But what did the emergence of rock 'n' roll in the late 1950s mean to you, the Beat writers and the wider culture. Did Elvis Presley and others shape your or their lives or art?

This harks me back to when I found myself an autonomous free spirit at Oxford from October 1954 through the rest of the 1950s, relishing my long-quested for, but first unfettered liberation from the heavy restrictions of family and school, coincident with my discoveries of jazz, rock, blues *et al.*, which virtually replaced the ultra-orthodox Jewish indoctrinations family and pretty conventional English middle-class mores grammar school had tried to impose.

Elvis, Bill Haley, Buddy Holly and their UK counterparts like Tommy Steele, Adam Faith and Cliff Richard were loud at parties and on café and pub jukeboxes, and so shaped my life and art developments in that they sound-tracked early sex and love interactions as well as cultural and intellectual interests.

But early rock 'n' roll did less for my male and female buddies than, on one hand just about all forms of both live and recorded jazz, on the other the gradually spreading round Britain R&B, scat, gospel, soul and other mainly Afro-American wordsounds of so many eloquent bands, groups and singer-guitarist-songwriters – including, to name but a quorum, Jimmy Rushing, Wynonie Harris, John Lee Hooker, Nat King Cole, Slim Gaillard, Sonny Boy Williamson, Big Bill Broonzy, Josh White, Champion Jack Dupree, Jimmy Witherspoon, Leroy Carr, Little Richard, Chuck Berry, Mahalia Jackson, Billie Holiday, Dinah Washington, Eartha Kitt, Aretha Franklin, Odetta, Howlin' Wolf, Bo Diddley, Otis Redding, Ray Charles and Nina Simone, along with the great blues artists Alexis Korner and Chris Barber helped to bring over – Sonny Terry and Brownie McGhee, Memphis Slim, Muddy Waters, Otis Spann, Sister Rosetta Tharpe.

What the emergence of rock meant to the Beats could in some instances have been parallel. But remember that the Beat Generation was to some extent (as Barry Miles has suggested in his commentaries on Allen Ginsberg) willed into existence by Allen, who along with some of the others made various definitions of its/their aspirations – from 'just a bunch of writers trying to get published' (Ginsberg) to his more grandiose designations, as toward the close of Part I of 'Howl' canonising the madman, bum & angel, as his heroes, 'beat in time', etc.

And in *On The Road* and other Kerouac texts, which mainly predated Elvis *et al.*, it's Lionel Hampton, George Shearing, Lester Young, Slim Gaillard and bebop I recall being celebrated – as in (earlier) Ginsberg, it's Ma Rainey, Thelonious Monk's 'loud key-bangs' and Ray Charles; in Burroughs, the lovely evocation of Duke Ellington's 'East St Louis Toodle-oo'; in Corso, Miles Davis, Charlie Parker and Gerry Mulligan. One of the hugely refreshing inputs these writers, and then of course their black associates LeRoi Jones (more latterly Amiri Baraka), Ted Joans, Calvin Hernton, Jayne Cortez as well as West Coast jazz poetry pioneers Kenneth Patchen and [Kenneth] Rexroth, Jack Micheline and Ferlinghetti and later Gil Scott-Heron and the Last Poets, was this growing embrace of oral and jazz an blues modes as at least as basic to both composition and performance of their rapidly evolving supra-literary innovations.

Then again, the open forms and 'Projective Verse' practices of Black Mountain College communards Charles Olson, Robert Creeley (who acknowledged his rhythmic masters as Alexander Pope and Miles Davis), Fielding Dawson, Jonathan Williams overlapped and inter-penetrated with the 'spontaneous bop prosody' hailed in Kerouac by Ginsberg – whose versification from 'Howl' on also drew intensively on Judaic liturgies, the 'Hebraic barbaric yawp' of Whitman and post-imagist documentary collages of his New Jersey neighbour and mentor William Carlos Williams. Allen in passing at the opening of 'Kaddish' ('... I've been up all night, talking, talking, reading the Kaddish aloud, listening to Ray Charles blues shout blind on the phonograph/the rhythm the rhythm...') and continually improvised over implicit or explicit musical resonances including every emergent phase, later jamming with Joe Strummer – see the text of 'Ghetto Defendant' in the *New Departures POP!* [Poetry Olympics Party] *Anthology* of 2000, transcribing their duologue on the 1982 Clash LP *Combat Rock*. Ginsberg adored and even briefly toured and recorded with Bob Dylan (Rolling Thunder Revue) and McCartney (Albert Hall London 1995/'Ballad of the Skeletons' CD). Various major collaborations with rockers got going later as with the evolutions of the Fugs, Doors, Dylan and associated formations, plus Patti Smith, Steven Taylor, Mike McClure with Ray Manzarek, Janis Joplin, *et al.*

Whilst Ginsberg drew on and celebrated many of the main rock groundbreakers: 'Portland Coliseum' from 1965, a spot-on exhilarated and exhilarating evocation of a massive Beatles concert in Oregon, is included in *The POM! Anthology* of 2001, and among other poems dedicated to his most beloved superstars is one addressed to Dylan I first read in *The Listener* – which begins by avowing and demonstrating Allen's adoption of Dylan's shorter lines – 'On Reading Dylan's Writings' from 1973 – Dylan in turn drew on various aspects of Ginsberg's and Kerouac's innovations in his song-writing, performances and recordings, as well as his published prose writings.

When Pete Brown and I met by chance at Beaulieu Jazz Festival in summer 1960, he had dug *New Departures* No. 1, and I'd been delighted by his punchy short poems in *Evergreen Review*. We immediately hitchhiked to Edinburgh Festival, improvising both soundpoems and jazzpoems en route, including an extended sequence of chase choruses (*à la* Wardell Gray/Dexter Gordon, Zoot Sims/Al Cohn and Jazz at the Phil, and also touched by Patchen, early Ginsberg, Ferlinghetti, Corso, and Kerouac's jazz-cadenced sequence *Mexico City Blues*), which grew and grew into 'Blues for the Hitchhiking Dead'.

As well as substantial chunks of my editorial 'Afterwords' to the 1969 Penguin *Children of Albion* Anthology accounting for the various live/*New Departures* developments of the previous decade, there's a detailed account of our earliest phases in the 'Jazz Poetry' issue of *New Departures* (No. 4, 1962) including some of this extended jazzpoem's closing choruses. Like most of our and some of our closest comrades' road-running round Britain (Christopher Logue, Adrian Mitchell, Spike Hawkins, Libby Houston, [Roger] McGough and [Brian] Patten), these and parallel experiments in oral and performance poetry drew delightedly and constantly on jazz (from New Orleans to bebop and beyond) and blues rather than rock. Brown and I regularly improvised and declaimed to the inspired accompaniments of Dudley Moore, Ronnie Scott, Stan Tracey, Dick Heckstall-Smith, Jeff Clyne, Laurie Morgan, Bobby Wellins, John Mumford, Ian Carr, Ginger Baker, Graham Bond, Bruce Turner, Joe Harriott, Shake Keane, Coleridge Goode, Don Rendell, Jack Bruce, Pete Lemer, Barry Fantoni, Ron Geesin, R.D. Laing, Lol Coxhill, Jeff Nuttall, Simon Wallace *et al.*, as well as fellow poet-musos Roy Fisher, Tom McGrath, Neil Sparkes and John Hegley.

I also collaborated with Emanuel Acquaye aka El Spedo (the Nigerian conga drummer beloved of Kenny Graham's Afro-Cubists and Georgie Fame's Blue Flames), the original Soft Machine (Daevid Allen, Robert Wyatt and Hugh Hopper – and gave them their first gig at the original Marquee Club in Oxford St in 1963), Ginger Johnson's drum bands, Guyanese flautist Keith Waithe, and with folk guitar virtuosi Davey Graham and John Renbourn. We also enjoyed hanging out, working and playing with some of the developing blues-into-skiffle-into-rock-into-reggae artists including Pete Townshend, Alexis Korner, Barbara Thompson, Peter Gabriel, John Mayall, Eric Clapton, Warren Ellis, Linton Kwesi Johnson, Valerie Bloom, Jean Breeze, Mervyn Africa and the various Ken Colyer, Cyril Davies and inter-genre groups like Nucleus, Colosseum and Paraphernalia.

But straight ahead commercial rock we tended to regard as threatening and pillaging the purer acoustic jazz continuum. I have, however, included over the years many artists who straddle diverse styles and sects, including one-offs such as Cornelius Cardew, Moondog, Fran Landesman, Kylie Minogue, the Waterson/Carthy families, Shusha Guppy, Patti Smith, Attila the Stockbroker, John Cooper Clarke, Damon Albarn, Gwyneth Herbert and Ayanna Witter-Johnson, and Blakean pop stars who also write poetry like Paul Weller, Nick Cave, Ray Davies and Jah Wobble, and folksinger-writer-musos like Martin Carthy, Julie Felix and Tymon Dogg, in Poetry Olympics and Jazz Poetry SuperJams.

The arrival of the Beatles gave British popular music a place on the global map. How did that affect what you did and what you wrote? Were they influential on you and other poets like Pete Brown and Adrian Mitchell?

Adrian [Mitchell] gave and published the first ever interview with the Beatles a bit before they hit bingo. He had always been a big music lover and his – and my – earliest blues/rock heroes and influences included Joe Turner & James Brown – the *New Departures POM!* [Poetry Olympics Marathon] *Anthology* of 2001 features Adrian's celebration of James Brown, as well as both song-lyrics and poems by Paul McCartney and Hank Wangford among others. All three of us – Adrian, Pete [Brown] and I – befriended the three Liverpool poets who were to become so mega-promoted and ubiquitous early on, and each of us would frequently perform and collaborate with them up north, whilst Adrian Henri, Brian [Patten] and Roger [McGough] would hook up with us down south. The introduction into our pieces on both stages & pages of more commercial song-like/chanter-crooner techniques helped break down the uptight barriers which had kept contemporary literature imprisoned in game-reserves of jealousy guarded by esoteric elites brandishing exclusion orders – 'No Trespassers unapproved by the official neo-academic marketing board'! These (r)evolutions naturally widened the appeal to ever more heterodox audiences and readerships, many of whose members might never have thought of paying any attention to poetry since leaving school – as well as appealing to plenty of children, students and teachers who in turn passed on the new musical poetry boogies.

The fact of the new British pop music, and just about equally of the gradual absorption of transatlantic and European experimental arts, especially Parisian and US Beat Generation activities, becoming much more widespread throughout the 1960s, of course affected each of us poets in different ways – Adrian [Mitchell] got more & more involved with many forms of (musical) theatre and song-writing (his play about William Blake, *Tyger*, for example, remains a continuing landmark of counterculture-into mainstream replenishment); Pete, more and more a highly original rock 'n' roller/singer/bandleader/producer; I, more and more publisher/ performer/impresario and much more still, latterly, musician via the duo with Stan Tracey and the William Blake Klezmatrix (with Pete Lemer, Annie Whitehead and Madeline Solomon) going from strength to strength. So, although none of us actually 100% embraced UK pop, its prevalence and commercial impact meant that the larger public was more open to emanations around its various fringes and overlaps such as our respective ones.

Adrian [Mitchell] became particular pals with Macca, toured with him occasionally and edited *Blackbird Singing*, McCartney's selected lyrics and poems, published in 2001.

I first met Lennon & McCartney at a London ICA [Institute of Contemporary Arts] do hosted by Colin MacInnes in around 1964; it was close to the time of Lennon's *In His Own Write*. They were matey and merry; then at Ginsy's thirty-ninth birthday party John and George and Cynthia [Lennon] and Pattie Boyd, they briefly chatted. I gradually befriended Macca more over subsequent years and presented him, at Queen's Theatre, London in October 2001, as part of the POM! Festival.

Quite a bit of influence came from the other side, as witness at Liverpool Art College Lennon produced *The Daily Howl*, and when in London in the later 60s Macca was living with Jane Asher's family he mingled with and picked up tips from all manner of experimental writers and artists, etc.

Could the Mersey poetry scene have arisen without the Beatles?

Pretty hypothetical/Rumsfeld area – unknown unknowns, etc.! The commercial apotheosis of Liverpool from the early 1960s on inevitably bestowed a marketing halo upon everyone and everything exploiting a Merseyside connection. McGough was writing poems before big Beatle things. Patten probably would have done too – he told me he was first most inspired to write and perform by the first jazz poetry he attended in his school cap, which Brown and I brought to the Crane Theatre in 1960 with Dick Heckstall-Smith some Scouse musos including drummer Ron Parry. We had also jammed with in the Edinburgh Cellars under the bus station in Live *New Departures* in August/Sept 1960/61, where Roger [McGough], Libby Houston, Alan Jackson, Jerry Rothenberg and Alan Brownjohn also read. Adrian Henri told me at the party after another early Live *New Departures* by Brown and myself, 'H'm, think I'll have a go at this poetry lark' – and he proceeded to push away at it, and, to adapt Christopher Logue's famous little poem, he flew ...

What was the relationship between the UK underground and the popular music of the mid-1960s? Was the Albert Hall event linked to a surge in the British pop arts or did it have a momentum of its own?

Relationships and interplays existed from the start, and particularly burgeoned after the 1965 Albert Hall Internationale and its continuing reverberations, especially via Peter Whitehead's *Wholly Communion* movie which captured selected highspots. In an interview Joe Strummer gave the Los Angeles LiveDaily on 14 August 2001, 16 months before his death aged 50, answering the question 'Was there something that dictated the direction his album Joe Strummer and The Mescaleros' *Global A Go-Go* – which he kindly dedicated to myself and Nina Simone! – would go in', Joe referred the interviewer to our first International Poetry Incarnation 1965 in the Albert Hall as: '... where you can mark the beginning of the British underground scene of the 1960s – it started on that particular night. Michael [Horovitz] still puts on something called the Poetry Olympics, and we played on one (The POP! [Poetry Olympics Party] Festival at London's Royal Festival Hall on my 65th birthday in 2000), and that gave me the vibe, because Pablo Cook and I went there stripped down, with just congas and acoustics. It was a kind of beatnik evening – there weren't any road managers or that kind of stuff. That really gave me the feeling of THIS IS THE WAY TO GO, let's relax. Sometimes you get tired of the big guitars and walloping drums and all that stuff, it can get boring. I was looking for a break in the weather, ways to change things up, and doing that beatnik Poetry Olympics evening gave us the feeling to go on to this record and try a bit of grooving around, whether we kept to it or not ...'

Joe of course became a pretty active protagonist of Poetry Olympics, notably in 2000 with his and Cook's inventive set at the Royal Festival Hall on 4 April 2000 (including an updated version of the Clash's 'London Calling' rewritten as a tribute to my achievements), and, in the autumn of 2000, with an equally open-spirited jam with Pablo, Tymon Dogg, Martin Carthy and Keith and Lily Allen at the London Astoria.

INTERVIEW 3

Larry Keenan, photographer of 'The Last Gathering of the Beats' in San Francisco in 1965

Larry Keenan was a photographer of international reputation based in the San Francisco Bay Area whose work is held by museums and private collections around the world. In 1964, while studying at the California College of Arts and Crafts, he became involved in a college project in association with one of his teachers, the poet Michael McClure. The project allowed him access to many of the city's poets and artists, friends of McClure, including Allen Ginsberg, Ken Kesey and others. These links were instrumental in his invitation to shoot the so-called Last Gathering of the Beats at City Lights bookshop in San Francisco at the end of 1965. The shoot saw many of the Beat writers convene – Ginsberg, McClure and Lawrence Ferlinghetti among them – and the appearance of Bob Dylan, on tour at the time, and his guitarist Robbie Robertson gave the occasion a special meaning. Keenan's images of the gathered Beats and a smaller group featuring Dylan and Ginsberg, McClure and Robertson have become a celebrated record of this moment. He established a significant career after his 1967 graduation, photographing the Beats frequently, rock bands and producing his own photographic artworks over many decades. Keenan spoke to me at his Emeryville home in July 2004.[1]

SW   **Tell me where are we, Larry?**

LK   Emeryville, California. Right by the bay. It's beautiful out here, God's country in a way, isn't it? It's beautiful, I love the water, it's wonderful.

---

[1]   Larry Keenan died after a long illness on 12 August 2012. See Simon Warner, 'Photographer who captured Dylan, Ginsberg and the Sixties counter-culture', *The Independent*, 28 August 2012, http://www.independent.co.uk/news/obituaries/larry-keenan-photographer-who-captured-dylan-ginsberg-and-the-sixties-counterculture-8082405.html [Accessed 16 December 2012].

SW **So is this part of Oakland?**

LK No, it's Emeryville, right next to Oakland. Between Oakland and Berkeley. It used to be a little tiny town built by one guy. Now, there's an IKEA, a lot of stores. Quite a lot of people who live in the city live here in this Watergate complex, a man-made marina with flats and offices that opened in the 1970s.

SW **And you're going to live here for a little while longer?**

LK Just a month. Then I either have to move out to a new place, or whoever buys could keep me as a tenant, possibly. Or I'll move somewhere else if isn't too far.

SW **Will you need the space to store all your gear and so on?**

LW I'll need space just as big as this place actually, could get a bit smaller that's for sure. I'll sell my archive, and give that to I dunno …

SW **Sell your archive?**

LK Yeah. I need the money.

SW **I'm sure that a museum would be interested in acquiring your archive.**

LK Hopefully for a lot of money. Let's hope so!

SW **Let's hope so! Absolutely. Well, let me just tell you, Larry, what I'm trying to do. I'm interested in investigating the relationship between the Beats, who weren't just San Franciscan, of course, but many certainly, in the 1950s and 60s, made their homes here. And I want to try and make some sort of assessment of how far there was a continuity between the Beats and, really, that more kind of serious rock artist that emerged after sort of 1965, 1966. I think this photograph, or this series of photographs, that you took at the end of 1965 outside City Lights bookshop, seems to be almost the sort of crossroads of this moment.**

LK Interesting that you mention that, yeah. There were some actors there as well. Many actors showed up. Garry Goodrow, for instance, from The Committee, the improv group. He's there.

SW **Oh right? So there were some actors there as well?**

LK A lot of people showed up. There were a lot of press.

SW **OK, let's start off by trying to establish why – you were young, still a teenager were you, then?**

LK I'd just turned 21.

SW **You were 21, OK. Just tell me a little bit about how you became involved in this extraordinary series of pictures. Why were you the person to photograph it?**

LK I was doing a book about my school because at art school you had no real projects to work on, you know. I did some portfolio work to try and get some real jobs, doing posters, album covers and books. So we also did a book about the school.

SW **Which school were you at?**

LK California College of Arts and Crafts. CCAC. And I wanted to be there because my parents thought it was bad news me being there. They wanted me in a more traditional environment, and I didn't wanna do that. So I went in another direction basically.

SW **Was there any tradition of taking photographs in your family?**

LK Not at all. My aunt's a pretty good artist, my mom's a pretty good artist, but that's it, you know. My dad's brother's still alive, he's good at art.

SW **So you went to college and photography became your main pursuit?**

LK I was actually an interior design major of all things. The only way I could get to art school was if I majored in interior design. My parents had disinherited me and didn't know what to do with me, so I had to major in interior design.

SW **So, interior design …**

LK Yeah, interior design, arts and crafts. Then of course, I wanted to be a photographer once I got there, so I took photo classes. But to be honest, I did all my photography on the side actually. I brought my portfolio into school and they taught me design, basically.

SW **So, had you graduated by the time the 1965 photographs were taken, or were you coming close to graduation?**

LK I was coming close to graduation. In 1966, I graduated, but I went back for two more years to be a teacher. I was there for six years altogether.

SW **So what was the background to the City Lights shoot?**

LK The college project came about the previous year. One of my teachers had a meeting and asked if I wanted to take some pictures of his friends, and I was, 'Who are your friends?' and he said, 'Well, you can come and meet my friends, basically'. And you know, I said, right! The friends were Allen Ginsberg, and all this, Lawrence Ferlinghetti, Ken Kesey, Bruce Conner and I was 'Oh my god, this is great!' One of my friends said, 'Going up?', and I was like, 'Yeah, I'm going up!' So then I started working with Michael [McClure], and everybody, and it was great.

SW **So Michael McClure was one of your teachers?**

LK Yes he was my teacher for a couple of years. I met him on our project. He was one of the few people who were poets who'd published any books that worked at our school. He had a lot of poetry experience. He'd published a lot of poetry books and he knew how to publish a book. He was the faculty adviser. He's advised me ever since. He's a great man, a wonderful writer, actually, terrific.

SW **I see. So was this earlier in 1965 that you had taken these first pictures?**

LK It was 1964 that McClure asked me if I wanted to work with him on this project. We met at his house in the Haight. My friend Dale Smith and I started shooting – we'd go to this place every Saturday. And we had a full-on call around to see who was available and we'd go and shoot them all day long and come back. There was a lot of stuff that got done. And back at school, we had a little contest, we had a little contest together, Dale and I, to see who was a better photographer. It was a tricky business, fun. It was neat.

SW **So, in December 1965 Michael McClure said to you, we've got this gathering happening, could you come and take some pictures?**

LK No, no, no. Lawrence Ferlinghetti [*of City Lights bookshop in San Francisco*] actually called that morning you know and I could do it. And Ginsberg was there and I met Dylan, too.

SW **So you'd already brushed shoulders with some of these subjects before? This was not the first time you'd photographed this group of people?**

LK I'd photographed a lot of them individually before. Michael and Allen, for example.

SW **Why did Lawrence Ferlinghetti organise this gathering at City Lights, I wonder?**

LK He wanted like a French photo of these nineteenth-century poets hanging out in France like at the Grand Guignol Theatre, with all these umbrellas in the rain. If you opened the umbrella up, it was great if you could catch it at the right time. All the main photographers were posted there that day. Tons of them. There were like 25 or 30 photographers there, too.

SW **Oh, so there were more photographers there than just you!**

LK Oh yeah, I only saw one of their shots and it was the one that was in the *San Francisco Chronicle*. That's the only one I've ever seen from it, so I don't know if they got money from it. I'm not certain, but my photos were all over the place, that's for sure. Dale was there too, but I didn't see any of his other stuff either. Yeah, it almost looks like a funeral, kind of real so sad looking. Then a fire truck came, a great big bright thing, Allen and McClure and everyone are all looking over, and it's because there's a fire truck coming.

SW **Oh, I see.**

LK Yeah, it was amazing. I think Ferlinghetti had called the fire drill himself. He pulled the alarm, but it was against the law, and they were 'You know it's against the law, don't you?' Of course he did.

SW **But why did he want to that?**

LK It was so dour. The whole thing was so dour he wanted to lighten the thing up.

SW **OK!**

LK   Yeah, and then some tourists started showing up, some sailors, all these people. They wondered what was going on there. And Dylan shows up, and he knew me and Michael and Allen, and we all went down the basement. And then the fans tried to break in the basement, so we all jumped out the window and ran down the alley.

SW   **In what was then Adler Place but what is now Jack Kerouac Alley?**

LK   Yeah, right.

SW   **So why do you think Bob Dylan turned up? What was going on?**

LK   He wanted to be with Allen – he wanted to be with the Beats. He wanted to have a photo for the album cover of *Blonde on Blonde*. We thought we could get a great cover.

SW   **Why didn't they use those photos?**

LK   Because so many people were taking those pictures, and then the crowd started threatening Dylan, he didn't know our names, he didn't know it was us. He didn't know what was going on. So he called the whole project off. But we were devastated that we couldn't include it in one way or another. I think it was Jim Marshall, he was there with photos, but someone said 'No-one take any photos, it's just these two guys' – Dale and I.

SW   **So was there a chance, then, that the Keenan photos might have appeared on *Blonde on Blonde*?**

LK   No, he didn't know who we were. He didn't know our names, or anything. He told Allen, Dylan said, 'I can't tell who these guys are.' So he just dropped the whole thing, which was really disappointing. Except they did appear in some of those Dylan books and stuff, and on some albums that've appeared anyway.

SW   **Which other albums might they have appeared on, then?**

LK   *Biograph*'s one of them.

SW   **How many photographs did you think you took that day? How many shots did you take?**

LK   Well, it's a very long story. Well, you know, I photographed Dylan right. My girlfriend at the time was visiting. I realised that I'd forgotten to put film in the camera and the whole time I was taking pictures there was no film in the camera! I was so pissed I couldn't believe it. I was devastated, I thought I'd lost the pictures of Dylan and all the people in those photographs. I'd spent all this time aligning these shots and there was nothing in the camera at all. I couldn't believe it.

SW   **But there were shots you took on another film?**

LK   Yeah, another camera had film in it, yes!

SW   **So one of the cameras didn't work, but the other did?**

LK   Right. I was so excited about Dylan being there and everyone, that

I didn't see there wasn't any film in. And Dylan said afterwards, 'Were you one of the guys taking my picture?' You know, I was there photographing him for like 20 minutes, and I said, 'Yeah, I was one of the guys taking your picture'. And it was like he didn't recognise me. But that's the kind of guy he was, that's OK, so that's alright. I understand it too, you know.

SW **So he could be quite a difficult subject?**

LK Oh yeah, yeah. But for this you know he showed up on time, he was nice with us, posing, he'd do any kind of pose you want, wonderful. Really good. Dale and I – Dale got good photos of that day actually.

SW **And it's interesting that the picture you normally see – I mean, obviously I've seen the famous picture outside City Lights – it's in a kind of portrait shape. And it's quite tight shot.**

LK Is that the horizontal version?

SW **Yeah, there's a horizontal version …**

LK Yeah, see how dour it looked, it looks so sad? Yeah. That's why I never show it.

SW **Oh, I see.**

LK Yeah, all the people are looking down, they all look kind of disappointed, like a bad bus stop, you know, it's terrible, so I never show it.

SW **I see. So, who was on this side of the picture who got cut off? Can you remember who was …?**

LK David Meltzer's in there, probably. I've probably got a better shot with him in there.

SW **Yes, I think Meltzer is actually hidden behind someone in the horizontal shot.**

LK Yeah.

SW **So, in essence then, Ferlinghetti wanted to do this Parisian sort of shot of poets and bohemians.**

LK It was a last gathering too. It was a last gathering. He definitely told me it was going to be a last gathering.

SW **He told you that?**

LK Yeah. He'll deny it, because he always forgets stuff. But my mind was like a sponge in those days, it's so crystal, it's right, right, right! Anything out of the ordinary I just sucked up and never forgot. That's why I've got such good detail of stuff.

SW **So this project was the last gathering? The Last Gathering of the Beats which is what's it come to be known as?**

LK Sure it was. Otherwise what would be the point of everybody being there, you know? It was the last gathering.

SW **And has Ferlinghetti since denied that's what it was?**

LK Well, he's said, 'Why do you do that?' and I said, 'Well that's what you said it was'. And he looked at me like – uhhh, Jesus. He burned me. Course I know, you know, I was there too, you know. The whole thing – everybody was dying, people were going to jail and stuff, and they wanted to be able to gather in one last photo because there were these new changes coming in.

SW **I see.**

LK The whole culture changed, everybody wanted to get the last photo before it all changed and they ran out of time.

SW **So, I mean, my theory then that this is the fulcrum of those changes, if you like …**

LK Sure it is. Yeah, yeah.

SW **Could be argued that Ferlinghetti has been, in more recent times, less keen to see it as this?**

LK Yeah, but that's Ferlinghetti. Ginsberg and McClure had the most sense of history, that's why. They just had the best sense of history of all. They wanted everyone to do this project, basically. Ferlinghetti called me, and he'd spoken to Dylan, Ginsberg and McClure about it too, and wanted it then because they knew it was changing and they wanted a little documentation of it, and it was great, you know. Sure. It was great for me, actually. A great shot.

SW **Do you think in some ways then, that the keys to the cultural castle, if you like, were passed over on this day? The Beats were passing the legacy to Dylan.**

LK I wouldn't go that far, no. Dylan was really there, Dylan was there and he was blown out of his mind. He didn't want to pose with them at all. Dylan and McClure and Ginsberg were real buddies, and he was doing it for them, I think, personally.

SW **I see. He did it for McClure and Ginsberg as friends?**

LK Yeah, yeah.

SW **And he didn't care too much about the other guys that were there?**

LK No, the other guys were just there but he didn't really care. He didn't want to be photographed with them for *Blonde on Blonde*, he wanted to be just with those two guys and also Robbie Robertson. I called Robbie out, Robbie just didn't look like he belonged there, so I took a separate shot, with all three of them, all four of them actually, together.

SW **So, Dylan wanted to be photographed with his friends, but he didn't of course take part in the large group shot.**

LK Not at all. They begged him. 'Come on, Bob! Come on Bob! Come on, come on, come on'. 'No, no, no'. He walked away. Good for you, man. It would have ruined this scene, because it was all about them, it wasn't about him anyway.

SW **So there was some tensions going on there?**

LK Well, there was a little tension, I thought. They were kinda pissed he wouldn't pose with them, but if he'd posed with them, it wouldn't have been about them. It would be about him, all the time, you know. He knew about that. It was a real smart move from him, actually, in that respect.

SW **Right.**

LK And after this gig, we went over next door to Vesuvio's which was another interesting thing that was going on. There was a huge table by the window, with about twelve of us sitting round the table. Everyone was ordering hard drinks, until it got to Dylan. Dylan ordered tea. Then everybody else ordered the tea. Anyway yeah, that was pretty funny, I thought, 'Oh my God, everyone's ordering tea, what a bunch of creeps'. I was so embarrassed for them – 'I'll have my booze too!', you know?

SW **Yeah!**

LK Everybody wanted to be Dylan so bad, it was amazing. Look at that photo over there of McClure and Dylan and Ginsberg. They all wanted to be Dylan so hard in that photo, it's incredible, you know?

SW **I was talking to Michael [McClure] and asking him, 'How did you feel about these rock gods appearing, were they straying on your territory, were they stealing some of your thunder?' And Michael's very clear, he didn't feel this was happening at all. He liked the idea.**

LK They put him in shows. Yeah, it was a good boost for him, actually. He got to be in things that he'd never been in before because they liked him. See, he didn't hang back and wait for it to happen, you gotta be there too, and he was there all the time. That's why he had the luck. He was the right guy, that's for sure.

SW **But, these shots that you took on that day in December 1965, they've become iconic, they've become world-famous. But clearly your body of work, even in the 60s, extends much more widely than that.**

LK Oh, certainly. You can only see them when I publish, most of it you'll never even notice, you know. I print them myself in the end.

SW **The great pictures you took of rock artists in the later 1960s in various settings, how did that happen? What's happened – did your career suddenly go into overdrive? What happened to you as result of those City Lights pictures?**

LK I got shooting Beats after that up until the next year, then the next year I went to Europe, in the summer of 1966. Before I went to Europe, for about five years or a little more, I was working with some rock groups of friends of mine, to get a lot of rock shots. With the popular guys, there were always too many cops around for that. It was too creepy, you know what I mean? I got too paranoid. I was teaching at a high school and, at the end of the day, if I'd had a drug bust that'd be the end of my career.

SW   **Who did you enjoy photographing through that time? What are your memorable moments there?**

LK   I was working for Frank Werber who managed the Kingston Trio. They named him 'the Dragon' – that was his nickname. When I met him, I thought, 'Oh my God! He *is* a dragon!' He had a meeting with Bill Champlin, of the Sons of Champlin, who Werber managed. He wanted to change the sound. There were five of them. He said to two people, 'You'd better leave now, we're gonna get another two and you'd better be gone'. Just 'cause he wanted to change the sound. That's the Dragon, man, that's heavy duty. These guys were like 19, 20 years old and that was really heavy, you know.

SW   **And, do you feel as if the characters who were the poets, the Beats, were they different people to the rock artists?**

LK   They all wanted to be rockers! I remember McClure saying that he and Bruce Conner wanted to be singing on the radio at midnight. That was great. I wish I'd seen that, too.

SW   **So there was this desire of the poets to be part of this scene?**

LK   Oh, sure. Someone told me that there were these tapes, Dylan was with Bruce Conner, amazing tapes, incredible tapes.

SW   **And obviously Bruce Conner is the artist. Where was the musical element in that?**

LK   Bruce Conner had this amazing tape recorder.

SW   **And did they do some musical things together?**

LK   Yeah, McClure would sing a song. Like a poem. They'd do poetry together. He wrote lines and lines and lines, you know? That was great, Conner was a great man. They made a tape together. There's one that I love that starts with these two, three beats, and they're reading a poem back and forth together. It was just amazing stuff. I love that stuff man, it's just amazing stuff.

SW   **This stuff has never really surfaced in a commercial sense?**

LK   I don't know, might have been. I don't know where they are. It should have been. Even then, it's just powerful stuff.

SW   **Because of course in recent times, you'll know very well that Michael has been working with Ray Manzarek and so on. So, do you think to some degree he has fulfilled some of his musical ambitions?**

LK   Oh, certainly.

SW **Through Manzarek?**

LK And other artists, you know. 'Mercedes Benz', the Janis Joplin song, he wrote that himself, you know. So he's been doing it a long time, writing songs and doing songs and working with others.

SW **When you say that the rock artists were different people, were they just younger, did they have different values?**

LK Oh, yeah, yeah. They had different values, for sure. They were into making it. The Beats were into just surviving and doing the best job they could. These guys were into making it. And they were more ruthless and more organised, with fights and stuff, you know. It was different. It was like rock 'n' roll was just different from poetry, for sure. One guy described me as being really soft-focused on hanging with the Beats, but he was hanging with the rockers, so it was different, different personalities. That's why I hung with them.

SW **So there was a different attitude, people were more interested in commercial success?**

LK The rockers were, that's for sure. I got told by one rocker that they just wanted to get laid, get some drugs and get some money. That's was the whole point. That was rock 'n' roll. That's what it was all about.

SW **So even those characters like the Grateful Dead, and the guys who were linked to – they seemed to be heirs to the Beats. You think they had a different take on life?**

LK The Dead?

SW **I mean, maybe the Dead were different, were they? I don't know …**

LK The Dead were different from anybody else. The Dead were more of a group thing, they were much more of a group hanging around. I saw them in some concerts. There were just so many bad concerts, I couldn't take it anymore. It was terrible stuff. It was terrible stuff. They had too many free concerts, too many drugs, too much shit that was going down. We stopped going to Dead concerts for quite a while. They got better. It did get better. They were really bad, for sure, but they're really good now.

SW **I mean, this drug element that you mention – you were talking about the fear of drug busts, and so on – obviously the Beats and the rock musicians used drugs, but did they use drugs for similar reasons? How would you read that?**

LK The Beats were different. I didn't do any drugs with the Beats at all. I was clean, I was under-age, about 20, 21. No drugs hanging with the Beats. Drugs came in hanging with the rockers, who always had drugs around. It was always soft stuff, cocaine and pot. No needles or any of that stuff at all. I had friends who were Hell's Angels who had problems with needles and stuff. That's another story, another book probably.

OBITUARY 1

Peter Orlovsky, 'Member of the Beat Generation, poet and lover of Allen Ginsberg'

The writer Peter Orlovsky, who has died aged 76 of lung cancer, spent more than four decades as the companion of Allen Ginsberg, arguably the highest profile US poet of the postwar years. Orlovsky's own literary legacy was modest in scale – his best-known collection was *Clean Asshole Poems and Smiling Vegetable Songs*, published in 1978 – and inevitably overshadowed by his lover's lofty stature and prolific output. But he still carved out a reputation that allowed him to be regarded as an active member of the Beat Generation, that community of experimental novelists and artists which emerged from Greenwich Village, New York, and North Beach, San Francisco, in the 1950s, to leave their creative influence on the counterculture of the psychedelic 1960s.

Orlovsky had experienced his own youthful dramas even before he encountered Ginsberg for the first time in San Francisco in 1954. He was born in New York's Lower East Side, to a Russian immigrant father, as the tentacles of the Depression squeezed the life from industrial America. His father's printing business failed, then his parents' marriage, and Peter, his mother, three brothers and a sister, moved to Queens, enduring several years of poverty.

When he was 17, his mother insisted he leave school and find work; she could no longer support him. His occupation as an orderly in a mental health institution was physically taxing and emotionally harrowing. The experience was a maturing one for this late adolescent but it would pre-empt a powerful and affecting strain in his future life: his brother Julius suffered psychological instability and Orlovsky would play a role in supporting his younger sibling long into adulthood.

Drafted in 1953, at the time of the Korean War, Orlovsky was marked out as a potential subversive by his communist-inclined reading matter. He was sent to

California to work in an army hospital, where he was befriended by a rising Bay Area artist, Robert LaVigne, who seduced him. When Ginsberg visited LaVigne's studio and saw a painting of a Pan-like boy, the artist told him that it was Orlovsky. Their relationship blossomed shortly afterwards and would last until Ginsberg's death in 1997.

But the association was far from straightforward. Ginsberg had, by now, abandoned any heterosexual pretence and, with his long poem 'Howl' in 1955, made an explicit attack on American values while also celebrating his own homosexuality. Orlovsky continued to express his attraction to women throughout their decades together. This tension would leave a mark on their friendship and there would be times when the two would separate, later to reunite.

In the early 1960s, with Ginsberg at the height of his powers and creative reputation, Orlovsky joined him on journeys to India, north Africa and Europe. As the US counterculture took shape, Ginsberg was a guru, guiding these forces for racial, political and sexual change. Orlovsky was usually by his side, writing, giving readings, and mixing with the movers and shakers of the day: Timothy Leary, Andy Warhol, Bob Dylan, John Lennon and Paul McCartney.

In 1969, Orlovsky collaborated with the photographer Robert Frank on a film entitled *Me and My Brother*, documenting Julius's mental illness. He contributed, too, to activities at Ginsberg's farm project at Cherry Valley in upstate New York (bought in part to wean Orlovsky off a methedrine addiction). Orlovsky later taught at the Jack Kerouac School of Disembodied Poetics at Naropa University in Boulder, Colorado, and joined Dylan's Rolling Thunder Revue concert tour. As the 1970s drew to a close, Orlovsky published his key verse collection, issued, suitably, by Lawrence Ferlinghetti's City Lights publishers, which had put out *Howl and Other Poems* more than two decades previously. In 1980 he produced a book with Ginsberg, *Straight Hearts' Delight: Love Poems and Selected Letters*.

After Ginsberg's death, Orlovsky's health gradually deteriorated. Chuck Lief, in latter years his guardian, says that: 'Peter was devoted to Allen for decades, but continued to struggle with his own demons. When Allen died, the removal of that anchor and reference point led Peter to become somewhat groundless.'

Peter Orlovsky, poet, born 8 July 1933; died 30 May 2010.

INTERLUDE B

All Neal: Cassady celebrated in downtown Denver

In 2007, I planned a celebration of the fiftieth anniversary of the publication of Jack Kerouac's *On the Road*. It was due to take place in the city of Leeds, where I work, and in the university's School of Music where I am based, a commemoration, in words and images, music and performance, of the arrival of this ground-breaking novel.

Among those who were slated to take part was the timeless and tireless Carolyn Cassady, a legendary figure herself in the story of the American Beat writers. But then I revealed to her that an unreleased movie simply titled *Neal Cassady*, a dramatic portrait of her husband, was to also form part of the programme.

Carolyn was very far from happy. In fact, she was quite disparaging of the new bio-pic, suggesting that if that screening remained in the schedule, she would have to seriously consider withdrawing from the event. For me, as organiser, the Sword of Damocles was briefly poised over my head.

Whatever the ins and outs of the matter – and, significantly, my event was frustratingly scuppered by a fire that ravaged my office just weeks before the celebration was due – there is no question that Neal Cassady remains a controversial and contested figure in the discourse of Beat history.

The reaction of his long-time partner was indicative that there is certainly no unanimity in the way we should make sense of this mercurial individual who, from his young life on the streets of Denver to his curious death by the tracks of a Mexican railroad, led an existence that was rich in experience, riddled with paradox, concluded in tragedy.

Lothario and tea-head, car-thief and raconteur, faithful friend and unfaithful partner, orphan and father, speed-king and spiritualist, literary inspiration and would-be novelist himself, Cassady is hero and villain, saint and sinner, toiling brakeman and reckless bum.

The fact that his fame – or infamy – stretched across some 20 years in the rise of the post-war cultural revolution and he was a principal player in the theatre of both Beat and hippy, from the late 1940s to the end of the 60s, made him an iconic figure, a symbol of liberation in a world that was only just wriggling from the straitjacket of social conformity and sexual repression.

Cast as Dean Moriarty in *On the Road*, Cassady appeared on the page as a fast-talking, jazz-loving, ever-optimistic magician of the roads, a supreme master of the steering wheel, his childlike wonder at the possibilities before them balanced by his rapacious sexual marauding.

By the time the writer Ken Kesey employed him to be the driver of his travelling troupe on the day-glo decorated bus dubbed Furthur, the line where the fictional character ended and the actual man began had been largely eroded by the mind-shaking effects of psychedelics and the harsh realities of jail after a set-up drugs bust when the law ensnared a larger-than-life individual whose escapades had been magnified by Kerouac's extraordinary prose.

Thus Cassady became a star of the emerging Beat fiction, as Kerouac immortalised him as free-wheeling wanderer and one of Norman Mailer's 'white Negroes', and then a hero to the hippies and a fellow traveller in their LSD adventures, episodes recounted by new journalist Tom Wolfe in *The Electric Kool Aid Acid Test*, a book published in 1968, the same year that Neal met his end.

The city where Cassady grew up will pay tribute to one of its more interesting sons, when the premiere Annual Neal Cassady Birthday Bash takes place in Denver, Colorado, on Sunday, 7 February 2010, close to, just one day before, the man of the moment would have chalked up his eighty-fourth year.

The occasion, staged in a well-loved and historic drinking haunt called My Brother's Bar, at 15th and Platte, promises an entertaining mixture of songs and readings and even attendance by members of the Cassady family, including, it is hoped, an in-person appearance by the matriarch of the clan.

Resident in London for many years, Carolyn, whose own autobiographical take on these lives and times was provided by her acclaimed 1990 memoir *Off the Road: Twenty Years with Cassady, Kerouac and Ginsberg*, plans to join the festivities.

The bar even has clear evidence that Neal Cassady had at least an occasional beer there: a prized and framed note, written from the state reformatory, which asks a friend if he'll cover a drinks tab he had built up there, is on display. 'I believe I owe them 3 or 4 dollars … please drop in and pay it, will you', it pleads.

Cassady lived life to the full – his hobo instincts delivered extraordinary adventures and also the carnage of relationships de-railed by that constant urge to seek more – and usually somewhere else. Even he and Kerouac had fall-outs and the powerful kinship they felt in the late 1940s was tarnished by the early 1960s, not unconnected to the jail term he served, at least in part, as fall-out from his literary reputation.

But Kerouac believed that Cassady was more than just an untameable livewire and irresponsible hedonist. He saw great qualities in his writing style and claimed to learn from his expression in letters, as electric and loose-limbed as his speech. But little survived the peripatetic rampaging and only *The First Third*,[1] an autobiographical novella published in 1971 after the author's death, has really seen the light of the day, apart from his *Collected Letters*.[2]

However, the legacy of this larger-than-life figure will be considered and applauded when My Brother's Bar unveils what promises to be merely the first of a yearly acknowledgement of Cassady's idiosyncratic contribution to a period of great change in the artistic and political consciousness of the USA.

---

[1] Cassady, 1971.

[2] Dave Moore (ed.), *Neal Cassady Collected Letters, 1944–1967* (London: Penguin, 2005).

Q&A 2

Mark Bliesener, rock band manager and a founder of Neal Cassady's memorial day in Denver

Mark Bliesener is a US rock band manager who has played a role in inaugurating and organising the Neal Cassady Annual Birthday Bash in Denver since its launch in 2010. Based in the city, he is director of BandGuru Management and Consulting. He has more than 40 years of daily experience in the music business: as a performer (1966–1976), music critic (1976–1978), publicist (1978-1988) and personal manager since 1989. Bliesener has received 16 Gold and Platinum record awards from artists whose careers he has managed including Alan Parsons, Lyle Lovett, Big Head Todd and the Monsters and the Nitty Gritty Dirt Band. He is the author of *The Complete Idiot's Guide to Starting a Band* (2004).

What do you see connecting the spirit of the Beats with the rock culture that has followed?

In a real sense the spirit common to both the Beats and rock culture is rooted in the notion of an American 'birthright' to mobility and independence. Prior to the emergence of rock 'n' roll, this was best represented by the cowboy and later the hobos, glorified by Woody Guthrie, and the emerging biker culture, hinted at by Marlon Brando in *The Wild One*. The living link however was Neal Cassady – through his collaboration with Ken Kesey in the development and propagation of the Acid Tests. Cassady's involvement in assisting the introduction of LSD to the American masses is of far greater influence on the rock generation(s) of songwriters than any of his most visionary early letters or literary works.

Neal's wide open, Western 'let 'er rip' lifestyle dovetailed with the hippy 'do your own thing' ethos in manner that was somehow foreign to the more educated, analytical East Coast Beats like Ginsberg and Kerouac. Neal lived both Beat and hippy lifestyles, though most likely he couldn't spot the differences. It was more a continuum. Yes, Allen Ginsberg ultimately attended more demonstrations and recording sessions than Neal, but Ginsberg spent most of his time watching. Never the observer, Cassady's life long quest for a spontaneous sort of knowledge – also called kicks – ensured that he was constantly in the moment. As well as in the driver's seat. Neal's maniacal embrace of life, and knowledge of all things cerebral and sensual, provided the bridge from Beat to hippy.

Do you feel there something in the art of the Beats that inspires artists like Dylan and Lennon, Waits and Patti Smith?

Yes. For Dylan, Waits, Smith and others, it was the Beats' shattering of the post-war myth of a 'Disney' America that was most profound. The 'American Dream' of a two kids, two car, happy family was in full bloom thanks in part to the concurrent accent of TV and its evil twin advertising. It was a sterile, safe place for Robert, Patti, Tom and their ilk to grow up in, a place most unwelcoming to weirdos or any deviation from the norm, a place they desperately wanted to escape from. The Beats provided the ride away from home for these teenage song-writing runaways. Books like *On the Road* and Ferlinghetti's *A Coney Island of the Mind* provided radical relief by painting vivid pictures of another reality existing just beyond suburban borders. Via this exposure to the real grit of life, these songwriters not only created a leaner more romantic lifestyle for themselves, but also discovered a cadence and freedom which illuminated the way to a much more American lexicon which would serve them well. No longer was pop music dominated by the Brill Building writers and the last vestiges of Tin Pan Alley which still, excluding R&B, dominated American popular music.

The Beats clearly pinned their colours to the mast of jazz but what do you think they made of rock 'n' roll in the later 1950s and the music that became rock from the mid-1960s? Can you see evidence in rock song-writing – lyrically, for example – of Beat influence?

There is direct evidence of the Beats as a primary source in the song-writing of Patti Smith, Bob Dylan and other luminaries. But the influence of the Beats on rock song-writing runs much deeper than their documented impact on these justifiably influential songwriters. Beat writers, in a sense, freed all of American song-writing and literature from the stale old world it was chained to. The Beats' timing was good. America was growing lazy and fat for perhaps the first time. Many who would go on to write the rock soundtrack of the 1960s and 70s were among the first to discover two books banned in most

American schools, *The Catcher in the Rye* and *On the Road*. Reading these was a part of the American rite of passage in the Eisenhower/Kennedy era. The 1960s youthquake and the rock song-writing explosion which was to follow could not have taken place without the direct and subliminal influence of these two books. Kerouac's romanticised notion of hitchhiking in *On the Road* accounts for untold thousands of road trips launched in the pre and early hippy time-frame. Though for most who would later pick up a guitar and a pen to express their feelings, the influence of the Beats was real, but more peripheral. All things Beat, from bongos to Burroughs, began to slowly stir itself into the American cultural stew. Notably it was television rather than Corso or McClure that brought Beat to the heartland. The nation's greatest exposure to Beat, and any resultant message contained therein, was delivered by Maynard G. Krebs the jive talking, dopey, 'beatnik' sidekick on popular TV sitcom *The Many Lives of Dobie Gillis*. Maynard was massive and weekly, while Kerouac struggled to draw a crowd for his live TV reading on the *Steve Allen Show*. But the authentic Beats contributed to, and certainly have a real place in the continuum of American music, that broad expanse of sounds and influences which they were so moved by.

Or is it more of a sociological issue – is it simply linked to anti-authoritarian resistance?

A bit of both I suppose. By kicking in the doors of American literature the Beat writers ensured that future generations of writers and songwriters would never have to endure the restraints imposed upon them prior to the1960s. In the process they helped define a liberated, more 'in-your-face' and, ultimately, more American style of writing than anything which had preceded it. This sea change occurred simultaneously with the igniting of the Civil Rights and anti-war and movements along with a counterculture deeply rooted in anti-authoritarian resistance.

To what degree might we regard Neal Cassady as an archetypal rock hero? He has been eulogised by the Grateful Dead, Tom Waits and many others.

Neal almost single-handedly invented the notion of the non-stop, 24-hour, sex and drugs and rock 'n' roll lifestyle, though he would have substituted jazz or classical for the musical component here. Neal personified action. He was the driver. He got you from here to there, an unforgettable, magnetic persona to those who encountered his frenetic force field. Back in the days before the music business was reduced to a series of talent contests – when real rock stars walked amongst us – they were a similar force to Neal. Again, Neal as master of all things cerebral and sensual.

What do you think Cassady made of the post-Beat culture of Kesey and the Acid Tests?

I'd speculate that Neal saw little difference between his years as Beat and hippy, though his hippy years were certainly more speed addled. Neal lived life in a series of moments: a continuation of the pursuit of kicks and some new place to find them in.

Did Cassady like rock music? Did he connect with it? What evidence may there be of this?

Though rock 'n' roll was staking its claim on American music and culture in this time-frame, evidence suggests that Neal didn't think any more or less of it than any other musical form. He loved all kinds of music, but preferred to groove with and find inspiration from jazz and its pure, improvisational nature. Or dig deep into classical music. Though his son John recalls Neal listening to Chuck Berry on the car radio and cranking up 'Maybelline' as he banged the dashboard to the beat. There was a natural affinity between the staccato phrasing and cars and girls centric lyrics of Berry and the Beats. Another link to an apparent appreciation of rock 'n' roll can be found in *On the Road*, Part Four. While in San Antonio, Sal and Dean pump nickels into the jukebox playing 'I Like My Baby's Pudding' by Wynonie Harris, the same Wynonie Harris whose 'Good Rockin' Tonight' would a few years later be covered by an unknown Elvis Presley. Did Chuck Berry read *On the Road*? Probably not, but Chuck and Jack and Neal dug Slim Gaillard. They were all swept along in the continuum of American music.

How have rock music or popular music, in all its forms, featured in the Neal Cassady celebrations you have organised?

The Neal Cassady Birthday Bash has more music each year. It's ranged from singer-songwriter Chris Carrington, singing his original Neal specific material, to David Amram jamming with renowned trumpeter Hugh Raglin. At the upcoming 2012 Birthday Bash, in February, we'll feature noted experimental guitarist Janet Feder and Jonny Five from platinum-selling, socially conscious hip hop band, the Flobots. Plus, David Amram will perform the music from the movie *Pull My Daisy*. As the event expands over the next few years to encompass a full weekend of activities, I'd like to feature artists like Patti Smith and Tom Waits. They'd both like to play the Denver Bash, they just don't know it yet...

His surviving family have certain musical tendencies. Can you say something about those interests? Have they played at the Neal Cassady birthday event?

Son John has played guitar since his teens. He's been in bands and still plays and writes. In 2010, he jammed on stage with some friends following the Bash in Denver.

What might Carolyn Cassady make of rock culture – does she have sympathies with it or does she link its rise in some way to the early demise of Neal?

I would never attempt speak for Carolyn, but doubt her estimation would be very high for most of what was to become known as rock. She is truly a genteel, almost plantation-reared Southern lady who's in possession of a rapier-like wit and self-assured knowledge.

Have you encountered musicians you've worked with or managed who have an affection for the Beats or see them as an inspiration?

Yes. And I think the Beats will continue to be a strong lyrical and lifestyle influence on a direct and subliminal level. Their impact is just beginning to reach a new, hungry post-rock 'n' roll generation via hip hop, rap, electronica and beyond. The great continuum of American music – now truly a world music – rolls on! And Neal's still in the driver's seat.

5 THE BRITISH BEAT: ROCK, LITERATURE AND THE UK COUNTERCULTURE IN THE 1960s

The mark that the Beat Generation writers left on the US at the end of the 1950s is hard to dispute. From the best-sellers lists, which saw Jack Kerouac's *On the Road* included for some weeks after the book's American publication in 1957, to the ructions that surrounded the obscenity claims against Allen Ginsberg's 'Howl' and the subsequent trial in the same year which would catapult an until then little-known poet into the national headlines, the Beats left their thumb-print on the consciousness of their homeland. They were hardly greeted with open arms by the mainstream, probably despised by much of the cultural establishment, but they were present on the radar: on TV chat shows, like that fronted by host and jazz pianist Steve Allen, where Kerouac would read,[1] or on middle-of-the-road, TV situation comedies which might feature a Beat character,[2] a butt of jokes, yes, but a recognised archetype in US homes as one decade moved towards the next.

Add to that, the vicarious interest of the weekly news photo magazines like *Life*[3] in the scenes surrounding those who followed in the wake of these writers – in Greenwich Village and North Beach, San Francisco – and the shorthand coined by Herb Caen – 'beatnik' – in a 1958 newspaper article for the *San Francisco Chronicle*[4]

---

[1] Kerouac appeared on the television show *Steve Allen* on 16 November 1959. See Miles, 1998, p. 263.
[2] Maynard G. Krebs was the resident beatnik on the 1959 TV sitcom *The Many Loves of Dobie Gillis*. See Henry Cabot Beck, 'From Beat to beatnik', *The Rolling Stone Book of the Beats: The Beat Generation and the Counterculture*, edited by Holly George-Warren (London: Bloomsbury, 1999), p. 95.
[3] For example, 'Kansas squares (Hutchinson, Kansas) vs. Coast beatniks (Venice, California)', *Life*, 21 September 1959.
[4] Caen claimed he didn't mean the word 'beatnik' in the pejorative sense and attempted to defend it to Kerouac himself. See Ann Charters, *Kerouac* (London: André Deutsch, 1974), p. 268.

that managed to elide both Beat and Sputnik – a recent arrival in the skies above Earth – and appeared to suggest that this subcultural crew were a terrestrial threat to American values just as the Soviets' orbiting satellite was an extra-terrestrial one, and we can see that the Beat Generation, while suspected and denigrated by core society, had made an impression.

Perhaps then it was little wonder that a rising crowd of young writers and musicians should feel some attachment to this rebel breed and its provocative ideas, this gathering of individuals who challenged the certainties of everyday politics and morality. Thus Ken Kesey and Richard Fariña, among the novelists, and Bob Dylan, Jerry Garcia and Roger McGuinn, among the singers and group members, to name just a small number of examples, would, by the early 1960s, be referencing their affection for the Beat axis and working through how they could incorporate some its style, some of its messages, into the prose they were writing, the songs they were penning.

But how did these issues, these cultural forces, characterise their presence in the UK? In this chapter I want to consider the ways in which British writing made strides in the 1950s, particularly with the rise of that body of fiction associated with the Angry Young Men, a movement that even attracted comparisons, if superficial ones only, with the Beat upsurge. Primarily though, I want to examine the quite different trajectory of popular music, an area of activity that saw the UK cower in the shadow of American domination during that decade, only to break out of this cultural stranglehold in dramatic fashion during the early years of the 1960s. As an extraordinary, and quite unpredicted, shift occurred, one that would see British songs and sounds actually challenge the previous omnipotence of US musical stars and their output, UK poets would be also able to carve out a new space that built on the successes of those home-based groups and singers. These innovative wordsmiths were provided with an opportunity to concoct a body of literature that bore closer resemblance to the products of the Beat eruption than the more conventional and restrained responses of the Angry Young Men.

Furthermore, the forging of an informal, social alliance between a rampant British musical scene from around 1964 and the practices of other creative and ground-breaking artists – painters, photographers, film-makers, playwrights and more – would lead to the emergence of a discernible and eclectic underground, one that would increasingly raise its head above the parapets during the remainder of the decade. In a time of economic prosperity, the liberalised and progressive tone of the period, often dubbed the Swinging Sixties, would encourage creative experiment and generate new opportunities to make connections with the fashionable mainstream. This UK phenomenon would bear comparison with the simultaneous surge of American energy that became known as the counterculture, that gathering of alternative renegades whose libertarian ideas would gain momentum from the mid-1950s onwards, first under a Beat banner and later as part of the hippy cavalcade.

In Britain, however, the conditions were quite different from those in the US and in crucial ways. While in America, the campaign for Civil Rights would give a focus and impetus to political radicalism during the first half of the decade and the demonstrations against the Vietnam War would inherit much of that earlier energy in the second half of a dynamic period, the UK was arguably more concerned with the exciting possibilities that full employment and consumer spending power might generate. Nonetheless, with a Labour government elected in 1964, this atmosphere of optimism re-kindled long-running debates about class and classlessness in a modern Britain. The startling rise of popular musicians, many of whom were drawn from the lower echelons of society, gave these questions fresh pertinence. Adding to this ferment of social fluidity were those engaged in the subterranean activities of the avant garde scene. Many such creatives would successfully cling to the coat-tails of the new, sophisticated rock music – hugely popular, mass consumed and increasingly politically engaged itself from the mid-1960s – to also make their presence felt on a number of the main stages of British life. As part of this survey, too, I want to assess to what extent there was actual evidence of the Beat spirit among the musicians who led this 1960s charge.

But, to backtrack a little, how were the areas of British fiction and poetry affected by the developments in New York and on the West Coast in the 1950s? Britain was most certainly a nation of literature for sure, even if those literary forms remained of a rather staid and conventional variety as the Second World War concluded. The written word was caught in the tides of an imposing history – from Shakespeare to Donne, Keats to Wilde, Wells to Waugh – challenged to some degree by the modernist scribes of the 1920s – James Joyce, Virginia Woolf and American émigré T. S. Eliot – then the new Socialist voices of the 1930s and their prime heir, George Orwell, from the 1940s. But the beating heart of conservatism, in both prose and verse, remained largely at the helm. However, from the middle of the 1950s, a wave of younger voices would challenge establishment notions of literary value. The Angry Young Men would produce new plays and novels that had something of the restless, resisting spirit of their Beat counterparts – challenging to accepted models of society, testing the seams of the social fabric – though the subjects they addressed and the ways they addressed them were somewhat different, as we shall see. It was also rather in their content than their form that they would take on long-standing bastions; the experimental tendencies of many Beats were rather less evident in the British canon of the AYM.

As for popular music, Britain, in the later 1940s and on into the 1950s, lived in the shadow of American domination, a product, we might argue, of a three-pronged assault. Firstly, Broadway, and its leading role in a young dramatic form known as musical theatre, had become pre-eminent since the 1920s, as both a setting for songwriters and composers and a source of material for singers and performers on New York City's Great White Way and beyond. Secondly,

Hollywood had become the means to transport that music and those songs across the US and around the world via its big screen romantic set-pieces and their accompanying soundtracks, still a relative novelty mid-century, as sound itself had only come to the big screen in 1927. Thirdly, we might cite a significant factor that had grown not out of industrial intent or strategic planning but rather out of global catastrophe: the presence of the US in Europe. Once President Franklin D. Roosevelt's troops had joined the war effort against Germany, here was a further means by which American popular culture, and its music specifically, could be effectively exported eastwards.

The fact that US soldiers would remain in Britain and on the Western continent for decades after the cessation of that landmark conflict added to this pervasive effect. For the British people, living with the very real possibility that the war might be lost, the American military assumed the role of would-be liberators on several levels, literally and symbolically. These transatlantic allies offered the genuine chance of victory in battle but also represented more besides. The stationing of the American troops generated a high level of local excitement but also offered the appealing spectre of cultural freedom. This combination proved a compelling attraction to those millions raised on the grey rations of a largely black and white island, during the dark days of the Blitz and then on into the austere early years of the next decade as post-war rationing persisted. The songs, the musicians and the dances, linked to the homeland of these military visitors, became more than just means of passing the time in a period of uncertainty and paucity; they emerged also as an emblem of liberty and escape, a metaphor of hope and a carrier of more glamorous possibilities. The lyrics, the melodies and the rhythms promised the tantalising prospect of more exhilarating experiences once Germany and her allies had been defeated and, in the 1950s, that war-time surge, that after-war promise, had hardly stalled.

In fact, by the end of the 1950s, the US's input, as exporter of popular cultural forms with a high quotient of glamour, was virtually undiminished, perhaps even magnified. American rock 'n' roll, emerging in full flood from the mid-decade in the shape of singers such as Elvis Presley, Bill Haley, Chuck Berry, Little Richard, Buddy Holly and Jerry Lee Lewis, thrilled a new generation of young Britons. Furthermore, there were few home-grown figures to challenge the appeal and the authority of that great wave of US talent. So how did pop music,[5] a term itself only coined around the middle of the century, stand within the British landscape at this time? In the UK, indigenously produced pop had little more than parochial impact. There *was* a British popular music, of course, one that could be charac-

---

[5] The shortening of the term popular 'gave the word a lively informality but opened it, more easily, to a sense of the trivial'. See Raymond Williams, *Keywords: A Vocabulary of Culture and Society* (London: HarperCollins, 1988), p. 238.

terised in three principal ways: light orchestral music, romantic ballads and the novelty songs attached to a music hall tradition. Light music would be heard on the BBC's Light Programme,[6] a middle of the road music-based service, inter-mingled with vocal or swing versions of American romantic songs that owed their debt to the prolific US assembly lines of theatre and film. Music hall material, more comedic and often risqué, was more likely to be heard live in theatres or communally sung around a pub piano. But all of these styles looked backwards – sentimental, nostalgic or simply outdated, they touched older, adult listeners, still idealising a pre-war idea of courtship and domestic normality. Yet, just as the US was beginning to experience various cultural shifts in the midst of its own consumer boom, a more repressed and straitened Britain was also registering readings on the Geiger counter of social change.

More subtle than the American model perhaps, this evolution could nevertheless not be ignored. If the rise of the teenager, with its attendant connection to fashion and location – sartorial looks, style choices and identifiable gathering places – occurred more slowly, if there was less spending power for British adolescents than their US counterparts, there was still a recognisable surfacing of that phenomenon known as teenage. This previously un-named stage – post-childhood but pre-adulthood – was by now being identified and discussed by commentators, from sociologists to newspaper columnists. Coffee bars became haunts of those not old enough to leave home and too young to visit public houses,[7] and those cafés also provided opportunities for a new generation of young artists to play live.[8] The new 45rpm, vinyl single – two-sided, plastic, 7″ discs, invented in the US at the end of the 1940s, which teens could afford to buy or certainly play on jukeboxes – contributed to this change, too. In addition, American movies cultivating images of adolescent life – from *Rebel Without a Cause* (1955) to *Rock Around the Clock* (1956) – crossed the ocean to London and Birmingham, Manchester and Glasgow. In the midst of these developments, localised subcultural strains began to take root, seeded, in some cases, by US style and attitude but, in other instances, distinctly British in mode. If the bikers, the ton-up boys of the late 1950s, were motorcyclists aware of movies like *The Wild One*, at least by reputation,[9] and loved

---

[6] Note that in 1967, in a major BBC shake-up, the Light Programme would become Radio 2 and the new Radio 1, a response to the rise of pirate broadcasting in the offshore waters of Britain, would become the UK's Top 40 station.

[7] Public houses, more colloquially 'pubs', are licensed to serve alcoholic drinks only those over the age of 18.

[8] In Soho, London, the 2i's Coffee Bar played host to artists like Tommy Steele and Cliff Richard at the end of the 1950s.

[9] *The Wild One* was released in the US in 1953 but was banned in the UK by the British Board of Film Certification until 1968.

American rock music, the Teddy Boys, who pre-dated them, were much closer to a home-grown tribe.

The Teddy Boys, or Teds,[10] affected an almost caricatured appearance based on upper middle-class Edwardian gentlemen of the 1910s, a working class bid to resurrect the days of Empire, though hardly articulated as a clear, quasi-political manifesto. The imperial golden age, which had stretched from sixteenth century Tudor times to the end of Victoriana and the first decade of the twentieth century, had seen England become a dominating force globally, militarily and economically, with the Union Jack planted, often aggressively, on every continent. Yet, the onset of the First World War in 1914 would set in train a remarkably speedy decline over mere decades. As Britain joined France, Germany and Russia in a brutal episode of apparent self-flagellation, those traditional European powers, most with extended track records as empire builders, engaged in four years of damaging conflict, as they strove to defend and retain their power-bases, continentally and further afield. The results were cataclysmic for most: Germany crushed and humiliated, Russia sent hurtling into a vortex of revolution and bloody civil war, and France and Britain traumatised by the horrors of human loss and the shattering financial blows inflicted by that near-Pyrrhic victory, hauled from the jaws of the savage trenches.

For England and Empire, the 25 years that followed the expensive triumph of the Great War would see the nation's prestige further undermined and, before the Second World War concluded in 1945, the long days of pre-eminence premised on a worldwide network of colonies – both rich in raw materials and also providers of markets for the abundant products of the industrial motherland – were nearing a close. The Teds, who had made appearances on British city streets by the turn of the 1950s, were, it seemed, dissenting voices against this decline: street level conservatives who railed, even if it was without any genuine coherence, against Britain's fading status. They regarded the street corner, the pub and the club as the battleground for their violent scuffles and drunken unruliness, but rock 'n' roll, when it arrived only a few years later, became their rallying call and their passion, too.

George Melly considers this sleight of hand that placed the fashion symbols of a more elevated class on the backs of these raucous rebels in this way: 'Immediately after the war, suspecting that upper-class young men-about-town might feel the need to express sartorially their dislike of the austerity-minded Socialist government, the smart tailors proposed a style based on the period of their grandfathers: the last golden moment for the British upper classes, the long

---

[10] The term 'Teddy' was drawn from Edward, King Edward VII, who would succeed his mother Queen Victoria in 1902 and sit on the throne until his own death in 1910.

Edwardian summer. There was certain amount of publicity around this style in the popular press, but the exact moment it was taken up by working class rebels (and of course immediately dropped by upper-class exquisites) is impossible to track down.' Yet, Melly adds, if this clothing 'bore no relation to past of *these* young men […] the whole thing jelled to look undeniably right. The arrival of rock 'n' roll was all that was needed. The first real pop movement was ready to explode.'[11]

But, if Britain felt like something of a popular cultural backwater during this decade, there would be, nonetheless, one intriguing musical upsurge, not, in essence, an original one but a surprising one, in which imitation could be legitimately regarded as a form of flattery. When skiffle, a near-obsolete off-shoot of pre-war New Orleans jazz, reared its head on the UK side of the Atlantic, briefly but unquestionably brightly, it gave a small community of British musicians the chance to take a national and international stage. Skiffle, historically, had been an informal, rough-and-ready interval music of some decades before, bridging the gap when the jazz trumpeters, pianists and percussionists took their break. In the UK, trad jazz, or traditional jazz to give it its more formal style, was the way the post-war British revivalists referred to their regenerated form of that older tailgate brand, born of the Delta and dating from the First World War and just after.

Trad jazz, which enjoyed a widening popularity in Britain in the decade and a half after 1945, was encoded with suggestions of black identity and creative authenticity, even if it was usually played by white, often middle-class and well-educated, players. It became a soundtrack to liberal student politics, too, in the final years of the 1950s and the start of the 1960s. Further, it helped to expose skiffle to audiences as a side-show to the main sets of established groups led by Ken Colyer and Chris Barber. Lonnie Donegan, who played banjo in major bands performing trad jazz, would re-introduce the skiffle element to those groups and, during this period, both skiffle and trad jazz would transcend the field of a mere esoteric appeal and achieve chart placings as well.

In fact, so appealing did skiffle become – guitars and banjos, improvised tea-chest basses, snare drums and kazoos replacing the brass and woodwind leads of the trad jazz circuit itself – that Donegan was able to branch out as a soloist in 1954. Taking tunes that formed part of the folk and blues world in the US – songs by Huddie Ledbetter, better known as Lead Belly, for example – this breezy singer-performer reincarnated them as Top 40 hits, mainly in the UK but also in the US. His 'Rock Island Line' was a chart-entry on both sides of the Atlantic.[12] Along the way, the skiffle boom inspired hundreds of young musicians to take up

---

[11] Melly, 1989, pp. 33–4.

[12] Lonnie Donegan's 'Rock Island Line' entered the UK charts on 6 January 1956 and reached No. 8. It achieved the same heights in the US charts, entering on 31 March just weeks later.

this do-it-yourself format and create groups of their own, the acts who, in many cases, would help produce Britain's verdant rock boom a handful of years later.

We might also usefully mention the contemporaneous folk revival, sometimes described as the second such renaissance as an earlier one had enjoyed currency in the closing years of the nineteenth century and at the beginning of the twentieth. The impartial historian or musicologist may have identified these 1950s musical trends, in some senses, as almost akin to parallel movements – folk and skiffle were both styles that tapped into older, historical, influences even if they had been drawn from opposing sides of the Atlantic. However, British folk music possessed a pedigree traceable for centuries, but one that had come under threat once the rural traditions of medieval England, Scotland, Ireland and Wales had been usurped by the Industrial Revolution during the long Victorian century. In that sense, it had a different, and much longer, past to the musics considered rustic folk by the Americans – such forms as blues and country or hillbilly. In short, the historical, ideological and political baggage attached to the post-Second World War folk boom in Britain was weighty: the new wave of folk singers was often connected to leftist political ideas. They regarded commercially-inclined pop music – and skiffle would be certainly bracketed under that heading once Donegan had adapted long-standing, US roots songs and taken them into the charts[13] – with large suspicion.

Pop, in the eyes of the committed folk core, best represented by the likes of the active Communist and songwriter Ewan MacColl,[14] was a mass manufactured commodity duping ordinary listeners with its trite and simple tropes and hypnotic accessibility; folk was seen as a pure and true music of an older land, upholding, in many instances, pre-industrial values, which had preceded this present era of the city and the factory, one increasingly obsessed with mass consumption and built-in obsolescence. In addition, post-war political tensions had seen the successful, war-time alliance of the capitalist US and the Communist USSR speedily collapse once the battle had been won. The relationship would rapidly degenerate into diplomatic stand-off then bitter Cold War, increasing the prospect of global destruction as the two superpowers contemplated unleashing their nuclear arsenals against the other. These global stresses were echoed in the attitudes of many of those on the British folk scene, who looked to the Soviets as a model of utopian hope, an operating system that rejected the profit-obsessed credo on the other side of the Atlantic.

---

[13] The UK charts, as Donegan struck, were a relatively new innovation. The pop weekly *New Musical Express* had launched the first such listing, a Top 12 based on the best-selling singles of the week, as recently as 1952.

[14] MacColl said: 'Skiffle took over, and then the machine took over the skiffle movement, castrated it and robbed it of all its energy.' See Robin Denselow, 1989, pp. 17–18.

In short, Americanisation was regarded, in some quarters, as a cultural danger, a symbol of an ethos that prized the dollar over human or communal values. Nor were these fears the sole province of the folk militants; its British critics were stretched across the ideological spectrum. In the UK, says Dick Ellis, '[t]his anti-American attack was primarily launched from the left and right wings of political opinion, with the left depicting America as a capitalist menace, and the right arraigning its déclassé democratisation ...'[15] Certainly, the kind of action the US establishment was taking in the post-war decade against those with socialist or Communist, worker or unionist leanings, from the late 1940s to the mid-1950s, was regarded by those on the British left as an anathema and an outrage, as artists and actors, film directors and playwrights, not to mention folk musicians such as Pete Seeger,[16] faced the approbation and condemnation of the investigations pursued under the authority of the House Un-American Activities Committee.

As for the more militant of the UK folkies, even if backwoods American music like skiffle shared some of the pure strains, rural precedents and cultural autonomy of British folk, they still regarded the style as a product of a social and political world which venerated capital first and even took concerted action against the philosophies of ordinary workers and those organisations that sought to represent them. The story was further complicated by the fact that the second folk revival in Britain had links to the work of Alan Lomax,[17] an American who had been collecting song recordings in the fields and on the stoops of the agricultural US from the 1930s. Lomax was an inspiration for MacColl and his fellow travellers, but the American ethnomusicologist became the subject himself of FBI enquiries in the 1940s, when he was suspected of Communist sympathies. He would, as a consequence, re-locate to the UK where he would spend the 1950s.

Yet, in the UK of the mid-1950s, if trad jazz and folk had their place, and often agendas that went some way beyond mere music-making, the popular musical mainstream aimed at the increasingly important teenage markets, was centred less on ideas of authenticity or issues of political expression and much more on notions of leisure, pleasure and entertainment. In that respect, it was the raw thrill and insistent energy of the new US pop that engaged its listeners most: that potent blend of black and white styles, spawning novel genres such as rhythm and blues, rock 'n' roll, rockabilly, doo wop and more. Engrained,

---

[15] R.J. Ellis, 'From "The Beetles" to "The Beatles": The British/Beat 1955–1965', *Symbiosis*, 4.1, April 2000, pp. 67–98 (p. 76).

[16] Seeger had to fight the possibility of a 10-year jail term after the HUAC subpoenaed him in 1955. See Denselow, 1989, p. 15.

[17] Alan Lomax was the son of John A. Lomax who was also a significant folklorist.

if unofficial, segregation that had dominated society in America for so long – and certainly in the fields of entertainment and music, film and radio – was slowly beginning to crumble. Race was still a deeply contentious issue in the conservative US mainstream but in the dynamic realm of the American teen, the older, entrenched colour coding was losing its grip; rock 'n' roll, viewed by some as an obvious and dangerous emblem of racial mixing, was feared by much of the white establishment for this very reason. On the other side of the Atlantic, in a country only just welcoming its first significant waves of non-white immigrants at the end of the 1940s,[18] such racial tensions were barely recorded. For British teenagers, meanwhile, the endemic and institutionalised racism of many parts of the US was very far from their day-to-day radar;[19] they could only hear the frenetic power of this hybrid American sound and flocked to immerse themselves in it.

As for practical, home-grown approaches to recording and performance, the prime thrust of British pop or rock 'n' roll in the latter half of the 1950s – and Donegan's flame had pretty well dimmed as that decade ebbed – was to imitate the best of the US acts. Tommy Steele blended Cockney cockiness with a chirpy, upbeat act, Cliff Richard started as a British answer to Presley – his superb debut, 'Move It', in 1958 had the ring of a genuine classic – and the stable of artist manager Larry Parnes introduced another string of re-christened singers – Marty Wilde, Vince Eager, Billy Fury and Tommy Quickly among them – who largely delivered anodyne versions of the American repertoire.

As the 1960s dawned, in northern English cities such as Liverpool and Manchester, hundreds of bands played youth clubs, dance halls and church halls but were little more than covers acts, recreating hit American compositions for local audiences. Certainly young, ambitious groups like the Quarrymen, then the Silver Beetles, eventually the Beatles, were scarcely more than a skiffle group, then a conveyor belt rock 'n' roll act, whose ability to copy the American style won them home city gigs and then, eventually, residences in Hamburg. There the mercantile community of a rumbustious port, echoing the sparky vivacity of Merseyside itself, also hungered for a passing imitation of the US sound to while away their late nights and early mornings in the bars of the infamous red light strip on the Reeperbahn.

Thus, if live popular music had a place in the British psyche, it was principally by way of copycat performers. Sometimes, bona fide US artists would hit these

---

[18] The *Empire Windrush* was the vessel that brought the first influx of post-war Caribbean settlers to the UK in 1948. See Mike Phillips, '*Windrush* – the passengers', BBC History, 3 October 2011, http://www.bbc.co.uk/history/british/modern/windrush_01.shtml [accessed 19 February 2012].

[19] It is, nonetheless, worth noting that the matter of race was not entirely absent from the British scene during this era. In London, the Notting Hill Riots of 1958 saw Caribbean arrivals in clashes with British protestors who claimed to fear the economic impact of the new intake, but there appeared to be more primal anxieties stirred by the skin colour of their neighbours.

shores – Bill Haley caused mayhem when the kiss-curled singer and His Comets played UK dates in 1956 and Jerry Lee Lewis was winning British fans galore until, in 1958, his relationship with a 13-year-old cousin saw him expelled from Britain, starting a moral backlash against the new rock 'n' roll that would last for the next couple of years. Certainly, the furore over this music and its implied gospel of immorality saw the Cavern in Liverpool, a jazz club at the time, ban rock for some considerable time after these tawdry revelations were exposed in the tabloid press.

There was also an interesting divide in Britain at the turn of the new decade, with a style like rock 'n' roll – which had a gallery of white stars at its heart – locking horns with genres like blues, rhythm and blues and jazz, forms perceived as closer to the real black American experience. In London the veneration of black musicians such as Muddy Waters, Howlin' Wolf and John Lee Hooker was led by blues players and aficionados like Alexis Korner, John Mayall and Cyril Davies. Not only did those UK musicians perform, record and tour their versions of this American sound, they also encouraged black bluesmen to play live in Britain, helping to organise gigs and playing host. For black musicians, marginalised and ghetto-ised to a large degree in their homeland, the respectful, often delirious, welcomes, from principally white audiences, were both surprising and gratifying.

If the capital became a hotbed for this piece of cultural exchange, Manchester was one city which also welcomed these exotic visitors. Liverpool, a more independent conurbation perhaps that had a long history as a racial melting pot, had its own distinctive musical agenda, it seemed. If, in the early 1960s, Liverpool clung to the attractions of rock 'n' roll – there were said to be 300 active bands in the city[20] at the start of the decade – London's hip crowd gravitated towards those earlier, more gritty, black styles. The outcome was an emerging British blues boom as groups, led by the more mature Mayall and Korner particularly, became the seeding ground for a whole generation of young new interpreters of American R&B. Mick Jagger, Charlie Watts, Eric Clapton, Jack Bruce, Peter Green and Mick Fleetwood were just a tip of that iceberg. The bands these musical graduates would form included the Rolling Stones, the Yardbirds, Manfred Mann, Cream and Fleetwood Mac. When the Beatles arrived in London in 1963, their brand of popular music – perceived as rock with a diluted black sound, closer to the nascent brand of Motown soul in Detroit – was considered to be more commercially oriented and thus less credible by the capital hipsters.

It would be a while before the Beatles managed to cast off the deep and long shadow cast by high profile US music-makers, white or black, abandon their core

---

[20] Bob Wooler, DJ at the club the Cavern, proposed this, c. 1961, in the pages of the local popular music newspaper *Mersey Beat*, though Mike Brocken, Liverpool-based historian and university lecturer, commented in an email to the author 27 December 2010: 'From my research the number is nowhere near that figure – lots of Battles of the Bands nights with groups adopting different names might have contributed to yet another Mersey urban myth!'

American rock repertoire, and find their own feet as national and international stars, though the traces would remain even then. Tunes like 'Twist and Shout',[21] an early Isley Brothers hit, 'Money (That's What I Want)',[22] co-penned by Motown founder Berry Gordy, Smokey Robinson's 'You Really Got a Hold on Me',[23] and Chuck Berry's 'Rock and Roll Music'[24] would all still feature on the group's early LPs. It is true to say also that, after this, the three composing members of the group, John Lennon, Paul McCartney and George Harrison, would quickly embrace the new cultural forces – in fashion and art, in film, technology and religion – that would proliferate from the mid-1960s. They would draw promiscuously on these energies to shape their own artistic identity. As the US, and audiences internationally, took the group to their hearts, their song-writing would gain in confidence and their studio work would take on an increasingly mature and inventive veneer, as poetry, the political and the rising drug culture impinged on their prolific creative instincts.

Underpinning the changing and expanding musical landscape of the UK was a powerful throb of evolving subcultural life. If university and art college students tended towards the cerebral styles of sophisticated modern jazz or the more dance-oriented tempos of trad, and the Teds and the rockers stuck rigidly to the sounds of rock 'n' roll, a new breed, the mods, provided an influx of fresh energy to the scene in the early 1960s. Jonathon Green comments: 'Like Teds, the mods emerged from the London outer suburbs [...] but unlike [...] the Teds they were more middle-class, often Jewish, the sons of middle-management, small businessmen or some equivalent [...] they began life as philosophers as well as dandies.'[25] Originally dubbed modernists – a result of their favouring innovative jazz giants like Miles Davis and John Coltrane – by the start of the new decade, this grouping had moved in favour of the rampant soul styles, the rootsy Stax label generally favoured over the hit factory of Motown, but they also found, amid the blossoming blues boom, a string of British groups to admire. The Who, the Kinks and the Small Faces became their UK idols. The mods adopted Italian fashions – jackets, suits ties – and the US army overcoat – the parka. Initially, they affected a liking for continental philosophy, European cinema and Beat writing, too. Green quotes mod Steve Sparks: 'Mod before it was commercialised was essentially an extension of the beatniks [...] it was to do with modern jazz and to do with [...] [a]mphetamine, Jean-Paul Sartre and John Lee Hooker.'[26] This

---

[21] The track was on the Beatles' LP debut, *Please Please Me* (1963).
[22] A song on *With the Beatles* (1963).
[23] *Ibid.*
[24] A cover version appears on *Beatles for Sale* (1964).
[25] Jonathon Green, *All Dressed Up: The Sixties and the Counterculture* (London: Pimlico, 1999), p. 41.
[26] *Ibid.*

subcultural community venerated black authenticity and danced at all-night but unlicensed clubs, replacing alcohol with speed. The mods rejected the grit and grime of the rocker and his motorbike, adopting clean-lined Italian scooters, Vespas and Lambrettas, as their mode of transport. By 1964 and into 1965 this diverging tribalism saw outbreaks of violence in South East English coastal resorts – Clacton, Brighton and elsewhere – as the mods and the rockers fought pitched Bank Holiday battles on seaside beaches. The ideological differences were based on appearance, class and musical choice, but the motivations for conflict were largely fuelled by adolescent testosterone at a time when the manacles of a disciplinarian society were loosening.

But, to what degree did the literary wave that had shaken up New York and San Francisco, and nascent bohemian cliques at many points in-between, have an effect on those in the UK? One thing we must say is that the mid-1950s did see some novelists and poets gradual move away from fawning deference to the past traditions of the English literary canon. At the onset of the 1950s, UK poetry and fiction remained very much in the hands of a conservative young breed who seemed to look backwards, a position typified by the Movement, formalists who wanted to clawback history rather than radically alter the future.[27] Yet there were some signs of a shifting mood, too. Voices outside the traditional stream or even the modernist and more radical caucus were making themselves felt. As we have hinted, Orwell's Socialist visions and his extraordinary satire on totalitarianism – *Nineteen Eighty-Four*, which emerged in 1949 – were setting a new tone and a fresh mood. By the mid-1950s, a pioneering wave of young writers was penning novels and plays about a post-war world in which nostalgic certainties had evaporated. To reiterate, Britain's imperial power and commercial domination of world trade had each taken serious setbacks in the critically damaging years of the Second World War and a small but bold group of rising writers would hold up a mirror to this denuded setting, this much altered state. But let us briefly step back another ten years.

The so-called Khaki Election of 1945 had marked a sea-change in British political life. Returning soldiers, in particular, had surprisingly rejected the war-winning hero, premier Winston Churchill and his upper-class, paternal and patrician Toryism. The electorate had plumped instead, in a remarkable landslide, for Labour under Clement Atlee, the first time this party, only founded at the start of the century, had ever held a clear Parliamentary advantage and the Socialist arrivistes would use this mandate with vigour. The radical innovations passed by

---

[27] Writers such as John Wain and Kingsley Amis and poet Donald Davie were among the Movement's order. American literary critic Leslie Fielder talked of the young British writer of this kind as 'able to define himself against the class he replaces: against a blend of homosexual sensibility, upper-class aloofness, liberal politics, and avant-garde literary devices'. See Alan Sinfield, *Literature, Politics and Culture in Postwar Britain* (London: Athlone, 1997), p. 80.

Prime Minister Atlee's regime – the formation of a welfare state coupled to the nationalisation of many of the nation's command industries, from coal to iron, shipbuilding and the railways – indicated that the older model of aristocratic government had passed its sell-by date. A democratised and more egalitarian Britain was promised and, if this manifesto pledge was hardly delivered in any wholesale sense, the effects of the wide-ranging moves Labour had initiated were too deep-seated and profound to be easily reversed. Thus when Churchill returned as PM in 1952, he could not roll back Atlee's tide of radical change in any meaningful way.

Such changes in atmosphere, with key legislation such as the reforming Education Act of 1944, a product of a war-time coalition administration, created an environment in which ordinary people – working class and lower middle-class young men, primarily – could at least consider, maybe even seize, opportunities for advancement. By the middle of the 1950s, if university entry remained very much a dream of the privileged sectors in society, there were glimmers of possibility and a number of young writers, several of whom had grabbed these chances and certainly witnessed some of these social changes at close hand, suggested through their novels and plays that transformation, of a deep and substantial kind, was underway. Dubbed the Angry Young Men – though few accepted the soubriquet with any enthusiasm – they told stories of a post-imperial Britain in which a new wave of ambitious working class and lower middle-class protagonists were making their way in a state forever changed by the scars of war and the political machinations of a visionary Labour administration.

Further, there was a fresh academic approach to culture and society in its broadest sense, as a group of bright young men who had faced the trauma of the war returned, hoping that the end of that global conflict would signal a new dawn: chances for ordinary people to prosper in a Britain that had felt the crude jolt of battle, at home and abroad, but was now awakening from that nightmare of despair – its lost sons, its battered cities – and dreaming of a brighter, better future, one in which professional and social mobility were not regarded as mere pie in the sky, the stuff only of fantastic utopias. Such individuals as Richard Hoggart and Raymond Williams who had faced the battlefront, returned and become involved with progressive adult education projects at English universities. As the 1950s neared their end, both had written and published books which preached a novel approach to understanding society, one that challenged the frozen stratification of class, aristocracy and elitism and, instead, discussed the everyday realities of the masses – their lives, their interests, their passions, their culture. Hoggart's *Uses of Literacy* (1957) proposed that working class culture had values that been too long under-valued and ignored, but also expressed reservations about mass culture swamping older cultural traditions. Williams suggested in *Culture and Society, 1780–1950* (1958) that the quotidian practices of the vast majority had been considered far too little in connection with the sphere of literary study. A little later, E. P. Thompson's *The Making of the English Working Class* (1963) related a history of Britain that was not based on kings, generals and bishops but on workers and their families, while Stuart Hall and Paddy Whannel's *The Popular Arts* (1964) broke new ground in seeing potential relationships between an increasingly high-profile range of popular cultural activities – in the visual arts, cinema and music – and the school curriculum.

Out of these seeds would grow an impressive philosophical moment, one that would lead, quite speedily, to the serious, scholarly study of everyday practices – culture as a way of life rather than a set of hierarchical behaviours pursued only by the high and mighty – and, in 1964, to the formation of the Centre for Contemporary Cultural Studies at the University of Birmingham, UK.[28] The centre would not only found a new field of intellectual engagement, eventually termed British Cultural Studies – a multi-disciplinary construct centred on the analysis of the world through the prism of power relations linked to class, race and gender – but also the recognition that the examination of mass and popular cultural forms – from music and television to the tabloid press and playground games – could also find a place within the hallowed portals of the academy. These breakthroughs nurtured the strong sense that popular culture could not be ignored, indeed should not be ignored. Such intellectual developments would cultivate a climate in which artistic practices outside the elite circuit – whether popular music or performance poetry, graphic art or agitprop theatre – could earn appropriate attention from the critics and, in time, the academy. Barriers of class and cash, which had been largely impenetrable before this cerebral revolution, would be cracked, dented and finally breached over the next decade, encouraging alliances to emerge between rock stars and Beat poets, bands and Pop artists, political novelists and radical film-makers, art photographers and avant garde choreographers, experimental playwrights and unconventional stages. This quite radical intellectual shift, the seeds of which would be sown slowly but deeply, would eventually bear rich fruit, a quiet accompaniment to the psychedelic trumpets blaring from TV and movie screens, theatre venues and music clubs.

The British *Zeitgeist* of the later 1950s hinted at this atmosphere of potential transformation and, alongside those fresh and far-sighted voices in the scholarly field, would rise a wave of almost contemporaneous new fiction and drama, produced by writers whom the press would characterise as the Angry Young Men. This loosely gathered literary force would critique the world of privilege and speak up for the common man, the new tier grammar schoolboys – principally boys – and challenge the pre-war certainties of empire and public school,

---

[28] Richard Hoggart, a key witness at the *Lady Chatterley's Lover* obscenity trial of 1960 as he defended the literary value of the book, became the first director of CCCS. The innovative institution would continue its work until its closure in 2002.

inherited fortunes and titles and power handed down. In the terrain of the novel and the stage, the new broom was wielded by writers and dramatists such as John Osborne and John Braine, Alan Sillitoe, Colin Wilson, Stan Barstow and Arnold Wesker and even, in time, women – a gender isolated, much as Beat women had been marginalised – like Shelagh Delaney and Lynne Reid Banks, who penned novels and stage plays which painted new images of the nation.

Some, like Osborne's 1956 play *Look Back in Anger*, railed against the dying imperial flame, the faded grandeur of a Britain that had collapsed under the ravages of war. Its presentation on the newly founded commercial television station[29] – another innovation that would test the BBC's monopoly and have a major effect on audience choice – offered a platform no play had ever enjoyed to that date. Braine published *Room at the Top* (1957), a tale of northern mill towns and striving lower-middle-class aspirants; Sillitoe issued *Saturday Night, Sunday Morning* (1958), an account of a working class factory operative whose drunken and adulterous behaviour was both shocking but also a sign that older moralities – the lynchpin of the faded, jaded and repressive system – could no longer be easily sustained; and *A Kind of Loving* (1960), Barstow's story of pregnancy outside wedlock, touched upon the fraying of long-standing codes, too. Shelagh Delaney from Salford, joined Braine from Leeds, Sillitoe from Nottingham and Barstow from Wakefield as part of a rising tide of regional talent from the north of England. Delaney's play *A Taste of Honey* (1958), which considered the social taboos and emotional traumas triggered by an inter-racial relationship, was part of a trend that saw working class literary talent not only aired, but new writers with non-metropolitan backgrounds challenging the received wisdom that London was the natural epicentre of the written word. The capital did, nonetheless, join this vogue for contemporary and unconventional narratives by younger voices. Lynne Reid Banks' *The L-Shaped Room* (1960) was another tale of unmarried pregnancy in a London setting, while Arnold Wesker brought the Jewish East End of the city ·to life in plays like *Chicken Soup with Barley* (1956).

Colin Wilson's *The Outsider* (1956) was also influential: a reflection on the existential possibilities of life, shaped by the French Left Bank thinkers of the 1940s, like Sartre and Camus and de Beauvoir, but also an echo of the kind of ideas of psychological liberation that the Beats were sharing in the US at a similar moment. There was even the first real novel of the new British youth subcultures, Colin MacInnes' *Absolute Beginners* (1959), which portrayed a vibrant, stylish and

---

[29] Granada Television in Manchester would transmit a live TV version of Osborne's play in 1956. In doing so, the elite confines of the theatre's proscenium arch, the province of the well-to-do, were dismantled. Such mass experience of a dramatic work would lay the ground for small-screen, kitchen sink productions like the soap opera *Coronation Street*, launched in 1960 and still running over 50 years on.

youthful London obsessed with American sounds, modes of dress that rejected the conservatism of suits and ties, and moral codes that reacted against long-standing notions of racial separation and class division.[30] Wilson and MacInnes aside, the Angry Young Men were not, however, by and large, proto-bohemians; they were upwardly aspirational even if the barriers to full and true social mobility remained persistently in place. They did not, as a whole, harbour a hunger for *nostalgie de la boue*; they were calling for ways in which the talented working and lower middle classes could take an up-escalator to status and influence and maybe reciprocal earnings and financial well-being.

MacInnes was a middle-class journalist and novelist who lived in – some may say slummed – in the rare English bohemia of Soho, the Italian-veined, inner London quarter, about which he often wrote. The young white people MacInnes described in his most celebrated books – *City of Spades* would pre-date *Absolute Beginners* by two years – were drawn to transatlantic style, particularly black Caribbean expressions, and might be usefully linked to that other subcultural strain that would come to prominence from the early 1960s, and one we have already touched upon – the mods.

Although few of this gathering of writers enthusiastically pinned their creative colours to any kind of unifying mast, the description of this diverse gang as Angry Young Men (the women came a little later, as we have said) by the mass media marked them as a group with a set of common intentions, even if this was just a helpful piece of shorthand. The fact that some feathers were ruffled by this over-arching denomination and that this distilled overview was incapable of describing the separations and differences – in class, politics and outlook of the members of this informal grouping – did not stop it being applied.

When Max Feldman and Gene Gartenberg co-edited a US collection called *Protest* and sub-titled *The Beat Generation and the Angry Young Men* in 1958, published in Britain the following year, the linking of these two transatlantic, and even more contrasting, communities was further sealed. Thus John Wain and Norman Mailer, Kingsley Amis and Kenneth Rexroth, found themselves gathered in a similar intellectual room and the collection – a diverse range of fiction and literary criticism, culture history and social commentary – proved to be a nourishing intellectual meal to readers in both the US and the UK. That said, once the elision of AYM and Beat was made, the coupling proved most difficult to un-link. Said the editors in their introduction to *Protest*:

In the United States of America, those 'new barbarians' who have chosen the present as the compass of their lives are the Beat Generation. In England,

---

[30] In 1986, MacInnes' novel would be brought to the big screen by director Julien Temple.

with certain differences, they are the Angry Young Men. Both the Beat Generation and the Angry Young Men are social phenomena which have found increasing literary expression, Because both represent a significant adaptation to life in mid-twentieth-century, the writings they have engendered possess an immediate value to us all. In the long run they may be the advance columns of a vast moral revolution, one which will transform man from a creature of history to a creature of experience ...[31]

Superficially there was a connection: here were writers of a similar age, largely in their mid-20s to 30s, trying to make sense of a post-war world but, of course, the national conditions were quite different. While the US cowered with fear at the possibility of nuclear annihilation, that same country enjoyed booming economic security; in the UK, the fiscal decline was immense, rationing remained in place – until 1954, in fact – and cities revealed the weals of destruction in weed-strewn bombsites, many left untouched and rotting for a decade and more after the German air-raids of the early 1940s. The introduction to *Protest* again:

> In England, World War II, which levelled tenement and manse in the common rubble of the night raid, produced the psychological levelling which made possible the victory of the Labour Party in their first peacetime election. Although the pressures of socialisation, higher income and inheritance taxes weakened the upper classes, the Socialists were generally blamed for the high cost of the war which, by necessity, had been borne into the years of reconstruction. Lacking the leadership possessing the boldness to overcome the disadvantage, the Labour Party was swept from office. In its place came the Tories, wearing the badges of accent, name and tie which have always symbolised rule to the English people. So there came into being – and remains today – the social anomaly of the Welfare State which must perpetuate itself on privilege.[32]

Feldman and Gartenberg maintain the theme, stating that it is against this background that the phenomenon of the Angry Young Men presents itself. They characterise the AYM as 'the sons of the lower middle and working classes who came of age with Socialism, had their bodies cared for by the government health programme and their minds nourished through government scholarships in red brick universities (though, now and then, Oxford). Prepared to seek their places in the new England that had been created by parliamentary revolution, they found

---

[31] Gene Feldman and Max Gartenberg (eds), 'Introduction', *Protest: The Beat Generation and the Angry Young Men* (London: Panther, 1960), pp. 9–17 (p. 10).
[32] *Ibid.*, p. 13.

they had nowhere to go.'[33] They did not, like the Beat Generation, seek to create their own subterranean world, but wanted entrance into the very real one on the surface where fortunes were made and power wielded.[34] In addition, the Angry Young Men 'had no common goal'[35] with John Osborne a old-fashioned, pre-war Socialist, Kingsley Amis, a lukewarm Labour backer, George Scott temporarily pinning his colours to a Tory mast and Colin Wilson formulating a religious existentialism.

But what actual impact did the news of stirrings Stateside have on the literary climate in Britain? How were the Beat signals translated? Hewison says that 'a romanticism of manner began to revive among the young as the austerities of the early 1950s eased: it was derived from images of Parisian Left-Bank bohemianism, Colin Wilson's Outsider, and increasingly from the style of the American Beats [...] although Wain, Amis, Wilson, Braine, Donleavy, Hinde, Scott and Osborne rather paled beside Kerouac and Carl Solomon, and especially Allen Ginsberg's poem "Howl". The Beat style fell in easily with jazz bands and CND;[36] the first British poet to pick up on the new manner was Christopher Logue, who experimented with poetry and jazz at the Royal Court...'[37] Logue would appear with several principal Beats at the International Poetry Incarnation at the Albert Hall in 1965. Ritchie also hints at the diluted character of British output when compared to the AYM as 'allied groups of anti-bourgeois rebels'.[38] He believes that only Colin MacInnes 'could stand comparison with the Beats' and comments that when Andrew Sinclair 'tried to use Beat attitudes and expressions' in his 1959 novel, *My Friend Judas*, 'the embarrassing result emphasised how alien the literature of Kerouac, Ginsberg, Burroughs and the rest really was'.[39]

Whatever intellectual commentators of the day or subsequent critics made of the AYM-Beat relationship, perceptions of what Beat might mean to a more mainstream audience were reflected in reports in Britain's sensationalist press. *The People*, a Sunday newspaper with a reputation for hard-hitting investigation, strove to expose the US Beat menace in a series of articles in summer 1960.[40] The

---

[33] *Ibid.*

[34] *Ibid.*

[35] *Ibid.*

[36] The Campaign for Nuclear Disarmament, a British organisation established in 1958, to lobby against nuclear weapons.

[37] Robert Hewison, *In Anger: Culture in the Cold War 1945–60* (London: Weidenfeld & Nicholson, 1981), p. 183.

[38] Harry Ritchie, *Success Stories: Literature and the Media in England, 1950–1959* (London: Faber, 1988), p. 51.

[39] Ritchie, 1986, p. 51.

[40] Peter Forbes, 'Blame these 4 men for the Beatnik horror', *The People*, 7 August 1960. See http://www.flickr.com/photos/29873672@N02/6897934379/sizes/o/in/photostream/ [accessed 22 February 2012].

pieces, read by several million readers, followed an outbreak of violence that had marred a jazz festival at the Beaulieu, stately home of Lord Montagu, the previous week. Blamed for this incident, though none was present at the musical event, were 'four strange men' who had been preaching 'a cult of despair'. The quartet in question were Kerouac, Burroughs, Ginsberg and Corso, 'beatnik "prophets" who do not themselves preach violence. But they do infect their followers with indifference or downright hostility to established codes of conduct'. The reporter Peter Forbes reveals that 'hobos' prophet' Kerouac is 'a talented writer' who has unfortunately 'devoted his great gifts to exalting the bums and jazz-maniacs of the New York jive cellars'; Burroughs, we learn, has 'freely admitted to being a drug addict for 15 years'; 'hate merchant' Ginsberg is 'a gifted poet' whose attitudes have 'infected some teenagers'; while Corso is dubbed 'the crank poet' who spreads his own messages of despair. In a feature peppered with stories of crime and violence, drugs and sex from the US Beat world, the writer concludes the report on a less threatening note. 'Fortunately', he comments, 'there is no encouragement of beatnik behaviour by ordinary people in Britain.'

Meanwhile, ordinary US citizens' concerns had been centred on reds-under-the-bed entryists who, it was feared, would hex the American dream forever. Not long before, Senator Joseph McCarthy's widely broadcast claims that the nation was being subverted by Soviet spies and infiltrators had brought into question the loyalty of government officials and prompted counter-claims of a witch-hunt. Britain's evolution and relationship to ideas of the left had been in some contrast. Socialism had left its lasting mark on the mixed economy and, rather than pursue the duck and cover, head-in-the-sand-ism of the American classroom, the British liberal lobby, supported by students in some numbers, backed the newly formed Campaign for Nuclear Disarmament (CND), an activist, pacifist movement that preached negotiated compromise – calls for discussion as opposed to bellicose threats – rather than the anti-Soviet, devils-in-our-midst paranoia of Washington.

In short, the literary responses of American Beats and British AYM were concocted and constructed in different places with different mind-sets, with contrasting economic backdrops and quite different class systems. So to lump them under one convenient book title of *Protest* was maybe a piece of over-simplified analysis too far. Ritchie is particularly critical of the cover of the 1960 paperback edition of the collection. He comments with a sardonic exasperation: 'Writing by the AYM now appeared under a cover depicting a group of tight-jeaned, crotch-thrusting drop-outs gathered in a back alley.'[41] This was hardly the

---

[41] Ritchie, 1986, p. 51.

métier of Osborne, Braine and all and he feels the combining of the two literary streams was 'ill-advised'.[42]

Yet, in the social realm, as we have hinted, those Beat influences – pro-peace, anti-war, refrains that permeated much of the US work – can hardly be separated from the emergence of CND, formed after a meeting at Oxford Town Hall in 1958 and led by a mixture of philosophers like Bertrand Russell, churchmen like Canon John Collins, progressive politicos such as Labour's Michael Foot, novelist J.B. Priestley and a rump of young enthusiasts – from universities and colleges, trade unions and the organised political parties – augmented by emerging musicians and artists, writers and poets. At the end of the decade and the start of the next, significant factions in the UK rallied to this cause. A march was staged to Aldermaston,[43] site of a nuclear weaponry facility 45 miles west of the capital, which cast a spotlight on the intense, and often secret, activity that was in progress to produce warheads to underpin the NATO strategy against the USSR and its satellite Warsaw Pact nations.

CND challenged the notion that the world's future should be allowed to totter on a knife edge, a belief that balanced nuclear war-chests, aimed menacingly at their ideological foes, would be the most likely way to maintain the peace. The campaign, aside from its gathering of largely middle-class radicals, also drew folk and trad jazz fans, and that smaller fringe of followers, now becoming aware of the Beats in the US, who adopted longer hair, grew beards and wore heavy duffel coats in the winter, open-toed sandals in the summer, and gravitated towards the newer forms of jazz like bebop. Ginsberg's barbed rhetoric in 'Howl' had already hinted at the American culture of paranoia, the undernote of social terror and the new environment of surveillance which appeared to echo the tensions of Cold War psychology. CND's ethos would then feed back into the Beat corpus with Corso's celebrated poem 'Bomb' – laid out on the page in the shape of a mushroom cloud – inspired, he said, by that very 'Ban the Bomb' movement CND had implemented and promoted. Not that alliances were simply sealed. When Ginsberg and Corso read in Oxford in Oxford in 1958, some local CND activists attacked 'Bomb''s frivolous character.[44]

Dick Ellis draws attention, too, to the differing situation in the UK and the delays in Beat messages reaching the UK. If *On the Road* had finally arrived in the UK in 1958, the year following its US debut, few in Britain were aware of the ongoing Beat developments over the water. He points out that the time-frames in Britain were quite different to those in New York and San Francisco:

---

[42] *Ibid.*

[43] Later marches travelled from Aldermaston itself to a massed Easter Monday rally in the heart of London – Trafalgar Square.

[44] Green, 1999, p. 36.

Interest [in the UK] before 1958 was limited primarily to word-of-mouth supporting [the] contention that the beginning of the British/Beat is linked to *On the Road*'s success in 1958/9 – even though 'Howl''s censorship troubles or sheer chance had led to some earlier 'pioneer' encounters [...] The late 1950s lift-off gives the British/Beat a different chronology to its American counterpart: the British/Beat had little contact with the first wave of Beat activity (roughly) 1945–1955.[45]

British individuals who would begin to absorb and share the American Beat impulse included the artist and jazz trumpeter Jeff Nuttall. Later a key contributor to the countercultural drama, he was author of the acclaimed text *Bomb Culture*, which would appear in 1968. The book would reflect both on the CND campaign and then on the subsequent rise of the UK underground, and gradually overground, frontline which would take the struggle forward on a variety of fronts – from anti-Vietnam demos to assaults on the drug laws. Another was poet Michael Horovitz, an Oxford graduate in English Literature of 1958, who initially pursued postgraduate study on his great hero William Blake then shifted to the then little-known Samuel Beckett – the reluctant Irish dramatist even wrote to him in a bid to dissuade him from undertaking such an academic enquiry – before abandoning those pursuits, too, in favour of ambitious, and realised, plans to create his own publication.

Horovitz's aim was to share both the new literary word – from Britain and the US and mainland Europe, too – but also, ultimately, forge fresh ways of marrying a literary, artistic and musical experience in a performance setting. At first he found his platform through the magazine he launched in 1959, *New Departures*. It was notable on several fronts, drawing attention to major avant garde figures from the UK and the continent who were still yet little known outside narrow educated and experimental circles. But, most pertinently here, it would also introduce various of the Beat writers to a British readership. Horovitz, who had made connections with Beat insiders as a result of Ginsberg and Corso's Oxford visit in 1958, was initially critical of the Beat writers but he would be won over to their cause quite quickly.[46] Through that Oxford visit and his spreading chain of contacts – Lawrence Ferlinghetti and William Burroughs, for example – he was able to generate a wide range of high grade work for his magazine, most of it subterranean and some way beyond the antennae of the transatlantic literary mainstream. The premiere issue would feature work by Kerouac and Burroughs, Beckett and musical avant gardist Cornelius Cardew.

---

[45] Ellis, 2000, pp. 70–1.
[46] Green, 1999, p. 37.

Horovitz was more than just publisher though; he had his own poetry ambitions, as well. When he met up with itinerant London poet Pete Brown at the Beaulieu Jazz Festival of 1960, they planned and realised a long poem inspired by their peripatetic lifestyles – hitching, readings, crashing on friendly floors. Entitled 'Blues for the Hitchhiking Dead', this was an exchange poem in which each writer devised calls and responses to the other, an echo of the friendly and competitive duels of lead jazz instrumentalists on, for example, Dexter Gordon and Wardell Gray's 1948 tune 'The Hunt', a work referred to by Kerouac in *On the Road*. This verse duetting emphasised both Horovitz and Brown's strong musical allegiance – to jazz and the blues – and their interest in poetry as a dynamic performing medium, rather than one frozen on the printed page. Says Brown: 'Mike and I were not instant friends, but from the beginning there was a creative chemistry between us that would last. We were in some way opposites – Mike had powerful academic credentials and I had none – but we both loved jazz, we were both Jewish and both had an ear for language and rhythm.'[47]

A further venture, reflecting these passions, would soon spring up alongside the ongoing magazine project. Live *New Departures*, which ran during the early years of the 1960s, became a platform for words, music, art and other performance styles. Within this creative framework, jazz poetry, with a distinctly British flavour, was a central ingredient. The live tours which saw Horovitz and Brown joined by poet Adrian Mitchell and a group of leading jazz musicians – pianist Stan Tracey, Bobby Wellins on sax, drummer Laurie Morgan, trumpeter Les Condon and bassist Jeff Clyne who formed the New Departures Quintet[48] – of the period were close in spirit and form to the kind of US experimentations that had occurred between Beat and Beat-linked poets and jazz players in the 1950s and even earlier. Kenneth Rexroth, Kenneth Patchen, ruth weiss, Lawrence Ferlinghetti, David Meltzer and Jack Kerouac had all presented performances where their written words were accompanied by jazz sounds on stage – and some had been committed to record, too. The New Departures Quintet backed Horovitz and Brown when 'Blues for the Hitchhiking Dead' was aired live for the first time. Horovitz also draws attention to 'the first large-scale informal poetry show in the North [of England]' when he and Brown and another poet Spike Hawkins performed at the Crane Theatre in Liverpool in 1960, accompanied by saxophonist Dick Heckstall-Smith and Art Reid's band.[49]

Live *New Departures*, based in London, travelled across England, to Wales and to Scotland – including the Edinburgh Fringe Festival where there were several

---

[47] Pete Brown, *White Rooms and Imaginary Westerns: On the Road with Ginsberg, Writing for Clapton and Cream – An Anarchic Odyssey* (London: JR Books, 2010), p. 43.
[48] 'A group of Britain's most adventurous modernists', said Michael Horovitz in his edited collection *Children of Albion: Poetry of the 'Underground' in Britain* (Harmondsworth: Penguin, 1970), p. 331.
[49] *Ibid.*, p. 328.

residencies – and established a reputation for lively innovation: an eclectic montage of art, politics and humour, experiment and avant garde activity. In Liverpool, where the beat music boom was gaining momentum, Horovitz and Brown would find a gaggle of kindred spirits. Liverpudlians Adrian Henri and Roger McGough and their younger friend Brian Patten were gaining a profile on the poetry café front, centred on a venue called Streate's. Henri, an artist and lecturer at Liverpool College of Art, had been among the first to bring the notion of 'the happening' to the UK and the city, inspired by the multi-media productions that Allan Kaprow had staged in the US at the end of the 1950s and early 1960s. McGough, an English Literature graduate of Hull University and teacher, was reading his own poetry. So was Patten, a 16-year-old trainee journalist on the local weekly newspaper the *Bootle Times*, who had already unveiled his own little poetry magazine called *Underdog* by 1963. Joining this key trio were other poets and writers like Spike Hawkins and Johnny Byrne. McGough describes the scene:

> Streate's Coffee Bar on Mount Pleasant, a candlelit, white-washed basement that wore a duffel coat and echoed to the sounds of modern jazz, was to poetry what the Cavern was to rock 'n' roll [...] Johnny Byrne, novelist and screenwriter, was then a mischievous young Dubliner with an encyclopedic knowledge of the American Beats who took up semi-residence there and began to organise regular poetry readings featuring Pete Brown and Spike Hawkins, a wild, charismatic southerner with an ambition to be an eccentric genius.[50]

The international ascendancy of the Beatles coupled to Ginsberg's 1965 visit to Liverpool would draw wider attention to this active grouping and see its national profile rise. The publication of *The Mersey Sound* in 1967 – a pocket volume in the Penguin Modern Poets series, showcasing Henri, McGough and Patten – would also be central in the spreading of this poetry gospel, while Edward Lucie-Smith's edited compendium of Mersey-based writing, *The Liverpool Scene*, from the same year, lent authority and identity to this new poetry world and also added to the sense of community and creative coherence in the city.

Alongside them, Horovitz and Brown, Mitchell, Hawkins and Byrne, Henri, McGough and Patten were others, like photographer John 'Hoppy' Hopkins and recent art school student Barry Miles, who would be further key catalysts in the unfolding of a British Beat version in the opening half of the 1960s. All were familiar with the American scene, and drew enthusiastically on it, but in the UK

---

[50] Roger McGough, *Said and Done: The Autobiography* (London: Arrow Books, 2006), p. 149.

there were different approaches and different outcomes, connected in part, we may argue, to the different time-frames unfolding on each side of the Atlantic but also to the contrasting social, political and cultural positions that separated the British and US experience in quite fundamental ways.

Meanwhile, at the start of the decade, the Beatles were striving to make a mark in the crowded room of their home city – so many acts were battling to be heard – and it would not be long before they took their expanding, American-heavy repertoire to the German port of Hamburg. Here, amid the sailors and prostitutes, drinkers and club-goers, the nocturnal roisterers of this lively waterfront scene, the group would hone their live performing skills and quickly become one of the hardest-working and most proficient acts in the city. By now, the group had, it appears, conceived their own tribute to the rising Beat tide, re-naming themselves in honour of this American literary uprising when, in 1960, the Liverpool-based Beat poet Royston Ellis proposed to John Lennon that a spelling change from Beetles to Beatles was in order and the alteration was agreed.[51] Lennon was aware of Ginsberg and 'Howl' at this point. His final schooldays, prior to entering Liverpool Art College in late 1957, had seen him produce a satirical, hand-drawn newspaper called *The Daily Howl*, which his headmaster had confiscated,[52] evidence enough, perhaps, that Beat inspiration had already struck him as a late teenage student and the name change for the Beatles seemed to further underline this interest. There was evidence, too, that the Beats had a presence in many college conversations between Lennon, the group's then bass player Stuart Sutcliffe and Bill Harry, a fellow student who would later found the magazine *Mersey Beat*. Frith and Horne report that they would sit for hours in a student pub 'discussing Henry Miller and Kerouac and the Beat poets, Corso and Ferlinghetti'.[53] Before long, Lennon would bring some of these influences to bear on his own art, his own writing, mainly through his music but also his lyrics and poetry. As the 1950s faded, the Beatles were on the cusp of a greatness that none of the group's members could possibly have anticipated.

Certainly, as the 1960s commenced, the British popular music scene was about to burst forth, regionally and nationally. The Beatles, returning to their home city from Germany, had secured a residency at the Cavern, a small but well-patronised cellar club in the heart of city in Mathew Street. Not long after, local businessman Brian Epstein, who owned the NEMS music store nearby, watched a lunch-time gig and asked if he could manage the four-piece. Within a short time, Epstein had

---

[51] Ellis, 2000, p. 67.

[52] Jonathan Clarke, *Can't Buy Me Love: The Beatles, Britain and America* (London: Portrait, 2007), p. 50.

[53] Philip Norman, *Shout!* (London: Elm Tree, 1981), p. 52, quoted in Simon Frith and Howard Horne, *Art Into Pop* (London: Methuen, 1987), p. 84.

helped clinch a recording contract with EMI subsidiary Parlophone and, in 1962, their first single 'Love Me Do' was released, hitting the lower reaches of the Top 20. This gentle start was a misleading augury – a nationwide and global splash was imminent. Within months, as 1963 unfolded, Beatlemania exploded across the UK, with number one singles and a debut album to follow. The eruption focused significant interest on Liverpool and the city's other musicians, writers and performers benefited from the slipstream of the Fab Four's momentum.

In February 1964, the Beatles made their first trip to the US, an extraordinary success and a move that would trigger the so-called British Invasion as UK pop and rock knocked down the metaphorical barricades and gained large-scale US attention as the decade accelerated. If British music had been deeply unfashionable and dated before the Beatles' rise, afterwards sounds that emanated from the UK became apparent passports to stardom, huge sales and a swelling fan base. The Dave Clark Five and the Rolling Stones from London, the Animals from Newcastle, and Herman's Hermits from Manchester were among the early beneficiaries of the astonishing post-Beatles effect. Others would soon follow: the Who, the Kinks, the Troggs and the Yardbirds to be succeeded by Cream and Led Zeppelin. The British Invasion's impact would barely decline for the next two decades as the new heavy rock bands – Black Sabbath and Deep Purple – then the progressive rockers – Pink Floyd, Yes, ELP and Genesis – the folk rockers – Jethro Tull, the Incredible String Band – singer-songwriters such as Donovan, Elton John and Cat Stevens, glam rockers – David Bowie and T. Rex – punks – the Clash and the Sex Pistols – and the New Romantics – Culture Club to Duran Duran – became successive kings of the American court, primarily because the Beatles had made British pop and rock credible and desirable in a manner no one could possibly have predicted at the 1950s.

But how did the newly powerful popular music of the early 1960s make closer associations with Beat culture? In the US, Bob Dylan's meeting with Allen Ginsberg,[54] at the close of 1963 was crucial to the launch of this new dialogue. Dylan's befriending of the poet would be followed by the singer's first meeting with the Beatles in summer 1964. Then, in May 1965, Dylan would bring Ginsberg and the Beatles together, inviting them all to join him in his hotel suite after an Albert Hall gig in London.[55] Thus, within a year and a half, the leading players in an increasingly influential generation of popular musicians would cross existing artistic boundaries to make positive contact with the most dynamic and high profile member of the Beat fraternity.

---

[54] Sean Wilentz, 2010, p. 69.
[55] See Barry Miles, *Ginsberg: A Biography* (London: Viking, 1990), pp. 369–70.

The slowly growing presence of a post-Beat subculture identified as hippy, often hippie,[56] was certainly significant here as informal links between musicians and poets developed. Hippy was a descriptor that had grown out of hipster, a term previously encoded with meanings that evoked the dangerous cultural fringes: it conjured notions of outsiderdom and transgression. Hipsters had connections to the world the Beat Generation writers inhabited, a terrain mapped out by Norman Mailer in 'The White Negro', an essay actually subtitled 'Superficial Reflections on the Hipster'. The derivation of hippy could also be connected to jazz-linked slang and terms such as hip, hep and hepcats. Hippies as a social group would be first documented in the US as early as 1965.[57] Drop-outs, outcasts and followers of an alternative lifestyle were described as such around the West Coast, and particularly San Francisco, before the middle of the decade. The area known as Haight-Ashbury in San Francisco would be one of the first neighbourhoods to attract communities of these individuals – longer of hair, often with moustaches and beards, and adopting clothing that had a colourful, carnivalesque quality, often incorporating elements of the historical or ethnic. Such details set them apart from the predominantly monochrome shades of Beat men and women. Yet many of their liberal values – on politics, drugs and personal relationships, for instance – had a common ring. In the US, these organic seeds, once planted, would bloom and proliferate as the decade unwrapped, climaxing, we may propose, at the legendary three-day music festival at Woodstock in August 1969.

The UK's hippy scene would also take shape within quite a similar time period but it would have a different, arguably more kaleidoscopic, genesis, gathering a spectrum of different tribes, subcultures and classes. Barry Miles was both part of the British eruption and has since become one of its most prolific historians. As he explains in a later account:

> The beginning of the hippie scene in Britain was quite different from that in the US [...] the underground scene came from the meeting of a number of different strands in youth culture [...] the mods, the rockers, the dollybirds of Swinging London, the Campaign for Nuclear Disarmament activists, the radical left students and the latest generation of art school graduates, most of whom were rock musicians.[58]

---

[56] While it is more usual to see the term hippie used to describe the subculture or an individual member of that community, I have tried, as far as possible, to apply some grammatical logic here and use hippy for the subculture or an individual member of the group and hippies for the plural.

[57] Terry H. Anderson, *The Movement and the Sixties: Protest in America from Greensboro to Wounded Knee* (Oxford: Oxford University Press, 1995), p. 170.

[58] Miles, 2003, p. 76.

There were various triggers that would see this somewhat disparate multitude gain a higher, and partially unified, profile. Miles adds: 'Then came the Beatles, followed rapidly by the Stones, and the whole explosion of beat groups that transformed rock 'n' roll […] in a year or so […] Between the rock groups, Biba's clothes shop, Mary Quant, the widespread introduction of the pill, full employment, pop art, satirical TV shows […], the growing availability of marijuana, LSD, books by the Beat Generation, American be-bop, Surrealism, French New Wave films, associations with West Indian communities of West London and myriad other factors, an underground culture emerged.'[59] Green is perhaps less convinced that this multi-coloured quilt was complemented by all its many parts. 'The groups that "came together" […] often overlapped – there were no bounds that restricted a given individual to a given group – but were essentially discrete entities, each working to achieve its own ends, and generally existing in its own self-absorbed world', he states. 'There was often a sense of like minds but not always a meeting. What linked them was an inchoate desire to "change the world", but the methods they proposed and the means they had available often kept them apart.'[60]

Nonetheless, whatever the debates about common purpose or shared manifestos, the central role of Miles, initially art student and little poetry magazine editor in Cheltenham and then bookseller, publisher and writer in London, in joining up many of these particular dots in the British capital, cannot be underestimated. Miles, friend of Michael Horovitz, John 'Hoppy' Hopkins and others on the growing underground scene, had been an early youthful correspondent with Ginsberg, Kerouac and others as he pulled together his own verse collections while still at college. When he arrived in London to work at Better Books, the city's first paperback book outlet, he was well situated to make links between published Americans and the new wave of British talent.[61] The blending and merging of various streams of activity, Miles has already described, but events of late spring and early summer of 1965 would see an increase in impetus and gravitas for the fragmented forces expounding the new arts and the possibilities of cultural change.

When Ginsberg arrived on UK shores after a global trek concluded by a European sojourn in May 1965, Miles played host. Shortly afterwards, when the poet, perhaps the most pro-active and social of the Beat Generation clan, attended Dylan's gig at London's Royal Albert Hall and met the Beatles, it was clear there was a great possibility of a dynamic network taking shape. Within days of the Albert

---

[59] *Ibid.*
[60] Green, 1999, p. 129.
[61] Says Michael Horovitz: 'Miles became very closely allied to Ginsberg, who, at first, as was often the case, had, I think fancied him […] [He] was very effective and became a sort of acolyte and representative of Ginsberg and Burroughs.' See Jonathon Green, *Days in the Life: Voices from the English Underground 1961–1971* (London: Pimlico, 1998), p. 44.

Hall gathering, Ginsberg had confirmed his genuine interest in the group by heading to Liverpool for a week, to meet poets, artists and musicians.[62] Returning in time to celebrate his thirty-ninth birthday in London, his guests included both John Lennon and George Harrison, both of whom left early after a celebratory but inebriated Ginsberg caused some offence by removing all his clothes.[63]

But the stimulus for a major breakthrough in the UK alternative poetry scene was barely a week or two away. With Ginsberg in London and Corso and Ferlinghetti about to arrive, Barbara Rubin, a film-maker and friend of Ginsberg, proposed that they should organise a reading in the capital, one on a scale never seen in the city, perhaps never even in the US. Miles, Horovitz and others in their circle were supportive though surprised when Rubin suggested that they secure the largest available venue they could. The Albert Hall was booked for ten days hence, at high expense and unquestioned risk, but work towards creating a programme and attracting an audience began in earnest. With three of the major names from the US Beat community present, there was already a headline bill of real status. But the organisers also wished to give British and European poets a chance to read, too. Horovitz, Adrian Mitchell and Pete Brown, were joined by other UK writers: Alexander Trocchi,[64] who would host the occasion, Christopher Logue, Harry Fainlight, Spike Hawkins and George McBeth, and poets from Europe, including the Dutch writer Simon Vinkenoog. The occasion, on 11 June 1965, drew a huge crowd of more than 7,000 to one of the city's great concert spaces and, even if Miles called it 'one of the worst poetry readings ever'[65] – Ginsberg had drunk too much, Corso was indulgent and Burroughs' voice, on tape, hardly discernible over the PA, though Ferlinghetti read well – there was a general sense that the event's significance outweighed the actual detail of the lengthy programme. Green said 'its importance and effect of the entirety far transcended that of its individual parts'.[66] In short, this extraordinary gathering of numerous fragments, many of whom recognised brotherly and sisterly spirit among the audience but had not actually met them until this time, suggested that London – like New York, like San Francisco – had a sizeable underground that had indeed been buried until this audacious, undoubtedly ambitious, one-off venture exposed the secret hoards to the light. It was also a key platform for confirming interest in poetry, as a live, oral form, but specifically Beat poetry, too. England's progressive activists – like Miles and Horovitz, Brown and Mitchell and

---

[62] See also Chapter 4.
[63] See Bowen, 1999, p. 64.
[64] The Scot Trocchi (1925–84) had been an early disciple of the darker ravages of Beat culture. Although he would produce several novels, his heroin addiction was virtually a life-long accompaniment.
[65] Quoted in Green, 1999, p. 139.
[66] Green, 1999, p. 139.

Nuttall, too, who also tried and failed to present a performance art piece of his own at the same Albert Hall occasion[67] – had, through a series of coincidences and some impressive risk-taking, established that, behind the tightly-drawn curtains of mainstream British life, there was a significant, resistant column, interested in radical literature, art and, by clear implication, an alternative politics too, perhaps. The International Poetry Incarnation had other names, as well: *Wholly Communion* was the title of the film that the UK film-maker Peter Whitehead shot and released, a short and grainy but evocative record of this seminal occasion, while *Poets of the World, Poets of Our Time*[68] is what it read on the tickets. Richard Neville, one of the founders of the underground magazine *Oz*, later described it as: 'Cosmic Poetry Visitation Accidentally Happening Carnally.'[69] Obscured until then by its splintered nature, the London gathering solidified hundreds, probably thousands, of individuals into a recognisable movement for social change which would continue its efforts through the 1960s and well beyond.

Yet, if we then wish to support the notion that popular music had now somehow commenced its public alliance with the clan of rebellious writers, it is hard to find crystal clear evidence at the Albert Hall. If Ginsberg had convened with Dylan and the Beatles just the previous month, there may be some plausibility in the claim that rock 'n' roll would now inevitably, and quickly, join the procession of poets and dance to the Beats. Yet the actual evidence was underwhelming. Miles, a reliable witness in these matters, recalls: 'I don't remember any rock musicians being there unless you count Julie Felix as one, more folk really. Ferlinghetti was staying in her Chelsea apartment. It's possible that Donovan attended as he was certainly at the Ginsberg reading at Better Books a few weeks before. John Dunbar says he was there, so maybe Marianne Faithfull was, since he was married to her at the time, but I've never heard her speak about it. But no, no Beatles, no Rolling Stones.'[70]

That said, if the Albert Hall jamboree represented the firing of the starting pistol of this new race, it would not be long before there were tangible signs of the burgeoning worlds of British rock and Beat influence lying down together. McCartney was the most important evidence of this. Although he had been regarded, by the media establishment, as a more stable and sensible individual than his somewhat caustic and controversial composing partner Lennon, it was Paul rather than John who would dip his toes in the waters of the avant garde first and with greatest enthusiasm. Lennon had married art student Cynthia Powell in 1962 but, by the mid-1960s, the couple were leading a suffocating domestic

---

[67] See Green, 1999, pp. 140–1.
[68] See John 'Hoppy' Hopkins, *From the Hip: Photographs 1960–1966* (Bologna: Damiani Editore, 2008), p. 102.
[69] Richard Neville, *Playpower* (London: Paladin, 1971), p. 25.
[70] Barry Miles, personal communication, email, 11 December 2009.

existence in a vast Surrey mansion, away from the crowds, the fans and press photographers, but cut-off from the hubble bubble and excitements of swinging London. He had shown a literary bent, however, producing two poetry collections – *In His Own Write* (1964) and *A Spaniard in the Works* (1965). While the publications were largely well-received and sold well, the work in them – verse and prose studded with puns and comic wordplay, illustrated by his own hand – owed more to the late nineteenth-century tradition of nonsense verse, from Edward Lear to Lewis Carroll, than the Beat style. But they nonetheless stressed that Lennon's talents were not confined to the three-minute pop song.

McCartney meanwhile was living in the heart of the capital and had become romantically attached to Jane Asher, an actress of impeccable middle-class credentials – her father was an eminent medic and her mother a prominent instrumentalist in a leading music conservatoire. Thus he was able to enjoy not only the fruits of the hippest city on the planet, as *Time* magazine were trumpeting at the height of the Carnaby Street hype, as a popular music star but also add to his experience as a concert and theatregoer. Among the events he attended in early 1966 was a lecture by the Italian avant garde composer Luciano Berio[71] and the same year he developed fertile connections with Ginsberg via their mutual associate Miles. When Miles needed support in his new project, the Indica Gallery, McCartney provided some cash and his own physical help; when the Beatle departed a bedroom in the home of the Ashers and secured his own house in the city, Ginsberg visited. Additionally, he became acquainted with William Burroughs, who had moved to London in late 1965, and members of his circle and provided some opportunities for the author to make use of various recording studio facilities which McCartney provided.[72] When the Beatles released their magnum opus *Sgt. Pepper's Lonely Hearts Club Band* in June 1967, Burroughs was one of the faces staring from the crowd assembled, at least photographically, by the UK Pop artist Peter Blake and his then wife, fellow artist Jann Haworth, in one of rock's most celebrated images.

There is scant dispute that the Beatles were at the heart of this cultural excitement – their creative standing and their economic clout ensured their role as leaders of this new surge of artistic energy. Within little more than a couple of years they had become national then global stars. Significant cultural commentators in the UK and key voices in the US were quick to acknowledge the critical importance of the group as harbingers of change and purveyors of a promise of liberation, social and cultural, even political. Jeff Nuttall remarks: 'The Beatles were [...] the biggest single catalyst in this whole acceleration in the development

---

[71] Barry Miles, *Paul McCartney: Many Years from Now* (London: Secker & Warburg, 1997), p. 234.
[72] Miles, 1993), pp. 175–6.

of the sub-culture. They robbed the pop world of its violence, its ignorant self-consciousness, its inferiority complex, they robbed the protest world of its terrible, self-righteous drabness, they robbed the art world of its cod-seriousness. They reflected the scene from which they came, where all this fusion of art, protest and pop had happened previously, in microcosm, for the world to follow; so that Allen Ginsberg, visiting Liverpool a year after the Beatles left, was moved to pronounce it "the centre of the consciousness of the human universe", a statement more perceptive than extravagant.[73] On the other side of the Atlantic, Ginsberg himself recognised very early the power generated and the possibilities triggered by the group: 'I remember the precise moment, the precise night I went to this place in New York City called the Dom and they turned on "I Want to Hold Your Hand", and I heard that high, yodelling alto sound of the OOOH that went right through my skull, and I realised it was going to go through the skull of Western civilisation. I began dancing in public for the first time in my life – complete delight and abandon, no self-conscious wall-flower anxieties.'[74]

McCartney's friendship with Ginsberg would persist over the latter part of the decade and the Beatle would lend further support to the wider Beat poetry project as the 1960s neared a close, when Ginsberg revealed a scheme to record poems by his hero, the great Romantic mystic, artist and poet William Blake, with the assistance of Barry Miles as producer. The poet describes the genesis of the idea:

[A]fter the Chicago convention of last year[75] [...] I began setting Blake's *Songs of Innocence and Experience* to music [...] they seemed the nearest thing to holy *mantra* or holy prayer poetry that I could find in my own consciousness, and also because, seeing that rock 'n' roll – the Stones, the Beatles, Dylan, even Donovan, even the Birds (*sic*), the Band, the Grateful Dead, the Fugs, Jefferson Airplane, all the lovely youthful bands that have been wakening the conscience of the world, really, were approaching high poetry and cosmic consciousness in their content, so I was interested in seeing if Blake's highest poetry could be vocalised, tuned, and sung in the context of the Beatles' 'I am the Walrus' or 'Day in the Life of' (*sic*) or in the context of 'Sad-eyed Lady of the Lowland' (*sic*) or 'John Wesley Harding' by Dylan. Also Dylan said that he didn't like Blake, so I thought this would be an interesting way of laying Blake on him.[76]

---

[73] Nuttall, 1970, p. 123.

[74] Allen Ginsberg, 'Yes, I remember it well', 20th anniversary celebration of Beatles appearance on *The Ed Sullivan Show*, *Rolling Stone*, 16 February 1984.

[75] Ginsberg was referring to the 1968 Democratic National Convention.

[76] Ginsberg, 'CBC broadcast on mantra', *Deliberate Prose: Selected Essays 1952–1995* (London: Penguin, 2000), p. 151.

The Beatles had reserves of cash they wished to invest speculatively in interesting proposals. Apple Records was the first of these visible ventures but money was also steered towards artists and creatives from many walks of life. The Fool, who specialised in clothing and had designed the original, then rejected, artwork for the cover of the album *Sgt. Pepper's Lonely Hearts Club Band* in 1967, had painted the images that adorned Apple's Savile Row headquarters in London. Other beneficiaries of the Fab Four float were left-field inventors and an array of talented, though unknown, musicians who would join the Beatles' own roster. James Taylor, Mary Hopkin and an early incarnation of Badfinger were among the initial acts to to be signed.

Apple now, with the particular enthusiasm of McCartney, agreed to form a spoken word label which would release the material through a new operation called Zapple: 'A is for Apple. Z is for Zapple',[77] as Lennon had quipped at one point. Launched in early 1969, the label promised much as a further symbol of coming together of poetic and musical representatives of the counterculture. Miles, friend to both McCartney and Ginsberg and proprietor of Indica, a radical London art gallery and bookshop, was a trusted associate of both poet and Beatle and seemed an ideal liaison on the venture.

Zapple appeared, at first, to be a concept with both momentum and ambition, with plans to produce spoken word records featuring a gallery of major American names. Ginsberg, and his Blake plan, would be joined, it was hoped, by Burroughs, McClure and Kesey, Ferlinghetti, Richard Brautigan and Charles Olson, Kenneth Patchen, Henry Miller and Charles Bukowski, Simon Vinkenoog, Ed Sanders and Anaïs Nin, Aram Saroyam and Anne Waldman.[78] During 1969, Miles spent time in the US recording Brautigan, Olson, Ferlinghetti and Bukowski and in the summer began taping Ginsberg's Blake cycle with musicians. However, the climate changed quite suddenly at Apple with a new managing figure in place, the hard-nosed American Allen Klein. Concerned about rising costs at Apple, there were mass firings and Zapple was a victim of the cull. It was 'folded without anyone even informing me',[79] recalls Miles who was left with hotel and recording costs unpaid before funds were eventually, if somewhat belatedly, negotiated.

This relatively minor setback in the Beatles chronology would soon be followed by much bigger crises, more damaging rifts, when, not long after in 1970, the group imploded with McCartney departing after disagreements about artistic policy and management arrangements, never satisfactorily resolved after Brian Epstein's death in 1967. Klein would, in time, be the man appointed to oversee the financial position of the other three band members, deepening

---

[77] Quoted in Miles, 2002, p. 247.
[78] Miles, 2002, p. 247.
[79] *Ibid.* p. 278.

the split with McCartney and leading to convoluted legal manoeuvres. Yet, if Zapple was one of the ideas that was crushed in the wake of this new fiscal probity orchestrated by Klein, Miles' efforts to create a spoken word series was not entirely in vain. A number of recordings found new label homes including Ginsberg's own Blake set which would eventually appear on MGM. The larger idea may have foundered on the rocks of Apple's financial crash but the fact that McCartney was keen to develop the venture – and Zapple was conceived to realise it – provided a clear sign that a major rock artist had been willing to back a poetry project of impressive vision, one with many Beat writers at its heart. That financial exigency extinguished the venture was less to with McCartney than the new holders of the purse-strings at the heart of a business that appeared to have spun out of control.

Lennon would later form a close relationship of his own with Ginsberg as the now ex-Beatle turned to politics, specifically the anti-Vietnam War campaign, and found a willing ally in the poet whose involvement with the peace push extended back to 1965. Such developments were trailed in 1969, when Lennon and Yoko Ono gathered a crowd of friends, musicians and other familiar faces in Montreal to record a track that would become a great anti-war anthem, 'Give Peace a Chance'. Ginsberg was one of the featured voices on the live chorus alongside Timothy Leary, and the poet also earned a mention in the song itself.

But how did other representative of the UK rock fraternity become embroiled with the Beat ethos? One band, Soft Machine, took their name from one of Burroughs' other acclaimed novels of the early 1960s, an appellation chosen by their founding member guitarist, Australian émigré Daevid Allen. He lived in the famed Beat Hotel in Paris at the start of the decade, a location where Ginsberg, Corso and Burroughs also made a home between 1959 and 1962. Although Daevid Allen departed the group quite quickly – he would re-emerge in the early 1970s with another art rock band with a radical twist called Gong – the band he had conceived would become musicians central to the impending countercultural drama.

In 1966, when *International Times*, later *IT*, the fortnightly newspaper of the UK underground conceived by Barry Miles, photographer John 'Hoppy' Hopkins, Jim Haynes and others, was unveiled at a launch at the Roundhouse in London on 14 October, Soft Machine along with Pink Floyd and the Crazy World of Arthur Brown were the principal performing attractions. It was an occasion that McCartney, alongside London's assorted radicals, freaks, artists and celebrities, would attend. The next year, on 29 April 1967, there was a further fund-raiser for *IT* at Alexandra Palace, London, entitled *The 14-Hour Technicolor Dream*. Again, Soft Machine, Pink Floyd and the Crazy World of Arthur Brown joined the musical stage alongside the Move, the Social Deviants and numerous other rock and blues acts. Poets were present, too – Michael Horovitz, Christopher Logue and Simon Vinkenoog, for example, who had all appeared at the International Poetry Incarnation two years previously. John Lennon and Yoko Ono – who presented a performance art piece of her own – also attended the event.

Liverpool's active poetic community would also join the musical upsurge with Roger McGough linking with McCartney's brother Mike – he chose McGear[80] as his stage name in a bid to jettison the inevitable Beatle-sibling tag – and actor-comic John Gorman in the Scaffold, a vocal pop group who blended singing, poetry and comedy in a short career that nonetheless earned them a series of Top 10 successes between 1966 and 1968 and many national television appearances. For the Liverpool Poets, as McGough, Henri and Patten would be collectively dubbed, 1967 proved a breakthrough year in the realm of poetry, too, as their joint collection, *The Mersey Sound*, became one Britain's best-selling verse collections ever. The success of this poetry volume could be credited to various intersecting factors: the Beatles effect could certainly not be discounted, and the general rise of Liverpool as cultural force has to be considered, too, as many singers and bands from the city attained a national and international standing in the wake of the Fab Four's emergence.[81] But it is hard not to see some genuine synergy between the converging forces of popular culture in the fields of music and words – an accessible popular poetry, a form of oral performance that had been directly inspired by the Beats, convening with the sounds of rock and pop.

There were other musical ventures, too, as Adrian Henri also became involved in projects that combined the poetic with performance, rock, blues and jazz. The Liverpool Scene, the name itself referencing, in part, Edward Lucie-Smith's celebrated book on the Merseyside cultural boom of the time, ran from 1967–1970 and incorporated various versatile musicians including guitarist Andy Roberts, saxophonist and one-time Clayton Square Mike Evans and Mike Hart, an ex-member of the well-considered Merseybeat act the Roadrunners, once described by George Harrison as his favourite band. In 1971, there was a further significant development when members of the Scaffold, the Liverpool Scene and the Bonzo Dog Band merged to create Grimms, a name which was an acronym of the original group members' names – John Gorman, Andy Roberts, Neil Innes, Mike McGear, Roger McGough and Vivian Stanshall. Combining music, poetry and comedy, Grimms would further expand into an eleven-piece, with Adrian Henri and Brian Patten adding their poetry skills and rock stalwarts like Michael Giles, who had played with King Crimson, much-travelled keyboardist

---

[80] McGear chose a fabricated name from 'gear' a popular Merseyside expression of approval of the day. He had also considered 'fab' but ultimately decided against the style McFab.

[81] Gerry and the Pacemakers, the Searchers, the Merseybeats, Billy Fury, Cilla Black and Billy J. Kramer and the Dakotas were among a number of the Merseyside acts who enjoyed UK and overseas success in the period 1963–6.

Zoot Money and Ollie Halsall, guitarist with Kevin Ayers, contributing at various points in an ensemble that lasted in a series of moveable incarnations until 1976.

There are other examples of the Beat-rock crossover in the UK we might identify, from Donovan to the Incredible String Band, the Rolling Stones and Van Morrison, Marianne Faithfull and Jethro Tull, David Bowie to King Crimson, all of whom either name-checked the Beats or wrote songs that drew upon the mythology of Beat or even attempted to bring the experimental Beat voice to that of the rock lyric. But most of these instances would come to the fore a little later, in the next decade or even after. Yet one poet, who had most certainly arisen from the British Beat scene and would establish himself as a significant contributor to rock's cause in second part of the 1960s, should be highlighted. Pete Brown, friend of Michael Horovitz and member of the Live *New Departures* crew from its inception, would eventually work with some of the most important artists and, in a particular, one of the most high profile UK bands of that era – Cream. He became a key contributor of lyrics to some of the trio's best-known songs – from 'Sunshine of Your Love' to 'I Feel Free' and 'White Room'. Furthermore he would form and lead bands of his own – the Poetry Band with jazz rock guitarist John McLaughlin,[82] before his Cream tour of duty and, post-Cream, with Pete Brown and His Battered Ornaments and Piblokto (a name borrowed from a Lawrence Ferlinghetti novel). He would also continue to work with Cream bassist Jack Bruce, even after the influential rock trio dissolved, and his poetic-musical excursions continue to this day. But his late 1960s work left its deepest and widest mark both in Britain and the US.

In fact, Brown, still active in 2012, just like his long-time, spiritual brother in arms Horovitz,[83] feels that he was one of the few individuals, maybe the only genuine example, who truly brought British Beat poetry and rock music together. Interviewed in 2009, he claimed: 'Well there was just me. There may have been a touch of it in Ray Davies and Pete Townshend. It was really more of an American thing, the Doors, for example.'[84] Interestingly, both Davies of the Kinks and Townshend of the Who, though they never pinned their colours to the Beat mast, would find literary grooves at a later stage – Davies published short stories under the title *Waterloo Sunset* (1998) and Townshend a similar collection, *Horse's*

---

[82] Yorkshire-born McLaughlin would become one of the world's great jazz guitarists, engaged by Miles Davis on his late 1960s jazz-rock experiemnets and later leader of the supergroup the Mahavishnu Orchestra.

[83] Michael Horovitz continues to perform as poet and act as a organiser for numerous events where poetry and music combine. In 2010, Damon Albarn's Gorillaz adapted part of one of Horovitz's verse works for the track 'Stylo' on their album *Plastic Beach*. In 2011, Albarn and Horovitz collaborated on a song supporting the cause of the Notting Hill Carnival, an event which faced possible sanction in the wake of the summer riots in London that year.

[84] Pete Brown, personal communication, email, 6 December 2009.

Neck (1985), at a time when the Who front-man was also serving as an editor at prestigious publishers Faber, home to an extraordinary cast of poets, from T. S. Eliot to Stephen Spender and Ted Hughes. We may even see Davies and Townshend as inheritors of the British, post-AYM flame, followers of MacInnes possibly rather than the more staid figures in that loosely-cast line-up.

In many ways, Brown, who had had an early love affair with the Beats and had had work published in the renowned US publication *Evergreen Review* as a very young writer, found as great a fascination with the way the English voice could find its own place in a rock context, especially as so much work by British acts had sought to recreate American sound and style, particularly through the lyrics they penned. He explained: 'The Beatles and Syd Barrett[85] fascinated me – they turned rock into something English, which was a huge breakthrough. They showed you could write rock songs that were English which really turned me on at the time. It was something I was trying to do.'[86] Through Cream and his subsequent recording and touring work he managed to bring his own voice, even one inspired by the US Beats, as an English poet and lyricist, very successfully into play.

One man who may well have seen his Beat association spread, had he survived, is Brian Jones, the Rolling Stones guitarist whose life was cut short in 1969 within weeks of departing the group. The year before, he had overseen and produced recordings by the Master Musicians of Joujouka, a North African drumming ensemble based in Morocco. The connection had been initiated by Burroughs' friend and collaborator, Brion Gysin, the mastermind of the cut-up method, to which he had introduced the novelist while they were both resident at the Beat Hotel in Paris at the end of the 1950s. Gysin had seen the Master Musicians of Joujouka with another associate of the Beats, novelist Paul Bowles, almost 20 years before, and he encouraged the Stone to hear then play. Jones recorded the ensemble in their home setting and then produced an album of their work. An early example, perhaps, of that rather later conception, World music, the 1971 release also included sleeve notes from William Burroughs among others.

Of the other Stones and their circle, Jagger, introduced to Ginsberg by Miles in 1967, would take a more than passing interest in the Beat stream. Miles comments: 'The Rolling Stones and their circle were familiar with the Beats, particularly Jagger who considered acting in Brion Gysin's script for *Naked Lunch* in 1972. There are many references to Dr. Benway in *Performance*, 1969, too.'[87]

A direct example of this cross-fertilisation occurred in 1967 in London, when Ginsberg was present at and participated in a historic Stones recording of the

---

[85] Barrett was a key early member of Pink Floyd who departed the group for his own solo projects in 1969.

[86] Brown, personal communication, email, 6 December 2009.

[87] Miles, personal communication, email, 29 November 2009.

song 'We Love You', a session that also saw Lennon and McCartney involved. The song was recorded as a tribute to Jagger and Richard in the wake of recent drugs charges that had seen the pair briefly jailed then released on appeal. The recording also formed part of a studio session where the song 'Dandelion' was laid down. Says Schumacher: 'Allen was delighted to be involved in a historic recording session involving members of the two most successful rock bands in the world.'[88] Furthermore, we might mention someone who was a long-time member of the Stones' entourage. Marianne Faithfull, whose first chart hit was a Jagger-Richard composition, 'As Tears Go By', in 1964 and who would enjoy a high profile relationship with Jagger up to 1969, later developed closer links with various Beat writers she had encountered during this phase. She became, for a time, a tutor at the Jack Kerouac School of Disembodied Poets, in Boulder, Colorado, and taught alongside Ginsberg, Burroughs and Corso.

The intertwining of Beat culture and the powerful push of British rock from the mid-1960s was undoubtedly evident yet the output, the enduring legacy, of this synergy is harder to quantify. The fact that both John Lennon and Paul McCartney invested time and interest in the Beat writers – as readers, as friends, sometimes supportively and vice versa – is almost enough to demonstrate the complementary forces at play. Perhaps it was their admiration for Dylan and his enthusiastic espousing of the Beat cause that prompted them to follow such connections, yet we have examples of an earlier Beat affiliation – from something as potentially significant as the change of group name to something more ephemeral such as Lennon's *Daily Howl* publication, a school project pre-dating the real rise to prominence of the band. As we have seen, McCartney's links to Ginsberg and Burroughs saw him act as patron to their creative projects – providing recording facilities to the *Soft Machine* author and his associates in London in the mid-1960s and carving out other opportunities to spread the Beat word, even if Zapple, the most ambitious of these ventures, stumbled for reasons beyond that individual Beatle's control. Down the line, Lennon would forge links with Ginsberg, particularly when his difficult US residency began, as he fought both the policies of the American government in Vietnam and then the immigration authorities to allow him to remain in New York City.

But how can we characterise the impact the Beats had on the Beatles' work? Were there discernible fruits of this high profile, transatlantic alliance? McCartney's musical output seemed to be little affected by the engagement. Setting aside the superficially psychedelic experiment of *Sgt. Pepper Lonely Hearts Club Band* in 1967, it is hard to pinpoint how Beat attitudes or influence changed or improved his work, a body of creativity based on a remarkable melodic sense

---

[88] Michael Schumacher, 1992, p. 485.

and words in the balladic tradition. That said, Lennon's key work on *Sgt. Pepper*, 'A Day in the Life', has something of an unconventional lyric style that owes more to memories re-evoked by poetry than a mere gathering of pop words, while the inventive and dramatic coda to the song speaks far more of the avant garde than Tin Pan Alley. Lennon's association, too, with wordplay and his stream of consciousness jousting on a song like 'I Am the Walrus', from later in 1967, may have owed as much to the English nonsense poetry tradition as Beat verse. Yet it is hard to see how, without the progressive artistic environment cultivated by the middle of the decade – by Dylan, by drugs, by the Beats, indeed, by the Beatles themselves, and a social climate in which the rules of cultural engagement were being re-written – such a song would have been recorded and released.

Lennon's relationship to the Beat spirit achieved an impetus later, too, and we could certainly make connections between the political campaigning of Ginsberg and the politicisation of Lennon as he entered the American phase of his life with Yoko Ono, herself a key member of the Fluxus art group in Manhattan before she married the rock star. Ono was an important catalyst for Lennon's avant gardism after 1968; Ginsberg was an influence, too, among a group of other hippy activists – Ed Sanders, Abbie Hoffman and Jerry Rubin were among others – who would inform the Beatle's idealistic, yet often dangerous, strategies as he mounted high-profile, anti-Vietnam campaigns and eventually took on the might of the US government. The fact though that Lennon raised his head above the parapet and took the battle to the streets of America, drawing the negative ire of the FBI along the way, has a potent irony when set against the near apoliticism of Ginsberg's other high profile rock partner, Bob Dylan, as the 1960s as historical period and utopian dream faded.

As for others who were drawn to the Beat flame, there were a number, some major, some bit part players, who would reference this scene or tap into its energies. We have mentioned the Rolling Stones – Jagger, Jones and Faithfull – and Pete Brown's contributions to Cream. It is hard not to argue that the Beatles, Rolling Stones and Cream were the three major British bands of that immediate time, so their close associations with the Beat community are important for that fact alone. Pink Floyd, a rising force who would become an enormous player on the scene in the early 1970s, were another act who clung to the coat-tails of a Beat aura, through their central links with the London underground, a movement which had *International Times* and Beat-linked figures like Barry Miles, Jeff Nuttall and 'Hoppy' Hopkins at its core, with the UFO club as its stage.

The poets attached to the British Beat scene never became the powerful cult heroes that Kerouac, Burroughs, Ferlinghetti, Corso and Ginsberg were, and continue to be, to the UK underground. Brown, through his Cream associa-tions, attracted an international reputation but it was for his lyrics rather than his poetry that his status was earned. Michael Horovitz,[89] Adrian Mitchell,[90] Spike Hawkins, Johnny Byrne and the Liverpool Poets – Adrian Henri,[91] Roger McGough and Brian Patten – busily ploughed quieter furrows, spent decades building smaller empires, publishing regularly and performing almost constantly, but once the extraordinary cultural tornado of the 1960s had subsided, they were never foregrounded in the way their 1950s American counterparts were. Yet it could be argued, I feel sure, that the reflected glory of British rock's extraordinary global splash helped to give stature and longevity to those subterranean scribes in the UK in the decades that followed. While Brown had sealed an impressive reputation with writing credits on several of rock's greatest tracks, and the poets of the Mersey, as we have described, found numerous opportunities, as well, to pursue pop and rock options on into the 1970s and beyond, an always energetic figure like Horovitz took the chance to build other long-running schemes, like his remarkable Poetry Olympics. Launched in 1980, this project would continue to bring poets of many cultures and popular musicians of the highest reputation – from Ray Davies and Paul McCartney to Paul Weller and Damon Albarn – into the same orbit, on stage, in anthologies and on recordings, deep into the opening decade of the next century. Without the momentum of the 1960s, when popular musicians and poets shared energies and ambitions in various ways, it is hard to see how those later alliances would have flourished in the way they have, and for so long.

That energy, cultural and radical, has enjoyed a longevity in a variety of ways but one pertinent example suggests a continuum. In July 1967, Allen Ginsberg attended an international congress in London on the 'Dialectics of Liberation'[92] which attracted politicos, philosophers and artists from both sides of the Atlantic, including Julian Beck of the Living Theatre, Emmett Grogan of the San Francisco Diggers, noted commentator Paul Goodman, Black Panther Stokely Carmichael and psychiatrist R. D. Laing. The occasion, staged at the Roundhouse, where *International Times* had been launched the year before, appeared to concentrate much of the multi-faceted dynamism of the new thinking and confirm the city as a centre of visionary debate. In February 2012, some of the same voices – Laing's colleagues Joseph Berke and Leon Redler, for example – gathered in the capital once more for 'Dialektikon',[93] a 45th anniversary return to the issues explored all

---

[89] Michael Horovitz was the subject of a 75th birthday tribute, *The Poetry Olympian*, BBC Radio 4, 4 April 2010, presented by the author.
[90] Adrian Mitchell died, aged 76, in 2008.
[91] Adrian Henri died, aged 68, in 2000.
[92] The full title of the 1967 event was the 'Congress of the Dialectics of Liberation for the Demystification of Human Violence in All Its Forms'. See the website, Dialectics of Liberation, http://www.dialecticsofliberation.com/ [accessed 1 March 2012].
[93] The later anniversary event was titled 'Dialektikon 2012 Violence and Liberation'.

those years before, in an event described as 'a re-birth of the congress' that was part conference, part theatre, part performance. Many of the key protagonists were no longer alive, their parts taken by actors, including Ginsberg himself. But Michael Horovitz, described as jazz troubadour, was present in person, sustaining the Beat flame in person in a bill that promised poetry and song, an echo of those very collaborations that Beats, both American and British, had helped engineer at the height of the 1960s.

INTERVIEW 4

Pete Brown, British poet and rock lyricist for Cream

Pete Brown has lived a number of lives as poet, lyricist and rock performer. His poetry appeared in *Evergreen Review* when he was still a teenager, but when he befriended another poet Michael Horovitz in 1960, they began an enduring and fruitful friendship. They wrote a long, Kerouac and jazz-inspired verse work called 'Blues for the Hitchhiking Dead' and toured together with Live *New Departures*, a stage version of Horovitz's poetry and art journal. He also participated in the International Poetry Incarnation at the Albert Hall in 1965. But it was when he linked with Jack Bruce and Cream in the mid-1960s to provide the lyrics to the band's signature songs, 'I Feel Free', 'Sunshine of Your Love' and 'White Room', his career moved into a higher gear. He then led Pete Brown and His Battered Ornaments and Piblokto! – a name taken from a Lawrence Ferlinghetti work – and has continued a varied career as singer, musician and producer ever since. I spoke to Brown by telephone at his London home in December 2009.

SW **How do you see the relationship between poetry and music?**

PB   Those poets of the 1950s – we can perhaps see them as jazz fans who all aspired to be musicians. Leonard Cohen was one. I was one of the other ones who became part of a band in the late 1950s. I liked jazz, blues and soul, swing, Coleman Hawkins, Duke Ellington, bebop, Dizzy Gillespie, Sonny Rollins – and I'm still in love with this music. In the 1950s a lot of the people we were listening to were a lot older. What Michael [Horovitz] and I were trying to do was some of what we saw as the techniques of jazz instrumentalists and composers. We wrote pretty collectively. 'Blues for the Hitchhiking Dead' was like a musical chase following the soloist and his theme.

Jack Kerouac had an interest, a love of jazz, but how superficial it was, I don't know. Bebop was a complex form of music, and not everyone could understand it. Some were superficially turned on to it. Bebop was an artist's music. It was the first time black musicians were not playing commodified music, not just playing for entertainment.

SW **How did you link up with musicians initially? And how did the Cream connection arise?**

PB I became a member of a working band, just wrote for them. I became a singer myself. I think of myself as a musician – I do play drums, percussion.

I always wanted to have my own band. I had one with [guitarist] John McLaughlin. I realised these guys were too good. I was not in their league. I wanted to get a band which was not quite as proficient. I would get more from working with people who were not better than me.

I always say that getting to see the Beatles film *A Hard Day's Night* was important to me, cause I had been in Liverpool a lot. I had rubbed shoulders with the Beatles and they had reached a vast audience. When the Cream chance came along, I grabbed it with both hands. I did not want to be a drunken poet who died in some sort of cheerful obscurity!

The Cream thing opened a lot of doors. I was a very minor celebrity on the party scene though I had done some quite big shows like the Albert Hall. When I got asked to write for Cream, it opened up opportunities, particularly in the US.

Ginger Baker had done some jazz/poetry gigs. I had been a poet for a long time. I had quite a lot of technique I could bring to writing 200 drafts of a song. On the first couple of things I was working with Jack. He had a broad musical language – Charles Mingus, classical training. The Mingus thing we had in common. His concepts were like poetic concepts, they were about creating atmosphere.

SW **After Cream you formed Pete Brown and His Battered Ornaments but that didn't end happily. Weren't you sacked from your own band? What happened?**

PB First, the guitarist Chris Spedding wanted to take over. Second, they were getting embarrassed by my lack of musical talent. The band's saxophonist George Kahn admitted later that they made a terrible mistake. I got more control of what I was doing. It was a kind of wake up call.

SW **How did the Beats shape your experience as a poet?**

PB I was not that familiar at first with Allen Ginsberg, but came through the traditions of blues poetry, Mingus and Ellington. I was better at lyrics than being a musician. I was not trying to do poetry. Some of the time I was using poetic forms found in blues and jazz.

I was a Beat poet, but I was totally in love with Mose Allison, Slim Galliard, Victoria Spivey, Wynonie Harris. Songs like Harris' 'Don't Roll Your Bloodshot Eyes' – they were just as interesting to me.

Michael Horovitz and I were the people who learned from Ferlinghetti and Ginsberg's work yet they were less important than the earlier people like [Robert] Creeley. And Corso, too. Lawrence Ferlinghetti – his British counterpart was Adrian Mitchell. Ferlinghetti put his money where his mouth was. Ginsberg was self-aggrandising and selfish. Ferlinghetti was 100% real. The band name Piblokto came from his novel called *Her*.

I initially encountered an environment where poets were not even allowed to read their own work. Actors used to do it for the BBC. Horovitz and me tried to promote the idea that poets could read, they could use their own voices. Spike Hawkins was another trying to do this.

SW **What is the association between poetry and lyrics? Are they the same thing for you?**

PB I don't set out to write poetry when I am writing a song. I am conscious of trying to get the song right. If the music is there first I almost act as a translator. Sometimes I would come up with something, a concept you might call poetry, write something very intense and use the tools of poetry. But for a long, long time I did not write any poetry. I have been writing poetry again for the last five years.

I write millions of lyrics, and also worked as a producer supplying lyrics. I am constantly doing things like that. I try to put together words that work but I would not call it poetry; I'd call it lyric-writing. Yet lyric-writing drove me back into the arms of poetry. It's a circular thing.

SW **You were part of the oral tradition of the poetry reading. What did you feel about that scene?**

PB Poetry readings – I really enjoy doing them. But that older literary scene does not exist. Mike [Horovitz] and I have never been accepted into any part of the mainstream. We are mavericks, discredited. Andrew Motion and all that shit – nothing to do with us! We have found our own little niche. But a bit of recognition in the UK would be nice. Awards in Germany, US and Japan but not Britain. I don't really give a fuck. But we should get a lot more recognition. I am an old socialist, left wing anarchist, like Michael.

SW **You've worked in poetry and rock. What do you feel connects the Beats and rock music?**

PB   I'd say it was much more evident in the US, with figures like Jim
      Morrison of the Doors, for example. You find a touch of it in Ray
      Davies [of the Kinks] and Pete Townshend [of the Who].

      The Beatles and Syd Barrett with Pink Floyd were very influential
      on rock lyrics. They turned the rock song into something English and
      that fascinated me for a time. 'Strawberry Fields', 'Penny Lane', 'See
      Emily Play' and 'Arnold Layne' were a huge breakthrough. They took
      it away from the transatlantic thing. You could write rock songs that
      were English. They were turning me on at that time. It was something
      I was trying to do, too. Spike Hawkins and me reading at the café in
      Liverpool, and Adrian [Henri] and Roger [McGough]. We brought
      an element of humour, a dark humour, from the blues and black
      American music. Lennon may well have been there, too. The Beatles
      and McGough also derived humour from the traditions of musical hall
      comedy.

Q&A 3

Jonah Raskin, Ginsberg biographer and cultural historian

Jonah Raskin came of age in the wake of rock 'n' roll and the writers of the Beat Generation. He entered Columbia College in New York in 1959, a decade after Allen Ginsberg graduated from the school, and took courses from some of the same professors, such as Lionel Trilling. In the mid-1960s he studied at the University of Manchester, then taught English and American literature at the State University of New York, and, since the 1980s, he has been a professor of communication studies at Sonoma State University in California. The author of 14 books, including *American Scream: Allen Ginsberg's "Howl" and the Making of the Beat Generation* (2004), he writes these days about movies, food, and popular culture for newspapers, magazines, and blogs and listens to the music of Ali Farka Toure, Lightnin' Hopkins and to the rock 'n' rollers of his youth: Chuck Berry, Carl Perkins, Ricky Nelson and more.

What do you feel rock music has taken from Beat culture?

Rock 'n' roll took the wildest of the Beats – the sex, the drugs, the gang of guys thing. A rock band is a mini gang; the Beats were a boy gang. The road is there in a lot of rock lyrics and much of the mythology of the road comes from Kerouac. Ginsberg's surrealism shaped Dylan's poetry, and Burroughs injected that extreme consciousness you get in the Stones, the Doors, the Beatles, too.

I was too young to be a Beat; but I was a beatnik when I was a teen and the Beats and rock 'n' roll were all over my teen years. I loved Elvis, Chuck Berry, and Carl Perkins and Ginsberg and Kerouac; I'd listen to rock 'n' roll and read *On the Road* – in 1957, 1958 – and read 'Howl', too. For me, the Beats and the rock 'n' rollers are members of the same family. I also listened to jazz and the blues – as did the Beats.

How can we best characterise the Beat/rock connection?

The Beats were artists; rock musicians are artists too, so I would say that art is a main connection – making art and performing art. The performance thing is major; the Beats were superlative performers and the Beatles and Dylan learned about performing from the Beats.

Where do you feel we encounter Beat influence in the rock music of the last half century or so?

I see it in Lou Reed, the Clash, Patti Smith, in John Lennon/Paul McCartney lyrics. I see it in Jim Morrison, who was a poet, and a surrealist and a performer who was shocking audiences, much as Burroughs and Ginsberg shocked them. I guess Kerouac shocked – or maybe it was more like surprised – audiences, especially when he waxed spiritual.

Do you think that the idea of the road that Kerouac and Cassady mythologised has been influential on musicians? Are there any examples you might share?

Yes, absolutely. For one thing, bands are often on the road. They live on the road and play on the road and the whole road experience of the Beats was passed on to musicians – either directly or indirectly. The road as a place of adventure, discovery, mystery, is something the Beats and the rock 'n' rollers share. Dylan's Rolling Thunder tour was a continuation of the Beats

What do you feel the Beats' take was on early rock 'n' roll?

They loved it and wanted to borrow from it. Kerouac wanted to change the title of his novel to *Rock 'n' roll Road*. Ginsberg has a direct, obvious reference to rock 'n' roll in 'Howl' – the phrase 'rocking and rolling'.

What do you think the Beats made of that post-Dylan/Beatles rock world?

Well, Burroughs was, for a while, a fixture of the rock world of the 1990s. Punk belongs to the great American underground, counterculture phenomena – it's a continuation from bohemian to hipster, to Beat to beatnik to hippy – to punk. That's what it feels like to me. When punk came along, I felt connected instantly and felt too that this was part of an on-going vital thread – or chord, shall we say.

What do you feel drew Dylan to Ginsberg – and Ginsberg to Dylan?

Dylan was drawn to Ginsberg as a poet, as part of the dissident American culture that went back to Whitman. Lineage is important to Dylan and connecting to Ginsberg was rooting himself in an American idiom. I think it's similar to his affinity for Woody Guthrie. Ginsberg loved stars and celebrities; he just naturally gravitated to them, and it was natural that he'd seek out Dylan.

In what way do you think the work of the Beats benefitted from their association with rock music and musicians?

In the second half of his life, Ginsberg played the harmonium when he read; he learned from rock and that music helped with poetry. Rock 'n' roll also rescued Ginsberg from his despairing world view – the words, the energy, and the whole youthfulness of rock 'n' roll made him more hopeful and accepting of himself and more optimistic about creating a humane world. Kerouac realised that a novel could be enriched with a soundtrack – with names of songs and musicians in the text so the reader would hear music while reading.

Burroughs seemed to have little affinity with rock music yet he was adopted as a guru from the early 1970s? Why was that?

Burroughs listened to rock. He liked the on-the-edge quality of the Stones, Mick Jagger – the darkness of the Stones and the sinisterness of the Stones. 'Sympathy for the Devil'. That sounds like Burroughs to me.

Who would you identify as a the key rock musicians who have drawn on the Beat legacy?

The Beatles, Patti Smith, Lou Reed, Dylan, the Stones.

Are there any particular tracks you feel personify this spirit?

Sgt. Pepper's Lonely Hearts Club Band has echoes of the Beats. I hear it in 'A Day in the Life'. I hear it in Dylan's 'Masters of War'.

A number of Beats – Ginsberg and Burroughs, Ferlinghetti and McClure among them – have made recordings with a rock flavour. What do you make of those experiments?

Ginsberg and Burroughs were exciting performers – rock amplified the intensity of their work. I've read with Ferlinghetti when he was accompanied by Sarah Barker, who sings and plays the blues. I read with a stand up bass player from

Canada named Claude Smith. I play with musicians as often as possible. I have heard McClure and Ray Manzarek and they're a very hip duo.

When rock has expressed itself politically in the last half century has it owed something to the original idealism or activism of the Beats?

Well, I'd say Woodstock was the Beat world of the 1950s magnified a zillion times. The Gathering of the Tribes or the Human Be-In in San Francisco in January 1967 had a Beat element to it, and was part of the cultural revolution of the day.

Is there a sense that the Beat spirit survives in rock music of today?

Musically speaking I'm a kind of dinosaur. I know the Beatles, the Stones, the Who, and the Kinks really well. I know the names of their albums, say *Abbey Road*, and the years they came out. Yes, I do also listen to new bands with young musicians regularly because my favourite radio station is KALX – the student station from the University of California at Berkeley, 90.7. The DJs play great contemporary music. I love it and I write down the names of the albums and the groups, too, hoping to go to Amoeba Records, the last of the great record/CD stores in San Francisco, but then I never go and buy them. I just turn on the radio and hear the music they play. I don't have any of the same familiarity I have with the rock groups of the 1960s and 1970s – and then also with groups like the Sex Pistols and the Ramones. Driving around, listening to KALX, I imagine Cassady and Kerouac driving and listening to KALX, too, and snapping their fingers and maybe even singing as I sing, 'Hail, hail rock 'n' roll/Deliver me from the days of old'.

6 THE SOUND OF THE SUMMER OF LOVE? THE BEATLES AND *SGT. PEPPER*, THE HIPPIES AND HAIGHT-ASHBURY

There appears to be an inextricable link between the so-called Summer of Love and *Sgt. Pepper's Lonely Hearts Club Band*, the Beatles album that first appeared in June 1967, a recording that frames a sequence of songs which seemed to provide a ubiquitous soundtrack to the artistic and creative, social and political events that came together during that auspicious season. George Martin, the production mastermind behind the record, even called his 1995 account of the LP's making *Summer of Love*.[1] But how much did the group's release actually owe to the spirit at large in that summer of 1967? Was *Sgt. Pepper* a catalyst, a mirror or merely a coincidental gathering of material which, it has been subsequently claimed, captured the flavour, distilled the mood, of those momentous months?

There are further contradictions and confusions, too, we might contemplate in respect of the enduring association between that ground-breaking record and that memory-saturated time, if only because the seeds of that celebratory summer had been sown not in Liverpool, the Beatles' birthplace, nor London, their *de facto* home by the time of the record's release, but in a city some 7,000 miles away: San Francisco, the Californian centre of the hippy movement where multiple threads – musical, sartorial, narcotic, erotic and spiritual – had been woven into a psyche-delic tapestry by members of an unconventional community located where the city streets of Haight and Ashbury intersected. In that Bay Area neighbourhood,

---

[1] George Martin with William Pearson, *The Summer of Love: The Making of Sgt. Pepper* (London: Pan, 1995).

a community that appeared to succeed, even supersede, the Beat settlements in North Beach in the late 1950s and early 1960s, had been established. Yet the connections between the bohemian poets of that earlier generation and the new wave of young artists and music-makers could hardly be avoided. While the hippies wore their hair longer and displayed a multitude of colour, when set against the more austere, often black, garb of the Beats, there was a powerful sense that the tribes setting up home in the Haight were the new, confident and more flamboyant heirs to that previous community of writers, artists and activists. If the styles had changed, the world had certainly changed also: the sound of the Cold War's low throb had been displaced by a higher profile and more vociferous chorus, one generated by masses gathering and demonstrators expressing a new and urgent mood. The early 1960s had seen righteous ethnic agitation as black Americans and their allies sought recognition and equality; by the mid-decade the playing field had shifted as the administration's call to arms, with military involvement in Vietnam intensifying by the month, posing the very real possibility of the draft for tens of thousands young adult male Americans, The theoretical, somewhat abstract threat, of nuclear annihilation had been overtaken, initially by largely non-violent calls for Civil Rights and then by an ever-more vigorous resistance to the strategies of the American war machine, brazenly uncurling its talons in the paddy fields of South East Asia. The young hippy nation, well exemplified by its principal Californian enclave and the anti-war Summer of Love it would call in 1967, would be important factors in the unfolding of a high-octane drama in the last few years of the decade. As Farrell describes this rising quarter of San Francisco around this very time:

> The vortex of the Summer of Love was Haight-Ashbury, a San Franciscan neighbourhood bordering on Golden Gate Park. Because of its low rents, the Haight had become an attraction for many young people [...] they developed a distinctive American subculture in the district, and they advertised it to America.[2]

In fact, the signs that Haight-Ashbury would become the focus of a new consciousness had begun to reveal themselves as early as 1965,[3] so there are certain curiosities that it took a further two years or so before there was a global recognition that the innovative ingredients, being mixed by a fresh-minded, post-war and baby boomer generation, had a broad sense of purpose, a

---

[2] Farrell, 1997, p. 218.
[3] Terry H. Anderson, *The Movement*, 1995, p. 170, quotes a *Time* report of July 1966 referring to the hippies as 'a wholly new subculture, a bizarre permutation of the middle-class American ethos' that had been emerging since the last months of 1965.

philosophical foundation and an identifiable manifesto. Furthermore, why was it in the UK that these characteristics were apparently made flesh, or at least vinyl, and linked so wholeheartedly to the Beatles' eighth LP?

The short answer may well be that, by the middle years of the increasingly sensational Sixties, where the Beatles led, the world's mass media, not to mention the planet's hundreds of millions of popular music fans, followed. If the Fab Four chose to pin their colours to a particular mast, a flotilla of journalists, photographers, film-makers and screaming adherents would be speedily in pursuit of the Merseysiders' flagship.[4] To use contemporary language, they were simply the most potent global brand of the time, irresistible, it seems, to both trend-seekers and opinion-formers. By adopting styles and embracing attitudes that had, until then, been seen as radical and revolutionary, distasteful and even dangerous, the band's ability to mediate between the extremes of insurrectionary contumacy and died-in-the-wool conservatism was extraordinary. Both heads of state[5] and the heads, the freaks, of the Californian communes seemed hypnotised by their charisma.

So, when the 39 minutes of music on *Sgt. Pepper*, the Beatles' most ambitious studio outing so far, appeared to draw upon various en vogue aspects of the cultural moment and re-stage them in words and sound, the project was bound to attract global media coverage, the interest of television, newspapers and magazines. In isolation, the colourful and eccentric hordes of Haight-Ashbury, with their non-conformist codes and countercultural associations, could only dream of attention on such a scale. The Beatles had an ability to cross boundaries, test convention, yet still appeal to the mainstream reporter or broadcaster and, by implication, their middle-of-the-road, mass audiences. This remarkable pop group were capable, it seemed, of transcending divisions of age, race and class, bridging the generation gap through their blend of musical originality and personable humour in a way that the Rolling Stones, determinedly uncouth, or Bob Dylan, relentlessly surly, could not.

But there is another factor to consider. If the Beatles had apparently alchemically frozen the spirit of the *Zeitgeist,* they had also achieved this sleight of hand at a distance. Even if England and, more specifically, London had been dubbed 'swinging' by the American press as early as 1966[6] and Carnaby Street had been

---

[4] In Clinton Heylin's *The Act You've Known for All These Years* (Edinburgh: Canongate, 2007), p. 5, the author quotes Lennon's remark in a 1980 edition of *Playboy*, which connects with this analogy: 'Whatever was blowing at the time moved The Beatles, too. I'm not saying we weren't flags on top of the tip. But the whole boat was moving'.

[5] For example, UK Prime Minister Harold Wilson awarded each of the group MBEs (Members of the British Empire) in 1965 (see Trynka, *The Beatles*, 2004, p. 170) and a visit to the Phillipines in 1966 caused local uproar when the President Ferdinand Marcos and wife Imelda were allegedly snubbed by the Beatles (*ibid.*, p. 208).

[6] On 15 April 1966, the US magazine *Time* published a celebrated account trailed on the cover as

crowned the epicentre of happening fashion,[7] the heart and soul of the new thinking still rested in the US. It was certainly on that side of the Atlantic, that the social movements and left-field subcultures, which had lit the blue touch-paper of an alternative lifestyle, continued to burn most brightly.

As we have hinted, at the seat of these developments were the earlier acts of often middle-class, frequently college-educated outsiders – literary figures like J. D. Salinger, Arthur Miller, Norman Mailer and the Beat Generation writers[8] – who, in the Fifties, identified a sickness in the US heartland, anxiously recoiling at the nuclear threat, vengefully revelling in the McCarthy-ite witch-hunts. These writers and commentators penned poems, essays, plays and novels which caught the imagination of thousands of younger readers who despised and challenged the reactionary and straitjacketed mind-set of middle America. Folk singers, too, like Woody Guthrie and Pete Seeger, who had championed socialist ideals from as early as the 1930s, had provoked the ire of the authorities once the Cold War had taken hold.[9] Yet the judicial procedures that took on the forces of the left in the decade after the Second World War could not douse the flames of change that these astute writers and acoustic troubadours had effectively fanned.

Such artistic gestures encouraged later political strategies, too. The Civil Rights campaign for Negro equality had a history of more than a decade[10] by the time *Sgt. Pepper* hit the racks of the record stores. More pertinently perhaps, the Vietnam War had reached a furious juncture by 1967 and the twin spectres of the military draft and the daily evidence of physical devastation in the war-zone – detailed reportage from the battle-front appearing on family TV screens each evening – concentrated minds more effectively than any brand of rock 'n' roll, however re-shaped and re-marketed, could possibly have achieved. The protests that gained momentum in US cities – whether in black ghettoes or on white campuses – may have occurred to a backdrop of, often thrilling, musical accompaniment – gospel, folk, blues, electric rock – but the true triggers were the visceral, stomach-churning realities of, on the one hand, social repression of a minority caste at home and, on the other, a government-sponsored conflict against political forces abroad.

Which of itself, raises a further paradox: why should winters of discontent, springs of desperation, autumns of exasperation, that had preceded 1967, certainly in the USA, suddenly sire a Summer of Love? How could the brutalising, sometimes

---

'London: The Swinging City'. See Green, 1999, p. 71.

[7] See Green, *ibid.*, p. 74.

[8] Salinger's *Catcher in the Rye* (1951), Miller's *The Crucible* (1953), Allen Ginsberg's *Howl and Other Poems* (1956), Mailer's 'The White Negro' (1957) and Jack Kerouac's *On the Road* (1957) exemplify some of these accounts. See also Chapter 1.

[9] See, for example, Denselow, 1989.

[10] Much longer, of course, if we include efforts that had crystalised in the NAACP (National Association for the Advancement of Colored People) founded as early as 1909 (see Wetterau, 1984, p. 540).

killing, of non-violent protestors in the American South, the murders of charismatic figureheads such as President John F. Kennedy and Black Muslim leader Malcolm X and the increasing tensions between pro- and anti-war forces across that nation, spawn a time when love – a spiritually-founded, emotionally-centred and increasingly anachronistic concept in an era of spreading mechanisation and accelerating secularity – was presented as the only weapon of response, of reform, of last resort, remaining?

This chapter will aim to identify the elements that we may regard as the central components and key signifiers of the Summer of Love and, further, examine how far these ideas may have been contained in or expressed by the Beatles' signature 1967 album. To what extent did the Summer of Love exist as a conscious construct and how far was it merely a convenient shorthand by the anti-authoritarian lobby to seek and achieve media approval or approbation? To what degree did the Beatles determinedly aim to condense the ideas and ideals of that moment into a long-playing record and how much was *Sgt. Pepper* merely a serendipitous reflection of the activities and actions of the time?

To begin then: how might we most usefully define the Summer of Love of 1967? Hamilton states that in the spring of that year 'hippie leaders in the Haight called for young people around the nation to journey to San Francisco and experience the good vibrations, the spiritual enlightenment'.[11] The call, however, caused some conflict within the community. 'Many hippies criticised it as a tactic developed by the hip businesses to make money, and they feared that the Haight, already beset with tourists who jammed its streets and sidewalks, would never be able to handle the expected crowds.'[12]

Nonetheless, the official hippy Council for a Summer of Love counselled against such fears. 'Food is being gathered', the body announced. 'Hotels are being prepared to supply free lodging…It is the will of God that His children will be met with Love',[13] stated extracts from the hippy-linked newspaper the *San Francisco Oracle*, striking a distinctly Biblical tone. The result was that '[a]ll summer long youth invaded – youngsters hitchhiked or arrived in vans be-decked with psychedelic Day-Glo images and they arrived in their tens of thousands.'[14]

Farber and Bailey describe an exodus to San Francisco in similar terms. '[T]housands of America's youths made a "pilgrimage" […] invited by Haight-Ashbury's Council for a Summer of Love and drawn by media coverage so intensive that people joked about bead-wearing *Life* magazine reporters interviewing

---

[11] Hamilton, 1997, p. 294.
[12] *Ibid.*
[13] Quoted in Allen Cohen, *The San Francisco Oracle, Facsimile Edition: The Psychedelic Newspaper of the Haight Ashbury, 1966–1968* (Berkeley, CA: Regent 1991), cited by Hamilton, *ibid.*
[14] Hamilton, *ibid.*

bead-wearing *Look* magazine reporters, more than 75,000 young people flooded into the district'.[15] Farrell though places the Summer of Love in a longer, historical context. He says that the Freedom Summer of 1964 'focused the ideas and institutions of the radical civil rights movement; the Summer of Love was a second freedom summer, but it demanded freedom, not just for African Americans, but for all Americans who had been caught in the gears of American society'.[16]

Yet, if the Summer of Love does seem to represent a genuine and organised attempt – here we have, after all, a co-ordinating committee – to gather like-minded individuals in the Bay Area, we should also note that another event that took place at the start of 1967 and was also a contributory factor in the story that would unfold in the subsequent months. The Human Be-In of 14 January, staged at Golden Gate Park, saw forces from various parts of that geographical region – San Francisco, Berkeley and its environs – join together. Charles Perry, who would later publish a history of the Haight,[17] recorded his reminiscences of the occasion ten years later. He saw the event as important because one of its purposes was to treat some of the rifts that had broken out between different sections of the broad counterculture with differing ideologies – the political and apolitical, the folk-oriented and rock-driven. Perry, who attended with his friends, speculates on the motivations of a gathering, which brought together electric folk – Country Joe McDonald – and acid rock – the Jefferson Airplane – and key figures from the Beat circle – Allen Ginsberg, Michael McClure, Gary Snyder and Lawrence Ferlinghetti – not to mention Timothy Leary, in his contribution to the *Rolling Stone* collection of memoirs, *The Sixties*:

> [W]e were living in Berkeley. Like most of the people we knew there, folkies, artists and dropouts from the radical-political scene, we were inclined to go on peace marches and pay some attention to the spokesmen of the Berkeley Left. But there was a dangerous narrowness about them, becoming more obvious as Berkeley became more narcissistic. Ever since the Free Speech Movement, which had brought a great blast of media attention, the politicos had come to think of fame as their natural right. But now the Haight was making the same claim, and that was a pisser. Berkeley distrusted rock and roll – throughout the McCarthy years rock had been the enemy and folk music was the true revolutionary music: pure, uncommercial, a little academic, a small pond not too over-crowded with the right size frogs. It distrusted drugs, though it had signed along on the sexual-freedom movement, which opened the door to

---

[15] David Farber and Beth Bailey, *The Columbia Guide to America in the 1960s* (New York: Columbia University Press, 2001), p. 249.
[16] Farrell, 1997, p. 218.
[17] Charles Perry, *The Haight-Ashbury: A History* (New York: Wenner Books, 2005).

every form of hedonism. But most of all, the Berkeley politicos despised the Haight's lack of politics and resented the fact that these nobodies [...] had stolen their thunder as young rebels and were cutting their recruiting among younger college students. The Be-In was intended, in some people's minds at least to heal the conflict. That was the meaning of the subtitle 'A Gathering of the Tribes'.[18]

The Be-In, which drew around 20,000 participants,[19] may be regarded then as a fraternal and pacifying precursor to the Summer of Love, a parley between different wings of the northern California scene and a moment when the historical divisions between the political and rock music were at least narrowed.

What though was the appeal of the invitation, to participate in a Summer of Love that followed? We can surely begin to explain that attraction by describing the ingredients that had, by as early as the previous year, started to provide the foundations of the growing Haight-Ashbury scene thought, by 1966, to be home to some 15,000 hippies.[20] Quoting one such hippy who attempted an overview of the community, its values and its concerns: 'The Haight-Ashbury had four or five grapevines cooking at all times, and the two words that went down the wire most in those days were *dope* and *revolution*. Our secret formula was grass, LSD, meditation, hot music, consolidation, and a joyous sexuality',[21] a gathering of ideas to which we will return in due course.

Hamilton also discusses the clothing that set the members of this exotic world apart. 'They wore mod styles, mini-skirts, Beatle boots, colourful paisley prints, Edwardian and velvet clothes, or perhaps Buddhist robes or flowing capes' but narcotic stimulants – 'marijuana smoke drifted around them' – and most specifically psychedelic drugs 'permeated the entire scene'. For the hippies, LSD or acid, was 'an avant garde tool – it elicited spontaneity, the ability to see previously hidden connections, and feelings of oneness with the universe. Hippies believed in spreading love, freedom, peace, sincerity, and creativity, and they considered acid essential in doing this'.[22]

Marwick agrees with the centrality of acid to the movement. 'What then distinguished a hippie? The essential ingredients were LSD and everything associated with it'.[23] But he also raises a different point about the definition of hippy and how far we should associate it with US society alone. He believes that there may have

---

[18] Charles Perry, 'The gathering of the tribes', *The Sixties*, edited by Linda Rosen Obst (New York: Random House/*Rolling Stone*, 1977), pp. 188–92.

[19] *Ibid.*, p. 192.

[20] Hamilton, 1997, p. 133.

[21] Cited in Hamilton, *ibid.*; his italics in each case.

[22] Hamilton, *ibid.*

[23] Marwick, 1998, p. 482.

been 200,000 hippies in America by the end of the 1960s but proposes that there may have been that many again in other locations around the world. Certainly his account – that of a British historian, after all – aims to provide a more international reading of the phenomenon. He asks:

> Was the hippie essentially an American invention? What was a hippie? […] The notion of the 'bohemian' is a useful one […] The bohemian is 'different', defies convention, but is not necessarily thereby engaged in trying to subvert 'bourgeois' society. The Beats of the fifties were particularly potent rebels in that the ideas and attitudes they generated continued to exert influence throughout the sixties, but they were bohemian in that their central commitment was to art, basically novels and poetry, not to social, still less political causes.[24]

Considering the etymology of the term hippy, he connects it to the language of Beat, 'hep' – as in 'most up to the moment'[25] – becoming 'hip' and then being adapted and attached to the later subculture here under consideration. Marwick adds: 'The linguistic origins are indisputably American. However, while recognising America as it birthplace, a French commentator highly critical of the whole hippie movement insisted that the European wave was originated in Britain by the Albert Hall underground poetry festival.[26] And in the American sources, […] we find the view being quite strongly expressed that the hip place to be is London.'[27]

Nonetheless, we should recognise, too, that the main focus of this cultural phenomenon remained in the US during 1967, with one of the defining moments of the Summer of Love occurring in another part of California on 16, 17 and 18 June when the Monterey Festival, the first outdoor music gathering of its kind, the precursor to the great end-of-decade festivals at Woodstock in 1969 and, in the UK, the Isle of Wight in both 1969 and 1970, convened, bringing together an extraordinary coalition of talent, familiar acts and those, as yet, little known: established artists such as the Mamas and the Papas, Otis Redding and the Who and the next generation of stars in Janis Joplin and Jimi Hendrix.

Lou Adler, record mogul and producer/manager of the Mamas and the Papas at the time, was a significant player in the organisation of Monterey, alongside John Phillips, a member of the very vocal group Adler was then steering. The pair involved a number of the highest profile musicians of the day in the planning

---

[24] Marwick, 1998, p. 481.
[25] *Ibid.*
[26] Staged in London on 11 June 1965. See also Green, 1999, pp. 138–41.
[27] Marwick, 1998, p. 481.

of the festival, Paul McCartney, Brian Wilson, Brian Jones and Rolling Stones manager Andrew Oldham among them. Says Adler:

[J]ust a few months before the gathering at Cass Elliot's house, someone – I think it was Paul McCartney – said it was about time that rock and roll became recognised as an art-form, instead of just a musical phase. Rock and roll had in fact grown up; we had experienced the Beatles and the Rolling Stones, and Dylan going electric. By the time John [Phillips] and I met again with the promoters and other artists, those three days at Monterey seemed like a great idea [...] We thought that any festival should be nonprofit [...] The promoters weren't geared to that thinking. Since it was a commercial venture, they were interested in producing a profit, naturally and rightfully so.[28]

In the end, a number of interested artists – Paul Simon and Johnny Rivers among them – agreed to split the initial cost and the event could proceed. Yet even then Adler reports that there were disagreements with the San Francisco bands – the Grateful Dead, Jefferson Airplane and Quicksilver Messenger Service – who believed that at the festival 'everything should be free [...] except, of course, their recording contracts',[29] a somewhat sarcastic remark on the nature of the negotiations that were eventually saved by the interventions of Bay Area promoter Bill Graham and *Rolling Stone* magazine lynchpin Ralph J. Gleason. However, Adler's comment is a clear indication that the share-all, peace and love ethos of the blossoming Summer of Love had already been pricked by the thorns of commercial reality. Adler's position also reveals a certain ambiguity to these processes. The co-founder of A&M Records, he talks about a desire for a non-profit event yet sees the aim of the promoters to achieve a profit as quite justified, an ambivalent position at best.

Preceding Monterey by a couple of weeks was the release of *Sgt. Pepper's Lonely Hearts Club Band*, issued to great fanfare by Parlophone, a subsidiary of the UK-based major EMI, the most powerful label in the world by this stage, on 1 June. Much anticipated, the LP had been trailed by a double A-sided single, 'Strawberry Fields Forever'/'Penny Lane' the previous February, two tracks that had originally been intended for inclusion on the forthcoming album. This extraordinary pair of songs, each bearing the distinct mark of the two group's principal songwriters, John Lennon and Paul McCartney, has significance as it offers clues regarding the original blueprint for the *Sgt. Pepper* collection. Both of these pieces, in their different ways, represented memories of childhood and, when the group gathered

---

[28] Lou Adler, 'Music, love and promoters', *The Sixties*, edited by Linda Rosen Obst (New York: Random House/*Rolling Stone*, 1977), pp. 204–7 (p. 204).
[29] *Ibid.*

in late 1966 to begin work on the next long player, MacDonald proposes that 'they were aiming at an autobiographical album developing the Liverpudlian resonances of records like "In My Life" and "Eleanor Rigby"'.[30] For 'Strawberry Fields Forever', Lennon had drawn on recollections of Strawberry Field (*sic*), a girls' reform school near his childhood home in Woolton,[31] while McCartney, in his piece, had re-visited schoolboy memories of the street and district of the city known as Penny Lane.[32]

However, and it is a significant qualification, neither of these titles, though schemed to appear on *Sgt. Pepper*, ever did. While George Martin has since suggested it was 'the biggest mistake of my professional life'[33] to eventually exclude the tracks from the album, these songs did not make it to final version for reasons linked to a standard British practice of the time that saw released singles not included on albums. Nonetheless, if this was the intention of the new record – to establish a theme and pen songs around that idea – then it plainly set out initially to be a record of nostalgia, a looking back, rather than a celebration of the contemporary, a comment on the particular style and spirit of that dynamic era unfolding as 1966 slipped into 1967.

If we are to move on to the songs that actually made the final cut, while we can still discern strands of the nostalgic within the record's song cycle – 'When I'm 64' and 'Being for the Benefit of Mr. Kite' fit this bill in various ways – there is scant evidence that the Liverpool autobiographical thread actually survived, once 'Strawberry Fields Forever' and 'Penny Lane' had been discarded for practical, commercial reasons rather than artistic ones. MacDonald remarks of the move: 'Apart from putting them back to square one with the new album, the decision killed the informal concept of an LP drawing inspiration from their Liverpool childhoods.'[34]

Let us now approach the finished article instead from a different position: how far can we recognise the values and concerns of the hippies of Haight-Ashbury and, by implication their Summer of Love project, in the album that was made publicly available? And to what extent are the songs on the record and, indeed, the Peter Blake-Jann Haworth conceived sleeve – such an integral part of this overall package – expressing ideas that are quite unconnected to the spirit of that time?

As templates for this consideration I would like to return to two quotes cited earlier in this piece – the view of a hippy who refers to the key importance of 'dope and revolution [...] grass, LSD, meditation, hot music, consolidation, and a

---

[30] Ian MacDonald, *Revolution in the Head, The Beatles' Records and the Sixties* (London: Pimlico, 2005), p. 215.
[31] *Ibid.*, p. 216.
[32] *Ibid.*, p. 222.
[33] Martin, 1995, p. 26.
[34] MacDonald, 2005, p. 228.

joyous sexuality',[35] and the summary that Hamilton provides: 'Hippies believed in spreading love, freedom, peace, sincerity, and creativity, and they considered acid essential in doing this.'[36]

To begin with 'dope' and 'grass', and the references in 'A Day in the Life' – 'I'd love to turn you on' (which would quickly lead to the BBC banning the song from its playlists) and 'Found my way upstairs and had a smoke/Somebody spoke and I went into a dream' could be construed as references to marijuana but there is no direct link beyond that one song. As for 'LSD', the song 'Lucy in the Sky with Diamonds' has become most famously connected to the hallucinogenic drug and the Lennon-penned lyric suggests a florid, multi-coloured odyssey that may well have been the product or record of an acid trip. That said, Lennon's interest in Lewis Carroll has been widely reported and the song certainly possesses nuances of Alice's adventures. Furthermore, he also claimed that the title of the song – with its apparently obvious nod to LSD – was inspired not by a drug but by a children's drawing. It begs the question why would Lennon have wanted to disguise the source of this song at all, even if his explanation appears to be rather disingenuous and ultimately banal? MacDonald comments that 'it was naturally assumed to be a coded reference to LSD. In fact, no such code was intended and, though the lyric explicitly recreates the psychedelic experience, the Beatles were genuinely surprised when it was pointed out to them'.[37] The death of a driver in 'A Day in the Life' – 'He blew his mind out in a car' – hints that the man who died – thought to be based on wealthy socialite and Beatles associate Tara Browne – had taken a drug that was mind-altering in some fashion, which also tarnished the public reception of the piece. There is a further suggestion of drug use in 'A Little Help from My Friends', with some readings assuming 'friends' is simply a euphemism for drugs and the line 'I get high with a little help from my friends' seems to at least, in part, support the case.[38] The track 'Fixing a Hole' has also attracted comment, in respect of its drug innuendo, as the title hints at the addict's use of the needle, though McCartney has discounted this.[39]

'Meditation' we can link to George Harrison's one compositional outing on the record. 'Within You Without You', with its sitar refrain, extra Indian instrumentation and Hindu inspired text, reflected that interest that was being expressed in matters oriental among the hippy generation, though it must be said that it was Buddhism and particularly Zen Buddhism – an inheritance from the Beat

---

[35] Quoted in Hamilton, 1997, p. 133.
[36] *Ibid.*
[37] MacDonald, 2005, p. 240.
[38] Interestingly MacDonald makes no mention of the word 'high'. He also mis-names the track 'With a Little Help from My Friends'.
[39] See McCartney's explanation in Heylin, 2007, p. 130.

writers like Ginsberg, Kerouac and Snyder[40] – that was engaging many young Californians by the mid- and later 1960s, a legacy, too, of the West Coast's links to Japan and the Pacific Rim, a trend prompted, at least in part, by that geographical proximity. The Beatles would, during 1967, take an active personal interest in the spiritual teachings of the Maharishi Mahesh Yogi, an association driven mainly by Harrison, but certainly consistent with a general feeling among many young Westerners that Eastern religions may offer possible spiritual answers to their own personal dilemmas. Of the one Harrison song on *Sgt. Pepper*, MacDonald says: 'Stylistically, it is the most distant departure from the staple Beatles sound in their discography and an altogether remarkable achievement for someone who had been acquainted with Hindustani classical music for barely eighteen months.'[41]

'Hot music' may be interpreted in various ways. Hot had become an adjective associated with upbeat, frenetic jazz by the 1920s, and there are strong suggestions that the term also connotes passion, sex even, though the phrase also has connotations of state-of-the-art or cutting-edge. By the mid-1960s, in Haight-Ashbury, the hot music of the time would almost certainly have been represented by a raft of emerging acid rock of bands, whose guitar players Jorma Kaukonen, Jerry Garcia and John Cippollina particularly, were coaxing amplified, electric sounds from their instruments which were frequently felt to signify sonic representations of the hallucinogenic experience in concert and also on record. We might certainly see some of the guitar experimentation of the Bay Area as having some effect on the subsequent inventions and histrionics of Jimi Hendrix, who came from Seattle, further north on America's West Coast, but had arrived in the UK by 1966. Nor should we ignore the experiments of British groups such as Pink Floyd and Soft Machine who, from the middle of the decade, had been producing sounds that drew in equal measure on electronics, improvisation and psychedelics.[42] How far did these forms of 'hot music' inform the content of *Sgt. Pepper*? It would seem quite little. While there is some outstanding rock guitar work on the album – for instance, McCartney's searing performance on the title track, a replacement solo for one Harrison had toiled seven hours to perfect only to see it end up on the cutting room floor[43] – there is scant sense that the sounds of California are permeating the Beatles' opus, even those more conventional vocal innovations that the Beach Boys had brought to *Pet Sounds* in all their multi-tracked glory in 1966, often regarded as the benchmark that the Beatles aimed to surpass with their next LP. The UK-centred innovations – which McCartney had certainly witnessed at

---

40 See, for example, Coupe, 2007.
41 MacDonald, 2008, p. 244.
42 For background see Heylin, 2007.
43 MacDonald, 2008, p. 233.

venues like the UFO and the Roundhouse – may be discerned to an extent on, say, 'A Day in the Life', but, again, there is little direct connection with the subterranean creativity that Syd Barrett and Daevid Allen and their groups had been working on.

There is some remarkable and memorable musical content on *Sgt. Pepper* – the exquisite chamber setting of 'She's Leaving Home', the head-spinning fairground re-creations of 'Mr. Kite', the sheer scale and scope of 'A Day in the Life' with its two quite distinct sections and extraordinary orchestral climax – but it is hard to equate the songs and sounds here with the styles that were causing excitement in San Francisco at the time. There are many more hints, perhaps, of an idiosyncratic English style – whether the orchestral settings, the music hall elements or the circus evocations – than blatant nods to contemporary American forms. Yet even these Anglicisms are rarely, maybe barely, of the ground-breaking character of those novel soundscapes that were being developed by British bands such as Pink Floyd and Soft Machine, highly inventive material that had been leaving such a strong live impression in the months prior to *Sgt. Pepper*'s minting.

Commenting on the music on the record, George Martin is a useful, if hardly disinterested, touchstone. In *The Summer of Love* he states: '*Sgt. Pepper* was a musical fragmentation grenade, exploding with a force that is still being felt. It grabbed the world of pop music by the scruff of the neck, shook it hard, and left it to wander off, dizzy but wagging its tail. As well as changing the way pop music was viewed, it changed the entire nature of the recording game – for keeps. Nothing even remotely like *Pepper* had ever been heard before'.[44] Perhaps though, he speaks for the production values, the technological innovations, more than for the songs themselves.

The idea of 'consolidation' provides some interesting points for consideration: the communalism of the hippies, the idea of strength *en masse* and the mutual support of the community's members is clearly regarded as significant within the hippy ethos of San Francisco. The Beatles by 1967 were, on the one hand, leaders of a cultural movement but, at the same time, rather distant figureheads. Retiring from touring in 1966, their studio-bound lives and membership of an elite metropolitan circle of artists, musicians and writers inevitably separated them – physically and psychologically – from the people at large. Yet *Sgt. Pepper* is an album that tries to resurrect some of the pleasure of their stage careers and also incorporates some of the sounds that connote not only a 'liveness' but also a desire to connect with an audience again, best symbolised by the title track and its reprise but also in other details of wildtrack – the orchestra tuning up at the start, audience applause at various stages, the suggestion that 'A Little Help From

---

[44] Martin, 1995, pp. 1–2.

My Friends' is an on-stage segue from a live opening number, and the relieving laughter at the end of the serious, solemnity of 'Within You, Without You'. All of these factors, however planned or contrived, hint that the group are wanting to make some link with a wider world, make a gesture of the ordinary, include the quotidian in the midst of their glamorous, star-crossed, yet rather isolated, existences. The Beatles may reach out only theatrically but at least they try to connect.

As for 'joyous sexuality' – and the release of the libido from its social and cultural handcuffs appears crucial to the hippy credo and a keystone to the Summer of Love – how much is that to be encountered in the grooves of *Sgt. Pepper*? In many ways, this is a perversely sex-less recording. There may be hints of platonic affection – 'When I'm 64' – or chummy attraction – 'Lovely Rita' – or even optimism for relationships that may have soured – 'Getting Better' – but the general tone of this album has little in common with the libertarian and intense physical feelings being vigorously played out in the Haight of the time. On the contrary, the album seems, all too often, to be fraught with an air of repression and frustration: the young woman escaping the provinces for the metropolis in 'She's Leaving Home' is not portrayed as a pioneer on the brink of adventure and salvation but a somewhat desperate escapee carrying a burden of sadness. Ultimately, the classic British restraint in sexual areas, the unease at expressing unfettered passion, characterises this collection much more than we might have expected: the liberated mood of the period in matters amorous is little evident in this Beatles collection.

What of Hamilton's own overview? 'Hippies believed in spreading love, freedom, peace, sincerity, and creativity, and they considered acid essential in doing this'.[45] To what degree can we perceive *Sgt. Pepper* to be aligned with such notions? 'Love', 'freedom' and 'peace' are touched upon only in the most passing or abstract of senses and barely in a celebratory fashion: the album provides no explicit and ringing endorsement of these values. Sincerity is more difficult still to identify. By the time of this record, the Beatles had adopted an alter ego of sorts – the fictional band of the title – which gave this LP its constructed and staged, even artificial, flavour.[46] Authentic feelings are not entirely absent – Lennon's 'A Day in the Life' and 'Good Morning', McCartney's 'Getting Better' and Harrison's 'Within You Without You' may possess elements of the autobiographical – but numerous of the pieces are closer to the model of McCartney's 'novelist' songs[47] ('Sgt. Pepper',

---

[45] Hamilton, 1997, p. 133.

[46] Andrew Goodwin, 'Popular music and postmodern theory', *Cultural Studies*, Vol. 5, No. 2, 1991, pp. 174–90, explores issues of authenticity and artifice in various key rock acts including the Beatles.

[47] MacDonald describes Lennon's scorn at McCartney's 'novelist' songs: 'These stories about boring people doing boring things – being postmen and secretaries and writing home. I'm not interested in third-party songs. I like to write about me, cos I *know* me' (2005, p. 239).

'Lucy', 'Rita', 'She's Leaving Home' and 'When I'm 64') than symbols of genuine, personal revelation.

As for 'creativity', we can hardly question the album's richness in this respect, building still further on the advancements of *Rubber Soul* (1965) and *Revolver* (1966). This *magnum opus* was the product of months of artistic imagination and technological experiment: the result of hundreds of hours of team-work between the Beatles themselves, George Martin and his principal engineers Geoff Emerick and Ken Scott. Yet, for all that, this was hardly a creative exercise of the sort that the hippies might have either realised or recognised. The group and their collaborators were working within congenial, if hardly state-of-the-art,[48] studio conditions sponsored by one of the most powerful entertainment businesses in existence, a high-end venture orchestrated by a major industrial conglomerate. The fact that label EMI – 'the greatest recording organisation in the world'[49] – owned the Abbey Road studios where the work was done produced an irresistible symbiosis. The Beatles, the leading name in global music-making at the time and a copper-bottomed certainty to produce a profitable outcome from their extended endeavours, had as much time as they needed to perfect their aesthetic vision, a luxury afforded to few acts, before or indeed since. While Lennon, McCartney and co. may have tipped their hats to traditional notions of the visiting muse or the spontaneous combustions of an individual, creative force, there is no question that *Sgt. Pepper* owed as much to the 'white heat of technology', to appropriate one of Prime Minister Harold Wilson's slogans of the time,[50] as to the auton-omous expression of the artist or the kind of organic romanticism and pastoral naturalism that many of the hippies had, by now, espoused.

The cover of *Sgt. Pepper* is a subject we cannot ignore in this consideration, as the sleeve – and the accompanying artefacts that were included within the package[51] – arguably goes further than the musical contents within as a vivid, visual realisation of the moment. The dazzling colour scheme – brilliant reds, yellows and the fluorescent shades of the band outfits – arguably speaks more eloquently of the optimisms of that summer than the songs themselves. The principal image, devised by Peter Blake and Jann Haworth from an original concept by McCartney then photographed by Michael Cooper,[52] is a potent distil-lation of the eclectic energy of that hippy summer. The Beatles adopt the guise of

---

[48] See Heylin's comment on Abbey Road's four-track recording facilities (2007, p. 10) but the ingenuity of the recording team stretched the technology's potential to the limit.

[49] A statement incorporated into EMI's own logo; see cover of *Sgt. Pepper*.

[50] See Brian Walden's account at 'The white heat of Wilson', BBC News, 31 March 2006, http://news.bbc.co.uk/1/hi/magazine/4865498.stm [accessed 12 October 2007].

[51] A card sheet featuring cut-out details from the Edwardian band outfits was included as an insert. The rear of the sleeve also included, for the first time, song lyrics.

[52] See Natalie Rudd, 2003, pp. 54–7.

turn-of-the-century bandsmen, albeit psychedelically re-tinted, a clear nod to the tendency of the hippy community to blend emblems of the natural and organic – characteristics included long-hair, bare-feet and jettisoning of the bra – with a set of carnivalesque references to the past: the Victorian and Edwardian, Art Nouveau and Symbolism. Add, too, that the collaged crowd who gather include Bob Dylan and Beat guru William Burroughs, a number of Indian mystics chosen by Harrison, pot plants and a reference to the Rolling Stones, the striking wax figure of Sonny Liston, a black sporting hero at the height of the Civil Rights push, and (an absent) Gandhi (who was meant to appear but was excised after legal advice) and we have a powerful concoction of the individuals and ideas informing the artistic, cultural, political and spiritual world of 1967. Yet, we shouldn't forget that in the midst of this fantastical convention lurks Adolph Hitler, conveniently hidden by the living, day-glo Beatles, suggesting that there was more than an air of a cheeky prank behind the making of the image and not merely a notion of phantasmagoric good vibes.

But to return to our key questions – was this creative product, in any real sense, a musical mantra to the Summer of Love and its expressions, to hippiedom and its subcultural value system, to the counterculture and its political concerns of that period? The Summer of Love would disintegrate almost as quickly as it had taken shape: the swallows of the gentle revolution would speedily fly off to other climes and times, with the more threatening invocations of the spring of 1968 to come. The idealism that may have lain at the root of the 1967 project was de-railed, in part, by its success. The media had played a part in distorting the ethos of the hippy cause – Farrell reports that *Time* magazine asked that their San Francisco reporters should compile a backgrounder on this 'controversial, cloud-cuckooland miniculture',[53] setting the tone for the mixture of ridicule and misinformation that shaped mainstream press accounts of the place and the venture – but the call to fellow travellers to come to the Bay Area also back-fired on the organising group as so many responded to the appeal. 'By the fall of 1967, the Haight had become so popular that it could not maintain its communitarian voluntarism', he points out.[54] Farber and Bailey comment that the new arrivals were not as able to adapt as those who had been there for some time, building this alternative community. 'Many if not most of the newcomers were poorly equipped for the task at hand. Hip businesses flourished but rape, disease, exploitation, violence and bad drug experiences skyrocketed'.[55] By the end of the summer the Diggers, that group most committed to creating a countercultural space in the Haight, had declared 'the

---

[53] Farrell, 1997, p. 221.
[54] *Ibid.*
[55] Farber and Bailey, 2001, p. 249.

death of Hippie'.[56] Hamilton puts it most directly: 'The Summer of Love crashed, many hippies fled the Haight, and as an alternative society, the district never recovered'.[57]

If we are to make direct connections between the Summer of Love, the Haight and the wider Californian scene and the Beatles, they do exist. As we have mentioned, McCartney was a mover behind the Monterey Festival and Harrison would, that year, actually visit the San Francisco quarter himself to see what was happening there.[58] But the so-called 'quiet Beatle',[59] joined by his then wife Pattie Boyd, endured an unhappy experience while among the residents of the hippy heartland. When Harrison, guitar in hand, proved less than accepting of an unsolicited drug offer, the crowd turned on him and the musician departed unimpressed and deeply unconvinced by the district's peace and love promises. Recalls Boyd:

> It was a slightly unfortunate situation because George and I [...] had taken a tab of acid and gone down to see what Haight-Ashbury was like, thinking it would be rather like the King's Road in London. And we walked down Haight-Ashbury and these people started walking towards us and they all looked quite beautiful. They all had flowers in their hair and long flowing robes, carrying babies. Then I realised they had a slightly mad look, pretty stoned and out of it. I know we were, too, but there was something quite odd about everybody being stoned. I heard a voice saying, do you want some drug. And George said, 'No, no, I'm fine'. And this man turned around to everybody and said: 'George Harrison turned me down'. At that point the crowd became nasty and angry.[60]

Ultimately though, despite these first-hand links – positive and negative – which the Beatles forged with the West Coast scene, *Sgt. Pepper* seems, in retrospect, a less than ideal representation of that broader period for the reasons we have described. Perhaps the best-remembered musical evocation of the time remains Scott McKenzie's 'San Francisco', with a lyric penned by Mamas and Papas member John Phillips, which not only carried the parenthetical legend 'Be Sure to Wear Some Flowers in Your Hair' in its subtitle, summing up quite brilliantly within that image the airy, sunny and fruitful possibilities that the Summer of Love appeared to promise, but also, along the way, enjoying significant commercial success on

---

[56] *Ibid.*

[57] *Ibid*, p. 294.

[58] Harrison's visit occurred on 8 August 1967 (see Trynka, 2004, p. 263).

[59] See 'George Harrison: The quiet Beatle', obituary, BBC News, 30 November 2001, http://news.bbc.co.uk/1/hi/entertainment/music/1432634.stm [accessed 18 February 2012].

[60] Pattie Boyd interviewed on *Woman's Hour*, BBC Radio 4, 27 August 2007.

the singles charts – a number one song in the UK and a Top 5 spot in the US – something that *Sgt. Pepper* itself was quite unable to generate, its intended golden musical nuggets, 'Strawberry Fields' and 'Penny Lane', issued in advance of the LP and destined never to even assume album track status.

Yet there is no little irony that, if the Beatles' highest profile long player was not genuinely able to embody the energy and excitements of the time, the group would, within slightly over four weeks of *Sgt. Pepper*'s unwrapping, write and perform a new piece for a global, satellite television broadcast that would express, in its three minutes or so, the core of the message the hippies had fought to impart over the previous months. Thus it was, a little after the main fanfare, we were able to experience conceivably the perfect song for the Summer of Love. 'All You Need is Love', the anthemic work unveiled in late June to an audience running into the hundreds of millions[61] and released as a single in July, represented, in many respects, the core theme of the original Haight-Ashbury campaign expressed in universal terms to a worldwide community. By then, although the Beatles' and Scott McKenzie's post-*Sgt. Pepper* releases would provide a mellifluous radio soundtrack for listeners across the UK and the US, the Summer of Love, at least that celebration forged in its founding city of San Francisco, had descended into over-populated chaos and the hopes that the Haight could form a regenerative model in the struggle against strife, domestic and international, had essentially crumbled.

Yet the remarks of Caroline Coon, British cultural and political activist, founder of the drug support agency Release, rock journalist with *Melody Maker* and later manager of the Clash, speaking on British radio on the 40th anniversary of the Summer of Love, provide a useful coda. If the original momentum of that campaign appeared to peter out all too quickly, she sees things with a different perspective and in a broader context. 'We won,' she states. 'Everything the hippy generation was fighting for in terms of green politics, gender politics, race politics, sex politics, is actually now the norm. There are still struggles, but the kind of authoritarian right wing, as we all know today, has had to come into the centre ground. And so the Summer of Love has an absolutely lasting and abiding influence.'[62] *Sgt. Pepper*, too, achieved an enduring reputation yet, as this account proposes the links between one subcultural demonstration and the other musical artefact are not as obvious, not as prevalent, as we may have expected. Further, we may see the Beatles' album as the beginning of the end for the grandiose rock statement. If it was also regarded as the first concept album and also a clear sign that the currency of the single had been superseded by the pre-eminence of the

---

[61] *Our World* was a live television show linking 24 countries and screened on 25 June 1967. See MacDonald, 2005, p. 261.
[62] Caroline Coon interviewed on *Woman's Hour*, BBC Radio 4, 27 August 2007.

long player, it was also a moment when some musicians began the trail towards a simpler, less complex approach to music-making, a gradual turn to a more primitive, back-to-basics strategy. The album that many in the following decade would cite as the most affecting on the punk and new wave movements would also emerge at the beginning of the Summer of Love, pre-dating *Sgt. Pepper* by a matter of weeks but unveiled to a far more muted fanfare. Released in April, *The Velvet Underground & Nico* was spare, minimal and dissonant in sound, a darker manifesto set against the peace and love credo of the hippies. While it would not strike commercial gold then, its impact on the generations of bands that would follow from the early 1970s would be arguably greater still than the Beatles' masterpiece, a remarkable technical triumph, yes, but less a snapshot of its immediate cultural times than has often been assumed.

Q&A 4

Levi Asher, founder of Beat website *Literary Kicks*

Levi Asher is the founder of *Literary Kicks*, the world's longest running book blog, and is the author of several new e-books including *Why Ayn Rand is Wrong (and Why It Matters)* and *Beats In Time: A Literary Generation's Legacy*. Levi works as a technology consultant for arts, culture and government websites, and splits his time between New York City and Washington, DC.

What do you feel rock music has taken from Beat culture?

Lots of things – a sense of pure, radical aestheticism, an appreciation of spontaneous fun. Many themes including political protest, awareness of nature, satire of popular culture.

Is there a lyrical connection there, a musical one or was it merely an anti-authoritarian stance?

Both, for sure!

Where do you see Beat influence in the rock music of the last half century?

The most obvious connection is Bob Dylan. He has made it explicitly clear at many points in his career that he wants his work to be seen as part of the Beat Generation continuum. He's proud of his Beat influence, and that says a lot.

What do you feel the Beats' take was on early rock 'n' roll?

As I understand it, Allen Ginsberg was an instant fan and 'got it' from minute one. Jack Kerouac was very fond of jazz and show tunes – his girlfriend Helen Weaver emphasises in her memoir how much the Original Broadway Cast recording of *My Fair Lady* meant to him.[1]

What do you think the Beats made of that post-Dylan/Beatles rock world?

Ginsberg was incredibly open-minded and agreeable by nature – and I admire this very much about him – and took to every kind of music. His recordings with the Clash are actually fun to listen to. His song 'Birdbrain', which to me resembles the clever work of Frank Zappa or solo John Lennon, is among his best work. Ginsberg totally got rock 'n' roll, and rock 'n' roll got him back.

Other than Ginsberg, I can't think of many examples to indicate that the Beats had a good understanding of rock music, though Ferlinghetti did appear in the Band's movie *The Last Waltz*.

Michael McClure has worked with Ray Manzarek of the Doors, and I caught one of their live shows at the Bottom Line in New York City. I think McClure is a great poet and a great Beat, but I was disappointed in this collaboration, especially when McClure read verses against Manzarek keyboard parts from actual Doors songs. This only emphasized the fact that McClure's poetry was not actually music. Jim Morrison is a hard act to replace. This is one case where I thought the Beat/rock collaboration didn't work.

Neal Cassady hung around with the early Grateful Dead, of course. But is there any evidence to indicate that he actually enjoyed listening to them?[2] He was a jazz fan, like Kerouac. Jerry Garcia had jazz chops, but they weren't so sharp in the early years. Neal Cassady probably would have liked the Dead's best work, which dated from the early to mid-1970s, if he could have lived to hear it.

I also didn't think Kurt Cobain's collaboration with William S. Burroughs amounted to much. I'm not sure if there was much specific chemistry between the Beats and rock music, but the question can only be answered on an individual level. Every case is different.

What drew Dylan to Ginsberg – and Ginsberg to Dylan?

---

[1] Dave Moore, personal communication, email, 28 May 2012, comments: 'Helen Weaver, in her memoir, also writes about Jack's love of rock 'n' roll during the late 1950s'.

[2] Dave Moore, personal communication, email, 28 May 2012, believes there is evidence that Neal enjoyed the rock music of the mid-1960s. In a letter of 30 August 1965 to Ken Kesey: 'I forgot to mention that Sunday night, after seeing Hell's Angel Frenchie, we, despite my protestations of fatigue, went to see a R. & R. group that Chan insisted on observing – well, who was it? that's rite – Signe & The HiWires or the Sextones or the Jefferson Hi Bandits, our pals, ya know; & they sounded great, esp. on one about a "Hi Flyin' Bird"'. (Note: The band would become better known as Jefferson Airplane). See Moore, 2005, p. 441. Also: 'went bar-hopping to hear some great Rock & Roll …', *ibid.*, p. 447.

As I understand it, Dylan was mainly into Kerouac. I think he really identified with *On the Road* and the other Kerouac books. I know he appreciated Ginsberg and Corso, too.

Burroughs seemed to have little affinity with rock music yet he was adopted as a guru from the early 1970s? Why was that?

Because he was so weird and cool and stylish, and a few rockers had great taste!

Who would you identify as the key rock musicians who have drawn on the Beat legacy?

Again, definitely Bob Dylan. Bob Dylan, in his mind, he *was* a part of the Beat Generation – the Beats' final phase. Interestingly, he eventually became even more popular and influential than any of the Beats ever did.

Are there any particular tracks you feel personify this spirit in Dylan?

I'd name 'Tangled Up In Blue', his great romantic song. There are no Beat references, yet I can only imagine that Dylan wrote this as a Kerouac novel. 'I lived with them on Montague Street, a basement down the stairs'. When the song swoops suddenly towards a book of Italian poetry from the thirteenth century, I feel Gregory Corso coming through.

When rock has expressed itself politically in the last half century has it owed something to the original idealism or activism of the Beats?

Absolutely! And I'm so glad this influence was there. Imagine how much poorer our classic rock would be without the political angle.

Is there a sense that the Beat spirit survives in rock music of today?

I can only say – yes! The music of today that I hear from my kids, their teens and early 20s, is just as folksy, rambling, punk, anarchist and crazy – BEAT – as ever. I'm also very impressed by the aestheticism of hip-hop: the emphasis on spontaneity, the romanticised autobiographies, the collaborative spirit. These features seem very Beat to me. I've written on *Literary Kicks* that Jay-Z resembles Jack Kerouac more than anybody else I can think of: like Kerouac's, his entire body of work adds up to a single never-ending autobiography.

INTERVIEW 5

Ronald Nameth, Beat film-maker and director of the film of the *Exploding Plastic Inevitable*

Ronald Nameth has worked in the field of experimental cinema in a career spanning more than 40 years, earning him an international reputation. Born in Detroit but today based in Sweden, Nameth's activities as film-maker and promoter of the alternative film culture continue. In the 1960s, his ground-breaking incorporation of electronics and video to create 'visual music' established him as an important innovator. That aspiration, to test and extend the boundaries of the medium, persists. In 1966, Nameth became closely involved with perhaps the most high profile multi-media event of an extraordinarily creative decade. Andy Warhol's *Exploding Plastic Inevitable*, a performance piece combining a dazzling array of art-forms – visuals, sound and light, film, dance and rock music with the Velvet Underground a central feature – had already attained a significant status in New York City.

When the production re-located to Chicago for a short residency, an opportunity arose to document the event. Nameth, by now based in that city, spent a week filming the show's performances at a club called Poor Richard's, eventually creating a widely acclaimed documentary that strove to capture the multiplicity of simultaneous features evident in the Warhol installation.

Later technology – the emergence of digital formats, primarily – enabled Nameth to re-produce his multi-perspective recording of the installation and construct an environment in which the film could be experienced by the viewer on a series of screens at the same time, replicating the multi-sensory components of the original 'happening'.

I first encountered this remarkable presentation in Seattle at the Experience Music Project popular music conference in spring 2005. Shortly afterwards,

Nameth's documentary became part of a major touring exhibition celebrating the artistic explosion of the 1960s. *Summer of Love: Art of the Psychedelic Era* was initially seen at Tate Liverpool and would move to Frankfurt and Vienna during late 2005 and early 2006.

It was at the Seattle screening of his documentary that Ronald Nameth and I first discussed the possibility of creating a film which might respond to the poem 'Howl' and its 50th anniversary in October 2005. The plan, to present a multi-disciplinary, commemorative event, *Howl for Now*, in the UK, provided a further catalyst to the film project which Nameth hoped to develop. While the celebration took place, as intended, at Leeds University and the event was filmed, the production process stands in abeyance. However, the discussions that arose as a result of this proposed collaboration were fertile.

In this interview, the film-maker discusses the impact of the Beats on his life as a teenage American, the emergence of an alternative film culture in the US of the Sixties, his involvement with the celebrated Warhol installation, and his thoughts on the creation of a film work which might reflect the spirit and energy of Allen Ginsberg's 'Howl'.

SW **How did the idea of a film linked to the 'Howl' anniversary emerge?**

RN It was really raised by our meeting in Seattle, when we were both attending the 2005 conference, at the Experience Music Project. You mentioned your plans for a project called *Howl for Now*, to celebrate the fiftieth anniversary of the inaugural reading of Ginsberg's poem 'Howl'. Your description of this celebration brought up a lot of old, almost forgotten memories of my own experience of reading 'Howl' for the first time, in the late 50s.

I was about 16 years old, living in Detroit, USA, and was in full rebellion. I had found in the writings of the Beats, a perfect mirror of my intense feelings at that time. They inspired me – primarily by the way they gave themselves the freedom to experience life intensely. Their search for themselves 'in the now' touched my own yearnings and I eagerly devoured everything I could read. As they threw themselves into their lives without reservation, their experiences opened the door in me to the possibility of a life lived fully.

Jack Kerouac and Allen Ginsberg had an especially strong impact on me. Their total abandonment to life was in stark contrast to the tied down, fear-filled life of middle-class society in the 1950s. Ginsberg's rage in that decade against the numbing and dumbing of society was a perfect mirror of my own feelings. Later in the 1960s, Ginsberg's presence and his activities became a major element in the emerging alternative life style. It was incredible to see his clear stance and lack of fear in facing off to the establishment. His actions were a powerful message to many people.

SW   **The Beats clearly impacted on you but how did you become involved in the creative arts yourself?**

RN   As the Beat was transformed into the hip, and the hippy and alternative movements expanded through the expanded consciousness of LSD, I became involved with making experimental films in Chicago. Working together in collaboration with other artists and musicians, many films were made as well as numerous trips to Mexico and San Francisco.

    Some years later, I moved to the Champaign-Urbana area south of Chicago, into a community filled with creative people of all types. The new emerging technology of electronics was utilized to create visual music. Working all night at the university's Electronic Music Studio (after the electronic music composers had gone home to sleep), electronically-generated sounds were utilized to create moving forms with colour. These were then transferred to film.

    This creative environment resulted in many collaborations with many creative people such as Steve Beck, the electronic synthesis engineer, Al Haung the Chinese Ta'i Chi master and dance performer, composer Salvatore Martirano, poet M. C. Holloway, John Cage, the musical inventor, the musician Michael Lytle, and many others.

SW   **There was evidently a hot-house of artistic talent gathered in Chicago but, of course, Andy Warhol's links were principally with Manhattan. How did you come to connect with his *Exploding Plastic Inevitable* project?**

RN   As I got involved in multi-media performances and light shows for music performances, I also created multiple-screen film environments – in particular for John Cage's first Musicircus and the Cage/Hiller HPSCHD music event in with 9,000 people participated. This work led to a contact with Andy Warhol's *Exploding Plastic Inevitable*, which was Warhol's most developed multi-screened multimedia environment.

    To create the *EPI*, Warhol collaborated with some of the most creative people in their fields. In music, he collaborated with the Velvet Underground, composed of some of the most advanced rock musicians of the time, including Lou Reed, John Cale, Sterling Morrison, Mo Tucker, and the singer/actress Nico. Once adjusted to the initial sonic blast of the Velvet Underground, the listener could hear the undertones of R&B, improvisations of free jazz as well as the musical avant-garde and the mystical drone of LaMonte Young.

    In November 1965, after completing several films in the dual-screen format, Warhol undertook to create his first multi-screened, multimedia environment for the Expanded Cinema Festival at the Film-makers' Cinematheque in New York. Warhol then recruited the professional film editor, Danny Williams, who later became involved in the design the light environment for the *EPI*.

It was in April 1966 that the first manifestation of the *Exploding Plastic Inevitable* took place at the Dom, a former Polish dance hall turned club in New York, attracting many people and a great deal of publicity and media. The film-maker Barbara Rubin and poet Allen Ginsberg were among the personalities participating, as was the well-known news anchorman Walter Cronkite, who came by to see what was happening, as did Jackie Kennedy and much of New York's society. It became a major culture happening as news crews reported on the scene.

Warhol said of this time: 'We all knew something revolutionary was happening. We just felt it. Things could not look this strange and new without some barrier being broken'.

SW **So Warhol's show was clearly making waves and attracting high profile interest. How did the film project itself get off the ground?**

RN Warhol's production then came to Chicago for a residency at Poor Richard's. During one week of performances of the *EPI* in June 1966, I worked every night filming, to make a comprehensive recording of the event. Because the *EPI* environment is a multiple screen projection environment, the film utilised multiple level super-impositions of imagery that sometimes reaches a depth of five layers. The film works extensively with the experience of time through its changing rhythms of motion. The film material was the only extensive motion picture document of the *EPI*. This film material was to create several versions in order to present as complete a document as possible – one version was for single screen projection while another version was for a 4-screen video installation that recreates the spatial experience and environment of the *EPI*. A photographic exhibition was also created.

SW **What sort of reaction was generated by the *Exploding Plastic Inevitable*?**

RN There are various critical and academic responses worth re-visiting, I think. Kate Butlers, a journalist wrote about the *EPI*, saying: 'The *Exploding Plastic Inevitable*, generated during the 1960s, has often been cited as the pioneering multimedia experience. Audiences were bombarded with floor to ceiling projections of Warhol films such as *Vinyl*. At centre stage, the Velvet Underground were transported with Warhol-directed lighting effects. Images filled the show that were disturbing and abrasive as Lou Reed's songs. Collaboration between artists and musicians had never before, or since, proved so influential despite its short life span.'

Later, Branden W. Joseph, the art historian at the University of California, wrote: 'The *Exploding Plastic Inevitable* remains as the strongest and most developed example of intermedia art. Although (other) productions [...] have since achieved greater technical dexterity on a visual plane, no one has yet managed to communicate a guiding spirit through the complex form as well as Warhol and the Underground.'

SW **How would you describe your own aesthetic approach to documenting this phenomenon?**

RN In filming the *EPI*, my intention was not to create a documentary, but instead to create a light/sound experience that would allow the viewer to experience, to some extent the actual event, without any verbal description. Since *EPI* was a multiple-screen, multi-sensory experience, and since I had only one screen (the film) I chose to use multiple levels of super-imposed imagery together, to come as close to the original experience as was possible.

There were also a number of technical limitations that would affect the making of the film. First, no artificial light would be used, as this would have destroyed the environment of lights and projected imagery. Yet, at the same time, film in the Sixties was not particularly light-sensitive. To solve this problem, I operated the camera at one third the normal speed, thus allowing more light to reach the film surface. Normally, when film is projected at 8 frames a second, instead of the normal 24 frames a second, it results in a choppy, speeded-up effect.

To avoid this, each frame of the recorded film was put into a device known as a contact printer, and each frame was then printed three times, thus creating 24 fames per second. This resulted in a kind of freeze-effect, in which normal motion is slightly frozen in a short space of time. This effect transformed 'normal' reality into a kind of other-worldly place – a slight warp of time and space. This time/space warp was then edited and super-imposed into a depth of five levels of imagery.

The cinematic style of *EPI*, and in most of my films is quite impressionistic – there seems a strong sense of atmosphere over form, suggestion over narrative, the implicit over the explicit. Atmosphere, suggestion, non-narrative, and the implied – all these are forms which allow one to go beyond the logical, rational mind, into realms that cannot be accurately presented with words.

When the technology of DVD discs became available, it was then possible to expand the original recordings of the *EPI* into a four-screen video environment, so that a space with multiple-screens could be created to provide a more intense experience of the original event.

SW **You have intentions to work on a film commemorating 'Howl' and its 50th anniversary. Could you describe how you might approach this project?**

RN For the planned production of the film to celebrate 'Howl''s 50th anniversary, the intention is to present a multi-faceted expression of the poem through the live performance *Howl for Now*. By presenting 'Howl' as a multi-faceted experience, via music, drama and monologue, the intention is to touch upon Ginsberg's original experiences and mirror the reality he projected in his original poem.

As with *EPI*, the *Howl for Now* production will work with multi-media and with a multi-disciplinary subject – spoken word, drama, music, imagery. Like *EPI*, it is intended to be in a single-screen form, as well as a multiple-screen video installation environment. Each of these forms will present 'Howl' in a way that is appropriate for that particular structure.

A lot of contemplation has gone into how to approach this work. There is a clear sense of what needs to be film, and what needs to be captured. At the same time, it is impossible to plan entirely – as reality always provides surprises. So, much reflection and contemplation will also be given while in the editing process. It is here that the creative process continues, and one finds the threads that will create the reality of the film and the form for the multiple-screen video installation environment.

Considerable thought has already been given to the form of the single-screen version. Several recordings are planned. The first will be of the live event, which sets the tone and mood for the dramatic aspect of the work, as the participants and performers will be in the space with a live audience.

In a second recording session, I plan to physically move into the space onstage and work directly in the performance space so that I can interact directly with the performers. They will thus be able to perform directly into the eye of the camera.

A third recording session is envisioned, in which the performers are moved from the stage, into the outside world – into streets and alleyways, again performing directly for the camera. Additional imagery will be gathered and edited into these recordings. This imagery will be indicative of the period of the Fifties and mirror the depth of experience in 'Howl'.

In film and video recording process, one works sequentially, first to gather together all the various elements necessary to the piece. One could perhaps compare it to the cooking of a meal. First, one must have all the necessary ingredients. When everything necessary is available; then comes the work of mixing everything. With traditional editing, conscious decisions are made to structure the material. One can also involve the use of chance operations (such as those of Burroughs or of Cage), so that the rational, logical, ego-mind is set aside in this process and thus allow unexpected combinations and juxtapositions to occur.

The single-screen version is most often shown in the context of a film projection environment, which means that people sit in chairs and watch the screen from beginning to end. That is, if they don't fall asleep of boredom or leave in exasperation or desperation! So, this aspect has to be taken into consideration.

The multiple-screen video installation environment offers a very different environment compared to traditional single-screen film viewing, since the viewer is free to walk freely in the space, and choose their own experience of how they wish to experience the space. This is similar to the act of viewing a painting in a gallery, or simply moving about in one's daily life. Here, there is no suspension of reality, as in the traditional film presentation. Instead, one is free in time and space to move and select one's own experience of the work.

In an environment with multiple screens, the use of a traditional visual language is not vital or necessary – one is free to allow juxtapositions of image, form and movement that would not work in a single-screen situation. Here, chance has a greater opportunity to play, and to allow the viewer to become the participant in the experience of the space. With the possibility of creating two very different experiences of Ginsberg's poem as presented in *Howl for Now*, the intention is to provide a multi-faceted, in-depth and varied experience of that will reveal the depth of Ginsberg's vision, and mirror the reality he experienced.

Author's note: *Howl for Now* was presented on 7 October 2005 at the Clothworkers' Centenary Concert Hall, School of Music, University of Leeds. The event, which took place half a century later to the night of Ginsberg's first reading of 'Howl' at the Six Gallery in San Francisco, featured a reading of the poem and six new musical works composed in tribute to the verse work. Although a DVD record of the occasion was produced, Ronald Nameth's scheme to adapt the material for a more ambitious, multi-screen production remains on the drawing board.

7 THE MELTZER CHRONICLES: POET, NOVELIST, MUSICIAN AND HISTORIAN OF BEAT AMERICA

In 1995–96, a major exhibition was mounted in the US, celebrating the Beat Generation and its legacy, showcasing among other prized artefacts, the vast paper roll on which Jack Kerouac had typed the original draft of his hugely influential 1957 novel *On the Road*. The exhibition, *Beat Culture and the New America: 1950–1965*, opened in New York in late 1995, then visited Minneapolis and San Francisco during 1996 and spawned a substantial and impressive hardback catalogue,[1] gathering images and essays reflecting on that moment in American letters when literature reached out to embrace art, cinema, music, theatre and life itself.

An early pair of photographs in the exhibition guide capture the social fracture of the times – the consumer-driven materialism of the nuclear family and the resistance of a new social formation. In the first, a brushed and gleaming Mom and Pop are framed with kids and dog in front of a brilliant, whitewood home; in the second, in a San Francisco alley, two hipsters in existential black are joined by their small son and an assortment of multi-racial street kids.[2] The pictures are potent enough, juxtaposing mainstream and marginalised America, the sunny hopes of consumerist materialism and the shadowy lives of the refuseniks, but the fact that the young man in the Beat shot, taken by Viennese documentary

---

[1] Lisa Phillips (ed.), *Beat Culture and the New America: 1950–1965*, exhibition catalogue, (New York: Whitney Museum of American Art, 1995).
[2] *Ibid.*, pp. 22–3.

cameraman Harry Redl in 1957, was a rising poet called David Meltzer is more interesting still.

David Meltzer was around the age of 20 when the picture was taken, newly arrived in the Bay Area from the East Coast, starting to make the acquaintance of the giants of the Beat world and their precursors – Allen Ginsberg, Lawrence Ferlinghetti, Kenneth Rexroth and so on – and appearing at the poetry bars and cafés in North Beach which were beginning to proliferate, as part of what became dubbed the San Francisco Poetry Renaissance. In the period that would follow, Meltzer's life as poet, then musician, would take its picaresque shape, performing and publishing, an active contributor to the subversive dramas of a new and rebellious America.

Some years on from the Redl sessions, in December 1965, Meltzer would appear in a more famous photograph – Larry Keenan's documenting of the Beat clan outside City Lights bookshop in San Francisco, featuring Ginsberg, the shop-owner Ferlinghetti, novelist Richard Brautigan, poet and playwright Michael McClure, and many other prominent names from this literary family. Often described as the 'Last Gathering of the Beat Generation',[3] Keenan's much-published image was taken as Bob Dylan visited the city on tour, an event that has been touched upon elsewhere in this collection. The pictures of the Beat group and those memorable images of Dylan with guitarist Robbie Robertson and Ginsberg and McClure, in what was much later re-named Jack Kerouac Street,[4] would become iconic portraits of a fascinating artistic encounter, between two generations who challenged the social establishment in distinctive fashions – through the spoken word, then through music.

Dylan's association with the poets and writers of the Beat Generation has been much commented on, including in this volume. Dylan was included in Ann Charters' substantial anthology *The Portable Beat Reader* (1992) to confirm his status as a Beat icon. Robert Shelton, the *New York Times* journalist credited with penning the earliest and most important reviews of this rising talent, wrote the acclaimed Dylan biography *No Direction Home* (1986). It provides a colourful and engaging overview of Dylan's Beat engagement and the effect of the movement's work on his own song-writing.

Yet the detail of Dylan's initial first-hand entanglement with the members of this literary school has not been widely reported. We know about his consumption of Ginsberg's 'Howl' and Kerouac's *On the Road* in Minnesota coffee houses in 1960,[5] all the way to the extraordinary scenes of the singer and Ginsberg perched at Kerouac's graveside in 1975 on the Rolling Thunder tour, material later utilised

---

[3] Steven Watson, 1995, p. 238.
[4] See Steve Turner, *Angel-Headed Hipster: A Life of Jack Kerouac* (London: Bloomsbury, 1996), p. 212.
[5] Richard Williams, 1992, p. 25.

in the sprawling semi-fictional documentary *Renaldo and Clara*,[6] but when did he first meet a member of the Beat circle? When was he first on speaking terms with a poet who we can regard as a resident of the Beat enclave? When did Dylan turn from being a reader of, a fan of, the Beat word and make personal contact with one of its purveyors and thus join the fringes of that literary coterie? This chapter aims to cast some further light on this matter.

Dylan biographers Anthony Scaduto, and the aforementioned Shelton and Williams[7] don't actually describe Dylan's first encounter with Ginsberg, for instance. However, Barry Miles and Michael Schumacher, approaching the topic from the Ginsberg angle in their biographies of the poet, make a more specific attempt to do so. Miles says that Ginsberg returned with Peter Orlovsky to New York in December 1963, after an extended time away, and would then, soon afterwards, stay at the home of his friend and business associate Ted Wilentz. 'One of their first visitors', Miles says, 'was the journalist Al Aronowitz, who showed up one day with his friend Bob Dylan.'[8] The date is hard to ascertain – a week on? a month after? – though clearly not long after that that December return to Manhattan. Schumacher suggests that the Dylan-Ginsberg meeting took place '[o]ne day in early 1964' when Aronowitz 'who had written the series about the Beat Generation for the *New York Post* stopped by Wilentz's apartment for a visit' with his friend Dylan in tow.[9] Wilentz's son Sean would provide a clearer insight in his 2010 volume *Bob Dylan in America*, when the date of the meeting was placed as 26 December 1963.[10]

But what of earlier encounters than this between Dylan and the Beats? This is where we should return to the part that David Meltzer would play in this important chain of events and his meeting with the singer that would pre-date, by some way, the more high profile liaisons we have touched upon. In late 1997, I was commissioned by the UK Beat Generation magazine *Beat Scene* to profile Meltzer as he set out a short tour of readings around the North of England. When we met, we talked about many things, about poetry, about Ginsberg, about Kerouac, about jazz, but when I asked him about the Larry Keenan photo sessions of 1965 he revealed some intriguing extra background about his early associations with Dylan.[11] Later he annotated these remarks in a correspondence with the author,[12] prefacing his expanded description of events with this comment: 'Much of the

---

[6] *Ibid.*, p. 137.
[7] Anthony Scaduto's *Dylan* (1973), Shelton's *No Direction Home* (1986) and Williams' *Dylan: A Man Called Alias* (1992).
[8] Miles, 1990), p. 333.
[9] Michael Schumacher, 1992, p. 405.
[10] Sean Wilentz, 2010, p. 69.
[11] See Simon Warner, 'David Meltzer', *Beat Scene*, No. 30, 1998.
[12] David Meltzer, personal communication, emails, 20 and 21 April 1999.

encounter I've kept under my hat; have tried to keep a low profile over the decades while mythographers and mythomaniacs concoct their epic narrative of "the good old days".[13] The account that follows draws heavily on both the 1998 interview and the 1999 annotations.

Unlike Dylan, Meltzer did not make it into Charters' *Portable Beat Reader* though she later expressed her regret at his non-inclusion in the UK Beat magazine *Beat Scene*, where she commented: 'I did forget good people. I forgot David Meltzer.'[14] So who was this 'good person' absent from that omnibus? We have already described the young Meltzer's arrival in San Francisco around 1957 and his poetry began to appear soon after in small press editions, and later through acclaimed imprints such as Black Sparrow Press. He also, in 1961, became joint editor, with McClure and Ferlinghetti, of *The Journal for the Protection of All Beings*, 'the era's most interesting periodical',[15] which was a collection noted not only for its writing but also its eco-consciousness, a prescient manifesto to be preaching over 50 years ago.

Meltzer was born in New York in 1937 to artistic parents and grew up in a post-Depression city that seethed with political and social tensions. Although the physical tremors of the Second World War were oceans away, the after-shocks of the Nazi death camps and the nuclear attacks on Hiroshima and Nagasaki left their psychological brand on young and old. He comments: 'From 1945 the world changed. The war was very important in terms of formulating a lot of my work. With the Atomic bomb and the Holocaust, there was a kind of rupture. Teenagers felt they had no future. Culture up to that point had been predicated on progress. When you don't have that as a social glue, other things happen.'[16]

Nonetheless, New York proved a highly educational experience for him. The quarter he grew up in – his family moved to Brooklyn in 1941 – was a rich mixture of 'working class immigrants, Jewish European immigrants, Italian Catholic immigrants. It was an interesting community of old world people and their progeny with their families. So you had the power of the old world with their religions but you also had the Communist Party in its US version, with second and third generations dealing with issues that were brought up by the Depression, the whole question of the Popular Front, the Cold War. On Friday nights, you either had the option of going to the synagogue or going to the CP meetings where

[13] Meltzer, email, 20 April 1999.
[14] Ann Charters quoted in Kevin Ring, 'Ann Charters – A Beat journey', *Beat Scene*, No. 16, 1993.
[15] Dennis McNally, *Desolate Angel: A Biography – Jack Kerouac, the Beat Generation and America* (New York: Random House, 1979), p. 298.
[16] Meltzer quoted Warner, 1998.

all these people in blue shirts, chambray, might bring on an authentic Negro to represent the idea of race relations.'[17]

Meltzer was a child performer who had sung on radio shows but his real musical development stemmed from a live encounter with Charlie Parker in the late 1940s at the Royal Roost on Broadway,[18] helping to cultivate a lifelong devotion to jazz. Yet if jazz was a growing passion, poetry was not far behind. A poem he wrote as an eleven-years-old schoolboy commemorating a Manhattan anniversary was published – 'it was free verse', he says, 'comparing the subway to the arteries of the human body'[19] – and encouraged him to work at his writing skills, too. When his parents, both classical musicians, split up, he headed with his father to California where the new television industries beckoned, making Los Angeles his home from 1952. By the mid-1950s, he recalls seeing the first City Lights publications when he was working on a news-stand in LA 'and then came "Howl" and *On the Road*'. Meltzer remarks: 'As an experimental writer, Kerouac has not yet been acknowledged. With Kerouac there was this notion, that appeals to so many young people today, of men in flight, from women, from problems, from the domestic sphere, that was being so heavily re-defined – the nuclear family and so on.'[20]

In 1956, with the promise of a job in a book warehouse, Meltzer headed north to San Francisco where the literary action seemed to be. He was not disappointed. 'I began to hang out at North Beach, did some poetry readings at the Cellar. It was an Italian community with low rents. They had no problem with people who were artists. In other sectors of American society they'd have set the dogs on us!' So whom did he meet in those early days? 'Ginsberg, of course, Ferlinghetti, Gregory Corso. You name any of those people – it's like the rolling of the titles … Robert Duncan, Gary Snyder, Jack Spicer. As a kind of arts community, people may have been ideologically opposed in terms of the practice of poetry, but there was still a certain amount of socialising and community.'[21] Did anyone make him feel, as a young man in an established grouping, at home? 'There was a lot of generosity when I started working at the Cellar, where people like Kenneth Rexroth, who is a very significant figure by the way, whose role as a conduit for so much of this has become under-valued and overlooked through time, represented part of this tradition of radical arts and politics. He was a Catholic anarchist, very involved

---

[17] Quoted in Warner, 1998.
[18] Jesse Crumb and Erica Detlefsen, 'David Meltzer', No. 30, *Beat Characters*, card collection (Northampton, MA: Kitchen Sink Press, 1995). Note that this source quotes Meltzer's first encounter with Parker as 1946. Dave Moore, personal communication, email, 28 May 2012, believes that Parker did not appear at the Royal Roost until 1948, the year the venue first staged live music.
[19] *Ibid.*
[20] *Ibid.*
[21] *Ibid.*

with other artists during the 1930s and 1940s, with the labour movement in San Francisco and the dock workers and general strikes.'[22]

'There was a sudden escalation in media attention and so many of the younger poets Rexroth had chaperoned into the light were suddenly getting all the publicity. This older man was being ignored because he wasn't young enough. It was an ego thing. Rexroth was like W. C. Fields; he could be a terrible blowhard yet he was a most generous man. But he was from a different period of history and a different politics.' So how did leftist politics fit into the mix by this time? 'Gary [Snyder], for example, came from the North West and his father had been involved with the Wobblies, the Industrial Workers of the World. And Allen Ginsberg, his mother was a Communist. So, many of these people had come out of a background of class-consciousness. Yet none of the people outside Snyder were actually working class. Ginsberg came out of a professional middle class family and Burroughs, of course, came out of the mandarin classes. So much of my difficulty with Burroughs is not that he's not brilliant at the writing but just that boredom was the impetus.'[23]

How then does Meltzer feel that Kerouac, who spent time on the West Coast at various points in the 1950s and early 1960s and attended the Six Gallery in San Francisco reading where Ginsberg's 'Howl' was premiered, may have fitted into this meeting of literature and political doctrine? 'Well, he *was* working class. He lived the life – he couldn't have gone to Columbia, an upper and middle class university, unless he had been a football player. He got one of those token awards given to those work-horses with athletic achievement. But Kerouac's bent was not athletics; it was literature and mysticism. He was a Catholic mystic, lamb-like in the Blakean sense, in the Christian sense, a sacrificial lamb in a sense. He was done in by success American-style. He killed himself systematically, drank himself to death. He was a victim, he had this martyrdom notion, but he was killed by society, by acceptance, a very cruel, parasitical notion of acceptance. Fame, especially in the USA, is manufactured by the whole concept of mass mediated, public relations-driven advertising. The rise of the advertising agency has been a major shaper of reality.'[24]

But surely Kerouac, the freewheeling literary outlaw distanced from society by attitudes and lifestyle, could have evaded such a web? 'He was involved with the myth of the writer as heroic individual', Meltzer states, 'which is a post-Romantic notion, where you get the whole idea of subjectivity. Suddenly, self is what you write about. You are no longer writing about the we, the us; it's the I, the isolated, heroic individual of Shelley and Byron. So he was reading that material and

---

[22] *Ibid.*
[23] *Ibid.*
[24] *Ibid.*

identifying as a kind of working class, abject, excluded, ethnic presence in the community. And the escape was through the imaginary realm of literature and also how you imagine a writer to be – as a kind of grand person.' So, was he unable to manage his own myth – or was it society that forced him, eventually, into that lonely and desperate corner? 'Kerouac was very shy. He was a kind of sacrifice for a post-war, postmodern media culture that essentially re-combined and recreated him in a way that tormented him and ultimately led to his death by fame, exacerbated by drink', he believes.[25]

Meltzer sees television as a crucial factor in the socio-cultural melting pot that the 1950s and 1960s threw up and a catalyst for many of the stresses and strains that artists and radicals faced from then on. 'From 1945, TV was inserted into the brain of the nation. It tripled, quadrupled, became a natural environment which could then, within a few months, neutralise any sort of social critique, whether it was the beatniks, the Black Power movement or the student politics of the Sixties. Ginsberg though was different. He was very comfortable with people. He was never being dishonest – that transparency, that was his great thing. Kerouac just wanted to write the books and feel the feelings, but Ginsberg understood TV at a time when no one really understood TV. He knew how to use it as a vehicle for his own presence and advancement and public de-stabilising tendencies.'[26]

Meltzer wrote poetry – his first published verse appeared in a collection with Donald Schenker in 1957 – and read poetry and performed his work in a jazz setting, the fruits of which were well-exemplified in a much later CD release, *Poet w/Jazz 1958*, not issued until 2006. Recorded at Club Renaissance, Sunset Boulevard, West Hollywood, with Bob Dorough on piano, drummer Chris Harris, trumpeter Ernie Williams and bassist Larry Hornings, it echoes the experiments that Ferlinghetti and Kerouac had embarked on at a similar time, marrying spoken word with musical rhythms. Said Meltzer, of the ten pieces that made up the album, in a letter to producer Jim Dickson: 'The poems on this record were written especially for presentation & interaction with a jazz group. They were written in a tentative language that would, when the music began, improvise & alter & revise and invent new words in dialogue with the music is (*sic*) sound & purpose. I'd bring a skeleton poem – a "head arrangement" of the words – & then would fill it in performance, improvising in the same spirit as the players.'[27] The same year of the jazz poetry recording, Meltzer would marry Tina, and the pair would enjoy collaborative music and poetry projects in the next decade. In 1959 he published a poetry collection entitled *Ragas*, the following year *The Clown*, and these would be the preface to half a century and more of versifying, essay

---

[25] *Ibid.*

[26] *Ibid.*

[27] Meltzer, 'Letter to Jim Dickson, 2 January 1959', CD sleeve notes, *Poet w/Jazz* (Sierra Records, 2005).

writing, novels and interview collections featuring other poets. *The Journal for the Protection of All Beings*, which made its first appearance in 1961 and saw Meltzer rub shoulders with well-established, fellow editors Ferlinghetti and McClure, featured an extraordinary gathering of talent between its covers: Snyder, Corso, Burroughs, Camus, Artaud and Bertrand Russell, Robert Duncan, Norman Mailer and Kenneth Patchen. Published by City Lights, the three editors penned a joint statement: 'We hope we have here an open place where normally apolitical men may speak uncensored upon any subject they feel most hotly & coolly about in a world which politics has made. We are not interested in protecting beings from themselves. We cannot help the deaths people give themselves, we are more concerned with the lives they do not allow themselves to live, and the deaths other people would give us, both of the body & spirit.'[28]

Yet, although it would be as a poet, writer and editor that he would make his cultural mark, Meltzer was also a folk singer, friend of and collaborator with a number of the musicians who would go on to leave an indelible footprint on the rock scene of the 1960s. Among his associates were David Crosby, soon to join the Byrds then, later in the decade, form Crosby, Stills and Nash, Jerry Garcia, an imminent member of the Warlocks quite quickly transformed into a group called the Grateful Dead, and Dino Valente, a songwriter who shared similar rock aspirations and would feature, in time, in the group Quicksilver Messenger Service.

But to step back to the early years of the decade, in spring 1962, almost three years prior to the Keenan Beat photographic session, when Meltzer first heard Dylan's self-titled debut LP, he recalls that he was impressed by the singer's initial recording. 'I remember being knocked out by Dylan's first album and really alerted by his second one. In response to them, I sent Dylan a couple of books of my poetry and wrote a cover letter praising the poetry I saw in his song lyrics.'[29]

He describes the setting at the time: 'Tina and I were part of the "folk revival" scene in San Francisco, mirrored in New York City and other urban centres like Chicago, Los Angeles. We performed either as a duo or with *ad hoc* string bands. During that time there was an influx of New York-based musicians like Eric Andersen, David Crosby, Dino Valente, Jesse Colin Young and Midwest blues people like Nick Gravenites, Charlie Musselwhite, Paul Butterfield, Michael Bloomfield and, from Port Arthur, Texas, came 20-year-old Janis Joplin.'[30]

Meltzer continues: 'Young banjo player, Jerry Garcia, came to the Coffee Gallery from Palo Alto. My playing mate, Jim Gurley, came out of a professional

---

[28] 'Editors' statement', *The Journal for the Protection of All Beings*, edited by Michael McClure, Lawrence Ferlinghetti and David Meltzer, No. 1 (San Francisco, CA: City Lights, 1961), p. 3.
[29] Meltzer, email, 20 April 1999.
[30] *Ibid.*

stunt-car racing background working for his father. He and I used to do experimental acoustic guitar improvisations at the Coffee Gallery before he, like many of us, went electric and became lead guitar for Big Brother. Janis, before electricity, used to sing at Coffee Gallery hootenannies; some of us backed her up while she stood still as a statue, hands clenched into fists stuck to her side and belted out Ma Rainey and Bessie Smith blues.'[31]

Having heard Dylan's premiere long player, Meltzer picks up the story and reveals what happened next. 'About a year later, when he came to San Francisco for his first tour, for which there was no entourage and virtually no audience, he was in some motel in some tacky area of the town and I was brought over by Dino Valente.'[32] Valente would go on to write a classic song of the period entitled 'Let's Get Together' for the Youngbloods, prior to finally joining one of the great Bay Area rock bands in Quicksilver in 1969 after lengthy delays involving a jail sentence linked to a marijuana bust mid-decade. Meltzer explains:

> As an 'outside' guitarist, I used to play behind Dino and he liked what I did. He also knew that I was a poet, which really intrigued him. A powerful presence, a forceful performer and heroic consumer of cannabis. Tina and I visited him at County Jail when he got busted. He sold all rights to 'Come on Everybody Let's Get Together' to Frank Werber, the manager of the Kingston Trio, to get bailed out. Dino was a colleague of Dylan's. When Dylan did his first SF concert, Dino took me to meet him at a cheesy motel off Van Ness Avenue. Dino introduced me as 'the guitarist' and Dylan murmured oblique greetings – but then my name lit up another sequence of correspondences and he asked me if I was the poet. Though I wanted to be the guitarist, I had to admit I was the poet. 'Yeah, man, I dug your books', Dylan said.[33]

He continues: 'A couple of days later, after his final concert, many folkies and marginals congregated at a dimly lit flat off Fillmore where Dylan previewed "Masters of War". When he finished, we talked some more. I was touched by the power and immediacy of the song and told him, "You song writers have the power now", or something equally and generously dramatic. "Oh no," he said, "you poets do".'[34]

Meltzer also recalls his attempts to spread the word on this fresh talent to other friends and contacts. 'I remember saying later to Michael McClure, "You should

---

[31] *Ibid.*
[32] Meltzer quoted in Warner, 1998.
[33] Meltzer, email, 20 April 1999.
[34] *Ibid.*

listen to this guy Dylan", and he said, "Oh, I don't know!" '.[35] He adds: 'I remember pushing Dylan's first two LPs to Michael. Michael had some success with *The Beard* and Ferlinghetti was a "best-selling" poet, a "star" just like Ginsberg was. At first McClure dismissed the recordings. But as "stars", they were smart enough to realise the potential of "the new thing" and wanted to affiliate with it.'[36]

He says: 'I think I was the conduit for Ginsberg and McClure to get in touch with Dylan. I suppose at that point I was the instrument. Ferlinghetti, McClure and Ginsberg wanted the cultural power of the music. They had that power to a point, but the music added to those possibilities. For Dylan, too, at that stage in his career, it was also expedient to be identified with them. It created this extended community.'[37]

Meltzer adds that 'years later, when the Band did their final concert' – the 1976 event at the Winterland Ballroom in San Francisco was captured on celluloid in the Martin Scorsese movie *The Last Waltz* – one of the event organisers 'Emmet Grogan called me and asked me to be one of the poets in between acts. I said "No". It was the music they were there for, not the middle-aged guys reciting verse. That time was done with, just as the Beats stomped out the formalist academic poetry of the post-war. Grogan said, "C'mon, man, it's a big event, a meeting of the tribes" '.[38] But the poet resisted his overtures though both Ferlinghetti and McClure did appear on the Winterland stage, joining a stellar bill of rock performers from Bob Dylan and Joni Mitchell, Eric Clapton and Neil Young, Muddy Waters and Van Morrison, Ronnie Hawkins and the Staples Singers, Neil Diamond and Dr. John, Paul Butterfield and Ronnie Wood, Ringo Starr and Stephen Stills, in paying a farewell tribute to the group. McClure read the introduction to *The Canterbury Tales* in Chaucerian dialect; Ferlinghetti read his own 'Loud Prayer'.

As for the inclusion of Dylan in Charters' *Portable Beat Reader*, Meltzer has this to say: 'By the time the anthology appeared, Dylan had appeared in a zillion photographs with Ginsberg, Burroughs and company. Though considerably younger, that is, nowhere near that "generation", in the public mind, he is seen as somehow part of it. When I met Allen, Ferlinghetti, Rexroth, Snyder in SF and Kerouac, via the mail, I was 20 and they were in their 30s. They were, gulp, "middle-aged" – not of my generation. Dylan was. All of this is neither here nor there. Ann's anthology is much more valuable in its range than Waldman's 1996 version[39] and is, academically, very serviceable [...] So, yes, why not Dylan in

---

[35] Meltzer quoted in Warner, 1998.
[36] Meltzer, email, 20 April 1999.
[37] Meltzer quoted in Warner, 1998.
[38] Meltzer, email, 20 April 1999.
[39] See Anne Waldman (ed.), *The Beat Book: Writings from the Beat Generation* (Boston, MA: Shambhala, 1996). Note that the title page ambiguously refers to a date of 1999.

the anthology? Especially the lyrics which, to my mind, link him to Kerouac's overlooked identifying with 1930s proletarian literature in much the same way young Zimmerman identified with Guthrie's Popular Front songs.'[40]

Meltzer's own musical trail would continue through the 1960s, eventually leaving behind jug bands, acoustic and folk music, to form, with his wife Tina, the amplified rock band the Serpent Power,[41] who released a single, eponymous album in 1967,[42] taking his poetry and placing it in a musical setting. Spotted by Ed Denton, manager of Country Joe and the Fish, at their first ever gig, a benefit for the Telegraph Hill Neighborhood Center in November 1966,[43] they were signed to Country Joe's label Vanguard Records. Reminiscent of the Great Society, Grace Slick's pre-Jefferson Airplane band, the group found a vogue-ish blend of folk-rock with psychedelic tinges. The debut LP featured Meltzer himself on guitar, harmonica and vocals, Tina Meltzer on vocals, Denny Ellis on rhythm guitar, David Stenson on bass, John Payne on organ and drummer Clark Coolidge,[44] plus an electric banjo player named J.P. Pickens who appeared only on the record's final track, 'a raga-rock epic'[45] entitled 'Endless Tunnel'.[46] A second album, credited to Tina and David Meltzer, called *Poet Song* would be issued in 1969. By the start of the 1970s, however, Meltzer the guitarist had largely returned to writing and his collection of interviews, *The San Francisco Poets*,[47] at the start of the new decade, was a clear attempt to place much of what had happened in that city's writing scene over the previous 15 years or so into a context and gave Meltzer a role as historian in the narrative, a place he has continued to occupy with authority.

Speaking in our original interview in 1997, Meltzer was neither nostalgic for the poetic past nor particularly happy about the fashion for re-shaping and

---

[40] Meltzer, email, 21 April 1999.

[41] The group's name had 'an echo of ancient yogic and tantric practice', says Jerome Rothenberg, 'Introduction', *David's Copy: The Selected Poems of David Meltzer*, edited by Michael Rothenberg (London: Penguin, 2005), p. xvii.

[42] When *Rolling Stone* named its 'Forty Essential Albums of 1967' in the second of its three fortieth anniversary special editions, 12–26 July 2007, *The Serpent Power* was placed at No. 30.

[43] See Alex Stimmel, 'The Serpent Power', *All Music Guide*, http://www.allmusic.com/artist/serpent-power-p143421/biography [accessed 22 December 2011].

[44] Coolidge published the book, *Now it's Jazz: Writings on Kerouac and the Sounds* (Albuquerque, NM: Living Batch Press), in 1999.

[45] Stimmel, *All Music Guide*.

[46] This track was produced by Samuel Charters, better known as Sam Charters, who produced Country Joe and the Fish between 1966 and 1970, and is also a noted writer on and historian of blues and jazz. He is married to Ann Charters, author of Jack Kerouac's first biography, *Kerouac*, published in 1973.

[47] *The San Francisco Poets* (New York: Ballantine Books, 1971), was followed by another Meltzer edited collection – *Golden Gate: Interviews with Five San Francisco Poets* (Berkeley, CA: Wingbow Press, 1976). Later, *San Francisco Beat: Talking with the Poets* (San Francisco, CA: City Lights, 2001) brought the two earlier volumes together in an updated edition.

re-making the history to create a mythology in more recent times. 'I've moved past it. I was there but I've moved past it. I'm not there, I'm here! Many people are still there and that's the level of my critique. I can't stand the idea of my peers making a career out of being there; it's grotesque. They are no longer that; they are old people ready for social security.'[48] Meanwhile, he has been re-inventing himself constantly, it appears, re-evaluating the Beat legacy, its heroes and its tragedies, but also broadening his widely-stretched canvas to incorporate every branch of post-war theorising from critical theory to feminism, radical politics to gender studies, movies and advertising, postmodernism to the riot grrrls, punk to hip hop.

Of Beat, he says: 'The legacy is hugely durable as it has become re-commodified to accommodate a youth market that, in a sense, is interested in the radicality of its grandparents. Invariably a younger generation finds the grandparents infinitely more interesting than the parents. That is part of that rebellion and that growth process.'[49] But if the legacy has endured, he is not convinced that the myth-building that has gone on alongside it is such a positive development. 'As it is turned into a commodity, it becomes a flight from the complex history so many of the Beat writers inhabited and were in resistance to, and were expressing their critique of.'[50] He recalls the Whitney Museum exhibition in New York, which would later arrive in San Francisco, too. 'I and some of the other survivors were wheeled out on our walkers,' he says mischievously, 'to bear witness. But I think that the catalogue is indicative of the kind of iconic way in which the subject is being dealt with. In fact, it is slightly distressing. As someone who was slightly younger than Kerouac and Ginsberg when I started, I find it bad history. There is this mytho-poetisising tendency.' In essence, Meltzer seems concerned about the dangers of turning Beat into a heroic side-show; transforming the movement into a commercial proposition is fraught with danger. He worries that 'it's not the books that matter, it's the looks. What essentially is being sold is not only the books but also a kitsch version of the Beats with the ubiquitous sunglasses, the berets, goatees, the bongos, all of that.'[51]

We should, rather, be reminded of the social criticism that Beat writers delivered against the background of those times. 'Poetry then offered this great uplifting to the masses, whoever they were – eccentrics, the battered, the disen-franchised and the people who were living, and often voluntarily, in marginal opposition to the stupefyingly uniform post-war abundance, consumerism and affluence. This was the great American revolution, the post-war economy and how

---

[48] Meltzer quoted in Warner, 1998.
[49] *Ibid.*
[50] *Ibid.*
[51] *Ibid.*

it manifested itself in the sort of desire to standardise reality, make it uniform and containable.'[52]

The last 40 years have not seen Meltzer assume the role of passive observer though, in any sense. Now approaching 75, Meltzer has remained an active figure on the Bay Area scene from, in recent times, his base in Oakland. He has taught in the humanities and the graduate poetics programme at the New College of California in the Mission district of San Francisco and has continued to publish – gathering existing work but also forging considerable bodies of new material as well. His poems have been collected in *The Name: Selected Poetry 1973–1983* (1984), and *Arrows: Selected Poetry 1957–1992* (1994) and *David's Copy: The Selected Poems of David Meltzer* (2005). Two edited collections reflect his passion for jazz – *Reading Jazz* (1993) and *Writing Jazz* (1999) – anthologising some of the best writing on the subject, but also including his own critical commentary. His own verse has continued to appear, too. His book-length verse homage to a great tenor saxophonist, *No Eyes: Lester Young*, was issued in 2000, a long poetic reflection on Beat, entitled *Beat Thing*, emerged in 2004 and, in 2011, the sixtieth volume in the famed City Lights Pocket Poets series was Meltzer's own *When I Was a Poet* – 'When I was a Poet/Everything was Possible/there wasn't Anything/ that wasn't Poetry'.[53]

What of the arc of poetry from the mid-1950s to the start of a new Millennium? Has the place of this art-form altered in that half century? Meltzer comments: 'In the '50s, people were actually listening to poetry. It was being taken out of the academy and into the coffee houses. It became a whole culture which eventually moved over to be replaced by the rock 'n' roll culture. Today, poetry is useless. So much conformity of American life is to do with the function of art – there is a puritan ethic which demands the utilitarian, the functional in all art. Art was always considered to be useless unless it was attached to functionalism.' Yet he adds a note of optimism, acknowledging the potency of a street poetry like rap. 'The most globalising art of all today is hip hop culture.'[54]

The East Coast boy who became the West Coast man, the young listener who was entranced by the rhythm of jazz, joined the Beat crowd on the streets and in the cafés and bars of San Francisco as a literary re-birth flowered, performed poetry and made folk music in the cafés, met Bob Dylan when few outside New York knew him and therefore played an intriguing role as a pre-emptive match-maker between the singer and Ginsberg, McClure and the wider Beat province, and made acid rock during the countercultural uprising, still appears to have his finger on the pulse. Says Michael Rothenberg, who edited *David's Copy*, the

---

[52] Meltzer quoted in Warner, 1998.
[53] Meltzer, 'When I Was a Poet', *When I Was a Poet* (San Francisco: City Lights, 2011), p. 15.
[54] Meltzer quoted in Warner, 1998.

2005 selected poems: 'When I read David's poetry, read his words, I think of alchemical conjuring, Zen, beat, jazz rhythms, prayer, the everyday in a moment-flash, historical overviews, urban and domestic reflections. Meltzer's work is sly and sardonic, twisted and awkward, non-doctrinaire, agit-smut in the face of love and desire, a commentary of the "real" that goes through a surreal/abstract filter, or *is* surreal.'[55] Of the collection itself, Rothenberg adds that it is 'a re-visioning of a poetic oeuvre, a selected moment in time, a songster's epic-journey, the journey of a "savage word slinger" rummaging relentlessly through iconic shards and celluloid of culture, pop, and hermetic images and language, tempered with humour and love.'[56]

---

[55] Michael Rothenberg (ed.), 'Foreword', *David's Copy: The Selected Poems of David Meltzer* (London: Penguin, 2005), p. xiii.
[56] *Ibid.*

REVIEW 1 – BOOK: DAVID MELTZER, *BEAT THING*

(Albuquerque, NM: La Alameda Press, 2004)

David Meltzer, wordsmith, novelist, jazz versifier, folk musician, frontman of psychedelic rock band the Serpent Power, has spent a life-time avoiding glib categorisation, determinedly ducking when critics and commentators have dubbed him a Beat poet. In fact, he has consistently railed against the mythography of the Beat Generation – 'it's the looks, not the books', he has said, attacking the triumph of style over content in the histories that have been told. But Meltzer, still active as writer and educator in the Bay Area that has been his home since the middle 1950s, seems to have softened his views, in some ways, on the misrepresentation of Beatdom.

He acknowledges there was a movement; he even appears to accept that he had a role in that community's evolution, despite his tendency, over the years, to keep such an interpretation at arm's length. It seems that it was only his youth – he was one of the youngest, one of the last, poets to ride the original North Beach roller-coaster as live verse resonated in basements and bars of San Francisco, before Beat became a little more than a tourist sham, as token bongos and hastily-sprouted goatees displaced the utopian visions of the first wave – or his modesty, that stopped him basking in the reflected limelight of Ginsberg, Ferlinghetti and co.

Yet Meltzer, despite certain shifts brought on, perhaps, by the mellowing of maturity, has not, in any real sense, swallowed the myth of Beat whole. His latest work, a long poem on a near-epic scale, doffs a cap to the movement – the piece is called *Beat Thing*, after all – but then proceeds in a 160-page torrent to challenge many of the premises of the Beat Generation, or at least those media-shaped assessments that have poured forth for the last half century. More pertinently, Meltzer is committed to seeing post-war experience as a great deal more than the cool, existential posturing of a new literature.

In a text that is dense, frenetic, spiky and often tangled in the roots and branches of the socio-political, the writer attempts a panoramic overview of America's later twentieth century, foregrounding movies and music, McCarthy and racism, the eye-ball searing flash of the H-bomb and the mind-scalding impressions left by the death camps. Beat bubbles behind the glass but Meltzer feels honour bound to set it in perspective and not over-privilege its part in recent decades.

Beat Thing is not a single, sustained blast – it comes in three sections and, like the very jazz Meltzer rapped and rolled over in the Cellar in the later 1950s, it is delivered in various forms, various voices: the rat-a-tat of the riff, the longer-lined elegance of the refrain, at times the angular abstraction of the bop solo. Sometimes there is a torrent of ideas folding over each other in waves; sometimes the poet stops to take breath and surveys a scene, a moment, coolly and carefully. Line lengths shift, blank verse transmutes into prose stanzas, then back again.

In the opening passage 'The Beat Thing Looms Up', Meltzer subjects the word, the concept, Beat to a relentless deconstruction, an unforgiving critique of Beat's use, its appropriation, its commercial exploitation, in the years that have followed the initial, and perhaps golden, age. 'Beat wax museums in Fisherman's Wharf downtown Lowell McDougal Street & Beat Thing Hall of Fame wing of Planet Hollywood on Sunset Boulevard' mouths Meltzer disparagingly, then adds: 'Beat superstar on MTV fastcut scratch 50s newsreel footage intercut w/ sitcom knows best voices over Kurt Loder asks Burroughs about killing his wife'. In fact, the writer rather economically, if elegiacally, sums up his own position when he says: 'don't wanna be forgotten but don't wanna be remembered in rememberings' dismembering'.

Yet the elongated account that follows is a warm, nostalgic and splendidly evocative re-telling of everyday Beat life as it was, contemplating writers in the ring – like Ray Bremser, Gary Snyder and Richard Brautigan – and musical compadres like Dino Valente, David Crosby and Nick Gravenites – and casual connections in the saloon and the lunch-counter, the lounging, ligging and loving, even an analysis of the genesis of jazz poetry. But it is when Meltzer wallows in the detail of the cafés and the cuisine of his Bay memories that the writing truly hits the taste-buds. 'What about Beat food?' he asks, then answers:

> … sushi especially wasabe bullet train blasting eyes into inland seas of kelp hurricane weep or shrimp cocktails at Swan Oyster Depot on Polk dip pink volt into red horseradish tomato karma lemon after rye toast soaked in Blum's sweet butter or linguine dreamy shimmer glazed with green Pesto paste …

Poetry as soul sustenance – and almost literally!

But the fare that follows is meatier and much, much darker. By the time 'Beat Thing: Commentary', a prequel in essence, commences, the shadows of a pre-Beat terror cast their dark and terrible shape:

it was the Bomb
Shoah
it was void
spirit crisis disconnect
no subject but blank unrelenting
bust time
no future
suburban expand into past
present nuclear (get it) family
droids Pavlov minutiae
it was Jews w/ blues
reds nulled & jolted
Ethel & Julius brains smoke
pyre of shoes & eyeglasses
weeping black G.I.s
open Belsen gates

The remainder of the poem, including the extended coda 'Primo Po-Mo' paints an extraordinary and deeply unnerving canvas, weaving threads as diverse as Hollywood and jazz, Holocaust and anti-Semitism, briefly pausing to state with calm and devastating assurance that, in the wake of nuclear typhoons and racial genocide, 1945 'closes Modernism's file; melts febrile glue of liberal humanism's Enlightenment's utopic elan & generosity; splatter into Nowheresville all socially sustaining (& framing) institutions & discourses.'

In short, *Beat Thing*, is a remarkably moving but also gravely pessimistic piece. While its language is charged with a frenetic energy, its imagery is jagged, fragmented and disquieting, a neo-expressionist description of civilisation's shattered and un-fixable mirror. Certainly, for those of us who placed faith in the liberal, anti-establishment projects that came in the wake of the Second World War, this contemplation is profoundly unsettling; it positions the impact of Beat and its humanist hopes in a very minor place. Quaint, convivial, charming in its way when young men gathered over beer and coffee to hear mystic visions through cigarette haze, its subsequent incarnations were merely shallow dilutions concocted by money-makers and their cheap lines of commodified relics.

As Meltzer, quite early in the piece, most potently declares:

Beat Gap line of chinos lumberjack flannel shirts Dr Dean beat shades Joe Camel unfiltered beat smokes Armani blue black basement zoots to suit up in & walk down to theme bar restaurant Coolsville chain owned by three publishers owned by a transglobal media conglomerate owned by a network of oil companies owned by a consortium of arms dealers owned by a clot of drug producers owned by a massive webwork of Swiss bankers & German brokers in silent partnership with Japanese alchemists in collusion with Chinese gerontologists as proxies for Reverend Moon

INTERVIEW 6

Bill Nelson, British rock guitarist and Beat follower

Bill Nelson has been navigating those choppy waters between rock and jazz, contemporary music and the avant garde, for more than four decades, never fully immersing himself in one style, always pressing on to find new means of expressing his musical voice. His career, documented in a recorded repertoire stretching to more than 50 released CDs, has embraced the blues and jazz, progressive and art rock, glam and the new wave, music for film and theatre, ambient soundscapes and drum 'n' bass.

From the late 1960s he strove to combine elements of popular music and the visual arts – he was both guitarist of reputation and a graduate of a British art school, sharing those characteristics with other major English rock stars from John Lennon to Keith Richards, Eric Clapton to Pete Townshend – seeking a synergy between his song-writing and the influences of those potent twentieth-century artistic impulses – from Futurism to Dada, Pop Art to US comic books – he had absorbed as a student.

Attracting the early attention of John Peel, the UK's most influential popular music broadcaster in his years on BBC radio from 1967 to his death in 2004, Nelson's recordings speedily gained national airplay and, when his band Be Bop Deluxe were signed by EMI, their sequence of four critically and commercially acclaimed albums revealed a distinctive marriage of inventive rock music and stylish album sleeve imagery, underlining their leader's keen interest in both sound *and* vision.

After enduring the pleasures and pains that accompany the life of the guitar hero – he was corroded rather than encouraged by the adulation and expectation, scarred by the rigors of the nascent US stadium circuit – he dissolved Be Bop Deluxe, formed a band with new wave nuances called Red Noise, and then settled into a long period of making music as solo composer, as label owner – his own

Cocteau Records ran in the 1980s – and collaborator, working with artists as diverse as Japan's Yellow Magic Orchestra, Channel Light Vessel and the American avant gardist Harold Budd.

The catalyst for the interview that follows was a project under consideration, to compose a soundtrack to a planned movie, based on 'Howl', by the eminent US film-maker Ronald Nameth. Here Nelson describes his attraction to the literature of the Beat Generation, how he approaches the process of composition, and offers some clues as to how he might deal with the challenge of creating a score to accompany Ginsberg's most celebrated verse work.

SW   **You have taken an interest in the Beat writers for many years. How was your interest in these novelists and poets sparked?**

BN   I was an art student in the mid-1960s, a period of positively optimistic cultural discovery, despite the fears generated by the Cold War and Vietnam. English art schools provided the perfect environment for creative exploration back then. I remember that, during my first year there, I was at Wakefield Art School in West Yorkshire, and the older students were of the generation that venerated the Beats. I was straight out of secondary modern school and fairly naive about such things but I recognised that these more seasoned students fitted the popular image of 'the beatnik'.

The senior students appeared as strong, independent characters to me, some of them colourful to the point of eccentricity. They often would stop what they were doing and recite strange poetry out loud and in a very dramatic, exclamatory fashion, oblivious to what anyone else might think of their behaviour. I was somewhat in awe of them, being little more than a shy schoolboy. Within a few weeks, however, I got to know some of them personally and picked up on their various influences and passions.

My own generation were mods, out of rock n' roll and moving towards the cusp of psychedelia. Bit by bit, we found our way into the emerging 'underground' music and art scene. I remember ordering, from a little Wakefield newsagent's shop, copies of *International Times*, the independently published countercultural newspaper, which regularly featured articles about Allen Ginsberg and William Burroughs. The publication was hardly known outside of certain circles at that time, at least in Wakefield, and reading it was like being let in on some exotic secret. I can recall reportage, in the publication, about the big poetry reading held at the Royal Albert Hall in London in 1965. The event featured Allen Ginsberg, Gregory Corso and Lawrence Ferlinghetti (amongst others) and created some interest and controversy in the mainstream media. I could only imagine, from the article and a couple of accompanying photos, how exciting it must have been. But it certainly kindled my curiosity even further.

William Burroughs had attended this event, although he hadn't given a live reading, and it was his *Naked Lunch* novel that became my first Beat Generation purchase. Of course, I was both intrigued and shocked by the book. It was perhaps the most radical thing I'd ever read, but I thought that the cut-up technique brought a strange beauty to material that might otherwise, at that time, have seemed sordid and prurient. It was the subject of much discussion amongst my fellow art students.

As the British counterculture grew and consolidated itself, I was able to discover more about its roots, which were, to some degree it seemed, entrenched in American soil. I'd had a strong interest in American pop culture for some time, starting out with super-hero comic books when I was very young, and popular films and music of course. At art school, I came across books in the library that referenced American 'underground' cinema and avant-garde music. I'd been a jazz fan for a while, being a young guitar player, but suddenly read about people such as John Cage and Harry Partch. Their creative ideas inspired me and I could see how there was a connected-ness to the world glimpsed in the pages of *International Times*. Yoko Ono was another discovery and the Fluxus group. None of this was exactly Beat Generation but, in some ways, it felt like a complementary force. I could sense kindred spirits. The American film experiments of Stan Brakhage, Jonas Mekas, Ron Rice, Ken Jacobs, Kenneth Anger, Jack Smith, Maya Deren, Harry Smith and others seemed connected to the Beats in some way too, though, for me, seeing anything other than stills in obscure art publications proved difficult.

In more recent years, I've re-visited all of these artistic territories, as one often does when one reaches a certain age. Naturally, my understanding has deepened with the passing years but I still find fresh inspiration from the writers, musicians and artists of that era.

SW **In what ways did they inspire or affect you?**

BN It's not always easy to pin-point exactly why some things make such an impact on one's life. It goes deeper than *liking* something, I suppose. There's definitely a feeling of kinship, of finding that one is not alone. A confirmation of sensibilities? There was also, for me at that time, a sense of being opened up to wider possibilities, an exciting, new-found freedom of expression. It was almost as if one had been given permission to dream in colour, instead of just black and white.

SW **How do you feel the influence of the Beats may have fed into your musical and wider creative work?**

BN   In general terms, the influence is part of an entire era that opened
       up many of my generation to our creative potential. It's a historical
       'passing of the torch' that moves from one artist to another. But, in
       more specific terms, Jack Kerouac's 'first thought, best thought' dictum
       is something I've held to for some time now. I'm a firm believer in
       allowing the subconscious a space within the work, a space in which
       it can make itself felt. I have to acknowledge the way that the Beat
       Generation's exploration of mysticism, particularly the Eastern variety,
       laid the foundations for my own investigations into that territory, even
       though some of it came second hand via the hippy route pioneered by
       Timothy Leary and Ken Kesey's Merry Pranksters. Not that I ever was
       brave enough to dabble with psychedelic drugs. I decided I had more
       than enough visions, dreams and nightmares to keep me awake at night
       without poking around in my even darker attic of demons!

SW   **Are you touched by the spirit? Or are you affected by the form?**
       Do you owe any kind of lyrical debt, for example, to the kind of
       techniques that Jack Kerouac, Allen Ginsberg, William Burroughs
       and other members of that literary community devised?

BN   Both, but perhaps the underlying spirit of it is more important to me,
       although quite a few rock musicians have tapped into Burroughs' – and,
       more accurately, Brion Gysin's – cut-up techniques. I've used variants
       of this in my lyric writing of the 1970s and early 1980s. Methods, in
       essence, of introducing chance into the work.
           Of course, John Cage devised various similar but different techniques
       to produce purely musical or sonic results, techniques aimed at
       bypassing the conscious mind of the artist. A different philosophical
       basis to Burroughs' approach, perhaps, but essentially a way of working
       with what appears to be chance. During my career with my 1970s era
       band Be Bop Deluxe, I recorded a piece called 'Futurist Manifesto'. It
       was, quite obviously, named after the document issued by the Italian
       Futurists at the beginning of the twentieth-century but the technique I
       used to create the lyrics owes a big debt to Burroughs and Gysin, rather
       than to Marinetti, Balla and Russolo.
           I picked up a copy of *Country Life* magazine that was lying around
       in the studio where the band were recording the album *Drastic Plastic*
       and, from an article chosen by simply opening the magazine at random,
       took the first word from the first line, the second from the second line,
       and so on, right through the article, until I had enough words to fit the
       piece. It wasn't a cut up or a 'fold in' as Burroughs and Gysin would
       think of it, but it was allied with their approach. It was also surprising
       what this technique threw up. There *were* some conscious adjustments

on my part afterwards though, just to get it to flow more interestingly in certain places, but not too many. I then made three tape recordings of the resultant text, speaking the words, rather than singing them.

These recordings were then played back on three tape recorders, deliberately out of sync with each other. This produced random audio juxtapositions of the text. The three tapes were then dubbed, whilst in this out of sync fashion, onto the main multitrack machine on which I'd previously created a music bed, again, using Cage's and Burroughs' concepts as inspiration to create the sounds. The finished piece had an otherwordly quality that might have escaped if I'd have used more orthodox means. The strangest thing was that it all appeared to have 'meaning'. It resonated with an authenticity that suggested a conscious impulse or 'hidden mind' was operating behind the work.

In more recent years, I've actually written songs dealing with various Beat-inspired ideas and also a song loosely around Jack Kerouac's celebration of the road journey as a kind of mythical quest. My 1995 solo album *After the Satellite Sings* provides the easiest reference to this kind of material, particularly tracks such as 'Streamliner', 'Flipside' and 'Memory Babe'.

SW **Have you drawn on literature in a wider sense when you come to compose? Are there characters or episodes, are there narratives or dramas on the printed page that have actually prompted you to pen particular musical or lyrical responses?**

BN I don't really use literature 'literally' in that respect. I generally don't write about characters from books or adapt fictional scenarios, although there have been the odd exceptions. I'm more often inspired by an author's honesty or willingness to open himself up to the experiences of his life, than any desire to take hold of his characters or subject matter and use it within my own work. I feel – and this is purely my personal approach here, no criticism intended of all those artists who adopt or appropriate fictional scenarios and characters – that I'm only properly equipped to comment on my *own* life and so my songs are, in the main, autobiographical, experiential, diary-like things. They are often loaded in symbolism or encoded in some way but, essentially, they are my life and dreams, hopes and fears, captured in sounds and words and pictures. Snapshots of a life. The music and form can become quite complex and multi-layered but the essence is simple and single-pointed. Perhaps selfish and self-obsessed sometimes too, I cheerfully admit. But this is what constitutes my 'prima materia', the stuff from which I attempt to transmute my philosopher's stone.

So, aside from considerations of pure aesthetics, I use my work to try to reveal myself to myself: it's an attempt to figure out some quite fundamental philosophical problems, often by examining the most ordinary and banal aspects of my existence. In this respect, Kerouac's work has shown me that this is nothing to be afraid of. Ginsberg's, too. His writing is as open and as direct as possible. Its honesty escapes the shackles of its beauty and stands naked and unashamed.

Every single person has a complex and emotional story to tell, or a song to sing. It's ultimately deserving of the mystical wonder that Kerouac saw in so many things. Something to be revered and respected. Of course, whilst life is enriched by the pursuit of such ideals, they ultimately don't save us from ourselves or our demons. If anything, this approach brings those demons into sharper focus. It's a difficult confrontation. Seeing them face to face can be a dangerous thing. I think Jack Kerouac's direct vision was a double-edged sword for him. It's the same for all artists, to one degree or another. Part of the price we pay for the privilege of *seeing*, perhaps? Lots of available theories about this, Freudian, Jungian, Reichian and so on ... it gets over-romanticised, too. 'The ever popular tortured artist effect' as someone once put it.

This is another interesting thing about the Beats' work for me: it explores the nature of the artist, the role of the imagination, the nature of *vision*. It seems perfectly natural that Ginsberg and Kerouac should find solace and inspiration in Buddhism – Tibetan in Allen's case, Zen in Jack's – and that Burroughs should be drawn to occultism. In their own ways, these were deeply *spiritual* men, the holy trinity of the Beats. Gary Snyder was, perhaps, the most 'authentic' in this respect though. At least initially.

SW **What are your feelings about a poem like 'Howl'? When did you initially encounter it?**

BN I can't remember *exactly* when I first read 'Howl'. It could have been the late 60s. I certainly remember reading *about* it before I actually read the work itself. Even back then, its opening lines were often quoted in alternative publications. When I actually got to read it, what initially came across was the sheer energy of the piece, the torrent of passion, anger and beauty that leapt from the page. For all its epic length, it was tight and focused, for all its sense of outrage and horror, it was elegant and aesthetically seductive, an undeniable masterpiece and a turning point for poetry in general at that time. God knows how it must have appeared to the uninitiated when it was first published. It's almost impossible to imagine the shock and controversy it would have caused back then, so much have public sensibilities changed in the intervening years. But it was, without a doubt, a *revolutionary* work. It's also a work that continues to resonate, that rewards re-investigation. I think you could easily say, 'timeless', despite the clearly defined cultural signifiers of that period.

SW **What approaches might you take if you compose a musical work which references a literary work in some fashion?**

BN The approach is generally dictated by two things, the work itself and my personal reaction to it. It's impossible to always 'get' the author's intention in its purest sense; one can only work from one's response to the writing. But the piece's history along with received knowledge about its author's inspiration are bound to colour one's responses to some degree. Essentially though, it's a subjective exercise. It's best if I'm moved in some way, emotionally, aesthetically, by the work. The intellectual content may or may not interest or connect with me, but if I can somehow 'feel' the core of the piece, then this isn't such an essential consideration.

With poetry, the *spoken* word is key to much of the music's composition. Meter, inflection, timing, tonality all contribute to the musical experience of a poem. Different readers will bring their own persona to bear on this, in much the same way that different musicians will interpret an individual composer's work. It's a little like jazz or improvised music in this respect. Until the actual performance, it's difficult to predict the final result.

I like to include hidden layers of meaning, reference points to time and place, the environment surrounding the creation of the poem, little signifiers that might be picked up by those who have studied the piece in more depth than the casual listener. At the same time, there needs to be an emotional, visceral charge that connects with and illuminates the work for even the most casual listener. It's tricky and can be hit and miss. You can spend a very long time trying out various avenues of possibility before hitting on the most appropriate approach. Then again, you can simply just 'go for it'. First thought, best thought!

SW **How might you attempt to make a musical response to a piece like the Ginsberg poem?**

BN Read and re-read the piece, make rough notes as to possible instrumentation and tonality. Research the circumstances surrounding the poem's birth, the music of the time, Ginsberg's own musical tastes, the political/social impulses that inform the poem's content. Try to see how much of this can be used as inspiration but not necessarily portrayed in a literal sense. It's a form of abstraction, a reduction of things to essentials without losing the plot, you might say.

It would also be good to use recordings from the era, music, sounds, news broadcasts, as background 'interference'. These could even be manipulated live by others at the appropriate points in the piece.

Ideally, there should be an opportunity to compose the music directly to a recording of the spoken word. The most effective way would be to record the poem being spoken by the actual person chosen to read it at the eventual public performance, then use their 'guide' voice as a template to create the music and assemble the sounds. My own preference would be to use a pre-recorded music bed with just a few live improvisations, rather than attempt a totally live, real-time musical score. There could certainly be elements of live improvisation though. Whilst the eventual public reading might vary to some degree (compared to the guide vocal), the recorded music would offer an appropriately structured response and also a 'map' of sorts for the reader to work with. I find that, no matter what plans one makes as to method, technique, etc., the end result is always something else, something that emerges through the moment by moment response to the materials at hand and the prevailing winds of the imagination. It's simply a matter of throwing oneself overboard and trusting that the muse will guide one to the shore. Sometimes, too much thinking and planning can close off more interesting and rewarding avenues of exploration. It should be a joyful adventure, not a scientific exercise or surgical dissection.

Author's note: *Howl for Now* was presented on 7 October 2005 at the Clothworkers' Centenary Concert Hall, School of Music, University of Leeds. The event, which took place half a century later to the night of Ginsberg's first reading of 'Howl' at the Six Gallery in San Francisco, featured a reading of the poem and six new musical works composed in tribute to the verse work. Although a DVD record of the occasion was produced, film director Ronald Nameth's scheme to adapt the material for a more ambitious, multi-screen production remains on the drawing board, as does Bill Nelson's soundtrack to the piece, discussed in the interview above.

Q&A 5

Jim Sampas, Beat record producer including *Kerouac: Kicks Joy Darkness*

Jim Sampas is Jack Kerouac's nephew.[1] He met his uncle when he was still a small child. A one-time singer-songwriter, he quickly turned to production and has, in the last decade and a half, delivered a string of recordings which have attracted widespread praise, from Beatles homages to a Bruce Springsteen tribute, *Badlands*. But his work on Beat-centred projects has formed a significant part of his activities. He created *Kerouac: Kicks, Joy, Darkness* in 1997, a collection which featured Patti Smith and Johnny Depp, Allen Ginsberg and William Burroughs, and *Jack Kerouac Reads On the Road* (1999), which saw Tom Waits interpret a Kerouac song. He has also made two albums with Lawrence Ferlinghetti, *A Coney Island of the Mind* (1999) and *Pictures of the Gone World* (2005). In 2009, he produced a documentary inspired by Kerouac's novel *Big Sur*, 40 years after the writer's death, which included contributions from Sam Shepard, Michael McClure and Carolyn Cassady. Here he talks about the genesis, evolution and success of *Kicks Joy Darkness*.

How did *Kicks Joy Darkness* come about? Was it your idea?

In my early 20s I had been producing and recording my own music at various studios in Boston and New York, with session musicians, experimenting with sounds, all culminating in a two week recording session in Woodstock, with a stellar group of players Jerry Marotta (Peter Gabriel), Gary Burke (Joe Jackson) and Graham Parker. During that time I became enthralled by the process of recording. Once the album was completed, I started playing the Boston music

---

[1] Stella Sampas, aunt to Jim, had married Kerouac, becoming his third wife in 1966. She outlived her husband by more than 20 years, dying in 1990 aged 71, and is buried in the same Lowell grave.

circuit with a band I had assembled. But after that experience, I became impatient, and found that my true love was the actual process of recording. So I started looking for a new recording project.

Jack [Kerouac] was my uncle, married to my father's sister Stella Sampas. So from an early age I had been exposed to his work and became a big fan. In my travels in and out of recording studios I found a seemingly endless list of musicians who had been dramatically influenced by his writings. I had a hunch there might be folks of all kinds of different art forms who had as well.

I thought of the idea of doing a spoken word tribute to Kerouac somewhere around 1994, but had problems with coming up with the right approach. After asking Allen Ginsberg, who was quite gracious in giving feedback, one thing I remember Allen saying emphatically though was 'Stay away from *On the Road* because it was overdone'. Around that time I started getting into Kerouac's poetry, and became completely caught up in the playfulness, simplicity, and beautiful rhythmic structure of his 'pomes' as he called them. They were self-contained and perfect for a four to five minute reading. This is what sealed the idea for me. I would seek to have the world discover Kerouac's 'pomes', and other obscure works like his novel *Visions of Cody*, through a diverse group celebrated artists, musicians, poets, actors and writers' voices.

Over the years, so many folks have commented on the musicality of Kerouac's writings. In the same way that jazz influenced Kerouac's 'spontaneous prose' method of writing, one can only imagine that when he composed poetry he had rhythm and cadence in mind, whether consciously or unconsciously. We can assume from the recordings of Kerouac that he really enjoyed reading the "pomes' out loud and it is surely by design that his 'pomes' flow so naturally when spoken.

Kerouac, like any other writer, had a strong desire to grab the readers' attention, and keep them engaged. My guess is that it was Kerouac's natural sense of rhythm, much like a musician, that made him instinctually understand that the key to maintaining a reader's interest was not just through clever word play but by the musicality of the words when either aloud or in one's head. The fact that the pomes have such an uncontrived natural tempo that begs to be read out loud is another example of Kerouac's genius. And, unlike a book on cassette, it was indeed the pomes' autonomy that I felt would make them similar to songs on a compilation, and thereby help to heighten the diversity of the many different voices on the album. I was inspired by Kerouac's work with great jazz artists David Amram, Al Cohn and Zoot Sims, musical accompaniment behind many of his readings. The idea certainly registered with the contributors – two of the poet/musicians of the group, Patti Smith and Jim Carroll, would actually go on to make the pomes into songs through singing the words with their own musical accompaniment. (This approach would later become an inspiration for a couple other Kerouac projects I would work on later, the Jack Kerouac/Tom

Waits song 'On the Road' for *Jack Kerouac Reads On the Road* and Jay Farrar and Ben Gibbard's *One Fast Move Or I'm Gone: Music From Kerouac's Big Sur*, wherein we would have Farrar make the prose of *Big Sur* into lyrics for a series of songs).

With all this in mind – and a desire to show to the world that hundreds of highly praised artists possessed dog-eared Kerouac books, and how that influence had, in turn, changed art culture as we know it today – I would create a great celebration of my uncle's work. Though I have to say, when working to explain this idea to others, I faced much resistance. 'Who is going to buy that?' people would ask. Which could be because back then Kerouac wasn't quite as popular as he is today, since that revival of his work in the late 1990s.

Was it a challenge to secure record label interest?

No, not really. What happened was I put a call into Dennis McNally, the Grateful Dead publicist and author of the Kerouac biography *Desolate Angel*, about the idea. He thought that the label to release the project should be Rykodisc. I was very familiar with Ryko's products, the magnificently packaged CD reissues by Frank Zappa, David Bowie and others. Logistically Ryko was also an ideal choice for me because they were based only an hour and half from where I lived, as opposed to many of the record companies in Los Angeles and New York. Dennis introduced me to David Greenberg and David ended up championing the project to president Don Rose. In an effort to entice David and Don even further, I created two live spoken word and music performances of Kerouac's works at the Middle East Café in Cambridge, MA, with artists Graham Parker, Mark Sandman of Morphine, poet Jim Carroll and others. I invited David and others at Ryko to both events which were nearly sold out. They received widespread coverage around Boston, including nearly every news publication in the area. David was impressed by both the concert, and the corresponding press acclaim, which helped to illustrate in real terms the substantial fan base for Kerouac. We signed a deal shortly thereafter.

And while it wasn't that difficult securing record company interest, it was a challenge for sure to get the budget I wanted. In fact I ended up financing most of the project myself, on credit cards, until I was later reimbursed by Ryko.

The title is a fragment from *On the Road*, isn't it? How did you settle on that?

The title is actually a mash up of the quote from *On the Road*. We mixed the words up a bit. David and I wanted a title that would grab folks and give them a feel for the project. *Kerouac – kicks joy darkness*, with the title in lower case without the commas as a tribute to Kerouac's own writing, which seemed to capture the essence of the project perfectly.

How did you manage to access such a rich range of material?

John Sampas, the executor of the Kerouac estate, and my uncle, kindly gave me access to materials in the Kerouac archive, including beautiful, never before seen, unpublished works such as dreams and essays.

How did you allocate it?

For the most part I gave artists three or four choices of works that I felt best suited their art and performance.

How did you attract the remarkable list of participants?

This is how it went, snowballing to include such a wonderful list of people as a direct result of Kerouac's vast diffusion into art and all its manifestations and forms. It was like a jigsaw puzzle to put together though. Kerouac's friend, the revered poet Allen Ginsberg, signed on right away, and then suggested Lee Ranaldo. I heard that Lee was performing in Cambridge and, luckily, I knew the manager of the club, Chris Porter, and asked him to introduce us. Lee enthusiastically jumped on board the moment I asked him and helped me get Eddie Vedder, who in turn helped attract so many other musicians simply by his presence in the effort. Having Allen Ginsberg also helped get me Patti Smith and getting Patti was instrumental in getting me Michael Stipe. Once I had those folks I knew I could go out to anyone and they would take the project seriously. And so I made a wish-list and started dialling phone of managers, agents, and the artists themselves, through phone numbers given to me by the folks already involved.

What attracted such an impressive cast, do you think?

First and foremost it was Kerouac's work that won the day. The project is a testament not only of the endurance of the writings, but of the widespread influence he had on people of all walks of life and varying art forms. Just imagine what the world would be like without Jack Kerouac, where the mélange of art culture would be, without that key ingredient. He taught a whole world of artists to stop thinking and over analysing too much, to make it real. As a result we have an artistic culture that I believe is far less contrived, and manipulated, than it would have been had Jack never set his 'spontaneous prose' to paper.

Did the two of you, Lee and yourself, actively direct the talent or did they essentially come to you with their interpretations?

It was a mix of both. Some sessions I attended and others I was unable to because of the budget I was working with. I would have many conversations with artists to help with the overall production and continuity.

Which tracks do you feel turned out best? Which are your favourites?

It's funny, I don't really have a favourite track. I love them all nearly equally as much. There isn't a dud on the album, all brilliantly conceived, and fascinatingly delivered performances, that I could listen to endlessly, thanks to the phenomenal talents of all involved.

Some of the participants have since died, of course – Mark Sandman and Joe Strummer, Jim Carroll and Jeff Buckley, Warren Zevon and Allen Ginsberg, too. Do you have particular memories of those individuals no longer with us?

One of the people who has since passed away was Rob Buck, the incredibly gifted guitarist for 10,000 Maniacs. Rob had a truly unique sound in a world where so many guitarists sound the same. We would hang out at his apartment in the East Village literally across the street from the famous gathering station of poets St. Mark's Church in New York. We'd have long conversations on the phone, he had a comedian's wit, such a joy to hang with, the most positive person I have ever encountered. I spoke with him only a few days before he died, and while he apparently was in the hospital at the time in need of a liver transplant, I had no idea. He may have said he wasn't feeling well but that was it. Positive until the end, so tragic is that loss.

Joe Strummer was an incredible influence on me as a kid. Chatting with him throughout the process of his creating the musical accompaniment for the Jack Kerouac recording was a real trip. Here was the guy whose every word I would hang on to, who helped me get through my teenage angst years, and not to be so absorbed in myself and see the world of politics outside of my city, my country, my small world, all through his music and ideas. I would later ask him to do an interview for a Mark Sandman documentary, and in the context of Morphine's seminal work, he graciously talked about how originality and progression was so essential to art. That you can't live in the past, need to dive into the future.

I got to know Mark Sandman a bit as well through my good friend Dana Colley, both of Morphine. I'm a huge admirer of Morphine's work, and so I was quite embarrassed when he and I got into a bit of a kerfuffle in the studio. Mark came out the control room after a captivating, spontaneous reading and performance of Kerouac's *Visions of Cody* with Mark reading and Dana playing sax and Billy Conway on drums at the legendary Fort Apache Studio in Cambridge. He pointed at the ADAT machine in the middle of the control room. 'What the fuck is that?' I said, 'An ADAT player,' which the engineer and I had set up in my effort to save money versus an expensive 2-inch analog tape. 'Why on earth would you use that?' and he continued to shout at me about the stupidity of using such a thin and fake sounding piece of technology. I listened to every word. I apologised and then, as calmly as I could, ejected the ADAT tape and handed it to Mark and asked him, 'How can I fix this?' He stormed out of the room, ADAT tape in hand. He would return in 20 minutes, after I believe talking to our mutual friend and his manager Deb Klein. He said it was okay, and explained that he hated the idea of using any digital recorders and that he lived by an eight-track, analog cassette player that he could have brought. He invited me to his house the next week. We first met at a local pub, had a pint, and then went this his loft/studio Hi 'N Dry and listened to the new recording at his house. I was completely blown away, at the astounding performance and recording from the cassette recorder! The thing to note about that track is that Mark recorded with the drums muted just watching the meters go up and down. He felt that this way there wouldn't be that contrived attempt to get each word to match the beat, and the approach works perfectly, sounds so natural. He and Hunter Thompson were the only ones who wrote a piece specifically for the project. Incidentally, I never worked with an ADAT recorder again.

I had a really nice time hanging out with Jim Carroll when he did my show in Cambridge. I picked him up at the train station and drove him everywhere. He was an incredibly intelligent guy, who talked with great excitement about creating his first novel, *The Petting Zoo,* and being outside of his wheelhouse with that mix of real life and fictional work.

I was so sad when Jeff Buckley passed, such an incredibly tragic moment in rock history.

When you look at this album what you see, with each and every person involved in it, is a true melting pot of talent and sway, who like Jack have been a great influence to so many people. So unbelievably sad that many involved are no longer with us, and I'm very appreciative of their work on the project, both from a creative but also historical standpoint. Again, it shows Kerouac's influence nearly 30 years after his death back in 1997.

How did the Japanese edition end up with a number of extra tracks?

The Japanese record label wanted some more material so I delved into the archive of spoken word performances at the Kerouac estate and came across that amazing reading from a Kerouac journal entry by Graham Parker. The UFO track had already been released in the US and I was aware of the recording and absolutely loved its mesmerizing soundscape behind Kerouac's reading. So when the label suggested we include it, I agreed right away.

Did everything you recorded for the album make the cut – or is there other unheard material that may emerge at some later point?

Yes, everything we recorded made the cut.

This was one of the most successful and, indeed, critically acclaimed spoken word albums. You must have been pleased by the responses; were you surprised?

I was truly astonished. Starting out with the project there were many naysayers and you start believing the idea that no one would be interested in 'spoken word' tribute. I can't tell you how many people have since told me how much they enjoyed this album, how it touched them so. It certainly has been a big help to me and my career as a producer.

The recording presents an amazing mixture of styles – artists drawn from the worlds of grunge and indie, punk and folk and more.

How do you think Jack Kerouac would have felt about this album?

That's a really tough question to answer. In all honesty, I just don't know. Perhaps he would have liked some tracks and not others, he was very opinionated from what I understand. But I do believe he would have really appreciated the effort, and be proud to see the multi-generational pull of his work.

8 VERSIONS OF CODY: JACK KEROUAC, TOM WAITS AND THE SONG 'ON THE ROAD'

Jack Kerouac enjoyed music of many varieties and styles. He liked to listen to jazz, of course, on record, on jukeboxes and live in bars and clubs, and even attempted to ape the winding solos of improvising saxophonists in his work, most notably in his long poem cycle *Mexico City Blues* (1959). He enjoyed the repertoire of popular songs of the 1940s and 1950s, romantic Tin Pan Alley frolics from the stage and screen.[1] And he also loved to sing, at least privately, a feature perhaps of his intrinsic shyness, that self-conscious manner in company which made him a rather quieter figure, in reality, in a public setting than the larger-than-life alter egos and impetuous freewheelers who inhabited his many stories. How do we know he liked to sing? Well, several examples of his vocalese came to light in the mid-1990s, contained in a batch of unidentified recordings that cast new light on the Kerouac legend, more than a quarter of a century after his early death.

In the mid-1950s, Jerry Newman, a recording engineer friend of Kerouac's, gave him a high-quality microphone. In the latter years of that decade and the early years of the one that followed, the novelist made extensive use of the mic, doing some studio-based recording with Newman himself, and on the home recording equipment he had in his possession. He enjoyed reading his own literary work – his fine speaking voice was well-suited to bringing his prose

---

[1] Dave Moore, personal communication, email, 28 May 2012, comments: 'Kerouac mentioned, in his letters and journal entries during 1957, various rock 'n' roll singers he admired, including Elvis Presley, Jackie Wilson, Frankie Lymon, and Screaming Jay Hawkins.' Moore also draws attention to an item in *The Kerouac Connection*, No. 22, Autumn 1991: 'Kerouac was also very fond of Frank Sinatra's music. On tapes recorded at home in Northport, 1960-1, for his girlfriend of the time, Lois Sorrells, Jack can be heard reading from *Doctor Sax, Old Angel Midnight* and *San Francisco Blues*, all with the Sinatra LPs, *No One Cares* and *In the Wee Small Hours*, playing in the background. At one point Jack stops reading and joins in singing with Sinatra for several numbers.'

and poetry to life as oration. But he also liked, in his less serious, more relaxed moments, to add his own singing track to existing instrumental recordings of Broadway and Hollywood favourites. The four examples that found their way on to the 1999 spoken word collection *Jack Kerouac Reads On the Road* are lively, if somewhat throwaway, examples of his talent as a singer.

Not only could he hold a tune but he was capable of presenting a warm and engaging personality in his performances: well-timed delivered with a jaunty humour and passable imitations of the kind of crooner who led the field, certainly in the pre-Presley era, from Frank Sinatra to Vic Damone and Tony Bennett. On the CD, Raymond B. Egan and Gus Kahn's 'Ain't We Got Fun'[2] (1921), Harold Arlen and Johnny Mercer's 'Come Rain or Come Shine'[3] (1946), the Bernie Hanighen, Gordon Jenkins and Johnny Mercer[4] work 'When a Woman Loves a Man' (1938), and George Handy and Jack Segal's 'Leavin' Town' (c. 1956)[5] make up the quartet of tunes which Kerouac takes on in his easy and impromptu manner. Douglas Brinkley, Beat historian and the pen behind the sleeve notes here, says that the novelist's rendering of 'Ain't We Got Fun' 'highlights the comic versatility that allowed Kerouac to play the distinguished Beat poet, TV showman and babbling raconteur all at the same time'. The performance is 'no more – or less – than a jolly jape, an only mildly ironic paean to good times and the eternal happiness of nostalgia'. On 'Leavin' Town', he says that Kerouac 'accentuates the lines like a nightclub pro, using clear diction and put on phrasing to make the standard his own'.[6]

These pieces are among a range of intriguing fragments from the Kerouac archive, which were re-discovered, long after the novelist's death in 1969, by representatives of the writer's estate in unmarked boxes. Among the other items that would make an appearance on the 1999 CD release was a long section from *On the Road* – his most famous novel, issued in 1957 – a sequence entitled 'Jazz of the Beat Generation',[7] one of the most celebrated sections from Kerouac's voluminous body of published writing, a brilliantly descriptive account that had first seen the light of day in copy of the literary magazine *New World Writing* in April 1955, merely carrying the signature Jean Louis, a passing nod to Kerouac's deep French, more accurately Canuck, roots. It was also thought to be an attempt to hide his true identity at a time when a paternity suit was being laid against him

---

[2] On the album notes the song is credited to Sammy Kahn.
[3] On the album the song title is rendered as 'Come Rain or Shine'.
[4] The sleeve notes credit the more formal version of lyricist's name, John H. Mercer.
[5] Establishing the date of this song, even identifying that this is the song described, has not been straightforward. Kerouac's loose extemporisation has proved hard to pin down with absolute certainty.
[6] Douglas Brinkley, CD sleeve notes, *Jack Kerouac Reads On the Road* (Rykodisc, 1999).
[7] Dave Moore, personal communication, email, 28 May 2012, points out that there are also 'separate, identifiable sections from *Visions of Cody*' drawn upon in this particular version.

by his second wife Joan Haverty who had borne a daughter called Jan[8] in 1951 but whose existence, or at least her blood relation to him, was virtually denied by her absent father.

'Jazz of the Beat Generation' is a dazzling tour de force – a frenetic, yet beautifully detailed and observed, rap on jazz musicians and their art, a torrent of roaring, spontaneous prose, a high octane prayer to the musical soundtrack that kept Kerouac's Sal Paradise and his compadre Dean Moriarty – a lightly veiled portrait of his great friend and inveterate adventurer Neal Cassady – up and ready during their criss-crossing tours of the US at the end of the 1940s. Yet this ground-breaking work that would trail the experimental vernacular from which Kerouac built a whole book, was not the only piece of 24-carat genius to find its way into that very special edition of *New World Writing*. Alongside pieces by Dylan Thomas – dead from the effects of drink by 1953 – and a poem by the rising critic A. Alvarez, work by the British poet Thom Gunn and a contribution from the German novelist Heinrich Böll, was part of a developing story called *Catch-18* by an unknown American wordsmith called Joseph Heller. By the turn of the next decade, Kerouac's *On the Road* and Heller's anti-war satire, by now re-named *Catch-22*, were among the most venerated examples of a new, post-Second World War, American literature.

The Kerouac reading then would form the core ingredient on the 1999 recorded collection, but there was more besides. Douglas Brinkley's sleeve notes capture the variety present on the disc when he states: 'This album […] is a nine-track showcase for the writer as romantic crooner, lonely vagabond, prose stylist, Tin Pan Alley cut-up, hobo poet and scat innovator'.[9] Further, *Jack Kerouac Reads On the Road* would also pay tribute to another artist linked to the Beat movement of the 1950s – the photographer Robert Frank, whose images would be utilised as part of the sleeve design. In 1959, Frank had produced a photographic collection called *The Americans*, a set of striking, and atmospheric, black and white images that captured something of the spirit of the ordinary, everyday USA from that period – the everyman and everywoman, children, too, framed by Frank, destined to become one of the legendary cameramen of the later century. If Frank's pictures distilled the spirit of the worker, the hobo, the frayed fringes of American society, they also seemed to embrace something of the spirit of Kerouac's writings of the time and there was a certain logic that the novelist should be asked to pen the introductory section to a book that, apart from that essay, relied merely on its

---

[8] Jan Kerouac would meet her father eventually and emerge as a novelist herself – *Baby Driver* (1981) and *Trainsong* (1998) were among her fiction publications – but she would die, following surgery, aged 44, in 1996.

[9] Brinkley, CD sleeve notes, 1999.

pictorial essay to tell its story. Kerouac with typical energy and a passionate enthusiasm responded to Frank's work:

> The humour, the sadness, the EVERYTHING-ness and American-ness of these pictures! Tall thin cowboy rolling butt outside Madison Square Garden New York for rodeo season, sad, spindly, unbelievable – Long shot of night road arrowing forlorn into immensities and flat of impossible-to-believe America in New Mexico under the prisoner's moon – under the whang whang guitar star – Haggard old frowsy dames of Los Angeles leaning peering out the right front window of Old Paw's car on a Sunday gawking and criticising to explain old Amerikay to little children in the spattered back seat – tattooed guy sleeping on grass in park in Cleveland …[10]

Forty years later, as Jim Sampas worked on the tribute album, he invited a well-regarded album sleeve designer to concoct the packaging. Frank Olinsky had worked on various Sonic Youth-linked graphic commissions including the band's *A Thousand Leaves* (1998) and another for member Thurston Moore, *Psychic Hearts*, in 1995. The fact that band guitarist Lee Ranaldo was joining Sampas as producer on the Kerouac disc was not irrelevant. The front cover showcased a Robert Frank image of Kerouac studying a jukebox, the back cover an evocative shot of the highway receding inexorably into a rain-filled sky. Explains Olinsky:

> Jim got permission for the Robert Frank photos. Someone told me the back cover photo of the highway was his choice for the original cover for *On The Road* book.[11] I was not allowed to crop the Frank photos so that was one of the factors that influenced my design. I love the detail photos of the tape reels with Kerouac's little drawings of fish, heart and so on, and encouraged their use. It was my idea to run Douglas Brinkley's liner notes vertically and set in a typewriter font as an homage to the original *On The Road* manuscript scroll.[12]

---

[10] Jack Kerouac, 'Introduction', *The Americans* by Robert Frank, in Kerouac, *Good Blonde & Others* (San Francisco, CA: Grey Fox Press, 1994), pp. 19–20.
[11] Dave Moore, personal communication, email, 28 May 2012, believes that 'the Robert Frank photo was not planned for an *On the Road* book cover, but for an *On the Road* LP cover. Kerouac recorded three LPs' worth of material for Norman Granz in March 1958, for release by Verve Records. Only one was issued at the time – *Readings on the Beat Generation*. Another was to be called *On the Road* but has never appeared.' In *The Kerouac Connection*, No.19, Spring 1990, record producer Bill Randle recalled: 'Robert Frank the photographer was the most real and dedicated of the people who hung around those sessions. We used a great picture of his for the *On the Road* album … that straight ending Western road at night pic … powerful.' Adds Moore: 'So Kerouac's "Jazz of the Beat Generation" recording was made in New York, March 1958, and was evidently intended to be part of that original *On the Road* album.'
[12] The Original Scroll Edition was Kerouac's first draft, written on a continuous teletype roll, for *On the Road*.

I also came up with the concept of the CD label covered with the pattern of typewritten words that aligns with the inside tray card.[13]

Another key player in this project was David Amram, who would emerge as a noted musician, composer and arranger from mid-century, and had been a friend of Kerouac's since before the release of his headline novel. Together they had informally conceived their own version of jazz poetry as performance art, Amram accompanying Kerouac's words on the various instruments he played – from French horn to piano and percussion. By the time *On the Road* had turned Kerouac's name into one of the hottest tickets in New York City, the pair had presented their act, in late 1957, at the Brata Art Gallery on East 10th Street and the Village's Circle in the Square Theatre. Later Kerouac linked with other jazz players at the Village Vanguard but the reviews were poor. Kerouac was already drinking too much and his nervous demeanour rendered his on-stage projection a blend of the wooden and the slapdash. However, the writer's association with Amram remained close – they would collaborate on the Robert Frank and Alfred Leslie movie *Pull My Daisy* in 1959 when Kerouac penned the screenplay and narrated while his erstwhile musical partner conceived the soundtrack. But their jazz poetry link-up itself never quite achieved what the duo believed was possible, nor was it documented via recording, so we will never know for sure how good this partnership was, nor how this on-stage relationship might have played out, in time, with more tender understanding and encouragement from the critics.

When the producer of the project, Jim Sampas, a nephew of the novelist by marriage, realised he had access to extended sections of his late uncle reading his own prose poems, he invited Amram, by now a veteran of many bands and orchestras, a sideman to Leonard Bernstein, Machito and Dizzy Gillespie over many years and a creator of symphonic, chamber and soundtrack works in his own right, to compose the musical accompaniment to these recordings. He proceeded to devise some outstanding arrangements that lent colour and depth to Kerouac's disembodied voice-track. 'Orizaba 210 Blues' and 'Washington DC Blues' are a pair of remarkable and extended work-outs in which Amram and his own jazz ensemble breathe life into reels that had been gathering dust for around 40 years. The settings – which integrate jazz and world, classical and baroque elements – fit the poetry like a glove, a strange experience when the oral and melodic components had been divided by so many decades.

Amram recalls the process: 'Jim [Sampas] sent me a copy of "Washington DC Blues" and a cassette of Jack [Kerouac] reading it. Jack sounded at his best. I felt like I was hanging out with him again.' He adds: 'As I listened […] I remembered

---

[13] Frank Olinsky, album sleeve designer, personal communication, email, 8 December 2008.

the gentle way Jack had of expressing himself. He was usually out-shouted by most of his friends, so he never blew out his vocal cords trying to out-shout them. His speaking voice was beautiful and he was a surprisingly good singer. When he wasn't reading aloud, scat singing, bashing at the piano, or hammering on the bongos, he would sit quietly in the middle of the pandemonium.'[14]

For the recording sessions, Amram devised a group with a neo-classical sound – including viola, bassoon, oboe and English horn – to approach the 'Washington DC Blues' account. It was the same orchestration style he had employed for the scored segments of *Pull My Daisy*. Remarkably he managed to gather the same instrumentalists who had played on the 1959 film soundtrack.[15] For 'Orizaba 210 Blues', he took a different approach. He explains that here he was looking for a 'jazz-Latin-World sound'.[16] The conga player he engaged for the recording provided another link to Kerouac's past – Candido had played with Dizzy Gillespie's band, an ensemble the novelist had seen in person.[17]

Amram undoubtedly brought an eclectic flavour to his updated takes on Kerouac's words and the results had much to recommend them. However, it is hard not to argue that the most interesting song on the album is one that reveals Kerouac as not only vocalist manqué, a prose and poetry stylist supreme, but also a man capable of writing an original song himself. The song 'On the Road' not only has a fascinating genesis, but is the subject, too, of a second version on the CD. Here, Beat aficionado Tom Waits and the Californian funk rock band Primus concoct a fresh take on Kerouac's self-composed blues. In this section, I would like to offer an archaeological trawl through a song-cum-poem that appears in numerous versions – both as a versatile vehicle for Kerouac's creative expression but also as a platform of various kinds for Waits as well.

The notion of versions, interestingly, has become part of the Kerouac legend as the writer was known not only to produce different editions of stories he wrote, but also extensively revise those variations. In fact, *On the Road*, definitively released by Viking Press, was actually just one incarnation of the same picaresque tale and one that the novelist himself was less than satisfied with. His earliest attempt to capture the spirit and energy of Sal and Dean's transcontinental journeys, was produced on a continuous teletype roll over three weeks in 1951. But this freeform rush of thought and deed, lacking even paragraph breaks, would be rejected early on in the commissioning process. Kerouac returned to the exercise several times in the period that followed and it would be actually six years later before a recognisable book – and one that the publishers would sign

---

[14] David Amram, *Offbeat: Celebrating with Kerouac* (New York: Thunder's Mouth Press, 2001), p. 194.
[15] Amram, pp. 192–3.
[16] *Ibid.*, p. 192.
[17] *Ibid.*

off – emerged. While the edition on the bookshop shelves would bring Kerouac significant sales, not a little cash and fame aplenty, it was never the book he had wanted to issue. The different versions that did exist would not see the light before the writer's alcohol-soaked death in 1969. Eventually, with the backing of his ever-supportive friend Allen Ginsberg, a posthumously published title called *Visions of Cody* was released in 1973. This was a highly experimental telling of the saga, one in which Dean Moriarty had now been renamed Cody Pomeray.

The re-cast edition not only featured long passages of spontaneous text, barely touched by the hand of an editor, the very approach that the radical artist in Kerouac found most appealing, but also transcripts of taped conversations that he and Cassady had shared, recollecting various aspects of their wanderings. What can be said is that the 1973 version, while a favourite among committed followers of the Kerouac canon, would not have seen the public light of day without the exciting reputation that the novelist had carved out through a dozen issued works and several volumes of poetry, too, in the interim. If *Visions of Cody* had been given the green light in 1957, its left-field format, its lack of respect for basic laws of syntax, would have been unlikely to garner the glowing review that Gilbert Millstein penned in the *New York Times*, on 5 September 1957, when he produced the key, breakthrough notice of *On the Road*, and nor would the public – that young, dynamic, and principally male, readership hungering for a story of freedom-seeking exuberance and one with a readable style and a conventional narrative – have been so easily recruited to what would rapidly become a significant Kerouac cult by the later 1950s and early 1960s.

Later, much later, in 2007, the Original Scroll edition of *On the Road*, that legendary version penned on the continuous roll, unfettered by many of the traditional niceties of written text – paragraph breaks, particularly, as we have mentioned – would finally become available to a general readership. The physical scroll had already become an object of general note following the purchase of the item for a world record figure by Jim Irsay, the super-wealthy owner of the National Football League franchise Indianapolis Colts, who acquired the document for $2.43m in 2001. A Kerouac fan, a rock music follower and plainly a committed sports backer, Irsay sent the scroll on a national, then international, tour, attracting crowds of visitors in museums around the world. The scroll narrative was not only unconventional in its style of expression; it also restored the genuine names of the novel's protagonists – Cassady, Ginsberg and so on – something that Kerouac had hoped would happen in the first place. But the legal offices of his publisher were nervous of stories that appeared to cross a line between fact and fiction, between factional recollections and genuinely actionable anecdotes, and it was inevitable that the players would need to be re-christened for the novel.

By the time the Original Scroll became available as a softback in 2007, virtually all the central *dramatis personae* were dead – Cassady by 1968, Kerouac a year later, Ginsberg and William Burroughs in 1997 – although, when I attended the opening of the Original Scroll exhibition in Birmingham, England, in December 2008,[18] there was at least one of the stars of the story present: the indefatigable Carolyn Cassady, Neal's wife, who was pleased to be present as one of the guests of honour at the unveiling, the first time that this totemic work had been on view in the UK. Carolyn Cassady, 85 at the time, has tended to play down the veneration of the Beats and subscribed to little of the mythology surrounding them, debunking some of their generational aura in her 1990 memoir *Off the Road: Twenty Years with Cassady, Kerouac and Ginsberg.*

As for the naming of actual names in the revised published text, the anxious concerns of mid-1950s publishers' lawyers were probably over-developed: the core cast of *On the Road* were hardly likely to turn litigious as their good friend secured publication of a saga that had been on ice for so long and was merely celebrating the diversely eccentric, often risqué, escapades that the Beats had indulged in, in Manhattan, in Denver, the deep South and Mexico and elsewhere, from the early 1940s to the end of that decade. That said, the inferences of drug use and abuse, sexual shenanigans and even homosexual diversions, would hardly have made for comfortable reading for those stiff-collared professionals with half an eye on the possibility of a libel suit.

So, when I refer to 'Versions of Cody' in the title of this chapter, you might perhaps excuse the wordplay – Kerouac's career, as we have shown, was peppered by such debates (during his lifetime and since) about what the definitive or favoured incarnation of a particular text may have been. There are other examples of books with different content to the edition that was published. *Big Sur*, for example, Kerouac's terrible, yet dazzling, delirium tremens-tinged confession, has sections that have never been seen outside the confines of the official archive.

Now though, I want to consider the blues work 'On the Road' as a Kerouac original and also as the subject of Waits' re-interpretation. I have identified at least seven versions of this composition, some that exist only in a literary sense, several that have a musical dimension, too, some attached to the original author-composer, others to Waits himself. Let us look initially at this poem-cum-song from Kerouac's perspective. To begin with the edition that was unearthed from the writer's archive, here was a home recording Kerouac had made, we have to assume, with his high fidelity microphone and tape recorder. Taking a lyric that rather mournfully commemorates a life of hobo-like travel, he sings the song in a manner that is full of atmosphere but short on tunefulness and lacking rhythmic discipline. In short, the performance reveals none of the confident jauntiness that he was able

---

[18] The Original Scroll was displayed at the Barber Institute of Fine Arts, Birmingham University from 3 December 2008–28 January 2009, its first exhibition in the UK.

to display on his recordings of the romantic standards to which we have earlier referred. Why is this? Several reasons may be put forward. Firstly, it seems likely that the earlier recordings, while amateurish and playful, did appear to benefit in some way from Jerry Newman's engineering skills. The recording of 'On the Road' instead appears much closer to a late night, almost certainly drunken, slice of melancholy: alcohol and self-pity both appear to be influencing factors in the version that is laid down. As Douglas Brinkley comments: 'Then there is the short lyric "On the Road" – a poem really – that Kerouac sings with a heart-wrenching melancholia, a sense of being lost in Thomas Wolfe's raw, vast America, that rootless land where salvation is always hovering around the next corner like a forgotten shroud. The listener can't miss the tender whisper in Kerouac's voice, as if offering confession to a Catholic priest, anxious for penance.'[19]

It seems likely, too, that the standards were committed to tape in the late 1950s when Kerouac's mood was much lighter. While the initial pleasures and then growing pains of fame were beginning to alter his life, his reliance on alcohol was less marked. By the start of the next decade though, when the song version of 'On the Road' was most likely recorded, drink was becoming a more central feature in the novelist's life. So when and where was the song recorded to tape? There seems strong evidence that Kerouac recorded this nocturnal ramble at his home in Florida around 1962. His life was always peripatetic: if he was not on the move as part of his roaming spirit, he was changing house on a very regular basis, decisions based around his mother's needs and wider family calls. Kerouac's base would range from New England to New York, Denver to Florida, as he followed – sometimes led – his surviving parent and sister to new properties across the US.

Bob Kealing, who is co-founder and board member of the Kerouac Project in Orlando, Florida, which works to celebrate the writer's legacy in that part of the States, comments: 'I suspect the recordings took place at Kerouac's Orlando home in 1961–62. I know he did other recordings there as well. This was a very typical block home in a new Orlando suburb, Kingswood Manor. He recorded some other material for his then-girlfriend Lois Sorrells.'[20]

Jim Sampas, overseeing the album's development with Lee Ranaldo, tends to concur. He believes that close listening to the recording reveals the sound of planes taking off or landing and he thinks that these could well have been from an airport near to Kerouac's Orlando base. However, he opines that the recording

---

[19] Brinkley, sleeve notes, 1999.
[20] Bob Kealing, Kerouac Project, Orlando, Florida, personal communication, email, 27 November 2008. Dave Moore, personal communication, email, 28 May 2012, remarks: 'I tend to agree with Bob Kealing that those recordings by Jack were from the same period as the other recordings he made for Lois Sorrells. I would suggest, though, that the location was Jack's home in Northport, Long Island, rather than Orlando, since poet LeRoi Jones was present for at least one session, and I don't believe that Jones ever visited Kerouac in Florida.'

in question may have been a little later than Kealing's, commenting: 'Kerouac also sounds a bit older to me. It could be even be the mid-1960s.'[21]

When Sampas came to consider how this song might feature on the album he was planning, he had a strong sense that the basic recording, while intriguing in its way, would need some extra work. He remarks: 'We had the solo version with Jack Kerouac singing *a cappella*. But we wondered how interesting that would be. We felt it needed a little bit of something. It was an amazing song but it was out of time.' It was at this stage that David Amram's band members came to the assistance of the project. 'What we decided was, we would record a backing at the studio in New York involving the David Amram Ensemble which included both guitarist Vic Juris and keyboard player John Medeski. They listened to it and then they took a stab. Vic Juris wrote the music. Vic and John played. They did a little bit of a practice run and then boom, they recorded it. They did it miraculously, a fantastic job.'

Guitarist Juris, who has also done work with Allen Ginsberg and Gregory Corso during his career, remembers the session, which took place on 24 and 26 October 1998, a little differently: 'I became involved with the Kerouac project through composer David Amram who was a personal friend of Jack's. They collaborated on the first jazz and poetry readings in the late 1950s. Jim Sampas discovered a few tapes and asked us to compose an accompaniment to Jack's singing. John Medeski added his personal touch at a later recording session.'[22]

Yet the home recording of the early to mid-1960s, and the revived version of 1999, were only part of the story of the lyric that Kerouac placed at the centre of his 'On the Road' song. In fact, the lyric had made a much earlier appearance in the novel *On the Road* itself, when, well into the account, Sal Paradise sings the song to himself as he awaits a hitched ride.[23] On this occasion the piece was only ten lines long, an abbreviated edition of the song. But Kerouac expanded the song lyric still further in a short story that would feature in the January 1958, Christmas special issue, of the magazine *Playboy*, a regular location, in its early years, for original fiction by the new writing talent of the day. In his tale 'The rumbling, rambling blues',[24] the writer – in his usual role of narrator – encounters a hobo Negro singer in a café in Des Moines. The full lyric is transcribed there for the reader but this still raises the question, is this an actual blues song? Is this an actual incident? Did Kerouac witness this episode and hear the song or did he fabricate it as a literary device? Kerouac's use of his own experiences, at least the basis of his experiences,

---

[21] Jim Sampas, producer of *Jack Kerouac Reads On the Road*, personal communication, email, 24 November 2008.

[22] Vic Juris, guitarist, personal communication, email, 24 November 2008.

[23] Jack Kerouac, *On the Road* (Harmondsworth: Penguin, 1972), p. 240.

[24] The story would be re-published in the 1993 Kerouac collection, *Good Blonde & Others* (San Francisco, CA: Grey Fox Press, 1998), pp. 40–4.

for yarn-spinning is widely recognised, so it is not impossible that the novelist did sit in a café somewhere and indeed encounter a visiting blues troubadour. But has he dreamt up his own blues lyric for the purposes of effect?

There are, of course, tens of thousands of blues lyrics but Dave Moore, an independent scholar of reputation and a foremost expert on Kerouac not to mention a close follower of the blues and its history, expresses a useful view on this matter. He remarks: 'I've heard a lot [of blues], including most of the old country blues songs. I have never come across those particular lyrics before. Kerouac had been exposed to blues recordings, both on record and live, in the 1940s and '50s, and was well aware of the format. It's my guess that he composed something "in the idiom" which found its way into both pieces of his writing.'[25]

So we might assume that Kerouac had shaped his own blues narrative in these self-penned words, then included it in two different pieces of fiction – novel followed by short story – before committing it, in *ad hoc* fashion, to his own tape archive. But what of Tom Waits' part in this story? How did he pick up the baton well over 30 years later? What brought him into this project and what did he now do with the lyric and the song that his novelist predecessor had conceived? First, perhaps, we should say something about Waits and his associations with Kerouac and the wider Beat ethos.

The Beat Generation writers have been long admired by Tom Waits. 'They were like father figures to me', he stated in a US National Public Radio interview in 2006 with broadcaster Robert Siegel. 'Because you have to have someone you can really look up to. And they were like pirates, real buccaneers. They struck out on their own, made a name for themselves'. Waits was a fan of Kerouac – his 'first true literary hero',[26] says Barney Hoskyns – and Ginsberg, Siegel knew, but did he also read Lawrence Ferlinghetti, the interviewer wondered. 'Ferlinghetti, no question about that. *Coney Island of the Mind*, I was a big fan. I remember that book very well. I got it signed when I was a teenager. I took the train to San Francisco, went to the bookstore.[27] And, you know, I went to a bar nearby where I heard that he hung out and I gave it to the bar tender and said, well if he comes in here, have him to sign it for me will you – and he did!'[28] So the singer, born at the end of the 1940s and an itinerant child as his parents split when he was young, was, even as an adolescent, drawn to the work of the Beats, by their writings but also their attitudes and lifestyle.

---

[25] Dave Moore, personal communication, email, 3 December 2008.
[26] Barney Hoskyns, *Lowside of the Road: A Life of Tom Waits* (London: Faber, 2009), p. 478.
[27] Lawrence Ferlinghetti was not only poet and publisher but was also proprietor of City Lights, a city landmark and one of the most famous independent bookshops in the world.
[28] Tom Waits quoted from 'Tom Waits: The whiskey voice returns', interview with Robert Siegel, *All Things Considered*, NPR, 21 November 2006, http://www.npr.org/templates/story/story. php?storyId=6519647 [accessed 29 November 2008].

As Cath Carroll comments: 'As soon as biologically possible, Waits also began to cultivate a goatee [...] At around the age of 18, he discovered Beat writers, absorbing the works of Jack Kerouac and Allen Ginsberg, of Charles Bukowksi and of the poet Delmore Schwartz [...] He found himself enthralled by the insidious musicality of the Beat poets' bare words.'[29] Says Waits himself: 'I guess everybody reads Kerouac at some point in their life. Even though I was growing up in Southern California, he made a tremendous impression on me. It was 1968. I started wearing dark glasses and got myself a subscription to *Down Beat*...I was a little late, Kerouac died in 1969 in St. Petersburg, Florida, a bitter old man.'[30]

Drawn to the vision of Beat experience as literary mode and as a blueprint for an existence he could cultivate at the enticing, if somewhat frayed, margins, Waits lived a life as bohemian troubadour from the late 1960s and certainly for the next decade. Humphries states: 'Waits boasted that he had "slept through the Sixties". This wasn't just irreverence, this was heresy. The icons and role models of the sixties stretched way into rock culture of the seventies and beyond, but Waits was typically out of step, determinedly harking back to earlier heroes.'[31] Humphries adds: 'Tom Waits soaked up Kerouac and got soused on Beat mythology. His favourite album of all time was Kerouac's 1960 collection *Blues and Haikus* and at his own New York debut in the mid-1970s, Waits was proud to include in his band saxophonist Al Cohn who had played on the album.'[32]

The road itself, the highway, was also a pervasive emblem in Waits just as it had been in Kerouac. Corinne Kessel dubs the novel *On the Road* 'an important thematic touchstone'[33] for the singer. She says that 'the lifestyles of Kerouac's rubber tramp characters [...] and his particular use of language have provided Waits with a framework for his own characters and language.'[34] She adds, in a manner that would have chimed with Kerouac and must still with Waits:

Highways are symbolic of many different freedoms and liberations for every individual who encounters them, whether as part of a spirit-revitalizing journey or as a necessary escape from mercilessly fatiguing constraints [...] Highways are highly conducive to the evanescent spirit of transients and vagabonds and are often places where lonely souls can be brought together for brief moments of interaction or crowded minds can be given space to refocus and meditate. Highways are places of movement; they are designed only to

---

29 Cath Carroll, *Tom Waits* (New York: Thunder's Mouth Press, 2000), p. 9.
30 Patrick Humphries, *Small Change: A Life of Tom Waits* (London: Omnibus, 1989), p. 15.
31 Humphries, 1989, p. 17.
32 *Ibid.*
33 Corinne Kessel, *The Words and Music of Tom Waits* (Westport, CT: Praeger, 2009), p. 65.
34 Kessel, 2009, p. 65.

facilitate travel from one place to another and thus offer endless possibilities to the wanderer.[35]

In his repertoire of jazz and blues, in bar-room balladry, in his shabby, crumpled glory, Waits seemed to personify a surviving beatnik style and ethos, long after the tide of psychedelia and long-hair had appeared to supplant those earlier monochrome times. His on-stage persona at least, from whiskey-scarred and nicotine-roughened vocals to a crushed pork pie hat, embodied the bruised romanticism of the travelling performer. Yet his musical heroes were James Brown and Ray Charles and Jimmy Witherspoon and he initially became embroiled in the eccentric fringes with Frank Zappa and Captain Beefheart as the 1960s fizzled out. By the early 1980s, as he married, forged a family and a song-writing partnership with his wife Kathleen Brennan, and settled down to some large degree, we might argue that his maintenance of the image of dishevelled vagrant, growling, groaning song-smith, is more mannered, less authentic maybe, than in the early days of his itinerant career. But the on-stage character has survived nonetheless.

Hoskyns writes: 'Waits gave vent to the influence of Beat writings and spoken word jazz verse in an early version of "Diamonds on My Windshield" that he read in a little storefront on the main business street in Venice.'[36] The lyric, which distilled much of the verveful spirit of Kerouac's road, would find a way onto his second album, *Heart of Saturday Night* in 1974, wrapped in a melancholic bebop-like keyboard dressing. Eventually, he would not only maintain this evident Beat allegiance but also include Kerouac and Cassady and their ilk in his own songs, most pertinently in the composition 'Jack and Neal' (1977) and also 'Bad Liver and a Broken Heart (in Lowell)' (1976), the latter paying tribute not just to the later, ailing days of the novelist but also the Massachusetts town where he would grow up and finally be buried.

Kessel, discussing Waits' 1975 live album *Nighthawks at the Diner*, says that the record saw 'the further development of Waits' drunken bohemian after-hours persona, which was an amalgamation of beatnik, vaudevillian and crooner quali-ties.'[37] Rather later, too, Waits would extend his active Beat participation when he worked on the William Burroughs project *The Black Rider*, a 1993 album linked to theatre director Robert Wilson's expressionist stage production in Hamburg, Germany.

So, in short, Waits' credentials to form a key ingredient in the *Jack Kerouac Reads On the Road* venture were hardly in doubt and Jim Sampas, who had also produced an earlier and acclaimed spoken word tribute to the writer in his 1997

---

[35] *Ibid.*
[36] Hoskyns, 2009, p. 68. Note that the reference is to Venice Beach, Los Angeles.
[37] Kessel, 2009, p. 3.

release *Kerouac: Kicks, Joy, Darkness*, was keen to bring the singer into the ring for this new production. Sampas states: '[Waits] was definitely interested, he was definitely fascinated. He was also unsure because of the influence Jack Kerouac had had on him and his admiration for Jack Kerouac was profound.' He sensed that Waits was striking a note of reticence even if he was drawn to the idea of adapting 'On the Road', the song, in his own manner. 'He wanted to be very careful. He was aware of the idea that if you screwed up it was not a good thing. He was very cautious. We had conversations. I sent the song to him and he listened to it. He called me back. Then I found a source for the lyrics. I sent them over to him. After a while he felt okay with it. He was wholeheartedly into it.' As for Waits' decision to include Primus on the session, hosted by Prairie Sun Recording Studios in Northern California, Sampas was, for his part, relaxed on this point. He comments: 'They were working together at the time. Primus bassist Les Claypool had worked with Tom on the Waits' album *Bone Machine* in 1992. My feeling was whoever Tom Waits wants to put on the Jack Kerouac song, he's going to have it. I was happy to give him artistic discretion.'[38]

The result could hardly have been more different to Kerouac's spare, late-night melodising even if it had now been annotated with some blues colourings by Juris and Medeski. Waits and Primus, in a vigorous swamp blues fashion, lent heft and drama to the piece, more rock than country, with the singer's gravelly tones forefronted, complemented with great atmosphere by muscular bass lines and a slide guitar line that suggested both a contemporary, rasping grind but hinted at the primitive sounds that the Lomaxes[39] might have tracked in the backwoods South as they gathered field recordings of, often ageing, musicians in the 1930s and 1940s. In short, Waits and Primus had created a concoction that spoke of the present *and* the past, a fine way to approach this most unusual of tasks: resurrecting a deeply private soliloquy in an electric band setting for public consumption. As Brinkley remarked on the sleeve: 'The producers hoped Waits would perform the song, and he jumped at the notion. [He] added a little melody and a few words of his own and recorded a moody, Bowery-tinged version of the song that exactly captures the rainy, subterranean ashcan essence of Kerouac's homeless lament.'[40] Kessel says this of the Waits take: '[Kerouac's] words pay homage to highway life and are layered overtop of the twang of the banjo, rollicking bass, scorching electric guitar, and amplified gritty harmonica.'[41]

Waits reflected on this exercise in musical revival in Hoskyns' 2009 biography, even if the various interpretations and how Kerouac came to lay down the original

---

[38] Jim Sampas, producer, interview with author, 20 November 2008.
[39] John A. Lomax (1867–1948) and his son Alan (1915–2002) were important folklorists, who gathered examples of the US's folk music heritage over much of the twentieth-century.
[40] Brinkley, CD sleeve notes, 1999.
[41] Kessel, 2009, p. 50.

were a little awry, with suggestions that the novelist's original version had been written and recorded as long ago as 1949. Waits comments: 'I guess Jack was at a party somewhere and snuck off into a closet and started singing into a reel-to-reel tape deck. Like, "I left New York in 1949, drove across the country …" I wound up turning it into a song.'[42] Further, says Hoskyns, Kerouac's namecheck for El Cajon, a suburb of San Diego, a city the singer had grown up near, perhaps brought the lyric close to home for Waits, and 1949 was also his birthyear, 'so there were places where I connected with that', the singer pointed out.[43] The father figure who haunts the song must also have had poignant echoes for Waits who had, at earlier stages in his life, conducted searches for that missing player in his own personal drama, a scenario that had clear reverberations of the track Neal Cassady had worn, yearning to re-connect with his own dad in the streets of Denver, episodes that became an integral part of *On the Road*'s fiction.

We should also note that the song 'On the Road' would make a further appearance, a different take it would seem from the Prairie Sun sessions, on Waits' triple album set of 2006, *Orphans: Brawlers, Bawlers & Bastards*. Further, Waits would include, on the same sprawling compilation gathering songs from various periods, another version of the song, this time entitled 'Home I'll Never Be', a pared down, solo arrangement with the singer accompanied on piano only.

This song, this interpretation, would feature in another important Beat setting when Hal Willner directed a tribute to the recently deceased Allen Ginsberg in Los Angeles in 1997. Steven Taylor, Ginsberg's long-time guitarist who was present, recalls the occasion: 'I was there. It was a memorial for Allen. I was under the impression that it was organised by Allen's cousin Oscar Janiger. Willner would have rounded up the musicians. Janiger was Allen's main Hollywood connection, and we usually stayed at his place in Santa Monica when we were in town. The actor Kevin Spacey read "White Shroud" to the accompaniment of a string quartet I had scored some years earlier for the poem. Johnny Depp made an appearance, and seemed to be "in character" for the role he played in *Fear and Loathing in Las Vegas*, which he must have been filming at the time. I remember Waits at the piano.'[44]

Thus, we witness Waits' varied engagement with the Beats – all of the great triumvirate of Kerouac, Burroughs and Ginsberg, not to mention Ferlinghetti – and evidenced in a number of ways. But it does seem that it is in the restless, probing, on-the-move compulsion of Jack that provides, for the singer, his most endearing and enduring template, and, in the song 'On the Road', Waits had the perfect opportunity to make a post-grave connection with his hero, an intimate

---

[42] Hoskyns, 2009, p. 479.

[43] *Ibid*.

[44] Steven Taylor, personal communication, email, 1 December 2008.

link with the writer's desires and fears, some of which had close parity with those of the musician himself. Speaking some years later, as a contributor to the 2009 documentary *One Fast Move or I'm Gone: Kerouac's Big Sur*,[45] Waits made some sympathetic remarks on the increasingly chaotic condition of his hero as, by the start of the 1960s, he sank into a mire of desperate, eventually morbid, alcoholic indulgence, spurred by the pressures of celebrity that his signature novel had generated. The 1962 novel *Big Sur* would be the acrid and scarred record of that psychological, then physical, decline as the bottle took its hold. Waits speaks warmly, if wryly. 'Well sometimes I read him and get sad. And I think, aaaww, man. Because nowadays we would just give you some Ritalin or something. Straighten your ass right out. Send you to AA, Jack. You'll be fine, man. You'll never write another word', he says breaking into a slightly bemused grin, 'But you'll be fine …'[46]

---

[45] The film was directed by Curt Worden and produced by Jim Sampas.
[46] Tom Waits, quoted in *One Fast Move or I'm Gone: Kerouac's Big Sur* (Kerouac Films, 2009).

9 FEELING THE BOHEMIAN PULSE: LOCATING PATTI SMITH WITHIN A POST-BEAT TRADITION

Patti Smith's multiple identities as musician and actor, artist, author and poet, have fascinated fans and critics, fellow performers, and the broader world of the left-field avant garde, in almost equal measure, since her artistic emergence at the beginning of the 1970s. Her ability to move through a range of creative practices and negotiate the evolving demands of her domestic life – marriage, motherhood and the loss of key significants – has seen her interweave her professional and personal résumés in a wide range of creative settings: candid, essentially autobiographical reflections presented in a number of fashions and formats over more than four decades – on record, in theatres, in interviews, on film and on the page.

We should also reflect on the fact that maturing, the onset of age, less usually considered in the realm of male practitioners, has also been addressed and managed with remarkable and admirable aplomb. When I witnessed a live appearance on her UK tour of spring 2007 in Sheffield, England,[1] I was struck by the extraordinarily youthful vivacity of the woman, impressed by the on-stage energy of a, by then, 60-year-old, one-time punk provocateur. It was hard not to believe I was witnessing a performance by a player at the height of her powers. She patently transcended any preconceptions that rock 'n' roll was no place for a middle-aged singer-songwriter to roam.

Perhaps Smith has pulled off the ultimate sleight of hand: the androgynous pose of her early career seems preserved in aspic. The unconventional, ambivalent appearance, frozen, for example, in photographer Robert Mapplethorpe's 1975

---

[1] The Patti Smith Group, live performance, Plug, Sheffield, 24 May 2007.

cover shot for her debut album *Horses*, has, we might argue, worn much better than the peroxided glamour of that other, and rather different, CBGBs goddess Deborah Harry. This is not to deride the attraction and appeal of the Blondie frontwoman, rather to argue that Smith's original persona has provided a more serviceable vehicle for this veritable Patti Pan: there is no sense that Smith's enduring kudos in the early twenty-first century is premised on nostalgia or revival, a rare feat of longevity in a musical terrain usually fixated on youth.

Smith's ideological position seems broadly wed to the bohemian impulse – that abiding spirit of subversive creativity that stretches from 1830s Paris to the Downtown traditions of New York City in the latter decades of the twentieth century and beyond. She cites guiding beacons as diverse as Arthur Rimbaud, Lotte Lenya and Jackson Pollock, reflecting this historical and geographical sweep. But her interest in the Beat Generation writers, the celebrated Greenwich Village bohemians of the 1940s and 1950s, is frequently evidenced.[2] Their confessional mode shaped Smith's poems and her lyrics to an extent that we might consider her an heir, in various ways, to Allen Ginsberg and William Burroughs. This paper will explore Smith's status as Beat or, indeed, post-Beat, an appellation her life and work has sometimes attracted. It will attempt to understand in what ways the term post-Beat has been applied and to what degree Smith can be identified as part of that later tradition or leaning. Further, it will reflect on the values and dangers of such association and absorb and test criticisms that such forms of appropriation lack substance and that name-dropping illustrious antecedents is a *modus operandi* that is not always positively acknowledged.

This chapter will draw on two principal sources: the main biographical texts by Bockris and Johnstone, Shaw and Tarr, and a body of newly collected primary materials, for which the author has drawn on ethnographic techniques, approaching a number of informants with insight into Smith and, particularly, her overlap with Beat culture. The latter includes interviews with surviving Beats and post-Beats (writers Anne Waldman, Joyce Pinchbeck and Steven Taylor, among them) exchanges with biographers (Victor Bockris and Philip Shaw, for instance), journalists and cultural historians (Holly George-Warren, Harvey Kubernik and Bart Bull), academics (Sheila Whiteley and Lucy O'Brien), and poets (Jim Cohn and David Cope), which explore the notion of transgenerational influence and also attempt to locate Patti Smith within this fluid field of activity, this matrix of interpersonal connection. What the essay will not attempt, for reasons of space, is a close examination of Smith's poetic and rock output in relation to Beat effect: this piece is about traces in her style and life and to what extent these traces are exaggerated or over-played, by her or by others.

---

[2] There are numerous Beat references in Smith's memoir, *Just Kids* (London: Bloomsbury, 2010).

However, I would like to begin this enquiry with some recent comments that have fired a number of critical arrows at Patti Smith, questioning her motivations for pinning her colours, so often and so enthusiastically, to the ethos of the Beat community and its output. These remarks will be utilised as a starting point for contextualisation, a platform from which established commentators are later able to provide their own readings and insights into Smith's status and behaviour, particularly in respect of the perceived homage that she has paid to this earlier gathering of writers.

Three web reviewers, considering Curt Worden's documentary *One Fast Move or I'm Gone: Kerouac's Big Sur*, all felt uncharitably disposed to Patti Smith's presence as an interview subject, a talking head, in this 2009 production, a feature which considered the circumstances surrounding Jack Kerouac's 1960 stay at Lawrence Ferlinghetti's Californian hillside cabin as he bid to escape his deepening alcoholism and, additionally, the novel called *Big Sur* that followed, a work which endeavoured to capture the asphyxiatingly depressing impact of the writer's, ultimately fatal, addiction during this period.

In *Slant* magazine, Joseph Jon Lanthier commented on the film-work:

> [...] a sincere, dumbstruck passion for Kerouac's rhythmic confessions pervades the majority of the interviews and, despite some spacey misinterpretations (who keeps inviting Patti Smith to these Beat docs?), the on-screen readers persuasively remind us of how the syntactical spell of *Big Sur* managed to hypnotize our impressionable, undergraduate selves in the first place.[3]

Lydia Kiesling, writing in *The Millions* about the same documentary, remarked: 'Patti Smith, whom I suspect [was] brought in because [she is] perceived as having a never-ending fund of "cred".'[4] Just over a year on, Bill Morris, also in *The Millions*, concurred with Kiesling about Smith's appearance in the production. 'That must be it', he said. 'It can't possibly be that anyone still cares that she used to have a crush on William S. Burroughs.'[5]

Why should three reviewers, two men and one woman, feel the need to be critical of the inclusion of Patti Smith in this film? Each had slightly different

---

[3] Joseph Jon Lanthier, '*One Fast Move or I'm Gone: Kerouac's Big Sur*', 'Movie Review', *Slant* magazine, 11 October 2009, http://www.slantmagazine.com/film/review/one-fast-move-or-im-gone-kerouacs-big-sur/4504 [accessed 20 July 2011].

[4] Lydia Kiesling, '*One Fast Move or I'm Gone*: A review', 'Screening Room', *The Millions*, 6 November 2009, http://www.themillions.com/2009/11/one-fast-move-or-im-gone-a-review.html [accessed 20 July, 2011].

[5] Bill Morris, 'Will you Beat hagiographers please be quite, please?', *The Millions*, 28 December 2010, http://www.themillions.com/2010/12/will-you-beat-hagiographers-please-be-quiet-please.html [accessed 20 July 2011].

takes on the subject – Lanthier was rather dismissive of her reading of Kerouac's words; Kiesling was somewhat dubious about her inclusion as an example of token credibility in the piece; while Morris insinuated that Smith's addition to the cast was merely because she had expressed feelings of affection towards Burroughs. But their comments, in all cases, framed a somewhat jaundiced view of Smith's presence in Beat scenarios. There was a real sense that these online writers felt uncomfortable with Smith's involvement in a celluloid celebration that looked back on a key moment in Kerouac's alcohol-soaked early 1960s, post-fame life through a documentary lens. I do not want to make direct comment on the trio's positions: journalists, particularly critics, are driven by many motivations, professional and personal. These individuals may not be fans of Smith; they may have felt a vocational need to find fault with the artistic project and justify that reservation; they may have wished to make small waves in their circle or within their readership. But the gathering of these comments made me wonder further about the Smith-Beat nexus and contemplate more general ideas about artists constructing an aspect of their own cachet on the attainments of the past. Is name-checking mere tribute, the valid gesture of a new generation tipping its hat to an older milieu, or can it be cloying, even exploitative?

So, firstly, what have biographers said about Patti Smith's Beat Generation tastes and affiliations? Victor Bockris' biography of Smith, which simply carries the artist's name, appeared in 1998. It is interesting to note how Bockris' account begins by stressing the presence and potency of poetry in Manhattan at the time that Smith was beginning to make a mark among New York City's radical subterraneans at the very start of the 1970s:

> In the early seventies in New York a poet was one of the coolest things you could be. You can't imagine how many people who are successful people now started their lives as New York poets – something that is almost unimaginable today. In those days the St. Mark's Poetry Project was on a par with Warhol's Factory, Mickey Ruskin's Max's Kansas City[6] and the Gotham Book Mart as a bastion of the influential underground art movements that were the emotional engines of New York, just as the city was on the verge of becoming the cultural capital of the world.[7]

So poetry, an obvious connection with many Beat writers (Ginsberg, Gregory Corso, Amiri Baraka, Lawrence Ferlinghetti, Gary Snyder, Michael McClure and

---

[6] Max's Kansas City was a bar located off Union Square in New York. Opened in January 1966 and named by the poet Julian Oppenheimer, it became a major hang-out for artists and subterraneans, then a live venue, during the later 1960s and early 1970s. See Sukenick, 1987, p. 203 and p. 217.

[7] Victor Bockris, *Patti Smith* (London: Fourth Estate, 1998), p. 1.

Kerouac, too, though one not generally made with Burroughs, interestingly[8]), is at the core of Smith's surge from her life as a novice harlequin painter-actor-journalist at the end of the previous decade to an existence as a rising versifier and spoken word practitioner. Her celebrated debut at the St. Mark's venue, arranged by project director Anne Waldman on 10 February 1971, when she first read her poetry live as a support to Warhol scenester Gerard Malanga, remained an oft-cited event by those present for decades afterwards. But its nervy verve and spiky power, nonchalant confidence and irreverent humour, was finally confirmed for a general listenership when it was eventually released on CD in 2006.[9]

Yet, in the midst of this 'obvious connection' with the Beat idiom, we should beware the dangers of building a seamless narrative history retrospectively: what we see, with the benefit of hindsight, is not always as continuous when we examine the contemporaneous details that are later shaped as a smooth, undisrupted stream of activity. Nonetheless, it appears that Smith had been impressed by an essay of the time by another poet Andrew Wylie,[10] published in the Philadelphia magazine *Telegrams*. Explains Bockris:

> [...] Wylie was direct and forceful in summing up where he stood on the poetry field [...] he could no longer relate to long works like Ginsberg's 'Howl' or Pound's *Cantos*. Living, he felt, in an extremely violent, fragile time, he was drawn to short, almost amputated works. The essay went on to express an intellectual's interpretations of the current vibrations he felt surrounded by, concluding that just to be alive in these times was an act of violence. The essay, which Patti received a copy of, most likely impressed her, as Wylie did, for its sense of urgency about making it now, about doing something *now*.[11]

But if Wylie may have deterred Smith to an extent from looking back to, say, an epic and masterful work like 'Howl', the tremors of which were still present on the US arts radar a decade and a half after its 1955 performed premiere, how can we identify ways in which the Beat legacy impacted on a newly recognised talent, the young woman who had made a mark at her St. Mark's reading?

One of the more intriguing clues that appear not long after are ideas she expresses to Bockris in an exchange he describes as 'her first in-depth interview'[12]

---

[8] There is an interesting consideration of Burroughs' debated status as poet in Oliver Harris' 'Burroughs is a poet too, really: The poetics of *Minutes to Go*', first published in *The Edinburgh Review*, 114 (2005), republished by RealityStudio in August 2010, http://realitystudio.org/scholarship/burroughs-is-a-poet-too-really-the-poetics-of-minutes-to-go/ [accessed 29 June 2011].

[9] Patti Smith with Lenny Kaye, *February 10, 1971*, CD (Mer Records, 2006).

[10] Wylie would become a leading literary agent in the years that followed.

[11] Bockris, *Patti Smith*, 1998, pp. 4–5.

[12] See Bockris, *Patti Smith*, 1998, pp. 63–4, p. 249.

as she published her verse collection *Seventh Heaven* in 1972. She makes reference here to Ginsberg, Beat follower Bob Dylan and Beat associate Frank O'Hara, plain evidence that they were on her radar, affecting her thinking as an artist. She remarks:

> I'm not a fame fucker, but I am a hero worshipper. I've been in love with heroes, that's what seduced me into art… But poets have become simps. There's this new thing: the poet is a simp, the sensitive young man always away in the attic, but it wasn't always like that. It used to be that the poet was a performer and I think the energy of Frank O'Hara started to re-inspire that. I mean, in the sixties there was all that happening stuff. Then Frank O'Hara died and it sort of petered out and then Dylan and Allen Ginsberg re-vitalised it, but then it got all fucked up again because instead of people learning from Dylan and Allen Ginsberg and realising that a poet was a performer they thought a poet was a social protestor. So it got fucked up. I ain't into social protesting.[13]

Smith's position here is expressed revealingly as she confesses a near-spiritual allegiance to certain figures of the past but she is keen to deflect allegations that it is merely the cup of fame she drinks of. Instead she appears to bow at the altar of some (she only hints at whom these may be[14]) and certainly acknowledges that Ginsberg and Dylan, perhaps the two most powerful figures in the original Beat then less defined post-Beat moments, are names she reveres. It is notable that 'social protestor' is a tag she rejects, especially as Dylan wrestled with similar tweaks of conscience in the mid-1960s as he moved from youthful Civil Rights troubadour to world-weary rock 'n' roller within months in 1965. Yet Ginsberg would surely have no problems with the epithet: he spent more than 40 years, to his death in 1997, on the political soapbox. Non-doctrinaire, perhaps anti-doctrinaire, the Beat guru fought issues with words – campaigns against the war, struggles against discrimination of all kinds – with a sustained vigour for most of his adult life.

But how do the historians of her life and surveyors of her output connect Smith to the Beat oeuvre? It does appear that Ginsberg and Burroughs are the principal members of this literary community to whom she turns for creative succour or artistic assurance.[15] It is not insignificant, for instance, that Kerouac is

---

[13] *Ibid.*

[14] There are certainly examples in Smith's work where we encounter litanies of praise to named individuals: the spoken section 'Dedication' on *February 10, 1971* or the song 'Piss Factory' (1974) on her debut single are peppered with such tributes. Ginsberg is an inveterate namer of names also: see the essay by John Muckle, 'The names: Allen Ginsberg's writings', *The Beat Generation Writers*, edited by A. Robert Lee (London: Pluto Press, 1996), pp. 10–36.

[15] Interestingly Gregory Corso is quite a regular presence in Smith's own 2010 memoir *Just Kids*.

not mentioned in either Bockris' or Tarr's account – the third corner of the most discussed triumvirate in the Beat canon is not present in these two overviews. We could speculate further on Kerouac's absence, although it is worth remembering that the author of *On the Road* had entered a period of self-exile in the 1960s, occasionally reappearing to share Republican, anti-hippy and even anti-counter-culture views, before his lonely and addicted death in 1969.[16] His star had sunk at the start of Smith's rise to prominence while Ginsberg and Burroughs – who had each experienced quite different relationships with the post-Beat, anti-Vietnam, hippy decade – would each become objects of veneration to the emerging punk scene in New York City of which Smith was a germinal seed.

To visit a number of biographies of Smith or written accounts of her recorded work, there is hardly a consistent thread or clear pattern: some make more of her Beat associations than others. Nick Johnstone's 1997 volume, *Patti Smith: A Biography*, opens with the claim that his subject 'has measured her own life against the lives of those who have influenced her'[17] and proceeds to demonstrate this trend with accounts of many examples of poets, artists and singers – from Arthur Rimbaud to Jean Genet and Jim Morrison – who have played muse to Smith's output but the Beats themselves are less frequent, less defined visitors to the narrative he offers. He makes reference to Smith's Chelsea Hotel period and introductions to Burroughs.[18] Later he discusses the influence of that author on the poem 'carnival! carnival!' which 'projects violent often anonymous sexuality against a backdrop of phrases that recall William Burroughs'.[19] Another important, if somewhat circumstantial, reflection on the Beat effect on Smith is also outlined when Johnstone points out that two of her greatest influences – Dylan and the Doors' Jim Morrison – had explicitly referenced Beat writers as shaping their own art. Thus we might argue that Smith has, by reifying the two singers, also paid her own homage, if once removed, to Kerouac, Ginsberg and others. As Johnstone explains:

> The rock 'n' roll influence was inevitable and when Patti became a renowned rocker and poet, she was following in the footsteps of other musicians who had also been published or whose lyrics were considered to have merged poetry with rock 'n' roll. Her primary rock influence was Bob Dylan, who has himself acknowledged Rimbaud as well as the Beat writers as influences [...] Secondary to his influence, but often more important, is the effect Jim Morrison had on Patti. Morrison was also a rabid Rimbaud fan and, like Dylan, name-checked

---

[16] See, for example, biographies by Charters (1974), McNally (1979) and Turner (1996).
[17] Nick Johnstone, *Patti Smith: A Biography* (London: Omnibus, 1997), p. 1.
[18] *Ibid.*, p. 38.
[19] *Ibid.*, p. 120.

the Beat writers [...] as influences. Patti's visit to Morrison's grave in 1972 was also the moment she claims to have committed her life to art.[20]

Johnstone further draws attention to Smith's involvement with a Kerouac benefit in the writer's hometown of Lowell in 1995, when she was joined by regular guitar collaborator Lenny Kaye and Sonic Youth's Thurston Moore, and also a then forthcoming collection which would pay tribute to the Beat novelist, *Kerouac: Kicks Joy Darkness*,[21] a spoken word venture incorporating rock contributions from Morphine, Lydia Lunch, Eddie Vedder of Pearl Jam and others. Released in 1997, this homage recording featured Smith reading the Kerouac-based work, 'The Last Hotel', when she was again joined by both Kaye and Moore.

Bockris' biography of Smith, which followed the year after Johnstone's in 1998, emerges from a different place, a different position. While Johnstone is a British rock journalist and biographer, Bockris, although born in England,[22] was, by the start of the 1970s, a writer and member of that very Manhattan scene from which Smith arose. He has been a friend of Andrew Wylie; he publishes some early Smith poems; and he is a noted documenter of the Downtown milieu through numerous histories. He therefore has the benefit of close proximity to the artist – an advantage in some ways, a disadvantage in others. This biographer may have the connections to the inner circle; he may also be too close to the flare of talent to be able to look beyond its hypnotic heat. That said, his volume sometimes, though not always, carries the franking 'unauthorised'[23] which at least moves it outside the sphere of simple hagiography: Smith has not had copy approval, so to speak, nor has she been a cooperative collaborator on the venture. Nonetheless his closeness to the epicentre, at crucial moments, must also allow him, we can perhaps presume, to build a convincing impression of the Smith persona. In that sense, his more conscious referencing of Burroughs and Ginsberg in his text may have a convincing ring: his role as an eye-witness may help to build a more plausible case for the reader as jury member. Bockris describes various connections between Smith and the two Beats – Ginsberg's attendance at the St. Mark's debut, for example, shared book signings and live appearances, a two-way conversation with Burroughs for a magazine, not to mention the impact on Smith of the two writers' deaths in the same year of 1997. But here, allow me to just home in on a few, more pertinent samples of evidence of Smith-Beat interaction.

At the height of Smith's engagement with the Chelsea Hotel crowd, from the end of 1969 and through 1970, she would encounter a visiting Burroughs and

---

[20] *Ibid.*, p. 123.
[21] Various Artists, *Kerouac: Kicks Joy Darkness*, CD (Rykodisc, 1997).
[22] Bockris was a child émigré to the US.
[23] US editions of the work are subtitled *An Unauthorized Biography* and the title is co-credited to Roberta Bayley.

he plainly had an impact, artistically and sartorially, on the nascent star. Bockris reports Smith's personal recollection of the celebrated author of such radical titles as *Naked Lunch* and *Soft Machine*.[24] 'Burroughs showed me a whole series of new tunnels to fall through. He was so neat. He would walk around in this big cashmere overcoat and this old hat. So of course Patti gets an old black hat and coat, and we would walk around the Chelsea looking like that. Of course he was never too crazy about women, but I guess he liked me 'cause I looked like a boy.'[25] Imitation, we can surely identify, as a form of flattery. Later Smith would attend, and contribute to, the Nova Convention,[26] a 1978 conference in New York City which paid tribute to Burroughs, and, in 1990, Burroughs would return the compliment by praising Smith's new collection *The Coral Sea*. 'It rings the bell of pure poetry', the older man said of the younger writer's verse.[27]

What of Ginsberg's presence in Bockris' account? As early as 1971, her biographer reports, Ginsberg was telling a journalist that he recognised something both original and engaging about Smith.

What Patti Smith seems to be doing may be a composite – a hybrid – of the Russian style of Declaimed Poetry which is memorized, and the American development of Oral Poetry that was from coffee houses now raised to pop spotlight circumstances and so declaimed from memory again with all the art-form – or art-song – glamour [...] Then there's an element that goes along with borrowing from the pop stars and spotlight too and that glitter. But it would be interesting if that did develop into a national style. If the national style could organically integrate that sort of arty personality – the arty Rimbaud – in its spotlight with make-up and T-shirt.[28]

Almost a quarter of a century later, in 1995, Ginsberg was still showing his support for Smith the poet when he invited her to join a sold-out benefit for Tibetan Buddhists in Ann Arbor, Michigan. Recent losses in Smith's life – her husband and brother – had left her bereft and Bockris believes that Ginsberg's gesture to include her was a bid to coax her back from the edge of emotional devastation. He told the audience that the second half of the show would include 'an important rock-and-roll poet who took poetry from the lofts, bookshops and gallery performances to the rock-n-roll world stage. We're really pleased

---

[24] There are inconsistencies in a number of names of key Burroughs texts. *Junky/Junkie* (1953), *The Naked Lunch/Naked Lunch* (1959) and *The Soft Machine/Soft Machine* (1961) are common, titular anomalies in the author's published catalogue.
[25] Bockris, *Patti Smith*, 1998, pp. 50–1.
[26] *Ibid.*, p. 153.
[27] Burroughs quoted in Bockris, *Patti Smith*, 1998, p. 72.
[28] Bockris, *Patti Smith*, 1998, p. 197.

and happy that Patti Smith is able to join us.' He generously added, because the event had been sold-out in advance of Smith's late involvement on the bill: 'I see we have a full house, and I think that's down to her charisma, glamour and genius.'[29] Prior to her reading, Smith had paid Ginsberg warm compliments, too, confirming the transgenerational bond. 'Allen is such a good man,' she remarked. 'Look at what he did for the Beat movement. He made sure the work of Kerouac and Burroughs wasn't lost in obscenity, or a heap of vomit. He's so unjealous, he wanted all of them to do well. He doesn't want to be a big kingpin writer. He just wants everyone who deserves to, to excel. He's so generous.'[30]

Shaw's later account of Smith, her life and art, is shorter but denser: a 2008 critical reading of the artist's creative powers – contemplating both catalysts and outcomes – with *Horses* as its ultimate fulcrum. He is not slow to claim her attachments to Rimbaud as crucial. Among 'several significant literary influences' he feels the French Symbolist poet is most notable: his 'provocative life, art and opinions provided a model of Smith's self-fashioning'.[31] But the author also talks about his young subject as 'a decadent beatnik type' while in college and cites a 1975 *Mademoiselle* article in which Smith is rendered thus: 'Black energy, black clothes. A skinny black jacket. A black shirt buttoned up to the neck. Black peg pants. Black hair, shaggy, coarse',[32] an archetypal Beat vision if there ever was one.

As for *Horses*, the album itself, Shaw offers an insightful summary of the binary oppositions at play within the record, tensions that have powerful echoes of the terrains that Ginsberg, Burroughs and Kerouac had boldly explored in an earlier period. The recording is 'concerned with testing limits: the boundaries of the sacred and the profane; between male and female; queer and straight; the poetic and the demotic; self and other; the living and the dead'.[33] In works from 'Howl' to 'Kaddish', *Naked Lunch* to *Big Sur*, to identify just a few obvious examples, the Beat writers, too, address these potent intersections of personal and psychological, sexual and spiritual paradox.

Further, the actual form of *Horses* is linked by Shaw to the practices of a wave of pre-modern and modernist artists who adopted bricolage methods as mirrors of a fractured age. He comments: 'In the literary sphere, Smith's heroes, Rimbaud,[34] Eliot[35] and Burroughs, had each attempted to create multivocal, layered forms of

---

[29] Quoted in Bockris, *Patti Smith*, 1998, p. 209.

[30] *Ibid.*

[31] Philip Shaw, *Horses* (New York: Continuum, 2008), p. 30.

[32] Amy Gross, 'Introducing rock 'n' roll's Lady Raunch: Patti Smith', *Mademoiselle*, September 1975, cited in Shaw, 2008, p. 75.

[33] Shaw, 2008, p. 98.

[34] For instance, poems in Arthur Rimbaud's 1873 collection *Une saison en enfer*.

[35] T. S. Eliot's 1922 poem 'The Waste Land' offers an example of the Anglo-American writer's technique.

expression. Via symbolism, collage and "cut-up", all three had sought to challenge the hegemony of conventional literary narratives, allowing for the eruption of unconscious connections, and for the creation of random, aleatory meanings.[36] He supports this analysis by quoting Tony Glover's review of the album in *Circus* in 1976, in which the journalist suggests it could be considered 'the aural equivalent of a William Burroughs book'.[37]

Yet Shaw is wary of undermining Smith's originality and talent by over-playing her sources, her guiding lights, whether Beat, rock 'n' roll or otherwise. He comments: 'But while Patti Smith's fame can be traced to her strategic place in a chain of makers and shakers, her vision remains unique, a product not merely of her times, but of the shaping spirit of her imagination.'[38] And he adds: 'For as much as Patti Smith is motivated by the spirits of Brian Jones, Jimi Hendrix, and Jin Morrison, her deepest love is reserved for the dead poets, the cracked actors, and the darkling *chanteurs*.'[39]

Tarr, too, returns to the notion of antecedents in his comprehensive survey of Patti Smith's recorded canon. He says that 'even as a star, she has found herself engrossed by the work of others'.[40] Smith, in a 2007 interview, reveals: 'I've always been an iconographer [...] I was always a big fan [...] By the time I was enjoying a certain amount of popularity I was 29 years old and so had already tasted what it meant to be a devoted fan, a documenter or reviewer of other people's work.'[41] Tarr comments on this idea:

Smith was never content to merely admire, however. Her obsessions with icons pushed her to become one herself. Although the imagining of fame has been played out countless times, it is mostly a fantasy of self-creation and identification. Rarely does the dreamer make it public through performance. It's even rarer that the dreamer makes any music or art of any significance. In the twentieth-century as music became the realm of professionals, most Americans settled for vicarious thrills with no risk involved. But although pop art is an extremely elite club, anybody can force their way through its doors, if they have enough verve, talent or chutzpah.[42]

As for key Beat references, Tarr homes in on two important later details on the album *Peace and Noise* from 1997: Smith's dedication of the album to the

---

[36] Shaw, 2008, p. 130.

[37] *Ibid.*, p. 130.

[38] *Ibid.*, p. 25.

[39] *Ibid.*

[40] Joe Tarr, *The Words and Music of Patti Smith* (Westport, CT: Praeger, 2008), p. 3.

[41] Smith interview with Paul Lester, 'Icon, me?', *The Scotsman*, 7 April 2007, cited by Tarr, 2008, p. 3.

[42] Tarr, 2008, pp. 3–4.

recently deceased Burroughs and her setting of Ginsberg's 'Footnote to Howl', itself a homage to the poet whose death had also been recorded a little earlier that year.[43]

So, a summary of some of the ways in which the Beat writers, and wider concepts of influence, have been addressed in biographically based works that attempt a consideration of Patti Smith as woman and artist. But what about more recent, more individual, reflections on the Smith-Beat confluence: its relevance and importance and the perceptions that might arise from that relationship. I contacted around 20 established figures who were linked in some fashion to this intersection of rock and literature, historically or critically – associates who knew or who had worked with Smith; academics and journalists interested in Smith as an artist and particularly as a female artist; and poets and novelists who had feet in either the original Beat camp or might be regarded as growing out of that earlier tradition. Most of those I approached were happy to comment on this link; in the end, more than half of my correspondents did share views.[44] The questions I raised were these: Where do you feel Patti Smith's art and life rest in relation to Beat culture? To what degree do you perceive Beat influence on Smith's work? Might we justifiably call Smith a post-Beat? To what extent might commentators critical of later musicians/artists associating themselves with earlier writers/movements have a valid case? The next section of this essay gathers an edited collection of answers that were gleaned.

Q.1 Where do you feel Patti Smith's art and life rest in relation to Beat culture?

One respondent Victor Bockris, commenting some 13 years after issuing his life story of the singer, recalls a seminal moment when the connection to the Beats and the cultural power the movement still possessed was patently expressed. He remarks: 'In 1974 from the stage of the St. Mark's Poetry Project at Second Avenue and 10th Street she asked the audience, "Do you know who just moved back to New York? William Burroughs just moved back to New York! Isn't that great … fucking great!" I remember thinking, "Thank God! This punk movement isn't going to have to kill their fathers, they're going to use them". And that was the beginning of the alliance between the Beats and Punks that put such firm ground under the movement. And turned it from a pretentious political movement to a movement based in tribal song.'

---

[43] Tarr, 2008, p. 84.
[44] A full list of correspondents, in respect of this chapter, appears in the 'Personal communication' section of the Bibliography on p. 498.

Philip Shaw, author of *Horses*, states: 'Through Dylan in the 1960s she was drawn to Rimbaud. Burroughs *et al.* presented Smith with a contemporary American take on Rimbaud's poetics: the "cut up", the interest in transgression, and the fascination with the outlaw figure can all be traced back to French avant-garde practices of the late nineteenth and early twentieth-century. Therefore, in this sense, Smith owes a great deal to the Beats. The poetry collection called *Kodak*, for example, owes much to Burroughs' "cut up" technique and you can hear this as well in the multi-tracked vocals of "Land" from *Horses*. But she also draws on other, non-Beat influences: rock 'n' roll and Pop Art. As for her life, the cultivation of an unkempt, roguish look is very much in the Beat tradition.'

Ginsberg guitarist for two decades, the New York-based musician and writer Steven Taylor, has also shared stages with Smith and expresses this view: 'She learned her trade and style from Rimbaud and Ginsberg and Corso and Dylan. She embraced that vagabond aesthetic, or outsider, marginal style, and the black–white crossover of the mid-twentieth-century, a major cultural trend in which the Beats played a part.'

Taylor adds: 'The whole poetry scene she emerged out of in the early 70s was heavily Beat influenced. Just the fact of getting up in a club and reading your poems to music is a Beat thing. She was in the same scene as Lou Reed, who had studied with Delmore Schwartz – a kindred spirit to the Beats, writing dark, post-Holocaust realist American fiction. And Richard Hell, who read Baudelaire and Rimbaud and the Surrealists. It was a whole complex of influences, a big atmosphere that was cooking downtown with connections back through the American moderns to the French avant garde.'

But he makes this further point about straightforward interpersonal reasons for this apparent artistic alliance. 'Also, it's personal – you walk into a cafeteria and Ginsberg offers to buy you a sandwich because you look hungry and broke (Patti relates this in her book[45]). People often miss that personal connection. Ginsberg was in the neighbourhood, and he knew everyone, or talked to everyone, like a chatty old aunt. It wasn't a grand academic tradition that you are supposed to get licensed into by some professor or critic. It was buying your groceries on First Avenue. As Allen would say, it was a matter of "gossip" or ordinary personal connections.'

Sheila Whiteley, formerly Professor of Popular Music at the University of Salford, UK, and gender specialist, comments: 'What I find interesting is that the Beats were men and she embraced a similar "on the road" attitude in her bohemianism. It's perhaps because she took on board the marginalised in society, the outsider, the misfit that aligns her with Beat culture. I think, too, that her

---

[45] Smith, 2010, p. 123.

androgynous body also challenged the sexual certainties of mainstream society, not least while with Mapplethorpe. Her move to New York in 1967 is obviously significant, in that its poetic communities were built around the existential values of Kerouac, Corso *et al.*, not least in the blend of anarchy and individualism found in Warhol.'

Poet-songwriter Jim Cohn, part of the gathering of contemporary versifiers who are linked to Ginsberg's Naropa Institute in Boulder, Colorado, and self-identify as 'Postbeats' says this: 'Patti Smith had strong affinities with Allen Ginsberg. After the death of her husband, Fred "Sonic" Smith, in 1994, her already established demotic and shamanic style took on a greater, generational significance, incorporating death, making death a meditation, bringing comfort to people, mainlining the essential energy of life. She was with Allen at the end of his life, with him when he died in 1997. Since then, she has performed with Philip Glass around the world, celebrating Allen's life and spirit, and evolving a spontaneous trust in herself as a channel from the Spirit World. She has lived a bohemian life as avant garde poet/songwriter/performer in the manner laid down by the Beats and, like many rock and rollers who came of age in the 60s, her art was deeply informed by the Beats.'

Rock journalist and biographer Lucy O'Brien has a particular interest in the place of women in popular music's history. She reflects: 'It is interesting that when she started out she presented herself as almost androgynous and asexual and most of her heroes (Camus, Dylan, Coltrane) were male. Probably a sensible move on a post-Beat scene that was still very male, viewing its women as muses or sex objects. Her feminism and sense of autonomy really stood out. She loved romantic poets like Rimbaud and William Blake, and took a Beat-inspired approach to her poetry – exuberant, spontaneous creativity with a cool swagger.'

Q.2 To what degree do you perceive Beat influence on Smith's work?

Victor Bockris responds: 'The point is that Patti Smith's art and life relates to Beat culture in a friendly way. Her poetry is not Beat poetry. Her prose is not Beat prose, but when she sings, "the boy looked at Johnny", she's channelling Burroughs. She's also advertising Burroughs. We need a new way to talk about these relationships. They don't fit into the academic form of artistic influence, it's more Warholian culture communication of signs and signals.'

Noted rock 'n' roll and spoken word historian Harvey Kubernik expresses this opinion: 'I do think there is a link of the legacy of the Beat to Patti. Perhaps in terms of the printed page to the audio/recording world and then the subsequent stage performance of her material. The aspect of improv that informs her work and particularly her live repertoire. In 2011, I had a series of conversations with Dr. James Cushing, a Professor of English and Literature at Cal Poly San Luis Obispo, and a long-time DJ on radio station KCPR-FM. All through the late 1970s and well into the 1980s we attended several Los Angeles and Hollywood Patti Smith recitals and heard her early Arista record offerings.'

He adds: 'Cushing told me in 2011 that *Just Kids* is authentic belated Beat literature in the same sense as Dylan's *Chronicles* or Ginsberg's *Death and Fame*. Belated in the sense that these books do not document the beginning of a sensibility as *On the Road* or "Howl" did, but authentic in the sense that the values these later works assume are Beat values, articulated in ways most associated with Beats: resistance to middle-class conformity, trust of the spontaneous, pursuit of altered states of consciousness, preference for termite-art over elephant-art, and above all the spirit of Whitman and his urban embodiment of Transcendentalism.'

Cohn remarks: 'Her poetry incorporates elements of Surrealism, free association, surprising juxtapositions, political consciousness and heartfelt emotion – going back to Ezra Pound's notion that "only emotion endures". She was part of the great '60s wave where rock and roll was seen, mostly as a result of Allen Ginsberg's advocacy, as "high art". One of Ginsberg's sense of Beat "effects" was this very fact – that Beat language arts and cultural life affected the lyric quality, the openness, critical social eye, visionary epiphany, that became the content of works of popular art that have transcended the immediate period of their creation.'

David Cope, another 'Postbeat' poet, says this: 'She is, as a true artist, fiercely original while maintaining those connections to the lineages of which her work is a part — and the Beats are among those lineages, along with Rimbaud, Whitman, Dickinson and others. Her work has its own savage experimental quality that breaks bounds as the Beat writings did in the '50s, but she is also part of a later generation that defined itself in terms of its own experiences, and, as a rocker, she has more in common with Bob Dylan, the MC5, Lou Reed or the Clash than with poet predecessors who dabbled in music rather than using it as the primary vehicle for the words.'

Beat commentator Holly George-Warren sees the influence 'particularly on *Horses* and *Radio Ethiopia*'. She explains: 'Burroughs' cut-up technique can be seen in Smith's lyrics; some of the homoeroticism of Ginsberg's work is also reflected here. In her artwork, you can find hints of Brion Gysin and another Beat influence, Jean Cocteau. Her live performances have always included spoken word/poetry – hearkening back to Ginsberg's reading of "Howl" at the Six Gallery.'

O'Brien states: 'It's very much there in her early work, particularly the album *Horses*, which combines jazz, rock and spoken word poetry. I interviewed her once about this, and she said that for the album she worked with a range of her poems, experimenting with words – "I was creating a sort of William Burroughs cut-up ..." Smith described working with producer John Cale as like "having two crazy poets dealing with a shower of words".

Taylor comments: 'Broadly, the idea that you can get up and read your poems in public, and with music, affiliates her with the oral poetry renaissance of the '50s. She's in the lineage of that, from Langston Hughes reading to jazz in the '20s, on down through Ferlinghetti, Ginsberg, di Prima, Baraka. It's a broad scene. I'm sure you could see connections by looking at her choice of words, her themes, her verse forms.'

Q.3 Might we justifiably call Smith a post-Beat?

Cohn says: 'I do. Although key poets such as Anne Waldman as well as musicians like Dylan and Smith are often identified by their relation to the Beats, if one considers the mid-'50s as the apex of the Beat period, with 1956 as the defining moment – I'm speaking of the Six Gallery or Six Angels reading where Allen debuted "Howl" – Patti Smith was ten, Anne Waldman 11 and Dylan an elder at 15 years old.[46] Clearly, they, like many younger people, were influenced. If one accepts the notion that these three artists were *part* of something generational, some kind of movement, it was something that would be more accurately described as *after* the Beats, based upon Beat influence, but ultimately, what I have argued is Postbeat.'

Cope remarks: 'All the outrider poets who came after the Beats were influenced by them, but the differences are just as significant. We "make it new", in Pound's words, but any poet worth his or her words knows that one builds a foundation out of the work of those who came before, as well as from the historical particulars and cultural influences from one's own time. Patti and other "post-beats" are children of the atomic age cold war, of King and Kennedy, of television, the Beatles and the Stones, and all the horrors of Vietnam; the Beats, by contrast, came out of the Great Depression, the Second World War, radio, jazz and the McCarthy era. We may share common concerns as writers and thinkers, but there are also very different historical or cultural influences at work in each generation and, notably, in each individual artist. Thus, if one needs such labels, she would certainly be a "post-beat" poet.'

Kubernik reflects: 'She might be viewed as a current Beat because she still puts words and her voice with a musical instrument like a drum that beats to

---

[46] Cohn's principal point is not disrupted by the fact that Patti Smith was born 30 December 1946, so would then have been eight years old; Anne Waldman was born 2 April 1945, so would have been ten years old at the time; and Bob Dylan was born 24 May 1941 and would have been 14 years of age when 'Howl' was read for the first time on 7 October 1955.

propel her long, hand-written lyrics and poems. Post-Beat? I like belated better than post. The Beat movement/moment is historical, approximately 1948–1961 (when did Maynard G. Krebs start up?), but these values go from Blake into the cyberfuture.'

Taylor comments: 'Not if that means turning against or in opposition to Beat. I saw her read a month ago. It could have been 1955. I think of the Beats as the last Romantics. She's right there. "Post" can get you into trouble, academic squabbles. Even the designation "Beat" is a problem. Who's in? Who's out? It's more fluid than that. These terms of convenience can get awfully stiff and fixed over time.'

Q.4 To what extent might commentators critical of later musicians/artists associating themselves with earlier writers/movements have a valid case?

Victor Bockris comments: 'I think it's great if musicians want to associate themselves with the Beats or other writers or movements. It's natural, it's recognition. Art is not pretentious; politics is, academia is, trying to be what is not. The greatest thing we had in 1977–82 in New York was cross-referencing between fields and generations. There was a wonderful openness and sharing. Today everybody is so scared they all stay in their own foxholes trying to not to be killed. No growth that way. I think Patti's vital contribution to the global culture was that she travelled around lighting a fire of inspiration and wide open celebration of the key artistic spirits: the Beats, the British Invasion, Warhol, the Counterculture.'

Magazine journalist and rock critic Bart Bull remarks: 'Patti Smith is the single biggest name-dropper in the history of rock 'n' roll. Bar none. But because the names she tended to drop early on were Rimbaud, Baudelaire, Blake, Bowles, Gysin, Godard, Bresson ... well, most of those she was talking to (or at, actually) didn't have a clue, other than the weightiness of name-drop's avoirdupois. You'd have to use a scale and a yardstick and a snow-shovel to see whether or not she was the single biggest name-dropper in the history of poetry, or whether that would be Allen Ginsberg.

He continues: 'But you'd definitely want to factor in Anne Waldman, who functioned as the Don-Doyenne of the St. Mark's Poetry Project and then of the Naropa Institute. These three all understood the accruable power that could come from fingering the rosary beads as loud as possible, that to publicly recite repeated litanies of the saints would serve to get you canonised yourself.'

Cohn says: 'Commentators can claim anything, but they would be hard pressed to explain Patti Smith's emergence as a significant Beat artist in her own right. As is well known, the women poets of the Beat Generation did not break out as did their male counterparts. Only Diane di Prima, Joanne Kyger and Janine Pommy

Vega made it in the white male poetry world. The Beat women were perhaps the last generation of women having to face a male world of patriarchal convention without comprehensive feminist theory, which did not really hit the mainstream until 1963 when Betty Friedan published *The Feminine Mystique*. Poets like Anne Waldman and Patti Smith were benefactors as much as agents of conventional change, implementers of feminist poetries, feministos. Their achievement really is at the heart of the realisation that times had changed and with them, new forces, forces of the Postbeat period, were at work.'

Cope states: 'I think those who try to cut themselves off from their predecessors in the name of some ephemeral "originality" are losing out on all those connections with elder brothers and sisters who came before. Allen's work, for example, is loaded with references to earlier writers and movements, and even the wildly original Whitman occasionally sounded his "barbaric yawp" with a nod to those who preceded him. Barring works that are mere slavish imitations of an earlier style, commentators who find fault with a poet acknowledging or associating with her/his elders really don't understand the nature of the art.'

He adds: 'Whitman and Dickinson can still speak to us as friends who bore their own struggles into words; all we have to do is read them aloud together, and they can instruct us as to how they made it through even as we learn to sing their songs. There's also the fact that already-established poets have always helped younger geniuses find their way: Pound helped Eliot and the Objectivists Reznikoff, Rakosi and Oppen, just as Allen "distributed monies to poor poets & nourished imaginative genius of the land", helping countless younger writers into print or with a helpful word that could sustain them as they grew. Thus, you could not have a Patti Smith without an Arthur Rimbaud or an Allen Ginsberg or a Bob Dylan to open the doors that made it possible for her to enter the next room and make it her own.'

George-Warren comments: 'Yes, Patti Smith lived the life of a Beat as a young artist, but has also retained her allegiance to the Beats and their heroes; her close relationships with Burroughs, Ginsberg (she was at his deathbed), and Gregory Corso reflect this. There's a great portrait of Patti (wearing what looks like a black leotard) reclining and reading *The Soft Machine*, with a pair of shades next to her, that says it all. I think that artists who wear their influences on their sleeves – and while doing so, bring the work of their own influences to a new generation/ audience – serve an important role. Obviously, those artists who use earlier writers' work as a jumping-off point, to create new work with a new vision/style/ voice, can create their own legacy, which can become just as important as those who came before them. Patti Smith has done this.'

Novelist Joyce Pinchbeck (née Glassman, then Johnson) is the author of *Minor Characters*, a Beat memoir detailing a romance with Jack Kerouac, and the author of a forthcoming Kerouac biography.[47] She says: 'I admire her as a performer, of course, and I hear that she has written a fine memoir, which I intend to read. I have to say that I do have some uncomfortable feelings about her portrayal of herself as someone who has taken on the mantle of Ginsberg, and I have it on good authority that she did not really have as close a relationship with Allen as she suggests. Frankly, I wish she would stop publicly weeping at the graves of departed male poets.

'She also of course keeps invoking Kerouac with whom she had no relationship at all. In the liner notes that accompany the DVD of the documentary *Big Sur*, in which she appears, she expresses her admiration for Jack as a writer who "simply spewed his words on paper". I can assure you that he did not spew, and that if he had, we would not be reading his works today. This is the kind of wrongheaded opinion that obscures Kerouac's artistic achievement. She also indicated that she herself has not read Kerouac, and that the reactions of her male friends were enough for her to go by. Really!! I throw up my hands! Such careless statements would have horrified Allen. But of course identifying with the Beats has been an excellent career move for Patti Smith. I am also troubled by the fact that Smith shows no interest in female artists, apart from herself. Apart from all these objections, she's obviously a very gifted woman.'

Taylor adds: 'To say that any artist doesn't have a right to draw upon or declare an ancestry is pure *dummheit*. That's how art happens. Artistic lineages don't come with a state-issued (or academic/critic sanctioned) licence. They're organic. It's a matter of personal commitments, influences, and who's around the neighbourhood. I mean, if Charlie Watts thinks he's channelling Gene Krupa, you going to tell him he's wrong?'

Some conclusions

I have attempted to contextualise Patti Smith's relationship with the Beat Generation writers and their cultural legacy by various means: reporting some recent critical commentary which has appeared online culture magazines; through a survey of a number of key biographical accounts; and via some newly generated interviews, primary materials in which contemporary opinion on the artist's status and stature has been invited. This provides us with both historical and current reflections on the links that join Smith and her Beat antecedents. There may, of course, be other ways in such a piece of analysis could be conducted – for example, close textual reading and interpretation of

---

[47] As Joyce Johnson, she published *The Voice is All: The Lonely Victory of Jack Kerouac* (New York: Viking) in 2012.

her poetic, musical and lyrical output. We would certainly find themes of the autobiographical and the confessional, work of candour, the search for spiritual and sexual truths, and a tendency to reference influential names, strains recognisable in the Beat ethos. But this particular exercise has been beyond the scope of a chapter of this length.

In terms of the conclusions we might draw from the information that has been presented, there seems little doubt that the Beats have had a bearing on Smith as a poet and rock musician, yet it is also important to stress that there are individuals – from the worlds of literature, art and music – who may be regarded as more significant still in shaping Smith's artistic vision, from Rimbaud to Dylan, Brian Jones to Jim Morrison, for example. If some recent web voices have been suspicious of Smith's willingness to attach her own creativity to the Beats and perhaps other writers, musicians and singers of the past, the voices of authority – from academics to journalists to other poets – seem to feel, in general terms, that there is little surprising, or dubious, about this artist's desire to see herself as part of a continuum, a carrier of a flame, a latterday vessel who may frequently cite her muses but one also capable of shaping fresh visions from that amalgam of influences. Whether Smith might be regarded as a Beat, a belated Beat, a current Beat or a post-Beat – all terms connected to her at points in this account – is a potential topic for a longer, more detailed work of lexicographical archaeology.

One thing we can perhaps say is that if Smith has shown, at times, a desire to link herself to that earlier era, a previous literary movement, it is surely not merely premised on efforts to attain fame by association. If we go back to her earliest steps – hesitant, uncertain, unfocused, if we can take her *Just Kids* recollections at face value – at the end of the 1960s, we can hardly identify an artist with a cynical or manipulative vision or strategy, a player with a clear career plan, determinedly scrambling up the ladder to recognition and success. Her progress as an actor or poet, as the 1970s commenced, seems to have been shaped, to a significant extent, by a series of accidents, perhaps most notably the connections she achieved in the Chelsea Hotel which allowed to her to interact with a network of emerging – and existing – underground talents. Chelsea residents with established reputations from Dylan associate Bobby Neuwirth to musicologist Harry Smith, poet Gregory Corso to Burroughs himself, found her engaging and encouraged her at a time when her intentions were still evolving. Her interest in art and writing was evident but the idea that she might sing, or use rock music as a vehicle, had barely germinated at this stage.

Further, we should stress the volume of work that Smith has achieved in her own right in the subsequent decades – on record, in book form, on tour and on film. There might be a counter-argument, based on that imposing creative résumé, that the Beats, since Smith's mid-1970s rise to critical and international acclaim, eventually had more to gain by their associating with her than vice versa.

We might well propose that by the 1990s, as Ginsberg and Burroughs entered their final years and Smith re-appeared in New York after her home-centred and reclusive 1980s in Detroit, the younger artist's reputation as multi-faceted writer-performer was now one that the older novelist and poets coveted, to some extent, and it was she who would add to their credibility quotient. Smith's appearance in the Kerouac *Big Sur* documentary which raised, as we have seen, a certain disquiet among web critics came, of course, long after the deaths of those two key Beats, so her contributions could hardly be seen as a concerted bid to curry favour with a literary grouping long shorn of most of its key participants (although Lawrence Ferlinghetti and Michael McClure did also make an appearance in the film in question).

Perhaps we could best complete this consideration by citing the thoughts of a woman and a poet who is often seen as a vital bridge between the original Beat caucus and the artistic spirit that has followed and survived in its wake. Anne Waldman, of a younger generation to Ginsberg, Burroughs and co., was nonetheless a close associate of the principal Beats, director of the St. Mark's Poetry Project from 1968–78 and therefore a crucial conduit between old and new, a sponsor of young New York voices like Smith and Jim Carroll, and a founding figure in the Jack Kerouac School of Disembodied Poetics at Naropa University in Boulder, Colorado, that saw Ginsberg bring his literary ideas and spiritual energy to an educational venture with deep Buddhist roots, from 1974.

What does Waldman makes of these debates? How does she see Patti Smith against the backdrop of the Beat community? She comments: 'Patti came up through a different trajectory, adjacent to these worlds and dropping in and out of them – her own amalgam of romanticism, Rimbaud (where every poet starts) and Blake – heroes of us all – siphoned thru Allen (later), and her increasing public stature which allowed her to recalibrate and invent herself in relation to various cultural icons and literary movements. She was not inside the Beat literary movement or culture in the early days, except thru encounters at the Chelsea much later that were not particularly literary. But yes, she's in the post-Beat pantheon. She takes what she can use (like Dylan too). Like all of us poets she's a magpie scholar.'

10 JIM CARROLL, POETRY PRODIGY, POST-BEAT AND ROCKER

It was, in contemporary terms, a relatively short life. But it was an extraordinary one. And one longer than many might have predicted when one of the great teen literary prodigies wandered on to the downtown New York scene in the heart of the 1960s. Jim Carroll, who died aged 60 on 11 September 2009, created a biography that extended across several key sections of the cultural underground. Because he began so young, the luminous moments of his career stretched from the height of Warhol's Factory around 1966 to the emergence of grunge at the turn of the 1990s and even beyond.

He was an adolescent who came to prominence during the early days of the St. Mark's Poetry Project on the Lower East Side and, 20 years later, he was still a leading player in that part of the new wave movement that valued the marriage of punk rock energy with dazzling street lyricism, short, sharp songs wrapped around vivid accounts of a life lived at the edge. He was, too, a bridge between Manhattan's art and music explosion centred on Pop Art, the Velvet Underground and the *Exploding Plastic Inevitable*, the fertile Lower East Side verse scene, with Allen Ginsberg its unofficial laureate, and the incandescent music that would erupt from Max's Kansas City, the Mercer Arts Center and, most importantly, CBGBs, from the early to mid-1970s.

Carroll was also aide and friend to various of the names who would light up the last quarter of the artistic twentieth-century. He knew fellow poet and rock star-to-be Patti Smith, the great photographer Robert Mapplethorpe and Sam Shepard, the most lauded of US playwrights since Arthur Miller, and Allen Lanier, the lyricist with the band Blue Oyster Cult. He worked in Warhol's film studio and he was an assistant to the painter Larry Rivers, whose magnificent *The Athlete's Dream* so aptly adorned the cover of the seminal Penguin Modern Classics version of Jack Kerouac's *On the Road*, and whose work is also a centrepiece in the foyer of the legendary Chelsea Hotel.

But, above all, and this is most pertinent to this piece, Carroll was a creator of poetry, prose and memoir that would mark him as one of the most important of the writers emerging in the wake of the Beat Generation. We can comfortably, I think, even though this is a contested category, consider him to be one of the principal post-Beats. Like a number of the original Beats, Carroll walked a very dangerous line between the experiment of living dangerously and the dire consequences of over-indulgence. By the time he was in his mid-teens, he had succumbed to the lure of the street and a taste for drugs.

Yet this was no ordinary story of a low life, teen hoodlum drifting into bad company and worse habits. Carroll had been born, in 1949, in the Lower East Side in modest circumstances. But his sporting skills and Irish spirit propelled him to a scholarship at an upper Manhattan private school called Trinity. His basketball skills were immense – he made the national High School All Star game and seemed destined for a rewarding sporting life. However, it wasn't only a youthful connection with the drugs scene that would mark this athlete as unusual. He was also a budding writer and one with definite potential. The schizophrenic life he led as star-sportsman-in-waiting and apprentice junkie provided the raw material for diaries that would eventually become the core of his most celebrated publication, *The Basketball Diaries*, in 1978.

By 1966, Carroll made his initial contacts with the new St. Mark's Project, a former church in the run-down Bowery area of the city, which would become the most significant crucible of the new poetry scene in New York City. Before very long, he had attracted the attention of Allen Ginsberg and other important writers were noting the presence of a prodigy. When Ted Berrigan, Jack Kerouac and William Burroughs read the boy's adolescent output they predicted great things. Kerouac, another one-time college athlete who chose a literary course, said of him: 'At 13 years of age, Jim Carroll writes better prose than 89 per cent of the novelists working today'. Burroughs dubbed him 'a born writer'.

By 1967, his first collection of poems, *Organic Trains*, had appeared. Three years later a second, *4 Ups and One Down*, would follow. But it was the appearance of passages, of what would eventually become *Living at the Movies,* in the pages of hallowed literary magazine *The Paris Review* that the buzz around Carroll became louder and insistent. Yet Carroll, ex-basketball rookie and now part-time heroin addict, was caught in a caustic cycle of remarkable levels of acclaim for his writing talents and the terrible physical fixation of junk. In 1973, he decided to escape the drug corners and shooting alleys of the island of Manhattan and run to California.

The switch was significant, not just geographically but personally, too, as he joined a community of artistically inclined individuals in Bolinas, north of San Francisco. He would marry his wife Rosemary Klemfuss and when Patti Smith asked her old friend to join her at a live music gig – she was now the premier purveyor of the rock poetry form with a hot group for company – Carroll charted a fresh future. Inspired by what he had experienced, he formed the Jim Carroll Band and, from 1978, carved out a reputation as a poetic voice with sharp rock 'n' roll tendencies. His early songs 'People Who Died' – a striking, if chilling, overview of the human loss that walked hand-in-hand with the threats and danger of the heroin world – and 'Catholic Boy' earned him a renewed reputation.

His poetry and his prose had already won him much admiration; his musical reincarnation allowed his intense and fierce lyricism to reach larger audiences, accompanied by the power of amplified guitars and drums, frequently a compelling chemistry on stage and on record. Yet some may argue that his efforts to maybe emulate his long-time associate and one-time lover Patti Smith, a raging one-off who had moved from stand-up poems in bars to rock stadium gigs around the world, was conceivably a mistaken one. Perhaps his stark and confessional verse work stood better alone, without the furious kinesis of electricity and power chords.

But the age in which Carroll came to maturity was too loud, too frenetic, too distracted, for mere words, it seems. Many of the poets who may, in earlier times, have carved a status as wordsmiths rather than singer-poets, took the rock road. The pulse of the music, exciting and instantaneously gratifying, outweighed the more cerebral notions of quiet contemplation. Bob Dylan and Leonard Cohen, Henry Rollins and Lydia Lunch, all possible heirs to the literary crowns that urban bards such as Ginsberg and Gregory Corso had worn, chose music to accompany their stanzas. And, of course, so many of the core Beats themselves – from Burroughs to Ferlinghetti and McClure – were drawn to work with rock artists, too. So Jim Carroll was, we might conclude, merely infused by the attractions and intoxications of the *Zeitgeist*.

So what did those individuals attached to the Beat movement and its wider circle make of the Carroll phenomenon? Poet Anne Waldman, long-time director of the St. Mark's Poetry Project and co-founder with Ginsberg of the Naropa Institute in Boulder, Colorado, commented: 'I saw Jim as a *poete maudite*, in the tradition of Villon, Rimbaud, not that he was dogged and cursed, but he did live somewhat outside society and the professionalisms and careerisms of poetry. He was the "real deal" – a true natural, an aspiring kid with a genuine yen for imagination in lyrical language, from his first setting foot in the mandala of the Poetry Project at St. Mark's, to his forays out to the Jack Kerouac School of Disembodied Poetics at Naropa where he taught classes in the "Socratic rap" mode, initiated by Gregory Corso.'

Steven Taylor, Ginsberg's guitarist for his last two decades of the poet's life, also provided accompaniment to Carroll on occasion. He remarked: 'Jim struggled, as they say, with heroin addiction for years. I went to see him play at Mabuhay Gardens in San Francisco with Ginsberg at one point. The Jim Carroll Band were great live. Jim seemed dizzy on stage, and said something about being sick, Allen bellowed "What?! – he was supposed to have moved to California to kick" '.

He added: 'Later, Jim sometimes taught in the annual Summer Writing Programs at Naropa. I recall him playing records for the poetry students. I feel he was the best poet among the rockers. He had a wonderful poetic eye and ear. He should have been famous for his poetry alone. His loss comes as a terrible shock.'

Levi Asher, founder of the leading Beat website *Literary Kicks*, said this: 'I liked him best for "People Who Died". I liked his plaintive voice and simple emotion. I saw him perform twice, once with Allen Ginsberg at the Bottom Line night club in Greenwich Village. That was a very special night. In a way I felt that Carroll was the "straight man" to Ginsberg's loopy wonderment. He was so sincere, so likeable.'

He went on: 'I then saw him perform again with Richard Hell at a Central Park Summerstage reading in the mid-1990s. I got a sense that his best contributions to the poetry scene (the scene that I think was closest to his heart) were contained within his mutually supportive friendships with other poets – that he was a person who made the scene warmer and more believable. He seemed satisfied and peaceful but I don't know if he ever seemed happy.'

Jim Carroll's funeral was held at Our Lady of Pompeii Roman Catholic Church on Bleecker Street in the West Village, at 9.30 a.m. on 16 September 2009. Steven Taylor shared this eye-witness account: 'There were about 100 people scattered in fives and sixes about the old Italian Baroque gaudiness. I recognised Rosemary Carroll – Jim's ex-wife and long-time attorney, and her husband, Danny Goldberg, as well as a number of poets, Simon Pettet, Brenda Coultas, Anselm Berrigan, and several generations of the staff of the Poetry Project. I went with Anne Waldman and her husband Ed Bowes.'

After the mass proper, and maybe a quarter of the crowd had communion, the priest invited anyone to speak, and Patti [Smith] and Lenny Kaye got up and did "Wing". And it was beautiful. Then the priest gestured for any other speakers, and Rosemary indicated that was it, and the priest blessed the long pale oak box, long and pale as the poet ever was, and a girl sang the *In Paradisum*, like to pierce your heart, and then we followed him out to the grey hearse in the cool morning occasional drizzle.'

OBITUARY 2

Jim Carroll, 'Poet and punk musician who documented his teenage drug addiction in *The Basketball Diaries*'

Jim Carroll, who has died of a heart attack aged 60, was a New York poet whose work and life linked several moments in the history of the US counterculture and its various literary expressions. He was one of the most important of the post-Beat generation writers, and became known to a wider public through *The Basketball Diaries* (1978), an account of his teenage years filmed in 1995 with Leonardo DiCaprio in the central, autobiographical role.

Yet Carroll was also closely associated with the Downtown scene in Manhattan at the start of the 1970s, which would eventually give rise to the club CBGBs and the emergence of punk, new wave and no wave. In time, he immersed himself in rock music, too. Carroll was thus a bridge between the art and music scene of late 1960s New York – exemplified by Andy Warhol and the Velvet Underground – and the frenetic, raw-toned, urban expression that grew out of it. His was poetry to be recited in the bar, and inspired by the sidewalk, rather than the rarefied verse of the academy. He was a true heir to Allen Ginsberg and the Beat tradition.

As the 1960s ended, and the pre-eminence of Warhol and the Factory gave way to a new cultural milieu premised on proto-punk and performance venues such as Max's Kansas City and the Mercer Arts Center, Carroll, along with other growing literary talents such as Patti Smith and Sam Shepard, was one of the young and shining stars. His streetwise style and life-on-the-edge experience gave him credibility from his early teens. But it was his writing that was the key to his reputation. He was unquestionably a prodigy.

Born on the Lower East Side of New York, he won a basketball scholarship to Trinity, an elite Manhattan private school. His sporting prowess, which owed something to his lofty ranginess, seemed destined to propel him to athletic stardom – he featured in the High School All-Star game in his chosen sport. Instead, he became engrossed in writing and enmeshed in the New York drugs scene. These experiences would form the basis of the notebooks that would eventually appear in print as *The Basketball Diaries*.

By the end of the 60s, after brief attendance at Columbia University, Carroll was working in Warhol's Factory and then in the painter Larry Rivers' studio, and he was well acquainted with other junior talents on the scene. He shared accommodation with Smith, with whom he had a relationship, and the photographer Robert Mapplethorpe.

But his abilities as a poet and writer were, by now, attracting attention from influential quarters. He became attached to the St. Mark's Poetry Project in the East Village from as early as 1966 and then became known to Ginsberg, the Lower East Side's unofficial laureate. Inspired also by Frank O'Hara, the young writer drew praise from figures such as Jack Kerouac and Ted Berrigan.

Carroll had already published teenage work through small presses: his first collection, a limited edition pamphlet, *Organic Trains*, was issued in 1967 when he was 16. In 1970, *4 Ups and One Down* followed, but it was the appearance of sections from a work-in-progress in the *Paris Review* that cemented his youthful reputation. Those extracts would be issued in the volume *Living at the Movies* (1973).

By then, Carroll's descent into drug addiction had led him to leave New York and settle on the west coast, in Bolinas, north of San Francisco, in a bid to kick his heroin habit. In 1978 he married Rosemary Klemfuss, but the relationship ended in divorce. After appearing on stage and reading with Smith's band, he formed a group of his own. The Jim Carroll Band had early success with songs such as 'People Who Died' – a litany to the singer-poet's deceased friends – and 'Catholic Boy', which touched on his Irish-American heritage (both from the group's 1980 debut album *Catholic Boy*).

His work as a poet-novelist and rock performer continued into the 1980s and 1990s, although the early glittering promise was never quite realised. Perhaps his decision to diversify into rock music distracted from his primary skills as a writer. His poetry came to take second place and his music, while always retaining a dedicated cult following, never really achieved mass acceptance or sales.

The New York poet Sharon Mesmer, who appeared on bills with Carroll on several occasions, commented: 'He brought a beautifully visceral poetic sense to prose, and a focused, hard, diamond-like quality to poetry via his lyrics. He really did rock.'

Steven Taylor, Ginsberg's guitarist for 20 years, remarked of Carroll: 'He spoke with the voice of a New York City street kid, as one would expect the son of Irish bartenders to sound. But he was very thoughtful and gentle in his manner, which came off as an odd combination. Everybody I know was very fond of Jim.'

He is survived by a brother, Tom.

James Dennis Carroll, poet, writer and musician, born 11 August 1949; died 11 September 2009.

11 ALL CUT UP? WILLIAM BURROUGHS AND GENESIS P-ORRIDGE'S BEATNIK PAST

I have known Genesis P-Orridge over a period of years and I consider him a devoted and serious artist in the Dada tradition. He instructs by pointing out banality through startling juxtapositions
WILLIAM BURROUGHS, AUTHOR *NAKED LUNCH*[1]

Genesis has the same spirit of humanism as the Beats in the fifties, and there's a great sense of humour there as was true of the Beatles and Rolling Stones as well. That sense of irony and fun
TIMOTHY LEARY, HARVARD PROFESSOR/AUTHOR[2]

Genesis P-Orridge, the British-born, New York-based poet and performance artist, rock 'n' roll renegade and art terrorist, has spent most of the last four decades expressing his transgressive codes through an extraordinary range of art-forms and media. As writer, painter, sculptor, choreographer, actor, installation artist, director of happenings, video producer and recording engineer, he has assumed a multitude of roles in the hinterland of radical creativity. Few performers have attempted so many practices and personae: as master/mistress of masquerade, as purveyor of subversive outrage, his output may not be equalled.

---

[1] Quoted in Genesis P-Orridge (ed.), *Painful but Fabulous: The Lives and Art of Genesis P-Orridge* (New York: Soft Skull Press, 2002), p. 1.
[2] *Ibid.*, p. 5.

But his most significant mark, in terms of public profile, has been left through his two rock bands – Throbbing Gristle, also referred to as TG, a group who dissolved in 1981 but actually played a final farewell gig in the UK in 2004,[3] and Psychic TV, his ongoing ensemble, who first emerged in 1982. His inspiration to the contemporary industrial music scene is widely acknowledged. Trent Reznor of Nine Inch Nails and Marilyn Manson are just two prominent figures who have paid tribute to P-Orridge's rock legacy. More left-field activists – Ministry, Coil and others – are almost direct beneficiaries of his artistic inheritance, keeping the TG flame burning bright. In 2004, his production work with cutting-edge New Yorkers the Yeah Yeah Yeahs continues to place P-Orridge at the heart of rock's avant garde.

In 2002, *Painful but Fabulous: The Lives and Art of Genesis P-Orridge*, a book that was neither autobiography nor biography rather 'the equivalent of a retrospective catalogue,'[4] a volume that certainly crossed all those terrains but carried the distinct mark of its subject's creative hand, was published. It provided a potent reminder – in text and visuals, interviews and commentary – of P-Orridge's eclectic portfolio, drawing on his writings, ideology, artworks and music to support a series of essays by Douglas Rushkoff, Carl Abrahamsson and Richard Metzger among others. Although, in essence, a celebration of P-Orridge's many and varied manifestations, it was not mere hagiography. The quotations carried in the preface to the volume balanced high praise with utter condemnation, a pattern of reception that has followed in the musician-artist's wake.

Yet, if P-Orridge's reception has been often entangled in headline-grabbing controversy and frequently searing antipathy, his determination to break new ground, test the bounds of convention, has never dimmed, not since, as an adolescent, he took slips of paper, each featuring single words, onto the streets of his respectable, boyhood town and invited passers by to re-assemble them as haikus, drawing the mystified attentions of his local newspaper,[5] right up to his present pursuits at the pioneering boundary of the visual and performing avant garde.

This piece is concerned with a number of entwined strands in the P-Orridge extravaganza – his own influences, specifically the Beat Generation and the friendships and collaborations he forged with William Burroughs and fellow cut-up pioneer Brion Gysin, and how experimental literature and innovative

---

[3] At an event called the Nightmare Before Christmas, Pontin's Holiday Camp, Camber Sands, Sussex, England in December 2004.

[4] Comment by Genesis P-Orridge, filmed interview with writer/researcher Jayne Sheridan, Columbia Hotel, London, 8 December 2004.

[5] See Simon Ford, *Wreckers of Civilisation: The Story of COUM Transmissions & Throbbing Gristle* (London: Black Dog Publishing, 1999), p. 1.2.

approaches to creating text have shaped his own rock and spoken word output. But it will also consider his latest project as artist, involving cut-up of a more extraordinary variety – a project to pursue a state he refers to as 'pandrogyny'. His body art concept, pursued through surgical reconstruction and re-shaping, will see him and his wife and partner, collaborator and fellow Psychic TV member Jackie Breyer, aka Lady Jaye, both adopt a shared and ambivalent fe/male identity.

It seems as if the notion of cut-up is an enduring pulse in much of what this performer does. He takes words and re-constructs them in his own semi-mystical language; he takes sound textures and samples and re-orders them in manners that are often dissonant, disorientating and disturbing; he takes his own life, his own flesh more accurately, and re-sculpts it in a fashion that almost satirises the contemporary Western obsession with plastic surgery – the quest for youth – but subverts it by adopting the sexual characteristics of the female – swollen breasts and narrowed waist – without claiming the slightest tendency towards transexuality. Rather P-Orridge and Breyer, his wife of nine years, are playing games with their own physical identities in the name of art alone. Pandrogyny, sometimes P-androgyny – an obvious play on androgyny, a melding of pan, as in the Greek for all, but surely in the mischievous puckish sense, too, and also *aner*, Greek for man, *gune* for woman[6] – is the manifesto he has penned and subscribes to, at times becoming andro*gen* in his own lexicon as he inserts a reference to himself in this adapted, corrupted version of the term.[7]

At the heart of this academic enquiry are two further threads – one personal, the other professional. In summer 2004, I met Genesis P-Orridge, a boyhood neighbour in an English suburb of Birmingham, for the first time in nearly 40 years. The interview I conducted with him, at this time, raises questions about the connection between different modes of creative expression – the interplay of music and written texts, the ambiguity of sexual identity in a rock context – but also about the relationship between objective research and intimate association with a subject.

In the middle of the 1960s, at the height of the UK's domination of the global rock scene, Neil Megson and I were at very different stages in our development. Megson was a loner teenager with existential tendencies, on the cusp of adulthood; I was a child, a pre-pubescent, eight-year-old primary school kid only just awakening to the power and possibility of pop music. In the same

---

[6] 'Androgyne', *Collins Dictionary of the English Language*, edited by Patrick Hanks (London: Collins, 1980), p. 53.
[7] 'Androgynous' can be regarded as a synonym for hermaphrodite – 'having male and female characteristics'. Note also gynandrous which also describes the hermaphroditic. In addition, with reference to pandro*geny*, androgenous means 'producing only male offspring', Hanks, *ibid*.

suburban street in Solihull, a dormitory town on the edge of England's second city Birmingham, Megson and I lived one house apart.

Divided by a family of Christian Scientists (who one day informed me, casually yet quite callously, that my innocent use of the quaint English phrase 'blimey' was a call on God to 'blind me'), this unlikely pairing, teen and child, made some contact with each other in the years between 1964 and 1966. My parents knew the Megsons – we were all from Manchester, refugees from our North West England homes, pulled to the Midlands by the father's work in each case. But why should a small boy find connection with an adolescent, dark-eyed, mysterious and distant? The answer was a train-set, a miniaturised, magical, electrified world housed in Neil's parents' loft.

In there, on a few isolated occasions, Neil would show me this transfixing little world of rails and papier-mâché mountains, tiny figures on train platforms, fir trees on mountain-sides, rolling stock and passenger carriages. 'Whether my teenage host saw this as an unwarranted intrusion I can't remember, but he seemed polite and welcoming enough.'[8]

By this time, the Beatles and the Rolling Stones had begun to carve up the pop kingdom. I knew the Beatles, of course, and had been bought my first single in 1963, 'She Loves You', a gift from my mother for accepting, without complaint, the fact I needed to wear spectacles. On the day I was to receive my reward (I must have *asked* for a 45rpm record), my mother and I stood together in the cramped listening booth in the store. First the assistant put on 'Not Fade Away' by the Stones, then the Beatles' song. Then my mother asked me which one I preferred but definitely, if gently, pressing me to choose the Fab Four, which I did.

Around this period, I also temporarily broke rank from the media-inspired Beatles versus Stones fracas. I briefly followed a much less fashionable, far more transient, fad, genuflecting not to Lennon and McCartney but to the drummer-led Londoners, the Dave Clark Five, also trail-blazing America on the wave of the British Invasion, ahead, it should be said, of the Stones in 1964. But it was, undoubtedly, the Beatles who would ultimately capture my favour, not to mention that of the broader constituency, as Beatlemania grew from a whisper to an ear-tearing scream. Even my parents – modest, Christian, respectable, conservative – liked the Fab Four: their vibrant pop and Merseyside manner – quick-witted, bright-eyed, jocular boys-next-door – combined traits in the great tradition of northern English entertainment, a sub-music hall manifestation of melody, on record and on-stage, and mirth, off-stage, talented music-makers with a comic touch.

---

[8] Simon Warner, 'Genesis and revelations: From the Midlands to Manhattan', 'Anglo Visions', *Pop Matters*, 12 March 2003, http://www.popmatters.com/columns/warner/030312.shtml [accessed 29 March 2005].

Meanwhile, the Rolling Stones were seen as the *bêtes noires* of the new British scene, the dishevelled disreputables fathers would instinctively protect daughters from, or so the mainstream press would have it. Longer of hair, rougher of dress, coarser of music, the Stones took American amplified blues and R&B and re-shaped it in a gutter-ish and urchin fashion, their London vowels emphasised and exaggerated, a working class assault on English as it should be spoken, all the stranger as lead vocalist Mick Jagger had enjoyed a middle-class upbringing and endured a period of study at the prestigious London School of Economics.

I doubt my parents had the slightest knowledge of the group's sources – Muddy Waters, Willie Dixon, Bobby Womack and Bo Diddley covers featured in a repertoire that was virtually all borrowed in the early years – but they had every suspicion of their output. Sexual, salacious, sordid, I recall disapproving tuts if Jagger and co. appeared on the minute, black and white TV that sat quite inconspicuously in the corner of the sitting room, on new UK teen shows like *Top of the Pops* and *Ready Steady Go*, which celebrated a rampant, fertile surge in indigenous popular culture. While the Stones' deeper, darker meanings were quite unrecognisable to this young boy, I now assume that it was Jagger's long-haired coiffure, voluminous lipped-pouting and its feminised ambiguity, that was particularly challenging to the values of the day.

So when we heard that the Megsons, father Ron and mother Muriel, daughter Cynthia and son Neil, were heading off to see the Stones play live, I recall that the whole matter utterly surprised and confused me. If my Mum and Dad saw something so demonic about the group, why would a similar parental pair be joining their two teens at such a performance? I could not work it out but never explored the matter beyond my own mind.

But for Neil Megson, an outsider who had earlier left his secondary school in Manchester in 1964 to enrol at Solihull's minor public school[9] and had quickly become the target of ostracism and bullying because of his northern accent,[10] the live sighting of the Stones would be transformational. At the Redifusion TV studios in Birmingham where *Thank Your Lucky Stars*, then a widely viewed rival to *Top of the Pops* screened on Independent Television, the BBC's commercial challenger, was taped, Megson not only saw his favourite band play on stage; he also had the good fortune to meet the group in person in the studio café between takes. The experience, possible because his father had a cleaning contract with the TV operation, would have a Damascene impact on the 16-year-old youth in that month of March 1966. The teenager was drawn to the rebel rowdiness of the Stones, to their music and their attitude, but he found one member of the band

---

[9] The public school in English parlance would be private school within the US system.
[10] Ford, 1999, p. 1.2.

totally magnetic. Brian Jones, who would die in 1969, became his beacon, his model, his inspiration, for subsequent decades to come. Sitting drinking coffee in the canteen with his heroes, he recalls the moment in the extended liner notes to his Psychic TV album, *Godstar: The Director's Cut*:

> What E do remember very, very clearly is how Brian Jones looked and how he looked at me. He seemed translucent, not fully materialised as if in an unguarded momeant when he wasn't fully focussed on being present, your hand might pass through him. It was as if thee particles that were intended to give him substance and represent thee physical body known as Brian Jones were dancing too freely, making it hard for him to maintain a human form. He was more apparition than person. Neither male nor female.[11]

GP-O continues:

> E made a promise to my SELF there and then, speaking to thee still forming person inside my head, and E locked it down with purity ov intent by using Brian Jones as thee hieroglyph to represent my dream with form. Why Brian Jones and not thee others? Intuition told me he was thee source, thee reckless explorer innovating with new instruments, new arrangements and most ov all perhaps new identities that transgressed taboos with abandon. Rightly or wrongly, E saw Brian Jones as a Romantic, flawed but daring, thee soul of thee group. He was thee first PANDROGYNE to enter my personal cosmology.[12]

It was an auspicious encounter, one that would shape his artistic and psychological future. The fact that the 2004 album, from which these remarks are drawn, was subtitled 'A film soundtrack based on thee life and times ov Brian Jones', tells its own tale of tribute, even if the movie, planned during the 1980s, was never made for lack of finance.

---

[11] Genesis P-Orridge, 'An over-painted smile … re-collections of mo-meants ov inspiration 1963–2004', CD sleeve notes to *Godstar: Thee Director's Cut* (Hyperdelic, 2004), p. 11.
[12] *Ibid*. Note: Genesis P-Orridge has used a language of his creation since the early days of his artistic emergence which draws attention to the sliding signifiers within words – for example, L-if-E, b-earthday, y-eras, movemeant – and also avoids the application of familiar pronouns like 'I' and 'me' replacing them with E and SELF. Called COUM speak or TOPI talk. (See Genesis P-Orridge, 'Full-length bio', the official Genesis P-Orridge website, http://www.genesisp-orridge.com/index. php?section=article&album_id=11&id=77 [accessed 3 April 2005]). The construction owes its inspiration to William Burroughs and issues of control related to language but also a system called E-Prime or English Prime which dispensed with the verb 'to be', Jason Louv, 'The GP-O Language', personal communication, email, 7 March 2005).

To these revelations, I will return, in due course, but my own personal connections with the evolving Megson would be cut short, not long after he enjoyed that highly affecting meeting with Brian Jones, for, at this point, in May 1966, my family uprooted and left Solihull to return to Manchester for my father's new job. It would be some time before I would become aware of Neil again. In fact, the author recalls the re-discovery in his *Pop Matters* 'Anglo Visions' column of March 2003:

> More than a decade later as I was completing my university studies, my mother contacted me to say that her friend Muriel Megson had been in touch and that Neil was now making a success in the rock world. As someone who, by now, was avidly consuming column miles of the music press each month, I was a bit shocked that I couldn't immediately place this new, young star. It soon transpired, however, that the adolescent Megson had taken on a fresh persona, and that the individual dubbed Genesis P-Orridge, and leader of a band called Throbbing Gristle, was the adopted alter ego of the teen who had long before offered me a guided tour of his model railway.[13]

Since then I have shared a curious, distant association with Genesis P-Orridge, or Gen, as he is known informally, or even Djin, a more recent signature on his emails, one that would not be re-kindled in any real sense for another 20 years after that, through letters and faxes in the later 1990s when an undergraduate popular music student of mine chose him as his final year dissertation topic, and, then again, not in person until 2004 when the book project I was working on would lead to our belated reunion in New York City that summer. Yet this account straddles a difficult path. My intrigue in P-Orridge is born of a slight childhood connection but it is, today, stimulated by a concern with his long-running links to members of the Beat Generation caucus. His collaborations with William Burroughs and Brion Gysin have become a key element in his journey, best represented in print by the special edition of San Francisco-based radical arts journal *RE/Search* which, not insignificantly, devoted itself to author, artist and the band TG in 1984.[14]

My account is not meant to be, in any way, a phony celebration of friendship – I am a fleeting figure in P-Orridge's past, he in mine. We may have belatedly restored our connection in quite surprising circumstances, but I am not feigning an intimate relationship. Nor is it a testimony of fandom – I am much more interested by P-Orridge's oeuvre than I am enamoured of it. But the fact that we have

---

[13] Warner, 2003.

[14] V. Vale and Andrea Juno (eds), *RE/Search #4/5, William S. Burroughs, Brion Gysin and Throbbing Gristle*, A Special Book Issue (San Francisco, CA: V/Search Publications, 1984).

a history makes my enquiry into his achievement less straightforward than the kind of research we might pursue as journalist or academic into the life and times of a popular musician from whom we are essentially detached. I cannot write a completely objective survey of this artist and the baggage he carries but I hope I can, to compensate, consider what occurs when that kind of personal interaction is part of a factual overview you are attempting to compile.

What this account certainly reflects on is the private and public, personal, psychological and artistic rollercoaster that P-Orridge has relentlessly ridden since his teens, when he determinedly embarked on a life that placed art at its heart and almost inevitably embraced the role of outsider, a part he has portrayed with a mixture of stoicism and perverse celebration since the mid-1960s. In his taking on the persona of 'a scapegoat' like his late hero Brian Jones,[15] he feels he is experiencing first-hand some of the trials and tribulations replicated in the lives of other subversive creatives who refused to toe the conventional line.

There is little doubt that a key catalyst in shaping Megson, the P-Orridge-to-be, was an experience in school when he was 14, one that had a strong bearing on his future activities but one that also lies at the heart of the arguments laid out in this thesis: that this artist owes much of his creative vision to the spirit of the Beat Generation writers. When we re-established our face-to-face connection in July 2004 he described an encounter with a teacher who had opened his eyes to a new body of literature. 'There was an English teacher at Solihull School whose nickname was "Bogbrush" because he had a moustache that stuck out, that was all bristly under his nose,' he explained. 'I'd have to look in an old school magazine to check his name what his real name was. And I handed him an essay for homework one day and got it back with ... I got a good mark but the thing was, it said "See me!" and I thought, "O-oh I'm in trouble again". So I had to wait till after the class, went to see him and he said "I really, really liked what you were writing and I think that you've a got a very unusual perspective on life and I'd like to recommend some writers that you should read." So he wrote them down for me ... he said you should try to find anything you can by Jack Kerouac and you should look for books by William Burroughs, no Jack Kerouac was the main one, it wasn't Burroughs ...'[16]

He continued: 'So I told my Dad that I'd been told I should try to get these books, *On the Road* in particular by Jack Kerouac, because he used to travel a lot with his work. He came back not long afterwards with a paperback copy of *On the Road*, Jack Kerouac, which I read straight through ... I loved it and I asked the teacher about it and what else there was and I started to seek out the

---

[15] Genesis P-Orridge, interview with the author, Brooklyn, New York City, 20 July 2004.
[16] GP-O, interview with the author, 2004.

other beatnik[17] writers because of that; I gave my father this list of names and I also realised that the Jack Kerouac books mentioned other people as fictional characters but they were actually really based upon other beatniks and that's how I got into the beatniks, through that. I was already writing my own poetry and my own creative writing, but that's the very specific sort of signifier of when I actually became consciously aware of the beatniks and started to look for them.'[18]

I wondered how that writing and reading that material had affected him? Did it influence the way he wrote poetry or wrote creatively? How in the years that followed did it impact on his artistic consciousness? 'There's no question that it affected the way I was writing. One of the things that most young artists do is they begin by mimicking the things they really like, same with rock bands, too. They'll start out trying to sound something like their favourite and so, because I didn't have a lot of support from my environment … it wasn't a good thing to do, to write poetry and want to be writer and an artist. The social environment was very much against that, so I was kind of on my own, so I would improvise and I had a couple of friends, […] just two or three people I knew, and we would spend the weekends trying to write our own beatnik poetry, and exchanging it with each other, reading out loud, basically being our own schoolboy version of the beatniks, the best we could. We'd drink wine and go in the park and fantasise that we were the beatniks. But what it did was, through doing that and immersing myself in the writing to that degree and especially the acting out in the theatrical way…the characters, the first thing I know that it did for me was it really made me aware of the sound of the poetry when it was spoken out loud.'[19]

While P-Orridge recalls that he and his proto-beatnik associates experimented with tape and did record some of their own poetry, I asked him if he actually heard anything of the Beats maybe reading their work? 'No. I'd never heard anything of that but the big impact upon me was definitely was learning to hear what I was writing, hear it as poetry and sound and song at the same time as I was writing it, instead of it being much more of an intellectual, academic exercise assembling words with meter and so on. I started to feel the actual natural rhythms of the words and the way that they were phrased and the sort of the pausing and the breaths, in a way not just the words, but also the non-words, the breath and the

---

[17] The term beatnik was coined by a writer on the *San Francisco Chronicle* in 1958. Herb Caen attempted to denigrate Beat Generation members or followers, often abbreviated to Beats, by adding the Russian suffix '*nik*'. In a climate of Cold War when the Russians were seen as the Communist enemy and at a time when the space race had witnessed the USSR's launch of their Earth-orbiting satellite Sputnik, Caen's device was a way of marking the Beats as a dangerous and subversive force, infiltrating American society. In our July 2004 interview, P-Orridge interestingly only used the more pejorative term beatnik, rather than Beat.
[18] GP-O, interview with the author, 2004.
[19] *Ibid.*

pacing and the slight hesitation and then all those sonic gestures, if you like, that one uses when you are doing things out loud, are not just another language of editing, which is one thing that they are, but it's also a whole extra language of connection between space and sound, the rhythmic aspect and, in a way, the emotional connections that come with hesitation or with loudness. All of that was suddenly made very real and very vivid for me.'[20]

Did that notion of the power of an oral style start to inform his work once he became involved in performance and theatre and song at the end of the 1960s and the start of the 1970s? 'I'm a great believer that everything you experience, everything you hear, everything you see, everything that you touch, that you have any interaction with mentally or physically, all of it influences what you create and people who kind of imply they have divine inspiration and what they make is unique and what they create, write or play or paint, that anything that they make is disconnected and a sign of their own personal genius, disconnected from things around it, I just think that's not true. I think that the great joy of creating art in any form is that the artist is the voice for the sum total of connections at any given moment, all their emotions which resonate with those of everyone and everything around them. That's why people can enjoy and be inspired by art; the reason is that they recognise themselves in it. So I've always felt that what you try to achieve is to build and project a voice which speaks for a person that doesn't exist in the usual sense, that person is the audience, which may be two or three or two thousand or two million, that you are actually just building a temporary fictional character that represents a common experience. So that was what I got from it on that level but the other really important thing was just the idea that when you were writing poetry, everything, again everything, could be included, that there was a journalistic, anecdotal aspect that I hadn't really understood before because growing up with Eng. Lit. where it's all about the classics and form ...'[21]

So, on the one hand there was a dominating, repressed, controlled form of expression, while the Beats showed him he could talk about personal experience and there was value to it. 'Personal experience, anecdotes, experiments, social and political things that are going on around you; they could all be included and referred to in the poetry and it was completely valid and in fact it gave us much more confidence ... it validates the experience of being an outsider in a way ...'[22]

Did he already feel like an outsider in the Midlands in England in the mid-1960s? 'Totally, I totally felt isolated and an alienated outsider and so when you read those books by the beatniks you see another possibility which is optimistic which is that somewhere out there in the wider world, there are others who may not be exactly

---

[20] *Ibid.*
[21] *Ibid.*
[22] *Ibid.*

the same as you, but they are enough like you or they perceive the world or they are experiencing life in a similar way, and that you can find them, so instead of having to accept your given family and your given social group, you can choose your own social group and your own extended family and that was very important for me as well, the idea that I could travel and go and seek out and find other people whose voices and whose experiences were more like my own and instead of being the outsider I could become at least affiliated with other people. I could recognise my kind, that something else was in there in the expression of life that would enable me to know when there were others who were more like me ...'[23]

Eventually, in 1968, he would escape the clutches of Solihull – his home, his family, his hated school – and headed off to the University of Hull, in Yorkshire, to study, ostensibly, Social Administration, Economics and Philosophy. But the odyssey would quickly switch track as 'he became connected with a group of kinetic/mixed media performers in 1969 known as Transmedia Exploration in Islington, England.'[24] Not long after, Megson, already beginning to function under the guise of Genesis,[25] became 'the Founding Artist and Theorist of seminal British Performance Art group COUM Transmissions in Shrewsbury, England ... [which] ... created and performed more than 200 art actions, installations, video work and street actions in Art Festivals and Galleries all over Europe and in America. The project was terminated in September 1976 with a final but now infamous show called *Prostitution* at the ICA Gallery in London.'[26]

Such controversy would never stray far from the P-Orridge doorstep in the years that followed: his courting, indeed shaping, of the insurrectionary fringe – in music, literature, art and philosophy – has frequently left him vulnerable to mainstream attack. On several occasions he has felt the forces of authority bring their powers to bear against him. Even before *Prostitution*, that notorious live/art show at the renowned Institute of Contemporary Arts (ICA), featuring exhibits and a debut Throbbing Gristle performance incorporating a striptease contribution from P-Orridge's lover-collaborator of the time Cosey Fanni Tutti,[27] a production that would lead to heated Parliamentary debate and a suggestion by MP Nicholas Fairbairn that these performers represented 'the wreckers of civilisation,'[28] P-Orridge's activities had drawn the attention of the law in 1975.

The phenomenon known as mailart, centred around the exchange of postcards, was at the core of P-Orridge's previous brush with the British courts. Mailart's roots

---

[23] *Ibid.*
[24] GP-O, 'Full-length bio'.
[25] Ford, 1999, p. 2.4.
[26] GP-O, 'Full-length bio'.
[27] Note that Cosey Fanni Tutti's real name is Christine Newby.
[28] Ford, 1999, p. 6.22.

lay in the activities of the New York-based art group Fluxus, a crucial gathering of US artists who strove to make the ordinary iconic and included Yoko Ono among its roll, which, for a number of years, encouraged its members and others to exchange communications by post – sending and sharing visual images of their own making through their letter-boxes, a pre-internet ritual that was cheap and also subversive as it relied on post office services across the globe to deliver its bounty. The products of this cottage art with a wider vision were sometimes eventually shown in galleries. 'Mailart contained no curator. Even during the height of the movement's popularity [in the 1970s], mailart galleries had an all-inclusive policy. Famous artist such as Ray Johnson and Fluxus-ian Ken Friedman were shown alongside obscure sendings from joe schmoe and his overseas pals. Mailart wasn't even about being an artist, stressing instead creative communication'.[29]

As for P-Orridge, 'while his work both within and without the postal medium has often dealt with erotic material, in the mid-1970s, he'd been combining images of pornography and royalty in his queen postcard series, citing "kitsch and the national sense of taboo", as his inspiration'.[30] Charged with indecency for his incorporation of Queen Elizabeth II's portrait into a series of juxtapositions, including one with a naked woman, the artist was prosecuted. He was fined a large sum (at the time) of £400 ($750, in current values) and given minimum time to pay under the threat of a 12-month jail sentence.

It is interesting that the collage or cut-up art should feature early in his history. Not long before, as a consequence of P-Orridge's involvement with mailart and the publications *File* and *Vile* (the titles each lampooned mainstream news magazine *Life*) which celebrated the form, he would first make contact with one of the principal figures linked to the writing of the Beat Generation, William Burroughs, whose cut-up approach to writing novels had become widely discussed and critically admired by the start of the 1970s. Although his debut work, *Junkie* (1953), had been built on a representational narrative, a thinly veiled autobiographical novel, his books *Naked Lunch* (1959) and *The Soft Machine* (1961)[31] were much more innovative in their approach. In these titles, he had experimented with the idea that texts could be written, taken apart and re-ordered to produce a new literary work. This form of deconstruction – and re-assembling – would pre-empt structuralism and poststructuralist theories of art and literature, developed and explored by French philosopher Jacques Derrida and others, which emerged in the 1960s and during the years that followed.

P-Orridge met Burroughs, based in London in 1972, as a result of an item the writer had placed in *File*. As part of the mailart network, Burroughs had invited

---

[29] Bengala, 'The intuitive lure of flesh: Genesis P-Orridge's erotic mailart', *Painful but Fabulous: The Lives and Art of Genesis P-Orridge*, edited by Genesis P-Orridge (New York: Soft Skull Press, 2002), p. 111.
[30] Bengala, *ibid.*, pp. 111–12.
[31] Note that these book titles have also appeared as *Junky*, *The Naked Lunch* and *Soft Machine*.

correspondents to send items that evoked 'camouflage for 1984', the musician recalled,[32] to his home address. 'I just thought, that can't really be William Burroughs' address but, just in case it was, I thought I'd write. So I wrote a very cheeky letter to the address which began with "I'm tired of you and Brion Gysin and Allen Ginsberg and everybody saying that you know me and please stop … you're just trying to be hip by saying that you know me". And, lo and behold, a few weeks later I got a postcard back from William Burroughs, a friendly postcard, so I began a correspondence with Burroughs. He just said whenever you're in London, cause then I was still living in Hull, just call me and come over and let's have dinner. I hitchhiked to London one weekend and rang the number and … [gravelly Burroughs impression] "Get in a taxi and come over" and I said, "I can't afford a taxi" and he just said, "I'll pay for it, just come over". So I went to Duke Street and there he was – Uncle Bill, William Burroughs. And he was ready for me – he had a bottle of Jack Daniels and his television with a remote so we could do cut-ups while we were talking. That's when we became friends. We drank the bottle of whiskey, he took me for dinner at the Angus Steakhouse, and we stayed friends until he passed away.'[33] It was the start of an association that would extend to the end of the novelist's life in 1997.

The link forged with one of his beloved 'beatnik writers', P-Orridge's interest in cut-up intensified and also drew him to the man whom Burroughs was quite willing to credit with devising the process – Brion Gysin. As Burroughs himself wrote in *RE/Search*: 'At a surrealist rally in the 1920s Tristan Tzara the man from nowhere proposed to create a poem on the spot by pulling words from a hat. A riot ensued and wrecked the theatre. Andre Breton expelled Tristan Tzara from the movement and grounded the cut-ups on the Freudian couch.'[34] He added:

> In the summer of 1959 Brion Gysin painter and writer cut newspaper articles into sections and rearranged the sections at *random*. 'Minutes to Go' resulted from this initial cut-up experiment. 'Minutes to Go' contains unedited unchanged cut-ups emerging as quite coherent and meaningful prose. The cut-up method brings to writers the collage, which has been used by painters for fifty years. And used by the moving and still camera. In fact all street shots from movie or still cameras are the unpredictable factors of passersby and juxtaposition cut-ups.[35]

---

[32] GP-O, interview with the author, 2004.
[33] *Ibid.*
[34] William S. Burroughs, 'The cut-up method of Brion Gysin', *RE/Search* #4/5, *William S. Burroughs, Brion Gysin and Throbbing Gristle*, A Special Book Issue, edited by V. Vale and Andrea Juno (San Francisco, CA: V/Search Publications, 1984), pp. 35–6 (p. 35).
[35] *Ibid.*

In the same issue of *RE/Search*, Gysin was interviewed by prominent UK rock journalist and P-Orridge associate Jon Savage, and also by P-Orridge with fellow Throbbing Gristle member Peter Christopherson. The conversations were part of a sequence that P-Orridge would edit into a collection of interviews, clearly making explicit the artistic alliance between the old guard of cut-up theory and the young Turks who were appropriating it. Gysin told Savage that the concept of cut-up had been 'an accident ... but which I *recognised* immediately as it happened, because of knowing of all the other past things – I knew about the history of the arts, let's say. And it seemed a marvellous thing to give to William [Burroughs] who had a huge body of work to which it could immediately be applied'.[36]

By the time P-Orridge and Christopherson's interview with Gysin took place in 1980, the band Throbbing Gristle were in their final throes and would actually play their last concert the following year.[37] Yet TG, formed in 1975 as an extension of the art group COUM and a band who played their premiere set at the *Prostitution* event, had, by then, left a significant mark on the fringes of the new music which erupted in the UK from the middle to the end of the 1970s. In fact, P-Orridge claims a vital part in launching the tide of punk, most usually linked, in Britain at least, to the rise of the Sex Pistols in late 1976, and tied in to the release of their first single 'Anarchy in the UK', the *Anarchy in the UK* tour and their expletive-charged appearance on the capital's regional ITV news show, *Today*, with presenter Bill Grundy, on 1 December, which won the group nationwide tabloid front page coverage the following day and, with it, ongoing notoriety.[38]

P-Orridge points out that TG had already appeared on Grundy's TV show six weeks earlier when *Prostitution* had been the controversial topic under the early evening spotlight. He states, too, that he was already immersed in TG activities a year before these two television items were aired. P-Orridge was rehearsing in the same building while Malcolm McLaren was attempting to forge a New York Dolls-like band in London. McLaren, who had managed the Dolls in their dying phases, tried, then failed, to lure Television refugee Richard Hell to England to front the new act.[39] Instead, he turned to a spiky-haired hanger-on who loitered in Sex, the clothes shop the entre-preneur-rock manager and his designer partner Vivienne Westwood ran in the Kings Road, Chelsea. In place of Hell, therefore, Johnny Rotten would become vocalist.

Yet there was more than just a rehearsal space to connect TG and the Pistols and the nascent style of punk. P-Orridge also temporarily became drummer in a band

---

[36] Gysin quoted in *RE/Search*, 1984, p. 55.
[37] Throbbing Gristle were dissolved in 1981 but they would take to the stage once again, more than two decades later, in December 2004 when a farewell performance saw them second on the bill to Mercury Rev at 'The Nightmare Before Christmas', a festival held at a UK holiday camp in Rye, Sussex, and curated by the controversial Britart brothers Jake and Dinos Chapman.
[38] Jon Savage, *England's Dreaming: Sex Pistols and Punk Rock* (London: Faber, 1991), pp. 257–75.
[39] *Ibid.*, p. 92.

that would well reflect the possibilities that the new musical form was providing for creative but untrained musicians. Mark Perry's Alternative TV were a minor moment in the punk chronology but their leader performed a more important role in the dissemination of the movement's aesthetic. Perry had, in addition, founded the fanzine *Sniffin' Glue*,[40] a rough and ready, roneo-ed comic which incorporated hastily written text, photo-copied images, cut-out, ransom-note-style headlines, a publication that would influence punk culture throughout the land, encouraging followers to launch their own determinedly slapdash accounts of the new scene in cities like Manchester (*City Fun*), Edinburgh (*Hangin' Around*) and Bradford (*Wool City Rocker*).

Throbbing Gristle, however, the project to which P-Orridge was to speedily return after his passing sojourn with ATV, were never going to produce the digestible soundbites that the Pistols ('God Save the Queen' and 'Pretty Vacant') and the Clash ('White Riot' and 'London's Burning') utilised, to induce slavish adherence in the burgeoning weekly music press of the time, and generate mass hysteria among the safety-pinned, ripped T-shirted fans who idolised them. Instead, P-Orridge's band 'created/explored an aural aesthetic frequently (although not exclusively) defined via extreme noise, and jarring splices of sound, randomly selected and presented, using the theories espoused by William Burroughs, Brion Gysin, and Ian Sommerville [*another Burroughs associate*] of the cut-up, tape viruses and infra-sound. The "musical" results of these sonic experiments range from the tranquil to the confrontational. Throbbing Gristle also utilised Gysin's adaptation of Hassan I Sabbah's credo: "Nothing is true. Everything is permitted".'[41]

The group appeared to combine intensely applied art theory – a fierce loyalty to the principles of the cut-up – with a parallel devotion to a version of anti-art incompetence which owed much to the Dada influence that P-Orridge has certainly been happy to credit as significant in his own creative development. At the same time, the quartet also laid down their anti-rock position: they appeared to despise punk's mere simplification of the rock sound, a cornerstone of the stripped down do-it-yourself ethic that McLaren had enthusiastically championed. That said, there are other arguments outlined in Savage (1991)[42] and Marcus (1989)[43]

[40] *Ibid.*, pp. 201–2.
[41] Jack Sargeant (ed.), *Naked Lens: Beat Cinema* (London: Creation, 1997), p. 184. Note: Hassan I Sabbah was an influential Middle East leader of the Ismalis from the eleventh-century. His followers, the Assassins, derived from *hachachin* (smokers of hashish), played a significant political role in the region for around 200 years. See 'The Last Words of Hassan Sabbah' by William S. Burroughs, http://www.interpc.fr/mapage/westernlands/Derniersmots.html [accessed 19 February 2012].
[42] Savage, 1991, pp. 23–36.
[43] Greil Marcus, *Lipstick Traces: A Secret History of the Twentieth Century* (London: Secker & Warburg, 1989), p. 19.

which reference the theories of Situationism, a later and more political outgrowth of Dada, speculating that these ideas had also been familiar to McLaren and had been applied to the band by the Sex Pistols' commercially shrewd, tactically astute and media savvy manager. So the presence of Dada sub-texts in *both* TG and the Pistols has been construed by some well-regarded commentators on both sides of the Atlantic.

P-Orridge succinctly described the template of TG in my interview with him in 2004:

> Throbbing Gristle, like all good bands when it works well, when the chemistry works, can only exist as the sum total of all of the four people involved – Sleazy[44] wanted, quite consciously…he wanted to find a way to incorporate the William Burroughs/Brion Gysin cut up techniques, so he used six cassette decks or Walkmans, when they first came out, and that was his instrument and later on he actually built his own hand-made sequencers so that he could play sequences. They would come though in rhythms (*suggests the beat of random electronic sounds*) but it was actually from cassette tapes, so his raw material was cassette tapes and he was able to use them so both sides of the cassette could be played at the same time – and stereo – so each tape had four sound sources. Those sound sources could be just him walking down the street or anything, so the six decks he had, 24 different sound sources, and you could sequence them or play them on a little keyboard one at a time or just run them, so that was his contribution. The sound began as a result of what we could do. I got a bass guitar because somebody had left it behind when they'd hitchhiked and stayed with us for a while and they had an old broken bass guitar which they left. I got Chris to fix it, he put humbucker picks ups in it, in a bass, two of those, and because I had grown up playing drums I wanted to do something rhythmic, so I played bass, and I basically started out hitting on rhythm. Chris made home-made synthesisers. His favourite band was Tangerine Dream, Kraftwerk, all that German stuff, so he built those old, big analog synths and so he brought his big, huge analog synths and then we just said, 'Well that means Cosey should play the lead guitar', cause the one thing we knew we didn't want, we didn't want a drummer because we thought that if you have a drummer, it becomes rock music. You can't stop it, somehow they can't help themselves; they do 4/4 and they just do rock drumming. So we cut that – no drummer. One thing we were sure of was to resist the rock formula and that's

---

[44] The nickname of Peter Christopherson, called thus because 'he was interested in the "sex" side of us', see Ford, 1999, p. 4.9.

how industrial music began…it was the result of what we did have available and what we refused to do.[45]

In Simon Ford's *Wreckers of Civilisation*, several contemporary reviews confirm a general inability to recognise TG's value as music-makers. Tony Parsons of *New Musical Express*, one of the main voices employed to write about punk on a paper that was enthusiastically backing the new sounds, was withering in his critique of the group's contribution to the *Prostitution* show:

> After Genesis finished his opening speech of doom and destruction, the band went into their, uh, music, which consisted of lots of weird, psychedelic taped sounds rolling around random keyboards played plink plonk style, lead guitar that Patti Smith would have been ashamed of and moronic bass on a superb Rickenbacker by old Genesis P-Orridge himself [...] Genesis seemed to be really enjoying himself but most of the audience were bored [...] I went back to the audience to check out why so many kids decked out in punk outfits had come along to the ICA tonight. Surely they weren't interested in this, uh, culture? 'NAH, MATE,' one of them told me while adjusting the safety-pin his carefully ripped tee-shirt. 'We've come along to see Chelsea. [Note: *A more conventional punk band of the day*]. They're on after the stripper.' [*Cosey Fanni Tutti*].[46]

It was by no means all negative and dismissive, however. Important critical voices did pin their colours to the TG flag, in the US and the UK. Richard Meltzer told *Village Voice* readers in 1978 that they were 'the Velvets of a "new age"'[47] and Paul Morley, writing in *NME* in 1981, commented: 'One day TG's music will sound rich and sweet. For now everything you feel about TG – septic, morbid, incomprehensible, gimmicky – think the opposite and wake up.'[48]

But for Genesis P-Orridge, positive reaction was not perhaps that crucial. The band were more about gesture and the use of a rock format to criticise the system; punk was a useful platform on which to climb. 'We didn't take punk massively seriously. It was just something we thought was interesting and went along with it,' he told journalist Jon Savage. 'Because it was rebellious and was antagonistic to the status quo.'[49] The ICA show would gain P-Orridge that slot on the same *Today* programme that would host the Sex Pistols several weeks later but his interest

---

[45] GP-O, interview with the author, 2004.
[46] Parsons cited in Ford, 1999, pp. 6.29–6.30.
[47] *Ibid.*, p. 0.3.
[48] *Ibid.*
[49] *Ibid.*, p. 6.29.

in punk was already waning. 'We hadn't thought of becoming part of the music business; we were a comment on culture, and hypocrisy and double values,' said P-Orridge.[50]

Yet if Throbbing Gristle, whose album releases included *20 Jazz Funk Greats* (1978) and *Heathen Earth* (1981), had assumed a prominent place in the mythology of indie rock and were capable of drawing crowds of many thousands to their US shows, P-Orridge decided, at one of those concerts, that it was time to pull the plug. He felt his anti-rock band were becoming part of the musical establishment, his own Industrial Records, which named the musical genre, an influential, if still small-scale, operation. The death of Throbbing Gristle suggested that the rock 'n' roll culture that had served his propaganda purposes well for five years would now be jettisoned, although this assumption would actually prove misplaced. Within two years, his musical persona would find a fresh outlet in a new band Psychic TV, whose 1987 single 'Godstar', a celebration of late hero Brian Jones, would become P-Orridge's most commercially successful 45 release.

However, during the early 1980s, P-Orridge's relationship with William Burroughs strengthened and was underpinned by some important developments which allowed him to explore other aspects of his artistic vision rather than merely his creative output. Although he had known the American writer professionally for nearly a decade and had received his personal backing when seeking Arts Council[51] support for COUM Transmissions in the early 1970s and a testimonial by the author in his favour when facing his mailart prosecution in 1976,[52] from 1980 the connection was bolstered in a number of significant ways.

Burroughs and Gysin had compiled a body of films during the 1960s and 1970s which recorded their lives and art in Tangier, at the so-called 'Beat Hotel' in Paris and in London. In fact, the celluloid documents, shot under the direction of another member of the circle Antony Balch, had been conceived as 'an epic "beatnik" movie'.[53] These three, plus Sommerville, were 'in all kind of cahoots together. Re-inventing and exploring with their constantly deepening experiments in deconstruction; writing; painting; sexuality; scientology; film; collage; audio tape; and, of course, neurobiology and pharmacology'.[54]

P-Orridge says that '[t]he result and legacy, with hindsight, is an incredibly significant and monumental celluloid archive. A body of documentary portraits that is truly unique. We have nothing that is so revealing, so experimental, so

---

[50] Quoted in Savage, 1991, p. 423.
[51] The Arts Council of Great Britain, founded in 1946, was the UK's public funding body for the arts (see Hewison, 1997, p. 29). It has been re-constituted since 1994 with the various member nations – England, Scotland, etc. – granted their own funding authority.
[52] P-Orridge, 1997, pp. 184–96 (p. 184).
[53] *Ibid.*
[54] P-Orridge, 1997, p. 184.

influential or so critically vital in preserving such important "Beat" figures and their unfolding, most radical ideas on film.'[55]

In 1980, Balch died of cancer, prompting Gysin to make an emergency call to P-Orridge from Paris. Gysin explained that the rent on Balch's Soho office had gone unpaid during an absence caused by his terminal illness. As a result the principal tenant of the rented space had decided to clear out all his effects. Among these were items from the filmed Burroughs-Gysin archive. P-Orridge explains that Gysin and his collaborators had agreed that, if he was able to save the materials from the dump, he could have them. Catching a taxi, P-Orridge arrived at the scene with little time to spare, but just managed to salvage the cans containing the film. There were 28 cans of reels of 35mm film which P-Orridge, with the help of a friendly taxi driver, was able to carry away. 'I called Brion when I got home,' he recalls, 'to give him the good news. He told me William [Burroughs] had been pleased I was saving what I could and fully supported my being the new proactive custodian of these films.'[56]

In the coming months, P-Orridge began a process of documenting the film materials in his possession. The important British film-maker Derek Jarman, who had directed the cult punk classic movie Jubilee (1977), was instrumental in helping him find the resources to study the footage. 'Then came the archaeological process. I sat for days […] and laboriously wrote a meticulous list of every single scene, every single edit section, in every single decaying can by noting as best I could a verbal description of what seemed to be happening visually.'[57]

These efforts bore fruit in 1982 when P-Orridge became further involved in a significant project with Burroughs. The Final Academy brought the two together in a live event involving readings, spoken word and musical ingredients. Commented P-Orridge: 'I told William that there were a lot of people who were inspired by Brion and William's idea of the cut-up and it would be a really great idea to put on an event and I'd already come up with the title, the Final Academy, because he mentions an academy in one of his books, it kind of comes into [the novel] The Wild Boys. And he basically said, "Fine if you can organise it, I'll take part". And so I got David Dawson, a friend of mine, and he then knew someone called Roger Ely, but basically David and I … somehow we pulled every string we could and we basically got it to happen…the nice part was that, because it was one of those wonderful upward spirals because of the attention the Final Academy drew to Burroughs and Gysin and their ideas, all of his books got re-published.'[58]

The production was seen at the renowned Haçienda club in Manchester during that winter. Out of this grew a major television documentary on the writer. Shown

---

[55] Ibid., p. 185.
[56] Ibid., p. 188.
[57] Ibid., p. 188.
[58] GP-O, interview with the author, 2004.

on BBC2,[59] in 1985, in the prestigious *Arena* strand, *Burroughs: The Movie* drew heavily on the very films that P-Orridge had saved and catalogued. But this fascinating episode – important for P-Orridge but also crucial in the telling of the Beat Generation history – had a disappointing conclusion. In 1991, P-Orridge's Brighton home was raided by the police after newspaper allegations that the musician had been central to a Satanist cult.[60] Although P-Orridge was in Tibet at the time, filmed material was seized, among it footage from the Burroughs-Gysin collection and items that Derek Jarman had produced while documenting the Final Academy proceedings. These films have never been recovered and are now thought lost or destroyed. The raid on P-Orridge's premises was a key factor in his decision to leave the UK and move to the US.

Yet that incident and the subsequent move to the States has, in no way, dented his desire to operate as an innovative and versatile artist – musician, writer, director, performer – ever pushing at the boundaries. All of those avenues he has continued to pursue, but arguably his boldest statement, in a life of bold statements, has seen him, in the early years of the new century, embark on a life-changing project. His interest in the concept of body art – the use of the artist's own physical being as artwork – has seen him join forces with his wife Jackie Breyer as his essential collaborator in the project. The pair now operate this creative coupling under the name Breyer P-Orridge.

Body art or body modification has a long and involved history stretching back to ancient times and lost cultures. Tattooing, piercing, branding and scarification have been a feature of cultures from all eras and all continents. But the more recent rise of a movement that has been dubbed 'modern primitive' has changed the emphasis of a practice that has been, in the past, linked to a cultural mainstream – the tribal, the ritual – to a contemporary one that marks the practitioner, or form of display, as *outside* the cultural mainstream. The book *Modern Primitives*, also published in the *RE/Search* series,[61] focuses on individuals who draw on a range of body art forms to express their identity to the wider world. The volume examines 'a vivid contemporary *enigma*: the growing revival of highly visual (and sometimes shocking) body modification practices.'[62] Genesis P-Orridge was one of the figures given attention in the publication.

Says Victoria Pitts: '*Modern Primitives* describes how individuals can create some form of social change [...] through creating visible bodily changes, while

---

[59] BBC2 was the second channel of the UK's principal public broadcaster. Launched in 1964, it became the outlet for more specialised programmes and documentaries, complementing BBC1's more mainstream broadcasts.

[60] GP-O, 2002, p. 40.

[61] V. Vale and Andrea Juno, *RE/Search* #12, *Modern Primitives* (San Francisco, CA: V/Search Publications, 1989).

[62] Vale and Juno, 1989, p. 4.

also asserting a radical message of self-invention [...] Modern primitivism does not replace, then, but rather *displaces* Western cultural identity and creates a subversive cultural style [...] the gestures of modern primitivism call into question the fixity of identity as such.'[63]

She also draws attention to Hebdige's theories of subculture which have 'much in common with the radical collage aesthetics of surrealism'.[64] Hebdige remarks that 'the radical aesthetic practices of Dada and Surrealism are [...] the classic modes of "anarchic discourse". Breton's manifestos (1924 and 1929) established the basic premise of surrealism: that a new surreality would emerge through the subversion of common sense, the collapse of prevalent logical categories and oppositions [...] and the celebration of the abnormal and forbidden.'[65] This makes, and emphasises, that pertinent link, as P-Orridge's interest in the Dadaists and Surrealists has been widely documented. He has claimed those artistic revolutionaries as influences and revealed his debt in his own creations. For example, in 1973, his work *Copyright Breeches* – a book which featured photographs signed by P-Orridge with the copyright sign – referenced Marcel Duchamp's pioneering work with ready-mades.[66] The same Dadaist would then inspire a 1974 performance piece called *Marcel Duchamp's Next Work*, in which bicycle wheels, an item Duchamp famously employed in an art-piece of 1913, were transformed into a musical instrument.[67] P-Orridge commented:

> When I was still at Solihull School the only things that excited me in art history [...] the two things that excited me were Surrealism and Dada, definitely, and, of those two, Dada I found the more satisfying, in the same way that Jack Kerouac and the beatniks excited me in the end, first of all, because their lives became integral to their art – it's pointless to try and separate them. In the same way with Dada and Surrealism, I enjoyed reading about their lives and their anecdotes about what they did as much as looking at the pieces they made [...] with Dada there was a certain realisation in the Dada movement that life, that their lives, ultimately, were as valid as a piece of art, a material item.[68]

The separation of those who utilise body modification as a sign of personal identity, however, and those who adopt the practice as a mode of artistic expression – like

---

[63] Victoria Pitts, *In the Flesh: The Cultural Politics of Body Modification* (Basingstoke: Palgrave Macmillan, 2003), p. 133.

[64] *Ibid.*

[65] Dick Hebdige, *Subculture: The Meaning of Style* (London: Methuen, 1979), p. 105.

[66] Ford, 1999, p. 2.21.

[67] Ford, 1999, p. 4.5–4.8.

[68] GP-O, interview with the author, 2004.

the performance artists Orlan[69] from France, and the Australian Stelarc[70] who are covered in Featherstone's edited collection *Body Modification*[71] – is a subtle one, raising more questions about the role and status of art in society, not to mention that of the individual and the use of the body as canvas. But P-Orridge seems to have made an early decision to include his own body in a holistic pursuit of his artistic oeuvre: for him, it could be argued, the subversive power of identity distortion *was* and *is* the artform.

During his time with COUM Transmissions, tattooing took on a talismanic quality – for instance, both he and Cosey Fanni Tutti had tattoos out of loyalty to a jailed associate[72] – and tattooing and piercing have become ongoing emblems of transgression in his résumé. Tattoos on the right shoulder, arms and lower abdomen – a snarling wolf's head on his right groin, providing a bestial emblem which echoes the sexual power of the penis – and body piercing – including genital decoration – have formed an intrinsic feature of P-Orridge's look for many years.[73]

P-Orridge talked in *Modern Primitives* about the concepts behind pandrogyny, while he was still involved in an earlier relationship with his then wife Paula. He said:

> Paula and I function as a symbiotic team when we do rituals and that is the Third Mind. We become fused as an androgynous being, or as we call it, a *Pandrogynous* being: P for power, Potency, and also for the Positive aspects of being blended male-female. And also because it then makes Pan, and Pan is also a good concept. Pandrogyny is one of my on-going investigations, and the other one is the idea that we're not an occult group, we're an *occulture*. Because my interest is in culture, but I approach it through occult means, if you like.[74]

In 2002, P-Orridge and Lady Jaye, a photographer and also performer as member of Psychic TV, the woman to whom he has been married since 1996, embarked on their experiment in pandrogyny, each pursuing, not a sex change, but a movement towards, what they describe as, a hermaphrodite state. This creative concept raises many issues about sex, gender, sexuality, identity and the part that art might play in annotating or obscuring those characteristics and their relationship to each other. So far, P-Orridge has undergone a number of surgical procedures

---

[69] See Orlan's website http://www.orlan.net/ [accessed 26 February 2009].
[70] See Stelarc's website http://www.stelarc.va.com.au/ [accessed 26 February 2009].
[71] Mike Featherstone (ed.), *Body Modification* (London: Sage, 2003), pp. 129–207.
[72] Vale and Juno,, 1989, p. 165.
[73] See Vale and Juno, 1989, p. 4, and GP-O, 2002, p. 22.
[74] Vale and Juno, 1989, p. 171.

– implanted breasts, a shrinking of the waist, work to cheekbones and lips – not to mention the installation of an impressive, and expensive, set of gold teeth.

We might also add that the tradition of gender play or gender bending or sexual ambivalence has a potent history within the field of entertainment – from boys playing women in original Shakespearean dramas to *castrati* of the Catholic choirs and the principal boys and dames of the *Comedia dell'Arte*-inspired pantomime. These theatrical antecedents have been particularly replicated in the field of post-war popular music – from Little Richard's outrageously camp stage style of the 1950s to the long-haired, feminised affectations of the hippy 1960s (the Stones have already been mentioned in this context) and onward to David Bowie, the New York Dolls, Boy George, Prince, Marilyn Manson and a large number of others (most often men, but sometimes women like Patti Smith, Annie Lennox and k.d.lang) who have resisted accepted notions of the masculine and feminine and turned those expectations on their head. It is important, I believe, that Genesis P-Orridge's transgressive patterns are considered in relation to that particular history, too.

Sheila Whiteley touches upon such ambiguities when she speaks of Mick Jagger as "'the king bitch of rock" [...] with a performing style derived largely from a careful scrutiny of Rudolph Nureyev and Tina Turner' and how he 'promised fantasy gratification of both the heterosexual and the homosexual'.[75] We have also already seen how P-Orridge's homoerotic celebration of Jagger's band rival Brian Jones – with his 'new identities that transgressed taboos with abandon' in the *Godstar* sleeve notes[76] – was a crucial juncture in his own artistic coming out.

Yet P-Orridge feels that for all these recent physical re-orderings, the bodily aspect of his art-making is not a stand-alone strategy, rather part of a pattern of creativity, reconstructing by reassembling texts, in the very widest sense, that stretches back to 'Beautiful Litter', his spontaneous haiku games on his own high street in 1968. 'My whole life before', he tells Bob Bert in *BB Gun* magazine, 'as an individual artist and musician was about experimenting with cut-ups in music, art, collaging in every possible way. Now I can see that I have always included my body in all of that as well in some form [...] Consciousness, body, sexual identity, perceptions, senses, and all those things that in some way add up to one thing that is called ME in one's head. All of that is now contributed as raw material to this new Breyer P-Orridge entity [...] It makes sense that we collaborated in the past with Burroughs and Gysin, that the invention of Industrial music grew from

---

[75] Sheila Whiteley, 'Little Red Rooster v the Honky Tonk Woman: Mick Jagger, sexuality, style, image', *Sexing the Groove: Popular Music and Gender*, edited by Sheila Whiteley (London: Routledge, 1997), p. 67.
[76] P-Orridge, 2004, p. 11.

a desire to find a way to apply cut-ups to contemporary music in a way that talked about modern times.'[77]

It seems that Genesis P-Orridge has spent the last 40 years constructing an alternative reality – an art-inspired parallel universe which challenges all notions of conventional organisation, whether musical, literary, visual or ethical, or the sexual categorising of the human being. However, at the end of it all, this programme of body modification, while it may be a dramatic course of action and a life-altering process, it is, for him, primarily an art project or art process, one that has attracted attention among the *cognoscenti* of cutting-edge art – whether that be makers or followers of performance art, installation art or body art – and will be seen as just that, with a documented record, compiled in photographs and film, mapping the evolution of the piece, to be exhibited in the future.

In fact, the very venture is also serving to stress P-Orridge's credentials as a maker of art, challenging his reputation as a renegade rocker. As he told writer-researcher Jayne Sheridan in an interview in England in 2004: '*Painful but Fabulous* [...] was very much concerned with me as an artist and not a musician and I really wanted to redress that balance, not be categorised as a musician because I don't feel that's what I am; I feel I am a multi-media artist. Everything I do I approach with the aesthetics of an artist, very much. I conceive an idea. I then explore and do research around the concept and if it seems valid to explore it and basically test it on the public, then I will. But I never do anything that I am not prepared to do to or for myself.'[78]

He also explained that as Lady Jaye 'edited all the photographs for the book, it became more and more apparent to us both – and for me it was quite a surprise – that within all the conscious projects that I've done in performance art, music, collage, painting, sculpture, that what was really central to all of them was an exploration of identity; it wasn't even just gender but it was identity itself. Who creates the person that we say we are? And it became more and more apparent, too, to me in fact everyone's identity is fictional and most of it is written by other people, that this is a narrative that we live and it can be re-written and we can actually usurp the outside world's control over our character, our identity, and we can begin to write the story for ourselves and be whoever we want to be.'[79]

But what happens when the investigator re-discovers the subject of this piece having known him in another time, another space? When the subject is Genesis

---

[77] Bob Bert, 'This is a story (a very special story) it's about ... Breyer P-Orridge', *BB Gun* magazine, Issue #7, 2004.

[78] Comment by Genesis P-Orridge, filmed interview with writer/researcher Jayne Sheridan, Columbia Hotel, London, 8 December 2004.

[79] *Ibid.*

P-Orridge, the question takes on extra pertinence especially when change of all kinds is a credo underpinning his activity, his life-long adventure. I had changed too, naturally – the eight-years-old boy had become the 48-years-old man – so the dislocation occurs on both sides of the fence but his pursuit of transformation seems to have been endemic; in my personal case, ageing alone could be blamed.

For me, meeting P-Orridge four decades after my initial encounters with him as Neil Megson was strange for many reasons. When I called him from close to the Brooklyn subway station – he had proposed meeting me there when I arrived – to let him know I was nearby, I asked how I would recognise him. 'I'll be wearing a white shirt and a blue, denim mini-skirt', he replied.[80] That was briefly disorientating but, when we met up just minutes after, we quickly connected. With a bob of peroxided hair, full lips and petite, he looked younger than his 54 years. He mocked me gently for my hippy-ish appearance. I was wearing a bandana and he suggested my stay in San Francisco in recent days had affected me. It broke the ice for both of us.

The afternoon and evening we passed together – my own partner Jayne Sheridan, who looked superficially, though still surprisingly, like P-Orridge, speedily befriended him, too, and later Lady Jaye joined us as we headed for a meal at Sea, one of the fashionable Williamsburg eateries – was comfortable and rewarding. I interviewed him on tape, was shown the only known sculpture, a self-portrait, that William Burroughs had created sitting close to the space where the Breyer P-Orridges have been planning a basement gallery, and shared our thoughts on a whole range of topics.

Genesis P-Orridge has pursued his personal metamorphosis for many years, but it seems that his association with Lady Jaye has given the quest for physical re-orientation a renewed and powerful momentum. He may be chasing this outcome in response to the sexual ambiguities he recognised in Brian Jones, and was so attracted to, when he met him in 1966. He may, as Pitts and Hebdige have proposed, be pursuing this extreme form of body modification for the same reasons he drew on tattoos and scarification in previous periods, as a subversive, cultural displacement activity. He may also have decided, in part, to strive to retain his Peter Pan-ish appearance for reasons of vanity, too – P-Orridge would not deny here the power and place of his own ego. But it seems that the intensity of the latest project has less to do with gender distortion or gender reassignment and more to do with sheer playfulness with the notions of identity – he refuses to be bound by his name, his culture, his own body and sees this refusal to comply, this disobedience, as the absolute moral obligation of his art and his artistry.

---

[80] GP-O, telephone conversation with the author, 20 July 2004.

There are other issues and paradoxes that we could explore, too. P-Orridge's fall from the window of an ablaze LA studio in 1995,[81] when he suffered such serious injuries including multiple fractures, might be regarded as the ultimate, if unplanned, cut-up. At the same time, his surgical procedures, conducted with planning and precision, could be regarded as the antithesis of cut-up: although the surgeon's knife literally slices the human tissue and re-constructs the body, the random laws of chance, seemingly central to the aesthetics of cut-up, appear to be removed from the equation. But those are speculations for further and future consideration.

For P-Orridge in 2005, while rock music and his spoken word pursuits – via Thee Majesty, a smaller ensemble also featuring Psychic TV personnel including Lady Jaye – will continue to feature in his portfolio of activities, it is his life as a maker of art, as an artist, as expressed through his bodily and identity alterations, that seems set to dominate his agenda now and in the years to come. His personal masquerade, as shared with his wife, will become the performance, the artwork, the process at the very centre of what he does. Yet there is also, at the heart, literally and metaphorically, of this pursuit an oddly old-fashioned commitment to his partner – the ritual they are enacting also has a strong under-current of a Romantic love pact. In the midst of these cut-ups, there is an older, healing, spiritual dimension which lends a mystical, almost anachronistic, quality to the avant garde anarchy of their *modus operandi*.

As Genesis P-Orridge remarks:

You know the old phrase that's my other half. Well we've taken it very literally and we are each other's other half and so we want to use the available resources of surgery and cosmetics to become more and more, at least on a basic gestural level, like each other physically. So it 's a cut-up literally – we are not just cutting up information, we are cutting up ourselves both our internalised consciousness self and our physical self in order to becomes mirrors of ourselves in order to see what happens, what unusual and remarkable things might happen when difference is removed and similarity becomes the objective.[82]

As for the enduring influence of the Beats, there is no question that William Burroughs and his artistic strategies remain central to P-Orridge's activities. He

[81] See Mark Kramer, '1998: The year in body modification', *Body Modification Ezine*, 1 January 1999, http://www.bmezine.com/news/softtoy/008/ [accessed 29 March 2005], and Deborah Mitchell and Beth Landman, 'All's fair in Love and Rockets', *New York Magazine*, 29 June 1998 (Add. reporting by Kate Coyne), http://newyorkmetro.com/nymetro/news/people/columns/intelligencer/2902/ [accessed 29 March 2005].

[82] Comment by Genesis P-Orridge, filmed interview with writer/researcher Jayne Sheridan, Columbia Hotel, London, 8 December 2004.

is unequivocal on this. 'My entire life is dedicated to quite literally my belief in, my faith in, the cut-up; even my body's a cut-up now quite literally and so I can't imagine anything that I do not being influenced by the cut-up. It's always there; I do collages, almost every week, certainly, I'm making collages. When I keep notebooks I always write them non-chronologically. I'll open them at whatever page is open – if that was my diary I'd just go "Okay, woops" and then I'd write on that page and then tomorrow I might write on that page and then sometimes I'll turn them the other way up and write back the other direction so all my diaries are cut-ups. Those are what I refer to when I'm writing lyrics.'[83]

But his interest in Burroughs' principal colleagues, Allen Ginsberg and Jack Kerouac, intense in his formative teenage period, has declined significantly. Of Ginsberg he told me: 'When you remove the bohemian trimmings, he is a very traditionalist, pretty much academic poet who was very self-conscious about placing himself in the Walt Whitman, American literary tradition and that that was his real ambition, to be seen as an academic and established poet even though his path to that was based on sensationalist, bohemian happenings and publicity. So I saw him as being innately conservative. His primary contribution I would say, apart from the fact that he wrote some okay poetry, was his championing of gay rights which I think one has to admire and give credit for. He did do an awful lot of important publicity for tolerance, tolerance of the gay life life-style and trying to get middle America to stop and think about the legal and social implications of and need for gay rights. For that, I think, he gets full marks. His poetry...I think "Howl" is a great poem, it's a really wonderful spontaneous outpouring that still stands up today. If you read it out loud it's fantastic and his other poetry is good poetry but for me it's not poetry … his work isn't something that I can take and apply to rock music or theatre or collage or a fine art gallery or streetlife/ popular culture and have it constantly reveal and re-value creativity. It's a frozen moment, it's a historical, specific, traditional piece of literary work, whereas Gysin and Burroughs, the cut-up and the ideas and the attitude that everything can be taken and re-worked and re-shaped and is malleable and forever, potentially life-changing. Culture is malleable and thought is just an incredible energised gift that can contribute to the evolution of the species. All of that I see in Burroughs and Gysin which just isn't in Ginsberg in the same way.'[84]

For Kerouac he has also revised his adolescent opinions, too. 'It seems that Kerouac was this wonderful inspirational manifestation for the adolescent and most people that I meet that have been inspired by Kerouac, it was when they were teenagers. By the same token most people when they return to Kerouac find him

---

[83] GP-O, interview with the author, 2004.
[84] *Ibid.*

a lot less satisfying when they are older and more mature so it seems that Kerouac captured an incredibly, vivid raw adolescence and in that capturing of adolescence, he also captured the utopian, idealistic, devotional love of the universe and potential which still happens when people first come across it and that's an amazing thing to have achieved, somehow encapsulating that adolescent love of potential but, in terms of its true literary worth, I know that it's studied at universities everywhere and they do all these books about it – he's the most written about of all of them in academia – but he just doesn't do it for me now, the magic event doesn't happen when I re-read it.'[85]

Note to reader: Jackie Breyer P-Orridge died in New York City on 9 October 2007. See her obituary: Pierre Perrone, 'Lady Jaye Breyer P-Orridge', *The Independent*, 23 October 2007, http://www.independent.co.uk/news/obituaries/lady-jaye-breyer-porridge-397604.html [accessed 16 December 2011].

Author's note: A version of this chapter formed part of the published proceedings of the biennial international conference of the International Association for the Study of Popular Music (IASPM), held in Rome, in July 2005.

---

[85] GP-O, interview with the author, 2004.

INTERVIEW 7

Steven Taylor, Ginsberg's guitarist and member of the Fugs

Steven Taylor was born in Manchester, England in 1955. His family emigrated to the US in the mid-1960s. After meeting Allen Ginsberg when he visited his teacher training college in 1976, he became a regular guitar accompanist to the poet for the next 20 years. In 1984 he became a member of the re-formed Fugs, a role he continues to play to this day. In the later 1980s he also fronted a punk band called the False Prophets. The detailed diary record he kept of that group and their US and European tours became a cornerstone of his successful, ethno-musicological doctoral thesis at Brown which was published in book form as *False Prophet: Field Notes from the Punk Underground* (2004). Now based in New York City, he has also taught at the Naropa Institute in Boulder, Colorado, where I interviewed him in July 2004.

SW   I think one of the first things that I would like to raise with you is that there is this interesting feature within recent popular music history, that the hippies and many of the rock musicians who formed part of that subcultural constituency, latched onto some of the Beat ideals. There seemed to be a kind of continuum between what happened in the 1950s, with the poets, and what happened in the 1960s, with the rockers.

Then, when punk came along in the early to mid-1970s, the punks tended to reject the hippy philosophies, the hippy manifestos. Yet, at the same time, punks and new wavers were still able to make some sense of, see some appeal in, the Beat manifesto.

This seems to me paradoxical. How were the hippies and the punks, who are in some kind of binary opposition – we might see a hippy set against a punk – both able to see something in Beat that made sense to them?

ST   Huge misunderstanding! Gosh, I don't know if I can answer that question – I think the punks were misunderstood. Not misunderstood; I think it was a class issue in one way. The hippies were seen as middle-class kids who were kind of over-realistic, over-romantic, on one level politicised, but on another level a kind of cultural narcissism, of middle-class self-congratulation, and relative economic prosperity, which the punks didn't have.

    You know, you had Margaret Thatcher and the worst economic conditions in Britain since the war and, similarly, under Reagan, the same thing happened in the United States. And so there was disillusionment and also the punks, that I talked to, thought that the hippies had sold out and just became lawyers rather than following through.

    But I think that a lot of the ideals were the same – a kind of anarchist ideal. But I think a lot of the material conditions were different. I think that the Beats, to over-simplify it if I say this, that the Beats, the hippies and the punks basically called their older generations on their hypocrisy and they have that in common. They said, what is this thing you were all talking about, about freedom: you get a bunch of control freaks talking about freedom. That is the paradox in the heart of America.

    You have this sort of control impulse that is going on and on and on about freedom, particularly now, and the more controlling and the more world dominating it becomes and the more narrowly ideological it becomes, the more they talk about freedom, there is a kind of inverse relationship between the ideal and the actual ideological base. I think that some of the punk people, as they got older, started to see some of the connections with the older generation, or the hippy generation.

    Like the guys I played with in the False Prophets, because they knew about the Beats, starting to see that the hippies had had those ideals. And also when one has more experience and one is political and one goes out into the world as a young person, a young punk, and becomes political, one educates oneself at a certain level, and learns that this is all coming out of the Civil Rights movement and we can all share that, as leftists, we can all share that base.

SW   **Just to get a sense of your own personal history – by the mid-1970s you must have been about 20 years of age.**

ST   I was 20 in 1975.

SW   **OK. So you were by then listening to music I'm sure, reading I'm sure. What kind of literature were you engaging in at that time? Were you a fan of the Beats by the time you were that sort of age or had you not encountered the Beats at that age?**

ST   I had read Kerouac. When I met Ginsberg I had read *The Dharma Bums*, *On the Road* and a piece of Ginsberg's poem 'Howl', called 'Footnote to Howl'. That was my experience with the Beats. Before that I had read a lot of novels, I had read all the way through the Russian novelists, just on my own, nobody telling me, just as a reader, sort of undirected reading. I read a lot of Russian novelists. I had some familiarity with American poetry but not a lot. Emily Dickinson was a favourite. So when Ginsberg came along, I did sort of understand the Beat thing from Kerouac and those novels.

SW   **When did you first meet Allen Ginsberg?**

ST   I met Allen Ginsberg when I was 21 years old in 1976, the spring of 1976, May.

SW   **We will certainly come back to that but, initially, to fill in the musical elements that you were absorbing as a late teenager and in your early 20s ... I guess that you were listening to rock music, were you? Were you listening to other kinds of music?**

ST   I had always been classically trained to the extent that one could be classically trained, given my class background. For example violin lessons at school in England. The choir, singing as one does, and then in high school, in America, studying clarinet and then guitar which very quickly won out. I took up the guitar at age 13 and by the age of 16 that became classical guitar, classical guitar training. So, very much a musician, in terms of practice, attached to the page with fairly sophisticated understanding of that, someone who read music well and so forth – not a great improviser but with a great interest of the music of the 1960s and, of course, I was living in Manchester in 1963 when the Beatles appeared on *People and Places*, their first regional television programme, and was completely swept away by that.

SW   **So as early as that? The Beatles?**

ST   It completely took over. It took over. It was huge. I mean you were there when that happened.

SW   **And I was feeling similar things, yes.**

ST   It was incredible. I remember walking home from school and singing those songs and the joy of that. Ginsberg talks about that in some of the interviews I did with him. That sense of joy, like 'I Wanna Hold Your Hand', this explosion. Suddenly everyone is dancing, you know. I saw that as a child. He saw that as an adult and was much more impressed by that as a phenomenon.

SW   **So even before you came to America in the mid-1960s, still as a boy, the new popular music, if we can call it, had been touching you?**

ST   It was hugely important. And as somebody who had taken up the guitar, you know, of course that is what you did. You know, Cream, the arrival of these bands on the scene were like huge events in your life and discovering The Who, discovering Cream, Jimi Hendrix…oh my God! What's that? You know.

And having not, I mean at that time, not knowing the background of that music, so it was like this phenomenon that exploded which must have been the experience in the mid-1950s of much of middle-class white America to see Little Richard. Like, what the hell is that, you know, and something like that. I had my own experience and so did my friends. And then sort of learning that way, at the same time, I had classical guitar lessons and initially had been studying with an old jazz guitar player called Vincent Delmonte who was an Italian-American guy, very old, and had been a big band guitarist. He was a superb musician, gave me correct technique, taught me to read, so made me quite a good guitarist, in that sense, as a kid.

But then the whole rock 'n' roll thing hit and that just took over and at the same time I am studying the Bach literature for the guitar, somewhat clumsily, and also simultaneously learning the Beatles tunes and copying licks from Eric Clapton, you know. It was a huge part of one's life.

SW **So you mentioned Cream, the Who, Hendrix and so on, How did the arrival of punk and new wave affect you in the mid-1970s? Did you quickly latch on to that or was it something you picked up on later?**

ST That is an interesting question. By the time I had finished music school, I was basically mostly interested in the music of myself and my friends plus a few favourite great artists who I listened to over and over again. By the time punk hit I was basically listening to John Coltrane, Jimi Hendrix and classical music, so quite limited, but over and over and over again, listening to those things. But also arranging, doing arranging work, doing some composing, doing a little bit of the alternative theatre work, music composing, accompanying poets a lot.

I was never a discophile and never had a big record collection and I never did sit around listening to a lot of music. There are probably a thousand bands that you could mention that most pop music fans would know that I would barely be familiar with. That is the kind of funny paradox of my becoming an ethnomusicologist, looking at pop music, because really, as in my book, I am looking mostly at myself and my friends. I don't have a huge history of that.

I will give you an example, and this is somewhat embarrassing but it illustrates the case. Ginsberg took me to meet the Clash and I had no clue who they were. It was at Electric Lady Studios in Greenwich Village and down in the basement of this studio with Joe Strummer and they were playing this music in the studio and Joe said 'Do you like this?'

SW **Was Ginsberg recording with them at this time?**

ST Yeah. They had asked him – it was 'Ghetto Defendant' the tune – to take part. They had told him they wanted the voice of God. And he had this big deep voice and they were sort of really interested in him plus he was also this great character and great company and had been a friend to several generations of rock musicians going back to the Beatles and Bob Dylan and so forth.

So, Joe says 'Do you like this music?' and I says 'Yeah this is really cool' because I thought it was theirs and I had no idea who they were and what they were doing. But of course, I very quickly learnt. Then though, I was kind of out of it.

So punk. Well first of all, when the Pistols came out with 'God Save the Queen', I just thought that was terribly offensive. But then so very quickly flipped and realised this was fabulous. And the bigger thing with punk rock was when I was on leave from college on a weekend – it must have been 1975 or 1976 – and somebody took me to a bar in Dover, New Jersey and it was crowded, it was full of all these people. I mean at this point, I was the kid from the suburbs with a classical music education.

I was in this bar and all these people with leather jackets which was immediately menacing and this band came on and it was like the lights went on and it was the Ramones, I'd never heard of them, they came on and it was like 'Oh my God. This is it. It's back. Rock 'n' roll is back'.

That was the moment when punk just hit for me, because I was just like, Bruce Springsteen, what is this crap, and the Beatles had broken up, Jimi Hendrix was dead, that was done, it was over as far as I was concerned. I was listening to jazz because, you know, that was finished, there was nothing going on.

SW **But the Ramones, really ignited something?**

ST Yeah, the Ramones – this is fabulous, that was great. And then I subsequently moved to New York City shortly after that.

SW **You were living in New Jersey at the time?**

ST I was living in New Jersey, going to school in New Jersey and left school in 1978, moved to New York City. I knew Richard, this is a funny paradox of my experience, I knew Richard Hell because he was my upstairs neighbour. But I never went to see the band.

SW **You never saw Television or, indeed, the Voidoids at CBGBs?**

ST I never went down to CBGBs. The only time I ever went down to CBGBs in the 1970s was when there was a benefit for the St. Mark's

Church held there. And that's when I saw Elvis Costello for the first time playing with Richard and I sat in with a bunch of musicians and played the banjo.

So there is a funny kind of thing: you live in the neighbourhood, this thing is exploding and you have no clue. You stay at home, writing music – and playing the banjo at CBGBs on a one-nighter! So I sort of missed it all until quite late in the game. I dug it though but didn't go out much but also was very busy making my living as a freelancer so not a person who liked to go to clubs a lot. But then I accidentally happened upon the False Prophets in 1988, and that's when I kinda got it, got clued in, and realised the power of it and what it had been and what it was.

SW   **So it was ten years or more later before …**

ST   Ten years on before I got it.

SW   **… and you'd been in the eye of the storm.**

ST   Yeah, I did hang out a bit with a band called the Stimulators in New York City who included Denise Mercedes, who was Peter Orlovsky's girlfriend but also a really good guitar player, who was also a friend of Mick Ronson and Bob Dylan.

Bob gave her a guitar and Mick gave her a Marshall amp and she went and played with Rat Scabies [of the Damned] for a while in England. And when she came back from England she had become a different musician and had become very powerful, probably from regular gigs in England and started this terrific band called the Stimulators with her nephew Harley Flanagan on drums who was at the time about 12 years old. He was a fabulous drummer who later became a notorious skinhead and I played with him once. It was like standing in front of a bunch of machine guns, I mean he was unbelievable and he became the Cro-Mags.

SW   **OK. So just to backtrack a little, you said you first met Ginsberg in 1976 but then you had been playing with some poets.**

ST   That was the beginning of it.

SW   **Which poets were you playing with?**

ST   Well I started with Allen.

SW   **You started with Allen?**

ST   Yeah. So I had been playing with like folk rock bands and solo stuff and very much thinking of myself as a singer. My father is a singer and singing is very much a kind of family business. Both sides of the family, my grandfathers had reputations as singers so I thought of myself as a singer and so doing that with the folk rock thing.

SW   **Singing your own and writing your own songs?**

ST   Some. Mostly covers and doing bar gigs and stuff like that, but then I'd
       been in school, wasn't happy with it, met Ginsberg and started playing
       with him and through him very soon met Ed Sanders, of the Fugs, who
       at the time had been thinking about getting back into music.

       At the time, actually, I became friends with Ed, he saw me with
       Ginsberg and the thing was that Ed had always wanted to have good
       vocals. With the Fugs, he had never had good vocals, he thought, 'I
       want good vocals'.

       He was obsessed with this vocal thing and he saw me singing with
       Allen and was impressed and he said, with my ability to ride the
       bucking bronco of Ginsberg's enunciation, in other words to sing
       in sync with him, he liked that and wanted to hire me as a singer
       initially.

       So I would go up to Woodstock and start working with Ed. And so,
       from working with Allen, very soon I was working with Ed Sanders
       and Anne Waldman and then when I was on tour with Allen, I would
       work with occasionally, very occasionally, with Andrei Voznesensky
       and a Japanese poet, once or twice, Kazuko Shiraishi – whoever was on
       the circuit who would like some company, I would sit in, travelling also.

       In the party that I was travelling a lot with, in the early days, was, almost
       always, Peter Orlovsky. I worked with him and often Gregory Corso.

SW   **So why did Allen Ginsberg ask you to play guitar with him?**

ST   He had been in the habit of going around picking up guitar players.
       Wherever he'd go, he would go to a college and he would have a college
       gig and he would say 'Is there a kid here who can play the guitar?' and
       then he would have an accompanist. So he asked the English professor
       who had organised the reading at my college to find him a guitar player
       and I was the only guitar player he knew.

SW   **So in a sense, good fortune?**

ST   Accident, right. But then when I sat in and started to play with Allen,
       I started to sing and that had never happened before, that I could
       actually harmonise with what he was doing on the spur of the moment.
       It blew his mind. He started to tremble and his voice took off and he
       got very excited.

       There is a recording of that at Stanford. I haven't heard it. May 1976.
       And so he was like totally inspired by the singing. So then he said
       'Next week I have a session with John Hammond at CBS in New York',
       because Hammond had started his own label with the idea of getting
       the stuff out of the vault and doing his own thing. Hammond originally
       recorded that Ginsberg session which I ended up playing on …

SW   **Yeah. Are these the ones on the 4 CD, Ginsberg box set?**

ST   Probably are now. I knew it as record called *First Blues* which was the
      second time they had used that title for a Ginsberg record. The first one
      was a folk recording by Harry Smith. But John Hammond liked the
      First Blues title and they used that, took it to Columbia and Columbia
      said 'Ginsberg, when are you going to start shaking your ass around?'

      Columbia didn't want the record. That may have been part of the
      impetus why John Hammond started his own label. I don't know
      whether his own label was in the works already or not.

      So I went with Allen. He said, 'Come to the rehearsal and meet the
      musicians'. So I went to the rehearsal and met the musicians. It was
      Jon Sholle, who's a wonderful guitarist, who was then recording on an
      alternative folk label, I can't remember, it was very well known. And
      also David Mansfield, who had been on Rolling Thunder and who
      played with the Byrds guys and Roger McGuinn. He had made a record
      with Roger McGuinn. He was a wonderful musician.

      So I went to the rehearsal. So Mansfield and Sholle said, 'Why
      don't you sit in with us, why don't you play the session?' So my first
      time in a recording studio was with John Hammond. It was quite
      extraordinary! And saying, you know, 'Move the microphone'. I got my
      first instructions on how to use a microphone from John Hammond.

SW   **The twentieth century's greatest A&R man!**

ST   He was a wonderful, gentlemanly, gentle man. He was a beautiful man,
      very kind and I knew him a while. In fact he once asked me to come to
      his office because he wanted to check me out. He said, 'Bring whatever
      you've got on tape and we'll check it out and we'll listen'. And you
      know this is the guy who signed Dylan and Billie Holliday. This is the
      guy that told Benny Goodman, 'You should get a band'. He said, 'You
      should bring your tapes'. So I bring my tapes and I am sitting there with
      my tape and John Hammond is listening and he says, 'Very nice, very
      nice'. That was it.

SW   **Nothing further really happened?**

ST   Not at the time. I still have those great regrets. I wish I had had my act
      together as a songwriter at 21 that I did when I was 41.

SW   **So how many sides, how many tracks did you lay down in those
      sessions for that second *First Blues* collection?**

ST   It must have been just, I would say not much, not very many more than
      one would need for the album, so it would have been maybe 12 tracks.
      But I really couldn't swear to it.

SW   **Quite a few of them do appear on that compilation collection
      because your name is on it.**

ST   Playing incompetent flute!

SW **You play flute?**

ST I play terrible flute but I liked it. It's a calypso tune and it was so sort of funky and primitive that they dug my flute-playing and kept it in the mix.

SW **OK. But in terms of accompanying Allen Ginsberg over the next 20 years, how many gigs did you play with Ginsberg?**

ST Hundreds. Literally hundreds.

SW **Around the world?**

ST Around Europe. I got as far as Israel, to the Far East is as far as I got with him. Mostly in Europe. The big numbers in terms of gigs, far more in Europe, because economically it made sense for me to travel with him in Europe, because we played five shows a week, 12 weeks at a time. Steady money, transport, a place to stay, so we would make money. In America, it made more sense for him to travel alone. It would be a one-off. He would fly to San Francisco for a gig to do it by himself. There was no reason for me to come out of college or stop what I was doing. They would have to come up with the money. So in the States, he tended to play by himself more often.

SW **Sure. And obviously you would have spent many, many hours, many, many weeks and months talking to Ginsberg about everything. I'm interested in knowing what Allen Ginsberg really made of rock music. As you say he dug the Beatles, he introduced you to the Clash, did he really make sense of this music?**

ST Yeah. I interviewed him. It was beautiful. I didn't use much of it but I've got it. He said it was the return of the body, he said it was the revenge of Africa on the hyper-intellectual West that had removed the head from the body and it was the revenge of Africa making the white people shake their ass. And it was great joy. And he saw it as a … he kind of had a punk view in a sense.

You know, you think of punk as sort of a rock 'n' roll purist in the sense that you see it as an alternative voice, a democratic voice, an opportunity for the underprivileged to speak. And he saw it that way too and he was much more articulate about it than I could ever be. So you know the opportunity for the young people to seize a voice and declare, seize a voice amidst the ruins of the capitalist culture, and declare a position. That kind of line.

SW **Sure. So he was powerfully attached to this …**

ST Yes. Primitive. A notion of a kind of neo-primitivism which he was interested in, where he would talk about, say the punk kids walking around with feathers in their ears, going back to a kind of native American sense or their understanding of neo-primitivist, anarchist politics and doing it, do it yourself, DIY. And which he connected, as I said in my book, to underground cinema of the 1950s and 1960s and to poetry, too. The idea that you don't need to take on the whole culture.

If you want to be a film-maker you don't need to go to Hollywood and take on the entire universe and get yourself a $40m budget. You can get yourself a wind up 16mm and shoot pictures of your friends and show it in coffee shops downtown. And that was this big explosion and it came out of independent cinema and it came out of what he called the oral poetry renaissance which started in San Francisco, the sort of signal event of which was the Six Gallery reading in 1955, which was the premiere of 'Howl'.

And then that sort of coffee shop poetry reading moved to New York and he said that when the…it was so unusual for there to be poetry reading in the bars and coffee shops as opposed to ladies' uptown literary evenings or ritzy salons or university literary lectures. To have it in the coffee shops and bars of downtown was so unusual that the New York *Daily News* ran a front page photograph of Jose Garcia and Peter Orlovsky, the poets who read in the coffee shops. How strange.

SW   **When was that, the early 60s?**

ST   Early 1960s, yes. There was a great book by Sally Banes called *Greenwich Village 1963*, where she takes just the Village, just in the year 1963, and says 'This is what's happening'. You know, alternative dance, people doing theatre performances in their apartments, you know, cheap little storefront galleries, it's all just exploding. And performance, always performance.

SW   **Completely different question, Steven, but connected. Obviously you encountered William Burroughs in the last ten or 20 years of his life, really. He was a man who was dubbed the Godfather of Punk and who wrote a column *Crawdaddy* of the early 1970s. Burroughs really didn't have much time for rock music did he?**

ST   I don't think so. He was a very private man, and a committed writer and content to read and write and associate with a small circle of friends and feel protected. I think William was a sort of wounded person, very kind in his way, very generous and sort of old fashioned, gentlemanly manners, coming as he did from St. Louis, old family upper crust. Very sweet man. Which doesn't come across in the public persona.

And I think the punk thing came from I would guess the sort of *Wild Boys* thing that he was describing. He was describing futuristic landscapes as in *Bladerunner*, his movie treatment *Bladerunner*, you know the crumbling buildings, the destroyed infra-structure, lack of government's ability to control anything, the underground economy, Dr. Benway operating in a washroom in a subway, you know, the kind of whole underground alternative thing in which there are these wild boy characters and I think that punk must have latched on to that.

SW **There is this kind of dystopian idea in what is later called cyberpunk, the William Gibson stuff, which grew out of, I suppose, Burroughs' science fiction stuff. Just to ask you about your involvement with the False Prophets in the late 80s early 90s. How much did the Beats inform you or them by then? Was Beat still an everyday thing for you? You worked with Ginsberg, you were involved with Naropa by then. But how much was Beat still a philosophy on the table of discussion among those later punks who you played with?**

ST Not much. Some, I mean like more literary characters like Richard Hell, of course, had a background as a poet and had an understanding that he was coming from the French Surrealists and the Beats to some extent. Deborah, who played guitar in the False Prophets, had a Master's degree from the Columbia University Journalism School and was making a living as a writer, or as an editor when she couldn't get writing work. She was actually ghost-writing business books for Simon and Schuster while she was playing in a rock band, so very literary, smart and actually knowing where it was coming from.

The others were sort of home-made, Brooklyn, newspaper readers, TV-based people. Some interest. One of the bass players, Anthony, had an interest in science fiction, so some sense of it, but not college people, not college graduates. So the American punk scene was not so literate, more TV babies I found.

SW **So by then you feel as if the literate-ness had faded, at least among the community with whom you were playing music?**

ST Yeah. And I don't know if it ever was. I mean I know that the literature tends to say that the American proto-punk types tended to think of themselves as artists, but I think that they thought of themselves as artists, not in a sense of intellectuals who had done their homework, but artists in the sort of romantic American sense of it, and a do it yourself sense of it. So that, you know, Patti Smith had some education and had educated herself and had read the Beats and had read Genet and had made a lot of those connections but they were not artists in the sense of the European intellectual who's in the medium and has read the background. You know, that kind of thing. I don't think it ever was like that and I think that is characteristic of American culture.

SW   **I'd like to spend the last few minutes of this conversation talking about the Fugs. When I contacted Ed Sanders a month or so ago, he didn't seem, he was quite modest, he said 'I don't feel as if the Fugs are really any kind of connection between Beat and rock'. Ed wants to play that down.**

       Was he right to play that down? Obviously you have played with the Fugs in more recent times so it is a little hard to go back to the 1960s when the Fugs were first making their mark, but how do they fit into this interesting history do you think?

ST   Well, he's huge. He's doing two things, I would say. One is, he is being modest and the other is, he is guarding his data stash. Man, that guy is not going to give you a whole lot, he has got a garage full of the history of the Sixties that is going to be dynamite of he ever gets it out. Ed is the guy, talk about do-it-yourself. He thinks he is going to write all the books, so he is not going to give you a whole lot, so it is partly modesty but it is partly protecting his research base. I am sure that is what it is. But I think the Fugs were a very important connection. This was a guy … OK, I keep going back to the Civil Rights Movement you know, I mean this is a guy who grew up in Missouri and who learned how to sing hymns with the Disciples of Christ. He turns on the radio: he's got rhythm and blues and he's got jazz, then all of a sudden he's got Elvis.

       He moves to New York City at the very beginning of the 1960s and he falls in with this whole bohemian culture, graduates from NYU with a degree in Classics. He'd started out wanting to do physics and wound up with a degree in Classics, joins the Civil Rights marches, swims out to the middle of the Connecticut river to board a nuclear submarine, gets himself arrested and starts to publish, because he publishes this poem from jail.

       Very much a sort of disciple of Ginsberg in the sense, that young man. I don't know how they met but I get the feeling he probably sought Allen out and connected with Ginsberg and was a kind of second generation Beat but also a disciple of Charles Olsen, with the idea that the poet is the historian and the preserver of a culture. Because a poet is the best equipped to deal with the language, he or she is the best equipped to preserve the best thought and to be the best social critic and be really the keeper of the flame of culture.

       He saw himself in that kind of Promethean role, the bearer of the flame, particularly with his background in the Classics, particularly with his knowledge of the Greek historians and the Greek poets and the Greek moral philosophers. I see him in that light, let's say, as in that lineage.

So then, when the Sixties thing starts to happen, the experimenting with music was one realm in a larger realm of experimentation – in dance and theatre and poetry and film-making. And all of those things that're happening at the same time as the Civil Rights thing and free jazz and all of this 'You can do it, you can do it', you know. And I mean the story that Ed told was that he and Tuli [Kupferberg] were at the Dom on St. Mark's Place which was the place to go because Stanley Tolkin was a local Polish bar owner and musician who, unlike his fellow expatriates, did not despise the young hipsters because he realised that he could sell them beer.

SW **This is where Lou Reed and Warhol spent time?**

ST All these guys went there, the young people who became the leading fashion designers of the period, the fashion designers, the theatre folk, the people who were studying the rag trade, the film-makers. They all hung out at Stanley Tolkin's bar.

Stanley opens the Dom, and there's a dance there. Ed said that there was a Robert Creeley poetry reading and they were all at the Dom after the reading, that had been at St. Mark's, and they were down in the basement and the Beatles come on and everybody just started dancing and Ed said, 'I looked at Tuli and said, you know, we could do this' and there's a sort of curious passage in this interview I did with Tuli that I think is in the book where he said, 'Well I thought that the Beatles weren't so good but that the music was great and we didn't understand where they would later go with the lyrics and that there would be this kind of political edge to it and we didn't realise that.'

But Ed, Social Democrat, Tuli an anarchist, as these committed people with backgrounds and political activism, and they saw everybody light up with this music and they looked at each other and they said we're poets, we are going to have great lyrics, we can do this, let's go. And that was the genesis of it. So it really was a sort of moment when the poets realise that they can make music again.

SW **This would have been about 1965?**

ST No, earlier than that. It was the winter of 1963 the Fugs got together; I believe the Fugs' premiere gig was like January of 1964, something like that, at the Peace Eye Bookstore.

And of course, it was in the air. Ed said there was a five block area of a very dynamic kind of cultural and alternative arts and Peace Eye Bookstore became a kind of neighbourhood hangout. So you would have Warhol, Bill Burroughs, the fashion models of the day, the painters of the day, the film-makers of the day, coming in the bookstore to watch the Fugs bang on cardboard boxes. It was like the place to be.

Norman Mailer, too. It went down like a who's who at the Fugs' first gig, it was like amazing. Andy Warhol, Norman Mailer, you know, all of these really happening people.

SW **When did you join the Fugs?**

ST 1984. And that was as a result of Ginsberg. We crashed a rehearsal. The band, I believe, had broken up in 1967 and Ed had moved out of the city, fearing really for the safety of his family I think. He had started to see increasing crime which probably, almost undoubtedly, coincided with a large scale, US Government Vietnam heroin connection which sent a crime wave through New York City and they saw people getting hurt on the street. And they had a young daughter and thought let's get out of here and so moved out.

So then, in 1970-something, I'd met Ed then and he'd seen me with Ginsberg but I hadn't started working with him. Then one day I am walking around the Village and there was to be a benefit at the Mudd Club, maybe 1982, and I am walking around the West Village with Ginsberg and he says, 'The Fugs are rehearsing, let's go crash the rehearsal', and I said 'OK'. It wasn't the Fugs, it was Mark Kramer who had a band called Shockabilly and who later became a very excellent and influential sort of underground record producer with a label called Shimmy-Disc. He's a genius, a marvellous guy to work with and he had hooked up with Sanders.

He was Sanders' main musical guy and they had a band called the Fred McMurrays and it was Coby Batty, Mark Kramer, somebody else and Ed. So they were rehearsing. Coby Batty was a guy who had a career as a singer as a child, he was a marvellous, marvellous singer, he was then playing drums with the band.

We walked in and they were singing a William Blake tune and Coby was harmonising it and I put on the third harmony, put on the tenor line. Once again the voice or the ability to harmonise and sync up and be in tune and it sounded like a magical moment. At that point the old manager of the Fugs had been Charlie Rothschild who had also been Judy Collins' manager, also worked with the Byrds and also with Odetta, and was Ginsberg's manager, and Charlie was there and Charlie said, 'You guys have got to work together.' So then we played the Mudd Club and a lot of people came out, Tuli Kupferberg was on the bill and Ed was on the bill, as separate acts, and a lot of people came out thinking that it was going to be the Fugs and we packed the house and we played our set and it was a big hit. That was when Ed decided to get the Fugs back together again.

So by the time it came around and we got it together and booked the gigs, it was 1984 and we played at the Bottom Line, a funny ensemble because the drummer was a French horn player, the bass player was a keyboardist, and I was a classical guitarist with not much experience of an electrical guitar, a little bit, doing this power trio bit, which was terrifying and wonderful but we had good vocals because Ed has a beautiful voice and now we had these two guys who could sing and so the Fugs have been doing that since 1984 now.

SW **Well, Steven, thank you very much for those answers.**

12 STEVEN TAYLOR: A BEAT ENGLISHMAN IN NEW YORK

When the Original Scroll of Jack Kerouac's *On the Road* was officially unveiled to British audiences for the first time early in December 2008, a new choral work, especially commissioned for the occasion, lent an appropriate musical note to a celebration that had the world's most valuable literary manuscript as its centrepiece.

In the concert hall of the Barber Institute of Fine Arts, a gallery based on the campus of Birmingham University where the scroll would go on show for the next two months, this choral piece drew on a range of Kerouac texts – from both his prose and poetry – and featured a score by an English composer whose whole adult life has been closely entangled with that of the Beat Generation.

In front of an audience that included Carolyn Cassady and British Beat bard Michael Horovitz, the Birmingham University Singers performed a world premiere of a song cycle which drew on *On the Road*, *Mexico City Blues* and *Some of the Dharma*. The composer Steven Taylor was thrilled to have his piece presented at such a significant moment. 'To have 25 people working with ·your music is wonderful. It did feel great', he said.

Steven Taylor has lived in the USA since the mid-1960s when he left the shores of Britain as a ten-year-old boy. Within a little over a decade of taking up this new life with his immigrant family, he had met Allen Ginsberg and, from that initial connection, launched a professional association that would last until the poet's death in 1997.

For just over 20 years, Taylor was guitar-playing accompanist to Ginsberg, touring the US and Europe and beyond, contributing to recording sessions, and establishing creative links across a wide front. Along the way the pair developed a close friendship that would also see this transatlantic émigré play a key role in the poet's educational venture, the Naropa Institute in Boulder, Colorado, over an extended period, too.

Now back in New York City after a lengthy residency in Boulder, Steven Taylor is currently penning a memoir of his time with Ginsberg and continues an active life as a musician, composer, writer and performer. In 2005, he devised a choral work to accompany fiftieth anniversary celebrations of the poet's most famous work 'Howl'. His setting of 'Footnote to Howl' was performed in the Big Apple's Tompkins Square by the Juilliard Choral Union.

The work that Taylor produced for that New York event – both the rehearsals and the actual performance – will eventually be included in a new documentary film on Ginsberg and 'Howl', presently in production under the direction of Rob Epstein, the film-maker behind the critically acclaimed 1984 movie *The Times of Harvey Milk*, the story of the man who would become San Francisco's first openly gay elected official and his ultimate murder.

It was, in part, because of this 'Howl' production that, when I was working on a 2007 commemoration of the half-centenary of Kerouac's *On the Road*, I invited the composer to repeat the feat and bring his skills to bear on a collection of texts by Ginsberg's great friend. Taylor proceeded to produce the piece but then disaster struck. I suffered a significant office fire just weeks before the event, sabotaging the celebration, and the plan was temporarily scuppered.

Thankfully, a year on, with the scroll arriving in Britain for the very first time, there was a further chance to premiere the choral work, now recognising the half-century since Kerouac's classic account first appeared in the bookshops of the UK in 1958. With that, Taylor was able to say that he had now penned substantial musical tributes to two of the Beat Generation's principal players.

Yet this is only part of what he does. When we spoke at the end of last year, he was able to report on a quite different project that had kept him musically active in recent months. Taylor has, since the early 1980s, been a member of the Fugs, that ground-breaking poetry and rock 'n' roll band who formed a key bridge between the world of Beat and rock culture and have often paid homage to that earlier community of writers.

Taylor, alongside founding members Ed Sanders – who famously joined Kerouac in a TV debate on the hippies in 1968 – and Tuli Kupferberg, has been hard at work on the Fugs' latest record, provisionally, and with typical tongue-in-cheek wit, entitled *The Fugs' Final CD, Part II*. Recorded in a studio in the Catskills, close to Woodstock in upstate New York, the new album gathers fresh material by all of the group's present line-up.

'We've laid down 14 songs so far but with more to be done', says Taylor. Has everyone been involved? 'Tuli, whose now 85, was sick for a while. He'd contracted pneumonia, so Ed recorded his vocals at home *a capella*.' Kupferberg's vocals were then incorporated into the recording sessions proper.

There will be at least two songs in the set by Taylor. His 'Hungry Blues' is a powerful political account. Is it a standard blues structure? 'Yes', he says, 'it's a tradi-tional blues, with the first couple of lines repeated and so on. I reckoned, here I am, this 53-year-old, white Englishman, I think I've probably just about paid my dues!'

The song has a poetic inspiration and a serious message. 'I thought of Allen as I was writing this. I loved his rubato vocal style, his simple blues, funny and clever. He had a real devotion to the blues.' So where does this particular song's theme come from? 'It's actually a personal lament. In the 1990s, 100 million starved to death. You could have saved all those people for the amount of money the military, globally, spends every two days!'

His second song for the new Fugs set, for which a release date is still to be agreed, is ambitious but draws on the band's previous form. 'They've used Greek poetry before, classical texts, Blake adapted for rock 'n' roll. So I've taken Homer, Alexander Pope's translation of *The Iliad*, and condensed the first two books into a six-minute pop song.'

Taylor now intends to dedicate some time to an autobiographical account of the Ginsberg years. His initial forays have already seen some material from the proposed volume appear within the alternative culture webzine *Reality Sandwich*.

So how did this remarkable adventure begin? How did this individual who spent his early years in Manchester with a bus-driving dad end up as a sideman to one of the most significant literary figures of the century? What was the trigger to this enduring friendship?

He initially met Ginsberg in the spring of 1976 when, as a 21-year-old student, Taylor was nearing the end of a teacher-training course at a college in New Jersey. His plan was to qualify as a high school music teacher and, for his working class, British parents, this seemed like the ultimate achievement.

'For my mother and father, this was a great step up. I don't think there was another profession that would have occurred to them. As for me, I did not like the training at all and I really felt as if I had no one I could speak to about this either', he recalls.

Ginsberg paid a visit to Glassboro State College, New Jersey, an institution that Patti Smith had also attended in the 1960s when she studied art. 'Allen toured, gave classes, performed. That's how he made a living', Taylor explains, 'and he came to the college to give a reading.'

'There was a talk, then a question and answer session and then later he gave a performance. Allen had the habit of picking up guitarists to sit in with him. Half way through, in came the professor who was hosting the event and said to me, "Go get your guitar".'

'Allen had his harmonium. I was able to watch his hands and get the changes. It was going quite well. Towards the end of the performance, I started singing. He'd never had that happen before. He got all inspired!'

'After the reading he said, "Don't leave." I rode back to the hotel with him. Two boys from the English department were the official escort. We sat in the back of the car and smoked pot. I got quite dizzy, and he talked me down. Then Ginsberg gave me his phone number and said that if I was ever in town I should give him a call', he recalls.

Not long after this, Ginsberg was going to record an album, eventually issued as *First Blues*, with the legendary Columbia A&R man John Hammond producing, and he asked Taylor if he wanted to join them in New York City. 'He thought I may like to come along and he invited me to the rehearsal. The band set up and then said, "Why don't you participate, too?"'

'Next day, I found myself in the recording studio with John Hammond!' Taylor still remembers with some excitement. Hammond had a track record second to none – he'd discovered a galaxy of popular music talent, from Count Basie and Billie Holiday to Bob Dylan and Bruce Springsteen. 'I was', Taylor confesses, 'blown away. Hammond was amazing and very nice. He said to me, "You have a wonderful voice. What's your name?"'

The singing had clearly made an impression on both Ginsberg and Hammond. I asked him how he had had the confidence to vocalise at the college session when he had first played with the poet. What had prompted that? 'I come from that place where everybody sang. My English family elders, they were always singing. My father was a pub singer. He was approached in the early 1950s with a contract to record and tour. He was a crooner like Bing Crosby. He sang Irving Berlin and the Gershwins. But my mother said that if he signed the contract she wouldn't marry him, so he gave it up. My mother's father also had a reputation as a singer.'

But did he know who Ginsberg was when he encountered him on that day? 'Yes, I did. My father had given me a book of poetry he'd got where he worked as a warehouseman at Dell Publishing in Jersey. It was a book called *Poets' Choice*. I've still got it. There was a piece in it from 'Howl'. Each poet contributed a poem and then there was an essay on each one.'

'So, I'd read some "Howl". I'd been reading a lot of Kerouac and had recently read Timothy Leary's book *High Priest*. Also Abbie Hoffman, Jerry Rubin and Richard Alpert's *Be Here Now*. But I'd been playing constantly in bands and I had much more knowledge of pop music than Beat poetry,' he explains.

Taylor continues: 'I wanted Allen to notice me. I was actually desperate, I was upset. I did not want to be a high school teacher. I went to the Q&A session and I asked lots of questions. Then we played together. I knew Blake. We sort of hit it off.'

Unquestionably, the meeting had an extraordinary impact on the arc of Taylor's life. A period of musical engagement commenced that would carry the guitarist into maturity, leaving far behind him those parental aspirations that he become a teacher.

'We probably did more than 200 shows in Europe alone, figuring four or five tours of up to three months at a time, playing five shows a week. We actually played more shows in Europe than in the US, because the European shows came in concentrated bunches, while his engagements over here tended to come one or two at a time', he points out.

Then there were the recording commitments with which he became involved. He features, for instance, on numerous of the tracks on the celebrated Ginsberg boxed set *Holy Soul Jelly Roll* including the cut 'Airplane Blues' taped in LA in 1981 with Taylor on guitar and Bob Dylan on bass. So how was that? 'Dylan is a man of few words. It was all business. He knew what he wanted in the studio, much to the engineer's dismay at times. He wanted to put Allen in the bathroom for the vocals, but the engineer said the plumbing was too noisy.'

'There was little in the way of sound separation in the studio. We all played in the same room, and there were sheets of Plexiglas duct-taped to the ceiling beams, if I remember correctly, and hanging down in front of the amps, makeshift.'

'When Bob arrived, we had already begun to put down "Airplane Blues". He said it was too slow, and in the wrong key. We started again, with Bob on bass, and the whole thing changed into a very cool reggae-like feel. Slightly a shambles, like a Dylan jam, which is what it was.'

Yet if teaching, in the conventional sense, had necessarily been jettisoned, education of a more radical from would eventually weave its way into the Taylor tapestry. Attending his first summer school as Ginsberg's assistant at Naropa in summer 1979, he returned there every year after that. 'I found a niche. As a trained musician I taught the poets music history', he says.

His journey was varied. When Ginsberg wasn't tapping into his talents, other musical projects took up his time and energy. Already part of the Fugs circle from the early 1980s, in 1988 he became a core member of the New York post-punk band False Prophets, trekked across America, and brought the group over here, too. 'We did those long European tours, playing 60 shows in 65 days, sort of thing. You get really good doing that', he remembers.

A band with a strong political ethos and a keen commitment to indie rock values and its communal codes, they made a mark on stage and on record but running a touring show on such egalitarian principles proved a massive strain on the group's personal relationships. Without the backing of a corporate major, False Prophets eventually succumbed to the strain of economic realities in the early 1990s.

Yet Taylor would reap a somewhat surprising reward from these experiences. Embarking finally on postgraduate study at Brown University as the band crumbled, he took ethnomusicology – a discipline centred on work in the field, close engagement with your subjects and often linked with, for example, the study of ethnic or tribal cultures – and produced a successful doctoral thesis that became a book.

False Prophet: Field Notes from the Punk Underground was published in 2004 and confirmed his academic credentials. Not that such confirmation was really required. In 1995, poet Anne Waldman, a Naropa stalwart herself, had offered Taylor a year's work. He took it and then continued at the Buddhist-inspired institute, home to the Ginsberg-founded Jack Kerouac School of Disembodied Poetics.

He remained at Naropa as a full-time staff member until 2008 when his wife Judy Hussie, a curator of dance and performance, secured work in New York and the family – including their son Eamonn, 12 – decided to head back to the city where Taylor had spent many of his most productive years, as Ginsberg's guitar man, friend and muse, as rocker, writer and poet.

He is now looking forward to Rob Epstein's Ginsberg documentary to which he contributes an interview. He also points out that the artist Eric Drooker – who provided illustrations for his own *False Prophet* volume – has been asked to contribute an animated sequence to the 'Howl' cinematic celebration. Drooker's style recalls German Expressionist woodcuts and should offer a fascinating extra commentary on that epic verse work.

Meanwhile, the memoir recounting his personal experience with the poet is gradually taking shape and will eventually add a further layer to the Beat literature as Taylor, who despite his long sojourn in the US remains a British citizen, plans to capture some of the detail and spirit of that two decade association.

So what are his enduring memories of the Ginsberg years? 'My favourite poem is "Song" from *Howl and Other Poems*. Allen told me that was [William Carlos] Williams' favourite poem, too. My take, finally, was that he was my best friend. He says, somewhere in a poem, "I refuse to say who my best friend is"; I take that as permission to say he was mine. He would probably have said Peter [Orlovsky] was his.

'There hasn't been another man in whom I can confide as I did with him. He was brilliant, very generous, and very patient with me, though not with some others. He was a beautiful human being. We had a lot of adventures, played a lot of music. He taught me many things. I think in a way he saved my life, because I was fairly unhappy as a young person.

'He just pulled me out of nowhere and took me to Rome to meet Luciano Berio, that sort of thing. One minute I'm wondering how I'm going to get out of this nowhere college in the New Jersey swamps, and the next minute I'm on stage at Carnegie Hall!'

Q&A 6

Pete Molinari, British singer-songwriter with Beat leanings

Pete Molinari is a UK singer-songwriter who has toured extensively in Britain and the US, has released three well-received albums – *Walking Off the Map* (2006), *A Virtual Landslide* (2008) and *A Train Bound for Glory* (2010) – and has acknowledged the impact Jack Kerouac has had on his work. Described by the magazine *Mojo* as 'one of the distinctive voices of his generation', he has also attracted high profile fans including Bruce Springsteen who, when asked by Ed Norton at the Toronto Film Festival what music he was listening to, he said, 'Pete Molinari – and if you don't know anything about him, he's great!'

You clearly have an enormous range of influences on your work, from the country and folk greats of the past, from Bob Dylan to Phil Ochs and so on, which you draw on to great effect. Tell me about your Beat interests and which writers have inspired you. Is it just Kerouac? Is it *On the Road*? Or are there others from that literary world who have also caught your attention?

I do I guess draw on a range of influences like you say and like any artist does. I don't believe much in scenes and try and look beyond them. I can see the need for them. For them to maybe label something and call it this or that but really I just either like a work and view it and judge it in a way that if it relates to me and has substance and content and comes alive in my mind and the atoms are still vibrant then I'm drawn to it. I guess Kerouac's *On the Road* and Guthrie's *Bound For Glory* were such books, as a child, that appealed to me because of the sense of freedom in them and I was an idealistic child. Still am to some degree, I guess, but see a little more through the illusion now. I like Steinbeck's works very much and something from most of those writers like Ginsberg and Ferlinghetti. Whitman I think was like early Beat. But there is so much spirit in his work. So much freedom.

How have you used that influence? Was it about inspiring you to become an itinerant troubadour? Are you drawn to the romantic notion of the travelling artist?

I guess I am drawn to it, yes. The word troubadour again is another label, though, for people to use. I guess I've always thought of myself as somewhat of a gypsy in the travelling and free sense of the word. My father too is from Egypt and it was only recently that I found out that the word gypsy originated from there. I guess we are all looking for something and are drawn to something romantic. It brings it alive, gives it glamour and colour. But there's is always illusion with these things so I try and get beyond them with music, literature, poetry, film, whatever ... I like to see the substance shine through. I love Chaplin and Keaton, early Marlon Brando pictures, etc. ... the theatre (when it's good). Most of all you have to let yourself shine through in your own work, to realise that you are not Kerouac or Guthrie. Maybe another link in a chain and perhaps we are all one if we want to look at the big picture spiritually and esoterically but let's just talk on a human level...we are our own unique personality. I'm from Chatham, Rochester in Kent and was brought up in a different surrounding with different influences and a different environment. But we are all the same in that we are human and have our love, anger, loneliness, joy and so on to express. We are all alone in that way but it is these things that bring us together. We are born alone and we die alone, but birth and death also brings us together. So as much as being inspired by other tales and other worlds I have to realise I have my own world. My own vision and my own path. My own voice.

Or is there some direct link between the art of Kerouac and the Beats which actually feeds into your work?

I don't think direct link but maybe a link. There always are links in a chain and it is these links that bring us together, as I said before. I like works of art or writing that show that we are vulnerable and human but I also like to see something that's beyond the intellect like William Blake or works from [Helena] Blavatsky and the Theosophical Society and the Arcane School and connected movements. I'm always searching. Searching myself and looking for answers. The answers are all there in the self and beyond the self. It would be great just to get a sense of what you have devoured, absorbed and how that material has triggered your creativity!Its all in the creative eye and spirit. To some degree they all have triggered something in me and I'm sure many others. Be it Tennessee Williams or Kerouac, [Billy] Childish, Wilde, Chaplin, but none so more than my own environment. The circles my soul moves in. The experiences we encounter everyday should be the biggest inspiration. Essentially that's what the Pre-Raphaelites, the Aesthetic movement, the Beats, punk, rock 'n' roll, folk, blues movements and many others do. It's the self that has to come through with art. It's not going to bring enlightenment. That has to be beyond the self.

13 RETURN TO LOWELL: A VISIT TO THE COMMEMORATIVE AND KEROUAC'S GRAVE

It is July of 2009. In a peaceful, public park in the heart of Lowell, Massachusetts, four early teenagers gather to chat and joke, one boy on a skateboard, three girls just sitting on one of the stone benches which form an integral part of the so-called Kerouac Commemorative. I enquire where they're from – or at least from originally. Three say Cambodia, one says India. Yet this quartet are patently all-American in this tranquil corner, shaded by trees, dedicated to a true all-American.

Unveiled in 1988, the Commemorative is the work of the artist Ben Woitena, a memorial to the life, death and work of Jack Kerouac, the local boy made good who returned, of course, to spend his last years in the town. The memorial features a series of triangular, granite pillars, replete with blocks of silver text from various Kerouac works – *The Town and the City* and *Doctor Sax*, *Mexico City Blues* and *Book of Dreams* among them. There is a striking simplicity to the arrangement which is unquestionably affecting.

I ask the group of teens if they know who Kerouac is. One girl, clearly amazed to hear an English voice, enthusiastically requests a high five before we talk further. They then reveal that they know something about the man remembered here.

'Isn't he a writer?' one says. 'Is he dead?' another asks. When I tell them that a Kerouac relative is in our midst, they are further intrigued. And the novelist's nephew Jim Sampas, just arrived from parking his car, speaks to them and reveals that he went to the same high school they will attend from this autumn, the adolescents are thrilled by this news. 'You went to our school?' one girl mouths, briefly wide-eyed at this information.

It is a fascinating moment in the continuing Kerouac saga – the immigrant, French-speaking, Canuck incomer who made the town his home with his family, took the place and made it in the setting – at least the opening sections – of his debut novel, is now recalled by a much later wave of arrivals: the children of a new generation of residents who have, at least, a vague sense of the man who has become Lowell's most famous son.

Not that it was always so. When I had last been in Lowell, more than 30 years before, few residents seemed to be even aware of Kerouac's existence. When we asked locals about him on that occasion, there were few hints of recognition at all. As that particular, late spring day wore into a darkening evening, a journalist from the *Lowell Sun* warned me and my travelling friend – both of us carrying shoulder-length hair, Stateside virgins paying our picaresque homage to the *On the Road* writer – not to visit Nick's Bar, the Sampas pub where Kerouac had drunk some of his final years away. 'It's too dangerous', the reporter advised. 'They won't welcome a couple of young hippies on Jack's trail'. Instead, he gave us a lift to a rural Greyhound stop and we took an overnight bus into Canada and escaped to further trans-America adventures.

Decades on, Jim Sampas, whose aunt Stella became Kerouac's third wife in 1966, agrees with the journalist's assessment of the time. He has few doubts that, then, the arrival of some unconventional visitors to his uncle Nick's pub would not have been greeted in a positive spirit. 'It was quite a tough place', he says. Today, Sampas, who actually met his uncle Jack Kerouac as a toddler, is an established record producer turned film producer. Jim, 43, began his career as a singer-songwriter and even made a debut album that also featured the great British vocalist Graham Parker, a figure who emerged where pub rock met the new wave and also became a high profile acolyte of the Beat legacy.

But Sampas largely said farewell the world of the performer to become, instead, the man behind the studio glass and, with rare access to the Kerouac archives – his blood uncle John largely oversees the author's inheritance – he has worked on several projects that have placed the great Beat pen-man in a musical setting.

In 1997 he was the producer, with Sonic Youth's Lee Ranaldo's support, of the album *Kerouac: Kicks Joy Darkness*, a splendid compilation of tributes to the author by a diverse range of Beat, rock, punk and folk figures – Ginsberg, Ferlinghetti and Burroughs, Patti Smith, Joe Strummer and Jeff Buckley, wordsmiths Hunter S. Thompson and Robert Hunter, and even cult movie stars such as Matt Dillon and Johnny Depp, each adding their take to the recording.

Two years later he was in charge again – this time Ranaldo took a co-producing role – as *Jack Kerouac Reads On the Road* provided an opportunity to hear long-lost Kerouac readings of his most famous volume plus unheard examples of the man himself singing a number of jazz standards. Tom Waits and Primus – who created a new song entitled 'On the Road' for the collection – and the great Beat composer and accompanist David Amram completed a rich and varied selection.

An arguably even more ambitious project saw Sampas produce a further musical collection in 2003, *Doctor Sax and The Great World Snake*, a new setting of Kerouac's phantasmagorical boyhood fiction, joined by an impressive musical and literary cast including Jim Carroll, Graham Parker, Robert Hunter and Lawrence Ferlinghetti.

But Sampas has, in recent times, moved into a fresh and exciting phase in his professional life. In 2005 he was recruited by Tango Pix, a company formed by an established film-maker Curt Worden, with a view to developing movie topics with a Beat inflection. Later this year, in autumn 2009, the first cinematic fruits of this collaboration will be released in the US and the UK. *One Fast Move or I'm Gone: Kerouac's Big Sur* is a fully fledged documentary on a scale that will justify a modest theatrical release before it is issued as a DVD. And, joining this hour and half account of one of the most dramatic but darkest periods in the Kerouac odyssey, will be a CD soundtrack inspired by both the book and the new film and concocted by two of the hippest young music-makers presently operating in the US.

Ben Gibbard, front-man of the band Death Cab for Cutie – a name taken from a song that Bonzo Dog Doo-Dah Band members Neil Innes and Vivian Stanshall perform in the Beatles' 1967 flick *Magical Mystery Tour* and then again from a fictional title that British literary critic Richard Hoggart conceived in his major 1957 study *The Uses of Literacy* – and Jay Farrar, of the groups Son Volt and Tupelo Honey, have produced a body of songs that brings elements of the Kerouac legend into the twenty-first-century and lends these episodes in the writer's story a contemporary indie rock cachet.

The DVD and CD will be issued through one of the most famous names in American music-making, Atlantic Records, part of the wider Warner Music group, and both Sampas and Worden are delighted that this labour of love, conceived over several years, will have some serious promotional muscle behind it when the material is finally unveiled.

Curt Worden, 59, who reveals that the film will have a premiere in 30 US cities in October, has long experience as a cameraman in the contrasting worlds of commerce and conflict. He filmed war-zones in Africa and the Middle East for NBC News at the end of the 1980s, before setting up a business that produced corporate films over the next decade or so. But his desire to bring his long-term experience and creative talents to the cinematic table, has been answered in this powerful *Big Sur*-inspired piece. The documentary involves the contributions of dozens of iconic Beat individuals and important commentators on this literary world.

Lawrence Ferlinghetti and Carolyn Cassady, Michael McClure and Sam Shepard are joined by Tom Waits, Patti Smith and the aforementioned Ben Gibbard and Jay Farrar, by Joyce Johnson, David Amram and narrator John Ventimiglia, Beat fan and one of the most in-demand character actors, a key player as Artie Bucco in the acclaimed TV series *The Sopranos*. And that is merely a selection of the faces and voices showcased in *One Fast Move or I'm Gone*.

The project has taken Sampas and Worden across the US several times, seeking locations and conducting many interviews. Worden is pleased with the outcome, a pleasing marriage of artistic and atmospheric images – from Bayside panoramas to the sheer canyons of Monterey, from stunning seascapes and forests to evocative details of the street, the bar, the road.

Over the summer, both Sampas and Worden agreed to meet up at their Rhode Island headquarters to discuss their collaborative venture. Jim, in fact, had generously promised some months previously that if I was in that part of the world any time, he would be pleased to take me to Lowell and show me the Kerouac-linked sites, including a visit to the author's grave, a landmark I'd signally failed to find on my first visit in 1978. First though we chatted about the documentary.

I asked why they had chosen *Big Sur* as their initial subject, a dramatic chapter indeed in the Kerouac odyssey but surely one of the most downbeat periods in the writer's resume, the once free-wheeling, life-loving hitchhiker cast to the psychological depths by a nightmarish cocktail of alcoholic dependency and delirium tremens? Explains Worden: 'We chose *Big Sur,* an evocative account of a time in Jack's life when he'd come undone, both emotionally and spiritually, because, fundamentally, it is a compelling story that has affected and inspired generations of readers. There were many voices to be heard, voices that just had to tell this amazing story.'

The original soundtrack to the piece has been broadly overseen by Sampas, after his years of close working with figures from the indie rock community. I asked him what listeners might expect from the accompanying album, which will carry the same title as the documentary. Sampas reveals that there are three songs from the CD that are actually employed in the film but there is extra material on the album. 'There are 12 songs, mostly written by Jay Farrar and a couple by Ben Gibbard, but all are drawn on from Kerouac's words from *Big Sur*. They use his prose verbatim to create the lyrics.'

Our conversation – the Beat Generation and jazz, the Beat revival among younger followers, rock tributes to Kerouac and much more – continued as the three of us began the journey from the pair's film studio base and headed for the place of Kerouac's birth and resting place. We wended our way through the long, flat, rural highways that connect Rhode Island to its New England neighbour Massachusetts. It's perhaps 90 minutes from Providence, the capital of the smallest US state, to Lowell, a one-time textile centre that went into dreadful industrial decline in the 1970s.

In fact, I even recall the UK town of Halifax, West Yorkshire, which was experiencing similar downturns around the same time, forging alliances of common concern with its US counterpart in the testing years that followed the terminal decline of the once global and mighty Anglo-American woollen and cotton businesses. Now though, Lowell, where Jim Sampas like Kerouac also grew up, has a worn-in but more comfortable air. Many of the old brick-built mills and warehouses have taken on new, post-industrial uses – apartments and small businesses and the like.

Some, almost quaint, cobbled streets remain and high street outlets include elegant restaurants, attractive bars and bohemian cafés. The old economic heartland of this place will never return but there seems to be a sense that the traumas of older shut-downs have at least been traversed, the commercial scars eventually healing if not yet disappeared.

We meet Paul Marion, editor of Kerouac's *Atop an Underwood: Early Stories and Other Writings*, in a café that says Greenwich Village or North Beach, San Francisco, rather than small-town America and the wholefood is fantastic. Marion is a long-time friend of Jim Sampas and there is much talk about past Kerouac celebrations and ones to come in the town. The era when the writer, a reputation tarnished by late-life controversy, was temporarily etched out of Lowell's history is long gone; today, in times when cultural tourism is a realm that has, at least partially, replaced the older, defunct blue-collar pursuits, Kerouac is a name that can draw regional, national and international visitors to this provincial yet appealing centre.

Marion leaves after lunch for his post in the local university, but Worden, Sampas and I make tracks for the Commemorative garden, a small number of blocks away. In the quiet calm of a warm, humid afternoon, I encounter the charming young Lowell-ites playing in the park, raising thoughts about the town's receding past and the potential energy of its multicultural present.

We then head by car to, I suppose, the holiest of the remaining Kerouac shrines in Lowell, his gravestone. But we drive via the extraordinary candle-lit, religious grotto and the row of statues recording the saints and the Stations of the Cross – glass cabinets, wooden painted figures, all in remarkably good order. These were the icons that Kerouac found so affecting as a boy and which Allen Ginsberg and Bob Dylan are seen wandering past in the epic tour movie *Renaldo and Clara*, scenes shot during the Rolling Thunder Revue trek of 1975.

When we do arrive at the vast Catholic cemetery, it is also hard not to forget Dylan and Ginsberg's sun-streaked autumn visit to the grave itself. The light now is cloudier, the day is cooler, but with Jim Sampas's assistance we track the inconspicuous tablet that records both Kerouac's passing in 1969 and the death of wife Stella in 1990. It is a moving moment, the last physical evidence that Kerouac was ever of this world and there are numerous mementoes already scattered on the spot – a MetroCard ticket from the New York subway, an empty bottle of Jack Daniel's, a guitar pick carrying a peace emblem among them.

Sampas says that fans leave similar items each and every week. We move the tokens, photograph the stone, and then restore the pieces as a simple tribute to the visitors who were keen to make some connection with the writer, long six feet under, 40 years since his premature death and the burial of a great writer in this unquestionably inauspicious plot.

The afternoon is fading and we eventually head away from Lowell. By early evening, we return to the handsome railway station in Providence where I say my goodbyes to Jim Sampas and Curt Worden to bring a fascinating, enriching and contemplative day to a conclusion. The Northeast Corridor train from Boston to New York City is ready to board, and I crumple into my seat. Penn Station and the dreaming spires of Manhattan, the birthplace of the Beats, awaits perhaps three and a half hours, some 180 miles, down the line.

REVIEW 2 – FILM: *ONE FAST MOVE OR I'M GONE: KEROUAC'S BIG SUR*

Director Curt Worden, DVD, Kerouac Films, 2009

Movies with a Jack Kerouac theme crop up every few years though the most-talked-about, an adaptation of *On the Road*, still, we understand, in production by Francis Ford Coppola's company under the direction of the cult Brazilian director Walter Salles, remains, at least to date, an elusive pipedream.[1] But a new documentary based on a very different period in the writer's life should whet the appetite of most Beat followers in the interim.

One Fast Move or I'm Gone: Kerouac's Big Sur re-visits a time when the author had experienced the heady elation of published success followed by the deflation of his drink-ravaged new celebrity. In 1960, in a bid to escape the attentions of the New York party crowd and the demon bottle, Kerouac made plans to stay in Lawrence Ferlinghetti's canyon-side cabin perched on the Monterey, California coast.

Intending to stay three weeks in solitude, an echo perhaps of his *Desolation Angels* mountain-top fire-watch summer of 1956, Kerouac hoped he could pull his disturbed psyche together, avoid alcohol, commune with nature and re-trigger his writing instincts in the thrilling isolation of a hidden, wooded glade above the crashing Pacific Ocean.

As with many moments in the arc of Kerouac's rarely straightforward life, these good intentions were quickly de-railed and, in more typical form, the sojourn on

---

[1] Note that the Walter Salles movie adaptation of Kerouac's *On the Road* was premiered at the Cannes Film Festival on 23 May 2012.

the West Coast was transformed into a sequence of chaotic incident: a short stay at the cabin, a return to the bars of San Francisco, a further time at the cabin, a series of social gatherings with poet friends – Ferlinghetti, Michael McClure and Lew Welch – and eventually a re-union with his greatest hero Neal Cassady alongside his family.

But, in the usual Kerouac manner, out of chaos – mental depression, fleeting sexual liaison and copious quantities of wine – came art and his extraordinary account of these episodes would form the heart of *Big Sur*, a book penned the following year and then published in 1962.

As Robert Hunter, Grateful Dead lyricist, comments in the documentary: 'As long as Jack is running, Jack is gonna live, and as long as Jack is living, Jack is gonna write. And we benefit from that hangover, those of us who love this particular book, this ugly, ugly book of ugly places in the mind, sordid places in the psyche. And Jack has to wring himself out like a greasy, wet dish-towel in this book, and he *has* to do it, he *has* to write this stuff …'

A shattering antidote to the free-spirited optimisms of *On the Road* and *The Dharma Bums,* this volume is a classic of a different kind: an extended piece of heart-searching fiction, a forensic examination of a soul in extremis, with the stunning coda of the poem 'Sea', in which the writer faithfully records the sounds of the eternal, rolling waves.

Film-maker Curt Worden recreates these frenetic short weeks in a powerful, 90-minute movie which employs the full arsenal of the creative documentary director and to most impressive effect: interviews with friends of Kerouac and surviving eye-witnesses to the Big Sur summer; archive black and white footage; an atmospheric soundtrack; and many lively and insightful reflections by biographers and contemporary writers, actors and musicians.

Ferlinghetti and McClure, Carolyn Cassady and Joyce Johnson make key contributions, playwright Sam Shepard and author S.E. Hinton are joined by Patti Smith, Tom Waits and the great Beat composer David Amram, and *Sopranos* actor John Ventimiglia, who narrates, also feature in a high-octane cast, lending anecdote and commentary in equal measure.

The soundtrack of the film, composed by contemporary indie rock artists Jay Farrar – of Son Volt and Uncle Tupelo – and Death Cab for Cutie's Ben Gibbard, adds an intriguing and evocative texture to the piece: rough and ready blues, dyed-in-the-roots grooves which draw on Kerouac's *Big Sur* prose verbatim for their lyrical texts.

Perhaps the most compelling ingredient of all though is the imposing geography against which all these dramas unfolded: the city panoramas, seascapes and forest vistas that potently capture the physical flavour of the world that briefly became this author's bolt-hole as he found himself at rock bottom, post-*On the Road* acclaim, post-new found fame, taunted by an unwanted level of attention, bedevilled by the terrors of delirium tremens.

'One fast move or I'm gone' is a haunting phrase from *Big Sur* itself, a statement that summed up Kerouac's personal crisis, his state of mind, his state of health. He felt that unless he did something drastic about his condition, his lifestyle, his speeding deterioration, he would indeed soon be a goner.

The fact that his 3,000-mile train journey west did not, ultimately, exorcise his demons and is now best known for spawning the dark, confessional novel that followed is maybe not that surprising: solitude and cold turkey were plainly not the solutions to the deepening Kerouac catastrophe.

Author's note: *One Fast Move or I'm Gone: Kerouac's Big Sur* had a limited cinema premiere in the US and the UK during autumn 2009. It is available on DVD, accompanied by a separate CD soundtrack, both released through Atlantic. See a trail at http://www.kerouacfilms.com

REVIEW 3 – CD: *ONE FAST MOVE OR I'M GONE: KEROUAC'S BIG SUR*

Music by Jay Farrar and Ben Gibbard

Executive producer: Jim Sampas

Released on CD by Atlantic Records, 20 October 2009

There has been a long and noble history of rock artists turning to the Beats for inspiration. Through several phases of popular music's post-Presley development, singers, songwriters and bands have found something compelling, alchemic even, about that group of writers and the approach they took to their art.

Bob Dylan, John Lennon and Paul McCartney lead this hierarchy of talent, but when we add the Grateful Dead, the Velvet Underground, David Bowie, Tom Waits, the Doors and Van Morrison, then punks and new wavers from Patti Smith to Joe Strummer and Kurt Cobain, Sonic Youth, U2 and REM, there is a pattern of association with this literary culture which is quite impossible to ignore.

So, to move into the early years a new millennium and discover that the same wheels continue to turn is not perhaps so great a shock. It may be half a century or more since Kerouac, Ginsberg and Burroughs made their extraordinary mark on US culture but the tremors from that radical eruption are still being felt and rock seems particularly responsive to its vibrations.

The latest rock musicians to pin their colours to this mast are two darlings of the US indie scene. Jay Farrar, once of Uncle Tupelo and now Son Volt, and Ben Gibbard, frontman of the hugely rated Death Cab for Cutie, have added their weight to a major project centred on Jack Kerouac and linked to the fortieth anniversary of the writer's death in October 2009.

Farrar and Gibbard are the featured creators of the soundtrack to the new documentary *One Fast Move or I'm Gone: Kerouac's Big Sur*, a 90-minute film which tells the remarkable story of the author's attempts to escape the spotlight of celebrity by fleeing to a remote Monterey cabin, high above the Pacific, owned by City Lights bookshop proprietor Lawrence Ferlinghetti.

The film offers a gripping account, marrying impressive interview footage, including eye-witness memories of the time, with stunning footage of the Bay Area, the Pacific coast and eye-catching coverage of the trails – and trials – that carried Kerouac from New York City to this extraordinary West Coast wilderness in the summer of 1960.

The music to this cinematic odyssey is available in two versions – as incidental and illustrative music in the DVD itself, of course, but also as a stand-alone, 12-track CD. It is also being released in a range of combinations – with the film, with the novel and also a collection of previously unseen Kerouac photographs – and in a spread of editions – including as a vinyl album.

The album, which carries the same title as the documentary – culled from a desperate phrase that Kerouac utilises in the book to characterise his alcohol-soaked condition and psychological frailty as the success of *On the Road* turned into an extended and destructive hangover – was pulled together by Jim Sampas, well-established record producer and a member of the wider Kerouac clan.

Sampas, Kerouac's nephew by marriage – his aunt was Stella and Jack's third and final wife – did meet his fading uncle as a toddler in the late 60s. For the last decade and more, though, he has become a key figure behind a series of albums that have celebrated the writer's talents in a musical context.

In 1997 he oversaw, with Sonic Youth's Lee Ranaldo, *Kerouac: Kicks Joy Darkness*, a well-received homage to the novelist, featuring a blend of high profile rockers – Patti Smith and Jeff Buckley among them – iconic movie stars – Matt Dillon and Johnny Depp – and surviving Beats, including Ginsberg, Burroughs and Ferlinghetti.

Two years on, he made the album *Jack Kerouac Reads On the Road*, with Ranaldo again on board and with Waits, Primus and the great Beat composer David Amram among the cast. In 2003, he was joined by poet Jim Carroll and the British singer Graham Parker for a dramatised account of *Doctor Sax and the Great White Snake*, a project combining spoken word and music.

Now working in close alliance with his colleague Curt Worden, the director of the documentary, in their joint venture Kerouac Films, based in Rhode Island, he was keen to ensure there was a strong music component when they first began discussions about the making of a *Big Sur*-based picture.

He'd worked with Jay Farrar previously on a Bruce Springsteen tribute CD entitled *Badlands*, so he had a good idea what the singer-songwriter would bring to the table. Most intriguing was the working method that Farrar would lend to this new collection of *Big Sur*-inspired originals, essentially a re-visiting of the old Beat principle of 'first thought, best thought', one which Kerouac particularly advocated.

As executive producer Sampas explains: 'I was fascinated by Jay's methodology, the way he worked in a spontaneous manner, a quick-shot style. He felt that the best songs he wrote were those he wrote quickly using a spontaneous prose approach.'

Farrar confirms the power that Kerouac has held over his creative ethos. 'He gave great rules to follow. Go with your first thought, stream of consciousness writing. Get your ideas down. He helps all those who are writing to get a style down that is ultimately more individualistic. Over all, his work resonates with the wanderlust and quest for self discovery that exists in all of us.'

He wrote all but one – the title track, penned by his musical collaborator Gibbard – of the songs on *One Fast Move* … but both players share a strong affiliation with Kerouac and his achievement even though the duo had never met before their San Francisco recording dates.

Comments Gibbard: 'I came across Kerouac at a really pivotal time in my life. I didn't know where I was going or what I wanted out of life. His work put me on a path in my life that I'm still very much on. I've translated his influence and world-view into the music I make. He'll always be one of my top three musical influences even though he's not a songwriter.'

Most interesting to Kerouac readers is that Farrar has taken actual lines, verbatim prose, from *Big Sur* to produce his lyrical texts. He tells the story in a broadly chronological way by choosing fragments from the story and then shaping them into song-words. Gibbard's title tune is more impressionistic, an artistic response to the novel and its dark threads.

Sampas and film-maker Worden were keen to avoid the usual musical reflections that are linked to Kerouac and his era – jazz and bebop specifically – to bring the legend of the writer and his work into a more contemporary context. Yet the songs that Farrar, mainly, and Gibbard have composed and perform here will not jolt the listener with more traditional notions of what Beat originally meant.

Blending folk and blues, roots and country – guitars, pianos, even steel guitar, well to the fore – this album brings to mind different nuances of the days when Kerouac was at the height of his powers, as traveller, observer and documenter of the four corners of North America.

Even though the songs are reminiscent of both the Californian songwriter fraternity of the late 1960s and early 1970s – Neil Young and Gram Parsons, perhaps – there are also flavours of later new country sounds – Steve Earle and Ryan Adams – which often reference the romance of the road. We can, too, within the new set, locate a loose continuity that stretches back to Dylan, Seeger and Guthrie and the traditions of the roaming troubadour. For sure, the current Americana scene happily tips its hat to many precursors.

The best tracks here are the title piece, 'California Zephyr' – an account of the train that Kerouac took West as he headed for Big Sur – 'Breathe our Iodine' – an insistent, bass-driven blues – and 'Final Horrors', a stark, sparse evocation of Kerouac's descending state in that fateful summer built on a simple, spidery guitar riff and a potent moan of a vocal.

While this CD is unlikely to draw mainstream audiences or attract the close attention of the chart-compilers, the ideas that like behind Farrar and Gibbard's collection will have, I think, for Kerouac followers more than mere curio value.

And, within the context of the documentary itself, the songs lend an evocative texture to a fascinating, if somewhat bleak, chapter in the sweeping Duluoz saga.

Author's note: Jay Farrar and Ben Gibbard's soundtrack to *One Fast Move or I'm Gone: Kerouac's Big Sur* is released in various formats – on CD and vinyl. It can also be purchased as part of a DVD and CD package in a number of editions.

Q&A 7

Chris T-T, British political singer-songwriter

Chris T-T has spent a decade and a half making fiercely independent and wryly personal music usually with a political edge. He played bass with indie band Magoo in the later 1990s but has been a solo artist for most of his working life. Described by the *Sunday Times* as 'a modern-day Blake', he also has a potent interest in the literary. He has released eight albums, the latest, *Disobedience*, a setting of the children's poetry of Winnie the Pooh creator A.A. Milne which formed the basis of his Edinburgh Fringe Festival show in summer 2011.

How did you discover the Beats?

I can't remember specifically but in my teens I loved two gateway cultures to the Beats: the drug-addled 1960s and then late-1980s and early 1990s alt-rock, as well as the (largely male) American literature of John Steinbeck, William Faulkner and J.D. Salinger.

Which Beat writers did you read and what texts?

I remember at school/sixth form reading *Naked Lunch* and Richard Brautigan's *Trout Fishing in America* and *The Abortion* first, alongside discovering stuff like Ballard and all the Salingers except *The Catcher in the Rye* – I've still not read *Catcher*, in a wilfully perverse kind of way, though I've read everything else Salinger published. Then for a while I was primarily into Bukowski and read *Post Office*, *Ordinary Madness*, etc. and only then, starting college, I found Ginsberg's *Mind Breaths* and *Howl and Other Poems* in their 'proper' City Lights editions quite cheap in the bookshop at the Royal Festival Hall. I then chased Corso and Ferlinghetti because of those – and I wonder now if I fell for their physical shape and conciseness as much as the content. But not – ever, really – Jack Kerouac's *On the Road*.

From that point on, and to this day, Ginsberg most resonated with me. Later I remember reading Harold Norse's *Memoirs of a Bastard Angel* which connected them all back to [Christopher] Isherwood.

What inspired you or excited you about their writing?

At first I was inspired by the crude, supremely honest, anti-establishment maleness of it – gritty. I guess these were the first books I'd read by people without comfortable lives 'outside' of their creativity. I loved how they were 'all in'; it coincided for me with discovering American punk rock – bands like Sonic Youth, Fugazi, Husker Du, Dinosaur Jr, Black Flag and Yo La Tengo – just at the moment this broke through as grunge, so my musical heroes were also outsiders who travelled around in scuzzy vans, became addicts, got beaten up, and so on! All very pre-Britpop.

Long-term, Ginsberg and Brautigan continue to inspire me – I think of Ginsberg's poetry as the greatest Beat work – that combination of hippy, gay, counterculture style with hardcore politics I love, alongside truly incandescent language. I'm not sure a lot of Beat writing is that brilliant, reading back, though maybe Burroughs is.

Did their influence feed into your own writing as a lyricist/songwriter? Was it direct or subliminal?

Broadly, literature influences my lyric-writing more than any other artform. The politics of *Mind Breaths* and 'Howl' fed directly into my early development as a lyricist and the travelling outsider narrative (real or myth) has hugely influenced how I see (and perhaps more relevantly how I narrate and mythologise) my life and career. I regret living so safely and statically the past few years but I have long blurred lines between lyric and life. Because/although I'm not capable of being a 'bad' male compared to some of the Beat writers, I have written violently bad perspectives a few times (such as employing violent imagery from morally ambiguous viewpoints). Meanwhile I guess my political lyrics (especially the invective) tend towards Ginsberg and away from Billy Bragg.

Despite big cultural differences I also connect the Beats with Bruce Chatwin (whose writing and lie-filled life I love), in terms of realised nomadic lives. Also, it's always surprising how influential Brautigan is today, particularly in hipster lit and indie music, despite being lesser known to wider public – and perhaps too rural or gentle to be a true Beat? I once got a bit obsessed with a whole set-up lifted from Brautigan in a Haruki Murakami novel, then, amazingly, got the chance to ask Murakami himself. And he said yes, it was a conscious reference – and that he's greatly influenced by Brautigan. In the very late 1990s, working in London, reading Brautigan's short story about thrown-away Christmas trees and meeting Lawrence Ferlinghetti. It was exceptionally powerful – like completing a circuit for me.

What links do you see between the Beats and rock culture – maybe the alternative, independent scene of which you are a part, or more generally.

It's not there in aspirational gangsta R&B, or post-Simon Cowell TV reality pop but it's there more than ever in the self-consciously destructive, and less professional than 10 years ago, alternative scenes. We were destroyed by, and are now rebuilding via, technology – and immediacy is a part of that. As MySpace and blogs grew, we switched from writing about ourselves in the third person, to directly communicating with fans in the first person. At which point the need to Beat up that narrative becomes vital.

We aren't rich, we scrabble, we have stuff to say but nobody is listening. Now we thrive on adversity and outsiderness. I guess any part of touring music world can connect itself to Beats if it tries – even inside the global corporatised juggernaut that is the Rolling Stones, there's a Keith Richards.

Do the Beats still touch you as an inspiration – for example, notions of artistic candour, ideas of the road?

Hugely. My last album, *Love is Not the Rescue* (2010), had a direct reference to the avoidance of responsibility and decision-making inherent in *On the Road*. But in more subtle ways the lyrical influence is constant and major.

Do the Beats still touch other younger generations of singer performers you encounter?

I don't know how widely read the Beats are now beyond the two or three key texts. I don't think Ginsberg is particularly influential. But if you include indirect influence and soaked-in mythology then they're still very important because the affectations, style and myths of the Beats have outlasted mere trends and become a core part of the language and dress-code of young alternative music.

OBITUARY 3

Tuli Kupferberg, 'Key figure in the US 1960s counterculture'

Tuli Kupferberg, who has died aged 86 after a long illness, was a key figure in the US countercultural campaign of the 1960s. As a publisher, poet, pacifist, singer and songwriter, he used his talents for writing and humour to attack the perceived repressions of his nation and its escalating military activities in South East Asia.

As part of that anti-war strategy, Kupferberg combined Beat writing sensibilities, folk whimsy and electric rock 'n' roll in the Fugs, the band that he formed in 1964 with fellow activist Ed Sanders. The group took their name from the toned-down expletive that Norman Mailer had been forced to adopt in his 1948 novel *The Naked and the Dead* to sidestep the true language of the Pacific front.

Born in New York and later a student at the city's Brooklyn College, Kupferberg got a job as a medical librarian, but submitted poetry and prose to publications including the *Village Voice*. He would go on to create poetry magazines of his own and one of them, *Birth*, founded in 1958, provided a home to work by numerous Beat writers of reputation – Diane di Prima and Allen Ginsberg included.

By then, Kupferberg had already been mythologised as part of the bohemian Greenwich Village community. He was the celebrated character, mentioned in Ginsberg's long poem of 1956, 'Howl', who 'jumped off the Brooklyn Bridge this actually happened and walked away unknown and forgotten'.

At a time when youth appeared to be ascribed a value above any material commodity, Kupferberg, who was already into his 40s, crept under the demographic radar to become a part of that frenetic scene which took on the establishment and its increasingly discredited politics. The Fugs provided a musical soundtrack to the forces of resistance as activists such as the Students for a Democratic Society took first to the soapbox, and then to the barricades, to be joined, in time, by more radical organisations such as the Yippies and the Black Panthers.

The band drew on satire and lampoon to ridicule their adversaries, in songs such as 'Kill for Peace', 'Supergirl' and 'Slum Goddess', often using language that drew controversy and censorship. But the band also paid tribute to their mystic hero William Blake in 'Ah, Sunflower, Weary of Time' on their 1965 debut LP, *The Village Fugs Sing Ballads of Contemporary Protest, Point of Views, and General Dissatisfaction.*

Kupferberg remained a poet, too, and his collaboration with Robert Bashlow, *1001 Ways to Beat the Draft*, became his most famous work. It was a literal, if absurd, listing of actions that might save you from conscription to the army. 'Say you're crazy', 'Marry your mother' and 'Get elected to the Supreme Soviet' were among the titbits of advice.

The Fugs were at the height of their powers in the later 1960s and released several albums, but faded from view, only to reform in 1985 with Kupferberg and Sanders still at the helm. Joined by Steven Taylor, Ginsberg's guitarist, among others, the band continued to make political capital that mixed caustic wit and street wisdom.

In recent years, Kupferberg's health faltered and his activity with the band declined, yet he continued to experiment with words, posting his punning aphorisms – he dubbed them 'perverbs' – online. A stroke in 2009 left him blind; a second, more recently, accelerated the end.

Ed Sanders praised his abilities with a melody: 'His songs were very nuanced and subtle, yet bold and daring at the same time, a genius in the footsteps of Stephen Foster and other major tunesmiths'. Steven Taylor also paid tribute to his band-mate: 'He was a friend, comrade, older brother, funny uncle, extra dad, all in one. All the Fugs loved him dearly'. Counterculture historian Jonah Raskin commented: 'Tuli was suave, a kind of sybarite. He was funny too; surviving the bridge fall had given him a way of viewing life comically, not tragically, a gift to us who followed him.'

He is survived by his wife, Sylvia Topp, his sons, Joe and Noah, and a daughter, Samara.

Naphtali 'Tuli' Kupferberg, poet and songwriter, born 28 September 1923; died 12 July 2010.

Q&A 8

Kevin Ring, editor of the magazine *Beat Scene*

In *Beat Scene*, the UK-based Beat Generation magazine he founded in 1988, **Kevin Ring** has assiduously charted the history and culture of this literary movement in over 60 regular issues of the publication over nearly a quarter of a century.

What do you feel rock music has taken from Beat culture over the decades?

Perhaps in the 1950s, or maybe even sooner, a sense of the outlaw, living outside society and those conventions. Instead of Pat Boone, it was Gene Vincent. They may also have taken the DIY ethic that appeared with the Beats in the 1950s, publishing themselves and bypassing the usual corporate avenues of getting a voice heard. All the little magazines, *Yugen* and so on. Of course, the punk era threw up a lot of little magazines – did they get that from the Beats?

Is there a lyrical connection there, a musical one or was it merely a railing against authority?

Well, if you listen to Bob Dylan or Michael McClure, they would cite the techniques of Jack Kerouac in, say *Mexico City Blues*. I think it is well documented that Bob Dylan felt that book spoke his language. And certainly well documented that Dylan took from Ginsberg's 'Howl', those extended lines. If you look at that Rykodisc CD, *Kicks Joy Darkness*, the reworking of Kerouac's words by musicians such as Patti Smith, Warren Zevon, Michael Stipe, Tom Waits and many others – I thought that was a most successful album. Good words are good words and combining those with imaginative interpretations made for something special.

In the case of Tom Waits, he made that move into the 'confessional' way of writing; his life and the characters he created became his myth. He made up words like Kerouac.

Where do you see Beat influence in the rock music of the last half century?

They helped ditch the 'moon in June' approach to rock music. Musicians read books, they even name their bands after writers and books, don't they? They see the rhythms that someone like Kerouac or Kenneth Patchen or Ginsberg create and they see the often open-hearted writing style and they copy it. How many confessional singer songwriters are there today! Possibly far too many.

But those Beats paved the way for them to write about their own lives and create art out of the everyday. Myth and legend out of the mundane. Just like some of the Beats did. And jazz and the Beats combined to create a whole new vocabulary. Think of Slim Gaillard.

Because of the Beats, San Francisco became this 'other' place, another country almost, where poetry thrived and it became a haven for the musicians who made the place famous. Obviously the writers and musicians mixed socially way back, Brautigan, McClure, even Snyder, Ginsberg. Jim Morrison couldn't make his mind up whether he was a musician or a poet. And, of course, SF was – and is – home to so many other musicians and poets, too many to list.

Do you think that the idea of the road that Kerouac and Cassady mythologised has been influential on musicians?

Oh yes. Such a powerful vision, an overused word I know when talking the Beats, but it truly was a vision. Someone like Chuck Berry picked up on that. It wasn't just Kerouac and Cassady of course: Chuck Berry was drawing on the blues, the travelling man, constantly going down to the station with a suitcase in his hand, his woman having left him. Or he was going to meet her?

But that idea of an almost endless road with infinite possibilities holds a sway over many musicians and, indeed, filmmakers. Think of *Easy Rider* in 1969: it revolutionised the way films were made. And that soundtrack as they travelled around America. It would be interesting to discover just how many impressionable young musicians and filmmakers left the cinema with their minds burning with ideas after that film.

That idea, or memory, Kerouac planted in the minds of so many was so evident later and while Kerouac would've protested the lifestyles of Dennis Hopper and Peter Fonda in the movie, he was a pivotal force in that development. Whether he liked it or not. Well, he resented it, didn't he? But given time and reflection he might have embraced all that. He liked Ed Sanders.

Looking back, and this is straying a little, it seems Kerouac's happiest time was as a 'Dharma Bum' with Gary Snyder. Without Kerouac there might not have been a 1960s as we recall it; his books and the life they evoked, real or myth, filtered through to the 1960s, opened a few minds to possibilities.

How do you feel the Beats felt about early rock 'n' roll?

There is a famous photo of Neal Cassady hunched over a jukebox in a café or bar somewhere. Putting his nickels in to play a tune. He looks relatively young in the photo, so I'm guessing it is early to mid-1950s. I wonder what he's playing? Is it jazz, or more likely, being America, country and western? No, it couldn't be. Maybe some Louis Jordan or Big Joe Turner to get the place jumping. Kerouac hardly mentions Elvis does he? Ginsberg talks jazz.

What drew Dylan to Ginsberg – and Ginsberg to Dylan?

In many ways, I think Bob Dylan saw Ginsberg as a connector to Jack Kerouac. He loved *Mexico City Blues* apparently. I think Michael McClure extolled the virtues of that book to Dylan when they met in 1965. It was unlikely that Dylan and Kerouac would have met up but Dylan, I'm sure, would've loved to. My limited knowledge of him tells me that he was always looking for mentor-like figures back then, Ramblin' Jack, Woody Guthrie *et al*. Ginsberg was another. Ginsberg could tell Dylan all about the real Kerouac. Sure he would have enjoyed that. Though you would hardly know, given that I can't recall Dylan ever smiling. I think it has emerged just how much Allen liked that rock-style life to an extent. Being with Dylan was a big kick for him. He possibly saw him as a young bardic musician in a long line from Blake, Whitman and a few others. A fellow poet.

Do you feel that the work of the Beats benefitted from their association with rock music and musicians?

You know I always liked Kerouac with Steve Allen. Everybody thinks Allen was so straight and corny and conservative and uncool. Just what was Kerouac doing with him, they ask? But Kerouac was straight and conservative in many ways, we've come to discover in the last thirty years. That tinkling Allen piano on the album, with Kerouac reading on Allen's TV show, it was so sympathetic, a word Kerouac used to telling effect on that very show. Whenever I read those lines of Kerouac's, I hear Allen's piano in the background. It fits like a glove.

Well, Allen Ginsberg and William Burroughs benefited greatly from associations with Dylan, Patti Smith and the whole host of rock bands and punk bands they connected with for whatever reasons. David Meltzer and Clark Coolidge seemed to have been helped by their time in the band Serpent Power.

Although Burroughs seemed to have little affinity with rock music, he was adopted as a guru from the early 1970s? What do you think drew musicians into his orbit?

He was from the dark side. The Darth Vader of literature. Certain musicians would be heavily drawn to such a persona. I get the feeling that was heavily orchestrated as well. David Bowie, Lou Reed, Debbie Harry, Patti Smith, Frank Zappa *et al.*, all come to the Bunker in NYC that was home for Burroughs back in the late 1970s & 1980s. To me it was a celebrity thing, possibly brought about by those around Burroughs; James Grauerholz, Victor Bockris maybe. Nothing sinister in it, just getting Burroughs a little press and raising his profile.

History tells us he really took off in a commercial sense at that point. But, of course, Bowie, Patti Smith, were reading his books and sensing things in Burroughs that filtered through into what they did. Bowie never lifted lines from Burroughs – or did he? – but his fascination with space and alien life mirrored that of Burroughs. That implacable image of Burroughs, his deadpan look, had a hold over these guys possibly. They could see his disdain for almost everything. A lot of the time it was just people posing with Burroughs, quite cynical really. Early celebrity nonsense.

Who would you identify as the key rock musicians who have drawn on the Beat legacy?

Tom Waits, Bob Dylan, Leonard Cohen (though many would hesitate to call Cohen a rock musician), Laurie Anderson. Tom Russell, he's hardly a household name, but to me he's drawn on Kerouac and Charles Bukowski to a great extent. Many musicians flirt with ideas from the Beats.

Are there any particular tracks you feel represent this spirit?

Well, there is that Tom Waits track on his wonderful *Foreign Affairs* album, 'Jack and Neal/California Here I Come'. It isn't the best track on the album but it is a kind of homage to Jack and Neal. I always liked Canned Heat's 'On the Road Again', track from 1968. That sense of travelling light. And the B-side to Scott McKenzie's 'San Francisco' – the lovely song that it is too cool for anyone to admit to liking. It's called 'What's the Difference'. A beautiful little song about just moving on, being young: 'Who's gonna miss us in a year or so/Nobody knows us or the dreams we've been dreamin'/So what's the difference if we go?"[1] I love it. That to me is a young Kerouac and Snyder.

A number of Beats – Ginsberg and Burroughs, Ferlinghetti and McClure among them – have made recordings with a rock flavour. What do you make of those experiments?

I'm particularly fond of Michael McClure's recordings. I find his 'beast language' experiments as baffling as the next person, though I think I can sense what he's trying to do there, just that it is a dead end, a little like the cut-ups of Burroughs. McClure works well with Ray Manzarek, they've made a number of albums together and they have it honed to a fine art.

Burroughs with Kurt Cobain, it does nothing for me, a squall of noise with Burroughs battling to be heard above the din. That's just a punk celebrity collaboration. Let's annoy the neighbours. Two outcasts against the world, the sentiments are fine, but would you have that on your jukebox? Ginsberg really wanted to be a rock musician didn't he?! Desperate. He took poetry with jazz along the way.

David Meltzer has also done some clever things, way back with his Serpent Power in the 1960s and more recently poetry with added music. Interesting. And while I can't get too deeply into his work, Brion Gysin has produced some unique recordings, playing around with sounds, investigating wordplay. I wish he'd done more. One of my favourites is Kenneth Patchen with the Alan Neill Quartet, but that's jazz I guess.

When rock has expressed itself politically in the last half century has it owed something to the original idealism or activism of the Beats?

That happens so little today. Wasn't there a point where a certain generation, say between 1966 and 1971, thought that music was a key component for social change? A song could be so moving, so anthemic, it would get across the message, it would unite, cross borders and boundaries.

Music is so fragmented now. Thirty or 40 years ago there were just a few camps. A musician who had a name could champion a cause – Joan Baez is almost as well recalled for her social campaigning as her music. I'm thinking the last real political stuff from musicians might have been the Specials and 'Free Nelson Mandela'. It seems a long way from Rock Against Racism. Because there are so

---

[1] See lyrics, Scott Mackenzie, 'What's the Difference' (1967), http://www.scottmckenzie.info/difference. html [accessed 23 December 2011].

many sub-divisions in music, it is almost impossible for a musician to crossover to a big enough audience in a political way.

But certainly if you reflect back and see how poets like Richard Brautigan, McClure, Snyder even, mixed with rock musicians freely at festivals, concerts and broadsides were hammered out, protesting this or that. Think of Ed Sanders and the Fugs, the archetypal rockers with a message. How has their legacy filtered down the ages?

Is there a sense that the Beat spirit survives in rock music of today?

Interesting question. Does rock music survive today even? I watched Lou Reed and Metallica play together on television recently. It was certainly a defiant idea of rock music, an absolute blitzkrieg of the senses. There was rebellion in it, nihilism. But they didn't get it from the Beats. Long ago and far away the Beats might have influenced *why* people made rock music.

REVIEW 4 – CD: *ON THE ROAD: ORIGINAL MOTION PICTURE SOUNDTRACK*

Original Score and Songs by Gustavo Santaolalla

Original Score featuring performances by Gustavo Santaolalla, Charlie Haden and Brian Blade

Released on CD by Universal, May 2012

On 23 May 2012 after a wait extending to well over half a century, a movie version of *On the Road*, Jack Kerouac's epic tale of picaresque adventure, was finally unveiled for the world to see – at least, that is, the insider crowd of the Cannes Film Festival – with a global general release to follow in the months to follow.[1]

So often has speculation about such a production arisen – ever since Kerouac himself made a vain bid, by letter, to attract Marlon Brando to such a film project within weeks of the book's 1957 publication – that there has been an air of excitement mingling paradoxically with a mild whiff of ennui, a sense of 'at last', but also a strong feeling of 'what took them so long?'

---

[1] The film received its UK premiere on 12 October 2012 and debuted in the US on 21 December 2012. See Simon Warner, '*On the Road:* Words beat pictures despite Salles' best intentions', *Beatnicity*, 20 October 2012, http://beatnicity.com/2012/10/20/on-the-road-words-beat-pictures-despite-salles-best-intentions/ [Accessed 16 December 2012].

Francis Ford Coppola, one of the great directors and Oscar winner for both of the first two *Godfather* movies, has been in the box seat – or so it has appeared – for most of the last three decades, critically holding the rights to the text and determined to bring the most high-profile and widely consumed of the Beat Generation works to the big screen.

I think it would be fair to suggest that most Kerouac followers – and perhaps cineastes, too – have had a certain faith in Coppola's project. Here is a San Francisco-based film-maker of scope and ambition whose place in that revered pantheon of independent movie directors, which broke the standard Hollywood studio mould as the 1960s expired, is secure. His Bay Area roots allowed him, too, to trump the glittering vacuum of LA.

Coppola's blend of maverick invention and aesthetic vision coupled to an ability to attain mainstream success, appeared to provide a most suitable combination to bring such a high risk venture to satisfying fruition: one that would be respectful to the spirit of the novel but also spread the word about *On the Road* to an audience beyond the committed and converted.

Yet the road, and we ought not perhaps labour this particular metaphor for too long, has been interminable, the subject of multiple diversions and heavily pot-holed at almost every turn. In fact, few movie concepts have lain so long on the drawing board, occasionally animated by briefly fevered newspaper hints that a start is to be made, casting is underway, and locations are being scouted. But the titbits have been just that, the scent usually cold within weeks of a report, the mirage of a sighting.

There is a bizarre, yet appealing, legend that when Leonardo painted *The Last Supper* he found an energetic and glowing young man to pose as Christ. Some while later, as the painter tracked his Judas, the same individual, now dissolute and marked by several years of over-indulgence, was sufficiently worn and torn to now suitably portray the part of Jesus' dark betrayer as well.

Ripe with speculation, the casting process for *On the Road* has felt a bit like that – the handsome Adonis of 1988 would be the life-lined middle-ager a decade on, the chiselled shoo-ins for the twentysomething travellers in 2000 would just be a fraction jaded as the clocked ticked forward and the plans remained ever on ice.

Thus names as high profile as Brad Pitt, Jim Carrey and Johnny Depp have all, at various moments, been hot hints for possible frontline roles in this film, with Sal Paradise – Kerouac's alter ego – and Dean Moriarty, the character based on his friend Neal Cassady, the most coveted, but with key parts as the fictionalised Ginsberg and Burroughs and the women in the principal protagonists' lives also up for grabs.

Yet time has inexorably moved on and a new wave of celluloid talent has edged into view, hoping that eventually and ultimately, *On the Road* might actually be on the screen. And now, it truly is, with British actor Sam Riley securing the

Paradise position, Garrett Hedlund cast as Moriarty and Kristen Stewart in place as Marylou, the flighty, sexy teenager who joins the two men on their journey.

Riley has secured a reputation for performances as rock singer Ian Curtis of Joy Division in the post-punk biopic *Control* (2007) and as Pinkie in a stylish re-make of Graham Greene's *Brighton Rock* (2010). Garrett Hedlund made both an acting and a musical contribution to the 2011 country music drama *Country Strong*, while Kristen Stewart is current darling of the vampire movie cycle *Twilight*.

Other key roles are taken by Tom Sturridge as Carlo Marx – based on Ginsberg – Viggo Mortenson as Old Blue Lee, Burroughs' cipher in the story, and Kirsten Dunst as Camille, an on-screen representation of Carolyn Cassady, Neal's wife.

Futhermore, if the cast is fresh, so has the managing group evolved, with Roman Coppola, son to Francis, furnishing the producing muscle and the experienced Brazilian director, Walter Salles, a man with a reputation for cultish excellence in pictures like *The Motorcycle Diaries* (2004), the creative brain behind the movie moves that will aim to bring this odyssey to believable life for us within the darkened womb of the cinema.

But as the coos of Cannes slowly die away and with the appearance of the movie beyond the Riviera's golden mile some small way off, let us think instead of the film's soundtrack. How has music been utilised to transport this saga of the printed page to the realm of the movie theatre? And the question is particularly pertinent, we might claim, as music is such a vein of silver in the original book.

Sounds, songs, music, accompany the wayward adventurers both on the sun-drenched highway and in their nocturnal stop-overs as Paradise and Cassady head west and west, and further beyond, looking for something to feed their appetites, their imaginations, in the great open trail that is mid-century America.

Radios waft tunes in their direction, jukeboxes blare hits of the day and in the bars where they park up or head out, remarkable real-life talents gild their ears, as blind pianist George Shearing sends Dean into raptures in a Denver club and arch showman Slim Gaillard delivers his delicious jump jive in downtown San Francisco.

In fact, between the book covers, there is a parade of recognisable names from the jazz world and a stream of popular ballads of the day, embroidering the trek and few examples better illustrate the driven urgency of two friends caught in a competitive search for kicks, for romance, for salvation, than Dexter Gordon and Wardell Gray's instrumental piece 'The Hunt', as two great tenormen duel their way through solo after challenging solo.

But there is no sign of Gordon and Gray locking metaphorical – or indeed literal – horns on the 2012 CD edition of *On the Road*'s *Original Motion Picture Soundtrack*, a shame and a missed opportunity we might well think, as both allegory and entertainment. Nor does Shearing show; accompanying these many miles, there's no Miles; Prez is definitely not present; Perez Prado's Latin mambo is quite absent; and Hampton chimes no times at all.

So how does Salles hope to add melodic and rhythmic verisimilitude to his contemporary staging of the *On the Road* myth? Well, he is mainly in the hands of the much-vaunted Argentinian composer Gustavo Santaolalla who has brought sufficient atmosphere to the soundscapes of *Brokeback Mountain* in 2005 and *Babel* in 2006 to hold two Oscars of his own for those earlier contributions, a feat of some rarity in itself and a most impressive calling card.

It is his incidental music that mostly fills the disc and it does possess sufficient warmth and shade, groove and lilt, a pulse of authentic life, to propose that the film itself is not going to be short of moments embellished by Santaolalla's colourful and coolly assertive musical manners. But let us consider what does actually feature on the soundtrack recording.

Kerouac's songs have been heard in certain contexts – generally private recordings unearthed long after his death – and the album opens with a short fragment of one of the novelist's own compositions, 'Sweet Sixteen'. Greg Kramer plays Mississippi Gene, one of the hobos whom Paradise meets on a flatboard truck heading to LA in the company of a number other hitchhikers. An upbeat, lightly romantic country blues, it features Gene's cracked and road-weary voice briefly joined by a small travelling chorus.

Coati Mundi, one-time member of Kid Creole and the Coconuts, a vibraphone player with multiple other instrumental skills, has a tricky furrow to hoe, cast as the mercurial and eccentric Slim Gaillard. Yet he carries off Slim's own tune 'Yep Roc Heresy' with huge flair and authority, a fine tribute to one of the great R&B originals.

'Roman Candles' is an elegant interplay, rhythmically taut, between Santaolalla's piano and Charlie Haden's strident bass-line, a jazz cameo – wordless, as all the principal composer's pieces on the CD are – responding to arguably the most quoted passage from the book: '… burn, burn, burn like fabulous yellow roman candles exploding like spiders across the stars'.

Dinah Washington's 'Mean and Evil Blues' is a brash R&B ballad arranged for big band, wrapped around a fluent saxophone solo, its vocal delivered with a brightly dismissive tone, the strong woman scolding the erring man. Yet the fact that the recording dates from 1953 and falls outside the late 1940s years when the *On the Road* journeys occurred raises the first question about the chronological credibility of the compiler's choices.

Santaolalla's 'Lovin' IT' – inspired by the ineffable, ephemeral 'it' that Paradise and Moriarty hope to find in transit – is a slow period piece for jazz quartet, the longest of the composer's works in the soundtrack collection. Terry Harrington's saxophone provides an evocative core to the item and makes a fluent nod to Lester Young.

Next is 'The Open Road', Santaolalla's painterly tale for trio – bass and drums, yes, but led here by the composer's own dulcimer and santur, a surprising and transfixing combination, as those stringed instruments, the latter of Middle Eastern origin, add an exotic flavour of World music to the mix.

Billie Holiday delivers a 1939 version of 'A Sailboat in the Moonlight', already around a decade old by the time the characters are journeying, and this pre-war recording lends an extra layer of nostalgia to the proceedings. As Paradise and Moriarty motor, the bebop revolution already established, this older tune suggests a lost past, receding, disappearing, in the rear-view mirror.

As for bebop, Charlie Parker's seminal 'Ko-Ko', a 1945 set-piece with Dizzy Gillespie on trumpet, Curley Russell on bass and Max Roach on drums, offers a perfect example. Laid down for Savoy Records in New York City, the instrumental became a cornerstone of the new musical wave and its verve fits comfortably here.

'Memories'/'Up to Speed' begins wistfully with Santaolalla employing a toy clarinet (shades of Ornette's plastic sax), as he has earlier on a fleeting passage called 'Reminiscence'. But this section takes on more muscular shape as frenetic percussion, including drummer Brian Blade, beefs up the canvas.

Ella Fitzgerald's 'I've Got the World on a String' takes a Harold Arlen song and delivers it with a smooth sophistication, a lush arrangement from 1950 that would surely have appealed to the sentimental side of Kerouac, then 'That's IT' follows, intimating the Perez Prado latin jazz stylings referenced in the novel, with pianist Mike Lang and Brad Dutz on percussion notably lighting the blue touch paper here on Santaolalla's capable pastiche.

On 'Keep it Rollin'', Santaolalla joins forces once more with drummer Blade and Haden on bass in a somewhat shapeless piece dominated by the upright and the leader's kora, a fragile embellishment usually, is hard to identify. Much more familiar is 'Salt Peanuts', from the 1945 Savoy session as Parker and Gillespie lead the team on a Dizzy and Kenny Clarke-penned romp, a cut heard to best effect, perhaps, on 'the greatest jazz concert ever' live 1953 recording in Toronto, *Jazz at Massey Hall*.

Then Slim Gaillard, this time in person, introduces from the concert stage a typically witty frolic as 'Groove Juice Special' but the track is credited in the sleeve notes as 'Hit that Jive Jack' from *Opera in Vout (Groove Juice Symphony)*. Built on some tough bass plucking and staccato guitar chords and a bout of comic scatting, this 1945 performance is delivered with expected pizzazz.

Santaolalla's 'God is Pooh Bear' and 'I Think of Dean' each tip their hat to phrases that have left an indelible mark in the novel's coda. First the composer combines church-like organ and African drumming patterns in a slightly jarring juxtaposition. The second piece is introspective, atmospheric, meditative: a glass harmonica wheezes the breeze before toy clarinet toots a winsome refrain. Dividing them is, 'Death Letter Blues', a grinding, growling, mournful, bottleneck hymn with Son House at the controls on this 1940 work-out, both dark and deep.

The album ends with a curiosity, not unfamiliar to close Kerouac followers but in a new version. The writer's own song, 'On the Road', self-recorded at home in the early 1960s, was re-imagined on the 1999 album *Jack Kerouac Reads On the*

Road as his ghostly voice was accompanied by Vic Juris guitar and John Medeski on organ, released 30 years after the novelist's death.

Here the same thin and haunted – and haunting – Kerouac vocal is the centre-piece but Santaolalla's guitar is barely discernible, lightly sustained chords as understated as they can possibly be, spectral echoes to the tired whisper of the lyrics, more spoken word than sung, an anguished litany to the harsh lure of the highway, a sombre but touching sign-off to the album.

So what might we make of the soundtrack as an entity? It is a production that eschews the predictable devices and skips the cliches: it could after all have simply drawn on the existing cues in the novel as its main template. Instead it uses some of those hooks but finds others and, if it doesn't entirely respect historical accuracy at all times, that is perhaps a pedantic reflection we can rise above.

Ultimately, I feel this album melds its own impressionistic, indeed plausible, portrait of the excitements and temptations, the rigours and the regrets, of these restless travellers and in Gustavo Santaolalla's original score – an eclectic and engaging affair which draws on different tempos and textures and a sonic palette that is far from predictable – possesses a set of sensitive tone poems to which we can, and will, return.

On the Road – the novel Songs, artists, recordings and performances mentioned in the 1957 book	*On the Road* – the movie soundtrack The 2012 album track listing
Charlie Parker – 'Ornithology'	Greg Kramer – 'Sweet Sixteen'
Miles Davis	'Roman Candles' (Gustavo Santaolalla)
Lionel Hampton – 'Central Avenue'	Coati Mundi – 'Yep Roc Heresy'
'Breakdown'	'Reminiscence' (Gustavo Santaolalla)
Billie Holiday – 'Lover Man'	'Lovin' IT' (Gustavo Santaolalla)
'Blue Skies'	'The Open Road' (Gustavo Santaolalla)
'A Fine Romance'	'Memories/Up to Speed' (Gustavo Santaolalla)
George Shearing	Ella Fitzgerald – 'I've Got the World on a String'
'Slow Boat to China'	'That's IT' (Gustavo Santaolalla)
Slim Gaillard – 'Cement Mixer'	'Keep it Rollin'' (Gustavo Santaolalla)
Slim Gaillard – 'C-Jam Blues'	Slim Gaillard – 'Hit That Jive Jack'
Freddy Strong – 'Close Your Eyes'	'God Is Pooh Bear' (Gustavo Santaolalla)
Dizzy Gillespie & Charlie Parker – 'Congo Blues'	Son House – 'Death Letter Blues'
Willis Jackson – ''Gator Tail'	'I Think of Dean' (Gustavo Santaolalla)
Lester Young	Jack Kerouac – 'On the Road'
Wynonie Harris – 'I Like My Baby's Pudding'	
Perez Prado – 'More Mambo Jambo'	
Perez Prado – 'Mambo de Chattanooga'	
Perez Prado – 'Mambo Numero Ocho'	
Duke Ellington	

APPENDIX

Kerouac and Cassady on record

Compiled by Dave Moore and Horst Spandler
A list of recordings which relate to Jack Kerouac and/or Neal Cassady.

The qualification for inclusion is that the item must either refer directly to Kerouac or Cassady, or quote from their work.

ARTIST	TRACK TITLE	DATE	JACK/NEAL	ALBUM (if any)
Dizzy Gillespie	'Kerouac' (improvisation on 'Exactly Like You', named in 1953)	1941	Jack	The Harlem Jazz Scene –1941
Allen Ginsberg	'The Green Automobile'	1954	Neal	Holy Soul Jelly Roll
Allen Ginsberg	'Howl' (for Carl Solomon)	1956	Neal	Holy Soul Jelly Roll
Allen Ginsberg	'Sunflower Sutra'	1956	Jack	Holy Soul Jelly Roll
Ella Fitzgerald	'Like Young'	1959	Jack	Get Happy

The Nervous Set cast	'Fun Life'	1959	Jack	*The Nervous Set*
Lenny Bruce, Steve Allen	'All Alone'	1959	Jack	*Swear to Tell the Truth* (movie soundtrack)
André Previn	*The Subterraneans* (movie soundtrack)	1960	Jack	*The Subterraneans*
André Previn	'Like Blue/Blue Subterranean' (from *The Subterraneans* movie)	1960	Jack	*Like Blue*
Linda Lawson	'Like Young'	1960	Jack	*Introducing Linda Lawson*
Don Morrow	'Kerouazy'	1961	Jack	*Grimm's Hip Fairy Tales*
Perry Como	'Like Young'	1961	Jack	*For the Young at Heart*
Charles Laughton	*The Dharma Bums* (extract)	1962	Jack	*The Story-Teller*
The Barrow Poets	*Mexico City Blues* (104th Chorus)	1963	Jack	*An Entertainment of Poetry & Music*
Paul Simon	'A Simple Desultory Philippic'	1965	Jack	*The Paul Simon Song Book*
David Amram	'Summer in the West' (from *Lonesome Traveller*)	1965	Jack	*A Year in Our Land*
Bob Dylan	'Desolation Row'	1965	Jack	*Highway 61 Revisited*
Bob Dylan	'Just Like Tom Thumb's Blues'	1965	Jack	*Highway 61 Revisited*
Eric von Schmidt	'Lolita'	1967	Jack	*Take a Trip with Me*
Paul Jones	'Tarzan, etc. ...'	1967	Jack	*Love Me, Love My Friends*
Joki Freund Quintett & Harald Leipnitz	'Mordsspektakel'	1967	Jack	*Amerika (Europa?) – Ich Rede Dich An!*
Joki Freund Quintett	'Charlie Parker' (240th Chorus)	1967	Jack	*Amerika (Europa?) – Ich Rede Dich An!*

Artist	Title	Year	Character	Album
Grateful Dead	'That's it for the Other One'	1968	Neal	Anthem of the Sun
Four Jacks And A Jill	'Master Jack'	1968	Jack	Jukebox Hits Of 1968, Vol. 2
David Amram, Lynn Sheffield	'Pull My Daisy'	1971	Jack	No More Walls
Allen Ginsberg	'On Neal's Ashes'	1971	Neal	Holy Soul Jelly Roll
Michel Corringe	'Kerouac Jack'	1971	Jack	En Public
Bob Weir	'Cassidy'	1972	Neal	Ace
Aztec Two-Step	'The Persecution & Restoration of Dean Moriarty'	1972	Jack and Neal	Aztec Two-Step
David Amram	'East and West'	1973	Jack	Subway Night
David Amram	'The Fabulous Fifties'	1973	Jack	Subway Night
Gary Farr	'Mexican Sun (?)'	1973	Jack	Addressed to the Censors of Love
Road	'Come Back Jack Kerouac'	1973	Jack	Road
Mott the Hoople	'The Wheel of the Quivering Meat Conception'	1974	Jack	Brain Capers
Willie Alexander	'Kerouac'	1975	Jack	Willie Loco Boom Boom Ga Ga
Doobie Brothers	'Neal's Fandango'	1975	Neal	Stampede
Al Stewart	'Modern Times'	1975	Jack	Modern Times
Jethro Tull	'From a Dead Beat to an Old Greaser'	1976	Jack	Too Old to Rock 'n' roll
David Amram	'Pull My Daisy' (live)	1976	Jack	Summer Nights, Winter Rain
Willie Alexander	'Kerouac'	1976	Jack	Live at The Rat
Tom Waits	'Jack & Neal'	1977	Jack and Neal	Foreign Affairs

Willie Alexander	'Kerouac'	1978	Jack	Willie Alexander & the Boom-Boom Band
Sylvain Lelièvre	'Kérouac'	1978	Jack	Sylvain Lelièvre
Pataphonie	'Kerouac' (instrumental)	1978	Jack	Le Matin Blanc
The Cooper Brothers	'Old Angel Midnight'	1978	Jack	The Dream Never Dies
Jack Nitzsche	Heart Beat (movie soundtrack)	1979	Jack and Neal	Heart Beat
Dexy's Midnight Runners	'There, There, My Dear'	1980	Jack	Searching for the Young Soul Rebels
Allen Ginsberg	'The Shrouded Stranger'	1980	Jack	In Wuppertal: Poems & Songs
Allen Ginsberg	'Pull My Daisy'	1980	Jack and Neal	In Wuppertal: Poems & Songs
Allen Ginsberg	'Prayer Blues: For John Lennon'	1980	Jack	In Wuppertal: Poems & Songs
Allen Ginsberg	'Howl' (incl. 'Footnote to Howl')	1980	Jack and Neal	In Wuppertal: Poems & Songs
Grateful Dead	'Cassidy'	1981	Neal	Reckoning
Godley & Creme	'Snack Attack'	1981	Jack	Ismism
Ramblin' Jack Elliott	'912 Greens'	1981	Jack	Kerouac's Last Dream
Mark Murphy	'Parker's Mood (including The Subterraneans extract)	1981	Jack	Bop for Kerouac
Mark Murphy	'Ballad of the Sad Young Men' (including On the Road extract)	1981	Jack and Neal	Bop for Kerouac
Emil Mangelsdorff Quartett	'Blues for Allen (i.e. Allen Ginsberg's 'Footnote to Howl')	1981	Jack and Neal	Das Geheul
Emil Mangelsdorff Quartett	'Rosengärten' (excerpt from Ginsberg's 'Howl')	1981	Neal	Das Geheul
Van Morrison	'Cleaning Windows'	1982	Jack	Beautiful Vision

Artist	Song	Year	Character(s)	Release
David Amram	'This Song's for You, Jack'	1982	Jack	This Song for Jack (movie soundtrack)
King Crimson	'Neal and Jack and Me'	1982	Jack and Neal	Beat
Wah!	'The Story of the Blues – Part 2'	1982	Jack	The Way We Wah!
Blue Oyster Cult	'Burnin' for You'	1982	Jack	E.T.I.
Charlélie Couture	'La Route (Oui Mais Kérouac est Mort)'	1982	Jack	Quoi Faire
David J.	'With the Indians Permanent'	1983	Jack and Neal	Etiquette of Violence
Graham Parker	'Sounds Like Chains'	1983	Jack	The Real Macaw
Steve Tilston	'B Movie'	1983	Jack	In for a Penny...In for a Pound
The Smiths	'Pretty Girls Make Graves'	1984	Jack	The Smiths
The Icicle Works	'When it all Comes Down'	1985	Jack	Seven Singles Deep
The Long Ryders	'Southside of the Story'	1985	Jack and Neal	Looking for Lewis & Clark (10'' single)
Van Morrison	'Cleaning Windows'	1985	Jack	Live at Grand Opera House Belfast
Bob Dylan	'Something's Burning, Baby'	1985	Jack	Empire Burlesque
King Crimson	'Neal and Jack and Me' (live)	1985	Jack and Neal	The Noise-Frejus 82
It's Immaterial	'Driving Away from Home' (Dead Man's Curve mix)	1986	Jack	Ed's Funky Diner (12'' single)
Minor Characters	'1972'	1986	Jack	Minor Characters (7'' EP)
Andy Summers	'Search for Kerouac' (instrumental)	1986	Jack	Down and Out in Beverly Hills
David Carradine	Reading from On the Road	1986	Jack and Neal	On the Road (double cassette)
East Buffalo Media Association	'Sea' (from Big Sur)	1986	Jack	Sea

Artist	Track	Year		Album
East Buffalo Media Association	'Mantra for Kerouac'	1986	Jack	Sea
Jesse Garon & the Desperadoes	'The Rain Fell Down'	1986	Jack	A Cabinet of Curiosities
The Go-Betweens	'The House That Jack Kerouac Built'	1987	Jack	Tallulah
Marillion	'Torch Song'	1987	Jack	Clutching at Straws
10,000 Maniacs	'Hey Jack Kerouac'	1987	Jack	In My Tribe
The Panic Brothers	'Bivouac'	1987	Jack	In the Red
Hobo	'Üvöltés ('Howl') – Carl Solomonért – részletek (Hungarian)'	1987	Neal	Üvöltés
Pierre Flynn	'Sur la Route'	1987	Jack	Le Parfum du Hasard
Richard Séguin	'L'Ange Vagabond'	1988	Jack	Journée d'Amerique
Beatnik Beatch	'Beatnik Beatch'	1988	Jack	Beatnik Beatch
David Amram	'Pull My Daisy'	1988	Jack	Pull My Daisy & Other Jazz Classics
Crash Harmony	'(Mexico) Jack Kerouac is Dead'	1988	Jack	Wesleyan University radio tape
Roger Manning	'Pearly Blues'	1989	Jack	Roger Manning
Billy Joel	'We Didn't Start the Fire'	1989	Jack	Storm Front
Eric Andersen	'Ghosts upon the Road'	1989	Jack and Neal	Ghosts upon the Road
The Washington Squares	'(Did You Hear) Neal Cassady Died?'	1989	Jack and Neal	Fair and Square
Mark Murphy	'San Francisco' (including Big Sur extract)	1989	Jack and Neal	Kerouac Then and Now
Mark Murphy	'November in the Snow' (including On the Road extract)	1989	Jack and Neal	Kerouac Then and Now

Artist	Title	Year	Subject	Release
Ramblin' Jack Elliott	'912 Greens'	1989	Jack	Legends of Folk
Jackson Sloane	'Jack Kerouac Said'	1989	Jack	Old Angel Midnight
The Beastie Boys	'3-Minute Rule'	1989	Jack	Paul's Boutique
Mike Heron	'Mexican Girl'	1989	Jack	The Glen Row Tapes
Robert Kraft	'The Beat Generation'	1989	Jack and Neal	Quake City
Steve Earle	'The Other Kind'	1990	Jack	The Hard Way
Everything But The Girl	'Me and Bobby D'	1990	Jack	The Language of Life
Adam Ant	'Anger Inc.'	1990	Jack	Manners and Physique
R.B. and the Irregulars	'Spy in My Brain'	1990	Jack and Neal	Local Man
Les David Vincent	'Kerouac Way'	1990	Jack	Ourouni
Tynal Tywyll	'Jack Kerouac' (in Welsh)	1990	Jack	'Jack Kerouac'/'Boomerang' (single)
Elliott Murphy	'Ballad of Sal Paradise'	1990	Jack and Neal	Affairs, etc.
Van Morrison	'On Hyndford Street'	1991	Jack	Hymns to the Silence
Pete Wylie and Wah!	'Don't Lose Your Dreams'	1991	Jack	Infamy
Allen Ginsberg	Reading from The Dharma Bums	1991	Jack	The Dharma Bums (double cassette)
A House	'Endless Art'	1991	Jack	I am the Greatest
John Gorka	'The Ballad of Jamie Bee'	1991	Jack	Jack's Crows
Suzanne Vega	'Cassidy'	1991	Neal	Deadicated: Tribute to Grateful Dead
R.E.M.	'Kerouac No. 4'	1991	Jack	Outtakes of Time (bootleg)
Mingus Dynasty	'Harlene'	1991	Jack	Next Generation Performs Mingus

Artist	Song	Year	Performer	Release
Terry Riley	'Mexico City Blues Suite: 224th, 204th & 216th-B Choruses'	1991	Jack	June Buddhas
Tom Parker	Reading *The Dharma Bums* (unabridged)	1992	Jack and Neal	*The Dharma Bums* (5 cassettes or 6 CDs)
Jerry Jeff Walker	'The Man He Used to Be'	1992	Jack	Hill Country Rain
Sweet Lizard Illtet	'Mutiny Zoo'	1992	Jack	Sweet Lizard Illtet
STS	'Unterwegs'	1992	Jack	Auf Tour
Everything But The Girl	'Me and Bobby D'	1992	Jack	Acoustic
Jasmine Love Bomb	'An Announcement'	1992	Jack	Fun With Mushrooms
Loudon Wainwright III	'Road Ode'	1993	Jack	Career Moves
Jawbreaker	'Boxcar'	1993	Jack	24 Hour Revenge Therapy
United Future Organization	'Poetry and All that Jazz'	1993	Jack	United Future Organization
Naked Soul	'You, Me & Jack Kerouac'	1993	Jack	Visiting Your Planet
Barrence Whitfield with Tom Russell	'Cleaning Windows'	1993	Jack	Hillbilly Voodoo
10,000 Maniacs	'Hey Jack Kerouac' (live)	1993	Jack	MTV Unplugged
"Ranger Will" Hodgson	'Smokin' Charlie's Saxophone'	1993	Jack and Neal	Unissued studio recording
Colin Vearncombe	'Call of the Narc'	1993	Jack	'Don't Take the Silence too Hard' (CD single)
Dashboard Saviors	'Sal Paradise'	1993	Jack	Spinnin On Down
Dave Graney 'n' The Coral Snakes	'Maggie Cassidy'	1993	Jack	Night of the Wolverine

Michael Smith	'Ballad of Elizabeth Dark'	1993	Jack	*Time*
The Zimmermans	'Love Saxophone'	1994	Jack	*Cut*
Peter Droge	'Straylin Street'	1994	Jack	*Necktie Second*
Weezer	'Holiday'	1994	Jack	*Weezer*
Bad Religion	'Stranger than Fiction'	1994	Jack	*Stranger than Fiction*
Hersch Silverman	'The Jack Kerouac Blues'	1994	Jack	*Channel Nine with Hersch Silverman*
Divine Comedy	'The Booklovers'	1994	Jack	*Promenade*
Lee Ranaldo	'Spring'	1994	Jack	*Envisioning*
Jawbreaker (outro: JK w. Steve Allen)	'Condition Oakland'	1994	Jack	*24 Hour Revenge Therapy*
Matthew Good	'Euphony'	1994	Jack	*Euphony*
Tom Parker	Reading *On the Road* (unabridged)	1995	Jack and Neal	*On the Road* (7 cassettes or 9 CDs)
Loudon Wainwright III	'Cobwebs'	1995	Jack	*Grown Man*
Dmitri Matheny	'The Myth of the Rainy Night'	1995	Jack	*Red Reflections*
Terrell	'Toystore'	1995	Jack and Neal	*Angry Southern Gentleman*
Graham Parker with David Amram	Reading from *The Town and the City*	1995	Jack	*A Kerouac ROMnibus*
Graham Parker with David Amram	Reading from *Visions of Cody*	1995	Jack and Neal	*A Kerouac ROMnibus*
Graham Parker with David Amram	Reading from *The Subterraneans*	1995	Jack	*A Kerouac ROMnibus*
Michael McClure	Reading from *Mexico City Blues*	1995	Jack	*A Kerouac ROMnibus*

Ann Charters	Reading from *Mexico City Blues*	1995	Jack	*A Kerouac ROMnibus*
Daniel Lavoie	'Nantucket'	1995	Jack	*Ici*
Eric Taylor	'Dean Moriarty'	1995	Jack and Neal	*Eric Taylor*
Jon Hassell	'Sulla Strada'	1995	Jack	*I Magazzini*
Reg E. Gaines	'Ode to Jack Kerouac'	1995	Jack	*Sweeper Don't Clean My Street*
Fatboy Slim	'Neal Cassady Starts Here' (with voice of Ken Babbs)	1995	Neal	'Santa Cruz' (12" single)
Tony Imbo	'Streaking The Days Asunder'	1995	Jack	*The Golden Age*
Cracker	'Big Dipper'	1996	Jack	*The Golden Age*
Graham Parker with David Amram	Reading from *Visions of Cody*	1996	Jack and Neal	*Visions of Cody* (double cassette)
Allen Ginsberg	Reading *Mexico City Blues*	1996	Jack	*Mexico City Blues* (double cassette)
Holy Barbarians	'Bodhisattva'	1996	Jack	*Cream*
David Byrne	'It Goes Back' (from 'Origins of Beat Generation')	1996	Jack	*Off Beat: A Red Hot Sound Trip*
Mike Heron	'Mexican Girl'	1996	Jack	*Where the Mystics Swim*
Aztec Two-Step	'The Persecution & Restoration of Dean Moriarty'	1996	Jack and Neal	*Highway Signs: 25th Anniversary Concert*
Fun Lovin' Criminals	'Come Find Yourself'	1996	Jack	*Come Find Yourself*
The Gathering Field	'Lost In America'	1996	Jack	*Lost In America*
The Gathering Field	'Are You an Angel?'	1996	Jack	*Lost In America*
The Gathering Field	'Midnight Ghost'	1996	Jack	*Lost In America*

I Mother Earth	'Hello Dave'	1996	Jack	Scenery & Fish
BR5-49	'Bettie, Bettie'	1996	Jack and Neal	Live From Robert's (EP)
Mike Plume Band	Various	1996	Jack	Jump Back Kerouac
Major Nelson	'Living Like Kerouac'	1996	Jack	Big Stir
The Bloodhound Gang	'Asleep At The Wheel'	1996	Jack	One Fierce Beer Coaster
Carolyn Cassady	Reading from Off The Road	1996	Jack and Neal	Women of the Beat Generation (4 cassettes)
ruth weiss	Reading from Nobody's Wife (by Joan Haverty)	1996	Jack	Women of the Beat Generation (4 cassettes)
Joyce Johnson	Reading from Minor Characters	1996	Jack	Women of the Beat Generation (4 cassettes)
Mary Norbert Körte	Reading from Trainsong (by Jan Kerouac)	1996	Jack	Women of the Beat Generation (4 cassettes)
Anne Waldman	'I Am The Guard!'	1996	Jack	Women of the Beat Generation (4 cassettes)
Holy Barbarians	'It Ain't Over Yet (For Jack Kerouac)'	1997	Jack	Beat.itude, A New Jazz Beat
Morphine	'Kerouac'	1997	Jack	B-Sides & Otherwise
Various Artists	Various readings from Kerouac's work	1997	Jack	Kerouac: Kicks Joy Darkness
Graham Parker with David Amram	Reading from Kerouac's unpublished journals 1949–50	1997	Jack	Kerouac: Kicks Joy Darkness (Japanese edition)
Matt Dillon	'The Thrashing Doves'	1997	Jack	Kerouac: Kicks Joy Darkness (Japanese edition)
Lydia Lunch	'How to Meditate + Mexican Loneliness'	1997	Jack	Kerouac: Kicks Joy Darkness (Japanese edition)

Belle and Sebastian	'Le Pastie de la Burgeoisie'	1997	Jack	3 .. 6 .. 9 Seconds of Light
Subincision	'Kerouac'	1997	Jack and Neal	Subincision
Silent Bear	'Kerouac's Child'	1997	Jack	River Drum Child
Patti Smith	'Spell' ("Footnote to Howl" by Allen Ginsberg)	1997	Jack and Neal	Peace and Noise
Bob Martin	'The Old Worthen'	1997	Jack	The River Turns the Wheel
Bob Martin	'Stella Kerouac'	1997	Jack	The River Turns the Wheel
RatDog	'Cassidy'	1997	Neal	Furthur More
Umka	'Kerouac (Treplo)'	1997	Jack	Dozhili, Mama
Various Artists	The Last Time I Committed Suicide (movie soundtrack)	1997	Neal	The Last Time I Committed Suicide
X Generation	'Sal's Paradise'	1997	Jack	Kerouac's Legacy
X Generation	'Nebraskan Dawn' (Dedicated to Cody)	1997	Neal	Kerouac's Legacy
Beat Hotel	'Beathotel'	1997	Jack	Beathotel
DJs Wally & Swingsett	'Smoking Up The Music'	1997	Jack	Dog Leg Left
Conrad	'Jack Kerouac'	1997	Jack	Conrad
The Dinner Is Ruined	'I Ain't No Neal Cassidy'	1997	Neal	Elevator Music for Non-Claustrophobic People
The Lord High Fixers	'Sal Paradise Delegation'	1997	Jack	Group Improvisation That's Music
Headswim	'Old Angel Midnight'	1997	Jack	Despite Yourself
Sportfreunde Stiller	'On the Road – Unterwegs'	1998	Jack and Neal	Thonträger

Dr. John	'John Gris'	1998	Jack (?)	Anutha Zone
Umka	'Kerouac (Treplo)' (live)	1998	Jack	Live in Fakel
Mike Heron & Robin Williamson	'Mexican Girl'	1998	Jack	Bloomsbury 1997
Jim Dunleavy	'Lonesome Travelers'	1998	Jack	Steady Rollin'
David Amram	'This Song's for You, Jack'	1998	Jack	Rebels (documentary soundtrack)
Tom Parker	Reading Big Sur (unabridged)	1998	Jack and Neal	Big Sur (4 cassettes or 5 CDs)
Jeremy Gloff	'Kerouac's Dead'	1998	Jack	Jeremy Gloff, 1998, Vol. 9
Beekler	'Dean Moriarty'	1998	Neal	In Layman's Terms
Richard Bicknell	'Dean Moriarty'	1998	Neal	Mayflower
Ron Whitehead	'The Other'	1998	Jack	Tapping My Own Phone
Ron Whitehead	'San Francisco, May 1993'	1998	Jack	Tapping My Own Phone
Ron Whitehead	'Asheville'	1998	Neal	Tapping My Own Phone
Five Iron Frenzy	'Superpowers'	1998	Jack	Our Newest Album Ever
David Nelson	'Kerouac'	1999	Jack and Neal	Visions under the Moon
Tom Waits with Primus	'On the Road'	1999	Jack	Jack Kerouac Reads On the Road
Guy Clark	'Cold Dog Soup'	1999	Jack	Cold Dog Soup
R.B. Morris	'Distillery'	1999	Jack	Zeke and the Wheel
Hot Sauce Johnson	'Jack Kerouac'	1999	Jack	Truck Stop Jug Hop
Richard Thompson	'Sibella'	1999	Jack	Mock Tudor
Patti Smith	'Spell' (live)	1999	Jack and Neal	Gung Ho Giveaway

Robert Briggs	'Lawrence Ferlinghetti, Jack Kerouac, Gary Snyder, Allen Ginsberg'	1999	Jack	*Poetry & the 1950s: Homage to the Beat Generation*
Michael Johnathon	'Kerouac Alley'	1999	Jack	*The Road*
Christian Brückner	'Beat-Glückselig' (from 'Origins of Beat Generation')	1999	Jack and Neal	*Brückner Beat*
Mary Gauthier	'Drag Queens in Limousines'	1999	Jack	*Drag Queens In Limousines*
Helen Shapiro	'32nd Chorus' from *Orlando Blues*	1999	Jack	*Jazz Poetry*
Ian Dury	'Skid Row Wine'	1999	Jack	*Beat Poetry* (2 CDs)
Anne Waldman	'Hymn'	1999	Jack	*Beat Poetry* (2 CDs)
Anne Waldman	'Pome on Doctor Sax'	1999	Jack	*Beat Poetry* (2 CDs)
David Alpher	'Tribute to Kerouac'	1999	Jack	*American Reflections*
Josh Lamkin	'Kerouac's Advice'	1999	Jack	*UNCA Music Biz*
Gregory Wiest *et al.*	'Chorus 172' (from *Mexico City Blues*)	1999	Jack	*Beat*
Frank Muller	Reading *On the Road* (unabridged)	1999	Jack and Neal	*On the Road* (10 CDs or 8 cassettes)
Alexander Adams	Reading *On the Road* (unabridged)	1999	Jack and Neal	*On the Road* (9 CDs or 8 cassettes)
Blue Room	'Jack Kerouac'	1999	Jack	*Into the Night*
Guy Forsyth	'Children of Jack'	1999	Jack	*Can You Live Without*
Jonathan Marosz	Reading *The Dharma Bums* (unabridged)	2000	Jack and Neal	*The Dharma Bums* (5 cassettes)
Grover Gardner	Reading *Orpheus Emerged* (unabridged)	2000	Jack	*Orpheus Emerged* (3 CDs)
Kevn Kinney	'Kerouac'	2000	Jack	*The Flower & the Knife*

Kurt Elling	'The Rent Party'	2000	Jack	*Live in Chicago*
Leona Naess	'Charm Attack'	2000	Jack (?)	*Comatised*
Umka	'Kerouac (Treplo)'	2000	Jack	*Dandelion Cinema*
Brian Hassett	'All of Us'/'Hearing Shearing' (including *On the Road* extract)	2000	Jack	Live at CBGB's, NYC, April 12th, 2000
Guy Clark	'Cold Dog Soup (live)'	2000	Jack	Austin City Limits performance
The Mighty Manatees with David Amram	'Smokin' Charlie's Saxophone'	2000	Jack and Neal	Live at Bitter End, NYC, April 22nd, 2000
Ralph	'Goodbye Jack Kerouac'	2000	Jack	*This Is for the Night People*
Ralph	'Pull My Daisy'	2000	Jack	*This Is for the Night People*
Cosmic Rough Riders	'Ungrateful'	2000	Jack	*Deliverance*
Matt Dillon	Reading *On the Road* (unabridged)	2000	Jack and Neal	*On the Road* (10 CDs)
Barenaked Ladies	'Car Seat'	2000	Jack	*Maroon*
Phased 4°F	'Jack-Off All Trades'	2000	Jack	*Painfield* (10" EP)
Allan Taylor	'Kerouac's Dream'	2000	Jack	*Colour To The Moon*
The Spanish Armada	'Baby Fever (Kerouac mix)'	2000	Jack	*Brave New Girl*
Shawn Mullins	'North on 95'	2000	Jack	*Beneath the Velvet Sun*
Bell X1	'Beautiful Madness'	2000	Jack and Neal	*Neither am I*
Flanagan Ingham Quartet	'Textile Lunch on Moody St' (suite – 4 tracks)	2000	Jack	*Textile Lunch*
David Amram et al.	'Various'	2001	Jack and Neal	*Spirit: A Tribute to Jack Kerouac*
Graham Cournoyer	'One for Jack'	2001	Jack	*One for Jack*

Anne Waldman	'Jack Kerouac Dream'	2001	Jack	Alchemical Elegy
John Gorka	'Oh Abraham'	2001	Jack	The Company You Keep
Michael Ubaldini	'Old Angel Midnight (Song to Kerouac)'	2001	Jack	American Blood
Tony Imbo	'Streaking the Days Asunder' (remix)	2001	Jack	Reinventing Man
Don Michael Sampson	'Come On Jack'	2001	Jack	Black Flower
Zwan	'Freedom Ain't What it Used to Be'	2001	Jack	'Honestly' (CD single)
Ron Whitehead	'Psychic Supper'	2001	Jack	Hozomeen Jam (EP)
Railroad Earth	'Railroad Earth'	2001	Jack	The Black Bear Session
Migala	'Kerouac'	2002	Jack	Diciembre, 3 a.m.
Dale Morningstar	'2000 Kerouac Girl'	2002	Jack	I Grew Up On Sodom Road
John Hasbrouck	'Kerouac Alone in Des Moines'	2002	Jack	Ice Cream
Guided by Voices	'Kerouac Never Drove, So He Never Drove Alone'	2002	Jack	Tropic of Nipples
Curse, with David Amram & Marc Ribot	'Pull My Daisy'	2002	Jack	'Pull My Daisy'/'Graveyard Shuffle' (single)
Valerie Lagrange	'Kerouac'	2002	Jack	Fleuve Congo
Our Lady Peace	'All For You'	2002	Jack	Gravity
David McMillin	'The Legend of Jack Kerouac'	2002	Jack	Where I Belong
Spitznagel	'Kerouac's Treehouse'	2002	Jack	Under the Plane
Kenn Kweder	'Jack Kerouac'	2002	Jack	Kwederology Vol. 1
Kenn Kweder	'Cassady's Bible'	2002	Neal	Kwederology Vol. 1

Chris Keup	'Close Your Eyes Maggie Cassidy'	2002	Jack	*The Subject of Some Regret*
BAP	'Schluss, Aus, OK!'	2002	Jack	'Schluss, Aus, Okay' (CD single)
Goodman County	'Kerouac Sings the Blues'	2002	Jack	*Pictures from a Moving Vehicle*
Richard Meltzer et al.	'Kerouac Never Drove, So He Never Drove Alone'	2002	Jack	*Tropic of Nipples*
Robert Creeley et al.	*Doctor Sax and the Great World Snake* (Kerouac's screenplay)'	2003	Jack	*Doctor Sax and the Great World Snake* (2 CDs)
Eric Andersen	'Beat Avenue'	2003	Jack	*Beat Avenue*
Allan Taylor	'The Beat Hotel'	2003	Jack	*Hotels and Dreamers*
Spitalfield	'I Loved the Way She Said L.A.'	2003	Jack	*Remember Right Now*
Steve Lacy	'Wave Lover' (from *Lucien Midnight*)	2003	Jack	*The Beat Suite*
Alfred Howard	'Kerouac Incarnate'	2003	Jack	*14 Days of the Universe in Incandescent Bloom*
Jack Shea, JD Caioulet & J Sanderson	'On the Road'	2003	Jack	*Who Owns Jack Kerouac?* (movie soundtrack)
Jack Shea, JD Caioulet & J Sanderson	'Jack Reaches God'	2003	Jack	*Who Owns Jack Kerouac?* (movie soundtrack)
Ron Whitehead & David Amram	'To Dream in Kerouac's Playground'	2003	Jack	*Kentucky Blues*
Ron Whitehead & David Amram	'Amram's Kentucky Rap'	2003	Jack	*Kentucky Blues*
Julie Geller	'The American Night (Kerouac's Song)'	2003	Jack	*This Road*
Mars Arizona	'Railroad Song'	2003	Jack	*Love Songs from the Apocalypse*

Artist	Song	Year	Character	Album
Reckless Kelly	'Desolation Angels'	2003	Jack	Under the Table & Above the Sun
Dayna Kurtz	'Just Like Jack'	2003	Jack	Postcards from Downtown
Rusted Root	'Jack Kerouac'	2004	Jack	Rusted Root Live
Seedy Gonzales	'Kerouac & Burroughs'	2004	Jack	Seedy Gonzales
Walter T. Ryan	'Burnin' (Like a Kerouac Coyote)'	2004	Jack	Underdog American Music
Max Joshua Klaooerman	'In Spiteful Dedication Jack Kerouac'	2004	Jack	This Side of Everywhere: Poet's Monday
Mark Boucot	'Cassady's Ashes'	2004	Neal	Mark Boucot
Mark Boucot	'Beatific Nights'	2004	Jack	Mark Boucot
Manual & Syntaks	'Sal Paradise'	2004	Jack	Golden Sun
Kevn Kinney	'Epilogue Epitaph In A Minor'	2004	Jack	Sun Tangled Angel Revival
Erin Jordan	'Road to Eureka'	2004	Jack	Land of Milk and Honey
Styrofoam (feat. Ben Gibbard)	'Couches in Alleys'	2004	Jack	Nothing's Lost
The Go-Betweens	'The House that Jack Kerouac Built'	2004	Jack	Live in London
Garagecow Ensemble	'I Never Slept with Allen Ginsberg'	2004	Jack	Saint Stephen's Dream
Tom Russell	'Border Lights'	2005	Jack	Hotwalker: Charles Bukowski & A Ballad For Gone America
Tom Russell	'Harry Partch, Jack Kerouac, Lenny Bruce'	2005	Jack	Hotwalker: Charles Bukowski & A Ballad For Gone America
Bap Kennedy	'Rock and Roll Heaven'	2005	Jack and Neal	The Big Picture
Bap Kennedy	'Moriarty's Blues' (with the voice of Carolyn Cassady)	2005	Jack and Neal	The Big Picture

Artist	Song	Year	Character	Album
Gang 90	'Jack Kerouac'	2005	Jack	*Sexual Life of the Savages*
Rock N Roll Monkey & the Robots	'Toss it Back Like Kerouac'	2005	Jack	*Detroit Trauma*
Ron Whitehead	'Searching for David Amram'	2005	Jack	*Closing Time*
Ron Whitehead	'Allen Ginsberg: The Bridge, Parts 2 & 3'	2005	Jack	*Closing Time*
Ron Whitehead	'From Hank Williams' Grave'	2005	Jack and Neal	*Closing Time*
Ron Whitehead	'Calling the Toads'	2005	Jack	*Closing Time*
Jimmy LaFave	'Bohemian Cowboy Blues'	2005	Jack	*Blue Nightfall*
Laura Ranieri	'Like Kerouac'	2005	Jack	*Southbound*
Sage Francis	'Escape Artist'	2005	Jack	*A Healthy Distrust*
The Clients	'Dharma Bum'	2005	Jack	*Straycat*
Denny Brown	'Kerouac "On the Road"'	2006	Jack and Neal	*No Middle Ground*
Haiku	Various tracks with a selection from Kerouac's haiku	2006	Jack	*The Kerouac Project*
Jeff Root	'Kerouac King Kong'	2006	Jack	*Kerouac King Kong*
Jim Dickinson	'Maggie Cassidy'	2006	Jack	*Fishing with Charlie and Other Selected Readings*
Jonathan Byerley	'I Got Over Kerouac'	2006	Jack	*Hymns and Fragments*
Mads Oustal	'På kjøret' (= *On the Road* in Norwegian)	2006	Jack and Neal	*På kjøret* (10 CDs)
Milagro Saints	'Kerouac'	2006	Jack	*Let It Rain*
Orko	'Hello Dean Moriarty'	2006	Neal	*Creating Short Fiction*

Artist	Title	Year	Character	Album
The Daisy Cutters	'Second Hand Kerouac'	2006	Jack	Lines and Sinkers (The EP Years)
The Hold Steady	'Stuck Between Stations'	2006	Jack	Boys and Girls in America
Tom Waits	'Home I'll Never Be'	2006	Jack	Orphans: Brawlers, Bawlers & Bastards
Tom Waits	'On the Road'	2006	Jack	Orphans: Brawlers, Bawlers & Bastards
Top Models	'Kerouac'	2006	Jack	To the Maximum
Beekler	'Dean Moriarty'	2007	Neal	In Layman's Terms
Jocelyn Arem	'Kerouac'	2007	Jack	What the Mirror Said
Mark Handley & The Bone Idols	'Jack Kerouak AKA Anywhere But Here'	2007	Jack	The Land of Song
Michael Hansonis	'Unterwegs' (= On the Road in German, abridged)	2007	Jack and Neal	Unterwegs (6 CDs)
Mudvayne	'On the Move'	2007	Jack	By the People, for the People
Steven Light & the Black Sand	'Cassady'	2007	Neal	Sweet Transmission
The Weather Underground	'Neal Cassady'	2007	Neal	Psalms & Shanties
Will Patton	'On the Road'	2007	Jack and Neal	On the Road (10 CDs)
Tim Minchin	'Inflatable You'	2007	Jack	So Live (DVD)
	On the Road (Penguin Readers simplified text)	2008	Jack and Neal	On the Road (Penguin Readers audio CD)
BAP	'Wat für e' Booch'	2008	Jack and Neal	Radio Pandora (plugged)
Blackwater Tribe	'Jack Realized Beat'	2008	Jack	Blackwater Runs Deep

Artist	Song	Year	Character	Album
Clifton Roy & Folkstringer	'Kerouac's Folksong'	2008	Jack	Where the Rock Meets the Rail
Danny Campbell	'Wake Up – A Life of the Buddha'	2008	Jack	Wake Up: A Life of the Buddha (5 CDs)
David Anderson	'Recollections of Neal Cassady'	2008	Neal and Jack	Layover in Reno
Five Iron Frenzy	'Superpowers'	2008	Jack	Proof That the Youth are Revolting
Individual	'Kerouac'	2008	Jack	Fantastic Smile
John Ventimiglia	'On the Road – The Original Scroll'	2008	Jack and Neal	On the Road (10 CDs)
Joy Askew	'Kerouac'	2008	Jack	The Pirate of Eel Pie
Ray Porter	'And the Hippos Were Boiled in Their Tanks'	2008	Jack	And the Hippos Were Boiled in Their Tanks (4 CDs)
Steve Allee Sextet	'Kerouac' (instrumental)	2008	Jack	New York in the Fifties (soundtrack)
Swallows	'Kerouac'	2008	Jack	Songs for Strippers (and Other Professions)
The Areola Treat	'Kerouac'	2008	Jack	The Areola Treat
The Five Corners Quintet, feat. Mark Murphy	'Kerouac Days in Montana'	2008	Jack	Hot Corner
The Maple State	'Starts with Dean Moriarty'	2008	Neal	Say Scientists
Tim Young Band	'Kerouac'	2008	Jack	The Cost
Van Bluus (vocal Horst Spandler)	'White Boy Blue'	2008	Jack	White Boy Blue
William S. Burroughs	'Speaking of Jack Kerouac' (various readings)	2008	Jack	A Spoken Breakdown
Yer Cronies	'Kerouac'	2008	Jack	When I Grow Up

Artist	Song/Track	Year	Reference	Album
BAP	'Unterwegs'/'Blue in Green'	2009	Jack and Neal	*Live und in Farbe*
BAP	'Wat für e' Booch'	2009	Jack and Neal	*Live und in Farbe*
Chris Hickey	'Kerouac'	2009	Jack and Neal	*Razzmatazz*
Frank Turner	'Poetry of the Deed'	2009	Jack	*Poetry of the Deed*
Jay Farrar & Benjamin Gibbard	Various tracks/*One Fast Move Or I'm Gone: Music From Kerouac's Big Sur* (movie soundtrack)	2009	Jack	*One Fast Move Or I'm Gone: Music From Kerouac's Big Sur* (movie soundtrack)
Tereu Tereu	'Neal Cassady'	2009	Neal	*All That Keeps Us Together*
The Low Anthem	'Home I'll Never Be'	2009	Jack	*Oh My God, Charlie Darwin*
Wreak Havoc	'Kerouac's Ghost'	2009	Jack	*Abandon Everything*
Chuck Perrin	'It Ain't Over Yet (for Jack Kerouac)'	2009	Jack	*Beat.titude – The Holy Barbarians*
Bob Martin	'Jack Kerouac'	2009	Jack	*Live tt The Bull Run*
Bob Martin	'Stella Kerouac'	2009	Jack	*Live at The Bull Run*
R.B. Morris	'Spy in the Brain'	2010	Jack and Neal	*Spies Lies and Burning Eyes*
R.B. Morris	'Father Fisheye'	2010	Jack	*Spies Lies and Burning Eyes*
Felix Goeser/Florian von Manteuffel	'Und die Nilpferde kochten in ihren Becken (Hippos)'	2010	Jack	*Und die Nilpferde kochten in ihren Becken* (4 CDs)
Billy Koumantzelis	Various narrations	2010	Jack	*On the Lowell Beat: My Time With Jack Kerouac*
The 757s	'Kerouac'	2010	Jack	*Last Laugh*
Papa Razzi & the Photogs	'Jack Kerouac Celebrated a Group of Irresponsible Dudes'	2010	Jack	*Songs About Great Literary Giants*
Brooke Fraser	'Jack Kerouac'	2010	Jack	*Flags*

Thieves and Villains	'Song For Dean Moriarty'	2010	Neal	South America
Frisco Jenny	'La Balada de Dean Moriarty'	2010	Neal	El Dolor del Escorpion
Andrew McConathy	'Dean Moriarty's Blues'	2010	Neal	Light of the Eye
Mort Weiss & Peter Marx	Readings of Kerouac	2011	Jack	Mort Weiss Meets Bill Cunliffe
Alanna Eileen	'Cassady and Kerouac'	2012	Jack and Neal	(single)
C.P. Carrington	'Phantom Thumb'	2012	Jack	The Valley
C.P. Carrington	'Neal Cassady, Parts 1 & 2'	2012	Neal	The Valley
C.P. Carrington	'Counting Tracks'	2012	Neal	The Valley
Spielgusher	'Kerouac'	2012	Jack	Spielgusher
Gustavo Santaolalla et al.	On the Road (movie soundtrack)	2012	Jack and Neal	On the Road: Original Motion Picture Soundtrack

Thanks to Ralph Alfonzo, Dan Barth, Adrien Begrand, Frank Bor, Richard Cooper, Diane De Rooy, Neil Douglas, Brian Hassett, John Low, Chris Moore, Frances Moore, Michael Powell, Stephen Ronan, and alphabetically last but by no means least, Horst Spandler.

To view online, visit: http://www.beatbookcovers.com/music/

Author's note: Thank you to compilers Dave Moore and Horst Spandler for granting permission to use this material.

BIBLIOGRAPHY

Adler, Lou, 'Music, love and promoters', *The Sixties*, edited by Linda Rosen Obst (New York: Random House/*Rolling Stone*, 1977), pp. 204–7.

Allis, Michael, *British Music and Literary Context: Artistic Connections in the Long Nineteenth Century* (Woodbridge: Boydell Press, 2012).

Amram, David, *Offbeat: Celebrating with Kerouac* (New York: Thunder's Mouth Press, 2002).

—*Upbeat: Nine Lives of a Musical Cat* (Boulder, CO: Paradigm Publishers, 2008).

—*Vibrations: The Adventures and Musical Times of David Amram* (Boulder, CO: Paradigm Publishers, 2010).

Anderson, Terry H., *The Movement and the Sixties: Protest in America from Greensboro to Wounded Knee* (Oxford: Oxford University Press, 1995).

Ankeny, Jason, 'Ani DiFranco – Biography', *All Music Guide*, http://www.allmusic.com/artist/ani-difranco-p38383/biography [accessed 28 February 2012].

Aronowitz, Al, *Bob Dylan and the Beatles: The Best of the Blacklisted Journalist, Vol. 1* (Bloomington, IN: Authorhouse, 2004).

Bangs, Lester, 'Elegy for a Desolation Angel', *The Rolling Stone Book of the Beats: The Beat Generation and the Counterculture*, edited by Holly George-Warren (London: Bloomsbury, 1999) pp. 140–3.

Banks, Lynne Reid, *The L-Shaped Room* (London: Chatto & Windus, 1960).

Barstow, Stan, *A Kind of Loving* (London: Michael Joseph, 1960).

BBC News, 'George Harrison: The quiet Beatle', obituary, BBC News, 30 November 2001, http://news.bbc.co.uk/1/hi/entertainment/music/1432634.stm [accessed 18 February 2012].

Beck, Henry Cabot, 'From Beat to beatnik', *The Rolling Stone Book of the Beats: The Beat Generation and the Counterculture*, edited by Holly George-Warren (London: Bloomsbury, 1999), pp. 95–105.

Bengala, 'The intuitive lure of flesh: Genesis P-Orridge's erotic mailart' *Painful but Fabulous: The Lives and Art of Genesis P-Orridge*, edited by Genesis P-Orridge (New York: Soft Skull Press, 2002), pp. 111–19.

Bershaw, Andy, 'Concert summary', The Rolling Thunder Revue Concert, Technical University (Lowell, MA), 2 November 1975, *Wolfgang's Vault*, http://www.wolfgangsvault.com/the-rolling-thunder-revue/concerts/technical-university-november-02-1975.html [accessed 5 September 2011].

Bert, Bob, 'This is a story (a very special story) it's about … Breyer P-Orridge', *BB Gun* magazine, Issue #7, 2004.

Birmingham, Jed, 'William Burroughs and Norman Mailer', 14 October 2009, *Reality*

Studio, http://realitystu.dio.org/bibliographic-bunker/william-burroughs-and-norman-mailer/ [accessed 16 October 2011].

—'Fuck You press archive', *Reality Studio*, http://realitystudio.org/bibliographic-bunker/fuck-you-press-archive/ [accessed 4 January 2012].

Bockris, Victor, *Lou Reed: The Biography* (London: Hutchinson, 1994).

—*New York Babylon: From Beat to Punk* (London: Omnibus, 1998).

—*Patti Smith* (London: Fourth Estate, 1998).

Bowen, Phil, *A Gallery to Play to: The Story of the Mersey Poets* (Exeter: Stride Publications, 1999).

Bradbury, Malcolm, *The Modern American Novel*, 2nd edn. (Oxford: Opus, 1992).

Braine, John, *Room at the Top* (London: Arrow, 1989, orig. pub. 1957).

Brinkley, Douglas, 'The American journey of Jack Kerouac', *The Rolling Stone Book of the Beats: The Beat Generation and the Counterculture*, edited by Holly George-Warren (London: Bloomsbury, 1999).

—CD sleeve notes, *Jack Kerouac Reads On the Road* (Rykodisc, 1999).

Brown, Pete, *White Rooms and Imaginary Westerns: On the Road with Ginsberg, Writing for Clapton and Cream – An Anarchic Odyssey* (London: JR Books, 2010).

Buckley, David, *Strange Fascination: David Bowie – The Definitive Story* (London: Virgin, 2005).

Burroughs, William S., *Junky* (Harmondsworth: Penguin, 1977, orig. pub. 1953).

—*Naked Lunch* (London: Flamingo, 1993, orig. pub. 1959).

—*The Soft Machine* (London: Corgi, 1970, orig. pub. 1961).

—*The Ticket that Exploded* (London: Calder & Boyars, 1968, orig. pub. 1962).

—*Nova Express* (London: Panther, 1968, orig. pub. 1964).

—*Queer* (London: Penguin, 2010, orig. pub. 1985).

—*Cities of the Red Night* (London: John Calder, 1981).

—*The Place of Dead Roads* (London: John Calder, 1984, orig. pub. 1983).

—'The cut-up method of Brion Gysin', *RE/Search* #4/5, 'A Special Book Issue: William S. Burroughs, Brion Gysin and Throbbing Gristle', edited by V. Vale and Andrea Juno (San Francisco, CA: V/Search Publications, 1984), pp. 35–6.

—*The Western Lands* (London: Picador, 1987).

Carr, Roy, Brian Case and Fred Dellar, *The Hip: Hipsters, Jazz and the Beat Generation* (London: Faber, 1986).

Carroll, Cath, *Tom Waits* (New York: Thunder's Mouth Press, 2000).

Carroll, Jim, *Living at the Movies* (New York: Grossman, 1973).

—*The Basketball Diaries* (New York: Penguin, 1978).

—*Forced Entries: The Downtown Diaries 1971–73* (New York: Penguin, 1987).

Carson, Rachel, *The Silent Spring* (Boston, MA: Houghton Mifflin, 1962).

Cassady, Carolyn, *Off the Road: My Years with Cassady, Kerouac and Ginsberg* (London: Black Spring, 1990).

Castaneda, Carlos, *The Teachings of Don Juan* (Berkeley, CA: University of California Press, 1968).

Caveney, Graham, *The 'Priest', They Call Him: The Life and Legacy of William S. Burroughs* (London: Bloomsbury, 1997).

Charters, Ann, *Kerouac* (London: André Deutsch, 1974).

—'Bob Dylan', *The Portable Beat Reader* (New York: Viking, 1992), pp. 370–9.

—'Foreword', *Girls Who Wore Black: Women Writing the Beat Generation*, edited by Ronna C. Johnson and Nancy M. Grace (New Brunswick, NJ: Rutgers University Press, 2002), pp. ix–xii.

Charters, Ann (ed.), *The Portable Beat Reader* (New York: Viking, 1992).
—*The Penguin Book of the Beats* (London: Penguin, 1993).
Charters, Sam, 'Jack Kerouac and jazz', '*On the Road*, 25th Anniversary Conference', Naropa Institute, Boulder, Colorado, 1982, http://www.archive.org/details/On_the_road__The_Jack_Kerouac_conference_82P261 [accessed 28 February 2012].
Clarke, Jonathan, *Can't Buy Me Love: The Beatles, Britain and America* (London: Portrait, 2007).
Cohen, Leonard, *Spice-Box of the Earth* (New York: Viking Press, 1961).
—*The Favourite Game* (New York: Viking Press, 1963).
—*Flowers for Hitler* (London: Cape, 1973, orig. pub. 1964).
—*Beautiful Losers* (London: Cape, 1970, orig. pub. 1966).
Cook, Bruce, *The Beat Generation* (New York: Charles Scribner's Sons, 1971).
Coolidge, Clark, *Now it's Jazz: Writings on Kerouac and the Sounds* (Albuquerque, NM: Living Batch Press, 1999).
Copetas, Craig, 'Beat godfather meets glitter mainman: Burroughs and David Bowie', *The Rolling Stone Book of the Beats: The Beat Generation and the Counterculture*, edited by Holly George-Warren (London: Bloomsbury, 1999), pp. 193–202.
Corso, Gregory, *Gasoline* (San Francisco, CA: City Lights, 1958).
—*Bomb* (San Francisco, CA: City Lights, 1958).
Coupe, Laurence, *Beat Sound, Beat Vision: The Beat Spirit and the Popular Song* (Manchester: Manchester University Press, 2007).
Cross, Charles R., *Heavier than Heaven: The Biography of Kurt Cobain* (London: Sceptre, 2002).
Crumb, Jesse and Erica Detlefsen, 'David Meltzer', No. 30, *Beat Characters*, card collection (Northampton, MA: Kitchen Sink Press, 1995).
Cunliffe, Marcus, *The Literature of the United States*, 4th edn. (Harmondsworth: Penguin, 1986).
—(ed.), *American Literature Since 1900* (London: Sphere, 1988).
Dalton, Stephen, 'Bill's excellent adventure', William Burroughs obituary, *New Musical Express*, 16 August 1997.
Da Sousa Correa, Delia, *Phrase and Subject: Studies in Literature and Music* (Oxford: Legenda, 2006).
Davies, Norman, *Europe: A History* (London: Pimlico, 1997).
De Beauvoir, Simone, *The Second Sex* (London: Vintage, 1997).
Delaney, Shelagh, *A Taste of Honey* (London: Methuen, 2006).
Denselow, Robin, *When the Music's Over: The Story of Political Pop* (London: Faber, 1989).
DeVeaux, Scott, *The Birth of Bebop: A Social and Musical History* (London: Picador, 1997).
Di Prima, Diane, *This Kind of Bird Flies Backward* (New York: Totem Press, 1958).
—*Memoirs of a Beatnik* (London: Marion Boyars, 2002, orig. pub 1969).
—*Revolutionary Letters* (San Francisco, CA: Last Gasp, 2007, orig. pub. 1971).
DJ Spooky, 'All consuming images: DJ Burroughs and me', *Naked Lunch @ 50: Anniversary Essays*, edited by Oliver Harris and Ian MacFadyen (Carbondale, IL: South Illinois University Press, 2009), pp. 233–7.
Doggett, Peter, *There's a Riot Going On: Revolutionaries, Rock Stars and the Rise and Fall of '60s Counter-culture* (Edinburgh: Canongate, 2007).
Dylan, Bob, album sleeve notes, *Bringing It All Back Home* (Columbia, 1965).
—*Writings and Drawings* (London: Panther, 1973).
—*Tarantula* (New York: St Martin's Press, 1994, orig. pub. 1971).
—*Chronicles: Volume One* (London: Pocket Books, 2005).

Elliot Fox, Robert, 'Review essay: *Kerouac: Kicks Joy Darkness*', *Postmodern Culture*, Vol. 7, No. 3, 1997, http://muse.jhu.edu/journals/postmodern_culture/v007/7.3r_fox.html [accessed 18 February 2012].

Ellis, R.J., 'From "The Beetles" to "The Beatles": The British/Beat 1955–1965', *Symbiosis*, Vol. 4, No. 1, April 2000, pp. 67–98.

Farber, David and Beth Bailey, *The Columbia Guide to America in the 1960s* (New York: Columbia University Press, 2001).

Fariña, Richard, *Been Down So Long It Looks Like Up to Me* (Harmondsworth: Penguin, 1983, orig. pub. 1966).

Farrell, James J., *The Spirit of the Sixties: The Making of Postwar Radicalism* (London: Routledge, 1997).

Farren, Mick, 'Rickie Lee Jones', *New Musical Express*, 9 June 1979, *Rock's Backpages*, http://0-www.rocksbackpages.com.wam.leeds.ac.uk/article.html?ArticleID=1554 [accessed 25 November 2011].

Featherstone, Mike (ed.), *Body Modification* (London: Sage, 2003).

Feldman, Gene and Max Gartenberg (eds.), *Protest: The Beat Generation and the Angry Young Men* (London: Panther, 1960).

Ferlinghetti, Lawrence, *Pictures of the Gone World* (San Francisco, CA: City Lights, 1995, orig. pub. 1955).

—*A Coney Island of the Mind* (New York: New Directions, 1958).

Fineberg, Jonathan, *Art Since 1940: Strategies of Being* (London: Laurence King, 2000).

Ford, Simon, *Wreckers of Civilisation: The Story of COUM Transmissions & Throbbing Gristle* (London: Black Dog Publishing, 1999).

Frank, Robert, *The Americans* (Manchester: Cornerhouse Publications, 1993, orig. pub. 1959).

Frith, Simon, *Sound Effects* (New York: Pantheon, 1981).

Frith, Simon and Howard Horne, *Art Into Pop* (London: Methuen, 1987).

George, Christopher, 'Allen Ginsberg in Liverpool' (For Adrian Henri 1932–2000), poem at http://chrisgeorge.netpublish.net/Poems/AllenGinsberginLiverpool.htm, originally published in *Electronic Acorn* 16 September 2004 [accessed 21 July 2006].

George-Warren, Holly (ed.), *The Rolling Stone Book of the Beats: The Beat Generation and the Counterculture* (London: Bloomsbury, 1999).

—'Introduction', *The Rolling Stone Book of the Beats: The Beat Generation and the Counterculture*, edited by Holly George-Warren (London: Bloomsbury, 1999), pp. ix–x.

Gillett, Charlie, *The Sound of the City: The Rise of Rock and Roll* (London: Souvenir, 1987).

Gilmore, Mikal, 'Allen Ginsberg, 1926–1997', *The Rolling Stone Book of the Beats: The Beat Generation and the Counterculture*, edited by Holly George-Warren (London: Bloomsbury, 1999), pp. 227–40.

Ginsberg, Allen, *Howl and Other Poems* (San Francisco, CA: City Lights, 1956).

—*Kaddish and Other Poems* (San Francisco: City Lights, 1961).

—*First Blues: Rags, Ballads of Harmonium Songs 1971–74* (New York: Full Court Press, 1975).

—'Songs of redemption', album sleeve notes, Bob Dylan, *Desire* (Columbia, 1976), sourced at 'Bard on bard, 1975', 9 June 2011, *The Rock File: Notes on the Rock Life*, http://therockfile.wordpress.com/2011/06/09/bard-on-bard-1975/ [accessed 6 September 2011].

—'Coming to terms with the Hell's Angels', *The Sixties*, edited by Lynda Rosen Obst (New York: Random House/Rolling Stone Press, 1977), pp. 160–3.

—'Yes, I remember it well', 20th anniversary celebration of Beatles appearance on *The Ed Sullivan Show*, *Rolling Stone*, 16 February 1984.

—*The Fall of America in Collected Poems 1947–1980* (Harmondsworth: Viking, 1985).

—'Beginning of a Poem of These States', from *The Fall of America in Collected Poems 1947–1980* (Harmondsworth: Viking, 1985), p. 369.

—'Hiway Poesy: LA-Albuquerque-Texas-Wichita,' *The Fall of America in Collected Poems 1947–1980* (Harmondsworth: Viking, 1985), p. 390.

—'Wichita Vortex Sutra,' *The Fall of America in Collected Poems 1947–1980* (Harmondsworth: Viking, 1985), p. 409.

—'Crossing Nation,' *The Fall of America in Collected Poems 1947–1980* (Harmondsworth: Viking, 1985), p. 499.

—'Ecologue,' *The Fall of America in Collected Poems 1947–1980* (Harmondsworth: Viking, 1985), p. 542.

—*Deliberate Prose: Selected Essays 1952–1995*, edited by Bill Morgan (London: Penguin, 2000).

—'CBC broadcast on mantra,' *Deliberate Prose: Selected Essays 1952–1995*, edited by Bill Morgan (London: Penguin, 2000), pp. 150–2.

—*Collected Poems 1947–1997* (London: Penguin, 2009).

Ginsberg, Allen and Louis Ginsberg, *Family Business: Selected Letters Between a Father and a Son*, edited by Michael Schumacher (New York: Bloomsbury, 2001).

Gioia, Ted, *The Birth and Death of the Cool* (Golden, CO: Speck Press, 2009).

Goddard, Seth, 'The Beats and the boom: A conversation with Allen Ginsberg,' published *Life*'s website, 5 July 2001, sourced at http://www.english.illinois.edu/maps/poets/g_l/ginsberg/interviews.htm [accessed 20 December 2011].

Goldman, Albert, *The Lives of John Lennon* (London: Bantam Press, 1988).

Goldstein, Richard, *The Poetry of Rock* (New York: Bantam, 1969).

Goodwin, Andrew, 'Popular music and postmodern theory,' *Cultural Studies*, Vol. 5, No. 2, 1991, pp. 174–90.

Gray, Michael, *The Bob Dylan Encyclopedia* (New York: Continuum, 2006).

Green, Jonathon, *Days in the Life: Voices from the English Underground 1961–1971* (London: Pimlico, 1998).

—*All Dressed Up: The Sixties and the Counterculture* (London: Pimlico, 1999).

Gysin, Brion, 'Brion Gysin interview,' conducted by Jon Savage, *RE/Search* #12, edited by V. Vale and Andrea Juno (San Francisco, CA: V/Search Publications, 1984), pp. 52–9.

Hajdu, David, *Positively Fourth Street: The Lives and Times of Joan Baez, Bob Dylan, Mimi Baez Fariña and Richard Fariña* (London: Bloomsbury, 2001).

Hall, Stuart and Paddy Whannel, *The Popular Arts* (London: Hutchinson Educational, 1964).

Hanks, Patrick (ed.), *Collins Dictionary of the English Language* (London: Collins, 1980).

Hamilton, Neil A., *The ABC-CLIO Companion to the 1960s Counterculture in America* (Santa Barbara, CA: ABC-CLIO, 1997).

Harris, Oliver, 'Burroughs is a poet too, really: The poetics of *Minutes to Go*', first published in *The Edinburgh Review*, 114 (2005), republished by *RealityStudio*, August 2010, http://realitystudio.org/scholarship/burroughs-is-a-poet-too-really-the-poetics-of-minutes-to-go/ [accessed 29 June 2011].

Harris, Oliver and Ian MacFadyen (eds.), *Naked Lunch @ 50: Anniversary Essays* (Carbondale, IL: South Illinois University Press, 2009).

Haverty Kerouac, Joan, *Nobody's Wife: The Smart Aleck and the King of Beats* (Berkeley, CA: Creative Arts Book Company, 2000).

Havranek, Carrie, *Women Icons of Popular Music: The Rebels, Rockers and Renegades*, Volume I (Westport, CT: Greenwood Press, 2009).

Hebdige, Dick, *Subculture: The Meaning of Style* (London: Methuen, 1979).

Helbig, Joerg and Simon Warner (eds.), *The Summer of Love: The Beatles, Art and Culture in the Sixties* (Trier: WVT, 2008).

Hell, Richard, 'My Burroughs: Postmortem notes', *The Rolling Stone Book of the Beats: The Beat Generation and the Counterculture*, edited by Holly George-Warren (London: Bloomsbury, 1999), pp. 216–29.

Henri, Adrian, Roger McGough and Brian Patten, *The Mersey Sound*, Penguin Modern Poets 10 (Harmondsworth: Penguin, 1982, orig. pub. 1967).

Hentoff, Nat, 'The pilgrims have landed on Kerouac's grave', *Rolling Stone*, 15 January 1976.

Hewison, Robert, *In Anger: Culture in the Cold War 1945–60* (London: Weidenfeld & Nicholson, 1981).

—*Culture and Consensus: England, Art and Politics since 1940* (London: Methuen, 1997).

Heylin, Clinton, *A Life in Stolen Moments – Day by Day: 1941–1995* (London: Omnibus, 1996).

—*Revolution in the Air – The Songs of Bob Dylan Vol. 1: 1957–73* (London: Constable, 2009).

Hishmeh, Richard E., 'Marketing genius: The friendship of Allen Ginsberg and Bob Dylan', *The Journal of American Culture*, Vol. 29, No. 4, December 2006, pp. 395–404.

Hoggart, Richard, *The Uses of Literacy* (Harmondsworth: Pelican Books, 1959, orig. pub. 1957).

Holmes, John Clellon, *Go* (New York: Thunder's Mouth Press, 1988, orig. pub. 1952).

Hopkins, Jerry and Danny Sugerman, *No One Here Gets Out Alive* (London: Plexus, 1982).

Hopkins, John 'Hoppy', *From the Hip: Photographs 1960–1966* (Bologna: Damiani Editore, 2008).

Horovitz, Michael, *Bank Holiday: A New Testament for the Love Generation* (1967).

—(ed.), *Children of Albion: Poetry of the 'Underground' in Britain* (Harmondsworth: Penguin, 1970).

—*Growing Up: Selected Poems and Pictures 1951–1979* (London: Allison & Busby, 1979).

—*Wordsounds and Sightlines: New and Selected Poems* (London: New Departures, 1994).

—*A New Waste Land: Timeship Earth at Nillennium* (London: New Departures, 2007).

Hoskyns, Barney, *Lowside of the Road: A Life of Tom Waits* (London: Faber, 2009).

Houen, Alex, '"Back! Back! Back! Central Mind-Machine Pentagon …": Allen Ginsberg and the Vietnam War', *Cultural Politics: An International Journal*, Vol. 4, No. 3, November 2008, pp. 351–73.

Humphries, Patrick, *Small Change: A Life of Tom Waits* (London: Omnibus, 1989).

Jameson, Fredric, *Postmodernism or the Cultural Logic of Late Capitalism* (Durham, NC: Duke University Press, 1999).

Johnson, Joyce, *Minor Characters* (London: Virago, 1996, orig. pub. 1987).

—*Missing Men: A Memoir* (New York: Viking, 2004).

Johnson, Ronna C. and Nancy M. Grace (eds.), *Girls Who Wore Black: Women Writing the Beat Generation* (New Brunswick, NJ: Rutgers University Press, 2002).

Johnstone, Nick, *Patti Smith: A Biography* (London: Omnibus, 1997).

Kandel, Lenore, *The Love Book* (San Francisco, CA: Stolen Paper Review, 1966).

Kemp, Mark, 'Beat Generation in the generation of beats', *The Rolling Stone Book of the Beats: The Beat Generation and the Counterculture*, edited by Holly George-Warren (London: Bloomsbury, 1999), pp. 415–19.

Kerouac, Jack, *The Town and the City* (London: Quartet, 1973, orig. pub. 1950).

—*On the Road* (London: Penguin, 1972, orig. pub. 1957).

—*The Dharma Bums* (London: Penguin, 2007, orig. pub. 1958).

—*The Subterraneans* (London: New English Library, 1972, orig. pub. 1958).

—'The Origins of the Beat Generation', *Playboy*, June 1959, http://xroads.virginia. edu/~ug00/lambert/ontheroad/response.html [accessed 9 November 2102].

—*Mexico City Blues* (New York: Grove, 1990, orig. pub. 1959).

—*Doctor Sax* (New York: Grove Press, 1959).

—*Book of Dreams* (San Francisco, CA: City Lights, 1961).

—*Big Sur* (London: New English Library, 1972, orig. pub. 1962),

—*Visions of Gerard* (New York: McGraw-Hill, 1976, orig. pub. 1963).

—*Lonesome Traveller* (London: Penguin, 2007, orig. pub. 1965).

—*Satori in Paris* (London: Quartet, 1973, orig. pub. 1966).

—*The Vanity of Duluoz* (London: Quartet, 1977, orig. pub. 1968).

—*Desolation Angels* (London, Panther, 1972, orig. pub. 1965).

—*Visions of Cody* (London: Granada, 1980, orig. pub. 1973).

—*Atop an Underwood: Early Stories and Other Writings*, edited by Paul Marion (New York: Viking, 1991).

—*Good Blonde & Others* (San Francisco: Grey Fox Press, 1994).

—'Introduction', *The Americans* by Robert Frank, in Kerouac, *Good Blonde & Others* (San Francisco, CA: Grey Fox Press, 1994), pp. 19–20.

Kerouac, Jack and William S. Burroughs, *And the Hippos were Boiled in Their Tanks* (London: Penguin, 2009).

Kerouac, Jan, *Baby Driver* (New York: Thunder's Mouth Press, 1998, orig. pub. 1981).

—*Trainsong* (New York: Thunder's Mouth Press, 1998, orig. pub. 1988).

Kerouac-Parker, Edie, *You'll Be Okay: My Life with Jack Kerouac* (San Francisco, CA: City Lights, 2007).

Kesey, Ken, *One Flew Over the Cuckoo's Nest* (London: Picador, 1973, orig. pub. 1962).

Kessel, Corinne, *The Words and Music of Tom Waits* (Westport, CT: Praeger, 2009).

Kiesling, Lydia, '*One Fast Move or I'm Gone*: A review', 'Screening Room', *The Millions*, 6 November 2009, http://www.themillions.com/2009/11/one-fast-move-or-im-gone-a-review.html [accessed 20 July 2011].

Knight, Brenda, 'Sisters, saints and sybils: Women and the Beat', in *Women of the Beat Generation*, edited by Brenda Knight (Berkeley, CA: Conari Press, 1996), pp. 1–6.

—(ed.), *Women of the Beat Generation* (Berkeley, CA: Conari Press, 1996).

Kramer, Mark, '1998: The year in body modification', *Body Modification Ezine*, 1 January 1999, http://www.bmezine.com/news/softtoy/008/ [accessed 29 March 2005].

Lanthier, Joseph Jon, '*One Fast Move or I'm Gone: Kerouac's Big Sur*', 'Movie Review', *Slant* magazine, 11 October 2009, http://www.slantmagazine.com/film/review/one-fast-move-or-im-gone-kerouacs-big-sur/4504 [accessed 20 July 2011].

Leland, John, *Hip: The History* (New York: Ecco, 2004).

Lennon, John, *In His Own Write* (London: Vintage Classics, 2012, orig. pub. 1964).

—*A Spaniard in the Works* (London: Vintage Classics, 2012, orig. pub. 1965).

—*The Lyrics of John Lennon* (London: Omnibus, 1997).

Lhamon, Jr., W.T., *Deliberate Speed: The Origins of a Cultural Style in the American 1950s* (Washington, DC: Smithsonian Institution, 1990).

Lindberg, Ulf, Gester Gudmundsson, Morten Michelsen and Hans Weisethaunet, *Rock Criticism from the Beginning: Amusers, Bruisers And Cool-Headed Cruisers* (New York: Peter Lang, 2005).

Literature and Music Research Group, Open University, http://www.open.ac.uk/Arts/literature-and-music/index.shtml [Accessed 16 December 2012].

Lucie-Smith, Edward (ed.), *The Liverpool Scene* (London: Donald Carroll, 1967).

MacAdams, Lewis, 'William S. Burroughs (1914–1997)', obituary, *The Rolling Stone Book of the Beats: The Beat Generation and the Counterculture*, edited by Holly-George-Warren (London: Bloomsbury, 1999), pp. 171–3.

—*Birth of the Cool: Beat, Bebop and the American Avant-Garde* (New York: The Free Press, 2001).

McCartney, Paul, *Blackbird Singing: Poems and Lyrics 1965–1999* (London: Faber and Faber, 2001).

McClure, Michael, *The New Book/A Book of Torture* (New York: Grove Press, 1961).

—*Love Lion Book* (San Francisco: Four Seasons Foundation, 1966).

—*Scratching the Beat Surface* (San Francisco, CA: North Point Press, 1982).

—*The Beard & Vktms: Two Plays* (New York: Grove Press, 1985).

—*Lighting the Corners: On Art, Nature, and the Visionary – Essays and Interviews*, (Albuquerque, NM: University of New Mexico Press, 1994).

—'Seven Things about Kenneth Rexroth', *Big Bridge*, http://www.bigbridge.org/issue10/elegymmcclure.htm [accessed 22 December 2011].

McClure, Michael, Lawrence Ferlinghetti and David Meltzer (eds.), *The Journal for the Protection of All Beings*, No. 1 (San Francisco: City Lights, 1961).

McGough, Roger, *Said and Done: The Autobiography* (London: Arrow Books, 2006).

MacDonald, Ian, *Revolution in the Head: The Beatles' Records and the Sixties* (London: Pimlico, 2005).

McNally, Dennis, *Desolate Angel: A Biography – Jack Kerouac, the Beat Generation and America* (New York: Random House, 1979).

—*A Long Strange Trip: The Inside Story of the Grateful Dead* (London: Bantam Press, 2002).

Mailer, Norman, 'The White Negro: Superficial reflections on the hipster', *Protest: The Beat Generation and the Angry Young Men*, edited by Gene Feldman and Max Gartenberg (London: Panther, 1960), pp. 288–306.

Maltby, Richard, *Hollywood Cinema* (Oxford: Blackwell, 1995).

Marcus, Greil, *Lipstick Traces: A Secret History of the Twentieth Century* (London: Secker & Warburg, 1989).

—*Invisible Republic: Bob Dylan's Basement Tapes* (London: Picador, 1997).

Martin, George with William Pearson, *The Summer of Love: The Making of Sgt. Pepper* (London: Pan, 1995).

Marwick, Arthur, *The Sixties: Cultural Revolution in Britain, France, Italy and the United States c.1958–c.1974* (Oxford: Oxford University Press, 1998).

Maslin, Janet, 'Singer songwriters', *The Rolling Stone Illustrated History of Rock & Roll*, edited by Jim Miller (New York: Random House, 1976), pp. 312–19.

Melly, George, *Revolt into Style: The Pop Arts in the 50s and 60s* (Oxford: Oxford University Press, 1989, orig. pub. 1970).

Meltzer, David, *The San Francisco Poets* (New York: Ballantine Books, 1971).

—*Golden Gate: Interviews with Five San Francisco Poets* (Berkeley, CA: Wingbow Press, 1976).

—*The Name: Selected Poetry 1973–1983* (Santa Barbara, CA: Black Sparrow Press, 1984).

—(ed.), *Reading Jazz* (San Francisco, CA: Mercury House, 1993).

—*Arrows: Selected Poetry 1957–1992* (Santa Rosa, CA: Black Sparrow Press, 1994).

—(ed.), *Writing Jazz* (San Francisco, CA: Mercury House, 1999).

—*No Eyes: Lester Young* (Santa Rosa, CA: Black Sparrow Press, 2000).

—(ed.), *San Francisco Beat: Talking with the Poets* (San Francisco, CA: City Lights, 2001).

—*Beat Thing* (Albuquerque, NM: La Alameda Press, 2004).

—*David's Copy: The Selected Poems of David Meltzer*, Michael Rothenberg (ed.) (London: Penguin, 2005).

—'Letter to Jim Dickson, January 2nd, 1959', CD sleeve notes, *Poet w/Jazz* (Sierra Records, 2005).

—*When I Was a Poet* (San Francisco, CA: City Lights, 2011).

Mesmer, Sharon, *Half Angel, Half Lunch* (Lenox, MA: Hard Press Editions, 1998).

—*Annoying Diabetic Bitch* (Cumberland, RI: Combo Books, 2008).

Miles, Barry, *Ginsberg: A Biography* (London: Viking, 1990).

—*William Burroughs: El Hombre Invisible* (London: Virgin, 1993).

—*Paul McCartney: Many Years from Now* (London: Secker & Warburg, 1997).

—*Jack Kerouac: King of the Beats* (London: Virgin, 1998).

—*The Beat Hotel: Ginsberg, Burroughs, and Corso in Paris, 1958–1963* (New York: Grove Press, 2000).

—*In the Sixties* (London: Jonathan Cape, 2002).

—*The Hippies* (London: Cassell Illustrated, 2003).

Miller, Jim (ed.), *The Rolling Stone Illustrated History of Rock & Roll*, (New York: Random House, 1976).

Mitchell, Deborah and Beth Landma, 'All's fair in Love and Rockets', *New York Magazine*, 29 June 1998 (Add. reporting by Kate Coyne), http://newyorkmetro.com/nymetro/news/people/columns/intelligencer/2902/ [accessed 29 March 2005].

Mitchell, Joni, *Joni Mitchell: The Complete Poems and Lyrics* (New York: Crown Publishing, 1997).

Moore, Dave (ed.), *Neal Cassady Collected Letters, 1944–1967* (London: Penguin, 2005).

Moore, Dave, 'Was Bob Dylan influenced by Jack Kerouac?', *Dharma Beat*, http://www.dharmabeat.com/kerouaccorner.html#Bob%20Dylan%20influenced%20by%20Jack%20Kerouac [accessed 29 August 2011].

Morgan, Bill, *The Beat Generation in New York: A Walking Tour of Jack Kerouac's City* (San Francisco, CA: City Lights, 1997).

—*The Typewriter is Holy: The Complete, Uncensored History of the Beat Generation* (New York: Free Press, 2010).

Morgan, Ted, *Literary Outlaw: The Life and Times of William S. Burroughs* (London: The Bodley Head, 1991).

Morris, Bill, 'Will you Beat hagiographers please be quiet, please?', *The Millions*, 28 December 2010, http://www.themillions.com/2010/12/will-you-beat-hagiographers-please-be-quiet-please.html [accessed 20 July 2011].

Morrison, Jim, *The Lords and the New Creatures* (London: Omnibus, 1985, orig. pub. 1969).

Mottram, Eric, 'American poetry, poetics and poetic movements', *American Literature Since 1900*, edited by Marcus Cunliffe (London: Sphere, 1988), pp. 237–82.

Muckle, John, 'The names: Allen Ginsberg's writings', *The Beat Generation Writers*, edited by A. Robert Lee (London: Pluto Press, 1996), pp. 10–36.

Neville, Richard, *Playpower* (London: Paladin, 1971).

Nolte, Carl, 'Kerouac Alley has face-lift', *San Francisco Chronicle*, 30 March 2007, http://www.sfgate.com/cgi-bin/article.cgi?f=/c/a/2007/03/30/BAG4NOUONC1.DTL [accessed 29 September 2011].

Norman, Philip, *Shout!* (London: Elm Tree, 1981).

Nuttall, Jeff, *Bomb Culture* (London: Paladin, 1970, orig. pub. 1968).

O'Brien, Lucy, *She Bop II: The Definitive History of Women in Pop, Rock and Soul* (London: Continuum, 2002).

Ono, Yoko, 'Memories of Allen', *The Rolling Stone Book of the Beats: The Beat Generation and the Counterculture,* edited by Holly George-Warren (London: Bloomsbury, 1999), pp. 275–83.

Osborne, John, *Look Back in Anger* (London: Faber, 1957).

Ostransky, Leon, *Understanding Jazz* (Englewood Cliffs, NJ: Prentice Hall, 1977).

Palmer, Robert, *Dancing the Street: A Rock & Roll History* (London: BBC Books, 1996).

Parsons, Tony, 'But mutilation is so passé …' *New Musical Express*, 30 October 1976, in *The Wreckers of Civilisation* by Simon Ford (London: Black Dog Publishing, 1999).

Paytress, Mark, *Break it Up: Patti Smith's* Horses *and the Remaking of Rock 'n' roll* (London: Portrait, 2006).

Perrone, Pierre, 'Lady Jaye Breyer P-Orridge', obituary, *The Independent*, 23 October 2007, http://www.independent.co.uk/news/obituaries/lady-jaye-breyer-porridge-397604. html [accessed 16 December 2011].

Perry, David, sleeve notes, CD box set, *The Jack Kerouac Collection* (Rhino Word Beat, 1990).

Perry, Charles, 'The gathering of the tribes', *The Sixties*, edited by Linda Rosen Obst (New York: Random House/*Rolling Stone*, 1977), pp. 188–92.

—*The Haight-Ashbury: A History* (New York: Wenner Books, 2005).

Peterson, Richard A., 'Why 1955? Explaining the advent of rock music', *Popular Music*, Vol. 9, No. 1, 1990, pp. 97–116.

Phillips, Lisa (ed.), *Beat Culture and the New America: 1950–1965*, exhibition catalogue (New York: Whitney Museum of American Art, 1995).

Phillips, Mike, 'Windrush – the passengers', BBC History, 3 October 2011, http://www. bbc.co.uk/history/british/modern/windrush_01.shtml [accessed 19 February 2012].

Pichaske, David, *The Poetry of Rock: The Golden Years* (Peoria, IL: The Ellis Press, 1981).

Pitts, Victoria, *In the Flesh: The Cultural Politics of Body Modification* (Basingstoke: Palgrave Macmillan, 2003).

P-Orridge, Genesis, ' "Thee Films": An account by Genesis P-Orridge', *Naked Lens: Beat Cinema*, edited by Jack Sargeant (London: Creation, 1997), pp. 184–96.

—(ed.), *Painful but Fabulous: The Lives and Art of Genesis P-Orridge* (New York: Soft Skull Press, 2002).

— 'An over-painted smile … re-collections of mo-meants ov inspiration 1963-2004', CD sleeve notes, *Godstar: Thee Director's Cut* (Hyperdelic, 2004).

— filmed interview with writer/researcher Jayne Sheridan, Columbia Hotel, London, 8 December 2004.

—'Full-length bio', the official Genesis P-Orridge website, http://www.genesisp-orridge. com/index.php?section=article&album_id=11&id=77 [accessed 3 April 2005].

Pountain, Dick and David Robins, *Cool Rules: Anatomy of an Attitude* (London: Reaktion Books, 2000).

Ranaldo, Lee, 'Interview – Beat Generation questions', Steve Appleford, 4 August 1998, Sonic Youth website, http://www.sonicyouth.com/symu/lee/2011/09/08/i-view-beat-generation-questions-1998/ [accessed 28 February 2012].

Raskin, Jonah, *American Scream: Allen Ginsberg's 'Howl' and the Making of the Beat Generation* (London: University of California Press, 2004).

Reed, Lou, 'Memories of Allen', *The Rolling Stone Book of the Beats: The Beat Generation and the Counterculture*, edited by Holly George-Warren (London: Bloomsbury, 1999), p. 278.

Reynolds, Frank and Michael McClure, *Freewheelin' Frank: The True Story of a Hell's Angel by a Hell's Angel* (London: New English Library, 1969).

Ring, Kevin, 'Beat culture and the new America and the Beat camera of Larry Keenan', *Beat Scene*, No. 26, 1996.

—'Ann Charters – A Beat journey', *Beat Scene*, No. 16, 1993.

—'Hey, Mr. Tambourine Man – Larry Keenan', Part 1, *Beat Scene*, No. 27, 1997.

—'Hey, Mr. Tambourine Man – Larry Keenan', Part 2, *Beat Scene*, No. 28, 1997.

Ritchie, Harry, *Success Stories: Literature and the Media in England, 1950–1959* (London: Faber, 1988).

Rolling Stone, 40th anniversary special edition, No. 2, 12–16 July 2007.

Rollins, Henry, 'You can't dance to a book', interview with Neddal Ayad, *The Modern Word*, 20 November 2005, http://www.themodernword.com/interviews/interview_rollins.html [accessed 28 February 2012].

Ronan, Stephen, *Disks of the Gone World: An Annotated Discography of the Beat Generation* (Berkeley, CA: Ammunition Press, 1996).

Rosen Obst, Lynda (ed.), *The Sixties*, (New York: Random House/*Rolling Stone* Press, 1977).

Rothenberg, Jerome, 'Introduction', David Meltzer, *David's Copy: The Selected Poems of David Meltzer*, edited by Michael Rothenberg (London: Penguin, 2005), pp. xv–xxi.

Rothenberg, Michael (ed.), 'Foreword', *David's Copy: The Selected Poems of David Meltzer* (London: Penguin, 2005), p. xiii.

Rudd, Natalie, *Peter Blake* (London: Tate, 2003).

Salinger, J.D., *The Catcher in the Rye* (Boston, MA: Little, Brown, 1951).

Sanders, Edward, *The Poetry and Life of Allen Ginsberg* (London, Scribner, 2002).

Sanders, Ed, *Fug You: An Informal History of the Peace Eye Bookstore, the Fuck You Press, the Fugs, and Counterculture in the Lower East Side* (Boston, MA: Da Capo, 2011).

Sargeant, Jack (ed.), *Naked Lens: Beat Cinema* (London: Creation, 1997).

Savage, Jon, *England's Dreaming: Sex Pistols and Punk Rock* (London: Faber, 1991).

Scaduto, Anthony, *Bob Dylan* (New York: New American Library, 1973).

Schumacher, Michael, *Dharma Lion: A Biography of Allen Ginsberg* (New York: St Martin's Press, 1992).

Scobie, Stephen, 'Ginsberg, Allen', 'The Bob Dylan Who's Who', *Expecting Rain*, 18 April 1997, http://expectingrain.com/dok/who/g/ginsbergallen.html [accessed 4 September 2011].

Serra, Richard, back page artwork, *The Nation*, 5 July, 2004.

Shambhala Sun, 'The late Allen Ginsberg and Beck in conversation: A Beat/Slacker transgenerational meeting of minds', January 1997, http://shambhalasun.com/index.php?option=com_content&task=view&id=2050&Itemid=244 [accessed 27 February, 2012].

Shaw, Philip, *Horses* (New York: Continuum, 2008).

Shelton, Robert, *No Direction Home: The Life and Music of Bob Dylan* (London: New English Library, 1986).

Shepard, Sam, *Rolling Thunder Logbook* (New York: Viking Press, 1977).

Siegle, Robert, 'Writing Downtown', *The Downtown Book: The New York Art Scene 1974–1984*, edited by Marvin J. Taylor (Princeton, NJ: Princeton University Press, 2006), pp. 131–153.

Sillitoe, Alan, *Saturday Night and Sunday Morning* (London: Grafton, 1985, orig. pub. 1958).

Sim, Stuart (ed.), *The Icon Dictionary of Postmodern Thought* (Cambridge: Icon, 1998).

Sinfield, Alan, *Literature, Politics and Culture in Postwar Britain* (London: Athlone, 1997).

Smith, Patti, *Just Kids* (London: Bloomsbury, 2010).

Stimmel, Alex, 'The Serpent Power', *All Music Guide*, http://www.allmusic.com/artist/serpent-power-p143421/biography [accessed 22 December 2011].

Stipe, Michael, *Two Times Intro: On the Road with Patti Smith* (New York: Ray Gun Press, 1998).

Stokes, Geoffrey, 'Trimming the sails', *Rock of Ages: The Rolling Stone History of Rock and Roll*, edited by Ed Ward, Geoffrey Stokes and Ken Tucker (Harmondsworth: Penguin, 1987), pp. 447–63.

Storey, John, 'Postmodernism and popular culture', *The Icon Dictionary of Postmodern Thought*, edited by Stuart Sim (Cambridge: Icon, 1998), pp. 147–57.

Strinati, Dominic, *An Introduction to Theories of Popular Culture* (London: Routledge, 1995).

Sukenick, Ronald, *Down and In: Life in the Underground* (New York: Collier Books, 1987).

Tarr, Joe, *The Words and Music of Patti Smith* (Westport, CT: Praeger, 2008).

Taylor, Marvin J. (ed.), *The Downtown Book: The New York Art Scene 1974–1984* (Princeton, NJ: Princeton University Press, 2006).

Taylor, Steven, *False Prophet: Field Notes from the Punk Underground* (Middletown, CT: Wesleyan University Press, 2004).

Thompson, E.P., *The Making of the English Working Class* (Harmondsworth: Pelican Books, 1970, orig. pub. 1963).

Thompson, Hunter S., *Hell's Angels: The Strange and Terrible Saga of the Outlaw Motorcycle Gangs* (London: Penguin, 2003, orig. pub. 1966).

Trager, Oliver, *Keys to the Rain: The Definitive Bob Dylan Encyclopedia* (New York: Billboard Books, 2004).

Trynka, Paul (ed.), *The Beatles: 10 Years that Shook the World* (London: Dorling Kindersley, 2004).

Turner, Steve, *Jack Kerouac: Angelheaded Hipster* (London: Bloomsbury, 1996).

Udo, Tommy, 'He was a great advertisement for doing everything you shouldn't do', *New Musical Express*, 16 August 1997.

Vale, V. and Andrea Juno (eds.), *RE/Search* #4/5, 'A Special Book Issue: William S. Burroughs, Brion Gysin and Throbbing Gristle' (San Francisco, CA: V/Search Publications, 1984).

—*RE/Search* #12, *Modern Primitives* (San Francisco, CA: V/Search Publications, 1989).

Verdant Press, 'Ed Sanders and the Fuck You Press', Verdant Press, http://www.verdantpress.com/fuckyou.html [accessed 4 January 2012].

Von Vogt, Elizabeth, *681 Lexington Avenue: A Beat Education in New York City 1947–1954* (Wooster, OH: Ten O'Clock Press, 2008).

Wade, Stephen, *Gladsongs and Gatherings: Poetry and Its Social Context in Liverpool since the 1960s* (Liverpool: Liverpool University Press, 2001).

Walden, Brian, 'The white heat of Wilson', BBC News, 31 March 2006, http://news.bbc.co.uk/1/hi/magazine/4865498.stm [accessed 12 October 2007].

Waldman, Anne, 'Foreword', *Women of the Beat Generation*, edited by Brenda Knight (Berkeley, CA: Conari Press, 1996), pp. ix–xii.

—*Fast Speaking Woman: Chants & Essays* (San Francisco, CA: City Lights, 1996).

—*Outrider: Poems, Essays, Interviews* (Albuquerque, NM: La Alameda Press, 2006).

—(ed.), *The Beat Book* (Boston, MA: Shambala, 1996).

Ward, Ed, 'The Fifties and before: Streetcorner symphony', *Rock of Ages: The Rolling*

Stone History of Rock and Roll, edited by Ed Ward, Geoffrey Stokes and Ken Tucker (Harmondsworth: Penguin, 1987), pp. 83–97.

Ward, Ed, Geoffrey Stokes and Ken Tucker (eds.), *Rock of Ages: The Rolling Stone History of Rock and Roll* (Harmondsworth: Penguin, 1987).

Wardle, Irving, 'American Theatre since 1945', *American Literature Since 1900*, edited by Marcus Cunliffe (London: Sphere, 1988), pp. 205–36.

Warner, Simon, *Rockspeak!: The Language of Rock and Pop* (London: Blandford, 1996).

— 'David Meltzer', *Beat Scene*, No. 30, 1998.

— 'Genesis and revelations: From the Midlands to Manhattan', 'Anglo Visions', *Pop Matters*, 12 March 2003, http://www.popmatters.com/columns/warner/030312.shtml [accessed 29 March 2005].

— 'Sifting the shifting sands: "Howl" and the American landscape in the 1950s', *Howl for Now: A Celebration of Allen Ginsberg's Epic Protest Poem*, edited by Simon Warner (Pontefract: Route, 2005), pp. 25–52.

— 'Raising the consciousness? Re-visiting Allen Ginsberg's trip to Liverpool in 1965', *Centre of the Creative Universe: Liverpool and the Avant Garde*, edited by Christoph Grunenberg and Robert Knifton (Liverpool: Liverpool University Press, 2007), pp. 95–108.

— 'Photographer who captured Dylan, Ginsberg and the Sixties counter-culture', *The Independent*, 28 August 2012, http://www.independent.co.uk/news/obituaries/ larry-keenan-photographer-who-captured-dylan-ginsberg-and-the-sixties-counterculture-8082405.html [Accessed 16 December 2012].

— '*On the Road:* Words beat pictures despite Salles' best intentions', *Beatnicity*, 20 October 2012, http://beatnicity.com/2012/10/20/on-the-road-words-beat-pictures-despite-salles-best-intentions/ [Accessed 16 December 2012].

— 'Amiri Baraka in Manchester', *Beat Scene*, No. 69, 2013.

Watson, Steven, *The Birth of the Beat Generation: Visionaries, Rebels, and Hipsters, 1944–1960* (New York: Pantheon, 1995).

— *Factory Made: Warhol and the Sixties* (New York: Pantheon, 2003).

Weaver, Helen, *The Awakener: A Memoir of Kerouac and the Fifties* (San Francisco, CA: City Lights, 2009).

Wenke, Joseph, 'Bob Dylan', *Dictionary of Literary Biography*, Vol. 16, 'The Beats: Literary Bohemians in Postwar America', Part 1, http://www.bookrags.com/biography/ bob-dylan-dlb/ [accessed August 2011].

Wesker, Arnold, *The Wesker Trilogy: Chicken Soup with Barley; Roots; I'm Talking about Jerusalem – Three Plays* (London: Jonathan Cape, 1960).

Wetterau, Bruce (ed.), *Concise Dictionary of World History* (London: Robert Hale, 1984).

Whitburn, Joel, *The Billboard Book of US Top 40 Hits – 1955 to Present* (New York: Billboard Publications, 1983).

White, Timothy, 'Rickie Lee Jones: The Great Disconnected's leading lady flirts with happiness', *Rolling Stone*, 6 August 1981.

Whiteley, Sheila (ed.), *Sexing the Groove: Popular Music and Gender* (London: Routledge, 1997).

— 'Little Red Rooster v. the Honky Tonk Woman: Mick Jagger, sexuality, style, image', *Sexing the Groove: Popular Music and Gender*, edited by Sheila Whiteley (London: Routledge, 1997), pp. 67–99.

— 'Patti Smith: The Old Grey Whistle Test, BBC2 TV, 11 May 1976', *Performance and Popular Music: History, Place and Time*, edited by Ian Inglis (Aldershot: Ashgate, 2006), pp. 81–91.

Wilentz, Sean, *Bob Dylan in America* (London: Bodley Head, 2010).

Williams, Paul, *Bob Dylan – Performing Artist 1960–1973: The Early Years* (London: Omnibus, 2004).

Williams, Raymond, *Culture and Society, 1780–1950* (New York: Columbia University Press, 1983, orig. pub. 1958).

—*Keywords: A Vocabulary of Culture and Society* (London: HarperCollins, 1988).

Williams, Richard, *Dylan: A Man Called Alias* (London: Bloomsbury, 1992).

Wilson, Colin, *The Outsider* (London: Gollancz, 1956).

Wolfe, Tom, *The Electric Kool Aid Acid Test* (London: Black Swan, 1989, orig. pub. 1968).

Discography

Author's note: This is a selective listing. See also **Appendix A**.

The Beatles, *Rubber Soul* (Parlophone, 1965).

—*Revolver* (Parlophone, 1966).

—*Sgt. Pepper's Lonely Hearts Club Band* (Parlophone, 1967).

Black Rebel Motorcycle Club, 'Howl' (Echo, 2005).

David Bowie, *The Rise and Fall of Ziggy Stardust and the Spiders from Mars* (RCA, 1972).

—*Diamond Dogs* (RCA, 1974).

William S. Burroughs, *Call Me Burroughs* (The English Bookshop, Paris, 1965).

William S. Burroughs, *Dead City Radio* (Island, 1990).

—*Spare Ass Annie and Other Tales* (Island, 1993).

William S. Burroughs and Kurt Cobain, 'The "Priest" They Called Him' (Tim Kerr Records, 1993)

William S. Burroughs and John Giorno, *William S. Burroughs/John Giorno* (Released by Giorno Poetry Systems Records, 1975).

William S. Burroughs with Gus van Sant, *The Elvis of Letters* (T. K. Records, 1985).

The Jim Carroll Band, *Catholic Boy* (Atco, 1980).

The Clash, *Combat Rock* (CBS, 1982).

Leonard Cohen, *The Songs of Leonard Cohen* (Columbia, 1967).

Gregory Corso, *Die On Me* (Koch, 2002).

Cream, *Fresh Cream* (Atco, 1966).

—*Disraeli Gears* (Polydor, 1967).

—*Wheels of Fire* (Polydor, 1968).

Death Cab for Cutie, *We Have the Facts and We're Voting Yes* (Barsuk, 2000).

—*Narrow Stairs* (Atlantic/WEA, 2008).

Ani DiFranco, *Ani DiFranco* (Righteous Records, 1990).

—*Living in Clip* (Righteous Babe Records,1997).

—*Revelling: Reckoning* (Righteous Babe Records, 2001).

—*Which Side are You On?* (Righteous Babe Records, 2012).

Donovan, *Beat Café* (Appleseed, 2004).

Bob Dylan, *Bob Dylan* (Columbia, 1962).

—*The Freewheelin' Bob Dylan* (Columbia, 1963).

—*The Times They are a-Changin'* (Columbia, 1964).

—*Another Side of Bob Dylan* (Columbia, 1964).

—*Bringing It All Back Home* (Columbia, 1965).

—*Highway 61 Revisited* (Columbia, 1965).

—*Blonde on Blonde* (Columbia, 1966).

—*Blood on the Tracks* (Columbia, 1975).

—'The Rolling Thunder Revue Concert', Technical University (Lowell, MA), *Wolfgang's Vault*, 2 November 1975, http://www.wolfgangsvault.com/the-rolling-thunder-revue/concerts/technical-university-november-02-1975.html [accessed 5 September 2011].

—*Desire* (Columbia, 1976).

—'Series of Dreams' (Columbia, 1991), YouTube, http://www.youtube.com/watch?v=AgqGUBP3Cx0 [Accessed 15 February 2012].

False Prophets, *Invisible People* (Patois, 1990).

Richard and Mimi Fariña, *Celebrations for a Grey Day* (Vanguard, 1965).

—*Reflections in a Crystal Wind* (Vanguard, 1965).

Jay Farrar and Ben Gibbard, *One Fast Move or I'm Gone: Kerouac's Big Sur* (Atlantic, 2009).

Lawrence Ferlinghetti and Kenneth Rexroth, *Poetry Recordings in the Cellar with the Cellar Jazz Quintet* (Fantasy Record, 1958).

Lawrence Ferlinghetti, *A Coney Island of the Mind* (Rykodisc, 1999).

—*Pictures of the Gone World* (Synergy, 2005).

The Fugs, *Village Fugs/First Album* (Folkways/ESP-Disk, 1965/1966).

Allen Ginsberg, *Howl and Other Poems* (Fantasy, 1959).

—*Allen Ginsberg Reads Kaddish* (Atlantic Verbum Series, 1966).

—*Songs of Innocence and Experience by William Blake* (MGM/Verve Forecast, 1969).

—*First Blues, Rags, Ballads & Harmonium Songs* (Folkways Records, 1981).

—*First Blues* (John Hammond Records, 1983).

—*Lion for Real* (Island, 1989).

—*Holy Soul Jelly Roll: Poems and Songs 1949–1943* (Rhino Word Beat, 1994).

—*The Ballad of the Skeletons* (Mercury Records, 1996).

Grimms, *Grimms* (Island, 1973).

Kerouac, Jack, *Poetry for the Beat Generation* (Dot/Hanover, 1959).

—*Blues and Haikus* (Hanover, 1959).

—*Readings by Jack Kerouac on the Beat Generation* (Verve, 1960).

—*The Jack Kerouac Collection* (Rhino Word Beat, 1989).

Rickie Lee Jones, *Rickie Lee Jones* (Warner Bros., 1979).

—*The Duchess of Coolsville: An Anthology* (Rhino, 2005).

King Crimson, *Beat* (EG Records, 1982).

Michael McClure and Ray Manzarek, *Love Lion* (Sanachie, 1993).

Material, *The Road to the Western Lands* (Triloka Records, 1999).

David Meltzer, *Poet w/ Jazz 1958* (Sierra Records, 2005).

Joni Mitchell, *Ladies of the Canyon* (Reprise, 1970).

—*Blue* (Reprise, 1971).

—*Court and Spark* (Asylum, 1974).

—*The Hissing of Summer Lawns* (Asylum, 1975).

—*Hejira* (Asylum, 1976).

—*Don Juan's Reckless Daughter* (Asylum, 1977).

—*Mingus* (Asylum, 1979).

Pete Molinari, *Walking Off the Map* (Damaged Goods, 2006).

—*A Virtual Landslide* (Damaged Goods, 2008).

—*A Train Bound for Glory* (Clarksville, 2010).

Bill Nelson, *After the Satellite Sings* (Resurgence, 1996).

New York Art Quintet, *New York Art Quintet* (ESP-Disk, 1966).
The Plastic Ono Band, 'Give Peace a Chance' (Apple, 1969).
Psychic TV, 'Godstar' (Temple,1986).
Psychic TV, *Godstar: Thee Director's Cut* (Hyperdelic, 2004).
Rage Against The Machine, 'Hadda Be Playing on the Jukebox' (Epic, 1996).
Gustavo Santaolalla *et al.*, *On the Road: Original Motion Picture Soundtrack* (Universal, 2012).
The Scaffold, *The Very Best of the Scaffold* (EMI Gold, 2002).
The Serpent Power, *The Serpent Power* (Vanguard Records, 1967).
Patti Smith, 'Piss Factory' (Mer, 1974).
—*Horses* (Arista, 1975).
—*Peace and Noise* (Arista, 1997).
—'Spell' (Arista, 1997).
Patti Smith with Lenny Kaye, *February 10, 1971* (Mer Records, 2006).
Gary Snyder, *Turtle Island* (Living Music Records, 1992).
Sonic Youth, 'Hits of Sunshine' (for Allen Ginsberg)' (DGC, 1998).
10,000 Maniacs, *In My Tribe* (Elektra, 1997).
—'Leaky Lifeboat (for Gregory Corso)' (Matador Records, 2009).
They Might Be Giants, 'I Should Be Allowed to Think' (Warner Bros, 1994).
Throbbing Gristle, *20 Jazz Funk Greats* (Mute Records, 1991, orig. released by Industrial Records, 1978).
Chris T-T, *Beat Verse* (Wine Cellar, 1999).
U2, *Achtung Baby* (Island, 1991).
—*Pop* (Island, 1997).
Anne Waldman, *Battery: Live at Naropa 1974–2002* (Fast Speaking Music, 2003).
Anne Waldman and Ambrose Bye, *The Milk of Universal Kindness* (Fast Speaking Music, 2011).
Various Artists, *The Nova Convention* (Giorno Poetry Systems Records, 1979).
—*10% File Under Burroughs* (Sub Rosa, 1996).
—*The Beat Generation* (Rhino Records, 1992).
—*Howls, Raps and Roars* (Fantasy, 1993).
—*Kerouac: Kicks Joy Darkness* (Rykodisc, 1997).
—*Jack Kerouac Reads On the* Road (Rykodisc, 1999).
—*Beat Poetry* (ABM, 1999).
—*Jazz Poetry* (ABM, 1999).
—*Doctor Sax and the Great World Snake* (Gallery Six, 2003).
The Velvet Underground, *The Velvet Underground & Nico* (Verve, 1967).
Tom Waits, *Heart of Saturday Night* (Asylum, 1974).
—*Nighthawks at the Diner* (Asylum, 1975).
—*Small Change* (Asylum, 1976).
—*Foreign Affairs* (Asylum, 1977).
—*The Black Rider* (Island, 1993).
—*Orphans: Brawlers, Bawlers & Bastards* (ANTI-, 2006).

Filmography

Don't Look Back, directed by D. A. Pennebaker (Leacock–Pennebaker, 1967).
Exploding Plastic Inevitable, directed by Ronald Nameth (Aardvark, 1967).

The Last Waltz, directed by Martin Scorsese (FM Productions/Last Waltz Inc., 1978).

The Life and Times and Allen Ginsberg, directed by Jerry Aronson (New Yorker Films, 2007).

No Direction Home: Bob Dylan, directed by Martin Scorsese (Paramount, 2005).

One Fast Move or I'm Gone: Kerouac's Big Sur, directed by Curt Worden (Kerouac Films, 2009).

Beat, directed by Gary Walkow (Millenium [*sic*] Pictures, 2000).

Pull My Daisy, directed Robert Frank and Alfred Leslie (G-String Enterprises, 1959).

Renaldo and Clara, directed by Bob Dylan (Lombard Street Films, 1978).

What Ever Happened to Kerouac?, directed by Richard Lerner and Lewis MacAdams (New Yorker Films, 1986).

Wholly Communion, directed by Peter Whitehead (Lorrimer Films, 1965).

Broadcasts

Pattie Boyd, interview, 'The 40th anniversary of the Summer of Love', *Woman's Hour*, BBC Radio 4, 27 August 2007.

Caroline Coon, interview, 'The 40th anniversary of the Summer of Love', *Woman's Hour*, BBC Radio 4, 27 August 2007.

Lawrence Ferlinghetti, *Lawrence Ferlinghetti: A Reluctant Beat*, 90th birthday tribute, BBC Radio 4, 15 March 2009.

Michael Horovitz, *The Poetry Olympian: Michael Horovitz at 75*, 75th birthday tribute, presented by Simon Warner, BBC Radio 4, 4 April 2010.

Tom Waits, 'Tom Waits: The whiskey voice returns', interview with Robert Siegel, *All Things Considered*, NPR, 21 November 2006, http://www.npr.org/templates/story/story.php?storyId=6519647 [accessed 29 November 2008].

Personal communication

Chapter 2 Chains of flashing memories: Bob Dylan and the Beats, 1959–1975
Dave Moore, independent Beat scholar, email, 26 August 2011.

Chapter 3 Muse, moll, maid, miss: Beat women and their rock legacy
David Meltzer, poet, critic and musician, email, 16 February 2009.
Sharon Mesmer, poet and novelist, email, 31 October 2011.
Anne Waldman, poet and critic, email, 28 September 2011.

Chapter 4 Raising the consciousness?: Re-visiting Allen Ginsberg's Liverpool trip in 1965
Jim Burns, poet and critic, letter, 15 July 2006.
Christopher George, poet, email, 6 and 7 July 2006.
Michael Horovitz, poet and publisher, email, 24 and 29 July and 7 August 2006.
Edward Lucie-Smith, critic and author, email, 4 July 2006.
David Meltzer, poet, critic and musician, email, 9 July 2006.

Brian Patten, poet, telephone conversation, 6 July 2006.
Jonah Raskin, biographer and academic, email, 5 July 2006.
Steven Taylor, musician and writer, email, 5 July 2006.

Chapter 5 The British Beat: Rock, Literature and the UK Counterculture in the 1960s
Michael Brocken, academic and musician, email, 27 December 2010.
Pete Brown, poet and lyricist, telephone conversation, 6 December 2009.
Barry Miles, author, email, 29 November and 11 December 2009.

Chapter 7 The Meltzer chronicles: Poet, novelist, musician and historian of Beat America
David Meltzer, poet, critic and musician, interview, 5 October 1997, Hebden Bridge, UK.
—email, 20 and 21 April 1999.
Dave Moore, independent Beat scholar, email, 28 May 2012.

Chapter 8 Versions of Cody: Jack Kerouac, Tom Waits and the song 'On the Road'
Vic Juris, guitarist, email, 24 November 2008.
Bob Kealing, Kerouac Project, Orlando, Florida, email, 27 November 2008.
Dave Moore, independent Beat scholar, email, 3 December 2008 and 28 May 2012.
Frank Olinsky, album sleeve designer, email, 8 December 2008.
Jim Sampas, producer of *Jack Kerouac Reads On the Road*, email, 20 and 24 November 2008.
Steven Taylor, musician/writer, email, 1 December 2008.

Chapter 9 Feeling the bohemian pulse: Locating Patti Smith within a post-Beat tradition
Victor Bockris, Patti Smith biographer and author, email, 3 February 2011.
Bart Bull, rock journalist with *Spin* and magazine writer, email, 7 February 2011.
Jim Cohn, 'Postbeat' poet and singer-songwriter, email, 8 February 2011.
David Cope, 'Postbeat' poet, email, 6 February 2011.
Holly George-Warren, journalist and editor of *The Rolling Stone Book of the Beats: The Beat Generation and the Counterculture,* email, 18 July 2011.
Harvey Kubernik, music journalist and author, email, 11 February, 2011.
Lucy O'Brien, rock journalist, author of *SheBop* and academic, email, 10 March 2011.
Joyce Pinchbeck, novelist and biographer, email, 10 February 2011.
Philip Shaw, academic and author of *Horses*, email, 2 February 2011.
Steven Taylor, musician and writer, email, 1 February 2011.
Anne Waldman, poet, email, 1 February 2011.
Sheila Whiteley, academic and author of *Sexing the Groove*, email, 22 March 2011.

Chapter 11 All cut up? Unwrapping Genesis P-Orridge's beatnik past
Jason Louv, 'The GP-O Language', email, 17 March 2005.
Genesis P-Orridge, rock musician/artist, telephone conversation, 20 July 2004.
—interview, Brooklyn, New York City, 20 July 2004.

Q&A details

Q&A 1 – Michael Horovitz, poet, publisher and British Beat, email, 2 January 2012.

Q&A 2 – Mark Bliesener, rock band manager and a founder of Neal Cassady's Memorial Day in Denver, email, 18 November 2011.

Q&A 3 – Jonah Raskin, Ginsberg biographer and cultural historian, email, 14 November 2011.

Q&A 4 – Levi Asher, founder of acclaimed Beat website *Literary Kicks*, email, 19 November 2011.

Q&A 5 – Jim Sampas, notable Beat record producer including *Kerouac: Kicks Joy Darkness*, email, 15 February 2012.

Q&A 6 – Pete Molinari, British singer-songwriter, email, 9 August 2011.

Q&A 7 – Chris T-T, British political singer-songwriter, email, 8 September 2011.

Q&A 8 – Kevin Ring, editor of the magazine *Beat Scene*, email, 21 December 2011.

INDEX